GOOD FISHI

COARSE FISHING

HEADLINE

First published in 1992
by HEADLINE BOOK PUBLISHING PLC

10 9 8 7 6 5 4 3 2 1

British Library Cataloguing in Publication Data
"Angling Times" Good Fishing Guide:
New Authoritative Guide to the Best Fishing
Locations in England, Scotland and Wales.
Coarse Fishing
799.1

ISBN 0-7472-7927-6

HEADLINE BOOK PUBLISHING PLC
Headline House
79 Great Titchfield Street
London W1P 7FN

Designed and produced by the Pen & Ink Book Company Ltd, Huntingdon, Cambridgeshire

Printed and bound in Great Britain by Richard Clays Ltd, Bungay Suffolk

Editorial and research by Bill Down, Roland Liiv and Helen Canning

Atlas section provided by GEOprojects (UK) Ltd, Reading, Berkshire

Cover design by Head, London W1

People who have kindly provided photographs
Paul Marriott, pp. 38, 50, 56, 60, 63, 66, 68, 74, 78, 79, 83, 86, 90, 94, 95, 104, 107, 110, 113, 114, 116, 118, 121, 122, 123, 124, 125, 127, 128, 129, 130, 131, 132, 133, 134, 137, 138, 139, 140, 141, 142, 143, 144, 145, 146, 149, 161, 162, 169, 175, 182, 210, 211, 213, 223, 227, 228, 233, 234, 241; David Pearson, title page, pp.120, 198; Chris Yates, pp. 6, 83, 96, 98, 105, 179, 192, 198, 208, 227, 236, 237, 245, 250, 251, 252, 260, 268, 274, 286, 287, 288, 290, 292, 293, 299, 313 and the photographic library of the *Angling Times*.

Foreword

by Chris Yates, current holder of the British record for Mirror carp at 51lb 8oz.

Chris Yates admiring a barbel from the Royalty.

Britain offers a wonderful variety of coarse fishing; from the slow peaceful rivers of the fenlands, with their wealth of bream and roach, to the faster streams of the south and west, with their great shoals of fat chub and dace; from the great reservoirs and gravel pits around London, jumping with giant tench and carp, to the wild lakes of Cumbria and Scotland, wherein lurk monstrous pike. There are ancient castle moats, municipal park ponds, disused canals, mighty rivers, winding brooks, mysterious woodland pools. And you can catch shoals of little fish one day and the monster of your dreams the next, especially if you know where to cast.

This book, more comprehensively than any previous guidebook, reveals to the casual and experienced angler alike the amazing amount of fishing that is available either free or for the price of a day, week or season ticket. It is a book I would have regarded as priceless in my youth, when I was scouring the southern counties, trying to catch my first tench and researching for waters that might hold carp. I would certainly have fished the Hampshire Avon sooner than I did had I access to the information this book provides.

There is too much secrecy surrounding productive fishing locations and young anglers in particular find this closed shop attitude slightly disheartening; but the fact is that there is so much truly splendid fishing available to everyone that secrecy is unnecessary. Despite the problems of pollution and abstraction, there has probably never been much such a diversity of location nor such a potential for big fish in the history of angling. Barbel are beginning to colonize the River Wye, enormous carp have been seen in the Thames, a record chub could be taken this season from the Hampshire Avon (after many years of decline the river is returning to its old, magnificent form), colossal tench are being caught from ponds that, previously, never produced anything remarkable. And while there will always be exclusive lakes beyond the means of most anglers, there are, as this book so graphically describes, more than enough readily available fisheries where even the most discerning piscator can enjoy delightful surroundings and cast for the fish of his – or her – dreams.

Chris Yates

Contents

Regions of the National River Authority

Scotland

North-umbria

North West

Yorkshire

Severn Trent

Anglian

Welsh Water

Thames

Wessex

Southern

South-West

Wessex Region
Rivers House, East Quay, Bridgwater, Somerset TA6 4YS; Tel. 0278 457333.
North-West Region
Richard Fairclough, Knutsford Road, Warrington WA4 1HG; Tel. 0925 53999.
Northumbria Region
Eldon House, Regent Centre, Gosforth, Newcastle-upon-Tyne NE3 3UD; Tel. 091 213 0266.
Yorkshire Region
21 Park Square South, Leeds LS1 2QG; Tel. 0532 440191.
Anglian Region
Kingfisher House, Goldhay Way, Orton Goldhay, Peterborough PE2 0ZR; Tel. 0733 371811.
Severn-Trent Region
Sapphire East, 550 Streetsbrook Road, Solihull B91 1QT; Tel. 021 711 2324.
Thames Region
Kings Meadow House, Kings Meadow Road, Reading RG1 8DQ; Tel. 0734 535000.
Welsh Region
Rivers House/Plas yr-Afon, St Mellons Business Park, St Mellons, Cardiff CF3 0EG; Tel. 0222 770088.

Southern Region
Guildbourne House, Chatsworth Road, Worthing, West Sussex BN11 1LD; Tel. 0903 820692.
South-West Region
Manley House, Kestrel Way, Exeter, Devon EX2 7LQ; Tel. 0392 444000.

Fishing in Scotland is under the general jurisdiction of the Department of Agriculture and Fisheries for Scotland, Pentland House, 47 Robb's Loan, Edinburgh EH14 1SQ; Tel. 031 556 8400.

Introduction

Welcome to the *Angling Times* 1992 Guide to Coarse Fishing, which has been designed with both the experienced – and the less experienced – angler in mind.

The Guide lists 1,000 coarse fishing venues located throughout England, Wales and Scotland, each of which should provide an exciting – and hopefully very productive – day's sport.

Although, originally, we designed the Guide to include only day-ticket fisheries, not all establishments provide such a facility and consequently a number of venues where reasonably-priced 'season-ticket-only' fishing is available have been included. Occasionally, membership of a local angling club or association may also be required before day tickets can be bought, and in such cases a contact name and/or telephone number is given.

The venues have been obtained from a variety of sources, including the NRA, tackle shops, commercial fisheries, recreational organisations, angling club secretaries and particularly the *Angling Times*, and we gratefully acknowledge the huge amount of help and guidance given to us by many people while we have been preparing the Guide. Of course, although we have included 1,000 venues, it's important to remember that the Guide was never intended as an exhaustive list of coarse fisheries in the UK, and any suggestions of venues for inclusion into later editions will be welcomed.

Although the venues have been recommended to us in various ways, of particular interest are the *Angling Times* 'Hotspots' – identified in the Guide by the 'Hotspot' logo. All 'Hotspots' have not only been recently fished by expert coarse anglers to verify their excellence, but also include 'Hotspot Tips' – suggestions by the expert which should help to provide a really good day's fishing!

A special thanks goes to the *Angling Times*, publisher Robert MacDonald; Editor, Keith Higginbottom; Technical Editor, Allan Haines who have provided articles, information and photographs used in the Guide.

We also gratefully acknowledge the help given by Stephen McCaveny, Development Chairman of the Scottish Federation for Coarse Fishing.

How to use the Guide

In order to make the Guide 'user-friendly', we have listed the entries within their respective National Rivers Authority (NRA) region (or Welsh Water Region and Scottish Water Authority as appropriate). Within each region, they are then listed separately by county, and their geographical location shown in the Atlas Section on pages 199–207.

The entry for each venue includes information such as size and appearance, brief details of 'how to get there', the type(s) of fish caught and their typical weights, recommendations and restrictions on items such as baits and tackle, plus any available facilities both on site and in the surrounding areas. The suitability of the venue for disabled and wheelchair anglers has also, whenever possible, been assessed. Finally, we have included the cost of day ticket fishing – plus how and where to buy the tickets for the large majority of venues.

Although all the information included in the Guide has been researched during late 1991 and early 1992, and is as up-to-date and as accurate as possible at the time of going to press, we appreciate that prices and conditions may since have changed, and would appreciate being informed of any such alterations whenever possible, in order to update later editions.

So, the Guide is now complete, and all that remains is for us to wish you a happy – and hopefully very productive – coarse fishing season!

Northumbrian Region

River Wear, Durham City.

NORTHUMBRIA

Good, quality roach.

The NRA's Northumbrian Region, which stretches from the Cleveland Hills near Middlesborough in the south, to Berwick-upon-Tweed and the Scottish Borders in the north, incorporates some 3,600 square miles of beautiful and rugged countryside which is interspersed with heavily industrialised areas.

Although in this region the sport is largely dominated by game angling, coarse fishing retains a flourishing and enthusiastic support. Among the region's waterways, coarse fishing is mainly confined to the lower reaches of most rivers, including for example, the Tyne and the Tees, as well as some sections of the Wear. On all these rivers, coarse angling provides both excitement and achievement, with large catches of good quality roach, dace, chub and perch, while for the specialist coarse fisherman there are plenty of large barbel and bream, plus – for that added spice – the occasional pike. And for the real enthusiast, that rarely-seen silver streak – the grayling – adds another dimension to Northumbria's coarse fishing scene.

Fortunately for the angler, coarse fishing in the region is not limited solely to the rivers. There are also plenty of well stocked ponds and lakes available in both urban and rural areas, many of which contain top quality coarse fish, including large carp, bream and perch.

All in all, Northumbria – with its blend of superb coarse fishing set amid wonderful scenery – offers the best of both worlds to the coarse angler.

ALBERT PARK LAKE
Atlas Page 205 E.3/1.5

A pleasant lake situated in a scenic park towards the north of Middlesborough, providing a good variety of coarse fish. Controlled by the local authority.

How to get there   From the city centre, drive north past the cathedral (on left) and follow signs to Albert Park and the lake. For further details, contact any local tackle shop.

Day tickets   Adult £1.25; junior/OAP £1. Available on the bank.

Best methods/baits   Use any recognised coarse technique and baits.

Restrictions   No lead weights under 1oz (except No. 8 or smaller). No night fishing.

Facilities   Toilets/cafe in the park. Nearest shops/pubs in Middlesborough.

Disabled facilities   Some swims suitable for disabled and wheelchair anglers.

AYCLIFFE POND
Atlas Page 205 E.9/1.5

A very well stocked coarse fishery a few miles north of Darlington. Expect most coarse species, and in quite large numbers!

How to get there   Leave the north-bound A1(M) just before Newton Aycliffe and follow minor road to Aycliffe village. Look for signs to the pond; car parking on site.

Day tickets   Adult £2; junior/OAP £2.

Best methods/baits   Use any recognised coarse technique and baits.

Restrictions   No lead weights under 1oz (except No. 8 or smaller). No night fishing.

Facilities   Nearest shop/pub in Aycliffe.

BOLAM LAKE
Atlas Page 205 E.9/1.6

A country park and lake north-west of Newcastle, with plenty of perch and pike, plus rudd and golden rudd.

How to get there Take the A696 north-west from Newcastle to Belsay (about 14 miles) and bear right onto minor road to Bolam Lake (about 3 miles on). Car parking on site.

Day tickets Adult £1.50; junior/OAP 75p. Season ticket: adult £4, junior/OAP £2. Available from the Warden's hut at the lake; Tel. 0661 881234.

Best methods/baits Use any recognised coarse technique and baits.

Restrictions No lead weights under 1oz (except No. 8 or smaller). No night fishing.

Facilities Toilets on site. Nearest shop/pub in Belsay.

Disabled facilities Some swims suitable for disabled anglers.

FELLGATE POND
Atlas Page 205 F.1/0.8

A 1½-acre fishery at Hebburn, well stocked with tench, roach, perch, bream, rudd and carp. Also some good-sized chub.

How to get there Take the A194 from Gateshead to Hebburn; the fishery is behind the Lakeside Hotel. Car parking on site.

Day tickets Adult/junior/OAP £2; available on the bank.

Best methods/baits Use general coarse techniques and baits.

Restrictions No night fishing.

Facilities Nearest shop in Hebburn (2 miles); nearest pub, The Lakeside Hotel.

Disabled facilities Some swims suitable for disabled and wheelchair anglers.

FIGHTING COCKS RESERVOIR
Atlas Page 205 E.9/1.7

A 10-acre reservoir a few miles east of Darlington. Expect moderate sport, with mainly perch, roach and bream, plus a few carp.

How to get there Take the A67 east from Darlington and turn right on minor road to Middleton St. George after about 3 miles. Follow signs to the reservoir; car parking on site.

Day tickets Adult £2; junior £1.50. Season tickets: adult £20; junior £10. Available from Allenden's tackle shop near fishery entrance.

Best methods/baits Use any recognised coarse technique and baits.

Facilities Nearest shop/pub in Middleton St. George.

Perch.

HARTBURN BRICK POND
Atlas Page 207 F.7/0.9

A former brick pond set in a rural area several miles west of Morpeth, providing a good variety of coarse fish and excellent sport.

How to get there From Newcastle, take the A1 north to Morpeth and turn left onto B6343 to Hartburn (about 10 miles). The Brick Pond is on the west side of the village. Car parking nearby.

Day tickets Free fishing.

Best methods/baits Use any recognised coarse technique and baits.

Restrictions No lead weights under 1oz (except No. 8 or smaller). No night fishing.

Facilities Nearest shop/pub in Hartburn village.

Tench.

Slowing down the pace.

HEMLINGTON LAKE
Atlas Page 205 F.3/1.6

A local authority-controlled lake fishery near Middlesborough, providing a good variety of coarse fish, mainly bream, tench, with good carp and roach.

How to get there   From Middlesborough town centre take A178 towards Stokesley, cross A171 and Hemlington is signposted on the right. Follow sign to the Recreation Centre. For details of access and parking, contact local tackle shops.

Day tickets   Adult £1.50; junior/OAP 75p. Available on the bank.

Best methods/baits   Use any recognised coarse technique and baits.

Restrictions   No lead weights under 1oz (except No. 8 or smaller). No night fishing.

Facilities   Nearest shops/pubs in Middlesborough.

KILLINGWORTH LAKE
Atlas Page 207 F.8/7.3

A fairly large lake in North Tyneside, located in a residential area. A very productive fishery, with some large pike, plus plenty of roach and perch. Fishing is generally best in the early morning, when it's quiet!

How to get there   In Newcastle, drive to Killingworth (North Tyneside); Killingworth Lake is directly alongside the main road. Car parking (free) nearby.

Day tickets   Free fishing.

Best methods/baits   Use general coarse techniques and baits.

Facilities   Nearest shops and pubs are in Killingworth (½ mile).

Disabled facilities   Good access to flat banks; some swims are suitable for disabled and wheelchair anglers.

KILLINGWORTH POND
Atlas Page 207 F.8/7.3

A small ½-acre pond, adjacent to Killingworth Lake, on North Tyneside. Good mixed coarse fishing, with Crucian carp plus roach, pike and perch. Fishes best in early morning.

How to get there   Drive to Killingworth, on North Tyneside; the main road runs between Killingworth Pond and Lake. Car parking nearby.

Day tickets   Free fishing.

Best methods/baits   Use general coarse techniques and baits.

Restrictions   No lead weights under 1oz (except No. 8 or smaller). No night fishing.

Facilities   Nearest shops and pubs are in Killingworth (½ mile).

Disabled facilities   Some swims are suitable for disabled and wheelchair anglers.

LEAZES PARK LAKE
Atlas Page 207 F.8/7.3

A park lake in the centre of Newcastle, providing good coarse fishing. Mainly carp, roach, tench, bream and perch.

How to get there   From Newcastle city centre head north on the A696 towards Jedburgh; Leazes Park is about ½ mile from the Tyne Bridge, on the right of the road. Follow signs to the lake and parking areas.

Day tickets   Adult £2; junior/OAP £2. Available from John Robertson's, Haymarket, Newcastle; Tel. 091 232 2018 or from Steve Smith's, Grey Street, in Newcastle.

Best methods/baits   Use any recognised coarse technique and baits.

Restriction   No lead weights under 1oz (except No. 8 or smaller). No night fishing.
Facilities   Toilets/cafe on site. Nearest shops/pubs in Newcastle.
Disabled facilities   Some swims suitable for disabled anglers.

MARDEN QUARRY
Atlas Page 207 F.8/7.3

A former quarry on the outskirts of Whitley Bay, providing good mixed coarse fishing, with mainly carp, roach and tench.

How to get there   Take the A191 from Newcastle city centre to Whitley Bay and follow signs to the quarry. For details of access and parking, contact Paul Armstrong; Tel. 091 274 9399.
Day tickets   Adult £1.50; junior/OAP £1.50. Available from Temples Tackle Shop, Whitley Bay.
Best methods/baits   Use any recognised coarse technique and baits.
Restrictions   No lead weights under 1oz (except No. 8 or smaller). No night

Rudd.

QUEEN ELIZABETH II PARK
Atlas Page 207 F.7/0.9

A country park at Ashington, near Morpeth. Good quality fishing for bream, roach, rudd, pike and perch in a pleasant country setting.

How to get there   From Newcastle, take the A1 north to Morpeth and turn right onto A197 to Ashington. Or, take A189 via Cramlington and Blyth. At Ashington, follow signs to the park and fishery. Car parking near the lake.

Day tickets   Adult £2.50; junior/OAP £1. For details of availability and access, contact R. Gair; Tel. 0670 520056.
Best methods/baits   Use any recognised coarse technique and baits.
Restrictions   No lead weights under 1oz (except No. 8 or smaller). No night fishing.
Facilities   Nearest shops/pubs in Ashington.
Disabled facilities   Some swims suitable for disabled anglers.

ROSSMERE PARK LAKE
Atlas Page 205 F.5/1.3

A local authority-controlled park lake, close to the centre of Hartlepool, and which contains a good variety of coarse fish.

How to get there   In Hartlepool town centre, follow signs to Rossmere Park and the fishery. Car parking on site.
Day tickets   Adult £2; junior/OAP £1. Available on the bank.
Best methods/baits   Use any recognised coarse technique and baits.
Restrictions   No lead weights under 1oz (except No. 8 or smaller). No night fishing.
Facilities   Toilets in park. Nearest shops/pubs in Hartlepool.

RYTON CURLING POND
Atlas Page 207 F.8/7.3

A small coarse fishing pond at Ryton, on the western outskirts of Newcastle. Good mixed fishing, but mainly roach and perch.

How to get there   From Newcastle city centre, follow the A695 west through Blaydon to Ryton; look for signs to the pond and fisheries. Car parking nearby.
Day tickets   Free fishing for limited numbers, but ticket required from Ryton Public Library.
Best methods/baits   Use any recognised coarse technique and baits.
Restrictions   No lead weights under 1oz (except No. 8 or smaller). No night fishing.
Facilities   Nearest shops/pubs in Ryton.
Disabled facilities   Some swims suitable for disabled anglers.

A good net of roach.

RYTON WILLOWS
Atlas Page 207 F.8/7.3

A small coarse fishery at Ryton, on the western outskirts of Newcastle and close to Ryton Curling Pond. Good mixed fishing, but mainly carp, roach and perch.

How to get there From Newcastle city centre, follow the A695 west through Blaydon to Ryton; look for signs to Ryton Willows and fisheries. Car parking nearby.

Day tickets Free fishing for limited numbers, but ticket required from Ryton Public Library.

Best methods/baits Use any recognised coarse technique and baits.

Restrictions No lead weights under 1oz (except No. 8 or smaller). No night fishing.

Facilities Nearest shops/pubs in Ryton.

Disabled facilities Some swims suitable for disabled anglers.

SHOTTON POND
Atlas Page 205 F.3/1.2

A prolific fishery just west of Peterlee, which contains carp (including Crucians), roach, rudd, bream, perch and tench.

How to get there From Middlesborough, head north on the A19 and at Peterlee, turn left on minor road to Shotton Colliery village. Follow signs to the Pond and park on site.

Day tickets Adult £1.50; junior/OAP £1.50. Available from Ian Proudfoot, 19 Lincoln Walk, Gt Lumley, Chester-le-Street; Tel. 091 389 2325. *Note*: a maximum of 6 day tickets is available each day.

Best methods/baits Use any recognised coarse technique and baits.

Restrictions No lead weights under 1oz (except No. 8 or smaller). No night fishing.

Facilities Nearest shop/pub in Shotton Colliery village.

SILKSWORTH LAKE
Atlas Page 205 F.2/0.8

A popular fishery on the southern outskirts of Sunderland, providing good mixed fishing, with tench, bream, roach, rudd, carp and perch.

How to get there From Middlesborough, take the A19 to just south of Sunderland and turn right onto the A690. Turn immediately right towards Silksworth and follow signs to the lake. Car parking on site.

Day tickets Adult £2; junior/OAP £1. Only limited numbers available to visitors; obtain these from the nearby Ski Centre.

Best methods/baits Use any recognised coarse technique and baits.

Restrictions No lead weights under 1oz (except No. 8 or smaller). No night fishing.

Facilities Nearest shop/pub in Silksworth.

Disabled facilities Some swims suitable for disabled anglers.

STARGATE PONDS
Atlas Page 207 F.8/7.3

A small pond at Ryton, on the western outskirts of Newcastle and close to Ryton Curling Pond and Ryton Willows. Good mixed fishing, with a good variety of species.

How to get there From Newcastle city centre, follow the A695 west through Blaydon to Ryton; look for signs to Stargate Ponds. Car parking nearby. For details, contact local tackle shops.

Day tickets Free fishing.

Best methods/baits Use any recognised coarse technique and baits.

Restrictions No lead weights under 1oz (except No. 8 or smaller). No night fishing.

Facilities Nearest shops/pubs in Ryton.

Disabled facilities Some swims suitable for disabled anglers.

Rivers
RIVER TEES

Despite pollution problems related to local industries, the Tees, over recent years, has fought back to become one the region's main fisheries, with the Piercebridge to Low Dinsdale section providing picturesque, varied river fishing. The imminent construction of a tidal barrage will also reduce the threat to the river's lower reaches. Six *Angling Times* Hotspots are located along this length.

BARNARD CASTLE
Atlas Page 205 E.7/1.7

A very picturesque stretch of the river, downstream from Stone Bridge to Thorngate footbridge (south bank only). Expect a good variety of fish, including grayling, dace, chub, roach and barbel.

How to get there From Darlington, take the A67 west (about 15 miles) to Barnard Castle. Park nearby. Access to the river is at various points within the town centre. Check with local tackle shops for details.

Day tickets Free fishing.

Best methods/baits Use any recognised coarse technique and baits.

Restrictions No lead weights under 1oz (except No. 8 or smaller). No night fishing. Taking of salmon is prohibited.

Facilities Nearest shops/pubs in Barnard Castle.

Disabled facilities Access is difficult, but possible, for disabled anglers at some swims.

PIERCEBRIDGE
Atlas Page 205 E.8/1.7

A fast stretch running over gravel and boulders. Average depth 2- 3ft, with occasional pools and glides on bends. Mainly dace, chub and grayling, but also recent roach and barbel catches. Chub nets over 30lb, plus good dace catches.

How to get there Take the A67 Darlington-Barnard Castle road; at Piercebridge, use the car park just past the George Hotel. Fish on the right bank, below the bridge, a 3-mile stretch to Manfield Scar.

Day tickets No day tickets; membership available through Yarm AC, Stockton AC, Thornaby AA, Darlington Brown Trout AA. Contact local tackle shops for details.

Best methods Streamy water – stick float with maggot or caster. Feeders are hit and miss. For chub – straight bomb with bread hookbait.

Best baits Casters, maggots; use big baits for chub.

Facilities Food/toilets at the George Hotel.

Hotspot Tips

- Waggler tactics are best in the wider, slower glides.
- The best swims are opposite High Coniscliffe village.
- The grayling sport here is always first-class.

The River Tees.

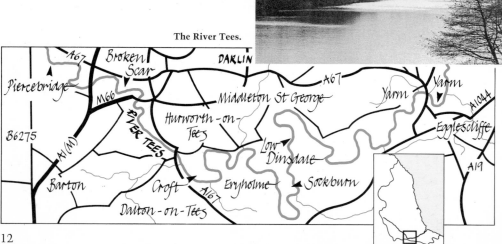

On the bank of the River Tees.

How to get there   At Croft, on the southbound A167 Darlington–Northallerton road. Park at Croft Working Men's Club (upstream) or Hurworth village hall (downstream).

Day tickets   Adult/OAP/junior £2; from D. Speight, 10 Stainsby Gate, Thornaby-on-Tees, Cleveland; Tel. 0642 672099.

Best methods   Mixed bags – waggler (stick in faster swims). Chub - leger (in cold months).

Best baits   Maggots, casters. For chub – bread or luncheon meat.

Facilities   Food/toilets at Croft Working Men's Club (check for availability).

Hotspot Tips

🐟 Swims below the bridge and island have performed best in recent matches.

BROKEN SCAR
Atlas Page 205 E.9/1.7

A 1-mile, left bank stretch, from Dam to Blackwell. Barbel sport is famous here, but other species are taken. Expect 10lb_ of grayling and dace, plus big barbel and chub – and 20lb+ pike!

How to get there   Follow the A67 Darlington-Barnard Castle road; shortly after leaving Darlington, the river runs just to the south of the road. Use the large car park.

Day tickets   Free fishing for Darlington residents only.

Best methods   Dace, grayling – stick float and waggler. Barbel - use big baits over a hemp bed.

Best baits   Chub – waspgrub (ideal), lobworm, luncheon meat, casters.

Hotspot Tips

🐟 Fish the groynes below the weir for grayling, dace and barbel.

CROFT
Atlas Page 205 E.9/1.7

A deeper section, 45 yards wide with less gravel and flat glides. Depths vary from 2–6ft; the bottom is silt or sand. Catches include dace, chub, roach, grayling, barbel, gudgeon, perch and pike. Expect 10lb-pleasure nets.

SOCKBURN
Atlas Page 205 E.9/1.7

A section of varying swims, streamy water, gravel shallows, glides and slow, deep areas. Average width 35–40 yards, with summer weed growth. Mostly dace and chub (2lb+), plus some grayling, roach and gudgeon. Typical pleasure nets are 15lb.

How to get there   Take the A167 Darlington–Northallerton road; at Croft (2 miles), bear left to Neasham village. Follow the signposts.

Day tickets   No day tickets; membership available through Yarm AC, Stockton AC, Thornaby AA, Darlington Brown Trout AA. Contact local tackle shops for details.

Best methods   Waggler or stick float according to conditions. Big chub, barbel – use big baits fished tight against the fish's cover.

Best baits   Casters, maggots, luncheon meat, bread.

Facilities   Shop in Neasham village.

Hotspot Tips

🐟 Depending on the conditions, a stick float offers better penetration in some swims.

🐟 Expect good chub and dace at Beverley Wood and the horseshoe bend – but it's a very long walk!

NEASHAM, DURHAM BANK
Atlas Page 205 E.9/1.7

A short stretch of the Tees, a few miles from Croft. Expect good catches of dace, grayling and chub. A typical Tees fishery.

How to get there   Take the A167 Darlington-Northallerton road; at Croft (2 miles), bear left to Neasham village. Follow the signs to the river. For details of access, contact Frank Flynn; Tel. 0642 672099.

Day tickets   Free fishing.

Best methods/baits   Use any recognised coarse technique and baits.

Restrictions   No lead weights under 1oz (except No. 8 or smaller). No night fishing.

Facilities   Nearest shop in Neasham village.

LOW DINSDALE
Atlas Page 205 E.9/1.7

A pretty, 25–40-yard wide stretch with a variety of swims (most are 2–3ft deep) and a weir upstream. Plenty of summer weed. Summer sport comprises dace, chub and grayling; winter sport is confined to chub and grayling. Mixed nets often reach 20lb.

How to get there   Take the A167 Darlington-Northallerton road; at Croft (2 miles), bear left to Neasham village, then towards Girsby. Park near the toll bridge.

Day tickets   No day tickets; open membership available from D. Dalziel, 357 Marton Road, Middlesborough, Cleveland.

Best methods   Waggler, stick float, swimfeeder or straight leger according to swim and conditions.

Best baits   Casters, maggots, waspgrub, bread, luncheon meat or worms.

Facilities   Shop in Neasham village.

Hotspot Tips

- For dace, fish light float gear between the streamer beds.
- For chub, fish the far bank, but you'll need heavy gear.
- Large barbel often appear in shallows above the toll bridge.

YARM
Atlas Page 205 E.9/1.7

A wide (40 yards), tidal stretch which switches banks. Depths from inches to 10ft according to tide. Little weed growth. Mainly roach, dace, chub and eels, plus bream, barbel, perch, gudgeon and carp. Fishing is even until first frosts; then expect chub at low peg numbers, with roach and dace downstream.

How to get there   Take the A67 from Darlington east to Yarm. The stretch runs from Lower Worsall (via B1264) eastwards to Egglescliffe golf course. Several parking points.

Day tickets   Adult £1.50; junior/OAP 75p; available from Frank Flynn's Tackle Shop, 12 Varco Terrace, Stockton-on-Tees; Tel. 0642 676473

Best methods   Stick float or waggler according to tide. Pole, feeder or straight leger as alternative.

Best baits   Maggots; also casters, waspgrub, bread (notably for chub). Cereal groundbait.

Facilities   Nearest shop Yarm village.

Hotspot Tips

- Local knowledge will help with constantly changing feeding habits and moving shoals.
- You'll need heavy feeding for big dace and roach shoals – so take plenty of maggots.

YARM, YORKSHIRE BANK
Atlas Page 205 E.9/1.7

A pleasant section, with depth varying according to tide. Expect good quality fishing, with plenty of roach, dace, chub, eels, bream, barbel, perch, gudgeon and carp.

How to get there   Take the A67 from Darlington east to Yarm. Fishing is on the Yorkshire bank; for details of access and parking, contact Frank Flynn's Tackle Shop; Tel. 0642 676473.

Day tickets   Free fishing.

Best methods/baits   Use any recognised coarse technique and baits.

Restrictions   No lead weights under 1oz (except No. 8 or smaller). No night fishing.

Facilities   Nearest shop/pub in Yarm village.

Rivers

RIVER WEAR

The River Wear – once the forgotten river of the north-east – is alive and flourishing, providing perhaps the region's top coarse fishing venue.The Wear's future is bright, with quality chub, barbel, plus many smaller species; enthusiasts speak of bream- stocking plans.

Day tickets are rare, but value-for-money open club membership is easily obtained with visitors most welcome. Six *Angling Times* Hotspots occur along the Maiden Castle to Chester-le-Street length of the Wear's banks.

The River Wear.

River Wear.

Atlas Page 205 E.8/1.4

Another shallow, generally fast-flowing stretch of the Wear set among the Pennines; expect good quality coarse fishing, with dace, chub, roach and barbel.

How to get there　From Bishop Auckland, take the A689 to Stanhope, then Eastgate (total about 18 miles). Access to the river is at various points; for details, contact Miss Bell; Tel. 0388 528414.

Day tickets　Adult £5; junior/OAP £2.50. Available from West End Filling Station, Stanhope.

Best methods/baits　Use any recognised coarse technique and baits.

Restrictions　No lead weights under 1oz (except No. 8 or smaller). No night fishing.

Facilities　Nearest shop, Eastgate; nearest pub, Stanhope.

SUNNYBROW TO PAGE BANK
Atlas Page 205 E.8/1.4

A very pleasant section of the river, set in countryside south-east of Willington. A good quality fishery, with plenty of roach, dace, chub and barbel.

How to get there　From Bishop Auckland take the A689 north-west about 2 miles, then turn right towards Hunwick and Willington. For details of river access and parking, contact Anglers Services; Tel. 091 384 7584.

Day tickets　Adult £2.50; junior/OAP £2.50. Available from Bonds Tackle Shop, High Street, Willington.

Best methods/baits　Use any recognised coarse technique and baits.

Restrictions　No lead weights under 1oz (except No. 8 or smaller). No night fishing.

Facilities　Nearest shops/pub in Willington.

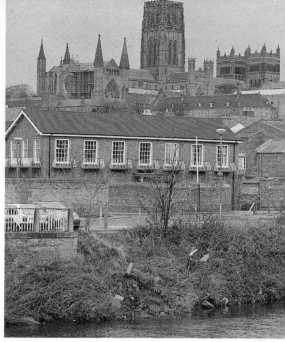

Cathedral length, River Wear.

 MAIDEN CASTLE
Atlas Page 205 E.9/1.2

A wide (35-yard) stretch, 3–4ft depth and pacey flow. Some summer weed, but not troublesome. Main species include grayling, roach, dace, chub and gudgeon, plus eels and an occasional bream or perch. Typical nets are 10lbs+, often with roach of 2lb, or chub of 3lb+.

How to get there　Upstream of Durham. Details given with club card.

Day tickets　None; Durham City AC open membership available from Martin Girwood, 62 Rosslea, Bournmoor Farm Estate, Bournmoor, Durham DH4 4PH; Tel. 091 385 4052; or from local tackle shops. Cost of membership: adult £30 and £10 entry fee; reduced rates for junior, OAP and disabled.

Best methods　Stick float and waggler rigs with light, strung- out shotting; bulk up shot in winter when flow is higher.

Best baits　Casters, maggots; large chub – luncheon meat or worms.

Hotspot Tips

✎ Try using a bomb feeder for chub and eels.

✎ Best swims are upstream of the footbridge and below the Rose Tree pub.

PREBENDS –
CATHEDRAL LENGTH
Atlas Page 205 E.9/1.2

A slow-flowing stretch, 40yds wide, shallowing downstream. Only minimal weed growth. Mostly dace, roach, gudgeon and barbel, plus an occasional bream; eels may be troublesome. Nets (dace to 12oz, roach to 2lb) often top 20lb; recent barbel match haul was 45lb.

How to get there   In Durham city centre. Prebends Bridge is halfway along the length, close to the cathedral.
Day tickets   None; Durham City AC open membership available from Ken Elleson, 32 St Monica Grove, Crossgate Moor, Durham; Tel. 091 384 1512.
Best methods   Feeder, waggler or pole according to conditions.
Best baits   Maggots, casters.
Facilities   Food/shops/toilets in city centre.

Hotspot Tips

- Keep your bait off the bottom to avoid the eels!
- Upstream of Prebends Bridge is the most reliable area (use the wall pegs).

FRANKLANDS
Atlas Page 205 E.9/1.2

This stretch averages 35yds wide and is deepest (most swims 8ft+) at its upstream end. Depths at the lower end average 3ft. streamer weed provides the fish with good cover. A prolific venue for dace and 3–4lb chub, with nets of 20lb+ quite common.

How to get there   Upstream of Durham. Details given with club card.
Day tickets   None. Durham City AC open membership available from Martin Girwood, 62 Rosslea, Bournmoor Farm Estate, Bournmoor, Durham DH4 4PH; Tel. 091 385 4052; or from local tackle shops Cost of membership: adult £30 and £10 entry fee; reduced rates for junior, OAP and disabled.
Best methods   Dace – float tactics (stick if possible, waggler if the wind is strong). Chub – feeder.
Best baits   Casters, maggots.

Hotspot Tips

- Fish for chub along the Clappergate length.
- Get the chub to feed and you could net a 50lb+ haul!

FINCHALE ABBEY
Atlas Page 205 E.9/1.2

A 2-mile stretch of the Wear, close to Finchale Priory, in very scenic surroundings. Good fishing, with roach, bream, dace and gudgeon, plus winter barbel.

How to get there   From Durham, head north on the A167 Chester- le-Street road and at Kimblesworth (about 3 miles), turn right onto minor road towards Finchale Priory (abbey).Follow signs to the river and park nearby. For details of access, contact Mr. Welsh; Tel. 091 386 6528.
Day tickets   Adult £2; junior/OAP £2. For availability, contact Mr Welsh (see above).
Best methods/baits   Use any recognised coarse technique and baits.
Restrictions   No lead weights under 1oz (except No. 8 or smaller). No night fishing.
Facilities   Nearest shop/pub in East/West Rainton.

CHESTER MOOR
Atlas Page 205 E.9/0.9

A steady-paced stretch, 35yds wide and average depth 4ft. Localised weed patches in summer. Mixed bags are common,

River Wear.

mostly dace and chub. Catches up to 14lb, but nearer 20lb if chub are feeding. Dace may also provide large nets – 33lb in a recent Championship match.

How to get there The site lies to the east of the A167, just south of Chester-le-Street.

Day tickets None; Durham City AC open membership available from Ken Elleson, 32 St Monica Grove, Crossgate Moor, Durham; Tel. 091 384 1512.

Best methods Dace and chub – stick float or waggler. Large chub - use heavy gear with a bomb or feeder.

Best baits Maggots, casters; chub – bread, waspgrub, meat.

Hotspot Tips

- In snaggy areas, heavy gear will be essential.
- For best hauls, fish just above or below the stream mouth.

Eels can be a nuisance.

CREIGHTON AVENUE
Atlas Page 205 E.9/0.9

A 35-yard wide stretch averaging 4–5ft in depth; some weed may appear, but is trouble-free. Catches consist mainly of dace, roach, chub, plus the odd barbel, gudgeon, perch or bream. Eels are a nuisance, but if using float tackle, nets can average 4–6lb.

How to get there Chester-le-Street. Park at the playing fields on Riverside Park, on the A167 heading out of town.

Day tickets Adult//OAP/junior £1.25; season ticket: Adult £15; junior £5; available from Armstrong's Tackle in Chester-le-Street town centre; Tel. 091 388 2154.

Best methods Ideal float fishing water; locals use waggler, but stick float is ideal in most conditions.

Best baits Maggots, casters.

Hotspot Tips

- Try for a big chub using legered bread, worm or luncheon meat.
- Keep your bait off the bottom to avoid the eels.
- For dace, look for a fast flow in summer, but a slower flow in winter.

LUMLEY BRIDGE
Atlas Page 205 E.9/0.9

A variable stretch of 30–35yds width. Above the weir are deep, slow-moving swims (up to 10ft); below the weir, water is shallower and more pacey, with good float fishing.Expect dace, roach, gudgeon, chub, eels, barbel, plus some bream or perch. Bumper nets are taken from deep water in winter.

How to get there In the centre of Chester-le-Street; park opposite Lumley Castle. The river stretch is upstream of Lumley Bridge, on the right-hand bank.

Day tickets Adult/junior/OAP £1.25; season ticket: adult £15; junior £5; available from Armstrong's Tackle in Chester-le- Street town centre Tel. 091 388 2154.

Best methods When water is low and clear, use stick float and waggler tactics; when water is up and coloured, use a pole, on the inside line.

Best baits Maggots, casters; chub, barbel – use bigger baits (bomb).

Facilities Food/shops/toilets in town centre.

Hotspot Tips

- Fish the shallow gravels downstream for barbel of 7lb+.
- In clear water, the waggler at range is the better method for starters.
- For reliable, good quality sport, swims between the bridge and weir are hard to beat.

Looking upstream towards the bridge at Chollerford on the Tyne.

WELLFIELD POND
Atlas Page 205 F.3/2.2

A quite large pond located at Wingate, a few miles west of Peterlee, which provides excellent coarse fishing. Expect good quality catches of bream, tench, carp, rudd, roach and perch.

How to get there   Take the A19 north from Middlesborough to Wheatley Hill (12 miles) and turn left onto A181 to Wingate. Follow signs to Wellfield Pond and park nearby. For more details, contact Alan Blackmore; Tel. 091 526 7327; or Ken's Angling, Tel. 0429 272581.

Day tickets   Adult £1.50; junior/OAP 75p; joining fee £7.50; annual membership £7.50. Tickets must be obtained through a member of Easington District Anglers. Some guest tickets are available; contact Alan Blackmore for details (see above).

Best methods/baits   Use any recognised coarse technique and baits.

Restrictions   No lead weights under 1oz (except No. 8 or smaller). No night fishing.

Facilities   Nearest shop/pub in Wingate.

Disabled facilities   Some swims suitable for disabled anglers.

The Barbel.

North-West Region

Fishing for pike at Bassenthwaite.

CHESHIRE

Atlas Page 204 D.2/4.3

BRIDGEWATER CANAL
A 15-mile stretch of canal from Broadheath Bridge, Altrincham, to Preston Brook, near Runcorn. Excellent fishing early morning or early evening, with plenty of carp, bream and roach. Also tremendous pike fishing.

How to get there From Altrincham, head west on the A56. Various access points and parking areas are available along the canal stretch. For details, contact Trev's Tackle, 16 Altrincham Road, Wilmslow, Cheshire; Tel. 0625 528831.

Day tickets Annual tickets only: £15 plus £15 joining fee. Available from Warrington Anglers, P.O. Box 71, Warrington, WA1 1LR.

Best methods Use any recognised coarse technique.

Best baits Most baits work well. Use bread punch for winter roach.

Restrictions No night fishing. No bloodworm.

Facilities Various shops and pubs along the canal stretch.

Disabled facilities Some swims suitable for disabled anglers (subject to access).

CAPESTHORNE HALL
Atlas Page 204 D.9/4.4
A small pond situated to the west of Macclesfield. Well stocked with small carp and tench, but limited peg numbers. An ideal venue for beginners and youngsters.

How to get there Take the A34 south from Wilmslow, through Alderley Edge towards Congleton. Capesthorne Hall is on the right, about 5 miles beyond Alderley Edge; look for signs to the lake and car park.

Day tickets Adult/junior/OAP £3. Available on the bank or from Mr Bradley; Tel. Siddington 861584.

Best methods/baits Use any recognised coarse technique.

Facilities Toilets on site. Nearest shop/pub Monks Heath.

Disabled facilities Some swims suitable for disabled and wheelchair anglers.

Long and narrow in shape, the North-West Region of the NRA stretches from the northern, mountainous re-gions of Cumbria, south through the heavily urbanised and indus-trialised districts of Man-chester and Liverpool, to the rolling, rural areas of Cheshire.

Such variety of scenery leads in turn to variety in coarse fishing offered. In Cumbria, for example, while the lakes and tarns of the Lake District are known for their quality roach and bream, it's the size, and ferocity, of their large pike that sticks in the angler's memory!

Further south, around Merseyside and Greater Manchester, the waterways are dominated by a network of slow-flowing canals, among which are the Leeds–Liverpool and the Bridgewater. These provide gentle, deep, slower-flowing waters which nonetheless produce exciting sport for the coarse angler, often with large catches of carp, tench and bream. The River Ribble offers some good quality fishing ranging from rural to motorway-side.

Moving further south still, to Cheshire and the tip of Derbyshire, river fishing is confined mainly to the Dane and Weaver, although the Macclesfield Canal offers some splendid coarse sport. In addition, a host of smaller lakes and ponds provide the angler with ample opportunity to pit his or her wits against some quality fish, with large carp and bream the main targets.

CHESHIRE FISHING, TATTENHALL
Atlas Page 204 D.2/4.8

A group of three lakes, midway between Chester and Nantwich. Depth varies from 6–8 ft, with 10ft holes; best fishing is in the deeper water. Plenty of roach, tench and bream, but sport is mainly carp, with commons and mirrors to 20lb. Typical nets are 20–45lb; the record is 170lb!

How to get there Take the M56/M53 to Chester and from the bypass head south on A41 towards Whitchurch. After 6 miles, turn left on minor road to Tattenhall. Drive to top of High Street, turn left towards Burwardsley. Cheshire Fishing is signposted on the left, after 1½ miles. Car parking on site.

Day tickets Adult/junior/OAP £6.50. Available on site (from 0800).

Best methods/baits Pole with maggots, sweetcorn or meat works best. Boilies generally produce poor results.

Restrictions No peanuts or tiger nuts. No fish over 1lb in keepnets.

Facilities Nearest shop/pub in Tattenhall.

Disabled facilities Some swims may be suitable for disabled anglers. For advice, Tel. 0829 70041.

CHORLTON WATER PARK
Atlas Page 204 D.9/4.1

A small lake in a town centre Water Park near Manchester, containing mainly specimen carp.

How to get there Leave the M56 at jct 3 and follow A56 towards Manchester, bearing left to Chorlton-cum-Hardy. The Water Park is situated near the southern cemetery in Chorlton; look for signs to the lake and car park (pay & display).

Day tickets Adult £3; reductions for juniors/OAPs. Available on the bank.

Best methods/baits Use mainly specialist carp techniques.

Restrictions No bloodworm.

Facilities Nearest shops/pubs in Chorlton town centre.

Disabled facilities Some swims suitable for disabled and wheelchair anglers.

Rivers

RIVER DANE

After rising in the Derbyshire hills, the River Dane meanders westwards through Cheshire, gaining in size before its confluence with the Weaver. The Dane was previously subject to flash-flooding, but has in many areas been tamed so that flow is often lacking. The Byley to Croxton section has long been recognised for excellent its chub and dace: now, the Dane holds good stocks of roach, gudgeon, barbel, carp and bream – plus an occasional surprise trout!

Five *Angling Times* Hotspots are located along this stretch of the Dane.

BYLEY ABOVE
Atlas Page 204 D.7/4.7

Upstream of Byley Bridge: a medium-paced stretch (except in spate); depth is 2–4ft, with marginal/streamer weed in summer. Summer sport centres on chub, dace and gudgeon, with more roach in winter. Typical pleasure nets 15lb, but closer to 50lb if the chub feed!

How to get there Leave the M6 at jct 18; take the A54 Middlewich road. After 2½ miles, turn right on the B5081 towards Byley. Cross the river bridge, park in the lane entrance. River access (both banks, **upstream**) is from the bridge (over stiles) A few pegs only available.

Day tickets £2; available from bailiffs on the bank or Dave's of Middlewich; Tel. 060684 3853.

Best methods Summer chub – use stick float (with shirt-button shotting) or Avon float (bulked 12" from the hook with large dropper shot).

Best baits Feeding chub – meat and bread, plus bronze/red maggots as change baits; casters are good in summer.

Hotspot Tips

- Quivertip gear can also be very effective for chub.
- Pegs 35, 36, 38 and 40 provide the best sport; in cold weather, Peg 40 is brilliant for dace.
- For a big, summer chub, try a big lump of meat under a stick or balsa Avon.

BYLEY BELOW
Atlas Page 204 D.7/4.7

Downstream of Byley Bridge: a medium-paced stretch; average depth 2–4ft; summer marginal/streamer weed. Summer sport centres on chub, dace and gudgeon, with more roach in winter. Typical pleasure nets 15lb, or 50lb when the chub feed – the match record here is 54lb!

How to get there   Leave the M6 at jct 18; take the A54 Middlewich road. After 2½ miles, turn right on the B5081 towards Byley. Cross the river bridge, park in the lane entrance. River access (both banks, **downstream**) is from the bridge (over stiles).

Day tickets   £2; available from bailiffs on the bank.

Best methods   Find the pacier water and use either float gear or the quivertip.

Best baits   Feeding chub – meat and bread, plus bronze/red maggots as change baits; casters are good in summer.

Hotspot Tips

✎ The glides above the rapids always hold large numbers of fish.

✎ Aim for Pegs 44 or 46 in winter, and 49–57 in summer; Pegs 59, 70 and 72 also provide good action.

CROXTON
Atlas Page 204 D.7/4.7

A left-bank fishery, slow paced, some summer weed growth. Expect a good variety of fish – chub, roach plus dace – 10lb+ nets of dace are quite common. Barbel and chub are large here and worth a try. In winter, the best pegs are just downstream from the footbridge.

How to get there   Leave the M6 at jct 18 and take the A54 to Middlewich. On leaving the one-way system, take 1st right (Croxton Lane) as far as the bridge; the fishery is on the right. The top length is accessed from King Street bridge.

Day tickets   £2; available on the bank.

Best methods   Roach, dace – stick float; chub, barbel – leger with meat.

Best baits   Barbel – hemp as feed plus meat hookbait; roach, dace – bronze maggots are best.

Facilities   Food/toilets in town centre.

Hotspot Tips

✎ The barbel hotspot is at the bottom of the weir.

✎ If the river is flooded, try just below the River Croco's mouth.

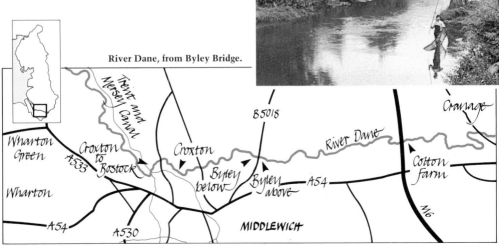

River Dane, from Byley Bridge.

The River Dane.

CROXTON TO BOSTOCK
Atlas Page 204 D.7/4.7

A far-from dramatic stretch, with marginal summer weed. The pace can become fairly high. The sport will be very varied, but expect roach, dace and chub for most of your catch. Summer bream and carp will probably put in an appearance.

How to get there   Leave the M6 at jct 18 and take the A54 to Middlewich. On leaving the one-way system, take 1st right (Croxton Lane) as far as the bridge; the fishery is on the right. Both banks are fishable; access to the right bank is easiest, via a towpath.

Day tickets   £2; available on the bank.

Best methods   Stick float or leger, according to your target!

Best baits   Roach – bronze maggot with hemp.

Disabled facilities   Good access to fishery via the towpath.

Hotspot Tips

- Legering is the most effective approach for good chub.
- Find some weed and the fish will keep coming for much longer!

COTTON FARM
Atlas Page 204 D.7/4.7

Depth here is up to 4ft, with a nice flow between beds of marginal weed. Mainly dace, roach and chub, with roach becoming predominant later in the season. A normal catch should top 15lb of dace and roach, but will quickly double if you find the chub.

How to get there   Leave the M6 at jct 18 and take the A54 Holmes Chapel road. Cotton Farm is situated close to the motorway.

Day tickets   £2; available from Cotton Farm.

Best methods   Stick or balsa float in the streamy swims. Chub – leger plus big bait (luncheon meat).

Best baits   Roach, dace, chub – maggots or casters.

Hotspot Tips

- Hemp can be a good holding feed for those bigger fish.
- Pegs immediately below the car park are usually provide the best catches.

KING GEORGE V POOL
Atlas Page 204 D.9/4.2

A small, shallow lake of about 3 acres, controlled by Trafford Metropolitan Council, and providing easy fishing. Mainly small carp, but some into double figures and some specimen fish of 20lb+.

How to get there   Take the A54 Manchester-Northwich road to Altrincham and follow signs to the pool. Car parking nearby.

Day tickets   Adult £1.40, evening 90p; junior/OAP 70p, evening 45p; season tickets: adult £23; junior/OAP £10. Available from the bailiff on the bank.

Best methods/baits   Use any recognised coarse technique or baits; carp methods advised.

Facilities   Nearest shops/pubs in Altrincham.

LYMM DAM
Atlas Page 204 D.5/4.3

A 15-acre lake near Warrington, containing bream, roach, pike and a few catfish, but most well known for a few huge carp – recent specimens of 30lb have been taken. A popular match water.

How to get there   From Warrington, head east on the A56 to Lymm (about 4 miles). Pass through Lymm; the lake is on the right. Parking nearby.

Day tickets   Weekday: adult £2; junior/OAP £1. Weekend: adult £2.50; junior/OAP £1.25. Available from bailiffs on the bank.

Best methods   Carp – use advanced carp methods. Other species - use any recognised coarse technique.

Best baits   Carp – high protein boilies.

Facilities   Nearest shop/pub in Lymm Village.

MACCLESFIELD CANAL
Atlas Page 205 E.2/4.5

A wide canal stretch in Macclesfield town centre, with fishing best in early morning or late evening to avoid large boat traffic. Mainly bream, roach and perch, plus a few carp.

How to get there   Take the A537 east from Macclesfield town centre towards Buxton. On leaving the town the road passes over the canal; fish either side of the bridge. Park on the road nearby.

Day tickets   Adult/junior/OAP £1. Available on the bank.

Best methods/baits   Use any recognised coarse technique or baits.

Facilities   Nearest toilets/shops/pubs in Macclesfield.

Disabled facilities   Some swims suitable for disabled and wheelchair anglers.

MARPLE LAKES
Atlas Page 205 E.1/4.2

A group of lakes in Marple, near Stockport. An excellent carp water, plus plenty of roach and tench.

How to get there   From Stockport, take the A656 east to Marple; on leaving Marple, look for signs to the lakes. Car parking nearby.

Day tickets   Adult £4; junior/OAP £2. Available on the bank.

Best methods/baits   Use any recognised coarse technique and baits.

Restrictions   Use barbless hooks only. No keepnets. No night fishing.

Facilities   Toilets/cafe on site. Nearest shop/pub in Marple.

MIDDLEWICH CANAL
Atlas Page 205 E.2/4.5

A canal stretch running from just north of Nantwich, north-east to Middlewich, in all about 8 miles long. Expect good catches of coarse fish, including bream, roach and lots of eels, despite heavy summer boat traffic. Also large carp, to 20lb+. In winter, expect more roach and gudgeon. Best fishing is at Cholmondeston, between Wardle and Church Minshull.

How to get there   From Nantwich, head north-west on the A51 about 4 miles to Wardle. Access to the canal is at various points along the canal between Wardle and Middlewich. Check with John Harding, the Water Board bailiff for best fishing spots and free parking; Tel. 0829 732748.

Day tickets   Adult £1.50; junior (12–16)/OAP £1. Also monthly tickets: adult £5; junior/OAP £2. Available on the bank or from local tackle shops.

Best methods/baits   Use general coarse techniques and baits. Castor is good for roach.

Restrictions Night fishing with permission only.
Facilities Various shops/pubs/toilets/food along the route.
Disabled facilities Some swims are suitable for disabled and wheelchair anglers; please phone the Bailiff for advice.

POYNTON POOL
Atlas Page 205 E.1/4.2

A long lake, with depth 2–10ft, providing excellent coarse fishing, a few miles south-east of Stockport. Expect large numbers of small fish (mostly roach) that are ideal for beginners, plus larger fish for experienced anglers. Also bream, carp and tench.

How to get there Take the main A6 south-east from Stockport towards Whaley Bridge. After about 5 miles, bear right on A523 to Poynton village; the pool runs alongside the main road, about ¼ mile north of the village centre. Car parking nearby, off South Park Drive.
Day tickets Adult £1.50; junior/OAP 65p. Also season ticket: £8.50. Available on the bank; day tickets permit fishing only from the *field* side.
Best methods/baits Use waggler, pole or leger with maggots. Groundbait is not needed here.
Restrictions No keepnets. No night fishing.
Facilities Nearest shop 1 mile; nearest pub in Poynton (¼ mile).
Disabled facilities Some swims suitable for disabled and wheelchair anglers.

REDESMERE
Atlas Page 204 D.9/4.4

A very large estate lake of 58 acres, containing large numbers of bream, pike, tench, Crucian carp, roach and perch, plus over 150 mirror and common carp of 10lb+ and over 40 at 20lb+. One of the best carp waters in the north west, but often difficult fishing.

How to get there Take the A34 from Alderley Edge towards Congleton; At Sidington (about 6 miles) look for signs to Capesthorne Estate and the fishery. Car parking on site.
Day tickets Season tickets only (also some guests). Available from Stoke-on-Trent A.S.; Mr S Broadgate, Lynton, 5 Kingsfield Oval, Basford, Stoke-on-Trent. Contact the bailiff for details; Tel. 0625 520061. Apply to Mr Broadgate, preferably with a sponsor who is a club member.
Best methods/baits Use any recognised coarse technique or baits; special carp methods may be required.
Facilities Nearest shop/pub in Siddington.

RUDYARD LAKE, NR. LEEK
Atlas Page 205 E.2/4.5

A large lake, a few miles north of Leek, which provides very good summer roach and bream fishing, plus excellent pike fishing in autumn/winter. A very popular match venue.

How to get there From Macclesfield, head south on the A523 towards Leek. Rudyard Lake is on the right, after about 7 miles; look for signs to the lake and car park.
Day tickets Adult/junior/OAP £2. Available on the bank.
Best methods/baits Use any recognised coarse technique or baits. Pole is preferred method.
Facilities Nearest shop/pub in Rudyard village.
Disabled facilities Some swims suitable for disabled and wheelchair anglers.

SALE WATER
Atlas Page 204 D.8/4.2

A mixed fishery on the south-eastern outskirts of Manchester, providing excellent facilities for a good day's fishing. Watersports on the water. Plenty of sport, with lots of carp, roach, bream, perch, tench and chub.

How to get there Leave the M63 at jct 8 and follow the signposts to Sale and Sale Water. Car parking on site.
Day tickets Adult £2.80, Sunday and Bank Holidays £3.40; junior/OAP £1.80. Available from main building; more expensive on the bank.
Best methods/baits Use any recognised coarse technique and baits. Legering is preferred method.
Facilities Cafe/bar/toilets/shop/pub all available on site.
Disabled facilities Some swims suitable for disabled and wheelchair anglers.

SANKEY CANAL, WARRINGTON
Atlas Page 204 D.5/4.2

A recently restored canal with no access for boats, providing good, quiet fishing. Stocked with trout during the spring, it holds good rudd and bream, fishes well for tench in the early part of the season. The carp run to 25lb, the pike close to 30lb.

How to get there   From Warrington, take the A57 to Liverpool and cross the canal shortly after leaving the town. There are various access points by turning either right or left at the first traffic lights.

Day tickets   Weekday: adult £1.50; junior/OAP 75p. Weekends: adults £2; junior/OAP £1. All tickets 50p cheaper in the winter. Available on the bank.

Best methods/baits   General coarse fishing.

Restrictions   No bloodworm, joker, live or dead bait or keepnets. Barbless hooks are recommended.

Facilities   Toilets are at various sites along the canal. Also plenty of shops and pubs in Warrington.

Disabled facilities   Access is fairly good for disabled and wheelchair anglers.

A good selection.

SHAKERLEY MERE
Atlas Page 204 D.5/4.5

A 17-acre mere, set in a country park close to the M6 motorway. A renowned carp fishery, with plenty of double figure mirrors and commons, plus a good head of mixed coarse species – tench, roach, perch, rudd and bream. Generally even fishing, but pegs 1–16 produce the best sport.

How to get there   Leave the M6 at jct 19, head towards Northwich on the A556 and turn left on B5082 (signposted Holmes Chapel). Continue to the B5081 junction and turn left; the lake is 1st right. Car park access is from the B5081.

Day tickets   Weekday: adult £2; junior/OAP £1. Weekend: adult £2.50; junior/OAP £1.25. Available on the bank.

Best methods/baits   Most methods work, but float with maggots is best.

Facilities   Nearest shop/pub in Byley.

Disabled facilities   Some swims may be suitable for disabled anglers.

SHROPSHIRE UNION CANAL
Atlas Page 204 D.1–D.5/4.5

The Shropshire Union Canal runs through some 25 miles of Cheshire countryside, from Ellesmere Port to Nantwich. Excellent coarse fishing all the way, with good catches of bream, dace, tench and roach, plus increasing numbers of carp. Summer hotspots include Chester Basin, Backford, Chester town and Waverton (Egg Bridge and Golden Nook). In winter, try Christleton, Tattenhall, Shady Oak and Bunbury Staircase locks for good sport.

How to get there   Access to the canal can be gained at various turnings off the main A51 Ellesmere Port to Nantwich road. For details of fishing places and free parking, contact John Harding, the British Waterways Bailiff; Tel. 0829 732748.

Day tickets   Adult £1.50; junior (12–16)/OAP £1. Also monthly tickets: adult £5; junior/OAP £2. Available on the bank or from local tackle shops.

Best methods/baits   Most methods and baits work well here, but bloodworm is very good for tench, and casters work well for roach, dace and bream.

Restrictions   Night fishing with permission only.

Facilities   Various shops/pubs/toilets/food along the route.

Disabled facilities   Some swims are suitable for disabled and wheelchair anglers; please phone the Bailiff for advice (see above).

STATHAM POOL, LYMM
Atlas Page 204 D.2/4.3

A 1-acre pool with average depth 4–5 feet, holding roach, rudd, a fair number of tench, bream, crucian and mirror carp to double figures.

How to get there   From jct 20 on the M6, follow the B5158 to Lymm. After 2 miles, at the junction with the A56, turn left and at the second bus stop on the left, turn right into Barsbank Lane. Follow the road under the canal, over the railway and to Statham Post Office. The pool is on the right.

Day tickets   Weekdays: adults £2; junior/OAP £1. Weekends: adult £2.50; junior/OAP £1.25. Available from Statham Post Office.

Best methods/baits   Loose fed maggots, the fish often take on the drop.

Restrictions   No groundbait, bloodworm, joker, live or dead bait. No keepnets. Barbless hooks are recommended.

Facilities   No toilets. Nearest shop is the Post Office; nearest pub, the Star Inn (¼ mile).

Disabled facilities   There is limited access for disabled and wheelchair anglers, two swims only being suitable.

STOCK POOL
Atlas Page 205 E.1/4.7

A very small (¼-acre) stock pond at Capesthorne Estate, containing plenty of small carp with some up to 15lb, and providing easy fishing. The ideal venue for the beginner or youngsters.

How to get there   Take the A34 from Alderley Edge towards Congleton; At Sidington (about 6 miles) look for signs to Capesthorne Estate and the fishery. Car parking on site.

Day tickets   Adult/junior/OAP £6 full day, £3 half day; under 15s require adult with them. Bookable in advance only from the bailiff, Mr Bradley; Tel. 0625 861584.

Best methods/baits   Use any recognised coarse technique and baits.

Facilities   Nearest shop/pub in Siddington.

Disabled facilities   Very suitable for disabled and wheelchair anglers.

TETTON LAKE
Atlas Page 204 D.8/4.8

A large lake caused by subsidence of former salt workings, near Middlewich. Tetton is the northern half of the lake, providing 4 acres of good quality fishing, with depths of 2–20ft. Expect large tench and bream, plus roach, small Crucian carp, perch and rudd. Big (20lb+) carp have also been taken here. Pegs 68 to 82 only are available.

How to get there   Leave the M6 at jct 17 and take A543 to Sandbach, then A533 towards Middlewich. At Elworth (chemical works on right), turn left over the canal bridge. The lake is on the left; car parking on site.

Day tickets   Adult £2.50; junior/OAP £2.50. Available on the bank or from Dave's of Middlewich; Tel. 060684 3853.

Best methods   Most methods work well here.

Best baits   Caster is best all-round bait. Bream, tench, Crucian carp – in summer, use sweetcorn or bread. Perch, roach – use maggot.

Restrictions   Fishing is only from the *west* bank.

Facilities   Nearest shop/pub in Elworth village.

Disabled facilities   Some swims may be suitable for disabled anglers.

VILLAGE POOL, WHITLEY
Atlas Page 204 D.2/4.3

A village pond of about ½ acre, well stocked with most coarse fish and some large carp ranging from 15–21lb.

How to get there   Leave the M56 at jct 10 and head south on the A559. Whitley village is on the right; look for signs to the pool and park nearby.

Day tickets   Lymm AC members only – £35 first year, £23 second year; reduction for juniors, ladies and pensioners. Available from Lymm A.C. Secretary, S. Griffiths, 18 Manor Way, Lymm; Tel. 0925 752763.

Best methods/baits   Use any recognised coarse technique and baits. Specialist carp methods may be needed.

Facilities   Nearest shop/pub in Whitley village.

Rivers

RIVER WEAVER

The River Weaver.

A 25-yard-wide section, with level bottom and average 9ft depth, drops sharply away nearside, but shelves gently up at the far bank. Steady flow, no weed growth, but some rush fringing. Mainly roach, with some bream; catches may top 30lb. Summer tench and carp are excellent (last year's best carp was 23lb).

How to get there   Follow the main A54 Winsford to Middlewich road. Just outside Winsford, take Rilshaw Lane and drive down to the river.

Day tickets   £1.50; available from the bailiff on the bank.

Best methods   For specimen fish, use quivertip-feeder combination plus brown crumb balls. Fish 2lb mainline with 12oz bottom and 22 hook.

Best baits   Maggots, casters and brown crumb, plus additives.

Hotspot Tips

🦐 Mini-boilies are great for tench and the odd carp.

🦐 Best fishing is from pegs 135 to 140.

The River Weaver, which drains the Cheshire plains, offers superb sport to anglers. The stretch between Rilshaw and Meadowbank is slow-moving and largely unaffected by flooding, but flow and level can vary widely according to the operations of local locks. The river's present mainstay is roach, with prime fish of over 1lb, while bream and tench can appear anywhere along its length. More recently, large carp – over 20lb – have added a further dimension to the river's sporting attractions.

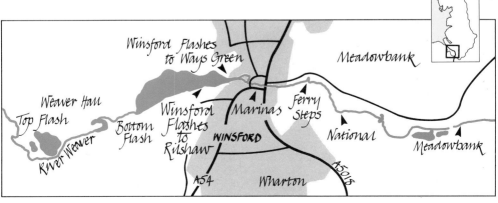

WINSFORD FLASHES TO WAYS GREEN
Atlas Page 204 D.5/4.7

Subsidence from local salt workings has produced this 250-yard- wide section, which is fed and drained by the main river. Flow and weed growth minimal, average depth 12ft. Summer – expect roach (to 1lb) and bream (to 4lb), plus 10lb+ carp; catches may reach 30lb+. Winter – expect roach and bream.

How to get there   Park at the marina alongside the main A54 road, and walk down to the section.

Day tickets   £1.50; available from the bailiff on the bank.

Best methods   Summer – waggler or sliding float; use a pole in 8ft swims, with 2lb main line, 12oz hooklength and 22 hook.

Best baits   Maggots, casters, brown crumb, plus additives.

Facilities   Food/toilets at the marina.

Hotspot Tips

- For good carp, try legering boilies at a distance.
- Peg 240 is noted for bream; Peg 244 is noted for carp, especially in heavy water.
- Heaviest catches are taken when fishing the feeder.

MARINAS
Atlas Page 204 D.5/4.7

A 25-yard-wide stretch; steady flow and even bottom, average depth 9ft and little weed growth. Roach all year, plus some gudgeon, bream or carp. Summer catches average 8lb, but in winter (when the stretch can be solid with fish), this rises to 15lb. A 3lb+ roach has been taken from these waters.

How to get there   The Marinas lie adjacent to the main A54 road, on the Middlewich side of Winsford. Parking is plentiful. Walk down-river from the car park to pegs under the road bridge.

Day tickets   £1.50; available from the bailiff on the bank.

Best methods   Waggler or stick float; fine tackle is essential.

Best baits   Summer – casters, maggots (tares in hot weather); winter – hemp, casters, bronze maggots to keep shoals feeding.

Facilities   Shops/food/toilets available at the Marinas.

Hotspot Tips

- Stepping up tackle strength will cope with those 10lb+ carp!
- Fish pack under the bridge in winter; Peg 194 is ideal.
- Loosefeed with bronze maggots (6 per cast) to keep fish feeding.

A respectable carp.

FERRY STEPS
Atlas Page 204 D.5/4.7

A wide (50 yards), curved section where flow is slow on the outside bend and there is no weed growth. Depth ranges from 8–12ft. Summer fishing includes roach (10lb catches) but centres on carp (up to 22lb) and tench (up to 6lb); winter sport centres on roach.

How to get there   Park in the Marina off the main A54 road and walk along the Red Lion section, down-river. Ferry Steps lies between Pegs 110 and 148.

Day tickets   £1.50; available from the bailiff on the bank.

Best methods   Roach – bronze maggot or caster on very fine tackle. Carp – hair-rigged boilies.

Best baits   Summer – bronze maggots, casters; winter – maggots.

Facilities   Food/shop/toilets at the Marina.

Hotspot Tips

- The carp have a taste for fruit-flavoured baits and fish-oil specials.
- Fish Pegs 142–148 for the best carp.

NATIONAL
Atlas Page 204 D.5/4.7

A medium-flow section of the river, 35 yards wide and average depth 10ft. Weed growth is minimal, and only on the nearside, shallow edge. Expect roach (with nets to 16lb), skimmer bream, tench (to 4lb) and carp (to 20lb) in summer, but roach only after the first winter frosts.

How to get there   Take the A54 from Middlewich; turn right onto the A533. After the railway bridge, take 2nd right, cross a second railway bridge. Turn left down track by scrapyard; continue ½ mile to the river.

Day tickets   £1.50; available from the bailiff on the bank.

Best methods   Fish the deeper water between the middle and near side. Use quivertip or slider float with fine tackle.

Best baits   Bronze maggots, casters in summer.

Hotspot Tips

🐟 Boilies are best for those specimen carp.

🐟 Aim for Pegs 105–110 for carp, or Pegs 74–78 and 90–94 for roach.

A bleak outlook on the Wear.

MEADOWBANK
Atlas Page 204 D.5/4.7

Average depth here is 10ft, with deeper regions nearside; the far bank is shallower. The medium flow can stop, or even back up. In summer, expect roach and tench, plus gudgeon and skimmer bream, with mixed catches of 30lb. In winter, Crucian carp – last year's best was 26lb – may appear with roach and gudgeon.

How to get there   At the Winsford town bridge roundabout on the A54, take the Whitegate turn along Bradford New Road. Go 2 miles past the ICI plant, turn right over bridges. The Pegs are upstream of this point.

Day tickets   £1.50; available from the bailiff on the bank.

Best methods   Using light tackle, pole-fish deep water on the inside, fishing over the ledge. Winter – use 12-metre pole, or leger.

Best baits   Summer – hemp, maggots, bronze maggots; winter - maggots or casters.

Hotspot Tips

🐟 Try Pegs 1–15 for roach, 20–25 for tench and carp; Pegs 55–60 are best in winter.

The River Weaver.

CUMBRIA

A fair sized pike.

BIGLAND HALL, NEWBY BRIDGE
Atlas Page 204 C.9/2.3

A 10–12-acre lake providing mixed coarse fishing, situated just south of Newby Bridge. The lake is full of perch, roach, tench (to 7lb), bream, carp (to 22lb) and eels, plus some fair-sized pike (to 15lb).

How to get there   Leave the M6 at jct 36 and take the A6, then A590 towards Barrow-in-Furness. At Newby Bridge (about 12 miles from M6) turn left to Brow Edge. Bigland Hall is at the T-junction after 1½ miles. Free parking on site.

Day tickets   Adult £4.50; junior/OAP £2 (two rods). Half-day (1400 onwards): adult £2.50; junior/OAP £1. Available from Bigland Hall County Sports, Backbarrow, Newby Bridge; Tel. 05395 31361.

Best methods   Most methods work; waggler preferred, two lengths out at shelf.

Best baits   Most baits work; maggots preferred.

Restrictions   No bloodworm. No livebait for pike.

Facilities   Toilets nearby. Nearest shop 1 mile; nearest pub 1½ miles.

Disabled facilities   Disabled and wheelchair anglers may fish with prior notice.

CLEABARROW TARN
Atlas Page 204 D.0/2.0

A small, picturesque, well-stocked lake a few miles east of Windermere, with large tench, crucian carp, rudd, plus common and mirror carp. Fishing in season only 16th June to 14th March.

How to get there   From north of Kendal by-pass, take the B5284 west via Crook towards Bowness-on-Windermere. The fishery is 4 miles on the right, just before Windermere golf club. Park on the roadside.

Day tickets   Adult/junior/OAP £3. Available from Carlsons Fishing Tackle, 64–66 Kirkland, Kendal; Tel. 0539 724867.

Best methods   Float fishing; also freelining.

Best baits   Maggots, sweetcorn, bread, boilies.

Restrictions   No spinning. No groundbait, loosefeed only.

Facilities   Nearest shop Windermere (2 miles); nearest pub, The Wild Boar, Crook (1½ miles).

ESTHWAITE WATER
Atlas Page 204 D.0/2.0

A very large (300 acres) peaceful lake lying between Windermere and Coniston Water, with specimen pike (to 36lb).

How to get there   Take the A593 south from Ambleside and at Clappersgate (1 mile) turn left onto B5286 to Hawkshead, then bear right onto minor road signposted to Newby Bridge; the lake is on the left when leaving Hawkshead. Free car parking on site.

Day tickets   Winter: adults £6.50; OAPs £3.00; under 12s free with adult. Summer: adult £9.50; OAPs £5.00; under 12s free with adult. Available from local tackle shops or Tel. 05394 36541 for details. Boat hire (rowing) available on site.

Best methods   Specialist pike fishing.

Best baits   Usual pike baits.

Facilities   Nearest shop Hawkshead (½ mile); nearest pub, Tower Bank Arms, nr Sawrey (2 miles).

Disabled facilities   Some swims suitable for disabled anglers; no wheelchair access.

GRASMERE
Atlas Page 204 D.0/2.0

A large, natural and very scenic lake just north of Windermere. Excellent perch and pike fishing with deadbait. Specimen pike to 30lb are common.

How to get there Take the A591 north through Windermere and Ambleside. The lake is on the left, just before Grasmere village. Park on the roadside.

Day tickets Adult £3.45; junior £1.75. Weekly ticket: adult £6.90; junior £3.45. Available from Carlsons Fishing Tackle, 64– 66 Kirkland, Kendal; Tel. 0539 724867.

Best methods Perch – leger with deadbait.

Best baits Deadbaits.

Restrictions No maggots or cheese. No livebaiting.

Facilities Nearest shop Grasmere (about 2 miles); nearest pub, Prince of Wales.

HOLEHIRD, TROUTBECK
Atlas Page 204 D.0/2.0

A small, picturesque lake situated near Troutbeck, north of Windermere. A very good mixed coarse fishing venue, with carp (to almost 20lb), rudd and chub.

How to get there Take the A591 north from Kendal and at Troutbeck Bridge turn onto A592 Patterdale road. The fishery is 2 miles on the right, in the Holehird Cheshire Home grounds. Free car parking on site.

Day tickets Adult/junior/OAP £2 per rod. Available on the bank or from Carlsons Fishing Tackle, 64–66 Kirkland, Kendal; Tel. 0539 724867.

Best methods Float fishing gives best results.

Best baits Maggots, bread, boilies.

Restrictions No keepnets. Maximum 10 anglers at pegs.

Facilities Nearest shop Windermere (2½ miles); nearest pub, Mortal Man, Troutbeck (1½ miles).

KILLINGTON RESERVOIR
Atlas Page 204 D.2/2.2

A large lake with about 4½ miles of bank for coarse fishing. Excellent sport all season, with large perch and pike. Fishing in season only 16th June to 14th March.

How to get there Leave the M6 at jct 37 and take A684 east towards Sedburgh. Take first right turn and continue for ½ mile, when the lane leads to the reservoir head. Park on the roadside.

Day tickets Adult £2; (junior £3 season). Weekly ticket: £4.50; available from Carlsons Fishing Tackle, 64–66 Kirkland, Kendal; Tel. 0539 724867.

Best methods Float or leger. Plugs for pike.

Best baits Maggots, worms.

Restrictions Maximum 3 rods per person.

Facilities Nearest shop Kendal (6 miles); nearest pub, Station Inn, Oxenholme (5 miles).

The Lancaster Canal.

LANCASTER CANAL
Atlas Page 204 D.2/2.2

A 2-mile section of the Lancaster Canal, from Stainton to Crooklands. Excellent coarse fishing for roach, perch, grass carp and pike, plus large tench, especially following raking swims and heavy pre-baiting!

How to get there Leave the M6 at jct 36 and take the A65 north towards Kendal. Drive through Endmoor (2 miles), continue 1 mile, then turn left to Stainton. Go through the village; the end of the canal is on the left. Various access points available; check at local tackle shops.

Day tickets Adult £1.20; junior/OAP 30p. Available from local tackle shops.

Best methods Float fishing gives best results.

Best baits Maggot, corn, punched bread.

Facilities Nearest shop Kendal (4 miles); nearest pub, Punch Bowl, Barrows Green (2 miles).

Disabled facilities Some swims suitable for disabled and wheelchair anglers at northern end of fishery.

RATHERHEATH TARN
Atlas Page 204 D.2/2.2

A shallow lake with two main arms, located a few miles north of Kendal. Most coarse species, including bream, tench, gudgeon and rudd. Fishing in season only, 16th June to 15th March.

How to get there Take the A591 Kendal to Windermere road; at Crook roundabout, take first left onto short dual carriageway. The car park is ¼ mile on the left; the fishery is on the *right* .

Day tickets Adult/junior/OAP £3. Available from Carlsons Fishing Tackle, 64–66 Kirkland, Kendal; Tel. 0539 724867.

Best methods Float or leger.

Best baits Maggots, sweetcorn, bread, worms.

Restrictions No wading. No groundbaiting, loosefeed only. Maximum 2 rods per person.

Facilities Nearest shop Kendal (1½ miles); nearest pub, Gateway, on Crock-Bowness road (½ mile).

Disabled facilities Some swims suitable for disabled and wheelchair anglers.

RYDAL WATER
Atlas Page 204 D.0/2.0

A large natural, scenic lake at the northern tip of Windermere. Excellent coarse fishing for perch, plus 30lb specimen pike.

How to get there Take the A591 north through Windermere and Ambleside. Rydal Water is about 2 miles beyond Ambleside. Free car parking at the fishery.

Day tickets Adult £3.45; junior £1.75. Weekly ticket: adult £6.90; junior £3.45. Available from Carlsons Fishing Tackle, 64–66 Kirkland, Kendal; Tel. 0539 724867.

Best methods/baits Legering preferred; use deadbait for pike.

Restrictions No maggots; no cheese. No livebaiting.

Facilities Nearest shop Ambleside (2 miles); nearest pub, Glen Rothay (lakeside).

ULVERSTON CANAL
Atlas Page 204 C.8/2.4

A 1½-mile canal stretch – the shortest, deepest and straightest in Britain! Produces good mixed fishing with most species, including large tench and pike – the latter mostly in basins.

How to get there Leave the M6 at jct 36 and take the A6/A590 west to Ulverston (about 25 miles). Approaching Ulverston, turn left in front of the pub and drive down the lane running along the bank. Park at the bank-side.

Day tickets Adult £1.75; junior/OAP 75p. Season ticket: adult £18; junior/OAP £9. Available from Carlsons Fishing Tackle, 64–66 Kirkland, Kendal; Tel. 0539 724867. Also details from Hugh Whittam, 29 Lyndhurst Road, Ulverston; Tel. 0229 52322.

Best methods Float, leger, pole.

Best baits All baits work well here.

Facilities Nearest shop Ulverston (½ mile); nearest pubs, Canal Tavern or Bay Horse (at each end of the canal).

Disabled facilities Some swims suitable for disabled and wheelchair anglers.

WHINFELL TARN
Atlas Page 204 D.2/2.2

A small lake on Borrans Farm, near Whinfell Beacon, north of Kendal. Good mixed coarse fishing with large tench and rudd, plus plenty of pike. The water tends to be weedy.

How to get there Take the A685 north-east from Kendal to Grayrigg (about 6 miles); Borrans Farm is approached via the the left turn there, which runs past Whinfell Beacon.

Day tickets Adult 75p; junior/OAP 75p. Available from the farmer.

Best methods Float fishing preferred.

Best baits Most baits work well here.

Facilities Nearest shop Kendal (3 miles); nearest pub, High Laverock House Hotel, Mealbank (1½ miles).

LAKE WINDERMERE
Atlas Page 204 D.0/2.0

A vast lake extending some 10 miles south from Ambleside. Very busy in parts, but also some very quiet fisheries, providing good sport for perch, plus some very large pike (up to 30lb). Fishing is best from a boat; there are plenty for hire at various points around the lake. Free car parking at the more secluded sites.

How to get there   From Windermere, head either north (A591) or south (A592) along the banks of the lake. Access to the lake is at various points; check with Carlson Fishing, 64–66 Kirkland, Kendal, Cumbria for details; Tel. 0539 724867.

Day tickets   Free fishing. For boat hire, enquire locally for rates.

Best methods/baits   Perch – use general coarse techniques and baits. Pike – use big plugs (diving plugs) and deadbait. Fishing is best from a boat.

Facilities   Various pubs and small shops around the lake.

Disabled facilities   Some swims are suitable for disabled and wheelchair anglers.

Lake Windermere, best from a boat.

DERBYSHIRE

COMBS RESERVOIR
Atlas Page 205 E.5/4.3

A very large, open reservoir, dammed at one end, just west of Chapel-en-le-Frith. Some very deep water, and 120 pegs produce a very good fishery, with excellent bream and roach catches taken over the ledge (20–60 yards out). Specimen hunters aim for the big pike.

How to get there   Take the A6 from Chapel-en-le-Frith west towards Whaley Bridge. The reservoir is on the left of the main road; look for signs to the on-site car park.

Day tickets   Adult £3; junior/OAP £1.50. Available on the bank.

Best methods/baits   Bream – use feeder; roach – use waggler and bronze maggot.

Facilities   Nearest shop/pub in Combs village.

Disabled facilities   Some swims suitable for disabled anglers; for advice; Tel. Robin Farley (0298 812186) or Simon Shepherd (0663 744854).

Patience and comfort.

LANCASHIRE

On the River Calder.

BAILRIGG LAKE
Atlas Page 204 D.1/2.7

A very popular lake, just south of
Lancaster, where carp fishing is the 'norm'
and specimens up to 20lb are common.
Also other species – roach, bream, rudd,
tench and eels.

How to get there   Approach Lancaster
from south on A6; turn left at Boot and
Shoe pub towards Hala, go up Hala Hill,
turn right at T-junction and go over
motorway bridge. Bailrigg is on the
right. No car parking.

Day tickets   Season tickets only; £24,
which permits fishing on Swantley Lake
also. Details from Charlton & Bagnall
Ltd., 3–5 Damside Street, Lancaster; Tel.
0524 63043.

Best methods   Float for most species;
leger for carp.

Best baits   Most baits work well here.

Facilities   Nearest shop/pub, Fox and
Goose (¼ mile).

BICKERSHAW OPEN CAST
Atlas Page 204 D.5/3.9

This 6-acre lake is located close to Leigh
town centre and offers good coarse fishing
all year round, with depths ranging from 3
to 10ft. The water was stocked with 4,000
carp in 1991, so future sport should be
brisk!

How to get there   Take the A580 west
from Manchester and turn off on A572
to Leigh town centre. Drive along Twist
Lane, turn right onto Wigan Road and
continue to Smiths Lane on the left. The
lake is about 400 yards on the left. Free
car parking on site.

Day tickets   Adult £1; junior/OAP 50p.
Available from Leigh & District A.A.,
Mr. Kelly, 70 Diamond Street, Leigh;
Tel. 0942 676291.

Best methods   Use general coarse
methods.

Best baits   Maggots, casters, sweetcorn,
breadflake.

Restrictions   No bloodworm or jokers.
No keepnets.

Facilities   Nearest shop, Smiths Lane;
nearest pub, The Red Cat, Wigan Road.

BOLTON-BURY CANAL
Atlas Page 204 D.8/4.8

A short canal stretch at Little Lever, near
Radcliffe. Expect only moderate fishing for
bream, roach and tench, with match nets
from 5–8lb.

How to get there   Leave the M62 at jct 17
and follow the road through Whitefield
and Radcliffe to Little Lever (about 4
miles). In Little Lever, access to the
canal is opposite the school. Car parking
(free) nearby.

Day tickets   Adult/junior/OAP £1.
Available from Mr. Swindles, 16 School
Street, Little Lever; Tel. 0204 706658.

Best methods/baits   Use pole, waggler or
leger. Most baits work well here.

Restrictions   No bloodworm from April
to November.

Facilities   Nearest shop/pub in Little
Lever.

Disabled facilities   Wide towpath
provides good access for disabled and
wheelchair anglers.

BRIDGEWATER CANAL, ALTRINCHAM
Atlas Page 204 D.9/4.2

A fairly long canal stretch, from
Altrincham to Castle Fields near
Manchester, with a towpath on one side
and mainly factories on the other. The
water is well stocked with bream and
roach, plus some tench. Also large carp
and pike for specimen anglers.

The River Calder.

How to get there   Access to the canal is at various points along the route; enquire about access and parking when purchasing day tickets.

Day tickets   Adult/junior/OAP £1. Available from Norman Hurst, Hornby Street, Wigan; Tel. 0942 36629.

Best methods/baits   Use general coarse techniques and baits.

Restrictions   No bloodworm from April to October.

Facilities   Shops and pubs at points along the route.

Disabled facilities   Some swims may be suitable for disabled anglers; for advice, contact Norman Hurst (see above).

BRIDGEWATER CANAL, LEIGH
Atlas Page 204 D.9/4.2

This stretch of the canal, about 6 miles, from Leigh Bridge to Trafford Park, Manchester, with typical depth in the 4 to 6ft region produces good catches of bream, tench, roach, perch and carp, with especially big nets – from 20–40lb – in the basins.

How to get there   Take the A580 west from Manchester and turn off on A572 to Leigh town centre. Drive over Leigh Bridge; the canal is on the left. Free car parking near the water.

Day tickets   Adult £1.20; junior/OAP 30p; season ticket: adult £14.50, junior/OAP £4.50 (covers 120 miles of canal). Available from Mr. Brown, 10 Dale Road, Golborne, Wigan; Tel. 0942 726917.

Best methods   Use general coarse methods. Pole is preferred method.

Best baits   Maggots, casters, sweetcorn, breadflake.

Facilities   Nearest shops and pub, the Bridge Inn, in St. Helens Road, Leigh.

Disabled facilities   Some swims are suitable for disabled and wheelchair anglers.

BURTON MERE
Atlas Page 204 C.9/4.4

Carp fishing on the main lake (specimens to 25lb+), plus general coarse fishing on the smaller lake on an estate at Burton Hall, near Ellesmere Port. Easy fishing for perch, rudd and roach, plus some large tench and carp.

How to get there   From Chester, take the A540 north-west; after about 8 miles, turn left on minor road to Burton village. Follow signs to Burton Manor and park near the lake.

Day tickets   Adult/junior/OAP £3.50. Half-day (weekdays only) £2. Available from Rod and Reel Tackle Shop, Enfield Road, Ellesmere Port; Tel. 051 356 0687.

Best methods/baits   Most species – use normal coarse techniques and baits, fishing close to the bank for best results. Carp – use modern tackle with boilies, with float in summer.

Facilities   Toilets on site. Nearest shop/pub in Burton village.

RIVER CALDER, BILLINGTON
Atlas Page 204 D.6/4.4

A small stretch of the River Calder, opposite Whalley Abbey, a few miles north-east of Blackburn. Holds plenty of chub and eels, plus an occasional brown trout.

How to get there   Leave the M6 at jct 31 and take the A59 east to Billington (about 12 miles). Follow the signs to Whalley and access point to the river. Free car parking near the swims.

Day tickets   Yearly tickets only; £25. Details from The Anglers Den, 17 Rosegrove Lane, Burnley; Tel. 0282 21837 or A. Balderstone; Tel. 0254 233517. The Accrington & District F.C., also control the River Calder at Martholme, Haggs Reservoir, and the

River Ribble at Sunderland Hall Farm, Balderstone. All these waters can be fished on the same season ticket.
Best methods Use coarse tackle, medium weight.
Best baits Maggots, worms.
Restrictions No livebait.
Facilities Nearest shop/pub 100 yards.

RIVER CALDER, DUNKIRK HALL FARM, READ
Atlas Page 204 D.6/4.4

A ¾-mile stretch of the river, with depth up to 5–6 feet. Not too quickly flowing, only where it shallows off to 18". Good heads of dace, roach and recently re-stocked chub.

How to get there Take the A671 Burnley to Whalley road. The farm is signposted on the left in the village of Read.
Day tickets See River Calder, Billingstone (above).
Best methods Use coarse tackle, medium weight.
Best baits Maggots, worms.
Restrictions No livebait.
Facilities Shops and pubs in the village.

RIVER CALDER, MARTHOLME
Atlas Pagem 204 D.6/4.4

A slightly longer stretch of the Calder, north-east from Blackburn, from the railway viaduct at Whalley to Cock Bridge. Expect a good head of chub, dace and eels, plus an occasional brown trout.

How to get there Leave the M6 at jct 31 and take the A59 east to Billington (about 12 miles). Follow the signs to Whalley and access point to the river. Free car parking near the swims.
Day tickets See River Calder, Billingstone (above).
Best methods Use coarse tackle, medium to heavy weight.
Best baits Maggots, worms.
Restrictions No livebait.
Facilities Nearest shop/pub ¼ mile.

CHERRY TREE LODGE
Atlas Page 204 D.8/4.8

An excellent fishing lodge, midway between Bolton and Bury. Deep water (8ft at the sides) which produces the Lodge's well known large perch (up to 3lb) and roach. Fishing here is generally best in winter.

How to get there Leave the M62 at jct 17 and follow the road through Whitefield and Radcliffe and bear right to Ainsworth (signposted). In the village, look for signs to the fishery; car parking is available on site.
Day tickets Adult/junior/OAP £1.50. Available from Dennis Eckershall at Radcliffe Angling Club; Tel. 061 724 6981.
Best methods/baits Use general coarse techniques and baits.
Facilities Nearest shop/pub in Ainsworth.

ELTON RESERVOIR
Atlas Page 204 D.9/4.8

A large reservoir (with up to 150 pegs), situated south-east of Bury, providing good catches of mainly bream, with catches of up to 100lb possible in summer. Also very good winter pike fishing.

How to get there Leave the M66 at jct 2 and follow the A58 through Bury towards Bolton. The reservoir is on the left, after about 2 miles; look for signs to Elton Sailing Club. Car parking (free) available on site.
Day tickets Adult/junior/OAP £2.40. Available from Elton sailing Club; Tel. 061 764 2858.
Best methods/baits Use general coarse techniques and baits.
Facilities Toilets/bar/sailing club on site. Nearest shops in Bury.

Perch

FARMER & DINGLES LODGES
Atlas Page 204 D.8/3.8

Two fishing lodges located at Radcliffe, a few miles south-west of Bury. Each lodge provides 30 pegs for good coarse fishing, with bream (to 7lb), roach and pike. Also an ideal water for the carp beginner, with many small fish.

How to get there   Leave the M62 at jct 17 and follow the road through Whitefield to Radcliffe. For details of access to the Lodges, enquire when purchasing day ticket. Car parking (free, but limited to 10 cars) is available on site.

Day tickets   Adult/junior/OAP £1. Available from Mr. Swindles, 16 School Street, Little Lever; Tel. 0204 706658.

Best methods/baits   Use general coarse techniques and baits.

Facilities   Nearest shops and pubs in Radcliffe.

FIGURE EIGHT POND
Atlas Page 204 C.8/4.2

A small pit (about ½ acre) just off the Birkenhead-Hoylake road, with big tench, plus Crucian carp, perch, bream and rudd. Carp of 18–22lb have been reported here. Fishes best in early season, and at night.

How to get there   From Birkenhead, take the A553 towards Hoylake; drive straight on at Bidston roundabout, the pond is on the right. Parking on site.

Day tickets   Free fishing.

Best methods/baits   Use any recognised coarse technique and baits.

Facilities   Nearest shops/pubs in Birkenhead.

FIRS PARK, LEIGH
Atlas Page 204 D.7/3.9

A very wide lake (50–60 yards) with average depth 4ft, close to Leigh town centre. Good coarse fishing all year round from 30 pegs, with large tench the most frequently caught fish. The match record is over 30lb; the best catches are taken in early summer.

How to get there   Take the A580 west from Manchester and turn off on A572 to Leigh town centre. Drive along Twist Lane, turn right onto Wigan Road, then left at Hulme Road. The lake is behind Wigan Road Working Men's Club. Free car parking nearby.

Crucian carp.

Day tickets   Adult £1; junior/OAP 50p. Available from Leigh & District A.A., Mr. Kelly, 70 Diamond Street, Leigh; Tel. 0942 676291.

Best methods   Use general coarse techniques.

Best baits   Maggots, sweetcorn, worms, casters.

Restrictions   No bloodworm or jokers.

Facilities   Nearest shop, 300 yards; nearest pub, Wigan Road Working Men's Club.

Disabled facilities   Some swims are suitable for disabled and wheelchair anglers.

FIR TREE FLASH, LEIGH
Atlas Page 204 D.7/3.9

A small lake close to Leigh town centre, with a good head of tench, carp, roach and perch, and which produces typical summer catches of about 20lb.

How to get there   Take the A580 west from Manchester and turn off on A572 to Leigh town centre. Drive along Twist Lane, turn right onto Wigan Road, then left at The Royal Oak pub. Carry straight on the water; free car parking nearby.

Day tickets   Adult £1.50; junior/OAP 50p. Available from Roger Newport, 8 Tunnicliffe New Road, Leigh; Tel. 0942 675403.

Best methods/baits   Use general coarse techniques. Pole tip or waggler is preferred method.

Best baits   Maggots, casters.

Restrictions   No keepnets to be used.

Facilities   Nearest shop and pub, The Royal Oak, in Wigan Road (¼ mile).

Disabled facilities   Some swims are suitable for disabled and wheelchair anglers.

HAGGS RESERVOIR
Atlas Page 204 D.8/3.4

A small, but very scenic pond, just off the main road in Accrington town centre. A good selection of coarse fish, including some large carp to 28lb. A very popular venue with local match anglers.

How to get there Take the A679 into the centre of Accrington; the reservoir is directly opposite the Asda superstore. Free car parking nearby.

Day tickets Yearly tickets only; £25. Details from The Anglers Den, 17 Rosegrove Lane, Burnley; Tel. 0282 21837 or A. Balderstone; Tel. 0254 233517. The Accrington & District F.C., also control the River Calder at Martholme, Haggs Reservoir, and the River Ribble at Sunderland Hall Farm, Balderstone. All these waters can be fished on the same season ticket.

Best methods Use coarse tackle, light to medium weight.
Best baits Most baits work well here.
Restrictions No livebait. Maximum 2 rods per person.
Facilities Nearest shop 100 yards; nearest pub 1 mile.
Disabled facilities Some swims suitable for disabled and wheelchair anglers.

A large pike.

HOLLINGWORTH LAKE
Atlas Page 205 E.1/3.7

A very large reservoir located right next to the M62 at Littleborough, about 6 miles north-east of Rochdale, and containing good stocks of roach, perch, tench, carp, pike and ruff.

How to get there Leave the M62 at jct 21 and follow signs to Littleborough and Hollingworth Lake (about 3 miles).
Day tickets Adult/junior/OAP £1.40; available on the bank.
Best methods/baits Use any recognised coarse technique.
Facilities Shop/toilets/food at the lake.
Disabled facilities Some swims suitable for disabled anglers.

HUDSON'S FARM
Atlas Page 204 C.8/3.3

A farm fishery in rural surroundings, about 10 miles east of Blackpool. Four separate lakes – one for carp, one for tench, one for pike and one mixed fishing. An exciting choice of angling sport.

How to get there Leave the M55 at jct 1 and take the A6 north to Churchtown; bear left onto the A586 and continue to St Michael's on Wyre. Turn right into Rawcliffe Road, turn right after 1 mile at sign to farm. Free car parking on site.
Day tickets Adult/junior/OAP £2.50; half-day £1.50. Available from the farm; for enquiries; Tel. 09958 654.
Best methods Float or leger on the mixed lake. Use carp or pike methods as appropriate.
Best baits Most baits work well here. Use deadbait for pike.
Facilities Nearest shop and pub, The Grapes, at St Michaels (1 mile). Food and instruction available on site.
Disabled facilities Some swims suitable for disabled and wheelchair anglers.

INCE BLUNDELL
Atlas Page 204 C.9/4.2

A very deep water (up to 20ft when levels are high) near Formby, a few miles north of Liverpool. Plenty of coarse fishing, including some very large tench and good-sized carp.

How to get there   Leave the M57 at jct 7 and follow signs for A565 (Southport). Turn off the Formby by-pass to Ince Blundell, go through village and follow the estate wall. Enter the fishery by the big green gates and use the free car park.

Day tickets   Adult/junior/OAP £2.50. Available from Mr Billy Aston on the bank while fishing.

Best methods/baits   Most methods work well, but sliding float is best when the water is deep. Step up lines for big tench and carp.

Facilities   Nearest shop, Formby village; nearest pub, Weld Blundell, on the A565.

Disabled facilities   Good banks provide suitable access for disabled and wheelchair anglers.

RIVER IRWELL, RADCLIFFE
Atlas Page 204 D.8/3.9

This town stretch of the river at Radcliffe has only a few fishable regions, but when these are located they can produce large catches of roach, rudd, gudgeon and chub, often to 30lb+. Fishing is best here after a flood.

How to get there   Leave the M62 at jct 17 and follow the road through Whitefield to Radcliffe. The river runs through the town centre; for details of access, enquire when purchasing day ticket. Car parking (free) nearby.

Day tickets   Free fishing at present, but for information on proposed charges, contact Elton Tackle, 47 Church Street, Radcliffe; Tel. 061 624 5425.

Best methods/baits   Use general coarse techniques and baits, but stick float is preferred here.

Facilities   Nearest shops and pubs in Radcliffe.

KEARNS ALLEN'S LODGES
Atlas Page 204 D.7/3.4

A smallish water situated at Baxenden on the southern outskirts of Accrington. Plenty of good carp (6–15lb) plus good general mixed coarse fishing.

How to get there   Head south from Accrington towards Haslingden on the A671; at Baxenden, the fishery is behind the Holland's pie factory. Free car parking nearby.

Day tickets   Yearly tickets only: £25. Details from The Anglers Den, 17 Rosegrove Lane, Burnley; Tel. 0282 21837.

Best methods   Use coarse tackle, medium to heavy weight.

Best baits   Most baits work well here; boilies for carp.

Restrictions   No livebait.

Facilities   Nearest shop/pub 100 yards.

LANCASTER CANAL – PRESTON TO KENDAL
Atlas Page 204 D.3/2.2–3.4

Over 21 miles of canal running from Preston, through Lancaster to Kendal in Cumbria. A very popular fishery, with favourite spots such as Salwick, Garstang, Lancaster and Kendal. Most species of coarse fish, but best for roach and bream.

How to get there   Travel northwards along the A6, from Preston to Kendal; the canal follows the road, with numerous access and parking points along the route. Check details with local tackle shops.

Day tickets   Adult £1; junior/OAP 50p. Available on the bank.

Best methods   Float, pole or leger. Use light tackle for best results.

Best baits   All baits work according to conditions.

Facilities   Numerous shop, pubs, cafes, toilets along the route.

Disabled facilities   Some swims suitable for disabled anglers.

LEEDS/LIVERPOOL CANAL, LEIGH
Atlas Page 204 D.7/3.9

A short canal stretch (about 2 miles) in Leigh town centre, with average depth just over 4ft. Fishing is best in early morning and evening, when things are quieter. Expect a good catch of bream, roach, tench, perch and carp, plus the occasional pike. The bream nets behind Plank Lane colliery are generally the biggest!

How to get there   Take the A580 west from Manchester and turn off on A572 to Leigh town centre. The canal runs behind Twist Lane, Firs Lane and up to and including, Plank Lane. Free car parking nearby.

Day tickets   Adult £1; junior/OAP 50p. Available from Leigh & District A.A., Mr. Kelly, 70 Diamond Street, Leigh; Tel. 0942 676291, or from local tackle shops.

Best methods/baits   Use general coarse techniques.

Best baits   Maggots, bread, casters, red worms.

Restrictions   No bloodworm or joker. No keepnets to be used.

Facilities   Shops in Twist Lane, Firs Lane and Plank Lane; nearest pub, The Sportsman, Firs Lane.

Disabled facilities   The Plank Lane fishery has some swims suitable for disabled and wheelchair anglers.

LEEDS/LIVERPOOL CANAL, CRANKWOOD LEIGH
Atlas Page 204 D.7/3.9

A short canal stretch at Leigh, running from Dover Lock to Crankwood. Quite shallow water (average 4ft), but reasonable stocks of roach, perch, bream and tench, with best fishing in the summer. Expect a top catch of about 10lb.

How to get there   Take the A580 west from Manchester and turn off on A572 to Leigh town centre. Drive past Twist Lane and Firs Lane, then turn into Plank Lane and continue to the Swing Bridge. Cross the bridge, turn right and use the car park nearby.

Day tickets   Adult/junior/OAP 50p. Also season tickets: adult £3; junior £1. Available from Mr. Brown, 10 Dale Road, Golborne, Wigan; Tel. 0942 726917.

Best methods   Use general coarse techniques. Pole and casters is the most popular method.

Best baits   Maggots, casters, worms.

Restrictions   No bloodworm.

Facilities   Nearest shop, Plank Lane; nearest pub, Nevison, Plank Lane.

Disabled facilities   Some swims are suitable for disabled and wheelchair anglers.

LEISURE LAKES COMPLEX
Atlas Page 204 C.8–D.3/3.4–3.6

A leisure complex incorporating many sports facilities, between Southport and Preston. Good coarse fishing all season, with excellent pike sport in winter. Some carp in the water, but these are rarely fished for.

How to get there   Leave the M57 at jct 7 and take the A565 through Formby and Southport towards Preston. Take the turning to Martin Mere (Wildfowl Trust) and follow signs to the Complex. Parking for anglers available on site.

Day tickets   Adult/junior/OAP £2 per rod. Available at the Complex.

Best methods/baits   Most species – use normal coarse techniques and baits. Pike – use livebaits and small plugs.

Facilities   Cafe/clubhouse/toilets/food available on site. Excellent summer family facilities. Shop and pub in the Complex.

Disabled facilities   Some swims suitable for disabled anglers.

LITTLEDALE HALL FISHERY
Atlas Page 204 D.2/2.7

A 1½-acre pond in a village just east of Lancaster, which is well stocked with carp (various types), rudd, roach, bream and tench. The ideal conditions for fishing here are overcast, with a slight ripple on the water.

How to get there   Leave the M6 at jct 34 and take A683 east to Caton (2 miles). In village, turn right by Station Hotel, continue to Black Bull Hotel, turn down Littledale Road (by pub) and drive 2 miles. The Hall is signposted; free car parking on site.

Day tickets   Adult £3; junior £1.50. Evening ticket: adult £2; junior £1. Available from local tackle shops.

Best methods   Use any method; float is most effective.

Best baits   Most baits work; maggots most effective.

Restrictions   No cereal groundbaits; no boilies.

Facilities   Nearest shop Caton village (2 miles); nearest pub, Black Bull (2 miles).

Disabled facilities   Level bank for disabled and wheelchair anglers, but very steep approach.

LOWERHOUSE LODGE
Atlas Page 204 D.8/3.3

A quite small, hard-to-fish section of water on the northern outskirts of Burnley. A good selection of coarse fish, including bream, tench and roach, plus some good-sized carp and pike.

How to get there Take the A671 from Burnley north-west towards the town outskirts at Padiham (about 2 miles); the fishery is at the bottom end of Lowerhouse Lane.Free parking nearby.

Day tickets Adult 50p; junior/OAP 20p. Available from The Anglers Den, 17 Rosegrove Lane, Burnley; Tel. 0282 21837.

Best methods/baits Use any recognised coarse technique.

Restrictions No livebaiting. Maximum 2 rods/person. Night fishing only by arrangement with the bailiffs.

Facilities Nearest shop 100 yards; nearest pub 200 yards.

NEWSHAM PARK
Atlas Page 204 C.9/4.2

A Liverpool City Council run public park, near Aintree. Expect good pleasure fishing, with 10lb match bags common, and big tench of 7- 8lb. Over 50,000 fish were introduced in summer 1991 after de-silting, so expect good sport in 1992!

How to get there Follow the M62 into Liverpool and continue onto the Ring Road into the city. Follow signs to Aintree and Newsham Park. Parking is available at the fishery.

Day tickets Free fishing.

Best methods/baits Use general coarse techniques and baits.

Facilities Shops and pubs are adjacent to the park and fishery; toilets on site.

Disabled facilities Some swims suitable for disabled anglers.

Inner city fishing in Liverpool.

NEWTON CANAL, SANKEY
Atlas Page 204 D.4/4.2

This 1½-mile length of disused canal, located near Newton-le-Willows, has now been blocked at each end. Expect some good quality coarse fishing, with chub, bream, carp and tench, and typical match catches of 20lb+; the 1991 match record was 26lb. Large pike (up to 20lb) have also been taken here.

How to get there Take the A580 west from Manchester towards Liverpool and after about 10 miles follow signs to Newton-le-Willows. Access to the fishery is at various points; contact local tackle shops or Mr. Grice of Newton Canal A.S. (see below) for details. Car parking available along the stretch.

Day tickets Adult £1; junior/OAP 50p. Also annual club membership: adult £13; junior £2.50; OAP 50p. Available from Mr. Grice, 10 Crown Street, Newton-le-Willows; Tel. 0925 222810.

Best methods Use general coarse techniques.

Best baits All baits work well here; casters and bronze maggot preferred.

Restrictions No bloodworm or joker. No keepnets to be used.

Facilities Nearest shop, 400 yards.

OLDHAM RESERVOIRS
Atlas Page 205 E.2/4.8

Two large reservoirs – Upper Strinesdale and Ogden – each containing mixed coarse fish, plus trout and carp. A difficult venue for good sport.

How to get there Leave the M62 at jct 20 and take A627(M) south to Oldham. Follow signs to the reservoirs, or for details of access and parking, contact Oldham United A.C., A. Dyson, & Raven Avenue, Chadderton, Oldham.

Day tickets Adult/junior/OAP £1. Season ticket: £10. Available on the bank.

Best methods/baits Use any recognised coarse technique and baits.

Facilities Nearest shops/pubs in Oldham.

OVERFLOW, BIRKENHEAD
Atlas Page 204 C.8/4.2

A 6-acre, former dry dock which now contains very deep (35ft) fresh water. Plenty of big perch (3–4lb) and eels (4–6lb) plus some good carp of 10lb+.

How to get there Take the A553 from Birkenhead to St. James' Church; turn right, then 1st left to Bidston Incinerator. Take next entrance and follow the dockside. Overflow is the furthest water. Park nearby.

Day tickets Free fishing.

Best methods Use any recognised coarse technique. Most carp are taken on the snaggy tip side (beware sunken cars!).

Best baits Use maggots or worm on light tackle.

Facilities Nearest shops/pubs in Birkenhead.

PARKER'S LODGE
Atlas Page 204 D.9/3.7

An agreeable fishing lodge, close to Bury town centre, providing good catches of roach, perch, bream, pike, carp and tench. All methods seem to work well here, all year round!

How to get there Leave the M66 at jct 2 and drive to Bury town centre. The Lodge is off Walshaw Road; for details of access and parking, contact Elton Tackle, 47 Church Street, Radcliffe; Tel. 061 724 5425.

Day tickets No day tickets; fishing available only on Bury A.C. Yearbook: £16 from Elton Tackle (see above for address).

Best methods/baits Use general coarse techniques and baits.

Restrictions No bloodworm from April to October.

Facilities Nearest shop, 300 yards; nearest pub, 200 yards.

PENNINGTON FLASH
Atlas Page 204 D.7/3.9

A pleasant fishing lake located in a country park complex, close to Leigh town centre. Expect quality fishing for bream, perch, roach and pike, plus some good-sized carp and tench. Bream catches are often surprisingly large here!

How to get there Take the A580 west from Manchester and turn off on either the A572 or A578 to Leigh town centre. Follow signs to Leigh Country Park and the fishery; free car parking on site.

Day tickets Adult £1; junior/OAP 50p. Available from Leigh Angling Centre, 261 Twist Lane, Leigh; Tel. 0942 670890.

Best methods Use general coarse techniques. Tip, pole and waggler are preferred for bream, roach and perch.

Best baits Most baits work well here.

Restrictions No bloodworm or boilies. No bream in keepnets. No livebaiting. No night fishing.

Facilities Toilets on site (in park). Nearest shops, Twist Lane; nearest pub, The Robin Hood, Pennington, or Nevison, Plank Lane.

Disabled facilities At present, no swims are suitable for disabled and wheelchair anglers.

PILSWORTH FISHERY
Atlas Page 204 D.9/3.7

A 9-acre lake situated near Bury, and controlled by Kevin and Benny Ashurst. Well stocked with most coarse fish, plus plenty of double-figure carp. A popular fishery, but sport can be moderate.

How to get there Take the M66 north from Manchester towards Bury and exit at jct 3; follow the minor road east towards Heywood and look for signs to pilsworth and the fishery. Car parking on site.

Day tickets Adult/junior/OAP £3.50. Available from the bailiff on the bank.

Best methods/baits Use any recognised coarse technique and baits. Specialist carp fishing methods may be required.

Facilities Nearest shops/pubs in Heywood.

QUEENS PARK LAKE
Atlas Page 205 E.1/3.8

A 3-acre lake, bequeathed to the people of Heywood, and set in parkland within the town, a few miles south of Rochdale. Most species, including perch and tench, plus carp to 10lb+.

How to get there Leave the M62 at jct 19 and drive north into Heywood; look for signs to Queens Park and the fishery, or enquire at Dave's Tackle Box, 211 Yorkshire Street, Rochdale; Tel. 0706 861219.

Day tickets Free fishing.

Best methods/baits Use any recognised coarse technique.

Facilities Nearest shop/pub/toilets in Heywood.

REDWELL FISHERIES
Atlas Page 204 D.2/2.7

A 4-acre lake, east of Carnforth, which is well stocked with most species, including mirror, ghost, grass, koi and crucian carp, bream, tench, rudd, roach and gudgeon.

How to get there   Leave the M6 at jct 35A and drive through Carnforth to join the B6254 Kirkby Lonsdale road. The fishery is about 1 mile on the right after passing through Over Kellet village.Free car parking on site.

Day tickets   Adult £4; junior (under 12) £3. Evening ticket: £2.50. Available from Redwell Fisheries, Kirkby Lonsdale Road, Arkholme, Carnforth; Tel. 05242 21979.

Best methods/baits   Use any recognised coarse technique.

Facilities   Toilets on site. Also fishing lodges under construction. Nearest shop Over Kellet (1 mile); nearest pub, Redwell Inn (150 yards).

Disabled facilities   Some swims suitable for disabled and wheelchair anglers.

Rudd.

Rivers

RIVER RIBBLE

Rising in the Yorkshire Dales and running to the Lancashire coast, the upper reaches of the Ribble provide a haven for game anglers, while in the lower sections, with their fast, shallow runs, deep glides and wide bends, there are plenty of superb coarse fishing waters. Although day-ticket facilities are limited, the Ribble offers a chance to practise a wide variety of fishing styles plus many species, including chub, barbel, dace, roach, bream and pike. Catches over 100lb are common when the river is in its best form.   Five *Angling Times* Hotspots are to be found along this section.

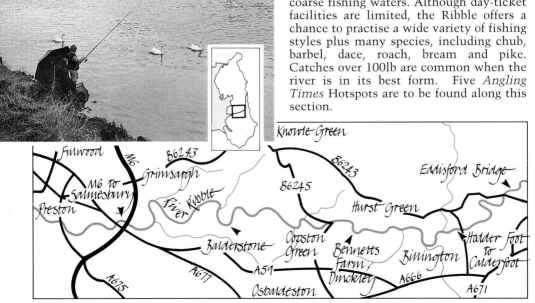

EDISFORD BRIDGE
Atlas Page 204 D.4/3.3

A straight, pacey, even-flowed section with a stoney bottom and average depth 4ft. A 15–20lb mixed bag of chub and dace is reasonable, but 50lb is possible under the best conditions.

How to get there From Clitheroe, take the B6243 towards Preston. At Edisford Bridge, use the large car park opposite the swimming pool.

Day tickets Adults £3.50; junior/OAP £1.75; available from Clitheroe Information Centre.

Best methods Stick float, or small balsa.

Best baits Maggots with float and loosefeed, plus hemp supplement; bread flake or crust best for legering.

Hotspot Tips

❧ If the fish are feeding well, you'll need four pints of maggots and hempseed.
❧ If float fishing is poor, try legering with a straight bomb.

In the shadow of the M6.

HODDER FOOT TO CALDERFOOT
Atlas Page 204 D.4/3.4

This narrow, powerful stretch has depths ranging from 2–6ft, plus summer weed growth which can cause problems in some swims. Winter fishing is best, with typical 20lb mixed nets of chub and dace, although the occasional 50lb net of chub is not unknown!

How to get there From Whalley, travel about 3 miles on the B6246 towards Longridge; turn left into the estate gates just before the river. Park as close to the river as conditions allow.

Day tickets £1; available nearby, from Mitton Hall Farm, Mitton.

Best methods Leger with straight lead or feeder.

Best baits Maggots, casters or bread.

Hotspot Tips

❧ Don't be tempted to fish too light – plenty of the chub reach 4lb.
❧ The early swims immediately below the Ribble:Hodder confluence are particularly productive.

SUNDERLAND HALL FARM, BALDERSTONE
Atlas Page 204 D.4/3.4

An even-fishing stretch that suits all tastes. Swims range from a deep pool to steady glides, plus areas of fast water.Expect chub (2–3lb) and large barbel to provide typical nets of 30–40lb. A good dace shoal has been known to produce a 25lb catch!

How to get there Leave the M6 at junction 31, then take the A59 east towards Blackburn. After about 4 miles, Balderstone is signposted on the left. Park at the farm.

Day tickets Yearly tickets only; £25. Details from The Anglers Den, 17 Rosegrove Lane, Burnley; Tel. 0282 21837 or A. Balderstone. Tel. 0254 233517. The Accrington & District F.C., also control the River Calder at Martholme, Haggs Reservoir, and the River Ribble at Sunderland Hall Farm, Balderstone. All these waters can be fished on the same season ticket.

Best methods Dace, chub – waggler; barbel and chub – legering plus feeder is best.

Best baits Hempseed and casters with float or swimfeeder.

Hotspot Tips

❧ For those larger specimens, try using meat, sweetcorn or bread as an alternative bait.

M6 TO SALMESBURY
Atlas Page 204 D.4/3.4

Plenty of big fish in this pacey stretch of the river. Mostly chub, but also plenty of barbel, with mixed bags of over 100lb in winter. An easy-to-fish section that provides excellent sport, but the enjoyment can be spoiled by constant traffic noise.

How to get there Close to junction 31 of the M6. Parking can be very difficult and the local police are very keen.
Day tickets £2; available from the garage alongside the Tickled Trout Hotel, just off the M6.
Best methods Waggler is best for big weights. Barbel – use feeder in main flow.
Best baits Maggots, casters, sweetcorn or bread; for feed, use hemp.
Facilities Food/toilets at the Tickled Trout Hotel.

Hotspot Tips

❧ Swims below the motorway are heavily fished, but others can produce big weights.
❧ Arrive early – many swims are occupied by first light!

River Ribble at the M6.

RISHTON PAPER MILL
Atlas Page 204 D.6/3.4

A mixed coarse fishery containing most species, but with particularly good carp, with specimens around 20lb.

How to get there From Blackburn head east on the A678 towards Rishton. Follow signs to the paper mill and park nearby.
Day tickets Members only. Adult £25; available from The Anglers Den, 17 Rosegrove Lane, Burnley; Tel. 0282 21837. Junior £5; available from A. Balderstone, 42 Towneley Avenue, Huncoat, Accrington; Tel. 0254 233517.
Best methods/baits Use any recognised coarse technique.
Restrictions No keepnets.
Facilities Nearest shop/pub Rishton.

ROCHDALE CANAL
Atlas Page 205 E.1/3.6

An 8-mile stretch of the canal running from the outskirts of Rochdale to Littleborough. Mixed species, including roach, perch, tench, bream, carp and pike.

How to get there From Rochdale, take the A6033 north-east to Littleborough. Access to the canal is at various points from Lock 36 (Summit) to Slattocks. Check details at local tackle shops.
Day tickets Adult/junior/OAP £2. Available on the bank.
Best methods/baits Use any recognised coarse technique.
Facilities Shops/pubs/toilets/food at various points.

ROWLEY LAKE
Atlas Page 204 D.9/3.3

A small but very popular lake in the centre of Burnley, used by pleasure and match anglers alike. A good roach and bream water, plus small tench. Also carp to 10lb, these are rare.

How to get there In Burnley town centre, at the top of Brunshaw Hill, on Brunshaw Road; ¼ mile from Turf Moor football ground. Free car parking nearby.
Day tickets Adult £1.20; junior/OAP 60p. Available on the bank or from local tackle shops.
Best methods/baits Use any recognised coarse technique. Evening fishing only by arrangement with the bailiff.
Restrictions Carp must not be kept in nets. Maximum 2 rods/person.

Facilities Nearest shop/pub ¾ mile.
Disabled facilities Two pegs suitable for wheelchair anglers.

SEFTON PARK, LIVERPOOL
Atlas Page 204 C.9/4.2

A city centre fishery in a park; very popular, with a good head of fish that are not tackle shy! Expect a good day's sport.

How to get there Follow the M62 into Liverpool and continue onto the Ring Road into the city centre. Follow signs to Sefton Park, near Liverpool's Garden Festival site. No car parking at the fishery.
Day tickets Free fishing.
Best methods/baits Use normal coarse techniques and baits.
Facilities Nearest shops/pubs in the city centre.
Disabled facilities Good access to the water makes some swims suitable for disabled anglers.

SPRING WATER FISHERY
Atlas Page 204 D.9/4.0

Two sheltered ponds (each with 30 pegs) located on Heaton Park golf course, to the south of Manchester. Both contain deep water (10ft at the edges) which produces plenty of roach and gudgeon, plus some very big perch and Crucian carp.

How to get there Leave the M63 at jct 12 and take A5145 towards Heaton Moor; bear right and follow signs to the golf course and fishery. Free car parking available on site.
Day tickets Adult/junior/OAP £2. Available from the bailiff on the bank (J. Greenwood; Tel. 061 724 7164) or at local tackle shops.
Best methods/baits Use general coarse techniques and baits.
Restrictions No boilies or bloodworm.
Facilities Toilets in park. Nearest pub, Heaton Park Hotel, 200 yards.

STARMOUNT LODGES
Atlas Page 204 D.9/3.8

Three small lodges (one opening in 1992) which form a fishing complex at Radcliffe. Deep water (10ft at the sides), producing mainly Crucian carp and roach at the small lodge; roach, Crucians, skimmer bream and large carp (to 20lb) and perch (to 2lb) in the middle lodge.

How to get there Leave the M62 at jct 17 and follow the road through Whitefield to Radcliffe. The fishery is in Bolton Road in Radcliffe; for details of access and on-site parking, enquire when purchasing day tickets.
Day tickets Adult/junior/OAP £1. Available from D. Eckershall, Radcliffe Anglers; Tel. 061 724 6981.
Best methods/baits Use general coarse techniques and baits.
Facilities Nearest shops and pubs in Radcliffe.

SWAN LODGE
Atlas Page 204 D.9/3.8

A shallow (less than 2ft) pond at Radcliffe, where fishing is dominated by large roach (2lb) and perch, plus plenty of small carp. Fairly quiet (30 pegs), with fishing generally best in the summer months.

How to get there Leave the M62 at jct 17 and follow the road through Whitefield to Radcliffe. The fishery is in Bolton Road in Radcliffe; for details of access and on-site parking, enquire when purchasing day tickets.
Day tickets Adult/junior/OAP £150. Available from J. Holbrook; Tel. 061 724 7492.
Best methods/baits Use general coarse techniques and baits, but pole and waggler are best.
Restrictions No boilies.
Facilities Nearest shops and pubs in Radcliffe.

SWANTLEY LAKE
Atlas Page 204 D.2/2.6

A fairly small, but very popular lake, just to the east of Carnforth. Mainly carp fishing, with specimens up to 15lb common. Also other species – roach, bream, rudd, tench and eels.

How to get there Leave the M6 at jct 35A, drive through Carnforth and take the B6254 towards Kirkby Lonsdale. At Over Kellet (about 2 miles), take 2nd turn on the right ; the lake is on the right. Park on the roadside.
Day tickets £2 Mon-Fri. Season ticket: £24 which permits fishing on Bailrigg Lake also. Details from Charlton & Bagnall Ltd., 3–5 Damside Street, Lancaster; Tel. 0524 63043.
Best methods Float or leger.

Best baits   Most baits work well here.
Facilities   Nearest shop and pub, Limeburner's Arms, in Nether Kellet (1 mile).
Disabled facilities   Some swims suitable for disabled and wheelchair anglers.

TWIN LAKES
Atlas Page 204 D.6/3.4

Two lakes at Croston, a few miles west of Chorley. The coarse lake (Willow) was opened in October 1991 and sport is developing well. Even-depth water (12–13ft) produces mainly roach and perch, but bream, tench and carp catches are sure to improve shortly.

How to get there   Leave the M61 at jct 8 and take A581 west through Chorley to Croston village. Drive through village, over the railway bridge, turn left and continue to the lake (on the left). Car park is adjacent.
Day tickets   Adult/junior/OAP £3. Available from the site lodge.
Best methods/baits   Quiver-tip and open-end feeder (crumb and maggot) and maggot hookbait works well. Waggler and pole also produce good sport.
Restrictions   No keepnets for pleasure fishing. No bloodworm or jokers. Groundbait must be limited.
Facilities   Toilets/food/bar on site. Nearest shop/pub in Croston.
Disabled facilities   Some swims may be suitable for disabled anglers; for advice Tel. 0772 601093.

A pole produces good sport.

VILLA ENTERPRISES, CARNFORTH
Atlas Page 204 D.2/2.6

A touring caravan site with two lakes, one for coarse fishing, only 2 minutes from the M6. Plenty of good fish, with carp (to 12lb), roach (to 2lb+), tench (to 5lb) and bream (to 3lb). An ideal site for the angler with a touring caravan.

How to get there   Leave the M6 at jct 35 and take the A6 north; turn right after 300 yards, signposted to Borwick. The fishery is 250 yards on the left. Free car parking on site.
Day tickets   Adult/junior/OAP £2.50. Half-day £1.25. Available from The Villa, Borwick Lane, Dock Acres, Carnforth, Lancs; Tel. 0524 732017.
Best methods/baits   Use any recognised coarse technique.
Facilities   Toilets on site (suitable disabled). Touring caravan parking. Nearest shop Carnforth (1¼ miles); nearest pub, Longlands (½ mile).
Disabled facilities   Some swims suitable for disabled and wheelchair anglers.

WALTON PARK
Atlas Page 204 C.9/4.2

A city-centre lake in Liverpool, with free – and surprisingly good – fishing sport, including large carp (10–17lb) and tench (10–11lb), plus some big roach and perch.

How to get there   Leave the M62 at jct 23 and take the A580 to Liverpool city centre. Continue along Queens Drive; the Park is in Walton Hall Avenue. Parking available on site.
Day tickets   Free fishing.
Best methods/baits   Use coarse techniques and baits.
Facilities   Nearest shop/pub in Walton village.
Disabled facilities   Good banks; access may be suitable for disabled anglers. For advice, contact Taskers tackle shop in Anfield; Tel. 051 260 6015.

WALVERDON LODGE
Atlas Page 204 D.9/3.4

A small reservoir at Nelson, due north of Burnley. Probably the best carp fishing water in the district, with many 10lb+ fish and 20lb fish imminent! Also tench (to 6lb) plus roach and bream. Best fishing in early morning, as water quickly becomes busy.

How to get there   Approach Burnley from the west via the M65 and follow signs to Nelson and Walverdon Reservoir via Railway Street and Brunswick Street. Free car parking near the fishery.

Day tickets   Adult £2.50; junior/OAP £1.25. Evening fishing: members only. Tickets available from Walverdon Lodge; Tel. 0282 66838, or from local tackle shops.

Best methods   Use any recognised coarse technique.

Best baits   Most baits work well; boilies are best for carp.

Restrictions   Carp must not be kept in nets. Maximum 2 rods/person.

Facilities   Nearest shop ½ mile; nearest pub ¾ mile.

Disabled facilities   Some swims suitable for disabled anglers.

WHITEHEADS LODGE
Atlas Page 204 D.9/3.8

A group of deep water lodges at Ainsworth village, near Radcliffe. Mainly bream, skimmer bream and roach, with pleasure catches reaching 60lb (mainly skimmers). Also some good pike in winter. Middle Lodge, with shallower water and plenty of small roach, is best for families.

How to get there   Leave the M62 at jct 17 and follow the road through Whitefield and Radcliffe and bear right to Ainsworth (signposted). In the village, look for signs to the fishery; car parking (50p) is available on site.

Day tickets   Adult/junior/OAP £1.50. Available from Dennis Eckershall at Radcliffe Angling Club; Tel. 061 724 6981.

Best methods/baits   Use general coarse techniques and baits.

Facilities   Nearest shops and pubs in Radcliffe.

WOODFOLD FARM FISHERIES
Atlas Page 204 D.3/3.4

A secluded farm fishery near Beacon fell, about 5 miles north of Preston. Good mixed coarse fishing, including roach, tench, bream, perch, carp (mirror, crucian, common and wild), rudd and chub, but no fish over 10lb.

How to get there   Take the A6 north from Preston; at 1 mile beyond M55 junction, turn right (at Roebuck Inn) onto B5269, signposted Beacon Fell. The fishery is signposted on the right after about 2 miles. Free car parking on site.

Day tickets   Adult/junior/OAP £3 (Mon-Sun). Second rod £1 per day. Available from John Cornthwaite, Woodfold Farm, Whitechapel, Goosnargh, Preston; Tel. 0995 40347.

Best methods   Floatfishing is preferred technique.

Best baits   Maggots, corn, bread.

Restrictions   Use only barbless hooks. No bloodworm, boilies or groundbait.

Facilities   Toilets available with consent. Nearest shop ½ mile; nearest pub 1½ miles.

WYRESIDE FISHERIES
Atlas Page 204 D.1/3.8

An excellent, well-run fishery about 8 miles south of Lancaster. Lots of carp (to 27lb) and large pike to provide a great day's sport. Recognised as a really good match venue.

How to get there   Leave the north-bound M6 at Forton Services (about 12 miles north of jct 32), drive over the motorway bridge. Follow the road round and take a right turn to Dolphinholme. The fishery is at Hampton Lane; parking on site.

Day tickets   Adult/junior/OAP £5. Available at the fishery.

Best methods   Carp and pike – use match techniques.

Best baits   Carp – boilies or maggots; pike – seafish deadbait.

Restrictions   No particle baits.

Facilities   Toilets on site; also tackle & bait for sale. Nearest shop/pub in Dolphinholme village.

Disabled facilities   Some swims suitable for disabled and wheelchair anglers.

Yorkshire Region

River Derwent at Stamford Bridge.

Coarse fishing in the Yorkshire NRA region offers great variety to the angler, with fishing available at all types of venue, from river to reservoir, from lake to canal.

The majority of the river fishing in the region focuses on the Swale, which after rising in the Dales, close to the Lancashire borders, flows rapidly south through Boroughbridge to the Humber Estuary. During its journey, the Swale provides excellent fishing at many venues, with large chub, barbel and bream the angler's main targets. Near Boroughbridge, the Swale joins forces with the Ure, itself a fast-flowing provider of good quality, coarse fish and fishing venues. Of course in addition to these river sites, Yorkshire also has its share of slower canal waters, with the eastern reaches of the Leeds–Liverpool, the Rochdale Canal and the Leven Canal providing most fishing on this type of water.

However, perhaps most popular among Yorkshire fishermen and visitors to the county are the stillwater fisheries – the lakes, reservoirs and ponds that are scattered throughout the region. Many of these are well organised, commercial fisheries, providing consistent, top quality fishing not only for the specialist carp or pike fisherman, but also for the enthusiast and beginner, with large catches of the more common species, including roach, tench and dace forming the bulk of the catch.

RIVER AIRE
KEIGHLEY TO STOCKBRIDGE
Atlas Page 205 E.5/3.2

A good stretch of the Aire, controlled by Keighley Angling Club. Mainly chub, plus an occasional brown trout. The best fishing is for very large pike.

How to get there   Head north from Keighley on the A629 Skipton road. Access to the river (left bank only) is from the A650 river bridge (Stockbridge) to Keighley golf club. Park nearby and walk to the river via bridge or side of Magnet Joinery, Royd Ing Ind. Estate.

Day tickets   Adult £1.50; junior/OAP 50p. Available from The Anglers Den, 17 Rosegrove Lane, Burnley; Tel. 0282 21837.

Best methods/baits   Use any recognised technique with heavy tackle.

Facilities   Nearest shop and pub 2 miles.

SILSDEN TO
MOTORWAY BRIDGE
Atlas Page 205 E.5/3.2

This stretch, from Silsden to Keighley golf course, is controlled by Keighley Angling Club. Mainly chub, plus large pike and the odd brown trout.

How to get there   From Keighley, take the A650 towards Skipton, then A6034 to Silsden. Access to river at Silsden is via stile at Steeton Bridge, or cross canal bridge, turn right, right again under culvert to the wooden bridge. Park off the road and go over stile to river.

Day tickets   Adult £1.50; junior/OAP 50p. Available from The Anglers Den, 17 Rosegrove Lane, Burnley; Tel. 0282 21837.

Best methods/baits   Use any recognised technique with heavy tackle.

Facilities   Nearest shop and pub 2 miles.

RIDDLESDON CRICKET CLUB TO
LAYCOCKS FIELD
Atlas Page 205 E.6/3.3

A good coarse fishing stretch which flows very quickly when in flood. Excellent chub bags, plus some fine pike fishing using deadbaits, and the occasional trout.

How to get there Follow the main A650 east from Keighley towards Bingley; the river is to the left of the road. Car parking is very limited. Enquire about access points at local tackle shops.

Day tickets Adult £1.50; junior/OAP Free. Available from The Anglers Den, 17 Rosegrove Lane, Burnley; Tel. 0282 21837.

Best methods/baits Use any recognised technique with heavy tackle.

Facilities Nearest shop 1½ miles; nearest pub 3–4 miles.

BAKER'S POND
Atlas Page 205 F.9/3.5

A privately-owned, 2½-acre lake a few miles east of Goole. Fairly deep (10–20ft) and snag and weed free, with plenty of Crucian carp and tench. Also well stocked with carp (to 20lb+).

How to get there Leave the M62 at jct 38 and head south-west on the B1230 to Newport village. The pond is in Thimble Hall Lane; parking on site.

Day tickets Adult/junior/OAP £1.00 per rod. Available from the owner on site. For availability, contact Bill Baker; Tel. 0430 440350.

Best methods/baits Use any recognised coarse technique and baits.

Facilities Nearest shop/pub in Newport village.

BIRKDALE FISHERIES
Atlas Page 205 F.7/2.8

A 4½-acre lake located about 15 miles north of York. Excellent carp fishing, some specimens to 20lb+. Fishing normally 0800–dusk, but night fishing can produce the *really* big carp!

How to get there Take the A64 north-east beyond York to Barton- le-Willows (about 12 miles) and turn left on minor road towards Flaxton and West Lilling, then bear right to Terrington. Look for signs to the fishery. Free parking on site.

Day tickets Adult £3 (£1 per extra rod; max 3). Night fishing by arrangement (max 6 rods). Tickets/bookings from Birkdale Fisheries, Low Mowthorpe, Terrington, N. Yorks; Tel. 065384 301.

Best methods/baits Use any recognised technique.

Restrictions Use only barbless hooks. No hard baits (peanuts); no boilies. No carp to be kept in keepnets.

Facilities Nearest shop/pub Terrington (1½ miles).

Disabled facilities Some swims suitable for disabled and wheelchair anglers.

RIVER CALDER, GANNY LOCK
Atlas Page 205/E.7/3.6

Located in Brighouse, West Yorkshire; good roach fishing, including chub, gudgeon and IDE – a rare British species which grows to well over 2lb in this river stretch.

How to get there From Leeds take the M62 west and exit at jct 25; take the A646 to Brighouse (about 2 miles). Look for signs to the River Calder and Ganny Lock.

Day tickets Season tickets: adult £7; junior/OAP £5. Available from local tackle shops.

Best methods Stick float or waggler.

Best baits Most baits work well.

Facilities Nearest shop 1 mile; nearest pub ½ mile.

CARLTON LODGE
Atlas Page 205 F.3/2.3

A good coarse fishing venue a few miles from Thirsk, providing – among others – excellent carp, tench, bream and pike. Fishing in season, from 15th June.

How to get there Take the A61 west from Thirsk to Carlton Miniott. Drive past the school (on left); the entrance to Carlton Lodge is on the left, approaching a slight right-hand bend. Look for the signs; free car parking on site.

Day tickets Adult £3; junior (under 18)/OAP £1. Evening ticket: adult £1; junior/OAP 50p. Season ticket: adult £50; junior/OAP £17.50. Available from Carlton Lodge, Carlton Miniott, Thirsk; Tel. 0845 522145.

Best methods/baits Use any recognised match-fishing technique.

Restrictions No groundbait.

Facilities Activity centre for young people, with associated facilities. Nearest shop ½ mile; nearest pub, Dog & Gun, or The Vale of York (½ mile).

Disabled facilities Some swims suitable for disabled and wheelchair anglers.

CASTLE HOWARD
Atlas Page 205 G.1/2.6

A 72-acre, quite shallow (max 14ft) lake situated within the grounds of Castle Howard. Well stocked with bream, tench, roach, perch, eels and huge pike (43lb, best in Yorkshire!). Fishing season begins 15th June.

How to get there Take the A64 east beyond York to Barton-le-Willows (about 12 miles) and follow signs on left to Castle Howard and the fishery (about 4 miles). Free car parking on site.

Day tickets Adult £2; junior/OAP £1. Available from the gamekeeper on the bank; Tel. 0653 84331.

Best methods Use recognised techniques.

Best baits Maggot, sweetcorn, worm.

Restrictions No groundbait. Maximum 2 rods for pike fishing and no livebaiting.

Facilities Nearest shop/toilets at campsite (50 yards); nearest pubs, three within 2 miles.

Disabled facilities Some swims suitable for disabled and wheelchair anglers.

CHATHAM RESERVOIR
Atlas Page 205 E.5/3.4

A small, well sheltered reservoir just to the west of Todmorden which fishes well and produces some good catches of small roach, perch, bream and carp. Open all year.

How to get there Follow the A646 east from Burnley; the reservoir is on the left hand side, just beyond the railway bridge on the outskirts of Todmorden. Free parking on site.

Day tickets No day tickets. Yearly ticket £24; available from local tackle shops.

Best methods Use any recognised coarse technique with light tackle.

Best baits Most baits work well.

Restrictions No bloodworms. No night fishing.

Facilities Nearest shop ¼ mile; nearest pub 100 yards.

COD BECK, DALTON
Atlas Page 205 F.3/22.3

A 2 mile (approx) stretch of the beck south-west of Thirsk, with excellent coarse fishing at points along its course. Expect a good head of chub and dace, plus some grayling, barbel and pike. Fishing in season, from 15th June.

How to get there From Thirsk, take the A168 south-west to Topcliffe (about 4 miles); access to the beck is at points from here due east to Dalton. Park (free) at Richmond Farm before Dalton. For details, enquire at Thirsk Anglers Centre, 7 Sowerby Road, Thirsk; Tel. 0845 524684.

Day tickets Adult/junior/OAP £2. Available from Thirsk Anglers Centre (see above). Fishing at any location is subject to the conditions of the day ticket purchased.

Best methods Use light feeder or pole.

Best bait Maggots.

Facilities Nearest shop and pubs, The Black Bull and The Angel, Topcliffe.

CUSWORTH HALL LAKE
Atlas Page 205 F. 6/3.9

A small lake located at Cusworth Hall in Doncaster, providing mixed coarse fishing.

How to get there At Cusworth Hall, Cushworth Lane, Doncaster. Take the A635 from the town centre and turn off on to the Sprotbrough road. Free car parking at the lake.

Day tickets Adult/junior/OAP £2 ;
available from Local tackle shops.
Details from R & R Sports, 40 High
Street, Bawtry, Doncaster;
Tel. 0302 711130.

Best methods/baits Use any recognised
coarse technique.

Facilities Toilets on site (limited access).
Nearest shop and pub, Ivanhoe Inn (1½
miles).

Disabled facilities Flat, easily-accessed
banks, but long walk to furthest pegs.

RIVER DEARNE, MEXBOROUGH
Atlas Page 205 F.6/3.9

A stretch of the Dearne a few miles north-
east of Rotherham. Well stocked with
tench, bream and eels; fishing is best in
warm, overcast weather, with excellent
nets during late summer/autumn.

How to get there From Doncaster, head
south-west on the A630 to Conisbrough
(3 miles) and turn right towards
Mexborough. Look for signs to Old
Denaby on the left. Access to the river
is at various points; check with local
tackle shops. Free parking at the river.

Day tickets Adult/junior/OAP 70p;
available from local tackle shops.

Best methods/baits Use recognised
coarse techniques. Pole and stick floats
preferred.

Facilities Nearest shop 1½ miles; nearest
pub, Reresby Arms, 1¼ miles.

Disabled facilities Access over
fence/stile may prevent disabled
angling.

DOE PARK RESERVOIR
Atlas Page 205 E.5/3.3

A small reservoir mid-way between
Halifax and Keighley. Excellent coarse
fishing, with roach, perch, bream, tench
and carp. The pike fishing here is
particularly good.

How to get there From Keighley, head
south on the A629 to Denholme (about
5 miles). Turn off at the sailing club;
free car parking on site.

Day tickets Adult/junior/OAP £2.30;
available from local tackle shops.

Best methods/baits Use recognised
coarse techniques.

Facilities Nearest pub ½ mile.

DYE HOUSE POND
Atlas Page 205 E.7/3.3

A small pond on the southern outskirts of
Bradford, with good mixed coarse fishing;
noted for roach, bream, chub, tench and
carp.

How to get there Head south from
Bradford towards Cleckheaton; at
Oakenshaw, turn left onto Dyehouse
Road. Free car parking available at the
pond.

Day tickets Season tickets only:
adult/junior/OAP £7; available from
local tackle shops.

Best methods/baits Use recognised
coarse techniques.

Restrictions No groundbait.

Facilities Nearest shop and pub 500
yards.

ELLERTON LAKES
Atlas Page 205 F.22/2.1

A 65-acre lake set in an old quarry just
east of Catterick. Deep water providing
good mixed fishing all year round – carp
(to 26lb), chub, bream, barbel, roach, tench
and perch, plus good pike fishing in
winter, with 28lb specimens taken.

How to get there From Richmond, take
the B1263 east and at Scorton, take
B6271 to Bolton-on-Swale. The lakes are
signposted after about 2 miles. Free car
parking on site.

Day tickets Adult £2; junior/OAP £1.
Available from Mr Thompson at the
lakes, or Tel. 0748 811373.

Best methods Use any recognised coarse
technique.

Best baits Most baits work well here.

Facilities Toilets/wash-basins on site.
Nearest shop/pubs Scorton (2 miles).

Disabled facilities Some swims suitable
for disabled and wheelchair anglers.

ELVINGTON LAKE
Atlas Page 205 F.7/2.9

A privately-owned lake of 3½ acres about 5
miles south east of York. A well stocked
lake, with roach, rudd, tench, chub, perch,
trout and recently stocked with barbel.
Also plenty of small carp, plus some 10-
15lb fish – and rumours of bigger
specimens!

How to get there   From eastern end of the A64 by-pass, take the B1228 south-east to Elvington village (about 4 miles). Follow signs to the fishery; car parking on site.

Day tickets   £2.00 for coarse; £3.00 for carp anglers. Available from the house on site. For details, contact Mr Britten, Lake Cottage, Elvington; Tel. 0904 608255.

Best methods/baits   Use any recognised coarse technique and baits.

Facilities   Toilets on site. Nearest shop/pub in Elvington.

Disabled facilities   Some swims suitable for disabled and wheelchair anglers.

EMMOTLAND
Atlas Page 205 G.9/2.7

Two lakes (gravel pits) at North Frodingham, near Great Driffield. Expect carp, tench, bream, roach, rudd and pike.

How to get there   Take the A166 east from York to Great Driffield (28 miles); then take B1249 south-east to North Frodingham. Look for signs to the lake, or contact Buckley's Angling Supplies, 6 Leading Post Street, Scarborough, N. Yorks; Tel. 0723 363202.

Day tickets   £2; available on the bank.

Best methods/baits   Use any recognised coarse technique.

Facilities   Nearest shop/pub North Frodingham.

FISHPONDS FARM FISHERIES
Atlas Page 205 H.0/2.7

Three ponds set in peaceful woodland; mainly carp (including Crucians), tench, bream, roach and perch. Open all year; 0700– sunset.

How to get there   Take the A166 east from York, via Great Driffield, to Bridlington (about 40 miles). For location, contact John Nadin for information;Tel. 0262 605873.

Day tickets   Adult/junior/OAP £2.50.

Best methods/baits   Use any recognised coarse technique.

Facilities   Nearest shop/pub Bridlington or surrounding villages.

Roach

FLEETS DAM, BARNSLEY
Atlas Page 205 F.1/3.9

An attractive, triangular-shaped fishery in pleasant surroundings, just north of Barnsley. Marginal deeps with shallow bar in centre. Most species, but fished mainly for carp and bream; the 5-hour match record is 92lb!

How to get there   Take the A61 north from Barnsley towards Wakefield. Turn left after the petrol station, into Smithies Lane and look for signs to Fleets Dam on the left. Free car parking on site.

Day tickets   Adult £3.50; junior/OAP £2.50. Evenings (1600–dusk) £2; available on the bank or from local tackle shops.

Best methods/baits   Carp – floatfish with luncheon meat, close in. Running line and waggler is best. Perch, roach, rudd – float with maggot, casters or bread. Bream, tench – use quiver-tip with red maggot.

Restrictions   No boilies. No livebaiting.

Facilities   Nearest shops Barnsley; nearest pub, The Woodman, 400 yards.

Disabled facilities   Some pegs palleted for easy use by disabled and wheelchair anglers.

Spawn-laden tench.

FLETCHER'S CARP LAKE
Atlas Page 205 F.3/2.3

An extended fishery near Thirsk, open all year round for good quality mixed coarse fishing. Expect mainly carp, plus tench, roach and rudd, and also possibly chub.

How to get there From Thirsk, head west on the A61 about 3 miles to Carlton Miniott; look for signs to the fishery.

Day tickets Adult/junior/OAP £4. Available from Thirsk Anglers Centre, 7 Sowerby Road, Thirsk; Tel. 0845 524684.

Best methods Use any recognised coarse technique.

Best baits Most baits work well here.

Restrictions No boilies. No heavy groundbaiting.

Facilities Toilets under construction on site. Nearest shop Carlton Miniott; nearest pub, Dog & Gun (2 mins walk).

Disabled facilities Some swims suitable for disabled and wheelchair anglers.

GRAFTON MERE CARP LAKE
Atlas Page 205 F.3/2.3

A very pleasant carp lake, just south of Boroughbridge, with plenty of large carp (to 20lb). Fishing available all year round.

How to get there Take the A1 north past Wetherby towards Boroughbridge; after about 10 miles, take right turn to Grafton village. Look for B&B sign, Prospect Farm, on the B6265 (York road). Free car parking on site.

Day tickets Adult/junior/OAP £5. Available from Prospect Farm, Marton-cum-Grafton, Nr Boroughbridge; Tel. 0423 322045.

Best methods Use any recognised carp fishing technique.

Best baits Luncheon meat, sweetcorn, bread. Surface bait should be limited in summer.

Restrictions No keepnets. Only barbless hooks to be used. Maximum 12 anglers, with maximum 2 rods per stand.

Facilities Holiday cottages/B&B available on site. Nearest shop/pubs, The Punchbowl, The Shoulder of Mutton, in village (few mins walk).

GROVE LODGE
Atlas Page 205 E.2/3.4

A mixed fishery, open all year round, located close to Todmorden, near Halifax. A small but very productive pond. Open all year.

How to get there From Halifax drive west on the A646 towards Hebden Bridge and Todmorden (about 9 miles). Littleborough village lies just outside Todmorden; look for signs to Grove Lodge, or enquire at local tackle shops.

Day tickets Yearly ticket only: adult/junior/OAP £24; available from local tackle shops; or The Anglers Den, 17 Rosegrove Lane, Burnley; Tel. 0282 21837.

Best methods/baits Use any recognised coarse technique; light tackle preferred.

Restrictions No groundbait. No night fishing. No keepnets in closed season.

Facilities Nearest shop and pub, ½ mile.

HAROLD PARK LAKE
Atlas Page 205 E.7/3.3

A mixed fishery producing good roach, perch, bream, tench, carp and pike. An abundance of small fish.

How to get there At Cemetery Road, Low Moor, Bradford, just off the Halifax–Huddersfield road.
Day tickets Adult 50p; junior/OAP 25p; available from local tackle shops.
Best methods/baits Use any recognised coarse technique.
Facilities Nearest shop 200 yards; nearest pub 500 yards.
Disabled facilities Some swims suitable for disabled and wheelchair anglers.

HAY-A-PARK
Atlas Page 205 F.1/2.8

A large (60 acres) gravel pit just outside Knaresborough. An open, clear water but quite weedy, providing good quality mixed fishing, with large specimens of bream, roach, rudd, tench, perch and pike, plus some big carp (to 25lb).

How to get there Leave the north-bound A1 a few miles north of Wetherby and take the A59 west to Knaresborough. The lake is in Chain Lane, on the edge of Knaresborough. Car parking on site.
Day tickets Adult £3.00; junior/OAP £3.00. Available from M&C Johnson Fishing Tackle, Briggate, Knaresborough; Tel. 0423 863065. Permits must be obtained before fishing.
Best methods/baits Use any recognised coarse technique and baits. Specialist carp methods may be required.
Restrictions Fish in season only, 1st June to end of February.
Facilities Nearest shops/pubs in Knaresborough.
Disabled facilities Some swims suitable for disabled anglers.

HORNSEA MERE
Atlas Page 205 H.2/3.1

A 350-acre lake, close to the east coast at Hornsea, north-east of Hull. Mixed coarse species, including roach and large pike. The Mere is controlled by Gordon Hood, The Boat House, The Mere, Hornsea; Tel. 0964 533277.

How to get there From Hull, head north on the A165 and turn onto the B1243 at South Skirlaugh (about 8 miles). Continue to Hornsea (about 8 miles); the Mere is on the right.
Day tickets Adult £1; junior 50p. Also boat hire available; £1/hour, £4/day (max 3 anglers).
Best methods/baits Use any recognised coarse technique.
Facilities Nearest shops/pubs in Hornsea.

KNOTFORD NOOK PIT
Atlas Page 205 E.8/3.2

A mature gravel pit with prolific fishing, in Wharfedale, about 8 miles north of Leeds. Particularly good sport during fine weather. Noted for its carp (to 30lb) and tench (to 7lb), plus many other coarse species.

How to get there From Leeds drive north on the A61 to Harewood (about 6 miles); turn left onto A659. The pit is about 4 miles on the right, just after Pool. Free car parking on site.
Day tickets Adult/junior/OAP £1.50; available from local tackle shops.
Best methods Carp, tench – leger; other species – waggler or feeder.
Best baits Use any permitted bait.
Facilities Nearest shop and pub, ½ mile.
Disabled facilities Some swims suitable for disabled anglers.

LEEDS – LIVERPOOL CANAL
Atlas Page 205 E.7/3.4

A 150-peg section of the canal at Ainsbury Avenue, Thuckley, near Bradford, from the locks to the railway bridge. Good mixed coarse fishing with carp, tench, roach, bream, perch, chub and some gudgeon.

How to get there Off Thuckley Road, near Greengates, Bradford.
Day tickets Season tickets only: adult/junior/OAP £7. Available from local tackle shops.
Best methods/baits Use any recognised coarse technique.
Facilities Nearest shop/pub 2 miles.
Disabled facilities Some swims suitable for disabled and wheelchair anglers.

LEVEN CANAL
Atlas Page 205 G.8/3.2

A short stretch of canal (about 3 miles) which runs from Leven, near Beverley, west to meet the River Hull. A very enjoyable fishing venue, with average width about 15 yards and depth 5–6ft. Quite heavy summer weed growth, but this causes no major problems. Expect roach, rudd, perch, bream, tench, pike and a few chub.

How to get there   From Kingston upon Hull, take the A165 north towards Bridlington. At Leven (about 14 miles) the start of the canal is to the left of the main road. Various access/parking points are available in the town centre and outskirts; for more details, check with local tackle shops.

Day tickets   Adult/junior/OAP £2. Available on the bank.

Best methods/baits   Use general coarse techniques and baits.

Facilities   Snack bar in Leven caravan site. Nearest shops/pub in Leven.

LIGHTWATER VALLEY
Atlas Page 205 E.8/2.5

A small lake forming part of a leisure park, about 5 miles north of Ripon. Good fishing for carp, tench, perch, roach and bream, with most sport in evenings and winter.

How to get there   From Ripon, take the A6108 north for 4 miles to North Stainley. Look for signs to the leisure park and fishery, just beyond the village. Free car parking on site.

Day tickets   Adult/junior/OAP £3. From the Leisure Park Office; advisable to check availability first; Tel. 0765 635321.

Best methods/baits   Use any recognised coarse technique.

Restrictions   Maximum 1 rod per person.

Facilities   Nearest shop/pub North Stainley.

LONG BOLTONS DAM
Atlas Page 205 F.1/3.5

A good mixed coarse fishery with carp, tench, chub, rudd, roach and perch.

How to get there   Alongside the Birstall Smithies to Batley road, just south of Morley, near Leeds. Free car parking near the fishery.

Day tickets   Adult/junior/OAP £1; available on the bank or from local tackle shops. Also Spenborough & District A.S. Yearbook holders.

Best methods/baits   Use any recognised coarse technique.

Facilities   Nearest shop 5 minutes; nearest pub 100 yards.

Disabled facilities   Some swims suitable for disabled and wheelchair anglers.

MANN DAM
Atlas Pag205 E.7/3.4

A small, shallow pond in the centre of Cleckheaton, near Bradford. Good summer evening fishing, with rudd, roach, bream, carp, tench and perch.

How to get there   From the centre of Cleckheaton, turn down the left side of the banks, opposite Fox's Wine Bar. Free car parking nearby.

Day tickets   Adult/junior/OAP £1; available on the bank or from local tackle shops. Also Spenborough & District A.S. Yearbook holders.

Best methods/baits   Use any recognised coarse technique.

Facilities   Nearest shop/pub 500 yards.

Disabled facilities   Some swims suitable for disabled and wheelchair anglers.

The wicked look of a large pike.

NAB END
Atlas Page 205 F.1/2.6

A stretch of the River Ure within Boroughbridge, north of Harrogate. Good fishing for bream, barbel, chub, dace, roach and perch, plus some large pike.

How to get there Take the A1 north from Wetherby about 12 miles to Boroughbridge; turn off the main road into the town (on the old A1) and drive to the river bridge. Park nearby. The stretch is from the bridge, downstream to the canal end.

Day tickets Adult £2.50; junior/OAP £2.50. Available from local tackle shops.

Best methods/baits Use any recognised coarse technique.

Facilities Nearest shop/pub in Boroughbridge (¼ mile).

NEW MILL DAM
Atlas Page 205 E.5/3.4

A smallish section of the Rochdale Canal in Todmorden, west of Halifax. Open all year and regularly stocked, with good carp (to 20lb) and bream, plus large tench (to 6lb).

How to get there From Halifax, head west on the A646 to Todmorden (about 12 miles). The Rochdale Canal runs through the centre of the town; the fishery is at Woodhouse Road. Free parking nearby.

Day tickets Yearly ticket only: £24; available from local tackle shops.

Best methods/baits Use medium to light tackle; most baits work well.

Restrictions No bloodworms; no groundbait. No night fishing. Maximum 1 rod per person.

Facilities Nearest shop/pub ½ mile.

Disabled facilities Some swims suitable for disabled anglers; also wheelchair access.

NEWSHAM PONDS
Atlas Pag 205 F.3/2.3

A small mixed coarse fishing lake on the western outskirts of Thirsk. Expect carp, roach and perch, plus some pike. Open all year round (except when frozen).

How to get there From Thirsk town centre, head west on the A61; at Newsham (after about 1 mile) look for signs to the fishery. Free car parking on site.

Day tickets Adult/junior/OAP £2. Available from Mr Bowes, The Dowlands, Newsham, Nr Thirsk; Tel. 0845 522932.

Best methods/baits Use any recognised coarse technique. Most methods and baits work well here.

Facilities Nearest shops/pubs in Thirsk (1 mile).

Disabled facilities A small number of swims are suitable for disabled and wheelchair anglers.

RIVER NIDD, LITTLE RIBSTON
Atlas Page 205 EF/2.9

A short stretch of the River Nidd running alongside the road, a few miles east of Harrogate. Plenty of chub, dace, eels, roach (2lb+ specimens), bream and barbel, plus some large pike.

How to get there From Wetherby, take the B6164 north-west towards Knaresborough; the fishery is at Little Ribston (about 4 miles). Free parking near the river. Check with local tackle shops for details of access points.

Day tickets Adult/junior/OAP £2.20; available from C.J. Fishing Tackle, 182 Kings Road, Harrogate; Tel. 0423 525000.

Best methods/baits Use any recognised coarse technique.

Restrictions No match fishing.

Facilities Nearest shop 2 miles; nearest pub ¼ mile.

RIVER NIDD, KNARESBOROUGH/SKIPBRIDGE
Atlas Page 205 E.8/E.9

A stretch of the River Nidd just east of Knaresborough. Good coarse fishing sport, including chub, dace, roach, bream and barbel.

How to get there Follow the main A59 east from Knaresborough towards York; the fishery is on the outskirts of the town. Park near the river. Check with local tackle shops for details of access points.

Day tickets Adult/junior/OAP £2.20; available from C.J. Fishing Tackle, 182 Kings Road, Harrogate; Tel. 0423 525000.

Best methods/baits Use any recognised coarse technique.

Facilities Nearest shop/pub in Knaresborough.

NORTHINGALES FISH PONDS
Atlas Page 205 F.7/3.3

Two privately-controlled lakes (2 acres and 1 acre) at Cawood, near Selby. Both contain tench, roach, bream, dace, trout and gudgeon, plus some carp, with large fish (to 15lb) in the larger lake.

How to get there   From York, take the A19 south and on city outskirts bear right onto B1222 to Cawood (about 10 miles). Follow signs to the ponds; car parking on site.

Day tickets   Adult £1.50; junior/OAP £1.50. Available from the house on site. For details, Tel. 075786 414.

Best methods/baits   Use any recognised coarse technique and baits.

Restrictions   Only 1 rod per person. No night fishing. Under 16s must be accompanied by an adult.

Facilities   Nearest shop/pub in Cawood.

4lb common carp.

NOSTELL PRIORY – UPPER LAKE
Atlas Page 205 F.1/3.6

A shallow 26-acre estate lake, maximum depth 8ft. Mostly tree-lined banks, plus reedbeds. Mainly bream (to 6lb), plus roach, perch and large tench (to 5lb). Also large pike and eels. Fishing in season only, 30th March to 28th February, open dawn to dusk (night fishing by arrangement only).

How to get there   From Wakefield, head south-east on the A638 for 5 miles; look for signs to Nostell Priory and the fishery. Free car parking on site.

Day tickets   Adult £2.75; half-day £1.75. Weekly ticket £15. Available from the Fisheries Shop (open 0700–1900 daily).

Best methods   Bream, tench – swimfeeder and long-range waggler on windy days. Pike – live and deadbait, lures.

Best baits   Bream – maggots, casters, worms. Carp – boilies. Tench – sweetcorn, bread. Eels – lobworms, deadbait.

Restrictions   Pike fishing Oct–Feb only.

Facilities   Fisheries shop/toilets/food on site. Touring caravans/tents welcome; also caravans for hire.

Disabled facilities   Some swims reached from platforms are suitable for disabled anglers.

NOSTELL PRIORY – MIDDLE LAKE
Atlas Page 205 F.1/3.6

A smaller, 7½-acre lake in the Priory gardens, well sheltered with good grass banks and depth 3–13ft. Mainly roach, perch, bream, tench, rudd, carp, pike and eels. Fishing in season only, 25th May to 31st December, open dawn to dusk.

How to get there   From Wakefield, head south-east on the A638 for 5 miles; look for signs to Nostell Priory and the fishery. Free car parking on site.

Day tickets   Adult £2.75; juniors/OAP £2. Half-day tickets: adult £1.75; junior/OAP £1.50. Weekly ticket £15. Available from the Fisheries Shop (open 0700–1900 daily).

Best methods   Most species – waggler, feeder and pole; use small hooks and light lines. Pike – live and deadbait, lures.

Best baits   Bream – maggots, casters, worms. Carp – boilies. Tench – sweetcorn, bread. Eels – lobworms, deadbait.

Restrictions   Pike fishing Oct–Dec only. No night fishing.

Facilities   Fisheries shop/toilets/food on site. Touring caravans/tents welcome; also caravans for hire.

Disabled facilities   Some swims are accessible by disabled anglers.

NOSTELL PRIORY – LOWER LAKE
Atlas Page 205 F.1/3.6

A very beautiful, 6-acre lake surrounded by mature trees and rhododendrons, many overhanging the lake. Depth 3-6ft with lots of lilies. Expect plenty of mirror and common carp (to 24lb) plus tench (to 6lb). Fishing in season only, 30th March to 31st December, open dawn to dusk.

How to get there   From Wakefield, head south-east on the A638 for 5 miles; look for signs to Nostell Priory and the fishery. Free car parking on site.

Day tickets   Adult £2.75; half-day tickets £1.75. Weekly ticket £15. Available from the Fisheries Shop (open 0700–1900 daily).

Best methods   Waggler, feeder and pole; use heavier tackle.

Best baits   Carp – boilies. Tench – sweetcorn, bread, mini-boilies.

Restrictions   Maggots and groundbait not allowed until October. No night fishing.

Facilities   Fisheries shop/toilets/food on site. Touring caravans/tents welcome; also caravans for hire.

Disabled facilities   Some swims are accessible by disabled anglers.

A pair of bream.

OXBOW LAKES
Atlas Page 205 F.3/3.4

A pair of oxbow-shaped lakes – both about 6 acres – surrounded by willows in a rural setting midway between Leeds and Castleford. Depth ranges from 3 to 20 feet, providing superb coarse fishing from 70 pegs. Expect large pike (28lb), magnificent shoals of bream (to 11lb), tench, perch and carp, plus rudd and Crucians. Recently re-stocked with over 6,000 fish! Fishing available all year round.

How to get there   Leave the M62 at jct 32 and take the A639 towards Rothwell; at Methley (about 4 miles), follow signs from Green Lane, taking the turning to Mickletow. Free car parking (60 cars) on site.

Day tickets   Adult £3.50; junior (under 16s)/OAP £1.50. Available either on site, or from The Paper Shop, 3 Lane End, Methley Road, Methley.

Best methods/baits   Use general coarse techniques and baits.

Facilities   Toilets under construction on site. Nearest shop and pub, Methley (½ mile).

Disabled facilities   Some swims are suitable for disabled and wheelchair anglers. Assistance always available from the bailiffs.

PATRINGTON HAVEN
Atlas Page 205 H.5/3.5

A stretch of land drain, between 12–15 yards wide and about 4ft deep, at Patrington, near Spurn Head and the Humber Estuary. An open but active fishery, with lots of skimmer bream and bream, perch, roach and some double-figure carp. Also an occasional flatfish in the lower regions nearer the Estuary.

How to get there   From Kingston upon Hull, head east on the A1033 through Heddon to Patrington (about 16 miles). Approaching the village, look for signs to the Haven and park (free) nearby.

Day tickets   Free fishing.

Best methods/baits   Use general coarse techniques and baits.

Facilities   Nearest shop and pub, The Stag, in Patrington.

RACECOURSE LAKE, RIPON
Atlas Page 205 F.1/3.5

A smallish gravel pit of about 1 acre, located just south of Ripon. Quite well stocked with carp, including several of 10lb+, together with bream, rudd, tench and roach.

How to get there   Leave the north-bound A1 near Boroughbridge and take the B6265 towards Ripon; the lake is near the racecourse, about 1 ½ miles south of Ripon town. Follow the signs and park on site.

Day tickets   Generally season tickets for locals only, but some day tickets are available for non-Ripon residents. Adult £3.00; juniors/OAP £1.50. For details, contact Mr R Looney, 12 Lower St. Agnes Street, Ripon; or P. Godden, 3 Oak Road, Ripon.

Best methods/baits   Use any recognised coarse technique and baits.
Facilities   Nearest shops/pubs in Ripon.
Disabled facilities   Some swims suitable for disabled anglers.

RAKER LAKES
Atlas Page 205 F.8/3.0

A newly-built lake, about 5 miles south-east of York. The fishery has been cleverly designed like a canal – 360 yards long, 25 yards wide and 9–10ft deep – and shaped like a horse-shoe so that nobody is fishing opposite! Good fishing, with lots of carp, roach, rudd, bream, tench, dace and perch – all in very pleasant landscaped surroundings.

How to get there   From the York bypass (A64) take the B1228 towards Elvington and after about 3½ miles (at Jake's Garage), turn right on minor road Wheldrake. The lake is on the second part of the sharp S-bend just before Wheldrake. Free car parking on site.
Day tickets   Adult £2.50; junior/OAP £2. Available on the bank (use the 'honesty box') or from Brian Pallister, The Lodge, Raker Lakes, Greengales Lane, Wheldrake, York; Tel. 0904 448793.
Best methods/baits   Use general coarse techniques and baits.
Facilities   Nearest shop and pubs, The Whenlock Arms (good food) or The Alice Hawthorn, in Wheldrake (½ mile).
Disabled facilities   Concrete standings have been specially prepared for use by disabled and wheelchair anglers.

ROCHDALE CANAL –
LOCK 36 TO LOCK 13
Atlas Page 205 E.5/3.4

A section of the Rochdale Canal in the centre of Todmorden, west from Halifax. The fishery extends from Lock 36 (Summit) to Lock 13 (Callis). Open all year; good fishing for roach, perch, gudgeon, rudd, tench, dace, bream, eels and pike, plus carp and chub to specimen size. A popular water, patrolled regularly.

How to get there   From Halifax, head west on the A646 to Todmorden (about 12 miles). The Rochdale Canal runs through the centre of the town; follow signs to Locks 36–13. Free parking nearby.
Day tickets   Yearly tickets only: £24. Available from local tackle shops.

Best methods/baits   Use any recognised technique; light to heavy tackle preferred.
Restrictions   No livebait. No bloodworms.
Facilities   Nearest shop/pub ¼ mile.
Disabled facilities   Some swims suitable for disabled anglers.

ROUNDHAY PARK, LEEDS
Atlas Page 205 F.0/3.3

A small lake situated in a park in the outskirts of Leeds. Open all year, and well stocked with quality roach and bream, providing good sport.

How to get there   Take the ring road anti-clockwise around the east side of Leeds and follow signs to Roundhay on the left. The fishery is ½ mile from the ring road, in the park. Free parking nearby.
Day tickets   Adult £1; junior/OAP 50p. Available from C.J. Fishing Tackle, 182 Kings Road, Harrogate; Tel. 0423 525000.
Best methods/baits   Use any recognised coarse technique.
Facilities   Shop//toilets/food in the park.
Disabled facilities   Excellent; some pegs are reserved for disabled anglers.

Dace.

ROYDS HALL DAM
Atlas Page 205 E..7/3.3

A fishery located in the southern outskirts of Bradford, providing high quality fish; good roach, with big bags both summer and winter. Also bream (to 7lb) and a few carp.

How to get there Off the Halifax–
  Bradford road, at Low Moor. Look for
  Abb Scott Lane and the fishery.
Day tickets Adult/junior/OAP 50p;
  available from local tackle shops. For
  details, contact Wibsey Angling Centre,
  208 High Street, Bradford:
  Tel. 0274 604542.
Best methods/baits Use any recognised
  coarse technique.
Facilities Nearest shop 200 yards; nearest
  pub 500 yards.
Disabled facilities Some swims are
  suitable for disabled anglers.

SCARBOROUGH MERE
Atlas Page 205 G.7/2.2

A rectangular lake of about 17 acres, split
into three sections by narrow islands, and
with an island ring in the centre of the
largest section. Good fishing, with large
carp (to 20lb+), good bream (many 5lb+)
and lots of roach. Also tench, rudd, perch,
chub and pike to add to the fun!

How to get there Approach Scarborough
  from either the west via the A64, or
  from the south via the A165.
  Scarborough Mere is signposted from
  either route, close to Seamer. Follow the
  signs and use the (free) car park.
Day tickets Adult/junior/OAP £2.
  Available on the bank.
Best methods/baits Use general coarse
  techniques and baits.
Facilities Toilets/cafe on site. Nearest
  shops and pubs in Scarborough.
Disabled facilities All swims are
  suitable for disabled and wheelchair
  anglers.

STAINFORTH CANAL
Atlas Page 205 F.6/3.9

A 2½-mile stretch of canal, from Bramwith
to Dunston Hill, about 6 miles east of
Doncaster. Fairly wide (15–30 yards) with
4ft at the edge and 10ft in the middle. A
pleasant fishery, with 200 pegs, producing
good chub and bream, plus roach and
perch.

How to get there Take the M18/M180,
  exit at jct 1 to Thorne and follow minor
  road to Stainforth. Access to the water
  is at varios points along the stretch;
  contact Tom Pickering Angling for
  advice; Tel. 0302 363629.

A good catch of roach and bream.

Day tickets Adult £1; junior/OAP 50p.
  Available on the bank or from local
  tackle shops. Also season ticket: £3.
Best methods/baits Use typical canal
  methods; most baits work well (notably
  squatts and pinkies). Hemp/caster is best
  late summer. For chub, use float or
  feeder, fished at the far bank.
Restrictions No bloodworm, jokers,
  waspgrub or cake.
Facilities Shop and pubs at points along
  the canal; phone for details (see above).
Disabled facilities Some swims may be
  suitable for disabled anglers; please
  phone for advice Tel. 0302 363629.

STAVELEY LAKES
Atlas Page 205 F.0/2.8

Two lakes (2 and 3 acres), located midway
between Knaresborough and
Boroughbridge. Both provide good mixed
coarse fishing with tench, chub, rudd,
perch and bream, plus quite large carp of
16lb+, and rumoured catches of 20lb+.

How to get there From Knaresborough,
  take the A6055 north towards
  Boroughbridge; after about 4 miles, look
  for left turn onto minor road to Staveley.
  Follow signs to the lakes; car parking on
  site.
Day tickets Open season tickets £26;
  available from Bradford City A.A. and
  Mr H Briggs, 4 Brown Hill Close,
  Birkinshaw, Bradford, West Yorks.
Best methods/baits Use any recognised
  coarse technique and baits.
Facilities Nearest shop/pub in Staveley
  village.

SUGDEN END RESERVOIR
Atlas Page 205 E.5/3.2

A large reservoir near Keighley, containing mixed coarse fish, including some very good tench, but recognised locally for its large carp.

How to get there Take the A60 north-west from Bradford towards Skipton, exit at Keighley and head for Keighley 'Crossroads'. Parking on site.

Day tickets Adult/junior/OAP £2. Season ticket: £10. Available from local tackle shops.

Best methods/baits Use any recognised coarse technique and baits.

Facilities Nearest shops/pubs in Keighley.

Disabled facilities Some swims suitable for disabled anglers.

Rivers
RIVER SWALE

A spate river which rises in the Yorkshire Dales north of Richmond, the Swale flows south through beautiful countryside before joining the River Ure, a few miles north-west of York. Along this stretch of the Swale lie a wide variety of excellent coarse fisheries, in both town and country environments, offering the angler a real challenge and the chance of superb fishing, mainly for chub, barbel and pike.

RICHMOND
Atlas Page 205 F.2/2.1

A pleasant stretch, often in spate, with clear, fast-running water over gravel beds, and overhanging willows. Mainly barbel (plenty of 10lb+) and large chub, plus excellent winter grayling. Also dace, perch, pike, trout, gudgeon and ruff.

River Swale.

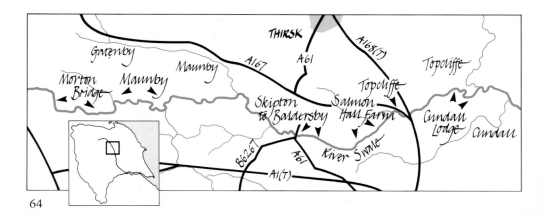

How to get there Take the A1 north from Boroughbridge and at Catterick follow the A6136 into Richmond town centre. Fishing is from Mercury Bridge downstream to the old railway bridge. Free parking according to fishery site. For details, contact Scott's, Market Place, Richmond; Tel. 0748 822782.

Day tickets Adult £3; junior/OAP £2. Weekly ticket: adult £12; junior/OAP £6. Available from Scott's (see above).

Best methods/baits Use any recognised coarse technique or baits. For winter grayling use red worm, red maggot.

Restrictions No spinning; no live or deadbait. Use single hooks only. Maximum 1 rod per person.

Facilities Nearest toilets/shops/pubs in Richmond.

Disabled facilities Some swims suitable for disabled and wheelchair anglers, but access is difficult.

CATTERICK BRIDGE
Atlas Page 205 F.2/2.1

A mainly shallow stretch of the river, but deeper (3–4ft) beneath the old railway bridge. A good mixed coarse fishery; expect mostly barbel, chub, dace, trout and grayling.

How to get there Take the A1 north from Boroughbridge and follow the A6136 into Catterick Bridge. Fish from the west bank (Brompton side), 150 yards upstream from Catterick bridge (opposite racecourse) to just beyond the old railway bridge. Free parking on the roadside. For details/advice, contact Scott's, Market Place, Richmond; Tel. 0748 822782.

Day tickets Adult £3; junior/OAP £2. Weekly ticket: adult £12; junior/OAP £6. Available from Scott's (see above).

Best methods/baits Use any recognised coarse technique or baits.

Restrictions No spinning; no live or deadbait. Use single hooks only.

Facilities Nearest shop Catterick village or Brompton village; nearest pub, Catterick Bridge Hotel (100 yards).

GREAT LANGTON
Atlas Page 205 F.2/2.1

A ½-mile long, shallow, fast-flowing stretch with shifting gravel beds that provide excellent barbel, chub, trout and dace fishing, plus tremendous winter grayling sport. Also an occasional large pike (to 20lb).

How to get there Take the A1 north to Leeming Bar roundabout and turn right onto A684 to Northallerton. Take B6271 north towards Richmond; Great langton is about 5 miles along this road. Park (free) on the roadside. Fish from the road bridge upstream, on opposite side from road. For details/advice, contact Scott's, Market Place, Richmond; Tel. 0748 822782.

Day tickets Adult £3; junior/OAP £2. Weekly ticket: adult £12; junior/OAP £6. Available from Scott's (see above).

Best methods/baits Use any recognised coarse technique or baits.

Restrictions No spinning. No live or deadbait.

Facilities Nearest shop Scorton (4 miles); nearest pub, The Wishing Well, Great Langton.

MORTON BRIDGE
Atlas Page 205 F.1/2.1

A 4½-mile stretch of the Swale, downstream from the bridge, on the left-hand bank to Far Fairholme. Fairly open, up to 60ft wide and 2–8ft deep, with some gravel banks. Expect bumper chub and barbel nets in summer (up to 60lb), with grayling – and double figure pike – in winter.

Netting the catch.

How to get there From Northallerton, head east on the A684 to just beyond Morton-on-Swale (about 3 miles); the fishery is just over Morton bridge (downstream). Use the large car park on the left.

Day tickets   Adult/junior/OAP £3;
available in Northallerton, either from
Terry Pratt Sports, Central Arcade; Tel.
0609 773398; or Andy Saife's, near the
bus station. Also from Mr Grainger's
house (on the right, approaching Morton
village).

Best methods   Stick float, waggler,
straight leger or feeder all work at times.

Best baits   Chub – casters, maggots,
bread, waspgrub, luncheon meat. Barbel –
meat, lobworm. Grayling – maggot,
sweetcorn, redworm. Cereal groundbait is
not recommended.

Restrictions   Fishing only from 1st May
to end of February.

Facilities   Nearest shop Morton village
(½ mile); nearest pub, Swaledale Arms
(100 yards).

Hotspot Tips

- Don't fish too fine – you'll need at
  least 2lb line to an 18 hook for the
  bigger fish.
- You'll need big hook and 4–6lb line to
  stop the big barbel reaching the tree
  roots and weeds.
- Look for the flow in summer,
  especially with tree cover; in winter,
  look for deeper, slower water.
- Shallower swims on the bends (over
  gravel) will hold fish beneath the
  willow cover.

MAUNBY
Atlas Page 205 F.1/2.1

A deeper stretch of the river, with more
sandy bottoms. Minimal bankside cover,
but shelves, channels and weed in some
swims. Expect chub, barbel, dace, bream
and gudgeon in summer, with double-
figure catches. Winter nets of chub,
grayling and pike (to 28lb) can top 100lb!

How to get there   Take the A167 south
from Northallerton; at South
Otteringham, turn right to Maunby.
Take road on right after Buck Inn and
park on the disused railway line. Fish
from the left bank, 3 miles upstream
(alternative parking further on, at Rush
Farm).

Day tickets   £1.75; available from the
Buck Inn in Maunby village.

Best methods   Use top and bottom floats
in long swims. Large chub and barbel –
use leger. Pike – deadbaits.

Best baits   Casters, maggots, hemp. Use
big baits for big fish.

Facilities   Toilets and food at the Buck
Inn, Maunby.

Disabled facilities   The long walk to the
river may deter disabled anglers.

Hotspot Tips

- You'll need at least a 2lb hook length
  to cope with the bigger fish.
- Mashed wasp nests work wonders for
  winter chub here!
- The glides with streamer weed and
  tree-covered swims hold plenty of
  chub.
- The deep holes on the bends are
  particularly good for pike.

5lb 12oz male tench.

SKIPTON TO BALDERSBY
Atlas Page 205 F.2/2.3

A fairly deep (5–10ft), slow moving river
stretch whose banks have been recently
replanted with trees. Good mixed coarse
fishing, with plenty of chub, dace, bream
(to 8lb), roach and barbel, plus some pike.
Fishing can be difficult here, with few
double figure nets.

How to get there   From Thirsk, take the
A61 west about 6 miles to Skipton-on-
Swale; the fishery extends along the
Swale banks from Skipton bridge to the
old railway bridge. Free parking near
Skipton bridge. Fishing is downstream
(pegs 1–34); for more details, contact
Thirsk Anglers Centre, 7 Sowerby Road,
Thirsk; Tel. 0845 524684.

Day tickets Adult/junior/OAP £2. Available from Thirsk Anglers Centre.

Best methods Stick float with maggot for small fish, or with casters for bigger fish. Use a leger in colder weather.

Best baits Maggots, casters, hemp for floats; big baits for leger. Use fishbaits for pike. Only wasp cake is effective as groundbait.

Facilities Nearest shops Skipton-on-Swale or Carlton Miniott; nearest pub, Dog & Gun (2 mins walk).

Disabled facilities Fences prevent access for disabled anglers.

Hotspot Tips

- Barbel prefer a still bait – so try a bomb or feeder first.
- For pike, try the pegs below Baldersby Buttress.
- Fish here tend to gather in channels and along ledges.
- It may pay to bulk-shot if the water is pushing through well.

The sensitive barbels.

SALMON HALL FARM
Atlas Page 205 F.1/2.6

A wide (60–70ft), quiet, slow and deep section of the river at Topcliffe, providing mainly chub, roach, dace, perch and some barbel, and 20–30lb nets. Bream stocking is currently in process and catches should improve in the coming seasons. Fishing available from 15th June.

How to get there From the A1 just north of Boroughbridge, take the A168 to Topcliffe (about 4 miles). Turn north onto A167 towards Catton; the fishery is upstream of Topcliffe Mill, on the east (left-hand) bank. Free parking on the roadside.

Best methods Float is best (waggler and stick). Use feeder or leger for big chub when float conditions are poor.

Best baits Bronze maggots, hemp for float. For chub, use legered bread, waspgrub or lobworm.

Restrictions No fishing on Sundays.

Facilities Toilet at farm (with permission). Nearest shop and pubs, The Swan or The Angel, Topcliffe (1 mile).

Hotspot Tips

- Don't overlook the pole – it can produce some very good fish!
- In mild conditions, bites may occur on the drop, with light, strung-out shotting the best method.
- The top cornfield is noted for producing chub on the feeder.

TOPCLIFFE
Atlas Page 205 F.1/2.6

A fast flowing, shallower section of the river, below the weir, gradually deepening off towards Topcliffe road bridge. Fishing on the right-hand bank, where depth is 2–12ft, and typical width 25 yards. Mainly barbel (to 18lb) and chub, with 50lb nets possible.

How to get there From the A1 just north of Boroughbridge, take the A168 to Topcliffe (about 4 miles). In the village, park (off- road) on the bend just above the bridge on the back road to Baldersby.

Day tickets Adult/junior/OAP £2; available from either The Angel (Tel. 0845 577237) or the Black Bull (Tel. 0845 577219) pubs, in Topcliffe.

Best methods Chub, barbel – use feeder. Use float for smaller fish.

Best baits Casters, maggots, hemp as small baits; meat or lobworm as big baits.

Facilities Toilets and food at the Black Bull.

Disabled facilities Access to the water may be possible for disabled anglers; for advice, contact the Black Bull pub.

Hotspot Tips

- The fish will stay near the far bank willows and roots, so heavy gear will be needed!
- As the fish get wiser, hair rigs may become essential tackle.
- The run-off above the bridge always holds chub and a few barbel.

CUNDALL LODGE
Atlas Page 205 F.2/2.2

A slow stretch, with depths of 10ft and width up to 90ft on the sweeping bends. Summer weed can cause problems but provides cover for the fish. Famous for large barbel, plus good quality chub and pike. Match nets can be 'patchy', but a very good pleasure fishing water.

How to get there From Thirsk, take the A168 south and exit at Asenby (about 4 miles) and follow minor road towards Helpersby. The fishery is on the left, immediately before Cundall village. Park in the fields, near the flood bank.

Day tickets £2; available from Cundall Lodge Farm.

Best methods Use heavy lines with bomb or feeder. Float and feeder work well for chub.

Best baits Use meat, lobworm or caster as hookbait. Take plenty of hemp for barbel.

Facilities Shop and pub in Cundall village.

Disabled facilities Vehicular access is available right along the fishery, close to the water.

Hotspot Tips

- Try lobworms when the water is coloured and fining, or hair rigs and big baits when levels are low.
- Lots of very good barbel and chub are caught from swims opposite the farm.
- For good winter chub, try either a float or a feeder – but be sure to use bread!

Bream.

THREE LAKES, SELBY
Atlas Page 205 F.7/3.3

A group of three lakes, one of 4 acres and two smaller lakes. Very good mixed fishing, with tench (to 8lb), eels (to 6lb), bream (to 11lb), plus large perch, roach and trout. Also large carp (to 20lb).

How to get there At Selby, due south from York. For details of access and parking, contact Paul Howgego; Tel. 0757 706065.

Day tickets Adult/junior/OAP: £2.50 for coarse anglers; £3 for carp anglers; £5 for night carp fishing. Available from Paul Howgego (see above).

Best methods/baits Carp – use normal carp fishing baits and methods; floaters do well (especially Pedigree Chum Mixer). Other species – use general coarse fishing methods.

Facilities Nearest shops/pubs in Selby.

TILERY LAKE, NR. HULL
Atlas Page 205 G.4/3.4

An open, featureless clay pit of 30 acres, containing over 400 carp averaging 18lb; plenty of 20lb+ specimens. Also a good head of pike, bream and roach.

How to get there Leave the M62 at junction 38 and take B1230 towards Newport. Take 1st left turn to Broomfleet; the lake is at the Broomfleet Tile factory. Park nearby.

Day tickets Club membership only (Hull & District A.A.; contact the Secretary, J. Holdenby, 1 Grebe Road, Thimblehall Lane, Newport. Annual membership £10; additional £20 covers night fishing (local anglers only).

Best methods/baits Use any recognised coarse technique and baits. Specialist carp tackle will be required.

Facilities Nearest shop/pub in Broomfleet.

ULLEY RESERVOIR
Atlas Page 205 F.1/4.2

A small reservoir located in pleasant countryside a few miles east of Sheffield. Well stocked with most coarse species and flat, easily-accessed banks. Also boating and water sports, but these do not interfere with angling.

How to get there Leave the M1 at jct 31 and head west towards Sheffield; bear right towards Aston, then Ulley. The reservoir is just to the west of the village. Free car parking on site.

Day tickets Adult/junior/OAP £2; available from the ticket machine in the car park.

Best methods/baits Use any recognised coarse technique.

Facilities Toilets on site. Nearest shop Aston/Aughton (½ mile); nearest pub, Royal Oak (¼ mile).

Disabled facilities Some swims suitable for disabled anglers; wheelchair access to some swims and toilets.

Rivers

RIVER URE

Rising on the North Yorkshire moors, the Ure flows swiftly through rapids and glides, over gravel and boulders, before running wide and deep from Middleham to Spennithorne. It then returns to a pacey flow before joining the Yorkshire Ouse. Along this variety of water lies a wealth of sport – chub, dace, grayling and barbel, plus big bream thought to have originated from Lake Semerwater, some miles upstream. On the Ripon to Boroughbridge section, *Angling Times* has selected six Hotspots.

River Ure.

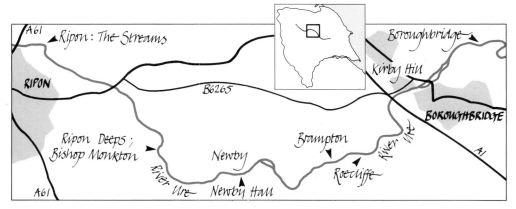

RIPON – THE STREAMS
Atlas Page 205 F.1/2.5

This section – Hutton Beck to Hewick Bridge (near the racecourse) – is wide, shallow and pacey, with little weed and 2–4ft depth. Expect large shoals of chub, plus dace, grayling and barbel. Most matches produce 20lb+ nets; pleasure nets can top 100lb!

How to get there The river runs to the east of Ripon; obtain route of access via the city centre when you buy a day ticket.

Day tickets Adult £3 (£8 weekly); junior £1.50; available from Wain's Newsagents, 82 Bongate; Ripon Angling Centre, North Road; Station hotel, North Bridge.

Best methods Chub, dace, grayling – light float rigs; barbel – swim feeder.

Best baits Casters – feed heavily for chub, lightly for dace and grayling. Keep big bait available for chub.

Hotspot Tips

- A caster/hemp combination can work well for barbel.
- Waspgrub can be 'overwhelmingly good' for chub.

River Ure.

RIPON DEEPS – BISHOP MONKTON
Atlas Page 205 F.1/2.5

A long, wide (up to 60 yards) stretch which begins streamy but rapidly slows and deepens to 6–12ft. Sport includes roach, perch, dace, chub, eels, bream, pike and barbel. Expect mainly chub and roach, plus a few bream, with match nets usually 10–20lb.

How to get there Left-bank access is at Foxham Farm or Ripon Yacht Club; right-bank access at Hewick Bridge, Canal Bridge and Bishop Monkton Bridge.

Day tickets Adult £3 (£8 weekly; yearly open membership £35); junior £1.50; available from Wain's Newsagents, 82 Bongate; Ripon Angling Centre, North Road; Station hotel, North Bridge.

Best methods Feeder and straight bomb; stick float and pole when river has extra water.

Best baits Maggots, casters.

Hotspot Tips

- Float fishing here means presenting a waggler rig in 6–12ft of water.
- Rely on the bottom field at Bishop Monkton for good roach, perch and chub.

NEWBY HALL
Atlas Page 205 F.2/2.5

A wide (45–60yd), slow-flowing section, but pacey above and below the weir. Fairly deep (8–18ft) with inside shelves and deep, central areas. A wide range of fish, mainly chub and perch, plus some winter roach. A typical day's net will be 5–8lb.

How to get there From Roecliffe (close to the A1), drive towards Bishop Monkton; access is next to bridging site bottom of Ripon waters, keep right of the stream through Holbeck Wood. Fish the right bank for 1 mile to lock house (opposite Newby Hall).

Day tickets Adult £2; 15 and under £1; available from Newby Hall Estates, Tel. 0423 322583

Best methods Chub – feeder or bomb cast to willow cover; other species – stick float on inside line or waggler in middle.

Best baits Maggots, casters; use big baits for chub.

Hotspot Tips

- Pike fishing here can be excellent on deadbaits.
- Try redworms for perch, bream and eels.
- The bottom cow drink is tops for chub, but keep to the canal mouth for pike!

BRAMPTON
Atlas Page 205 E.6/3.3

A wide, variable section, with slow-flowing shallows and deeper areas, with depth 8–9ft. Plenty of summer weed – and boats! Chub and bream feed here all year, so 40lb+ nets are quite common. Roach, dace, perch, eels and barbel also appear.

How to get there   From the A1, head for Newby Hall; turn left just before the Hall gates. Follow the lane to Brampton Hall Farm; park on the roadside and walk to the pegged left-hand bank.

Day tickets   No day tickets; open membership available (Bradford City AA) £26. Contact Ian Weston, 50 Wrose Mount, Wrose, Shipley. Tel. 0274 582516

Best methods   Chub – block-end feeder; mixed bags – waggler down the middle.

Best baits   Maggots, casters, waspgrub, bread, meat, worms.

Hotspot Tips

&   Waspgrub or bread will often sort out those large chub.

&   Peg 1 can produce big chub nets, but pegs 7–10 are more consistent.

ROECLIFFE
Atlas Page 205 F.1/2.7

A mostly very deep (8–18ft) stretch; short lengths of shallows and slow flow. Some weed, some shelves – and plenty of summer boats. Most coarse species, with bream unpredictable and roach improving later in the season. Mixed bags from 10–20lb, but much bigger when the bream are feeding.

River Ure.

How to get there   The right-bank stretch below Boroughbridge. For the bottom section, above and below the A1 bridge, park at Langthorpe and walk – but it's a long way!

Day tickets   £2.35; available from The Anchor Inn, Boroughbridge.

Best methods   Chub – swimfeeder with maggot, caster or waspgrub. Bream – open-end feeder with groundbait plus double caster hookbait.

Best baits   Chub – bronze maggot; hemp, casters, waspgrub, bread, worm or luncheon meat alternatives.

Disabled facilities   Limited; access via Langthorpe is by a long walk.

Hotspot Tips

&   The chub are mainly found under far bank cover; the bream are mainly in the middle.

&   A pole on the nearside will produce a good mixed bag.

&   For bream in the middle, on a moving bait, you'll need a sliding float.

BOROUGHBRIDGE
Atlas Page 205 F.1/2.6

A fairly wide stretch, up to 20ft deep in places, slightly weedy, with the flow picking up downstream of the town. A wide variety – roach, dace, chub, perch, eels, gudgeon, bream, pike, bleak and barbel. Expect double-figure nets .

How to get there   At the village of Aldborough, just south-east of Boroughbridge; it extends from the village cricket field to Old Arms Lane.

Day tickets   £2.50 on Harrogate Waters, £2 on Boroughbridge; available at Boroughbridge Post Office and The Three Horseshoes; Tel. 0423 322314. No day tickets on Sundays.

Best methods   Float is preferred but extreme depth causes problems; otherwise pole.

Best baits   Maggots, casters; big baits for chub.

Hotspot Tips

&   If a moving bait is advantageous, use a sliding float.

&   For roach, the deeper swims are best after the first frosts.

&   Waspgrub is always worth a try for that really big chub!

WALSDEN PRINTING COMPANY
Atlas Page 205 E.3/3.5

Two dams which create a fishery adjacent to a printing works at Walsden, just south of Todmorden. Mixed coarse fishing, with decent carp, tench and roach. Open all year.

How to get there From Halifax head west on the A646 to Todmorden, then turn left onto A6033; Walsden village is about 2 miles further on. Look for Ramsden Wood Road and the fishery. Free car parking nearby.
Day tickets Yearly tickets only: £24. Available from local tackle shops. Details from The Anglers Den, 17 Rosegrove Lane, Burnley; Tel. 0282 21837.
Best methods/baits Use any recognised coarse technique.
Restrictions No bloodworm. No night fishing.
Facilities Nearest shop/pub ¼ mile.

WENTWORTH LAKES
Atlas Page 205 F.3/4.1

Two coarse lakes totalling just over 2 acres, located to the north-west of Rotherham. Mixed species, with bream and tench (each to 7lb), roach and perch (each to 3lb), plus large pike (20lb) and even larger carp (to 29lb)!

How to get there From Barnsley drive south on the A633 and bear right (about 5 miles) onto B6089, then right again onto B6090. Wentworth is about 3 miles further on. Look for signs to the lakes.
Day tickets Permit only, available only from Wentworth Estate Office, Clayfields Lane, Wentworth, Rotherham, Tel. 0226 742041. Single rod permit £35; double rod £60; junior £15.
Best methods/baits Use any recognised coarse technique.
Facilities Nearest shop/pub Wentworth village.

RIVER WHARFE, POOL
Atlas Page 205 F.0/2.9

A 5-mile stretch of the Wharfe, about 10 miles south of Harrogate. Varying flow from gravel bottom with dace and grayling to deep, slower water with very good chub. Also an occasional 5lb+ brown trout! Best fishing when the river is fining off after a fresh.

How to get there Take the A61 south from Harrogate; after 3 miles bear right onto A658 towards Bradford and continue to Pool (about 6 miles). Access to the river is at various points; check with local tackle shops. Free parking nearby.
Day tickets Adult/junior/OAP £1.50; available from C.J. Tackle, 182 Kings Road, Harrogate; Tel. 0423 525000.
Best methods Stick float or waggler.
Best baits Most baits work well here.
Facilities Nearest shop/pub in Pool.

WHITEFIELDS RESERVOIR/ ROBERTS PONDS
Atlas Page 205 E.4/3.2

A fishing 'complex' comprising a reservoir and a small pond, near Keighley. Expect good mixed coarse fishing, with tench, roach, perch and pike, plus some large carp in both waters.

How to get there Take the A60 from Bradford north-west towards Skipton and exit at Keighley (about 12 miles). Access to the reservoir/pond is difficult; enquire at local tackle shops for details.
Day tickets Adult/junior/OAP £2. Season ticket: £10. Available from local tackle shops.
Best methods/baits Use any recognised coarse technique and baits.
Facilities Nearest shops/pubs in Keighley.
Disabled facilities Some swims suitable for disabled anglers.

WOLDGATE FISHERY
Atlas Page 205 G.9/2.6

A group of four or five different ponds set in beautifully maintained woodland surroundings just outside Bridlington. Expect mostly roach, rudd, tench, carp, bream and Crucian carp in the main pond, but some very big carp in the specialist carp pond. Be prepared for a really large fish!

How to get there Approaching Bridlington from the north via the A165, the fishery is signposted as 'Civic Amenities Fresh Water Fisheries'. Follow the signs and use the free car park near the lakes.
Day tickets Adult/junior/OAP £2.50. Available on the bank.

Best methods/baits Use general coarse techniques and baits.

Restrictions No keepnets. Use only barbless hooks. No groundbait or hemp. Use *minimum* 8lb breaking strain line when fishing for carp.

Facilities Nearest shops and pubs in Bridlington.

Disabled facilities Swims on the first pond are suitable for disabled and wheelchair anglers.

WOODALL'S POND
Atlas Page 205 G.0/3.5

A small pond at Newport, near Goole. A popular day ticket fishery, with plenty of coarse fish and well stocked with carp (to 20lb).

How to get there Leave the M62 at jct 38 and head south-west on the B1230 to Newport village. Turn right at the shop into Canalside East. The pond is 200 yards on the right.

Day tickets Adult £1; junior/OAP £1. Available from Mr and Mrs Woodall, 27 Canalside East, Newport.

Best methods/baits Use any recognised coarse technique and baits.

Facilities Nearest shop/pub in Newport village.

WORSBOROUGH RESERVOIR
Atlas Page 205 F.1/3.8

A large reservoir with distinct deep (14ft) and shallow (2ft) ends, situated within a country park, with a working mill, about 3 miles south of Barnsley. Good mixed coarse fishing in a pleasant environment; particularly well stocked with bream about 2lb. Ideal for children and family outings.

How to get there Leave the M1 at jct 36 and take the A61 towards Barnsley. Drive downhill towards Worsborough; the reservoir is on the left after about 2 miles. Park (free) at the Red Lion pub on the left and walk to the water past the Mill Museum. Also free parking in the Mill car park.

Day tickets Adult/junior/OAP £2; available from the machine or the bailiff on the bank.

Best methods/baits Summer – polefish with sweetcorn, maggot or caster (sensitive quiver-tip recommended). Winter – use groundbait swim-feeder, with accurate casting.

Restrictions No hemp, bloodworm or joker. No livebaiting.

Facilities Toilets at the Mill; food in the Mill car park. Nearest pub, The Red Lion (35 yards). Gift shop at mill.

Disabled facilities Some pegs are designed for use by disabled anglers.

Pike.

Severn Trent Region

River Trent, Nottingham embankment.

Among the NRA regions, Severn Trent contains perhaps the most variety among its coarse fisheries, with rivers, canals, reservoirs and gravel pits, plus a host of lakes and ponds which are available to the angler.

Among the rivers, the region is dominated by the Severn and Trent, each with its own character and type of fishing. Rising in the Welsh Hills, the Severn flows rapidly through mainly rural areas around Shrewsbury and Worcester before entering the Bristol Channel, at the same time providing excellent coarse fishing, with top quality chub and barbel in its upper to middle reaches. In contrast, the slower-flowing Trent rises in Staffordshire and runs east through the industrialised areas of Nottingham and Newark to the Humber Estuary, providing good catches of coarse fish including roach, dace, perch and pike.

River fishing here, however, is not limited to the Severn and Trent. The River Teme, which rises near Ludlow and joins the Severn near Worcester, and the upper reaches of the Avon, near Stratford-on-Avon, both produce good chub and dace in large numbers – and in very pleasant surroundings.

Canal fishing – so popular in the Severn Trent region – centres largely on the Grand Union from Birmingham towards Northampton, but many smaller canals in the Midlands area also provide many miles of good quality fishing for most coarse species. The Montgomeryshire Canal, near Welshpool, also provides some excellent coarse fishing. And if the many smaller – and not so small – stillwaters, including lakes, pools and ponds is taken into consideration, Severn Trent clearly offers the coarse angler almost limitless opportunity to test his or her skills to the full.

The Grand Union Canal.

74

DERBYSHIRE

AMERICAN THEME PARK
Atlas Page 205 F.3/5.1

An excellent fishery at the Theme Park near Heanor, Derbyshire, where fishing begins when the fun ends in autumn. Plenty of roach, bream, carp and tench, plus some large pike (to 25lb). A first-class winter fishing venue.

How to get there From Nottingham, take the A609 west to Ilkeston, then the A6007 north-west towards Heanor. The Theme Park is on the A6007, approaching Heanor – you can't miss it, just follow the trail signs! Plenty of car parking on site.

Day tickets Adult £5; junior/OAP £2.50. Available on site.

Best methods/baits Roach – use pole or waggler, with plenty of loosefed maggots. Bream – use open-end feeder with worm or maggot.

Restrictions Fishing only 23rd September to 13th March (open daily from 3rd November).

Facilities Plenty of toilets/cafe/bars/shops/amusements on site.

Disabled facilities Some swims are suitable for disabled anglers; please phone for advice; Tel. 0602 637921 or 0533 848922.

BUTTERLY RESERVOIR
Atlas Page 205 F.3/4.8

A large reservoir near Alfreton, north of Derby. A pleasant venue, with summer sport provided by carp and specimen tench, while winter fishing includes mainly bream and roach.

How to get there Leave the M1 at jct 28 and take the A38 through Alfreton, then B6016 to Swanwick. Follow signs to the Midland Railway Centre; the reservoir is adjacent to the Centre. Free car parking on site.

Day tickets Adult/junior/OAP £2. Available on site.

Best methods/baits Use general coarse techniques and baits.

Facilities Nearest shop and pub, the Cross Keys, at Swanwick (less than 1 mile).

Disabled facilities Platforms have been constructed for use by disabled and wheelchair anglers.

CATTON PARK FISHERY
Atlas Page 205 E.7/5.9

Situated about 8 miles north of Tamworth, Catton Park fishery is about 10 acres, and provides general coarse fishing 7 days a week. Well stocked, with large carp of 10lb+ as well as other mixed species.

How to get there Take the A38 south from Burton upon Trent; after about 9 miles, turn left onto A513 Tamworth road. Pass under the railway bridge and take 1st left; the fishery is 1 mile on the left. Free car parking on site.

Day tickets Adult/junior/OAP £7. Available from the caravan at the fishery; for details, Tel. 0283 716876.

Best methods/baits Use any recognised coarse technique. Use specialist tackle for carp.

Restrictions No groundbaits. No keepnets.

Facilities Toilets on site. Nearest pub, White Swan (2 miles).

Disabled facilities Some swims suitable for disabled and wheelchair anglers.

RIVER DERWENT, WHATSTANDWELL
Atlas Page 205 E.9/4.7

A ½-mile, tree-lined stretch of the Derwent, between Belper and Matlock. Depth variable, from shallow gravel runs to deep running water (15ft). Excellent grayling, plus a bonus of chub, dace, trout and roach. Generally, fishing is best at the top end, where the water is faster.

How to get there From Derby, head north on the A6 to Belper, then Whatstandwell (about 5 miles from Belper). Look for the Derwent Hotel and park on the roadside nearby. Fishing is either side of the foundry.

Day tickets Adult/junior/OAP £1.50. Available from the Derwent Hotel.

Best methods Most methods work, but feeder fished and trotted baits are best. Use bomb or feeder in deep water.

Best baits Grayling – use maggots, worm, casters.

Restrictions No float fishing in close season.

Facilities Toilets/food at the Derwent Hotel. Shops in Whatstandwell village.

Disabled facilities For advice, please phone the Hotel; Tel. 0773 856616.

HARTSHORNE DAMS
Atlas Page 205 F.1/5.6

Two lakes located at a farm north of Swadlincote. One lake (1½ acres) contains only carp (to 20lb); the second lake (1 acre) contains mixed coarse species, including wild brown trout.

How to get there   Take the A50 east from Burton upon Trent and turn left at the 1st roundabout to Hartshorne. Go through the village and turn right at Bulls Head pub. The fishery is on the left. Free car parking.

Day tickets   Adult/junior/OAP £3. Available from Mr David Burchall, The Farmhouse, Manor Farm, Hartshorne, nr Burton upon Trent; Tel. 0283 215769.

Best methods/baits   Use any recognised coarse technique. Use minimum 8lb line on carp lake.

Restrictions   No groundbait.

Facilities   Nearest shop Hartshorne; nearest pub, Bulls Head (1 mile).

HIGHAM FARM
Atlas Page 205 F.3/4.9

A 4-lake fishing complex, each of about 3 acres, at a farm in pleasant surroundings near Alfreton. Water is quite deep (up to 12ft) and contains little weed. Expect most species – tench, chub, roach, bream – plus large carp (to 20lb+).

How to get there   From Derby take the A38 north to Alfreton, then A61 to Higham (about 3 miles). Look for Higham Farm within the village and park near the lake.

Day tickets   Adult ££5.50; junior/OAP £5.50. Available ££ on the bank.

Best methods   Use any recognised coarse technique; carp methods may be required.

Best baits   Boilies best for carp.

Facilities   Toilets/food at the hotel. Also village shop.

Disabled facilities   Some swims suitable for disabled anglers.

SWARKESTONE GRAVEL PITS
Atlas Page 205 F.1/5.3

A series of very large gravel pits due south-west of Derby. Plenty of roach, bream, tench, perch and pike, but only very few carp, though these can reach a good size.

How to get there   From Derby take the A5132 south through Swarkestone towards Willington. The gravel pits are visible from the road; look for The Rising Sun pub and follow signs to the fishery. Parking on site.

Day tickets   Weekly permits only £5 from Derby AA, PO Box 167, Derby DE3 7UE or local tackle shops.

Best methods/baits   Use any recognised coarse technique and baits.

Facilities   Nearest shop in Willington; nearest pub, The Rising Sun.

THE COPPICE WATER
Atlas Page 205 F.3/5.1

A 5-acre lake situated at Shipley Park, near the American Theme Park, north of Ilkeston. Good coarse fishing, with tench, roach, perch and pike, plus some large carp of 25lb+.

How to get there   From Derby, take the A6096 to Ilkeston, then A6007 north towards Heanor. The fishery is close to the Theme Park on the A6007; parking on site.

Day tickets   Adult/junior/OAP £3 per rod. Available from The Coppice Inn & Restaurant, Shipley Park; Tel. 0773 712606.

Best methods/baits   Use any recognised coarse technique and baits.

Facilities   Toilets/food/shop/bar available on site.

Disabled facilities   Some swims suitable for disabled anglers.

GLOUCESTER

GLOUCESTER AND SHARPNESS CANAL
Atlas Page 200 F.6/2.7

A long canal stretch (about 14 miles) running from the dismantled railway bridge at Sharpness, north-east to Hempsted Bridge, just south of Gloucester. Over 1000 pegs in all, providing deep, wide, regularly-dredged, weed-free water. Mainly roach, bream, chub and perch, plus some pike. Nets can reach 100lb!

How to get there   Follow the A38 south-west from Gloucester; access to the canal is via minor roads on the eastern side of the road. For details of access, contact Cheza Sports, 10 Kingsmill Road, Dursley (southern end); Batemans of Stroud (centre); or Gloucester Angling Centre, nr. Hempsted Bridge, Gloucester (northern end). Free parking is available at every bridge.
Day tickets   Free fishing.
Best methods/baits   Use general coarse techniques and baits.
Facilities   Various shops, pubs and toilets along the stretch.
Disabled facilities   Good towpaths for wheelchair and disabled anglers; fishing from the car is possible at some swims.

LYDNEY BOATING LAKE
Atlas Page 200 F.1/3.2
A busy town boating lake, quite large (5 acres) with a large island, children and boats (restricted to one end). A good mixed fishery, with roach, tench, bream, rudd, eels and barbel, plus some good common carp (to 9lb) and some mirrors (to 20lb). Fishing is best here at night, when things quieten down!

How to get there   Take the A40 Gloucester-Ross-on-Wye road and at roundabout bear left onto A48 towards Chepstow. At Lydney (about 20 miles) turn left (opposite Woolworth's), then right when past the houses. The boating lake is on the river side of the town. Park nearby.
Day tickets   Season ticket only: £10 (may increase) Day ticket £3; available from the sports shop in Lydney High Street.
Best methods/baits   Float fishing preferred. Only basic carp methods required.
Facilities   Nearest shop/pub in Lydney.
Disabled facilities   Some swims suitable for disabled anglers.

WATERSMEET
Atlas Page 200 F.6/3.7
Two mature pits, close to a guest house near Gloucester. A pleasant environment, with plenty of roach, tench, rudd and bream, plus some common carp (to 10lb) and some mirrors (to 20lb). Fishing is best here at night.

How to get there   Take the A40 Gloucester to Ross-on-Wye road and turn right after 1 mile onto A417 towards Ledbury. At Hartspury (about 5 miles) the ponds are on the left, next to Watersmeet Guest House (white-painted). Park nearby.
Day tickets   Adult/junior/OAP £2, £5 weekly, £11.50 season. Available from Mr & Mrs Ring at the Guest House. Tickets also available to residents.
Best methods/baits   Most species – use any recognised coarse technique. Carp – use advanced methods.
Facilities   Nearest shop in Hartspury.
Disabled facilities   Some swims suitable for disabled anglers.

HEREFORD & WORCESTER

A.C.R. FISHERIES, EVESBATCH
Atlas Page 200 F.5/1.9
Two lakes – one large, one small – in a popular fishery west of Great Malvern. The large lake is carp only, with specimens to 20lb+; the small lake contains general coarse fish of mixed species.

How to get there   Take the A4103 south-west from Worcester for about 11 miles and turn right on minor road to Evesbatch. Look for signs to the fishery and car park.
Day tickets   Adult/junior/OAP £3 winter, £3.50 summer. Available from Alans Fishing Tackle, St. Johns, Worcester. *Note* : tickets must be purchased *before* fishing.
Best methods/baits   Use any recognised coarse technique and baits.
Facilities   Nearest shop/pub in Evesbatch.
Disabled facilities   Some swims suitable for disabled anglers.

ARROW LAKE
Atlas Page 202 A.4/2.6
A medium-sized lake near Redditch, providing very good coarse fishing for tench, roach, rudd and some large bream; also some double-figure carp. Very heavily fished at weekends, but much quieter on weekdays.

How to get there   At Redditch, south of Birmingham. The lake is located at the site of the Shakespeare Tackle Company. For details of access and parking, contact the local tackle shops.

Day tickets   Adult/junior/OAP £2.80; junior/OAP £1.50. Available from the Warden at the property, John Lewis; Tel. 0527 68337.

Best methods/baits   Use any recognised coarse technique and baits.

Facilities   Nearest shops/pubs in Redditch.

EASTNOR CASTLE
Atlas Page 200 F.4/3.3

A beautiful lake (about 5 acres), surrounded by trees, just outside Ledbury. Some areas are thickly covered by lilies, making fishing impossible. Expect mainly roach, rudd, bream, tench and carp, with mirrors and commons to 15lb+.

How to get there   From Tewkesbury, drive west on the A438 towards Ledbury; Eastnor is on the left, about 1 mile before Ledbury. The entrance to the fishery is on the left; follow the signs to the car park.

Day tickets   Adult/junior/OAP £3. Available from the bailiffs on the bank.

Best methods/baits   Use any recognised coarse technique and baits. Most carp are caught at the dam end, or near the lilies.

Facilities   Nearest shop/pub in Eastnor village.

Disabled facilities   Some swims suitable for disabled anglers.

Common carp.

GOLDEN VALLEY
Atlas Page 200 F.6/3.3

A dammed-type estate lake, situated on open common land at Castlemorton, near Ledbury. A high, open water providing good catches of Crucian carp, roach, perch and bream, plus some common carp in the 6–8lb range. Most fish are caught here at night.

How to get there   From Tewkesbury, drive west on the A438 towards Ledbury; after about 6 miles, turn right onto B4208 and continue 1 mile. A lane on the left runs to the common; the lake is on the right. Park nearby.

Day tickets   Adult/junior/OAP 50p. Available from the bailiffs on the bank.

Best methods/baits   Use any recognised coarse technique and baits. Some specialist carp methods may be needed. No keepnets.

Facilities   Nearest shop/pub at Castlemorton.

Disabled facilities   Some swims suitable for disabled anglers.

HAYE FARM FISHERY
Atlas Page 200 F.6/1.2

A recently-dug but small farm pond near Snuff Mill on the River Severn at Bewdley. Although a new venue, a good head of quite large carp (15lb+) and other coarse fish ensure entertaining fishing here.

How to get there   At Bewdley, follow signs to the River Severn and Snuff Mill. For details of access and parking, contact the local tackle shops.

Day tickets   Adult/junior/OAP £3. Available on the bank.

Best methods/baits   Use any recognised coarse technique and baits.

Facilities   Nearest shops/pubs in Bewdley.

HERRIOTS POOL
Atlas Page 200 F.8/1.7

A small pool, near Droitwich, containing most coarse species.

How to get there   Leave the M5 at jct 5 and take A38 to Droitwich, turn left at traffic lights by Chateaux Impney, follow road to swimming pool. Herriots Pool is on the left; park by the pool.

Day tickets   Adult/junior/OAP 85p from bailiff on the bank.

Best methods/baits Use any recognised coarse technique and baits.

Facilities Nearest shops/pubs in Droitwich.

Disabled facilities Suitable for disabled and wheelchair anglers.

MOORLANDS FARM
Atlas Page 200 F.6/1.2

Six lakes, near Kidderminster, all suitably stocked for match fishing with nine species in each lake.

How to get there Take the A449 from Kidderminster to Worcester, after 6 miles you cannot fail to see the 6ft fish signposting the fishery.

Day tickets Adult/junior/OAP £3; junior/OAP £2.50 weekdays. Night fishing by appointment only.

Best methods/baits Use general match fishing techniques and baits.

Restrictions No cereal groundbait, boilies or bloodworm. No keepnets.

Facilities Toilets, a permanent snack bar on the site, two pubs and a shop in Hartlebury.

Disabled facilities The lakes are readily usable by disabled and wheelchair anglers, with regular matches held there. Disabled toilet facilities also available.

POOLE HALL
Atlas Page 200 F.6/1.2

A six-lake complex, five of which are used for coarse fishing, near Kidderminster. Expect roach, carp, tench, rudd, gudgeon and bream in most pools. A consistent fishery, with best fishing in deep water in the winter months.

Mirror carp.

How to get there From Birmingham, take the A456 west to Kidderminster and turn north onto the A442, towards Bridgnorth. Poole Hall is on the left after about 2 miles; follow signs to the fishery. Parking available on site.

Day tickets Adult/junior/OAP £3 for general coarse fishing; £4 for specimen fishing. Available on site. For further information; Tel. 02997 458.

Best methods Most methods work well here. Paste baits (fruit- flavoured), bread, sweetcorn and maggots all work well.

Restrictions Use only barbless hooks.

Facilities Toilets on site. Nearest shops/pubs in Kidderminster.

Disabled facilities Some swims suitable for disabled and wheelchair anglers; please phone for advice (see above).

SNUFF MILL
Atlas Page 200 F6/1.2

A very small, old pool near the River Severn at Bewdley, providing reasonable quality coarse fishing for tench, roach and bream, plus some good quality carp of 15lb+.

How to get there At Bewdley, follow signs to the River Severn and Snuff Mill. For details of access and parking, contact the local tackle shops (see below).

Day tickets Adult/junior/OAP £2. Available from S. Lewis Tackle, Severnside South, Bewdley; Tel. 0299 403358.

Best methods/baits Use any recognised coarse technique and baits.

Facilities Nearest shops/pubs in Bewdley.

WELLFIELD POOL
Atlas Page 200 F.6/1.2

This small pool is close to the Severn, about 6 miles due north of Bewdley. Good quality coarse fishing, with tench, bream and roach; carp here are mainly small – but growing well!

How to get there From Bewdley, head north-west on the B4194 and bear right onto B4363. After about 2 miles, turn right onto B4555 and follow road round to Highley. Look for signs to the fishery and car park.

Day tickets   Adult/junior/OAP £2.
  Available from S. Lewis Tackle,
  Severnside South, Bewdley;
  Tel. 0299 403358.
Best methods/baits   Use any recognised
  coarse technique and baits.
Facilities   Nearest shop/pub in Highley
  village.
Disabled facilities   Some swims suitable
  for disabled anglers.

WILDEN POOL
Atlas Page 200 F.6/1.3

A fair-sized pool, close to the River Stour,
just east of Stourport-on-Severn. Variety of
coarse fishing here is limited, with few of
the main species, but expect some good
quality carp, many small, but with the
occasional fish to 10lb+.

How to get there   From Kidderminster,
  drive south on the A449 and after about
  3 miles take minor road on right towards
  Wilden village and the River Stour.
  Follow directions to the pool and car
  park.
Day tickets   Adult/junior/OAP £2.50.
  Available on the bank.
Best methods/baits   Use standard float or
  leger tactics, with recognised baits.
Facilities   Nearest shop/pub in Wilden
  village.

Grand Union Canal.

WITLEY FRUITS FISHERY
Atlas Page 200 F.7/1.8

Three pools, one with a few specimen carp
to 20lb, otherwise a carp pool with mixed
fish, one with crucian and golden Orfe, the
other mixed competition fish. Set in the
country with ample space between them,
and a few miles from Worcester.

How to get there   From Worcester take
  the A443, go through Little Witley, turn
  right by some green houses to Shrawley.
  The pools start 1 mile on the left.
Day tickets   Adult £3 weekdays; £4
  weekends; junior with adult/OAP £1.50.
  Half-day tickets also available. From
  Frank Colwill, Dingle Farm, Little
  Witley, nr Worcester; Tel. 0299 896600.
Best methods   Use good coarse fishing
  methods and baits.
Restrictions   Use only barbless hooks.
  No boilies, hemp or groundbait.
Facilities   Mrs Colwill is going to start
  providing snacks at the bank. Also pick
  your own fruit nearby. Nearest
  shop/pub in Gt Witley (3 miles).
Disabled facilities   Very suitable for
  disabled and wheelchair anglers.

LEICESTERSHIRE

GRAND UNION CANAL
Atlas Page 202 B.9/2.1

A 5-mile stretch of the canal near Market
Harborough; well stocked with carp (to
about 10lb) plus a good head of roach,
tench and bream.

How to get there   From Market
  Harborough, access to the canal can be
  made at various points along minor
  roads to the north-west and west of the
  town. Check with local tackle shops for
  details.
Day tickets   Adult £1; junior/OAP 50p.
  Season ticket: Adults £8, junior/OAP
  £4. Available from bailiffs on the bank,
  or from Sports Shop, 7 St. Mary Road,
  Market Harborough; Tel. 0858 464046.
Best methods/baits   Use any recognised
  coarse technique and baits.
Facilities   Various shops/pubs along the
  stretch.
Disabled facilities   Access for disabled
  anglers is possible at some locations;
  check with bailiffs or local tackle shops.

MAKIN FISHERIES
Atlas Page 202 A.9/2.2

A five-lake complex just north of Coventry. Lakes range from beginners, with plenty of small/medium mixed fish to specimen waters containing carp into double figures. An enjoyable fishery which can suit all levels of angler.

How to get there   Leave the M69 at jct 1 and take B4112 to Wolvey village. In the village, turn down Bulkington Raod (opposite Subaru garage) and turn right at sign to Bramcote (¾ mile). The fishery is 300 yards on the right. Free car parking.

Day tickets   From 16th June–31st October: adult £5; junior £3; disabled/OAP £2. From 1st November–14th March: adult £3; junior £2; disabled/OAP £1. Evening tickets half-price all season. Available on site.

Best methods/baits   Use general coarse techniques and baits. Heavy feeding is best in summer.

Restrictions   No keepnets. Use only barbless hooks. No matches or bookings. Any amendments to fishing times will be published on the banks.

Facilities   Toilets/food (mobile) on site. Nearest shop and pub, The Blue Pig, in Wolvey village (1 mile).

Disabled facilities   Most swims have concreted positions suitable for disabled and wheelchair anglers.

NANPANTAN RESERVOIR
Atlas Page 202 B.4/2.2

A small reservoir of about 5 acres, located a few miles from Loughborough. Drained several years ago and stocked with mirror carp which now range from 10–20lb. Also bream, tench, roach and perch.

How to get there   From Loughborough, follow the B5350 south-west towards Nanpantan; follow signs to the reservoir and park on site.

Day tickets   Adult £2; junior/OAP £1. Available from W.H. Wortley, 45 Baxter Gate, Loughborough; Tel. 0509 212697. Limited numbers only (see below).

Best methods   Use any recognised coarse technique and carp methods as required.

Best baits   sweetcorn, luncheon meat for carp.

Restrictions   No groundbaiting. Maximum 30 anglers per day. No night fishing. Part of the reservoir is closed to anglers.

Facilities   Nearest shop/pub in Nanpantan.

Rivers

RIVER SOAR

The Soar is one of Britain's slowest flowing rivers, for many years nick-named 'gudgeon alley' and ignored by most anglers due to the predominance of these tiny fish and lack of good sport. However, today, the river has taken on a new lease of life, with a wide choice of swims, easily-accessed banks (though a long walk may be needed), plus plentiful numbers of roach, dace and chub.

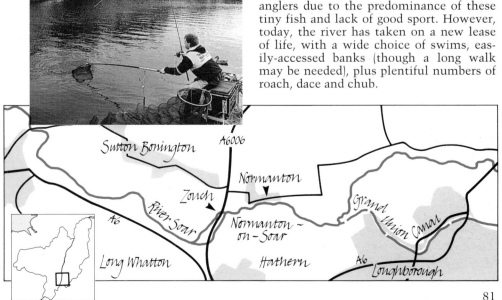

NORMANTON
Atlas Page 202 B.9/1.3

A slow-flowing section; depth 10ft beyond nearside 10-yard shelf, 6ft at the far bank. Some weed growth. Fishable side is clear of cover; moorings opposite. Mainly roach, gudgeon, perch, chub, skimmer bream. Expect a 10lb net – gudgeon first, roach and chub later.

How to get there Take the A6006 west from Melton Mowbray. After about 16 miles, look for Normanton-on-Soar on the left. Follow signs to the river and park carefully.

Day tickets Adults £2; junior/OAP 75p. Available in advance from local tackle shops.

Best methods Most species – waggler or pole (with a light styls rig) tactics. Loosefeed with maggots – sparingly.

Best baits Maggots (bronze or red), hemp.

Facilities Food/toilets at the village pub.

Disabled facilities Access is good but involves a long walk.

Hotspot Tips

- If the river is off-form, try using a very light leger.
- Start fishing against the far bank with a waggler, but be prepared to change to an inside line pole.
- The best swims are opposite the pub.

ZOUCH
Atlas Page 202 B.9/1.3

A clear, easily-fishable bank with some trees and bushes. Depth is variable, but expect 8ft in most swims. There are some ledges, so plumb around. An even-fishing stretch, with mainly roach and chub (nets of 15lb+) or gudgeon and dace (nets of 10lb).

How to get there Follow the A6006 west from Melton Mowbray via Normanton-on-Soar (about 16 miles), then Zouch. Park on the roadside and walk upstream towards Normanton.

Day tickets Adults £2; junior/OAP 75p. Available in advance from Loughborough tackle shops.

Best methods Roach – standard light styl rig with 22 hook; chub - waggler at the far bank.

Best baits Maggots (bronze and red); hemp for loosefeed.

Hotspot Tips

- For big roach, feed with bronze maggot/hemp, but use red maggot hookbait.
- Keep shot down the line and expect bites on the drop.
- The swims with far bank cover provide more scope.

River Soar.

LINCOLNSHIRE

A brace of common carp.

HOLME LAKE, MESSINGHAM
Atlas Page 205 G.5/4.5

A 15-acre lake containing large carp (up to 27lb), plus bream (9lb), roach (2lb), rudd, perch and dace. Fishing in season only 15th March to 16th June.

How to get there Take the A15 north from Lincoln; at Kirton in Lindsey (about 18 miles) look for B4100 on left to Messingham (about 8 miles).

Day tickets Adult £3 (12 hours) or £5 (24 hours) Fri, Sat, Sun only. Enquiries for permits to Alan Barton (Tel. 0724 850917) or on the bank.

Restrictions No keepnets to be used.

LOWFIELDS COUNTRY HOLIDAY FISHING RETREAT
Atlas Page 205 G.1/4.9

A holiday retreat in beautiful surroundings, with 3 small lakes providing fishing sport. A good mixed fishery, with perch, roach, bream, tench and eels, plus plenty of large carp (to 20lb).

How to get there From Newark-on-Trent take the A1133 north about 10 miles and take right turn on minor road to North Scarle. Follow signs to the Holiday Retreat (which was formerly known as 'The Poplars'). Parking on site.

Day tickets Fishing available only to resident holiday-makers. Enquiries Tel. 0522 77717.

Best methods/baits Use any recognised coarse technique and baits.

Facilities Toilets/self-catering accommodation on site. Nearest shop/pub in North Scarle village.

Disabled facilities Some swims suitable for disabled anglers.

NOTTINGHAMSHIRE

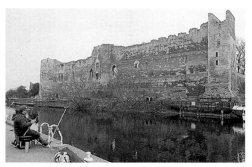

Newark Town Centre.

A1 PIT
Atlas Page 205 G.1/4.9

A very large, 40-acre gravel pit which occasionally floods from the River Trent, located a few miles north of Newark. An excellent mixed fishery with most species, but also very well stocked with large carp up to 20lb+.

How to get there Turn off the A1 at North Muskham, just north of Newark-on-Trent. In the village, the entrance to the pit is just by the railway crossing.

Day tickets Adult/junior/OAP £2.50; 24-hrs ticket £4; weekend ticket £7. Available on the bank.

Best methods/baits Use any recognised coarse technique and baits.

Facilities Nearest shop/pub in North Muskham.

Disabled facilities Some pegs are suitable for disabled and wheelchair anglers.

ATTENBOROUGH SOUTH
Atlas Page 205 F.6/5.2

A vast (114-acre) gravel pit, just south of Nottingham, and close to the River Trent. Mainly mixed coarse fish, plus a few carp. A 1½-mile stretch of the Trent is included in this fishery and provides good carp sport.

How to get there From Nottingham, head south-west to Long Eaton. At Station Road, take New Hythe Street (opposite Horshoe Sports) for 1 mile to municipal car park.

Day tickets Adult £1.50; junior/OAP 75p. Available from 'Wotsits' Tackle Shop, 8 Archer Road, Nottingham; Tel. 0602 396096.

Best methods/baits   Use any recognised coarse technique and baits.
Restrictions   Fishing dawn-dusk only; no night fishing. River fishing only when no matches are being held.
Facilities   Nearest shops/pubs in Long Eaton.

CLUMBER PARK LAKE
Atlas Page 205 F.6/4.8

A huge lake in a National Trust-controlled park, lying between Worksop and Mansfield. Good mixed coarse fishing, with plenty of bream, skimmer bream, roach and perch.

How to get there   Various approaches: from A57 east of Worksop; from A614 south-east of Worksop; from B6005 Worksop-Ollerton road. Follow signs to various car parks around the lake.
Note: some areas are designated non-angling zones.
Day tickets   Adult £2.50; under 12's/OAP £1.50. Available from the bailiff on the bank.
Best methods/baits   Use any recognised coarse technique.
Facilities   Nearest shops/pubs Worksop, Norton, Cuckney, Carburton (according to location).
Disabled facilities   Disabled angling platforms at Hardwick village end of lake (though vehicular access is not possible).

DANESHILL LAKE
Atlas Page 205 F.6/4.6

A small lake at Torworth, just north-west of East Retford. A moderate fishery, with most coarse species, including some large carp which were stocked in 1984 (at 11lb) and are now achieving specimen size!

How to get there   Leave the north-bound A1 at Blyth (just north of East Retford) and turn right onto A634, then B6045. Look for right turn to Torworth village; the lake is in Daneshill Road, near the mainline railway. Parking on site.
Day tickets   Adult £2; junior/OAP £1. Season tickets: adult £15; junior/OAP £12. Available on site.
Best methods/baits   Use any recognised coarse technique and baits.
Restrictions   No night fishing.
Facilities   Nearest shop/pub in Torworth.

RIVER IDLE
Atlas Page 205 F.7/3.9

An almost 3-mile, north bank, stretch of the Idle, between Cornley Lane and West Stockwith pumping station, with flow from east to west. Mainly bream, skimmer bream, roach, gudgeon and pike, plus some chub.

How to get there   From Doncaster, head south on the A638 to Bawtry. Then various access points: from the A161 at Haxey Gate bridge and on unclassified road behind Haxey Gate Inn (upstream); from the A161 at Haxey Gate bridge and North Carr Road; by footpath past West Stockwith pumping station. Park on or near the river bank according to location.
Day tickets   Adult £1; junior/OAP £1 Available from the bailiff on the bank.
Best methods/baits   Use any recognised coarse technique.
Facilities   Nearest shop/pub West Stockwith.
Disabled facilities   Limited access/ suitability for disabled anglers.

NORTH MUSKHAM FISHERY
Atlas Page 205 G.1/4.8

A fishing complex comprising three lakes and a section of the River Trent, a few miles north of Newark. Expect a good mixed bag of roach, chub, bream, dace, tench, pike, bleak and gudgeon, plus plenty of good carp about 5lb. In No. 1 lake, there is also the chance of very big carp, to 25lb+!

How to get there   Turn off the A1 at North Muskham, just north of Newark-on-Trent. In the village, follow signs to the fishery and park on site.
Day tickets   Adult £2.50; junior/OAP £2.50. Available on site; Tel. 0636 702457.
Best methods/baits   Use any recognised coarse technique and baits.
Facilities   Nearest shop/pub in North Muskham.

SANDHILL LAKE
Atlas Page 205 F.5/4.4

A permanently-pegged pleasure fishing lake (except for school and OAP matches) in Worksop town; owned by Bassetlaw District Council and controlled by

Worksop & District Angling Society. Mainly rudd, tench, roach and bream, plus some chub, pike and perch.

How to get there In Worksop, turn off Gateford Road (the old A57) into Gladston Street; take the 4th turn on the left, just before John street. There is ample car parking in controlled zones.

Day tickets Adult £2; junior/OAP £50p. Available from the bailiff on the bank.

Best methods/baits Use any recognised coarse technique.

Facilities Nearest shops/pubs in Worksop.

Disabled facilities Some pegs are suitable for disabled anglers on canal-side car parks. No disabled angling platforms.

SAPPHIRE LAKE
Atlas Page 205 G.1/4.8

A widely publicised fishery due to its very big catches, about 7 miles north of Newark. Most species present, including bream, perch and eels, but huge carp are the attraction, with 25lb+ fish quite common and 35lb+ monsters rumoured.

How to get there Take the A1 north of Newark and turn left at Cromwell (just after North Muskham roundabout). Follow the minor road to Norwell; the lake is signposted along this road. Parking on site.

Day tickets Carp lake: adult/junior/ OAP £6; Coarse lakes: adult £3,; junior £2. Available on site; for details; Tel. 0636 821131.

Best methods/baits Use any recognised coarse technique and baits.

Restrictions Line of less than 10lb breaking strain is banned in some areas. Night fishermen must leave car keys with owner.

Facilities Toilets on site. Nearest shop/pub in Cromwell village.

Rivers

RIVER TRENT

After drastic anti-pollution treatment by the former Trent River Board, the Trent has now begun to glisten again, with streamer weed beginning to grow, gravels to glisten, and virtually every species of coarse fish beginning to flourish. Among others, chub, barbel, bream and carp have colonised the water in abundance to provide the premier match- and pleasure-fishing venue in the country – a true 'gem'. The Trent Embankment to Hoveringham stretch of the Trent contains six *Angling Times* Hotspots.

THRUMPTON
Atlas Page 205 F.6/5.2

A pleasant section of the Trent, a few miles south-west of Nottingham, and downstream of Radcliffe Power Station. Excellent fishing for chub, roach and skimmer bream in the deep, slow-moving water.

How to get there Leave the M1 at jct 24 and take the A453 towards Nottingham. After about 3½ miles, look for left turn on minor road to Thrumpton village and the river. The fishery is close to a caravan site; free car parking nearby.

Day tickets Adult/junior/OAP £2. Available on the banks.

Best methods/baits Use general coarse techniques and baits.

Facilities Toilet facilities at the caravan site. Nearest shop and pub, in Clifton village (1 mile).

Disabled facilities Some swims suitable for disabled and wheelchair anglers.

BARTON ISLAND
Atlas Page 205 F.6/5.2

A very wide, very slow-moving section of the Trent, with very deep water on the wide side of the island. Excellent fishing on the shallow side for roach in winter. Bream are often taken in the wider sections, but try the peg 57 region for some good-sized chub.

How to get there Leave the M1 at jct 24 and take the A453 towards Nottingham. Take the third turn on the left after Radcliffe Power Station (about 5 miles), into Barton village. Follow signs to the river; free car parking nearby.

Day tickets Adult £2; junior/OAP £1. Available on the bank.

Best methods/baits Use general coarse techniques and baits.

Facilities Nearest shop and pub in Barton village.

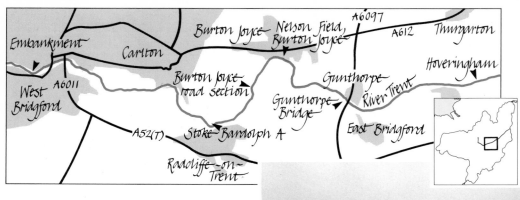

CLIFTON BRIDGE
Atlas Page 205 F.6/4.2

A very deep, slow-moving stretch of the Trent, about 5 miles south-west of Nottingham. Fishing is best here when the weather is warm, with excellent catches of chub, plus a wide variety of other coarse species.

How to get there   Leave the M1 at jct 24 and take the A453 towards Nottingham. Continue for about 6 miles, then turn left to Clifton village. Follow signs to the river; free car parking nearby.

Day tickets   Adult/junior/OAP £2. Available on the bank.

Best methods/baits   Use general coarse techniques and baits.

Facilities   Nearest shop, Clifton village; nearest pub, The Crusader, on the A453.

BEESTON WEIR
Atlas Page 205 F.6/4.1

The river near Beeston Weir provides a great variety of coarse fishing. Above the weir, expect good winter roach and big summer bream. Below the weir, expect good catches of chub, large barbel (to 11lb) and roach, plus pike in the weir pool. The Wattonians – the stretch to Clifton Bridge – regularly produces 60lb nets, mainly of chub.

How to get there   Leave the M1 at jct 24 and take the A453 towards Nottingham. Continue for about 6 miles, then turn left to Clifton village. Follow signs to Clifton Grove and Beeston Weir (anyone in the village will give you directions!). Free car parking nearby.

Day tickets   Adult/junior/OAP £2. Available on the bank.

River Trent, Nottingham embankment.

Best methods/baits   Use general coarse techniques and baits.

Facilities   Nearest shop, Clifton village; nearest pub, The Crusader, on the A453.

NOTTINGHAM
Atlas Page 205 F.6/4.1

A stretch of varying depth (5–8ft), very shallow close in, with heavy summer weed growth. Mainly roach and silver bream in summer, plus barbel and bream mid-stream; chub are more evident in winter. Typical mixed catches are 10lb+, but barbel hauls may top 30lb.

How to get there   At the junction of the A52 and A453, look for signs to Wilford Toll Bridge. The stretch is located between the toll bridge and Trent Bridge, Nottingham.

Day tickets   Free fishing

Best methods   Summer – block-end feeder fished two-thirds across. Waggler (with caster) in slow, inside-line water.

Best baits Hemp, casters or tares as summer hookbaits.

Facilities Food/shops/toilets in Nottingham.

Hotspot Tips

- A long-line, 6–8-metre pole with seed bait and a very light float can produce excellent roach.
- Use a stick float when the river is carrying extra water.
- The best swims are opposite the boat ramp, just below Wilford Flats.

EASTWOOD SECTION
Atlas Page 205 F.6/5.2

A Nottingham town-centre section of the Trent, with 30 pegs providing some good coarse fishing. The wide, slow-moving water is well known for its roach, and also for some big chub which are often taken near the bridge.

How to get there Leave the M1 at jct 24 and take the A453 to Nottingham. Follow signs towards Nottingham Forest football ground and Lady Bay Bridge. Access to the river banks is clearly marked; free car parking nearby.

Day tickets Adult/junior/OAP £2. Available on the bank.

Best methods/baits Use general coarse techniques and baits.

Facilities Shops, pubs and toilets nearby, in the town centre.

Disabled facilities Tarmac path along the river bank provides suitable fishing for disabled and wheelchair anglers.

NOTTINGHAM EMBANKMENT
Atlas Page 205 F.6/5.2

A deep, slow-moving section of the river, upstream of the town centre and including four bridges. Expect chub catches near the bridges, plus plenty of roach and other coarse species – for which the fishery is renowned – in other areas.

How to get there Leave the M1 at jct 24 and take the A453 to Nottingham. Follow signs towards the town centre and locate Trent Bridge. Access is available to the embankment on both sides of the river; free car parking available nearby.

Day tickets Free fishing (for about 300 pegs).

Best methods/baits Use general coarse techniques and baits.

Facilities Shops/cafes(3)/toilets along the embankment; there are two pubs (with good food), one at each end of the bridge.

Disabled facilities Some swims suitable for disabled and wheelchair anglers.

HIGGIN TRENT
Atlas Page 205 F.6/5.2

A deep, slow-moving stretch, at Lady Bay Bridge, near Nottingham town centre. Fishing is from 60 pegs (beginning at peg 30) downstream from the bridge. Expect a wide variety of good coarse fish, but especially good quality roach.

How to get there Leave the M1 at jct 24 and take the A453 to Nottingham. Follow signs towards the town centre and Lady Bay Bridge; car parking nearby. For further details of access/parking, contact local tackle shops.

Day tickets Adult/junior/OAP £2. Available on the bank.

Best methods/baits Use general coarse techniques and baits.

Facilities Various shops and pubs in the town centre.

BARDOLPH A SECTION
Atlas Page 205 F.6/5.2

Inside line flow is poor here, but rises a quarter of the way across. Expect shoals of bream and silver bream in summer, plus roach, chub, dace and good carp and barbel. Chub are more common in winter, but roach, dace, barbel and carp all available. Catches reach 20–30lb, or 50lb+ if carp are feeding.

The calm and eerie Trent.

How to get there   By car, take the upstream track from the Ferry Boat Inn at Stoke Bardolph. Park next to the weir, and walk through the lock-keeper's yard and clapper gates until you reach the river (at Peg 341). Walk upstream to the hotspot.

Day tickets   Adult £2; junior/OAP £1 available from the bailiff on the bank.

Best methods   Feeder is supreme. Summer bream–casters and groundbait with open-ended feeder, and red maggot or worm on hook. Winter – block-end feeder.

Best baits   Casters, hemp, maggots, red worms and sweetcorn; winter – bronze and red maggots.

Hotspot Tips

- Try fishing a waggler 3–4 rod-lengths out for roach and skimmer bream.
- The best swims are around Peg 374.

BURTON JOYCE ROAD
Atlas Page 205 F.6/5.2

A fairly wide section, with steady pace and 6–8ft depth. Mainly chub and roach, plus some bream. Roach all year; chub and gudgeon appear at the end of the season. Typical catches are 10lb+ in summer, 20lb+ in winter. Sport is very good after flooding, when the water is coloured.

How to get there   Take the A612 from Nottingham towards Newark on Trent. Follow signs to Stoke Bardolph, and take road to Burton Joyce village. The road runs alongside the river.

Day tickets   Adult £2; junior/OAP £1 available from the bailiff on the bank.

Best methods   Use pole to feeder; summer – casters fished with hemp; winter – short whips and maggot fished with 1.5 gram olivette rigs.

Best baits   Summer – casters, hemp; winter – stewing steak (hookbait with large waggler or balsa float) and mince (groundbait) for chub.

Hotspot Tips

- Use a block-end feeder for chub, especially from peg 260 upstream to the outfall.
- Try stewing steak as hookbait for winter chub.
- Best pegs are: chub, 260–277; roach, 240–270; gudgeon, 265- 272; bream, 235–245; bleak, 272–277 (flood only).

NELSON FIELD, BURTON JOYCE
Atlas Page 205 F.7/5.2

A wide stretch with strong, even flow on the inside and a 'snaggy' bottom. Barbel provide the best sport, with 6lb+ fish possible. Poor day catches exceed 10lb; 50lb+ catches are common. Skill is required – wily barbel only respond to hooklengths of 1½–2lb.

How to get there   On the A612, at the Lord Nelson pub, between Lowdham roundabout and Colwick Loop Road. Park at the pub and walk through the railway crossing gates towards the river. Follow the pegs downstream.

Day tickets   Adult £2; junior/OAP £1 available from the bailiff on the river bank.

Best methods   Block-end feeder, fished 3 rod-lengths out.

Best baits   Hemp, casters, maggots; luncheon meat as hookbait.

Facilities   Food/toilets at the Lord Nelson pub.

Hotspot Tips

- Keep on groundbaiting to hold the barbel on the boil!
- Peg 187 is the prime barbel spot on the stretch.

GUNTHORPE BRIDGE
Atlas Page 205 F.7/5.2

A stretch with depth to 8ft and average pace. Lilies provide marginal cover in summer. Mainly chub and large bream in summer; large fish are rare in winter unless water is coloured. Catches are excellent all year; 30lb is common in winter; 70lb of chub has been taken on a stick float and maggots!

How to get there   Gunthorpe Bridge lies on the A6097, between Lowdham and Bingham. Parking is difficult in summer; spaces are limited, so arrive early!

Day tickets   Adult £2; junior/OAP £1; available from the bailiff on the river bank.

Best methods   Various methods, including float and feeder; use pole downstream of the bridge (bream, roach and gudgeon respond to a 5–6-metre whip).

Best baits Maggots, hemp with pole or running line. Red maggots, redworms hookbaits.

Hotspot Tips

- Pegs 2a and 3 are chub hotspots; pegs 6–9 are great float angling sites (notably for bream).
- For bream, try beet and brown sliced crumb, with a dash of Brasem, plus casters in an open-end feeder.

HOVERINGHAM
Atlas Page 205 F.8/5.2

A fairly shallow stretch, normally under 6ft deep right across. A small shelf under the inside bank supports summer weed growth. Chub (1–4lb), small roach and silver bream (up to 4lb) are taken in both summer and winter. Nets of 20lb are realistic; 30–40lb nets are common; 60lb has been reached.

How to get there Hoveringham village lies just east of the A612 Nottingham to Southwell road, and north-east of Caythorpe.
Day tickets Adult £2; junior/OAP £1; available from the bailiff on the bank.
Best methods Long-range feeders provide good mixed catches; roach – waggler in summer, stick float in winter.
Best baits Maggots ideal; casters, hemp for large chub and bream.

Hotspot Tips

- The best swims are at pegs 120–130; peg 128 seems to be in top form.

NEWARK-ON-TRENT
Atlas Page 205 G.1/4.9

This deep, wide, slow-moving river stretch of the Trent, which extends from Newark Castle, upstream to the weir, provides some very good fishing, with mainly chub and some big carp. Also barbel, roach and bream in the deeper water by the castle.

How to get there Take the A1 north beyond Grantham and turn left on the A6065 (or via the A17) to Newark-on-Trent. Access to the river bank is in the town centre, near the castle. Free car parking is available near the river. For further details of access/parking, contact the local tackle shop.
Day tickets Adult/junior/OAP £2. Available on the bank.

Best methods/baits Use general coarse techniques and baits.
Facilities Various shops/pubs/toilets/food in the town centre.
Disabled facilities Some areas of the bank, opposite the castle, have been concreted for use by disabled and wheelchair anglers.

Rivers
THE UPPER TRENT

An early evening catch.

Considered by many enthusiasts as the jewel in the Midland's angling crown, the Upper Trent is a wide, powerful river with mostly even-paced sections, interspersed with the occasional very fast-flowing stretch. It can – at times – surprise even its regular anglers with its prolific early season catches, which comprise many good chub and barbel. However, these are quickly rivalled by the large numbers of roach which appear along with the first frosts of autumn.

CUTTLE BROOK
Atlas Page 205 F.1/5.4

A mainly fast, shallow section providing summer chub, roach and dace, plus a few barbel. Some swims in the wood (permanent pegs 40–50) provide deeper water; the best swims are at the top end.

How to get there Leave the M1 at jct 25 and take the A52 to Derby. From the ring road, follow signs south to Swarkestone. Enter the car park through the farm ¼ mile before Swarkestone Bridge. The fishery is downstream.
Day tickets Weekly permits only: £5 from Derby AA, PO Box 167, Derby DE3 7UE, or from local tackle shops.

The scenic Upper Trent.

Best methods   Most species – stick float; waggler and feeder in the wood. Barbel – feeder.

Hotspot Tips

& Look for big barbel on the high bank at low peg numbers.

& Strong end tackle is vital for barbel – they are often 5lb+.

CREWE AND HARPUR
Atlas Page 205 F.1/5.4

A stretch with a fast-flowing top end, and a much steadier bottom end. Depth varies from 3 to 6ft. Mainly roach and chub, with 50lb nets common later in the season.

How to get there   Leave the M1 at jct 25 and take the A52 to Derby. From the ring road, follow signs south to Swarkestone. Park in the Crewe and Harpur car park, next to the bridge.

Day tickets   Weekly permits only: £5 from Derby AA, PO Box 167, Derby DE3 7UE, or from local tackle shops.

Best methods   Roach – stick float (especially after Christmas).

Hotspot Tips

& Top pegs are best early season, bottom pegs later on.

INGLEBY TO SWARKESTONE BRIDGE
Atlas Page 205 F.1/5.4

A shallow stretch with a few deeper pegs just above Swarkestone Bridge. Summer sport is mainly chub, roach and dace, plus some barbel. Expect 20lb+ nets in most places. The best match net is 106lb! Barbel seldom show later in the year.

How to get there   Leave the M1 at jct 25 and take the A52 to Derby. From the ring road, follow signs south to Swarkestone. Enter the car park through the farm ¼ mile before Swarkestone Bridge. The fishery is upstream.

Day tickets   Weekly permits only: £5 from Derby AA, PO Box 167, Derby DE3 7UE, or from local tackle shops.

Best methods   Most species – stick float; barbel – feeder.

Hotspot Tips

& Don't forget your strong end tackle for the barbel!

& The best pegs are 12, 19, 28 and 29, or the beach at the bottom of the stretch.

JOHN THOMPSON
Atlas Page 205 F.1/5.4

A fast, shallow section which produces good numbers of chub, roach and dace. Some big barbel are taken in summer. Most pegs will net 4–6lb.

How to get there   Leave the M1 at jct 25 and take the A52 to Derby. Take the turning from ring road south to Swarkestone bridge. Turn right, drive 2 miles to John Thompson pub. Use the bottom of the car park.

Day tickets   Weekly permits only: £5 from Derby AA, PO Box 167, Derby DE3 7UE, or from local tackle shops.

Best methods   Most species – stick float;
barbel – feeder.
Facilities   Food/toilets at the John
Thompson pub.

Hotspot Tips

~ Try pegs 42 and 42a for 40lb+ catches.

WILLINGTON POWER STATION
Atlas Page 205 F.1/5.4

This fast, shallow stretch produces mainly
chub, roach and dace, plus some barbel.
Most pegs provide double-figure nets; 40lb
is common in matches.

How to get there   Leave the M1 at jct 25
and take the A52 to Derby. Take the
turning from the ring road south to
Swarkestone bridge and turn right
(A5132) before the bridge. Park on the
verge, before the power station.
Day tickets   Weekly permits only: £5
from Derby AA, PO Box 167, Derby
DE3 7UE, or from local tackle shops.
Best methods   Most species – stick float;
barbel – feeder.

Hotspot Tips

~ The best pegs are 47, 58, 61, 62, 70, 87,
90, 94, 95 and 101.

METALWORKS LANE
Atlas Page 205 F.1/5.4

A shallow stretch, less pacey than other
Upper Trent fisheries. Plenty of chub,
roach and dace, plus good-sized barbel in
summer and early autumn. Pegs opposite
the wood can produce 50lb+ nets.

How to get there   Leave the M1 at jct 25
and take the A52 to Derby. Take the
turning from ring road south to
Swarkestone bridge and turn right
(A5132) before the bridge. Drive past the
power station into Willington, then
towards Repton. Turn right before the
river bridge.
Day tickets   Weekly permits only: £5
from Derby AA, PO Box 167, Derby
DE3 7UE, or from local tackle shops.
Best methods   Most species – stick float;
barbel – feeder.

Hotspot Tips

~ The best pegs are from 15 to 30.

VICKERS WATER, CLIPSTONE
Atlas Page 205 F.5/4.8

A small but very pleasant fishery, a few
miles north-east of Mansfield. Plenty of
double-figure carp here, plus some recent
reports of good-sized bream catches.

How to get there   Leave the M1 at jct 28
and take the A38 through Mansfield and
pick up the B6030 towards Ollerton. At
the shops in Old Clipstone (about 5
miles from Mansfield), follow signs to
Vickers Water, which is located just
before the colliery. Free parking on site.
Day tickets   Adult/junior/OAP £2.
Available on the bank.
Best methods/baits   Use general coarse
techniques and baits.
Facilities   Nearest shop/pub in Clipstone
(½ mile).
Disabled facilities   Some swims suitable
for disabled and wheelchair anglers.

WOODSETTS QUARRY POND
Atlas Page 205 F.5/4.4

A former quarry near Worksop, owned by
Bassetlaw District Council and controlled
by Worksop & District Angling Society,
providing pleasure fishing only, with
tench, carp and pike, plus some roach,
rudd and skimmer bream.

Netting a catch on the Trent.

How to get there Located alongside the new A57 Worksop ring road, at the (roundabout) junction of the Worksop-Sheffield and Worksop-Dinnington roads. Car parking on site.

Day tickets Adult £2; junior/OAP 60p. Available from the bailiff on the bank.

Best methods/baits Use any recognised coarse technique.

Facilities Nearest shops/pubs Dinnington/Anston/Worksop.

Disabled facilities Some special car-park angling platforms for disabled anglers.

POWYS

Bream.

LLYN CLYS POOL
Atlas Page 204 C.7/5.4

A small, but very beautiful, 1½-acre lake on a farm, near Llanymynech, about 4 miles south of Oswestry. Exceptional coarse fishing, with skimmer bream and roach, plus some enormous pike. A specimen bream taken last year weighed 14lb!

How to get there From Welshpool, take the A483 north towards Oswestry; shortly after crossing the A483/A495 junction at Llynclys, look for signs to Llynclys Farm on the right (about 300 yards after the crossroads. Free car parking on site.

Day tickets Adult £2; junior/OAP £1. Available at Llynclys Farm.

Best methods/baits Use general coarse methods and baits.

Facilities Nearest shop, Spar in Pant (1 mile); nearest pub, The White Lion (at the crossroads).

Disabled facilities Some swims are suitable for disabled and wheelchair anglers.

LLYNDU POOL
Atlas Page 200 E.3/0.4

A small (1½-acre) lake which is surrounded by trees, yet close to Welshpool town centre. Quite deep water (up to 12ft) so expect some giant roach and tench, plus pike and big eels. Also some perch and rudd to add to the variety!

How to get there In Welshpool town centre, park behind the Gateway supermarket. Access to the pool is on the far right side, over a stile. Follow the fence to the trees; the lake is on the right.

Day tickets Adult/junior/OAP £2.50. Available only at Bond's Tackle Shop in Welshpool.

Best methods/baits Use general coarse methods and baits.

Restrictions No night fishing.

Facilities Nearest shop, Gateway; nearest pubs are in the town centre.

MONTGOMERYSHIRE CANAL, LLANYMYNECH TO POOL QUAY
Atlas Page 204 C.6/5.6

A 9-mile, uninterrupted canal stretch, midway between Oswestry and Welshpool. Plenty of reeds on the banks, and plenty of tench, bream, perch, pike and eels to provide the sport.

How to get there Take the A483 south from Oswestry to Llanymynech (about 6 miles). The canal runs south, close to the A483 to Pool Quay (about 9 miles); access to the water is available at various points along the route. For information on where to fish, contact Bryan's Tackle & Bait Supplies, Canalside, Llanymynech; Tel. 0691 830027.

Day tickets Free fishing.

Best methods/baits Use general coarse methods and baits. Sweetcorn works well here – but no cans on the banks!

Facilities Nearest shops and pub, in Llanymynech.

Disabled facilities Some swims are suitable for disabled and wheelchair anglers; contact Bryan's Tackle & Bait Supplies for advice.

MONTGOMERYSHIRE CANAL, POOL QUAY TO WELSHPOOL
Atlas Page 200 E.3/0.4

A shorter (about 5 miles) stretch of the canal, from Pool Quay to just south of Welshpool. Predominantly roach here, plus tench, bream, chub, perch and eels. Bream here are especially large, with several double-figure fish taken.

How to get there   From Pool Quay, continue south along the A483 towards Welshpool. The canal runs close to the road; access to the water is available at various points along the route. For information on where to fish, contact Bryan's Tackle & Bait Supplies, Canalside, Llanymynech; Tel. 0691 830027.

Day tickets   Adult £2.50; junior/OAP £1.50. Available from Bryan's Tackle & Bait Supplies (see above).

Best methods/baits   Use general coarse methods and baits. Sweetcorn is best in summer (no cans on the banks).

Facilities   Nearest shops and pubs, in Welshpool.

Disabled facilities   Some swims nearer Welshpool are suitable for disabled and wheelchair anglers; contact Bryan's Tackle & Bait Supplies for advice.

MONTGOMERYSHIRE CANAL, LLANYMYNECH
Atlas Page 204 C.7/5.4

A short (¾-mile), reed-lined stretch of the canal, in a village setting, a few miles south of Oswestry. Only minimal boat traffic. Heavily stocked with carp, tench and roach, providing top quality fishing.

How to get there   Take the A483 south from Oswestry to Llanymynech (about 6 miles). The canal runs through the centre of the village; access to the water is available at several points. For information on where to fish, contact Bryan's Tackle & Bait Supplies, Canalside, Llanymynech; Tel. 0691 830027.

Day tickets   Adult £2.50; OAP £1.50; junior £1. Weekly ticket £7. Available from Bryan's Tackle & Bait Supplies.

Best methods/baits   Use general coarse methods and baits.

Restrictions   Use only barbless hooks. No keepnets to be used.

Facilities   Toilets within 100 yards. Nearest shop and pub, The Cross keys, in the village.

RIVER SEVERN, LLANDRINIO
Atlas Page 204 C.7/5.4

A very pleasant section of the Severn, quite wide (15 yards) and deep, but not fast moving, located about 8 miles north-east of Welshpool. Expect good sport, with large numbers of barbel, chub, roach, bream, dace, gudgeon and pike.

How to get there   Take the A483 north from Welshpool towards Llanymynech and just before the village turn right onto the B4393 towards Shrewsbury. Llandrinio is about 1 mile further on. Park (free) on the roadside; access to the river is about 50 yards to the right of the road bridge.

Day tickets   Adult £2.50; junior/OAP £1.50. Available from Bryan's Tackle & Bait Supplies, Canalside, Llanymynech; Tel. 0691 830027.

Best methods   Use general coarse methods.

Best baits   Barbel and chub – feed heavy hemp and bronze maggots; use luncheon meat if the water is coloured.

Facilities   Nearest shop and pub, in Llanymynech (2 miles).

RIVER VYRNWY, GREAT DYFFRYD
Atlas Page 204 C.7/5.4

A short stretch of river near Llanymynech, providing mixed coarse fishing for chub, dace, roach, grayling and perch. The barbel here can reach 12lb – the Welsh record fish was taken here in 1990. Fishing can be unproductive in winter, after flooding.

How to get there   Take the A483 north from Welshpool to Llanymynech and turn right onto the B4398 towards Knockin. Turn right at the signpost for Great Dyffryd and bear right until the big double farm gate. Drive through the gate and park (free) under the trees. Access to the river is on the right and left.

Day tickets   Adult £2.50; junior/OAP £1.50. Weekly ticket £10. Season ticket £15. Available from Bryan's Tackle & Bait Supplies, Canalside, Llanymynech; Tel. 0691 830027.

Best methods/baits   Use general coarse methods and baits.

Facilities   Nearest shop, Llanymynech; nearest pub, The Black Horse (good food), in Maesbrook (1 mile).

SHROPSHIRE

APELEY POOL
Atlas Page 200 F.3/0.3

A mixed coarse fishing pool at Shawbirch, near Telford. Expect mainly carp (to 6lb) plus some roach. Typical match weights are about 40lb.

How to get there   Leave the M54 at jct 4, and take the A442 to Whitchurch. Drive straight over the roundabouts, ¾ mile after the 4th pool behind a wall. Park in the lay-by.

Day tickets   Adult £2; junior/OAP £1; available on the bank.

Best methods/baits   Use any recognised coarse technique.

Facilities   Nearest shop/pub Shawbirch.

BACHE POOL, NR. LUDLOW
Atlas Page 200 E.9/1.2

A long, narrow 1½-acre lake, with lots of lillies, set in deep countryside. Very coloured, opaque water providing excellent coarse fishing for most species, with plenty of very big carp – commons and mirrors. A very popular fishery among Midlands anglers.

How to get there   Take the A49 north from Ludlow and turn right onto B4365 after 2 miles. After about 3 miles, bear left along minor roads towards Craven Arms. Look for signs to the pool and park nearby.

Day tickets   Adult/junior/OAP £2. Available on the bank.

Best methods/baits   Floaters preferred for carp. Most baits work well here.

Facilities   Nearest shop/pub in Craven Arms.

BAYLISS'S POOL
Atlas Page 200 F.3/0.3

Two pools near Shifnal, just east of Telford. Mixed coarse fishing, but mainly carp, bream and roach.

How to get there   Leave the M54 at jct 4 and take the A464 to Shifnal. Turn left immediately to the pool.

Day tickets   Adult £3; junior/OAP £1.50. Available on the bank.

Best methods/baits   Use any recognised coarse technique.

Facilities   Nearest shop/pub Shifnal.

BEECHES POOL
Atlas Page 200 F.3/0.3

A pleasant, 1-acre pool near the Ironbridge Gorge, providing general coarse fishing with carp of 15–20lb quite common.

How to get there   From Telford, take the A442 south and follow signs to Ironbridge. For details of access to the fishery and potential sport, contact Rod & Gun, 3 High Street, Dawley; Tel. 0952 503550.

Day tickets   Adult/junior/OAP £1.50. Available on site.

Best methods/baits   Use any recognised coarse technique and baits.

Facilities   Toilets on site. Snacks available, breakfast on the bank! Nearest shops/pubs at Ironbridge.

BOLDINGS POOL
Atlas Page 200 F.6/0.5

Several small pools near Bridgnorth, offering good fishing sport, with plenty of medium-sized carp, tench, bream and roach.

How to get there   Drive through Bridgnorth High Town past Leisure Centre, and turn right into Stanley Lane. The pool is 3 miles on left.

Day tickets   Adult £2; junior/OAP £1; available at the house.

Best methods/baits   Use any recognised coarse technique.

Facilities   Nearest shop/pub Bridgnorth.

A respectably-sized common carp.

CASTLE POOLS
Atlas Page 200 F.3/0.3

Three separate mixed coarse fishing pools at Little Dawley, near Telford. All pools contain large numbers of tench, roach and Crucian carp. There are also some bream and carp in the mid–2lb weight range.

How to get there   At Little Dawley, near Telford, turn left past the Unicorn pub and continue to the bottom of the road. Park nearby.
Day tickets   Adult £2; junior/OAP £1; available on the bank.
Best methods/baits   Use any recognised coarse technique.
Facilities   Nearest shop/pub Shawbirch.

DELL POOL
Atlas Page 200 E.9/0.3

A tree-lined farm pool at Sundorne Farm, just outside Shrewsbury. Fishing is only on one side of the lake, so pegs are limited. Typical depth 3–5ft. Most coarse species, with large carp near the lily pads. Expect a 5–20lb pleasure catch.

How to get there   From Shrewsbury, take the A53 towards Market Drayton. On the outskirts of Shrewsbury, turn right after Loosemore's Skip Hire and drive down the lane to the farm. Free car parking on site.
Day tickets   Adult £1; junior/OAP 50p. Available on the bank.
Best methods   Float, light feeder or pole.
Best baits   All baits work well; use boilies for large carp.
Facilities   Nearest shop 1½ miles; nearest pub, the Dog in Lane, Shrewsbury.

HAWKSTONE PARK LAKE
Atlas Page 200 E.9/0.3

A very long (1¼ miles), narrow lake in a park near Wem, north of Shrewsbury. Well stocked with most coarse species plus large common and mirror carp, though the lake's immense size can make finding the fish difficult!

How to get there   Follow the A53 north from Shrewsbury to Hodnet village (about 13 miles) and turn left onto A442. Hawkstone Park is on the left; follow signs to the Park and fishery and park on site.
Day tickets   No day tickets. Fishing available to members only: £14 from Crewe Pioneer Angling Club, 83 Underwood Lane, Crewe; Tel. 0270 255999.

Best methods/baits   Use any recognised coarse technique and baits. Specialist carp methods may be required.
Facilities   Toilets on site. Nearest shop/pub in Hodnet.
Disabled facilities   Some swims suitable for disabled anglers.

KYRE POOL
Atlas Page 200 F.0/1.4

A small lake near Tenbury Wells, south-east of Ludlow. A good mixed fishery, with pike, eels and carp (to well over 20lb).

How to get there   From Ludlow, take the A49 south and turn left (about 6 miles) onto A456 to Tenbury Wells. For details of access to lake, contact S. Lewis Fishing Tackle, Bewdley.
Day tickets   Adult/junior/OAP £3; available from S. Lewis Tackle, Severside South, Bewdley; Tel. 0299 403358.
Best methods/baits   Use any recognised coarse technique and baits.
Facilities   Nearest shops/pub in Tenbury Wells.

Pike.

LONGFORD FARM
Atlas Page 204 D.5/5.5

Two ponds (recently converted from trout fishing) at a farm just south of Market Drayton. Plenty of roach and tench, mirror and Crucian carp to 10lb+, but much bigger carp also available. Expect a day catch of 10–20lb.

How to get there   From Shrewsbury, take the A53 towards Market Drayton. At Ternhill roundabout (about 17 miles) turn left towards Whitchurch. Look for the fishery sign 50 yards on the right. Free car parking on site.

Day tickets   Adult/junior/OAP £4 (2 rods); £2.50 (1 rod). Available from the farm. For details; Tel. 063083 295.

Best methods   Small fish – light waggler or pole; large carp - use specialist gear.

Best baits   Maggots, casters, pinkies, squatts; boilies for carp.

Restrictions   No night fishing.

Facilities   Toilets at the farm (with permission). Nearest shop, Ternhill.

MOSS POOL, NR. NEWPORT
Atlas Page 204 D.7/5.2

A pleasantly-situated pool of about 2 acres, containing some large bream and tench, plus a few large carp. Fishing can be difficult here; ask at the local tackle shop for advice on best sport.

How to get there   From Telford, take the A518 north-east to Newport, then A518 Eccleshall road to Forton (about 2 miles). For details of access to the pool, contact the local tackle shop: Rod & Gun, 3 High Street, Dawley; Tel. 0952 503550.

Day tickets   Adult/junior/OAP £2. Available on the bank.

Best methods/baits   Use any recognised coarse technique and baits.

Facilities   Nearest shop/pub in Forton village.

NEWPORT CANAL
Atlas Page 204 D.7/5.2

A 2-mile length of disused canal, at Newport, near Telford, offering a good level of sport, with Crucian carp, roach, tench, carp, bream and perch.

How to get there   At Newport, turn left in the High Street, go past the church to crossroads. Turn right in to Water Lane (200 yds), and turn left on apex of corner to canal. Fish the basin or towpath.

Day tickets   Adult/junior/OAP 50p. Fishing here is shared by five clubs but day tickets are also available on the bank.

Best methods/baits   Use any recognised coarse technique.

Facilities   Nearest shop/pub Newport.

Rivers
RIVER SEVERN

River Severn at Bewdley.

From its source in Wales, the Severn rushes through picturesque countryside to Bewdley, forming long, shallow runs interspersed with deeper pools. Beyond Bewdley the river changes dramatically, widening and deepening to provide a host of fishing experiences. The scenery, coupled with the many species available and an explosion barbel numbers, makes the Severn an angler's dream. The Quatford to Tewkesbury stretch of the Severn is the site for six *Angling Times* Hotspots.

EMSTREY
Atlas Page 200 E.9/0.3

A section of the Severn just outside Shrewsbury town. Excellent fishing, with big barbel (to 9lb), plus dace and chub. Expect match nets of 10–50lb, but pleasure nets of 100lb are possible if the barbel feed well!

How to get there   Take the main A5 London road from Emstrey Island through Shrewsbury: the fishery is at the first farm on the left. Free car parking on site.

Day tickets   Adult/junior/OAP £2. Bookings available from Terry Jackson; Tel. 0743 245613.

Best methods   Barbel – feeder; chub, dace – float.

Best baits   Hemp, casters, maggots, meat, bread.

Facilities   Nearest shop/pub Shrewsbury.

SHREWSBURY
Atlas Page E.9/0.7

Three adjacent fisheries, the Quarry, County Ground and Monkmore. Mainly roach and chub, with match catches of 10–20lb and pleasure catches of 15–30lb when the fishing is good. In general, fishing is best after September when the water is at winter level.

How to get there   Take the main A49 north into Shrewsbury and follow signs to the quarry. Park in Frankwell car park (50p).

Day tickets   Adult/junior/OAP £1.50. Available on the bank, or bookings from Shrewsbury & Atcham Borough Council.

Best methods   Stick float, waggler floats (mid-river), straight lead (inside line). Use feeder at Monkmore.

Best baits   Bronze maggots, casters, hemp, meat.

Facilities   Toilets at Quarry. Nearest shop Shrewsbury; nearest pub, Anchor Inn in Frankwell car park.

Disabled facilities   Some swims suitable for disabled and wheelchair anglers.

ATCHAM
Atlas Page E.9/0.7

A fast-flowing section of the river, about 5 miles east of Shrewsbury. Fishing is best in summer, though weed can cause problems. Excellent barbel and chub catches with day nets well over 100lb reported in 1991.

How to get there   Follow the main A5 from Telford towards Shrewsbury. Atcham bridge crosses the river about 4 miles before Shrewsbury. Park (free) near the river and walk to the fishery.

Day tickets   Adult/junior/OAP £2. Tickets available from the garage near Atcham Bridge (A5), next to Mytton & Mermaid pub.

Best methods   Standard feeder tackle; 'beefed-up' float tackle.

Best baits   Hemp, meat, casters, maggots.

Facilities   Nearest shop Atcham; nearest pub, Mytton & Mermaid (on site).

SOUTH OF BRIDGNORTH
Atlas Page F.6/0.5

A town water section which produces good mixed catches of chub, barbel, dace, roach, eels and pike. Also an occasional trout.

How to get there   In Bridgnorth, head down Hermitage Hill; turn left and take 2nd right (about 300 yards) to car park (pay & display). Walk (½ mile) to the river.

Day tickets   Free fishing.

Best methods   Chub, dace – stick float; barbel – leger; pike – livebait.

Best baits   Hemp, casters. Use meat for barbel.

Facilities   Toilets at caravan site downstream. Nearest shop/pub, Shrewsbury (10 mins walk).

QUATFORD
Atlas Page E.9/0.7

A straight, left-bank stretch with fords, tree-lined, steep banks. Quite shallow (3–4ft); deeper stretches above/opposite Eardington village. Expect chub and barbel all season, with summer barbel nets of 65lb (100lb in right conditions). Roach nets of 20lb are also likely.

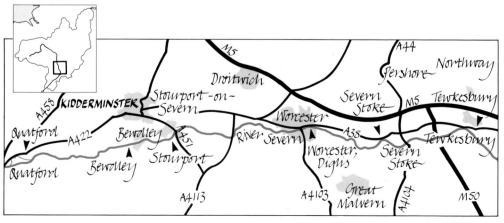

How to get there   From Bridgnorth, take A442 south towards Kidderminster. After 3 miles, look for Allens Cafe on the left; park on roadside and take footpath to and beyond caravan site behind the Little Chef.

Day tickets   Not available; Birmingham AA, members only; contact F A Jennings, BAA, 100 Icknield Port Road, Rotton Park, Birmingham B16 0AP.

Best methods   Chub, barbel – swimfeeder with caster and hemp or maggot; stout tackle is essential for barbel (6lb line straight through). Roach – stick float, tares or hemp in summer; for dace, try a small waggler or stick.*Best baits* Summer – maggots, casters, hemp, tares and sweetcorn; winter – luncheon meat.

Facilities   Food/toilets at Little Chef or Allens Cafe.

Hotspot Tips

- In winter, or at high water, luncheon meat is best for barbel.
- For chub and barbel, fish well out with a large waggler or a balsa.
- For summer roach, use seed baits and casters; in winter, switch to maggots.
- The best swims are in the willow trees, 200 yards from the access point.

Bewdley.

BEWDLEY
Atlas Page 200 F.7/1.2

This section has shallow fords, glides and deep, even-flowing stretches. Summer weed is dense. Barbel in summer/autumn, roach in autumn/winter, chub all-season. Look for pike in steadier swims. Mixed nets with swim-feeders are often 50–60lb; float fishing hauls may be 30lb.

How to get there   Take A456 west from Kidderminster. At Bewdley, the right-bank Kidderminster DAA water is accessed via the riverside car park; walk upstream or from Dowles Lane, off Bridgnorth road. Or, access the Winterdyne stretch via Lax Lane in town, or downstream from the B4195; park on the roadside.

Day tickets   Not available; yearly honorary membership cards £11 from local tackle shops. Day tickets for opposite bank available from Stan Lewis' tackle shop on riverside, below the bridge at £2 or £3 on the bank.

Best methods   Summer and autumn barbel – large and medium block-end feeders with casters, hemp & maggots, with maggot or caster hookbait. Roach – seed bait in summer, casters and maggots in winter.

Best baits   Maggots, casters and hemp (tares in summer); try luncheon meat at high water for chub.

Hotspot Tips

- Sweetcorn, steak or luncheon meat baits can provide good pleasure angling.
- Don't forget – in faster water, you'll need extra lead to anchor the swimfeeder.
- Good shoals of big roach lurk in steady, deep water in front of the cottages at Dowle and in the middle at Winterdyne; a stick float should ensure a good catch.
- Barbel often shoal tightly at the head of, or just below, the fords.

STOURPORT
Atlas Page 200 F.6/1.2

A wide stretch, steady flow, 5–10ft depth. Winter roach are superb, plus dace, perch, chub and pike (to 20lb). Barbel provide excellent summer/autumn sport. Roach often 2lb+ in autumn and winter. Match nets (roach and dace) often top 20lb; pleasure nets can top 70lb.

How to get there   Lyttleton AA water (right-bank section: access is via the B4194 Bewdley Road; park on the roadside (4 places) or walk from the bridge car park. Access below the bridge is via a footpath. Park in the town, near the bridge. Birmingham AA water is on the left bank, above the bridge.

Day tickets Day tickets for Lyttleton AA must be purchased in advance from John White Tackle, Raven Street, Stourport; Tel. 02993 71735. Adults £1.50; junior/OAP 80p.

Best methods Float or leger/feeder methods according to conditions. Waggler in shallow areas, or to reachmid-river shoals. Small hooks are essential; size 22–26 tied to 12oz bottom is common for roach and dace.

Best baits Chub, roach and dace – maggot and casters plus hempseed; hemp or tares in hot weather.

Restrictions Birmingham AA water is members-only (see Quatford). Handbooks are available from tackle shops or BAA HQ.

Hotspot Tips

- Use bigger baits, such as sweetcorn or luncheon meat – plus bigger hooks – for barbel and chub.
- In coloured water, use a stick float with 18–20 hooks and casters and maggots for roach and dace.
- In flood water, fish for roach close to the near bank using a light link leger .

WORCESTER, DIGLIS

Atlas Page 200 F.7/1.8

An 'even-fishing' stretch, with 6–7ft depth. Dense weed growth, and reeds at the edges. Fishing is best in summer/autumn, with chub and barbel (12lb+), plus roach, dace and bream, many feeding well into winter. Expect pleasure hauls of 80lb+; match hauls of 50lb+.

How to get there In Worcester city, on the right bank; the 50-peg fishery starts 300 yards below the weir. Access is via Weir Lane, off the A449 Great Malvern road.

Day tickets Not available; Worcester DUAA honorary membership cards cost £15; 14-day permits £10; from local tackle shops.

Best methods All methods work here – a waggler in the middle, a stick close in, a swimfeeder or light leger. Stick floats and seed baits for summer roach. For bream, use an open-end feeder.

Best baits Maggots, casters, hemp or tares; luncheon meat, steak or sweetcorn for winter chub and barbel.

Facilities Shops/food/toilets in city centre.

Hotspot Tips

- The most popular match method for barbel and chub is a waggler, with plenty of hemp and maggot or caster hookbait.
- Put enough weight on your swim-feeder to keep it in one spot and pull the shoals into a tight area.
- For good bream on the bend pegs, try an open-end feeder with red maggot or worm.
- Pegs 37–40 produce good chub and barbel; pegs 10 and 20 are best for wagglers.

SEVERN STOKE

Atlas Page 200 F.8/2.0

A wide, very deep (to 20ft), slow-moving, left-bank fishery. The 5–6ft-deep shelf below the opposite cliffs is ideal for chub. Also dace, roach and bream all season, plus large summer barbel (10lb+) and an occasional 10lb+ pike. Expect pleasure nets over 30lb.

How to get there Take the A38 from Worcester south towards Tewkesbury. At Severn Stoke (7 miles), turn right at the war memorial; use the riverside car park. From the south, take the M5, exit at jct 8 to M50 and A38 to Severn Stoke.

Day tickets Not available; Birmingham AA club members only (see Quatford).

Best methods Chub – use powerful feeder rod and heavy end tackle. Fish for barbel at the near bank, using a feeder with hemp and casters.

Best baits Maggots, casters and hemp; sweetcorn, meat, bread or cheese all work well for chub. Bream – groundbait near the feeder.

Hotspot Tips

- You'll find bream in deeper, mid-river water – use an open-end feeder with maggot or worms.
- Long, accurate casting is vital to miss overhanging bushes.
- For dace, try a stick float with maggot, just above the car park.
- Just upstream of the car park is often the best barbel stretch.

TEWKESBURY
Atlas Page 200 F.8/2.3

A pleasant section, average 10ft depth, uneven bottom and steady flow that increases in shallows below the weir. Deeper areas further downstream, plus marginal reed growth. Bream, chub and roach are good in summer, with barbel (to 10lb) in summer/autumn, plus pike to 20lb. Pleasure nets reach 60–100lb.

How to get there Travel to Tewkesbury via the A38, M5 or M50. In the town, approach the river via Key Street and footbridge over the Mill Avon near Healing's flour mill, or via Mill Bank, opposite the abbey. *Note*: it's a long walk!

Day tickets Not available; Tewkesbury Popular AA honorary membership cards cost £10; 14-day permits £5.50 from local tackle shops.

Best methods Bream – open-ended swimfeeder; fish one-third across. Chub, barbel – waggler tactics. Roach, dace – pole or stick float (size 20–22 hooks).

Best baits Roach, chub, barbel – maggot and casters with hemp; bream -red maggot, worm and caster (all season), plus brown/white crumb with squatts, casters or maggots in the feeder.

Disabled facilities The swim is a long distance from the car park.

Hotspot Tips

- A straight leger and balled groundbait can also produce a good bream haul.
- In hot weather, roach respond better to seed baits.
- The Severn-Mill Avon confluence is a good bream area, especially during flooding.
- The best barbel and chub will be found in shallow swims close to the weir.

STIRCHLEY POOLS
Atlas Page 200 F.3/0.3

Two mixed coarse fishing pools at Hinkshay, near Telford. Good fishing, with mainly carp (to mid–20lb region), bream, tench, perch, roach and some Crucians.

How to get there From Telford town centre take B4373, and after 1 mile, turn left into Hinkshay Road. Just before the White Hart pub, turn right down to the pools. Park nearby.

Day tickets Adult £2 per rod; junior/OAP £1. Available on the bank.

Best methods/baits Use any recognised coarse technique.

Facilities Nearest shop/pub Hinkshay.

TEE LAKE
Atlas Page 200 F.3/0.3

A shallow lake at Dothill, near Telford, offering good fishing sport with skimmer bream, tench, roach and crucian carp. Also some large carp to 20lb.

How to get there From the A442/A5223 roundabout north of Telford, head towards Telford. At the next roundabout turn right, turn right again at the school, take next left, right at T-junction, next left, follow long sweeping road to the end. The pool is on the left.

Day tickets Adult £1.50; junior/OAP 75p. Available on the bank.

Best methods/baits Use any recognised coarse technique.

Facilities Nearest shop/pub Dothill.

Rivers

RIVER TEME

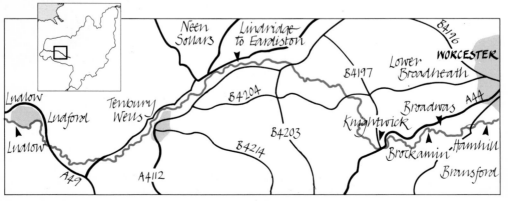

Rising on the Wales/Shropshire borders, the Teme meanders through beautiful countryside, and past the towns of Knighton and Ludlow, eventually joining the Severn near Worcester. With tree-lined stretches and overgrown banks, it flows through fords, shallow gravels, steady glides and deep pools. Although classed as a game river, the Teme is packed with coarse fish, including chub, roach, dace, barbel and grayling.

LUDLOW
Atlas Page 200 E.9/1.2

A 1-mile stretch, weedy, but deeper lower down (10ft in places), with a slower flow. Tree-lined, often steep, banks. Mainly chub, dace and roach, plus bream, barbel and grayling. Expect good pleasure hauls of 10lb+, and the occasional 50lb net.

How to get there   The fishery is upstream of Ludlow town. Five access points, each with parking facilities. Use both banks.

Day tickets   Open membership: contact Bob Deakin, Dale View Cottage, Hayton, Ludlow SY8 2AX.

Best methods   Stick float in deeper downstream section.

Best baits   Roach, dace – maggot or casters; chub – waspgrub, luncheon meat, breadflake.

Hotspot Tips

&   A waggler fished under the trees on shallow water works well for chub.

&   Pegs 20–25, where shallow water deepens, produce all season.

&   A swimfeeder scores well with chub, but try straight legering too!

LINDRIDGE TO EARDISTON
Atlas Page 200 F.4/1.4

A 4-mile, left-bank fishery with heavy bankside growth and trees sheltering the middle reaches. Shallow glides, fast-flowing channels, placid stretches; very weedy in parts. Mainly barbel and chub, plus dace and roach in summer; chub and roach in winter. Barbel can reach 9lb, chub 4lb.

How to get there   The river runs parallel to the A443 Worcester-Tenbury Wells road. Access is via car parks at either Eastham bridge, Lindridge or Eardiston.

Day tickets   No day tickets; Birmingham AA members only; see River Severn.

Best methods   Most swims – swimfeeder with maggots, casters, hemp; stick float and waggler where there is more room to work.

Best baits   Most species – maggots, casters, hempseed; chub - cheese, breadflake. Groundbait is rarely used.

Hotspot Tips

&   On shallower runs and glides try straight legering with sweetcorn or luncheon meat.

&   The pools at the end of fast runs usually produce most fish.

&   This tranquil setting demands a very quiet approach.

KNIGHTWICK
Atlas Page 200 F.5/1.8

A 3-mile, left-bank stretch with many bends and variable depth and steep, often overgrown banks. Large areas of streamer weed in the shallows. Expect barbel, chub, dace in summer and autumn; chub and roach in winter. Regular bags are 20–30lb.

How to get there   Take the A44 Worcester-Bromyard road. Near Knightwick, park in one of 4 signposted lay-bys. Or turn right at Knightwick bridge to Talbot Inn; park at the footbridge, fish upstream to the weir.

Day tickets   No day tickets; membership open to all (Worcester DUAA)

Best methods   Chub, barbel – small waggler on shallower runs; roach, dace – stick float on or round the bends.

Best baits   Most species – maggots, casters, hemp; chub, barbel - big baits.

Facilities   Food/toilets at the Talbot Inn.

Hotspot Tips

&   Try a straight leger with meat or sweetcorn for large chub and barbel.

&   You'll need very stout feeder tackle to land the big barbel.

&   There are good swims on the bends, but go for those with plenty of cover.

BROCKAMIN
Atlas Page 200 F.7/1.8

A newly-acquired, ½-mile, right-bank section. Fast gravel runs, deeper glides, channels into pools and some 'beach'. Tree-lined, overgrown banks are easily accessed. Plenty of barbel (to 9lb) and chub (to 3lb), plus roach and an occasional

How to get there   Take the A4103 Worcester-Hereford road. Cross the Teme at Bransford; turn right to Leigh and Brockamin. At Brockamin, turn right (Dingle Road), then 2nd right past carp pools to the river. The designated car park is the only access.

Day tickets   No day tickets; open membership is available from Birmingham AA, 100 Icknield Port Road, Birmingham, B16 0AP.

Best methods   Barbel, chub – swimfeeder; otherwise stick float.

Best baits   Most species – maggots, casters, hempseed; chub - big baits.

Disabled facilities   Good access to banks.

Hotspot Tips

- The bottom end is good waggler water.
- The steady water midway along is excellent stick float territory.

BROADWAS
Atlas Page 200 F.5/1.8

A very twisty, left-bank stretch covering 4 meadows. Often shallow and weedy but with deeper pools, glides and fords. Plenty of bankside rushes and reeds. Mostly barbel (often 7lb), chub (4lb) and dace in summer and autumn; roach and dace in winter.

How to get there   Take the A44 Worcester-Bromyard road. Between Broadwas and Cotheridge, look for two signposted car parks – either opposite Hilltop Farm, or further downstream.

Day tickets   No day tickets; open membership available (Worcester DUAA); contact local tackle shops.

Best methods   Barbel, chub – swimfeeder tactics, or try big baits (meat, corn, worms) for big fish.

Best baits   Most species – maggots, casters, hemp.

Hotspot Tips

- The barbel are very big – you'll need strong tackle.
- Pegs either side of the brook near the downstream car park are renowned for barbel and chub.

HAM MILL
Atlas Page 200 F.8/1.8

A streamy, even-paced, 1¾-mile, left-bank stretch with lots of trees and steady runs 4–8ft deep. Shallow fords and weedy patches where barbel lurk. Mostly barbel, chub, roach and dace in summer and autumn; roach and dace in winter. Pleasure nets often 50lb+, with 30lb roach nets also possible.

How to get there   Take the A449 Worcester-Malvern road. Just outside Worcester, park near Powick old road bridge; walk upstream to the Worcester DUAA notice board.

Day tickets   No day tickets; open membership available (Worcester DUAA); contact local tackle shops.

Best methods   Chub, roach, dace – waggler and stick float.

Best baits   Most species – maggots, casters, hemp; try luncheon meat or sweetcorn as big baits.

Hotspot Tips

- The swimfeeder is very effective for barbel here.
- The bottom 15 swims throw up big catches – up to 60lb!

TRENCH AND MIDDLE POOLS, TELFORD
Atlas Page 200 F.3/0.3

Two pools at Telford: Trench Pool (18 acres) contains plenty of roach and tench, plus large bream and carp (to 30lb+). Middle Pool (10+ acres) contains roach, bream and tench, plus carp to 20lb.

How to get there   For Trench Pool, leave the M54 at jct 4, A442, take second exit left to roundabout, take third exit, 200 yards turn left into Wourbridge Road, After 300 yards by (Bridge Inn) turn left into Teagues Crescent, take second left and immediately turn right down to the Blue Pig Inn; the pool is in front of you. For Middle Pool, leave the M54 at jct 4 and take A442 towards Whitechurch. At roundabout, take 2nd exit, then 1st exit. Continue 200–300 yards and turn left. Follow the road to the T-junction, turn right. The car park is ¼ mile on the right, with access to the pool.

Day tickets   Adult £2; junior/OAP £1. Available on the bank.
Best methods/baits   Use any recognised coarse technique.
Facilities   Nearest shop/pub Telford.

WITHY POOL
Atlas Page 200 F.3/0.3

A single mixed coarse fishing pool at Hinkshay, near Telford. Very big carp (to over 30lb) plus large catfish (to 20lb+). Also roach, bream and Crucian carp.

How to get there   From Telford town centre take B4373, and after 1 mile turn left into Hinkshay Road. Carry on as far as the gate; the pool is on the other side on the left.
Day tickets   Adult £2 per rod; junior/OAP £1 per rod. Also season tickets. Available from Mrs M. Buttery, 21 Webb Crescent, Dawley, Telford; Tel. 0952 506392.
Best methods/baits   Use any recognised coarse technique.
Facilities   Nearest shop/pub Hinkshay.

STAFFORDSHIRE

On the canal banks.

BROCKAMIN POOLS
Atlas Page 200 F.6/1.8

A group of pools about 5 miles west of Worcester. Best fishing is when conditions are cloudy with a breeze blowing. Mixed fishing, but mainly carp, bream and roach, with 50–60lb catches common.

How to get there   From Worcester, head south-west on the A4103 towards Hereford; after 4 miles turn right, signposted Leigh and Brockamin. Look for signs to the fishery. Parking (charged) near the pools.

Day tickets   Adult £3.50 (half-day £2.50); junior/OAP £2.50. Available from Alans Fishing Tackle, 26 Malvern Road, St Johns, Worcester; Tel. 0905 422107.
Best methods   Most methods work well.
Best baits   Maggots, casters, sweetcorn.
Facilities   Nearest shop ½ mile; nearest pub 1½ miles.
Disabled facilities   Some swims suitable for disabled and wheelchair anglers.

EVESBATCH FISHERIES
Atlas Page 200 F.2/1.9

Two pools of total area about 2 acres, located mid-way between Worcester and Hereford. Plenty of roach, chub, rudd and tench, plus many large carp (to 28lb) taken by carp specialists. Pleasure catches here can reach 100lb!

How to get there   From Worcester, head south-west on the A4103 towards Hereford; the turn for Evesbatch is on the right after about 10 miles. Free car parking on site.
Day tickets   Adult £3.50; half-day £2.50. Available from Alans Fishing Tackle, 26 Malvern Road, St Johns, Worcester; Tel. 0905 422107.
Best methods   Most methods work well.
Best baits   Maggots, casters, sweetcorn, bread, meat.
Facilities   Nearest shop/pub 2 miles.
Disabled facilities   Some swims suitable for disabled and wheelchair anglers.

FRADLEY CANAL
Atlas Page 202 A.4/1.5

A small canal located just north of Lichfield, providing good mixed coarse fishing with most species, plus plenty of carp (when they can be found!).

How to get there   From Burton-upon-Trent head south-west on the A38 about 10 miles to Fradley. For details of various access points to the stretch, contact the local tackle shops.
Day tickets   Adult/junior/OAP £1; season ticket £12.50. Available from local tackle shops.
Best methods/baits   Legering with boilies produces good results.
Facilities   Nearest shops/pubs in Alrewas or Lichfield.
Disabled facilities   Access for disabled anglers is possible at some swims; check with local tackle shops.

RUDYARD LAKE
Atlas Page 205 E.3/4.8

A very big, 180-acre reservoir, north-east of Leek, which feeds the Caldon Canal. Good mixed fishing for bream, roach and perch, plus a few carp and pike (to 30lb+). Catches of large fish have declined as water levels have been lowered for dam repairs.

A good pike.

How to get there   From Leek, take the A523 north-west towards Macclesfield. For the dam end, turn left onto the B5331 (about 2 miles); for the railway side, continue on the A523, turn left at sign for Congleton, then immediately left before crossing the feeder stream. Park along the track.

Day tickets   Adult £2; junior/OAP £1.50. Available on the bank.

Best methods   Normal conditions – use pole or waggler; use mini-feeder with maggot at low water levels.

Best baits   Bream – redworm, maggots (chopped worm in feeder). Roach, perch – casters.

Restrictions   Fishing only on the railway side; very few pegs are available by the dam.

Facilities   Nearest shop/pub in Rudyard village.

Disabled facilities   Some swims may be suitable for disabled anglers; for advice; Tel. 0538 33280.

STAFFS & WORCESTER CANAL – BRIDGES 55–56
Atlas Page 202 A.5/1.9

A short section of the canal on Wolverhampton's outskirts. Mainly bream, roach, perch, gudgeon and eels, plus some larger carp (to 10lb).

How to get there   Take the A454 from Wolverhampton towards Bridgnorth; on leaving Wolverhampton, turn left at The Mermaid pub; access to fishing on the canal is 50 yards, left or right.

Day tickets   Free fishing (unless water occupied by fishing club).

Best methods   Float (at far bank), or leger (in middle).

Best baits   Maggots; loosefeed with pinkies or squatts. Use meat when legering.

Facilities   Nearest shop/pub, The Firs (10 mins walk).

Disabled facilities   Some swims suitable for disabled and wheelchair anglers.

STOWE POOL
Atlas Page 202 A.5/1.5

A large (4-acre) and very busy lake in the centre of Lichfield town. Expect to see most coarse species, with some surprisingly large carp (20lb+), but fishing can be difficult here.

How to get there   In Lichfield town centre, follow signs to the pool and park nearby.

Day tickets   Adult £1.40; junior U16/OAP 70p; season ticket: adult £14; junior/OAP £7. Available on the bank.

Best methods/baits   Use any recognised coarse technique and baits.

Facilities   Toilets/cafe on site. Nearest shops/pubs in Lichfield.

Disabled facilities   Some swims suitable for disabled anglers.

TRENT & MERSEY CANAL – BRIDGES 28–42
Atlas Page 205 E.9/5.5

A very long canal stretch which contains plenty of fish, from gudgeon to double-figure carp! Excellent fishing all year round.

How to get there   Take the A38 for about 8 miles either side of Burton upon Trent; the canal runs parallel to the road. Access to the fishery is at various points; check with local tackle shops for details.

Day tickets   Adult/junior/OAP £1 (half-day £1). Also season tickets: adult £5; junior £2.Available from Mullarkey & Sons, 184/185 Waterloo Street, Burton-upon-Trent; Tel. 0283 66777.

Best methods/baits   Long pole with worm and joker; also rod and line with pinkies.

Facilities   Shops/pubs/toilets at various points.

Disabled facilities   Some swims suitable for disabled and wheelchair anglers.

WARWICKSHIRE
Rivers
THE WARWICKSHIRE AVON

The Warwick Avon.

The Warwickshire Avon, with its steady flow and fairly even depth, is a Mecca for pleasure and match anglers alike. The river is slow to rise in hot weather, yet prone to flooding, when its steep banks can become treacherous. The Bidford to Eckington stretch offers excellent mixed coarse fishing, where the waggler and stick float can provide outstanding summer sport, while those anglers adopting swimfeeder and leger tactics will take plenty of good fish from the deeper areas.

HAMPTON LUCY
Atlas Page 202 A.7/2.9

A pleasant Avon fishery, about 3 miles north-east of Stratford- upon-Avon, but parking is very limited and the walk to the water very long. Expect good catches of chub, roach, dace and gudgeon, with pleasure nets of 20lb+ common. Often used for club and open contests.

How to get there   From Warwick, head south on the A46, then A439 towards Stratford-upon-Avon; after about 3 miles, turn left at crossroads on minor road signposted Hampton Lucy. In the village, access to the fishery is by the drive from the bridge. *Note:* no parking outside the fishery or opposite the council houses.

Day tickets   No day tickets, but Open Membership of Warwick & District A.S. available from the General Secretary; Tel. 0926 494201.
Best methods/baits   Use general coarse techniques and baits.
Restrictions   No bloodworm or jokers. No waspgrub.
Facilities   Nearest shop, Hampton Lucy (¾ mile).

STRATFORD LIDO
Atlas Page 202 A.7/2.9

A very picturesque, 80-peg, river section just north of Stratford-upon-Avon, which fishes best when the water is coloured and mild. Depth ranges from 3–9ft, producing mainly chub, roach and gudgeon. The occasional barbel has also recently been reported.

How to get there   From Stratford-upon-Avon town centre, take the A439 (Old Warwick Road) north towards Warwick. The fishery is near the main road, about 1 mile upstream from Stratford town centre. Look for signs to Stratford Lido and the (free) car park.
Day tickets   Adult £1.70; junior/OAP 80p. Available from Mr. Archer, Hon. Sec., Royal Leamington Spa A.A.; Tel. 0926 334185.
Best methods/baits   Waggler, stick float and small feeder all produce good results. Most baits work well here.
Restrictions   No bloodworm or jokers.
Facilities   Barbecue facilities on site. Nearest pub, 1 mile towards Stratford-upon-Avon.
Disabled facilities   Selected swims are suitable for disabled and wheelchair anglers.

BIDFORD, MARLCLIFF AND CLEEVE PRIOR
Atlas Page 202 A.4/3.0

An even-flowing stretch, with some push at the top right bank and in channels below Marlcliff Weir. Average depth 5–6ft; some marginal weed and clumps. Fish right-bank pegs for chub; left-bank pegs for roach and dace. Barbel/chub catches may top 100lb at Marlcliff; 40lb chub nets are common at Bidford and Cleeve Prior.

How to get there   Bidford is on the A439 Evesham to Stratford upon Avon road. For right bank, turn left at traffic lights,

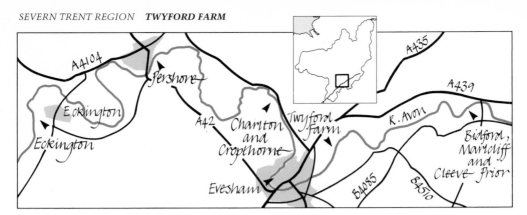

park in Birmingham AA's car park, behind church. Left bank section is approached over the bridge; park at recreation ground. Cleeve Prior and Marlcliff are approached further along the Cleeve Prior road; a No Through Road leads to the river.

Day tickets   None; Birmingham AA open membership is available for £14; see River Severn, Quatford.

Best methods   Stick float or waggler (latter for chub feeding at distance), with small hooks and light hooklengths.

Best baits   Maggots, casters; hemp and tares are best for summer roach. For larger fish (on feeder) use sweetcorn, luncheon meat or bread.

Hotspot Tips

- Swimfeeder tactics are best in turbulent water below the weir.
- The five pegs above the Arrow mouth are brilliant for chub.
- Fish from the island below Marlcliff Weir for barbel and chub.

TWYFORD FARM
Atlas Page 202 A.3/3.1

This 1¼-mile Avon stretch provides superb fishing. Some deep swims are 12ft, most are 6ft, shelving to 4ft close in. Chub (to 5lb), bream (to 5lb) plus quality roach, perch and dace all season, with match nets of 20lb+ and some 50lb+ bream catches. Winter pike are an added bonus. Also available is a stocked pool, 1½ acres with carp to 18lb, roach to 2¼lb, rudd, skimmers, bream and chub from the river, which feeds the lake.

How to get there   At Twyford Country Park, 1 mile north of Evesham, on the A435 Alcester road. Park on the riverside if the ground is dry.

Day tickets   £2 on the river; £3 on the pool; available from Mrs May Vince at Twyford; Tel. 0386 446108.

Best methods   Chub – waggler from middle to far bank; small hooks/light lines are essential. Bream – swimfeeder (also for chub in adverse weather).

Best baits   Bronze maggot (or caster) with wagglers; luncheon meat and sweetcorn are also effective (mainly in summer).

Restrictions   Waspgrub, bloodworm, jokers and raw meat are banned on the river . No groundbait, hempseed, boilies or any high protein bait on the lake.

Hotspot Tips

- Good catches of summer roach and dace are possible with a pole, using hemp and tares.
- Fish pegs 19–23 for good bream; fish pegs 1–24 (on the island) for chub.

EVESHAM
Atlas Page 202 A.3/3.1

A popular, even-flowing loop, 30 yards wide in places, and 4–14ft deep; some weed in the margins. Two excellent adjacent sites – Crown Meadows and Hampton Ferry. Main species are chub, roach, dace and perch, plus bream; carp and barbel appear occasionally; pike may be taken in winter.

How to get there   Crown Meadows is approached via a slip road near the town centre road bridge; Hampton Ferry is approached via a lane, signposted from the A435.

Day tickets   Crown Meadows: £1.80 excluding car park; juniors/OAPs half price; available on the bankside; Hampton Ferry: adult £2, OAP £1.50, under 16s free fishing; available from the riverside cafe.

Best methods   Chub – waggler in middle or further across; stick float and pole tactics are best for smaller fish.

Best baits   Maggots, casters (hemp and tares in summer); pleasure anglers do better with luncheon meat and bread.

Hotspot Tips

- Big perch may fall to dace anglers using a stick float.
- Crown Meadow's upstream pegs are best – as are the shallow bend pegs at Hampton Ferry.
- Look for bream in deep water on the left bank; if you're successful, use a feeder.

Roach.

CROPTHORNE AND CHARLTON
Atlas Page 200 F.9/2.1

A steady-flowing, even-bottomed stretch; water deepens to 12ft above Charlton weir, shallows (to 8ft) below, and deepens again towards Cropthorne. Expect good winter chub above the weir, and bream all season, plus some roach and dace. Top match catches (both sites) reach 50lb; typical float bags are 10lb.

How to get there   For both sites, take the A44 from Evesham towards Pershore. After 2 miles, turn right to Charlton village; use the Birmingham AA car park. For Cropthorne, follow signs to village and continue towards Fladbury; use the BAA car park on the right, before the bridge.

Day tickets   None: open membership to Birmingham AA is available for £14.

Best methods   For chub above Charlton weir, use a half-depth waggler in the middle; use a stickfloat or waggler for mixed bags.

Best baits   Cropthorne: caster or worm for bream. Charlton: bread for summer and autumn bream.

Hotspot Tips

- For Charlton summer bream, use a swimfeeder below the weir.
- At Charlton, the best chub pegs are above the weir; the best bream pegs are immediately below!

PERSHORE
Atlas Page 200 F.9/2.1

Above the weir waters are slow-moving, dropping from 16ft to a 5ft shelf close-in. Below the weir, waters shallow and quicken, then slow and deepen by the bridges. Mainly bream, chub, roach, dace and barbel in summer/autumn; typical right-bank chub nets reach 50lb. Vast hauls of barbel, chub and bream are taken below the weir. Winter pike also provide excellent sport.

How to get there   Pershore is 6 miles west of Evesham, on A44 Worcester road. Free fishing between the two bridges, and on right bank for three meadows behind swimming pool and by sports ground. Park by bridges or in town. (*Note*: Birmingham AA water is left bank above and below the weir, and right bank below the bridges.)

Day tickets   Limited free fishing; otherwise Birmingham AA members only (membership £14).

Best methods   Use swimfeeder below the weir; stick float and waggler above. Use leger or swimfeeder to reach deeper water.

Best baits   Maggots and casters; hemp and tares in summer.

Hotspot Tips

- There is excellent float fishing for chub below the bridges.
- The best swims are below the weir, and on the right bank below the bridges.

ECKINGTON
Atlas Page 200 F.9/2.1

Excellent bream fishery, with slow pace, average 15ft depth and fairly even, gently sloping bottom. Deepest water may be very close in on some pegs. Sport can be patchy, with mainly bream (to 6lb) all season; nets of 40–50lb are common. Plenty of roach, plus 4lb+ chub and good pike.

How to get there   Take the A44 from
  Evesham to Pershore; turn south
  (A4104), then B4080 to Eckington
  village. Fish from the stone bridge down
  to the rowing club (opposite bank);
  access by a track from the village or
  from the bridge.
Day tickets   Solihull AC members only;
  annual ticket £14, plus joining fee.
Best methods   Summer bream – open-
  ended swimfeeder with groundbait plus
  breadflake hookbait. Winter bream –
  groundbait plus caster, worm or red
  maggot. Small hooks and fine bottoms
  are essential in clear water.
Best baits   Roach – maggots, or hemp or
  tares in hot weather.
Facilities   Shops in Eckington village.

Hotspot Tips

 Use a stick float and pole for roach, but
  also consider a waggler.
 Chub are taken most regularly below
  the Cock Inn.

BISHOPS BOWL LAKES
Atlas Page 202 A.9/2.6

A four-lake complex, formerly a limestone
quarry and now a nature reserve, a few
miles south-east of Leamington Spa. Good
general coarse fishing, some trout and big
pike, bream and tench. Dinosaur's Dip,
Mitre Pool and Blue Pool are especially
good for carp. Green Hill Lake is
especially good for pike.

How to get there   Leave the north-bound
  M40 at jct 12 and turn right onto the
  B4451 to Bishop's Itchington village.
  Look for signs to the lakes and park
  nearby.
Day tickets   Membership £10, plus £4
  day ticket or £6 day ticket for non-
  members. Half day: £2.50 and £3.50
  respectively; junior/OAP – members
  prices. Available on site; for details of
  availability; Tel. 0926 613344.
Best methods/baits   Use any recognised
  coarse technique and baits. Specialist
  carp methods may be required.
Restrictions   No night fishing.
Facilities   Nearest shop/pub in Bishop's
  Itchington or Southam (3 miles).
Disabled facilities   Some swims suitable
  for disabled anglers.

FOXHOLES FISHERY
Atlas Page 202 B.4/2.3

Three lakes located in the village of Crick,
about 5 miles east of Rugby. Expect good
general mixed coarse fishing, including
good-sized carp and tench.

How to get there   Leave the M1 at jct 18
  and head east on the A428 to Crick
  (about ½ mile).The fishery is signposted
  in the village; car parking on site.
Day tickets   Adult/junior/OAP £3 per
  rod. Available from Roger Chaplin;
  Tel. 0788 823967. Open 16th June–30th
  October.
Best methods/baits   Use any recognised
  coarse technique and baits.
Facilities   Nearest shop/pub in Crick
  village.

GRAND UNION CANAL, CALCOTT LOCKS TO WARWICK
Atlas Page 202 A.8/2.6

A long canal stretch, from the outskirts of
Warwick, west to Napton – about 14 miles
in all. A traditional Midlands canal in a
rural setting, providing plenty of small
fish, including roach, skimmer bream,
perch and bream, plus tench in the basin
areas.

How to get there   From Warwick, follow
  the A425 east towards Southam and
  Napton on the Hill (about 14 miles).
  Access is at various points, including
  the Birmingham road (A41) at Warwick,
  the A423 at Long Itchington, and from
  Calcott Locks to Napton marina on the
  A425. Free parking is available at the
  bridges along the stretch. For any
  further details, contact Mr. Archer (see
  below) or local tackle shops.
Day tickets   Adult £1.60; junior/OAP
  £1.60. Available from Mr. Archer, Hon.
  Sec., Royal Leamington Spa AA;
  Tel. 0926 334185.
Best methods/baits   Float fish (rod and
  line) or polefish in early morning or
  evening to avoid boat traffic. Caster fish
  where tree cover is on far bank.
Restrictions   No bloodworm or joker.
Facilities   Various shops/pubs/toilets/
  food to be found near the water, along
  the whole stretch, according to location.
Disabled facilities   Swims at selected
  locations are suitable for disabled and
  wheelchair anglers; for advice, please
  contact Mr. Archer (see above).

JUBILEE POOLS
Atlas Page 202 A.9/2.2

Two lakes – Island and Horseshoe – located on a farm at Ryton-on-Dunsmore, a few miles south-east of Coventry. Excellent mixed fishing, with prolific tench and carp catches, especially during the summer months.

How to get there   Take the A45 east from Coventry towards Northampton. At Ryton-on-Dunsmore, just after the junction with the A445 Leamington Spa road (about 2½ miles), look for the lane to Manor Farm and the fishery (access is only available from one side of the dual carriageway). Car parking on site: £1.

Day tickets   Adult £1.50; junior/OAP 80p; available only to Royal Leamington Spa AA members. Fee £13 from Mr Archer, Hon. Sec.; Tel. 0926 334185.

Best methods/baits   Use general coarse techniques and baits.

Restrictions   No bloodworm or jokers. Keepnets must be staked at all times. All fish over 3lb must be returned to the water. Groundbait to be used only in moderation. Fishing only from 0600 onwards.

Facilities   Nearest shop, Ryton village, (1 mile); nearest pub, Ryton British Legion, 300 yards.

Disabled facilities   Some swims on Island Lake are suitable for disabled and wheelchair anglers.

KINGSBURY WATER PARK/ GIBSONS LAKE
Atlas Page 202 A.6/1.7

A group of several old pits, in a pleasant setting near Tamworth. One lake (3 acres) is for carp specialists only, with 20lb+ fish common; plenty of tench, roach, rudd, bream, perch and pike in the other lakes.

How to get there   Take the A4097 from Birmingham towards Tamworth and take right turn signposted 'Bodymoor Heath'. Continue for 1 mile; the fishery is on the left. Car parking on site (£1 per day).

Day tickets   Coarse lakes, £1.20; carp lake, £2.30; tickets from the machine in the car park.

Best methods/baits   Use any recognised coarse technique and baits. Specialist carp methods may be required.

Restrictions   No live bait for pike. No lead weights. A keep net is implemented for the first six weeks of the season

Facilities   Toilets/cafe on site. Nearest shops/pubs in Fazeley or Tamworth.

Disabled facilities   Some swims are suitable for disabled and wheelchair anglers. Check with the Visitor's Centre for the best swims; Tel. 0827 872660.

NAPTON RESERVOIR
Atlas Page 202 A9/2.2

Two-lakes (one of 20 acres, one of 4 acres) near Southam, Coventry which are joined by a narrow channel. A good head of bream, roach, tench and perch, plus some large carp (mirrors over 20lb) – mainly in the smaller lake. Excellent fishing, particularly in the summer months and when the water is coloured.

How to get there   From Leamington Spa head east on the A425 to Southam, then Napton on the Hill. The reservoir is on the left, beyond the village. Parking (free) on site.

Day tickets   Adult/junior/OAP £4. Available from bailiffs on the bank.

Best methods/baits   Use general coarse techniques and baits. Casters and normal summer baits are best fished using float tactics. Specialist carp methods may be required in the small lake.

Restrictions   Night fishing by special permit only.

Facilities   Nearest shop/pub in Napton village (1 mile).

Disabled facilities Some swims are suitable for disabled and wheelchair anglers.

NEWBOLD QUARRY
Atlas Page 202 B.4/2.3

A pit fishery just north of Rugby, providing very good tench fishing, plus bream and roach. Also excellent winter pike fishing, with 20lb+ specimens each year. Limited pegs (about 40) and very exposed in bad weather. Nets of 40lb are always likely here.

How to get there   Leave the M6 at jct 1 and turn south on A426 to Rugby. After about 2 miles, turn right at roundabout onto minor road to Newbold on Avon; in the village, the Quarry is on the left. Follow signs to the water and car park.

Day tickets   Adult £3; junior/OAP £1.50. Available on the bank. Also season tickets: adult £10; junior/OAP £4.

Best methods/baits   Tench, bream – use sweetcorn. Roach – maggots.

Restrictions   No bloodworm or jokers. No tins to be taken on site.

Facilities   Nearest shop/pub in Newbold village.

Disabled facilities   Banks are very unprotected, making access difficult.

WEST MIDLANDS

Bracebridge Pool.

ARBORETUM LAKE
Atlas Page 202 A.5/1.9

Also known as Hatherton Lake, this picturesque, tree-lined and very popular lake is close to Walsall town centre, and provides some very good coarse fishing. Expect bream, roach, perch, carp, pike and an occasional chub. Very deep in some areas, so caution is required when fishing here.

How to get there   Leave the M6 at jct 10 and take the A454 into Walsall town centre, then the A461 towards Lichfield. The fishery is at the roundabout where the A461 meets Broadway (about 1½ miles). Car parking is available in Arboretum Road.

Day tickets   Adult £1; junior/OAP 50p. Available on the bank.

Best methods/baits   In summer, fish on the drop with squatts, pinkies or hemp. In shallow areas, use float or pole with caster, maggot or bread. In deeper areas, use swimfeeder and slider.

Facilities   Snack bar on site in summer. Shops/pubs/toilets all within walking distance.

Disabled facilities   Some swims may be suitable for disabled and wheelchair anglers; please contact Bentley Bait Box for advice; Tel. 0922 29454.

BAILEYS POOL
Atlas Page 202 A.5/1.9

A pretty, rush-lined pool at Willenhall, just outside Walsall town centre. Depth ranges from 2–11ft and weed growth is dense in some areas, but fishing is good, with excellent summer tench which may reach 5lb. Also large carp (to 20lb), bream (to 4lb), roach, perch and pike (to 21lb).

How to get there   Leave the M6 at jct 10 and take the A454 into Walsall town centre. After about 1 mile, turn left onto A34 towards Cannock, then left again (after 3 miles) onto A4124 towards Wolverhampton. The pool is on the left, just before the canal. Car parking available nearby.

Day tickets   Adult £1; junior/OAP 50p. Available on the bank.

Best methods   Use float, pole or swimfeeder for most species.

Best baits   Floating baits are best for carp; use sweetcorn, bread, worms, casters or maggots for other species.

Facilities   Shops nearby on Moseley Estate; nearest pub, on Sneyd (walking distance).

Disabled facilities   Some swims may be suitable for disabled and wheelchair anglers; please contact Bentley Bait Box for advice; Tel. 0922 29454.

BLACKROOT POOL
Atlas Page A.5/2.1

A 12-acre estate lake at Sutton Park, just north of Birmingham. A well stocked lake with most coarse species and some good-sized pike, plus some very large carp, including several 20lb fish and (at least) two of 30lb+.

How to get there   Leave the M6 at junction 6 and follow the A453 towards Sutton Coldfield. At the Ring Road, take first left; the park is straight ahead. Parking (free) on site.

Day tickets   Adult £2; junior/OAP £1. Available from bailiffs on the bank.

Best methods/baits   Use any recognised coarse technique and baits.

Facilities   Toilets/cafe on site in summer. Nearest shops 1 mile/plenty of pubs surrounding the park.

Disabled facilities   Some access points for disabled and wheelchair anglers.

BONEHILL MILL
Atlas Page 202 A.6/1.7

Three lakes, totalling 20 acres, just south of Tamworth, which are heavily stocked with only small common carp (2–5lb), although some double-figure fish may appear.

How to get there   Follow the A5 towards Tamworth; Fazeley village is just south of Tamworth. Look for signs to the Mill; car parking on site.

Day tickets   Adult/junior/OAP £3. Available on the bank.

Best methods/baits   Use any recognised coarse technique and baits. Specialist carp methods may be required.

Restrictions   No night fishing.

Facilities   Nearest shop/pub in Fazeley village.

BRACEBRIDGE POOL
Atlas Page 202 A.5/1.9

A quite large (16-acre) lake at Sutton Park in Sutton Coldfield, near Birmingham. Plenty of coarse fish here, with roach, pike, tench, bream and even a few 20lb+ carp! Large catches of bream are also taken regularly in summer – up to 60lb is possible.

How to get there   Leave the M6 at jct 6 and follow the A453 to Sutton Coldfield. At the Ring Road, take the 1st left turn and drive straight on to Sutton Park. Use the (free) car park and follow signs to the fishery.

Day tickets   Adult £2; junior/OAP £1. Available on the bank.

Best methods/baits   Use general coarse techniques and baits.

Facilities   Toilets/cafe in the park. Nearest shop, less than 1 mile; there are plenty of pubs surrounding the park.

Disabled facilities   Some swims are suitable for disabled and wheelchair anglers.

THE BRIDGE POOL
Atlas Page 200 F.8/0.6

A small, 1-acre lake with 20 pegs, holding carp to 18lb, bream to 6lb, tench to 6 lb, perch to 3lb and roach to 2lb. The carp are normally caught at the opposite end to the bridge and the tench by the fallen tree and winter-lilies.

How to get there   Take the A454 from Wolverhampton to Bridgnorth, turning right to Pattingham after 5 miles. Bear right in the village centre and Patshull is on the right. Car parking by the lodge.

Day tickets   Adult £2.50; junior/OAP £1.50. Available from Patshull Park Fisheries, Patshull Park, Burnhill Green, Wolverhampton; Tel. 0902 700774.

Best methods   Use general coarse methods and baits.

Restrictions   No keep-nets. No hemp seed or groundbait.

Facilities   There is very easy access for disabled and wheelchair anglers.

BUMBLE HOLE
Atlas Page 200 F.9/0.9

A 5-acre ash pit, 3–12ft deep in places, at Darby End near Netherton. A good coarse fishery, with roach (to 2lb), perch, Crucian carp and tench.

How to get there   From Dudley, take the A450 Pedmore road towards Merry Hill and Netherton. Free car parking on site.

Day tickets   Free fishing.

Best methods/baits   Use any recognised coarse technique.

Facilities   Nearest shop/pub Darby End.

CALF HEATH RESERVOIR
Atlas Page 200 F.5/0.5

A 50-acre reservoir adjacent to the A5 and only a few miles north-west of Birmingham. Some coarse fish present, but mainly plentifully- stocked carp, with several 20–30lb fish taken recently.

How to get there   Leave the M6 at jct 12 and head west on the A5 towards Telford. The reservoir is on the left; park nearby.

Day tickets   Annual permits only: adult/junior/OAP £9. Available from the bailiff's house on the A5 bank.

Best methods/baits   Use any recognised coarse technique and baits.

Facilities   Nearest shop/pub in Horsebrook or Stretton (about 2 miles).

COOMBE ABBEY LAKE
Atlas Page 202 A.9/2.3

A delightful 70-acre lake set in park and woodland surroundings, about 3 miles east of Coventry. Depth ranges from 2–5ft, and there is very good access to the banks, which hold 100 pegs. Fishing is the only sport here, with most species present, but bream predominating, with bags approaching 100lb during the summer.

How to get there   From Coventry city centre, take the A428 east towards Rugby and on the city outskirts, bear left onto the B4027 towards Brinklow. Look for signs to Coombe Abbey and the fishery on the left, after about 2½ miles. Free car parking on site.

Day tickets   Adult £1.80; junior/OAP £1. Holders of Coventry City Council 'Passport To Leisure' 60p. Available from Coventry City Council, Leisure Services, Rangers Dept., Coombe Abbey Park, Brinklow Road, Coventry; Tel. 0203 453720.

Best methods/baits   Use general coarse techniques and baits.

Restrictions   Fishing is restricted to the west bank.

Facilities   Nearest shop, towards Coventry (1 mile); nearest pub, the Craven Arms (1 mile).

Disabled facilities   Some swims are suitable for disabled and wheelchair anglers.

CUTTLE MILL
Atlas Page 202 A.5/2.0

Two lakes (one 5 acres with carp, one 2¾ acres with carp, tench, bream, dace, chub and roach), just east of Sutton Coldfield. A very popular fishery, with plenty of carp in double figures and many of 20lb+.

How to get there   From Birmingham, take the A4091 north towards Tamworth; after about 4 miles (at jct with A446, near the National Golf Centre) turn left to Wishaw. Follow signs to the fishery and park on site.

Day tickets   Carp lake: adult/junior/OAP £10. Coarse lake: adult £5; junior/OAP £4. Maximum two rods per person. Available from Tony Huggins (owner) at the mill; Tel. 0827 872253. Fishing from 0700 – dusk (0700–1900 in winter).

Best methods/baits   Carp – use advanced methods/rigs. Best results with high protein boilies on hair rigs and floating baits. Other species – use any recognised coarse technique.

Restrictions   Use only barbless hooks. No keepnets. No seed, nut, pea or bean baits. No night fishing.

Facilities   Nearest shop/pub in Wishaw.

DONKEY POOL
Atlas Page 202 A.3/2.0

A 2-acre clay pit with an island at Dudley, in the suburbs of Birmingham. The pool provides mixed coarse fishing, with perch, roach, carp and bream, plus very good tench, but is heavily fished. Sport is generally best early morning before things get busy.

How to get there   From Dudley, follow Birmingham New Road from Burntree Island to the King Arthur pub; the pool is behind the trees, opposite the pub. Free car parking nearby.

Day tickets   Free fishing.

Best methods   Float (for tench) or feeder.

Best baits   Bread, maggots, corn (for tench).

Facilities   Nearest shop 400 yards; nearest pub, King Arthur (opposite).

EARLSWOOD LAKES
Atlas Page 202 A.5/2.5

Two lakes, located midway between Solihull and Redditch, which provide fishing from either the bank or the dam walls. Plenty of roach and bream (to 5lb), with fishing best in the summer months when the water levels are low.

How to get there   Take the A34 south from Birmingham and at Shirley (about 2 miles before the M42) turn right onto the B4102 to Earlswood Crossroads. Follow signs to the lakes and use the (free) car park on site.

Day tickets   Adult £2; junior/OAP £1. Available from the bailiff on the bank.

Best methods/baits   Float and leger tactics both work well here. Most baits work well.

Facilities   Nearest shop, Earlswood Crossroads (300 yards); nearest pubs, Reservoir Hotel (200 yards); Red Lion (300 yards).

Disabled facilities   Some swims at both lakes are suitable for disabled and wheelchair anglers (with assistance).

FARMERS POOL, PENSNETT
Atlas Page 205 A.3/2.0

A small, ½-acre pool at the Fens Pool Centre. Heavily weeded, but only 8 pegs for fishing. Mainly tench, with specimens to 5lb, plus perch and small pike (only 4lb).

How to get there   Drive from Dudley via A4101 Kingswinford Road past Russells Hall hospital and go down the dirt track at the back of the houses. Park by the metal bollards and fish from the left hand bank.

Day tickets   Free fishing.

Best methods   Float fishing preferred.

Best baits   Bread.

Facilities   Nearest shop/pub Kingswinford.

10lb 12oz tench.

FENS POOL, PENSNETT
Atlas Page 205 A.3/2.0

A 10-acre gravel pit, 1–20ft deep, part of the canal feeder system in Dudley. Provides good all-round coarse fishing, with excellent tench (average size 3–4lb, some 6lb+), plus large pike (to 25lb). Best fishing is early on, using a feeder on the shallow side.

How to get there   Drive from Dudley via A4101 Kingswinford Road, past Russells Hall Hospital. Turn left onto the housing estate and follow the signs to Fens Pool Centre. Free parking at the centre.

Day tickets   Free fishing.

Best methods   Feeder; otherwise float.

Best baits   Maggots, bread, corn.

Facilities   Nearest shops on housing estate (½ mile); nearest pub, Red Lion, Chaple Street.

GROVE POOL, PENSNETT
Atlas Page 205 A.3/2.0

This 4½-acre, very shallow pool is also part of the canal feeder system in Dudley. Good all-round coarse fishing, mainly tench (average size 3–4lb), roach, perch and carp, plus large pike (to 25lb). Best fishing is early on, using a feeder in shallower areas.

How to get there   Drive from Dudley via A4101 Kingswinford Road, past Russells Hall Hospital. Turn left onto the housing estate and follow the signs to Fens Pool Centre. Free parking at the centre.

Day tickets   Free fishing.

Best methods   Feeder; otherwise float.

Best baits   Maggots, bread, corn.

Facilities   Nearest shops on housing estate (½ mile); nearest pub, Red Lion, Chaple Street.

HIMLEY HALL
Atlas Page 205 A.3/1.9

A man-made, 8-acre lake, 3–12ft deep in places. Probably the best fishery in the Dudley area, well worth a visit. Expect large bags of tench, crucian carp (to 50lb+!) as well as mirrors and commons to 20lb. Also large grass carp (10lb+).

How to get there   From Dudley (Eve Hill), take the B4176 Himley Road for 4 miles past the Bulls Head pub to the main gates of the Hall. Free parking at the Hall for anglers.

Day tickets   Adult £3.15; junior/OAP Mon-Fri £1.55, weekend full price. Available on the bank. Night syndicate tickets £59.60 annually from Dudley Leisure Services; Tel. 0384 456000, or the Himley Hall Warden; Tel. 0902 324093.

Best methods   Float, leger, feeder. Specialist long-range tackle may be required.

Best baits   Maggots, bread, corn, boiled baits, paste.

Restrictions   No keepnets.

Facilities   Toilets/food available on site. Nearest pub, Dudley Arms (½ mile).

Disabled facilities   Some swims suitable for disabled and wheelchair anglers.

ISLAND POOL
Atlas Page 202 A.1/1.9

A 4-acre pit at Baggeridge Park providing good mixed coarse fishing, with perch, roach, carp and tench.

How to get there   From Dudley take the B4176, then at Himley take the A449, (right) to Wolverhampton. At the next roundabout take the A463 to Sedgeley. The park entrance is signposted in Gospel End village.

Day tickets   Adult £2.50; junior/OAP £1.80. Available from the Visitor's Centre on the site.

Best methods/baits   Use any recognised coarse technique.

Restrictions   No night fishing.

Facilities   Toilets/food available on site. Nearest pub, Dudley Arms (½ mile).

KEEPERS LAKE
Atlas Page 202 A.5/1.9

A small (1-acre) lake at Sutton Park in Sutton Coldfield, near Birmingham. A pleasant fishery, with some quite large pike (to 20lb) plus lots of skimmer bream, perch, and some big roach.

How to get there   Leave the M6 at jct 6 and follow the A453 to Sutton Coldfield. At the Ring Road, take the 1st left turn and drive straight on to Sutton Park. Use the (free) car park and follow signs to the fishery.

Day tickets   Adult £2; junior/OAP £1. Available on the bank.

Best methods/baits   Use general coarse techniques and baits.

Facilities   Toilets on site. Nearest shop, less than 1 mile; there are plenty of pubs surrounding the park.

Disabled facilities   Some swims are suitable for disabled and wheelchair anglers.

LEASOWES CANAL
Atlas Page 202 A.4/2.0

A very heavily weeded ½-mile section of canal, near Halesowen, from the footbridge at Leasowes Park to Mucklow's Hill. Very weedy and not a lot of fish here, but still well worth a try, because some very large carp, tench, roach and perch have been taken from these waters.

How to get there   From Halesowen, drive up Mucklow's Hill and turn right onto Leasowens Park. Use the car park and walk to the pool.

Day tickets   Free fishing.

Best methods   Float, leger, feeder. Strong tackle is essential.

Best baits   Maggots, bread, boilies.

Facilities   Toilets/children's playground in park. Golf course. Nearest shop Halesowen (1 mile).

LEASOWES POOL (BREACHES POOL)
Atlas Page 202 A.4/2.0

A pretty, tree-lined 4-acre lake at Mucklow's Hill, near Halesowen, with lily pads and abundant wildlife. Best fishing is in early morning when bankside disturbances are least. Expect perch, roach, carp and eels.

How to get there   From Halesowen, drive up Mucklows Hill and turn right onto Leasowens Park. Use the car park and walk to the pool.

Day tickets   Free fishing.

Best methods   Float, leger, feeder.

Best baits   Maggots, bread, boilies.

Facilities   Toilets/children's playground in park. Golf course. Nearest shop Halesowen (1 mile).

Hook retrieval from a pike's mouth.

MIDDLE POOL, PENSNETT
Atlas Page 202 A3/2.0

A 12-acre gravel pit, the third part of the canal feeder system in Dudley, located in a Site of Special Scientific Interest (SSSI). A nice fishing water, but in the middle of a housing/industrial estate! A good head of tench (to 7lb), plus roach (2lb), bream (5lb) and pike. Potentially a good carp water, with lots of 15lb+ specimens taken so far.

How to get there   Drive from Dudley via A4101 Kingswinford Road, past Russells Hall Hospital. Turn left onto the housing estate and follow the signs to Fens Pool Centre. Free parking at the centre.
Day tickets   Free fishing.
Best methods   Feeder; float/leader for carp. Long-stay fishing may be required for carp.
Best baits   Maggots, bread, corn.
Facilities   Nearest shops on housing estate (½ mile); nearest pub, Red Lion, Chaple Street.

NETHERTON RESERVOIR
Atlas Page 202 A.3/2.0

A 12-acre reservoir just south of Dudley, near Saltwells Nature Reserve. A good fishery, very open and windswept. Mainly roach, perch and carp, with good-sized catches, plus large pike and eels when using a specialist approach. Best fishing in the early morning, before the boating traffic builds up!

How to get there   From Dudley, take the A450 Pedmore road towards Merry Hill; turn left at Island, through the Enterprise Zone to the reservoir. Free parking at the lake.
Day tickets   Free fishing.
Best methods   Float or leger; also specialist pike tackle.
Best baits   Maggots, worms.
Facilities   Nearest shops on housing estate (½ mile).

OLD HALL POOL
Atlas Page 202 A.3/1.9

This very popular pear-shaped fishery (also known as Irish Pool) is located in the centre of a housing estate close to Walsall town centre and the M6, yet produces some excellent coarse fish. Depth is variable, from 14ft in parts to shallows which are very weedy in summer. Expect carp (up to 26lb), tench, bream, roach, perch and eels, plus chub which are always 3lb+.

How to get there   Leave the M6 at jct 10 and take the A454 towards Aldridge. Take 1st left (Bloxwich Lane), then 1st left (Churchill Road) over the motorway and turn right into Poplar Avenue. The fishery is on the left; park alongside the pool, behind the Old Hall pub.
Day tickets   Adult £1; junior/OAP 50p. Available on the bank, but very popular, especially in summer.
Best methods   Pole, waggler and legering all produce good catches.
Best baits   Use floating baits for carp. Use maggots, casters, bread or sweetcorn for other species.
Facilities   Shops nearby (walking distance); nearest pub, the Old Hall, by the car park.
Disabled facilities   Some swims are suitable for disabled and wheelchair anglers; please contact Bentley Bait Box for advice; Tel. 0922 29454.

PARK LIME PITS
Atlas Page 202 A.3/1.9

Two former lime pits now controlled by Walsall Leisure Services, located in a secluded, wooded area at Daw End near Aldridge, east of Walsall. A very busy venue with anglers, ramblers and picnickers. The large lake is very deep (up to 30ft) with clear water, making fishing difficult, but expect roach (to 2lb), bream (to 6lb) and perch, plus some large pike and carp.

How to get there   Leave the M6 at jct 10 and take the A454 to Aldridge. At the B4154 junction head for Barr Common and Bosty Lane and follow signs to the fishery. Car parking available on site.
Day tickets   Adult £1; junior/OAP 50p. Available from Rangers on the bank, or from the Lodge.
Best methods/baits   Use general coarse techniques and baits.
Restrictions   No fishing in the small lake.
Facilities   Nearest shop/pub/toilets are about 2 miles away.
Disabled facilities   Some swims may be suitable for disabled and wheelchair anglers; please contact Bentley Bait Box for advice; Tel. 0922 29454.

PATSHULL PARK
Atlas Page 200 F.8/0.7

A very picturesque fishing complex, just west of Wolverhampton, with fishing on two lakes – Great Lake (75 acres) and Bridge Pool. Great lake contains large pike (to 34lb); best fishing is at the Scout Hut or Lodge Bay exit. Bridge Pool contains carp, tench, bream, roach and perch; best fishing is at the far bank.

How to get there   Take the A41 north-west from Wolverhampton about 5 miles and turn left on minor road to Pattingham. Follow signs to the golf course; the fishery is nearby. Car parking (free) next to the fishing lodge.

Day tickets   Bridge Pool: adult/junior/OAP £2.50. The Great Lake: adult/junior/OAP £4.50 (£5 including boat hire). All tickets available on site.

Best methods/baits   Use a 5-metre pole or waggler with red maggot or caster. For pike, use specialist methods with livebait/deadbait.

Restrictions   No hemp or groundbait. No keepnets in summer. No spinners or plugs for pike fishing (Great Lake).

Facilities   Toilets/cafe at fishing lodge. Nearest shop/pub in Pattingham.

Disabled facilities   Some swims may be suitable for disabled anglers; please phone for advice; Tel. 0902 700774.

6¾lb bream.

POOL HALL
Atlas Page 200 F.8/0.7

This popular, heavily-fished, large (25-acre), mainly carp fishing lake lies to the west of Wolverhampton. Excellent carp sport is virtually guaranteed, with plenty of 20lb fish (mostly commons); also some roach. Best fishing is in warm weather.

How to get there   Take the A454 west from Wolverhampton towards Bridgnorth. Just before Trescott (after about 4 miles), turn left on minor road to Lower Penn and follow signs to Pool Hall and the fishery. Parking available on site.

Day tickets   Adult/junior/OAP £2; half-day £2; weekend £2.50. Available on the bank.

Best methods   Floating baits preferred. Leger in winter.

Best baits   Boilies, hemp, Chum Mixer, luncheon meat, sweetcorn.

Facilities   Nearest shop/pub in Castlecroft (1 mile).

Disabled facilities   Some swims suitable for disabled and wheelchair anglers.

POWELLS POOL
Atlas Page 202 A.5/1.9

An 18-acre lake at Sutton Park in Sutton Coldfield, near Birmingham. Lots of quite large pike (to 15lb) plus skimmer bream and roach. A large head of tench also inhabit the lake, but are hard to locate. Fishing is best on either side of the Beefeater Restaurant, or along the dam wall.

How to get there   Leave the M6 at jct 6 and follow the A453 to Sutton Coldfield. At the Ring Road, take the 1st left turn and drive straight on to Sutton Park. Use the (free) car park and follow signs to the fishery.

Day tickets   Adult £2; junior/OAP £1. Available on the bank.

Best methods/baits   Use general coarse techniques and baits. Open-end feeder and maggot produce the best results.

Facilities   Toilets at Bracebridge Pool, in the park. Nearest shop, less than 1 mile; there are plenty of pubs surrounding the park.

Disabled facilities   Some swims are suitable for disabled and wheelchair anglers.

PRIMROSE HILL TO STOURBRIDGE CANAL
Atlas Page 202 A.3/2.0

A 3-mile section of the Stourbridge Canal, 3–4ft deep, which provides very good early morning fishing, with good catches of perch, gudgeon, roach, tench and rudd.

How to get there   From Dudley, take the A450 Pedmore road towards Merry Hill and Netherton. Free car near the canal.

Day tickets   Free fishing.

Best methods/baits   Use any recognised coarse technique.

Facilities   Nearest shops on housing estate (½ mile).

SALFORD PARK
Atlas Page 202 A.3/2.1

A busy, 12-acre town fishery, close to 'Spaghetti Junction' in Birmingham. Good (but often difficult) mixed fishing, with roach, perch and tench, plus carp which average 13lb, with some topping 20lb.

How to get there   Leave the M6 at jct 6 and take the A38 towards Birmingham city centre. Look for signs to the reservoir. For details of access/parking, contact the local tackle shops.

Day tickets   Adult £1.40; junior/OAP 90p; UB40 45p. Annual carp licence £11.50. Available on the bank. For details; Tel. 021 327 1419.

Best methods/baits   Use any recognised coarse technique and baits.

Restrictions   No night fishing.

Facilities   Toilets/food/shops/pubs – plenty in the Birmingham area.

Disabled facilities   Some swims suitable for disabled anglers.

SCHOOL POOL
Atlas Page 202 A.3/1.9

A gravel-bottomed pool near Walsall town centre. The water is also used for school activities (windsurfing, yachting, etc.), so fishing is best in early morning or late evening when things quieten down. Expect good bream, roach, perch, Crucian carp and the occasional tench and carp.

How to get there   Leave the M6 at jct 10 and take the A454 into Walsall town centre. After about 1 mile, turn left onto A34 towards Cannock, then left again (after 3 miles) onto A4124 towards Wolverhampton. Turn right (Vernon Way) just before the canal; the pool is behind the comprehensive school. Car parking nearby.

Day tickets   Adult £1; junior/OAP 50p. Available on the bank.

Best methods   Use waggler, pole or feeder.

Best baits   Use sweetcorn, casters, maggots, worms; bloodworm is best in winter.

Facilities   Shops nearby on Moseley Estate; nearest pub, on Sneyd (walking distance).

Disabled facilities   Some swims may be suitable for disabled and wheelchair anglers; please contact Bentley Bait Box for advice; Tel. 0922 29454.

SNEYD RESERVOIR
Atlas Page 202 A.3/1.9

A reed-lined pool, at Willenhall, close to Walsall town centre and the M6. Even depth up to 6ft, providing straightforward fishing for tench (to 5lb), roach, perch and the occasional carp.

How to get there   Leave the M6 at jct 10 and take the A454 into Walsall town centre. After about 1 mile, turn left onto A34 towards Cannock, then left again (after 3 miles) onto A4124 towards Wolverhampton. Turn right (Vernon Way) just before the canal; the reservoir is on the left. Park near the Sneyd pub or Moseley Estate shops.

Day tickets   Adult/junior/OAP £1. Available on the bank.

Best methods   Float fishing is best with a waggler or swimfeeder.

Best baits   Use sweetcorn, bread, worms, casters and maggots.

Restrictions   Fishing only on two banks (bird sanctuary on other two banks).

Facilities   Shops on Moseley Estate; nearest pub, on Sneyd (near the car park).

Disabled facilities   Some swims may be suitable for disabled and wheelchair anglers; please contact Bentley Bait Box for advice; Tel. 0922 29454.

SOMERS PACKINGTON COARSE FISHERY
Atlas Page 202 A.7/2.1

A 5-lake complex fishery totalling 23 acres, situated mid-way between Coventry and Birmingham. A sixth (5-acre) lake is currently under construction. Plenty of fish for everyone, including carp (to 30lb), tench (to 7lb) and big pike, nudging 40lb! Caters for all types of responsible angler.

How to get there   Take the A45 Coventry-Birmingham road; at signpost 'Meriden' (opposite Little Chef), turn into Birmingham Road, then right again into Somers Road. Continue for 1½ miles; the fishery entrance is on the right. Free parking on site.

Day tickets   16th June – 31st October: adult £4; junior/OAP £2. 1st November – 14th March: adult £3.50; junior/OAP £1.75. Half-day ticket £3 (all season). Available from the Fishery, Somers Road, Meriden; Tel. 0676 23833.

Best methods   Most methods work well here.

Best baits   Sweetcorn, luncheon meat, boilies, hemp.

Restrictions   No tiger nuts, peanuts or seed baits. Limited ground baiting. Carp and pike to be returned immediately to the water. Livebait must be purchased on site.

Facilities   Toilets/food/bait and groundbait available on site. Nearest shop and pub, The Bulls Head, in Meriden (1 mile).

Disabled facilities   Some swims suitable for disabled and wheelchair anglers.

Common carp.

WIDEWATERS CANAL
Atlas Page 202 A.3/2.0

A ¾-mile section of the canal feeder system in Dudley, which has been cleaned out in the last two years. Best fishing is in the early morning, when big shoals of roach are present, plus big tench (to 6lb), carp (to 10lb), perch (to 2lb) and medium-sized pike (10lb).

How to get there   Drive from Dudley via A4101 Kingswinford Road, past Russells Hall Hospital. Turn left onto the housing estate and follow the signs to Fens Pool Centre. Free parking at the centre.

Day tickets   Free fishing.

Best methods   Float is preferred; also leger.

Best baits   Maggots, bread, corn.

Facilities   Nearest shops on housing estate (½ mile); nearest pub, Red Lion, Chaple Street.

WORDSLEY BASIN TO DUDLEY BOROUGH
Atlas Page 202 A.3/2.0

A 1½-mile section of the Staffs and Worcs Canal which provides plenty of roach, perch, rudd, gudgeon and some large carp (to 10lb+).

How to get there   Head east from Dudley on the A4101, then turn south on A449 to Wordsley. Access to the canal is near the Stuart Crystal glassworks. Free parking nearby.

Day tickets   Free fishing.

Best methods/baits   Use any recognised coarse technique.

Facilities   Nearest shop/pub Wordsley.

WYRELEY AND ESSINGTON CANAL, PELSHALL
Atlas Page 202 A.3/1.9

A very 'reedy', 70-peg canal stretch located in open heathland near Wood Common, a few miles north-east of Walsall. The water becomes very clear in winter as boat traffic subsides. Good-sized roach and perch form the major part of any catch here.

How to get there   Leave the M6 at jct 10, take the A454 into Walsall town centre and after 1 mile, turn left onto A34 towards Cannock, then right (after 3 miles) onto A4124 towards Lichfield. Turn left down Wood Lane and park close to the shops and Free Trade Inn.

Day tickets   Adult £1, junior/OAP 60p; season card: adult £5, junior/OAP £3; available on the bank.

Best methods/baits   Use general coarse techniques. Squatt, pinkie, breadpunch and bloodworm are best for roach and perch.

Facilities   Shops and pub, The Free Trade Inn, near the car park.

Disabled facilities   Some swims may be suitable for disabled and wheelchair anglers; please contact Bentley Bait Box for advice; Tel. 0922 29454.

WYRELEY AND ESSINGTON CANAL, LANE HEAD BRIDGE

Atlas Page 202 A.3/1.9

A short canal length, just west of the M6 in Walsall. Mainly a summer fishery due to the high clarity of water in winter; expect good catches of roach (nets of up to 20lb), plus perch, tench, bream and carp.

How to get there   Leave the M6 at jct 10 and take the A454 towards Aldridge. Take 1st left (Bloxwich Lane), then 2nd left (Bentley Lane) over the motorway and continue to the A462 junction. Access is at various points between the Bridge Inn and the United Kingdom pub. Car parking nearby.

Day tickets   Free fishing.

Best methods   Use general coarse techniques.

Best baits   Maggots, casters, bread and seed baits all work well here.

Facilities   Shops at various points along the stretch; nearest pubs, the Bridge Inn and United Kingdom (walking distance).

Disabled facilities   Some swims may be suitable for disabled and wheelchair anglers; please contact Bentley Bait Box for advice; Tel. 0922 29454.

A good catch as the sun sets on the River Trent.

119

Anglian Region

River Nene, Peterborough embankment.

Among the NRA regions, Anglian is the largest, extending north-south from the Humber to the Thames Estuary, and east-west from Buckinghamshire to the East Anglian coast. Despite the region's size, its waterways fall into two categories – those draining the low Fenlands around The Wash, and the rivers, lakes, reservoirs and ponds of the 'higher' ground.

The 'drains' are largely man-made straight, deep, slow-flowing drainage channels in which water levels are controlled by pumps. The Fen Drains and the Lincolnshire Drains are good examples, operating in connection with natural rivers, such as the Welland and the Witham. Despite such potential drawbacks of changing levels, the waters offer good coarse fishing – especially in winter – with plenty of bream and roach, but pike and zander never very far away!

Further afield, the region's river fishing focuses on the trio of the Cam (near Cambridge), the Nene (from Northampton east through Peterborough and Wisbech to The Wash), and the Great Ouse (from Bedfordshire east through Huntingdon and Ely to The Wash at King's Lynn). All provide excellent coarse fishing, with good catches of bream, roach, dace and tench, and in a variety of both rural and urban surroundings. Plenty of good fishing is also available in East Anglia, where the Norfolk Broads and the Rivers Yare, Thurne and Bure offer good sport despite continued problems of boat traffic and pollution.

Stillwater lake and pond fishing is also popular in the region, especially in Lincolnshire, Cambridgeshire, Bedfordshire and Suffolk, with many former gravel pits and reservoirs now used as commercial fisheries specialising in large carp, although there are always good numbers of smaller fish around to provide consistent sport!

BEDFORDSHIRE

AMPTHILL RESERVOIR
Atlas Page 202 C.5/3.3

A delightful reservoir, only ¾ acre in size but with variable depth – 20ft in places. Summer weed can cause problems but can also provide an advantage to the angler. Expect roach and Crucian carp.

How to get there   Take the B530 south from Bedford to Ampthill; the reservoir is set in Ampthill Park (signposted).
Day tickets   Members of Ampthill A.C. only; £17.50 from Dumpleton's; Tel. 0582 582715.

Best methods Floatfishing (preferably near the weeds); leger if this fails.

Best baits Carp, roach – bread, maggots, or worms if these fail.

Restrictions There is no fishing on some parts of the reservoir.

Facilities Food/toilets in Ampthill Park.

GIRTFORD, RIVER IVEL
Atlas Page 202 C.9/3.0

The River Ivel is a deep, slowish-flowing river which was dredged during the 1988/89 season but fishes well. Heavy weed growth generally limits sport until later winter months. Mainly roach, chub and dace; pike fishing here is also well worth a try.

How to get there Located just off the A1 at Sandy, Bedfordshire.

Day tickets £1.50; Vauxhall A.C. members only; £20 from Dumpleton's; Tel. 0582 582715.

Best methods Floatfishing is preferred, using static bait. Laying on can provide interesting sport.

Best baits Maggots.

Facilities Shops/food/toilets in Sandy.

RIVER GREAT OUSE
PAVENHAM
Atlas Page 202 C.6/2.9

A very pleasant ¾-mile long stretch of the Ouse, surrounded by a small spinney. Variable depth, but 15ft in places. Heavy summer weed can cause bait presentation problems. Mainly chub, roach, perch, dace and pike.

The River Great Ouse.

How to get there Take the A6 north from Bedford; drive about 3 miles to Clapham and take minor road on left to Pavenham.

Day tickets Members of Ampthill A.C. only; £17.50 from Dumpleton's; Tel. 0582 582715.

Best methods Stick float and feeder.

Best baits Chub, roach – worm, maggots; hempseed can also produce good results.

Restrictions Fishing is only allowed on the left bank.

Facilities Shop in Pavenham village.

BIDDENHAM
Atlas Page 202 C.4/3.0

A 1-mile long section of the Ouse, enveloped by beautiful, wooded areas. Water depth varies from swim to swim, with flooding occurring after heavy rain. Expect mainly chub and roach.

How to get there Take the A428 west from Bedford; after about 1 mile look for signs to Biddenham on the left. Drive through the village; access to the river is near the church.

Day tickets Members of Luton A.C. only; £12.50 from Dumpleton's; Tel. 0582 582715.

Best methods Float or feeder; also, occasionally, a bomb.

Best baits Maggots most of the season; in warmer months use hempseed for roach and chub. Use large baits with the bomb.

Facilities Shop in Biddenham village.

RADWELL
Atlas Page 202 C.5/2.9

An excellent mixed Ouse fishery in pleasant countryside. Shallow gravelly runs, slower, deeper glides and no boat traffic! Profuse summer weed growth can cause problems; heavy winter rain can cause flooding. Expect chub, roach, bream, dace and pike.

How to get there Radwell is a small village about 8 miles north of Bedford.

Day tickets £1.50; Vauxhall A.C. members only; £20 from Dumpleton's; Tel. 0582 582715.

Best methods Leger or float.

Best baits Chub, roach, dace – maggots all year; seed baits in summer. Barbel, chub – leger with large baits in faster flowing water.

Facilities Shop in Radwell village.

NORTH HOUSE LAKE
Atlas Page 202 C.9/2.9

This 5-acre lake lacks scenery but more than compensates by its fishing. Average depth is 10–12ft. Expect mainly Crucian carp.

How to get there   Take the A1 north of Sandy (about 6 miles); look for signs to Wyboston Lakes Leisure Complex. North House Lake is set in a hollow close to the Wyboston complex.

Day tickets   Members of Luton A.C. only; £12.50 from Dumpleton's; Tel. 0582 582715.

Best methods   Floatfish with waggler, or use long pole with elastic fitted.

Best baits   Maggots, worms; use punched bread if bites are finicky.

Restrictions   No night fishing. Keepnets are only to be used when necessary.

Facilities   Club House/bar/toilets at Wyboston Lakes.

SHARNBROOK, PIT NO. 2
Atlas Page 202 C.6/2.9

The second largest of a four-pit complex; depths vary from swim to swim. Expect bream, tench, roach and perch – the Vauxhall AC perch record fish was caught here. If you feel like it, some pike fishing always adds fun to the day!

How to get there   Take the A6 north from Bedford towards Sharnbrook (signposted, 6 miles). Look for signs to Radwell village and pit complex. Free parking close to swims in some areas.

Day tickets   £1; Vauxhall A.C. members only; £20 from Dumpleton's; Tel. 0582 582715.

Best methods   Bream – feeder and groundbait; roach – floatfishing.

Best baits   Maggots, worms.

Facilities   Shop/food in Sharnbrook village.

Mirror carp.

BUCKINGHAMSHIRE

BLACK HORSE LAKE
Atlas Page 202 C.2/3.1

A large, open gravel pit, a short distance from the M1, with some board-sailers. Contains large tench (10lb+), bream (8lb+) and pike (30lb+), as well as roach, eels and specimen carp of over 30lb. Many mirrors here are in double figures.

How to get there   Leave the M1 at jct 14 and take A509 towards Newport Pagnell. Turn left at 1st roundabout, right at 2nd, left at T-junction. Go under bridge, over mini-roundabout and turn right into 'Linear Fisheries'; park on the right.

Day tickets   Adult: dawn–dusk, £3 per rod; 24 hours, £4 per rod; junior/OAP £2 and £3 respectively. Season: £30, dawn–dusk; £40, 24 hour. Available from Linear Fisheries, 2 Northcroft, Shenley Lodge, Milton Keynes; Tel. 0908 607577.

Best methods/baits   Use any recognised coarse technique and baits.

Restrictions   No night fishing. No sacking of carp.

Facilities   Nearest shops/pub in Newport Pagnell.

Disabled facilities   Some swims suitable for disabled anglers.

CALDECOTTE LAKE
Atlas Page 202 C.2/3.3

A 90-acre lake consisting of two parts – the North and South Arms – in Milton Keynes. Depth varies from 2–15ft, and summer weed growth can be excessive. Fishing is limited to about 80 pegs, with good bream (3–4lb), perch and roach, plus some large pike, for which fishing is best near the dam wall end. Best bream are caught near the bridge.

How to get there   Leave the north-bound A5 at Milton Keynes and take roadway H10 east (Bletcham Way) to roundabout with V10 (Brickhill Street). To fish the North Arm, turn left, then left again and park on left. To fish South Arm, follow signs back underneath H10 to car park.

Day tickets   Adult/junior/OAP £2. Available on the bank.

Best methods   Pole, float or leger all work well.

Best baits   Roach – coloured maggots. Perch – worm. Summer bream – bread. Pike – deadbait.

Facilities   Shops/toilets/food/pubs in Milton Keynes.

Disabled facilities   Some swims may be suitable for disabled anglers; please phone for advice; Tel. 0908 649446.

REDHOUSE LAKE
Atlas Page 202 C.2/3.1

A pleasant lake in a fishing complex near the M1 at Newport Pagnell. Some very large coarse fish – bream (to 8lb), tench (to 6lb+) and pike (to 20lb+). Also good-sized roach and perch, plus plenty of double-figure carp.

How to get there   Leave the M1 at jct 14 and take A509 towards Newport Pagnell. Turn left at 1st roundabout, right at 2nd, left at T-junction. Go under bridge, over mini-roundabout and turn right into 'Linear Fisheries'; park on the right.

Day tickets   Adult: dawn–dusk, £3 per rod; 24 hours, £4 per rod; junior/OAP £2 and £3 respectively. Season: £30, dawn–dusk; £40, 24 hour. Available from Linear Fisheries, 2 Northcroft, Shenley Lodge, Milton Keynes; Tel. 0908 607577.

Double-figure carp at Redhouse Lake.

Best methods/baits   Use any recognised coarse technique and baits.

Restrictions   No sacking of carp.

Facilities   Nearest shops/pub in Newport Pagnell.

Disabled facilities   Some swims suitable for disabled anglers.

ROCLA LAKE
Atlas Page 202 C.2/3.1

An attractive, but irregularly-shaped lake within a fishing complex at Newport Pagnell. Large bream, tench, pike, roach and perch, and always the opportunity of a very big carp around the island in these waters.

How to get there   Leave the M1 at jct 14 and take A509 towards Newport Pagnell. Turn left at 1st roundabout, right at 2nd, left at T-junction. Go under bridge, over mini-roundabout and turn right into 'Linear Fisheries'; park on the right.

Day tickets   Adult: dawn–dusk, £3 per rod; 24 hours, £4 per rod; junior/OAP £2 and £3 respectively. Season: £30, dawn–dusk; £40, 24 hour. Available from Linear Fisheries, 2 Northcroft, Shenley Lodge, Milton Keynes; Tel. 0908 607577.

Best methods/baits   Use any recognised coarse technique and baits.

Restrictions   No sacking of carp.

Facilities   Nearest shops/pub in Newport Pagnell.

Disabled facilities   Some swims suitable for disabled anglers.

HAVERSHAM LAKE
Atlas Page 202 C.2/3.1

Stocked with tench to 8lb, carp to 27lb, pike to 30lb. Very good roach, 2lb+, good bream and lots of perch.

How to get there   Leave the M1 at jct 14 and take A509 towards Newport Pagnell. Turn left at 1st roundabout, right at 2nd, left at T-junction. Go under bridge, over mini-roundabout and turn right into 'Linear Fisheries'; park on the right.

Day tickets   Adult: dawn–dusk, £3 per rod; 24 hours, £4 per rod; junior/OAP £2 and £3 respectively. Season: £30, dawn–dusk; £40, 24 hour. Available from Linear Fisheries, 2 Northcroft,

Shenley Lodge, Milton Keynes;
Tel. 0908 607577.

Best methods/baits   Use any recognised
coarse technique and baits.

Restrictions   No sacking of carp.

Facilities   Nearest shops/pub in Newport
Pagnell.

Disabled facilities   Some swims suitable
for disabled anglers.

BRADWELL LAKE
Atlas Page 202 C.2/3.1

Bags of roach up to 80lb, pike into the 20s
and bream to almost 8lb.

How to get there   Leave the M1 at jct 14
and take A509 towards Newport
Pagnell. Turn left at 1st roundabout,
right at 2nd, left at T-junction. Go under
bridge, over mini-roundabout and turn
right into 'Linear Fisheries'; park on the
right.

Day tickets   Adult: dawn–dusk, £3 per
rod; 24 hours, £4 per rod; junior/OAP £2
and £3 respectively. Season: £30,
dawn–dusk; £40, 24 hour. Available
from Linear Fisheries, 2 Northcroft,
Shenley Lodge, Milton Keynes;
Tel. 0908 607577.

Best methods/baits   Use any recognised
coarse technique and baits.

Restrictions   No sacking of carp.

Facilities   Nearest shops/pub in Newport
Pagnell.

Disabled facilities   Some swims suitable
for disabled anglers.

RIVER OUSE AT LINEAR FISHERIES
Atlas Page 202 C.2/3.1

Three miles of bank, with barbel up to
13lb, chub over 5lb, good roach and pike,
and recently stocked with grayling. A few
very good carp if you can find them.

How to get there   Leave the M1 at jct 14
and take A509 towards Newport
Pagnell. Turn left at 1st roundabout,
right at 2nd, left at T-junction. Go under
bridge, over mini-roundabout and turn
right into 'Linear Fisheries'; park on the
right.

Day tickets   Adult: dawn–dusk, £3 per
rod; 24 hours, £4 per rod; junior/OAP £2
and £3 respectively. Season: £30,
dawn–dusk; £40, 24 hour. Available
from Linear Fisheries, 2 Northcroft,
Shenley Lodge, Milton Keynes;
Tel. 0908 607577.

Best methods/baits   Use any recognised
coarse technique and baits.

Restrictions   No sacking of carp.

Facilities   Nearest shops/pub in Newport
Pagnell.

Disabled facilities   Some swims suitable
for disabled anglers.

TEARDROPS, LOUGHTON LAKES
Atlas Page 202 C.2/3.3

A stillwater complex of three lakes, each
of 2 acres and average depth 6ft, at Milton
Keynes. Expect a good head of roach,
bream, perch, tench and chub, with best
fishing in No. 1 lake and best swims near
the bridge. Also some small carp and a few
catfish for variety!

How to get there   Leave the M1 at jct 14
and turn onto Milton Keynes roadway
M5 Portway to Watling Street. Turn left
at the next roundabout; the fishery is
located behind the Milton Keynes Bowl
sports complex. Parking available
nearby; follow the signs.

Day tickets   Adult/junior/OAP £3.
Available on the bank.

Best methods   Pole and light float are
best methods.

Best baits   Roach, perch, bream, rudd –
bronze or red maggot as hookbait. Chub
– worm.

Restrictions   No bloodworm or joker.

Facilities   Shop/pubs/food/toilets at the
sports complex.

Disabled facilities   Some swims may be
suitable for disabled anglers; please
phone for advice; Tel. 0908 649446.

A proud catch, tench.

CAMBRIDGESHIRE

Rivers

ALWALTON LYNCH
Atlas Page 202 C.8/1.8

Located on the River Nene upstream of Orton Staunch. Good mixed fishing, excellent chub and roach. Pike in winter.

How to get there   In Alwalton village; turn off the A605 Peterborough-Oundle road.Free parking available.
Day tickets   Adult £2; child/OAP £1; available on the bank.
Best methods   Float, leger.
Best baits   Maggots, casters, bread, luncheon meat.
Facilities   Shop/Post Office in Alwalton village; food/toilets at Wheatsheaf pub, 1 mile in village.

BRAMPTON
Atlas Page 202 C.9/3.4

A group of waters ranging from larger lakes to small brooks plus two river venues; the pit on the A1 is most popular. Mainly good quality carp, bream and tench; also some roach and pike.

How to get there   From Huntingdon, take the A604 west to Brampton village, or approach from the east via the A1/A141. Free car parking at all sites. For details of various access points to waters, contact Tim's Tackle, 88 High St, Huntingdon; Tel. 0480 450039.
Day tickets   Adult £2; junior/OAP £2 (per year). Available from Tim's Tackle.
Best methods/baits   Use any recognised coarse technique.
Restrictions   No bloodworm.
Facilities   Nearest shop/pub, The Dragoon, Brampton (5–10 mins walk).
Disabled facilities   Some swims suitable for disabled and wheelchair anglers at A1 pit.

RIVER CAM

The Cam is a river of two parts. On its upper reaches above Cambridge, it is a winding, natural river, with comfortable banks along which most species are found in the many gently flowing swims. However, beyond Cambridge, it changes character, with the comfortable tree-lined towpaths being replaced – as it begins to flow through the flat Fens – by a typical Fenland river, with slow-flowing, deeper regions. Surprisingly, despite these changes, the Cam provides excellent sport, with good roach, chub and bream being taken along its length. Along the Grantchester to Dimmocks Cote length, there are six *Angling Times* Hotspots.

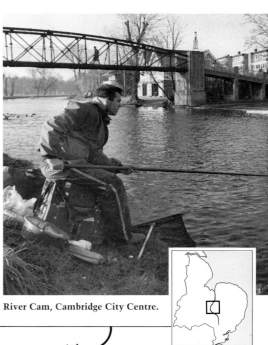

River Cam, Cambridge City Centre.

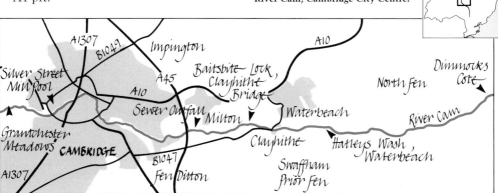

GRANTCHESTER MEADOWS
Atlas Page 202 D.4/2.8

A winding, west-bank stretch; bushes and overhanging trees. Summer flow steady, pacier in winter. Depth 4–12ft, 6ft in most swims. Summer weed heavy. Mostly chub, roach, dace, bream and pike; typical mixed nets 10lb; summer chub nets often 50lb+. Specimen fish of all species are likely.

How to get there   Leave the M11 at jct 12 and take the A603 towards Cambridge city (look for Newnham); turn into Grantchester Road, then Grantchester Meadows. Park on the verge at the road end.

Day tickets   Free fishing.

Best methods   Chub – waggler at the far bank; use a 3lb mainline and 2lb hooklength.

Best baits   Casters, hemp, cheese, flake and maggots.

Hotspot Tips

- In weedy swims, the straight leger on heavy gear is best.
- The deep water on bends (or clear areas just above or below bends) provides the best swims.
- Feed heavily at first for roach and dace – and the chub will move in!

SILVER STREET MILL POOL
Atlas Page 202 D.4/2.8

A kidney-shaped pool between two sluices; overhanging trees, moored punts; little weed growth. Average depth 8ft, shallower areas in the sluice runs. Many specimen chub, roach, bream and carp (many 10lb+). Fishing consistent in winter, but summer boats prevent worthwhile angling.

How to get there   Follow the southern ring road to the 'Backs' of the University area; parking is difficult (pay & display; best early morning). Cross Silver Street Bridge (220yds); river access is via the Anchor pub.

Day tickets   Free fishing.

Best methods   Chub – leger at the side or tail of the flow from the sluices.

Best baits   Chub – cheese paste, luncheon meat or bread flake; bream – worms.

Facilities   Shops/food/toilets in the city centre or at the Anchor pub.

Hotspot Tips

- When the flow is light, try fishing immediately in front of the sluice gates.
- The chub often hide under the moored punts.
- You'll find the fish feeding much better in early morning and late evening.

SEWER OUTFALL
Atlas Page 202 D.4/2.8

A 300-yard stretch from Baitsbite Lock upstream, below the A45 road bridge. Average width 30–35yds, depth 7–8ft; level bank and towpath. Flow is slow, but quickens near the outfall. Plenty of roach and bream (often 4lb+) all season; 10lb+ nets are common along this stretch.

How to get there   Approach Cambridge on the A10 Fen Road via the village of Milton. Look for signposts to Baitsbite Lock. Drive over the level crossing and down to the river; park on the verge. Walk upstream, past Baitsbite Lock.

Day tickets   £2; available from local tackle shops or the lock-keeper. Or £3 from the bailiff on the bank.

Best methods   Bream – leger halfway to two-thirds across, in the swims near the outfall. Cage feeders are popular. Roach – waggler (2AAA or 3AAA) or pole rig (.75 gram), held back in the flow.

Best baits   Summer – hemp and tares, casters, maggots and bread; winter – punched bread, maggot and hemp.

Hotspot Tips

- For really good results, use cereal groundbait, little and often.
- In winter, fish overdepth and present a still bait.

BAITSBITE LOCK TO CLAYHITHE BRIDGE
Atlas Page 202 D.4/2.8

A popular stretch; often sluggish flow, pacier near the locks. Average depth 8ft, weed growth until frosts. Near bank has towpath; far bank has trees, overhanging bushes and boats. Mainly roach, with 10lb+ catches, but chub numbers are rising. Bream are elusive here.

How to get there Access to the Baitsbite Lock end is as for the Sewer Outfall (see page 126). For Clayhithe Bridge, take the A10 north and turn right through Waterbeach towards Horningsea. Drive over the level crossing; park in the layby before the bridge. Access to the fishery is at the Bridge Hotel.

Day tickets £2; available from local tackle shops or the lock-keeper. Or £3 from the bailiff on the bank.

Best methods Summer – use a pole; fish holes between the weedbeds; winter – waggler.

Best baits Summer – hemp and tares, casters and maggots; winter – punched bread, hemp, bronze maggots and casters.

Facilities Food/toilets at the Bridge Hotel.

Hotspot Tips

- The shallow bend downstream of the car park is good for chub.

HATLEYS WASH, WATERBEACH
Atlas Page 202 D.4/2.8

A much wider, featureless stretch; average depth 4–5ft, marginal weed at both banks. Summer sport includes bream and roach, plus some good chub and pike (to 20lb); a typical summer net (mostly bream) may be 20–30lb. Roach fishing improves in winter, with nets often into double figures.

How to get there Turn off the A10 into Waterbeach village; follow signs to Bottisham Lock via Barvold Road. Park at the lock, cross the footbridge over Bottisham Drive to Hatleys Wash. The first peg is at the drain's mouth.

Day tickets £2 in advance from local tackle shops; £4 from the bailiff on the bank.

Best methods Bream – leger in the middle channel; roach – pole or waggler.

Best baits Summer – bread, casters and hemp; winter – punched bread or maggot.

Hotspot Tips

- Use bronze maggots to pick up good chub.
- Try spinning for smaller pike in this stretch.
- Peg 1 is best for summer bream; Pegs 7, 8 and 9 are best for winter chub.

DIMMOCKS COTE
Atlas Page 202 D.4/2.8

A typical Fenland river stretch, average 6ft depth; pronounced shelves 3–12ft out. Marginal weed in summer. Catches include roach and bream all season, plus the odd pike. Roach nets reach 10lb+ all year; bream can be hard to find – expect a really good net if you're successful!

How to get there Take the A1123 from Stretham towards Wicken; the road crosses the river at Dimmocks Cote. Park on the verge beside the bridge; the fishery is on the west bank only, and extends upstream and downstream of the bridge.

Day tickets £1.50 in advance from local tackle shops; £3 from the bailiff on the bank.

Best methods Bream, roach – float with straight waggler set for 5ft. Bream – fish overdepth with a static bait.

Best baits Summer – hemp and casters; winter – maggots.

Hotspot Tips

- If boat traffic is heavy, try fishing the far side.
- Use brown crumb groundbait for bream, but avoid it if you're looking for roach!
- White maggot is by far the best bait for bream here.
- The willows upstream of the bridge is a great spot, but it's a long walk!

A good catch of bream.

DECOY LAKE
Atlas Page 202 C.9/1.8

A fair-sized gravel pit (almost 4 acres) a few miles east of Peterborough. Excellent fishing, with enormous catches routine. Mainly bream, tench and rudd, plus some roach, but carp numbers are vast, with over 11,000 commons and mirrors stocked in recent years, and now reaching 4–6lb.

How to get there   From the north-bound A1 turn right via A605 to Whittlesey and continue towards March for about 1½ miles. At Eastrea, Decoy Farm is on the left, opposite some white silos; parking on site.

Day tickets   Adult/OAP £5; junior £3 – for 9 hours' fishing. *Note*: Club booking and matches only. Available from Peter Band (Tel. 0733 202230) or Tony Hudson (Tel. 0733 203428).

Best methods/baits   Use any recognised coarse technique and baits.

Restrictions   Keepnets are supplied. Use only barbless hooks. No night fishing. No fishing by children.

Facilities   Nearest shop/pub in Eastrea or Coates.

Disabled facilities   Some swims suitable for disabled anglers.

Rivers

THE FEN DRAINS

The Fen Drains that comprise this maze of waterways are invariably straight, with steep banks, pronounced ledges and are deepest at their centre. Those of the Middle Level are deepest – the Twenty Foot River, the Sixteen Foot, Forty Foot, Popham's Eau, the Old River Nene and the Middle Level Main Drain itself. All are mainly still, flowing only when water is pumped from them into the tidal reaches of the Great Ouse. Main species include roach, though bream have recently returned; tench may appear in early summer. For specialist anglers, pike and zander provide excellent sport during autumn and winter.

Black Ham Drain, Yaxley.

SIXTEEN FOOT, STONEA
Atlas Page 202 D.4/2.0

A straight, wide (25 yard) stretch with little edge weed growth and some lilies. Swims are 7–8ft deep at 6 yards out – an ideal starting place. Lots of roach all season, plus tench early on and the odd rudd in summer. A typical summer's day catch is 1lb of roach per hour. Pike and zander provide excellent winter sport.

Large early season tench.

How to get there   Take the B1098 Chatteris to Upwell & Outwell road to Stonea. The road runs alongside the fishery; parking is on the verge, behind your swim.

Day tickets   £2.50 on the bank; £2 in advance at local tackle shops.

Best methods   Use a 4-metre whip; fish any depth. Roach – single maggot on small hook plus cloud groundbait. Tench – lay hook in bottom or fish breadflake. Deadbait rigs for pike and zander.

Best baits   Maggots, bread are unbeatable; seafish deadbait for pike.

Hotspot Tips

- Mornings are best for pike; dusk is best for zander.
- Any bankside feature – reeds, lilies, side drain outfalls – are worth a try.
- Most fish are taken in the bottom layers of the water.

SIXTEEN FOOT, BEDLAM BRIDGE
Atlas Page 202 D.4/1.8

A 25-yard wide stretch, still or slow-moving (except in pumping), with some marginal reeds and lilies. Typical depth 12ft, with 7ft at the rod tip. Mostly roach and bream in summer, plus an odd rudd. Roach, pike and zander in autumn and winter. Bream can reach 6lb; catches can reach 100lb!

How to get there   Near March, Cambridgeshire; where the B1099 March to Christchurch road crosses the drain. Park on the verge close to the bridge, or on verge opposite river.

Day tickets   £2.50 on the bank; £2 in advance at local tackle shops.

Best methods   Leger close to far bank. Roach – fish inside line with pole.

Best baits   Squatts, casters as groundbait; worms, maggots as hookbait. Roach – loosefed pinkies and maggot hookbait.

Hotspot Tips

- Always use elastic tackle in case you hook a big bream!
- Bronze and red maggots are the best in this stretch.
- For good bream, try the ten pegs just south of the bridge.

MIDDLE LEVEL, THREE HOLES BRIDGE
Atlas Page 202 D.7/1.9

A deep (12ft), very wide stretch (100ft), still in summer but 'drifty' in windy weather. Flow can be very strong in winter pumping, or after heavy rain. Mainly bream in summer (and mild winters); roach, pike, zander, some perch and rudd. Bream may reach 5lb+; nets can be large – recently, 75lb in 3.5 hours!

How to get there   At Three Holes village, where the A1101 Wisbech to Welney road crosses the drain. Park in the lay-by near the bridge; fish from the east bank, either side of the bridge.

Day tickets   £2.50 on the bank; £2 in advance at local tackle shops.

Best methods   Bream – leger the far bank (use a bomb for accurate casting); roach, skimmer bream – pole-fish the near bank.

Best baits   Casters, squatts as groundbait; worm, casters as hookbait. Pinkies are best for roach.

Hotspot Tips

- Try laying on with a pole for good bream and tench, but stay well out – over 6 yards.
- Breadflake can be a big scorer in hot weather.

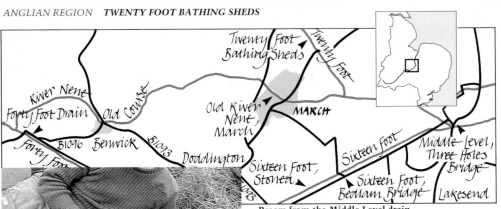

Bream from the Middle Level drain system.

TWENTY FOOT BATHING SHEDS
Atlas Page 202 D.4/1.6

A 25–30yd-wide stretch, 12ft deep with minimal flow (except during pumping). No pronounced ledges; lilies and reeds provide the bankside features. Expect roach, bream (up to 5lb) and tench in summer; pike and zander in autumn and winter. Early season can be poor, but 20lb catches are common from July onwards.

How to get there   Turn right off the A141 March to Wisbech (signposted Elm). The road runs alongside the river; the site is on a slight bend. Park on the river side, close to your swim.

Day tickets   £2; available from the bailiff on the bank.

Best methods   Leger for bream; never groundbait over a feeding shoal.

Best baits   Hookbait – casters; worm for big fish. Roach - caster in clear water, pinkies or maggots if coloured.

Hotspot Tips

- In warm weather, fish a 6ft tail to pick up bottom-feeders.
- Don't slam your car door – you'll scare fish from your swim.

OLD RIVER NENE, MARCH
Atlas Page 202 D.4/1.8

This largely town-centre stretch may reach 15 yards in width, with an average depth of 3ft, range 3–5ft. There is minimal marginal weed, and few pronounced shelves. Expect roach, especially in winter; catches may reach 1lb per hour in flowing water, but are often poor in still water. Skimmer bream, dace and rudd may also appear.

How to get there   In March, Cambridgeshire. Access is from the A141 by-pass or from the town centre. Parking is difficult at the latter point.

Day tickets   Free fishing

Best methods   Roach – waggler in the main channel; pole allows perfect bait presentation.

Best baits   Maggots for loosefeed; maggots, pinkies or punched bread as hookbait.

Restriction   No bloodworm or jokers.

Facilities   Food/shops/toilets in the town centre.

Hotspot Tips

- For good bites, you'll need to experiment with your bait depth.
- Bait trotted down under a waggler will often pick up more fish.
- Pegs near the by-pass are best in summer; those near the town improve in winter.
- Small quantities of cloud groundbait are vital to keep the fish feeding.

FORTY FOOT DRAIN
Atlas Page 202 D.3/1.8

A straight stretch, 25 yards wide, maximum depth 10ft, and plenty of lilies. Normally still, but flows during pumping. No pronounced ledges, but 5ft at the rod tip. Mainly roach, bream (to 7lb) and tench; the pike are good in winter. An even-fishing stretch, with nets of 20–30lb, but with a good bream shoal, 50lb+ is possible.

How to get there   From Ramsey, Cambridgeshire, take the B1096 towards Chatteris. At the village of Ramsey Forty Foot, the road runs alongside the drain. Park opposite your swim.
Day tickets   £1.50; from bailiffs on the bank, or in advance from Wades, Great Whyte, Ramsey; Tel. 0487 813537.
Best methods   Roach – 6-metre line close to marginal lilies. Bream – leger to the far bank.
Best baits   Bream – worm or bread; roach – maggots in coloured water, casters in clear.

Hotspot Tips

- In hot weather, use a hemp and tares combination.
- Roach may be poor in early season, but improve in July.
- For bream, look for rolling fish, or drop in on areas of coloured water.

FERRY MEADOWS LAKES
Atlas Page 202 C.9/1.8

A large lake complex lying within a public park just west of Peterborough; one of the best summer bream waters in Britain, plus good roach all year.

How to get there   Take the A605 west from Peterborough towards Oundle; Ferry Meadows Lakes are well signposted about 3 miles from Peterborough. Car parking on site (chargeable at weekends only).
Day tickets   Adult/junior/OAP £2. Available from bailiffs on the bank (daily visits). For match bookings, contact Walter Yates; Tel. 0733 67952.
Best methods/baits   Bream – small groundbait feeders or bomb with casters and red squatt; red worm or red maggot as hookbait.
Restrictions   No lead weights to be used. No bloodworm or jokers.

Facilities   Cafe/toilets/food/information available on site. Nearest shop Orton (1 mile); nearest pub, The Granary (½ mile).
Disabled facilities   Some swims suitable for disabled and wheelchair anglers.

HINCHINGBROOKE COUNTRY PARK
Atlas Page 202 C.9/2.4

A large (156 acres) country park on the western outskirts of Huntingdon, with a very large, open, deep and often very weedy lake. Excellent fishing for roach, bream, tench, carp, pike and some chub. Also some very big eels. Fishing from pegged swims only.

How to get there   From the north-bound A1 at Brampton roundabout, turn right on the A604 to Huntingdon; Hinchingbrooke Park is signposted on the left, just before the town. Follow the road to a mini-roundabout, turn left, park (free) after 100 yards; walk 400 yards to the lake.
Day tickets   Adult £2; junior/OAP £1 (dawn-dusk). Available from Tim's Tackle, 88 High Street, Huntingdon; Tel. 0480 450039.
Best methods   Leger or waggler; weed may need clearing before fishing.
Best baits   Maggots, worms, hemp, sweetcorn.
Restrictions   Opening times of the park are limited; check at local tackle shop.
Facilities   Toilets at the Visitor's Centre. Food/drinks available on summer Sundays. Nearest shops Brampton/ Huntingdon (¾ mile); nearest pub, Black Bull, Brampton (¾ mile).

Hinchingbrooke Country Park.

Rivers

THE GREAT OUSE

The middle reaches of the Great Ouse, in addition to being scenic as they meander through rolling countryside before entering the Fen flatlands, provide some excellent fishing, though summer boat traffic can cause problems. The river has a steady flow which can vary intermittently as the locks are used, but with such a wide choice of swims and species, many local anglers rate this section of the Great Ouse as one of the rapidly improving fishing stretches in East Anglia. Between Ely and the Wash, the Great Ouse is wide, deep and slow moving, with few natural features in the open flat Fen countryside. The river is a match and pleasure fisherman's paradise – renowned not only for its excellent bream, but also for large catches of quality roach, while the pike and zander, although fewer in number, grow very large in these waters.

River Ouse, Huntingdon Centre.

EATON SOCON
Atlas Page 202 C.9/2.7

A wide section, with generally slow-moving water and some deeper areas, just upstream from St. Neots town centre. Expect even fishing, despite occasional difficult boat traffic, with most species including carp and big pike. Good barbel (up to 4lb+) are often taken in the faster flowing water near the weir.

How to get there   Leave the A1 at Eaton Socon and follow the A45 towards St. Neots town centre. After about ½ mile, turn right (by the church) to the Rivermill (signposted); use the car park and walk across the weir. On the right, fishing is as far as the A45 flyover; on the left, fishing is as far as the town.

Day tickets   Adult £2.50; junior/OAP £1.25. Season tickets: adult £20; junior £6.50; OAP/disabled £5. Available on the bank.

Best methods/baits   Use general coarse techniques and baits.

Facilities   Nearest shop, Eaton Socon village (1 mile); nearest pub, Rivermill Tavern, by the car park.

Eaton Socon, Rivermill.

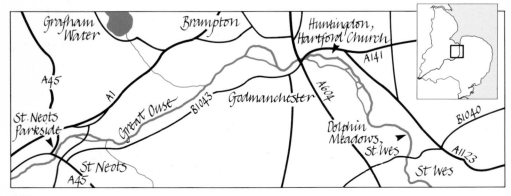

EYNESBURY
Atlas Page 202 C.9/2.7

A wide, slow-moving section with deeper regions, close to St. Neots town centre. Weekend boat traffic can cause problems, but generally good fishing, with most species, plus good-sized carp and pike.

How to get there   Leave the A1 at Eaton Socon, follow the A45 into St. Neots town centre and turn right at 2nd traffic lights. Follow road to the Coneygeare pub and use the car park (free). Cross the bridge and fish to the left or right.
Day tickets   Adult £2.50; junior/OAP £1.25. Season tickets: adult £20; junior £6.50; OAP/disabled £5. Available on the bank.
Best methods/baits   Use general coarse techniques and baits.
Facilities   Toilets on site. Nearest shops/food/pubs in Hardwicke Road (about ¼ mile).

River Ouse, Parkside.

ST. NEOTS PARKSIDE/ EATON FORD
Atlas Page 202 C.9/2.7

A fairly wide, slow-moving river section, quite deep in places, within walking distance of St. Neots town centre. Boat traffic can cause problems, especially at weekends, but expect a wide variety of species, including a few carp and some really good pike. A very even-fishing stretch, providing good quality sport.

How to get there   Leave the A1 at Eaton Socon, follow the A45 towards St. Neots town centre. At the river bridge, park in the Riverside Park (signposted). The fishery extends for about 1 mile to the right.

Day tickets   Adult £2.50; junior/OAP £1.25. Season tickets: adult £20; junior £6.50; OAP/disabled £5. Available on the bank.
Best methods   Use a pole at 8–9 metres, just over the near ledge, or a waggler down the middle.
Best baits   Use maggots and casters all season. Hemp and tares are best for summer roach.
Facilities   Toilets at Riverside Park. Nearest shops, St. Neots town centre (¼ mile); nearest pubs, at least 3 in the market square, near the bridge.
Disabled facilities   Some swims close to the car park are suitable for disabled and wheelchair anglers.

Hotspot Tips

- In extra water after rain, try a leger or a stick float.
- When the river is very coloured, use a small feeder for bream.
- The first four swims above the bridge are 'bankers'!

LITTLE PAXTON
Atlas Page 202 C.9/2.7

A slow-moving, wide and fairly deep river section water, just downstream from St. Neots town centre. Expect some boat traffic (mainly weekends), but good fishing for with most coarse species including carp and big pike.

How to get there   Leave the A1 at the St. Neots turn-off and follow the signs to Little Paxton. In the village, park (free) by the paper mill and fish up to and beyond the sewage farm. For more details, contact St. Neots Angling Centre, 28B Hardwicke Road, St. Neots; Tel. 0480 212108.
Day tickets   Adult £2.50; junior/OAP £1.25. Season tickets: adult £20; junior £6.50; OAP/disabled £5. Available on the bank.
Best methods/baits   Use general coarse techniques and baits.
Facilities   Nearest shop and pub, Little Paxton (½ mile).

HUNTINGDON, HARTFORD CHURCH
Atlas Page 202 C.9/2.4

This wide (30yd) stretch of the Ouse has a steady flow, 3–4ft deep close in, but 6ft two-thirds across. Weed growth close in.

Boat traffic is not a problem. Mostly roach, rudd, dace, perch and eels, plus skimmer bream and chub.

How to get there   Take the A141 north from Huntingdon. Hartford church is signposted on the right; use the parking area close to the church.

Day tickets   £2; available on the bank, or from local tackle shops. Weekly ticket £4. Free fishing from the concrete area.

Best methods   Summer roach – 5-metre whip with hemp and tares, or waggler two-thirds across with bronze maggot.

Best baits   Hemp, bronze maggots.

Hotspot Tips

❦ Bring the fish high in the water with hemp loosefeed and use a waggler on the drop.

❦ The best areas are on the concrete, near the church.

DOLPHIN MEADOWS, ST IVES
Atlas Page 202 D.1/2.4

A varied stretch with some buildings early on but tree cover upstream. A good bank with many comfortable swims. Variable depth (4–6ft) and width (20–40 yards), with weed growth in bays. Expect summer roach, bream and perch, plus chub and pike in late season.

How to get there   From the A604 Huntingdon-Cambridge road, take the B1040 to St Ives. Access is by the old river bridge, close to the Dolphin Hotel. Fishing is upstream towards Hemingford Grey.

Day tickets   Adult £1; junior/OAP 50p; available from bailiffs on the bank, or St Ives Angling Centre; Tel. 0480 301903.

Best methods   Summer – waggler; autumn onwards – leger at the far bank.

Best baits   Maggots, hemp, tares in summer; bread or punched bread as change bait. For chub – worms, maggots or cheese plus loosefeed.

Facilities   Food at the Dolphin Hotel; pubs/shops in town centre.

Hotspot Tips

❦ Pole methods catch plenty of fish.
❦ When rain swells the flow, a stick float can be very effective.
❦ The popular swims are at pegs 50–70 at the marina end.

River Ouse, Ely Centre.

ELY CENTRE
Atlas Page 202 D.7/2.2

A 40–50-yard-wide, even-fishing west bank section of the Great Ouse with slow to zero flow; depth 9ft, with marina/boat moorings opposite. Mainly roach (up to 1½lb), with best fishing in winter. Expect a 30lb+ catch.

How to get there   Approach Ely on the B1382 from the north-east; turn right after the river crossing, park in public car park at Cutter Inn pub. Or, go through market, down hill, turn left, park on grass. Fish between the road and railway bridges.

Day tickets   Free fishing.

Best methods   Waggler down the middle in still flow, with bulk shot two-thirds down. Or, block-end feeder on the float line. Use large floats.

Best baits   Maggot, plus hemp/maggot feed; avoid cereal groundbait.

Facilities   Food/toilets at the Cutter Inn pub. Shops/toilets in city centre.

Hotspot Tips

❦ Start with size 17–20 hooks, but size up to 16 if better fish show.
❦ Try fishing at the far bank – you might pick up bonus fish!
❦ If the flow is strong, move inside to a more comfortable line.

LARK MOUTH
Atlas Page 202 D.7/2.2

A wide stretch, 15ft deep with slow to zero flow (except after rain) and a nearside shelf and lilies. A renowned bream hotspot in summer, with 30lb nets likely; good roach nets in winter. Also noted for pike (20lb) and zander (7lb).

How to get there   Take the B1382 north-east from Ely; after 1 mile, cross the railway, turn left. The road runs alongside the river; park on the verge lose to the Ouse-Lark confluence.

Day tickets   £2; available from Tight Lines, 36 Forehill, Ely.

Best methods   Bream – leger with swimfeeder; roach – waggler in summer, pole and feeder in winter.

Best baits   Bream – maggot, worm, bread; roach – maggots, hemp.

Facilities   Shops/toilets at Littleport.

Hotspot Tips

- For good roach, try fishing the nearside shelf.
- Deadbaits and livebaits both score well with predators.
- The roach show all along the stretch; look for predators in the Lark mouth.

BLACK HORSE
Atlas Page 202 D.7/2.2

A typical Great Ouse section, up to 60 yards wide and 16ft deep. Often slow flow, with 6ft swims, a ledge at 5 yards and good, flat banks. Renowned for winter roach (many 10lb+ nets November on), plus some large bream and pike.

How to get there   Sandhills Bridge, Littleport, just off the A10. Park on the roadside; fish downstream of the bridge (70 pegs).

Day tickets   £2; available from Colebys, Granby St, Littleport; or the Black Horse pub, by Sandhills Bridge.

Best methods   Pole (min 6 metre), with 5ft of line between pole tip and float. Or, swimfeeder. Avoid waggler and stick float in extreme depth.

Best baits   Roach – hemp, tares in summer; maggot/hemp in winter, plus loosefeed. Bream – worm with caster or red maggot.

Facilities   Shops/toilets in Littleport; food/toilets at the Black Horse pub.

Disabled facilities   Good access to water via flat banks.

Hotspot Tips

- Only use cereal groundbait in an open-ended feeder and in summer.
- When the river is pulling, you may need a 2oz weight to hold bottom.

TEN MILE BANK
Atlas Page 202 D.8/2.0

A wide (40–50 yards) Great Ouse section, 16ft deep in the middle, 20ft at the Wissey mouth. Slow flow except in floods and when Denver Sluice is opened. Ledge 3–15 yards out, plus good flat banks. Expect roach, bream in summer and winter, plus pike and zander.

How to get there   Take the A10 Ely-Downham Market road; after 10 miles turn left, follow signs to Denver Sluice, take road alongside river, pass under railway bridge. Park on roadside, with chapel on right.

Day tickets   £2; season ticket: adult £12.50; junior £3.50; available from the Windmill pub, Ten Mile Bank; Denver Post Office; RJA Tackle, Runcton Holme; Colin Stevens Tackle, 55 London Rd, King's Lynn; Tel. 0553 775852.

Best methods   Roach – fish nearside shelf with 5–6 metre pole and 2 gram float. Or leger from middle to nearside, with block-end feeder (open-end feeder if bream show).

Best baits   Roach – maggots, hemp; bream – casters, hemp.

Facilities   Shops/toilets at Denver; food at the Windmill pub.

Hotspot Tips

- For good bream – there's nothing to beat a straight leger over a groundbait carpet!
- On hot summer days, breadflake can tempt those bream.
- Just downstream of the Wissey outfall is the best area for bream.

HILGAY BRIDGE
Atlas Page 202 D.8/1.9

This featureless stretch of the Great Ouse is 35 yards wide, with 12ft depth, no ledges but some reedbeds. Flow is slow, can be two-directional. Mainly roach, bream, zander and pike, with best fishing when the water is coloured (after Christmas). Recent catches here have reached 150lb!

How to get there   Just off the A10, about 1 mile south of Downham Market. The Cut-Off Channel is 200 yards north of

the Wissey (which the road crosses).
Use the car park at Fordham
village.

Day tickets   £2; season ticket: adult
£12.50; junior £3.50; available from
Bridge Stores, Hilgay; RJA Tackle,
Runcton Holme; Colin Stevens Tackle,
55 London Rd, King's Lynn.

Best methods   Waggler, or pole (7 metres
with long line) near the bridge when fish
are feeding well. Or, leger for good
bream and roach.

Facilities   Shops at Fordham village.

Disabled facilities   There is good access
to banks.

Hotspot Tips

- ☙ If you fish a waggler, run the float
  down the middle of the river.
- ☙ Pike and zander hotspots are close to
  the bridge.
- ☙ Look for bream around the bend, above
  the bridge.

ST GERMANS
Atlas Page 202 D.8/1.4

A very wide (80 yard+) section, average
depth 13ft. Normally gently flowing, but
fierce if sluice gates open. Plenty of roach
in summer/autumn (15–20lb nets), catches
slow when first frosts appear. Bream are
best at Stow Bridge, with 60lb nets
possible. Pike and zander are often
slow.

How to get there   Take the A10
Downham Market-King's Lynn road;
after 7 miles, turn left to St Germans
village. There is easy access to the Relief
Channel; use the car parks at the bridge.

Day tickets   £2; season ticket: adult
£12.50; junior £3.50; available from John
Baxter, 6 Edinburgh Place, St Germans;
St Germans Central Stores; RJA Tackle,
Runcton Holme; Colin Stevens Tackle,
55 London Road, King's Lynn.

Best methods   Float, 3–4 rod lengths out,
or pole. Leger for bream, straight or over
cereal groundbait carpet or open-end
feeder.

Best baits   Roach—maggots, hemp, plus
loosefeed. Bream – worm, bread plus
maggot.

Facilities   Shops at St Germans village.

Disabled facilities   Good access to swims
at the bridge.

Hotspot Tips

- ☙ Bream sport is always best here in
  windy conditions.
- ☙ Always look for coloured water – that's
  where the fish will be!
- ☙ Try fishing the bottom first – but be
  prepared to find fish in midwater.

LEE'S BROOK
Atlas Page 202 C.9/2.4

A narrow stream in which depth can reach
9ft in places, located among fields on the
outskirts of Godmanchester, near
Huntingdon. Plenty of good fishing from
80 pegs, providing good-sized chub and
roach, plus lots of bleak and gudgeon.
There are some bream here too, but
they're very elusive!

How to get there   From Huntingdon ring
road, head towards Godmanchester and
take the B1043 signposted Offord
Cluny/Offord Darcy. At the first bend
after leaving the town, turn right into
Duck Lane and drive down to the river.
Free (but limited) parking near the
water.

Day tickets   Adult/junior/OAP £1.50.
Available from Stanjay Fishing Tackle,
7 Old Court Hall, Godmanchester,
Huntingdon; Tel. 0480 453303.

Best methods   Pole, stick or leger
methods all work well here. Leger is
best for chub.

Best baits   Seed baits, casters, worms,
luncheon meat; maggots are good for
bleak and gudgeon.

Facilities   Nearest shop and pub,
Godmanchester (1 mile).

LITTLE PAXTON FISHERY
Atlas Page 202 C.9/2.7

A commercial fishery located in a 5-lake,
30-acre complex near St. Neots. An
excellent mixed fishery with bream, tench,
roach, rudd, perch and pike, plus large
(20lb) carp in all lakes. The 'car park' lake
has plenty of 15–20lb carp.

How to get there   Leave the A1 just north
of St. Neots and follow road to Little
Paxton (B1041). Turn left at sign 'Paxton
Quarry' and drive about ¼ mile to the car
park. No parking elsewhere on site.

Day tickets Available only on two lakes. Adult £2; junior/OAP £1. Evening ticket £1. Available from the site office at the car park. *Note*: tickets must be purchased before fishing, except at weekends when fishing can begin before 0800 and tickets bought later. Also season tickets: for details, contact Ian May Tel. 0480 212059.

Best methods Use any recognised coarse technique. Specialist carp methods may be required.

Best baits Maggot, casters, hemp, boilies, deadbait.

Restrictions Fishing from 0730–sunset (but advance day ticket holders may fish sunrise until dark). No night fishing. No sacking of carp.

Facilities Nearest shop/pub in Little Paxton.

Milton Ferry Bridge, downstream.

MORTON'S LEAM
Atlas Page 202 D.4/1.8

A narrow, straight drain near March, full of roach, skimmer bream, bream, tench, pike and a few carp. Best fishing is for winter roach and pike, but summer bream sport can be good too! Some very big pike (to 30lb) also inhabit these waters. Fishing here can be badly affected by water from the Nene influxing through a sluice gate.

How to get there Take the A141 from Huntingdon through Chatteris and the March by-pass. At Ring's End (about 4 miles from March), turn left, next to the Fisherman's Haunt pub. Park next to the water.

Day tickets Adult/junior/OAP £1.50. Available from the bailiff on the bank.

Best methods Pole is best method, but waggler is good too. Groundbait is essential; fish just inside the far shelf for best results. Use standard tactics for pike.

Best baits Roach, bream – use bronze maggot in summer; pinkies in winter.

Restrictions No bloodworm or jokers.

Facilities Nearest shop in Guyhirn; nearest pub, the Fisherman's Haunt.

Disabled facilities Some swims may be suitable for disabled anglers.

Rivers

RIVER NENE

The 12-mile stretch of the Nene around Peterborough from Wansford to the tidal sluice near Whittlesey is one of the slowest-flowing rivers in Europe. It contains a wide variety of coarse fish, offers a rich variety of swims and produces good fish throughout the season.

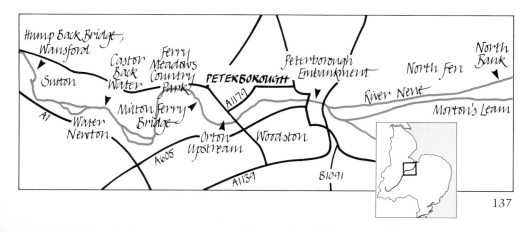

Wansford, upstream.

HUMP BACK BRIDGE, WANSFORD
Atlas Page 202 C.5/1.6

A much-improved section with good chub (4lb+) all season (best after August) and roach. Some very big bream are taken here. Swims vary in depth and degree of tree cover. Pleasure nets regularly top 20lb.

How to get there   From the A1, at Wansford (7 miles south of Stamford), take the A47 east for 1 mile. Park in the layby close to the river, or in the side road to the left. *Note:* there is no parking in Sutton village.

Day tickets   £2. Also season tickets: adult £15, junior/OAP £3. Available from bailiffs on the bank.

Best methods   Roach – stick float on the inside, or pole when seed fishing or using caster/maggots. Chub – waggler within inches of the far bank.

Best baits   Roach – hemp, tares; chub – bronze maggots, casters, worms or bread.

Facilities   Shops at Wansford village.

Hotspot Tips

- When fishing for chub, keep shotting down the line and expect fish on the drop.
- An alternative chub method is a feeder, close to the far bank.
- Try to find a spot where there is overhanging tree cover.

CASTOR BACK WATER
Atlas Page 205 C.6/1.7

A very attractive section, with a wooded island on the far bank. Some swims have tree cover; open areas are prone to downstream wind. Mainly roach and big bream (5lb+), plus chub where tree or weed cover exists. Expect a pleasure net of up to 80lb.

How to get there   Take the A47 west from Peterborough or east from the A1. At Castor, turn down Splash Lane (farm access, so park carefully). Walk from lane end along field boundary to railway bridge; the river is just beyond the bridge.

Day tickets   Adults £1.75; juniors/OAPs £1.50; all year £12. Available from bailiffs on the bank.

Best methods   Bream – leger with feeder, or straight if fish get finicky. Chub – waggler or block-end feeder at the far bank. Roach – pole, stick float or waggler.

Best baits   Bream – bread, casters/worm cocktails. Chub, roach – casters, bronze maggots.

Facilities   Shop in Wansford or Sutton villages.

Disabled facilities   Some swims suitable for wheelchair access.

Hotspot Tips

- If you're after bream, be prepared to switch to straight legering if the fish get finicky.

MILTON FERRY BRIDGE
Atlas Page 202 C.8/1.8

A picturesque stretch, with wooded bank opposite pegged meadows. Deep swims downstream (some 13ft+), others 10–12ft. Mainly roach and chub, plus some bream and skimmer bream. Winter catches often top 40lb from any swim. *Note:* fishing from the wooded (far) bank is only allowed midweek.

How to get there   Access at Milton Ferry bridge on the A47, opposite Ferry Meadows (limited parking), or take the sliproad from the A47 and park in Thorpe Wood golf course car park (opposite the Greenkeeper pub); take the footpath alongside the course to the river (600 yards).

Day tickets   Downstream: available from the bailiffs on the bank: adults £1.75; juniors/OAPs £1.50; all year £12. Upstream: free fishing for 2 miles.

Best methods   Chub – waggler with slow-falling bait on the far shelf. Roach – mid-river waggler or stick float two rod-lengths out, or use pole.

Best baits   Bronze maggots, casters are consistent. Avoid groundbait for chub.

Facilities   Food/toilets at the Greenkeeper pub, or cafe/shop/bar at Ferry Meadows.

Hotspot Tips

☞ For chub, big baits such as cheese or luncheon meat are fine.
☞ Block-end feeders can be very effective for chub.
☞ The swims in the bushes are good autumn and winter hotspots for roach and chub.

ORTON STAUNCH
Atlas Page 202 C.9/1.9

On the River Nene, downstream of Nene Park; also two small lakes. Mainly roach, bream, chub and pike. Large carp (10lb+) have been caught in the area.

How to get there   Located on the A605 Peterborough-Oundle road. Free car parking.
Day tickets   Adult £2; junior/OAP £1. Available from Peterborough DAA bailiffs on the bank.
Best methods   Float fishing with stick or waggler; leger.
Best baits   Maggot, casters, breadflake.
Facilities   Shop/toilets/food available on site. Also Gordon Arms pub within ½ mile.
Disabled facilities   Swims accessible for disabled and wheelchair anglers.

ORTON UPSTREAM
Atlas Page 202 C.9/1.9

A north bank fishery, along the edge of Thorpe Wood golf course. Weekend boating activity opposite can cause problems. Average width 30 yards, depth 9–12ft. Mainly roach, dace and chub (4lb+), plus lots of skimmer bream in summer.

How to get there   Take the A605 west from Peterborough towards Oundle; take turning to Nene Valley Steam Railway station (signposted). Use the car park(s) next to the station, cross the river at the locks and turn left.
Day tickets   Adult £2; junior/OAP £1; available from bailiffs on the bank.
Best methods   Chub – use feeder under moored boats or waggler on same line. Skimmer bream – fish mid-river. Roach – mid-river or pole/stick float in good flow.

Best baits   skimmer bream – white maggot (early season), squatts, brown groundbait. Chub, roach – red/bronze maggots, seed baits.
Facilities   Food/toilets at Nene Valley Railway station.

Hotspot Tips

☞ For chub, try some hemp feed and caster hookbait.
☞ Just above the locks is a good area for skimmer bream.
☞ The big chub often lurk under the big, black-hulled boats.

Peterborough Embankment on the River Nene.

 ## PETERBOROUGH EMBANKMENT
Atlas Page 202 C.9/1.9

A very wide, concrete, canal-like section, with sluggish flow. Popular boat moorings in summer. Expect mostly bream (up to 5lb, especially in winter), but also roach and skimmer bream. Sport can be very good when the river is receding after flooding.

How to get there   In Peterborough city centre, between the old town bridge and the new Eastern Industry Parkway route. Park (pay & display) nearby and walk to the river.
Day tickets   Free fishing.
Best methods   Bream – groundbait in open-end feeder, or waggler with bait slowed down. Roach, skimmer bream – waggler with heavy shot.
Best baits   Bream – worm/caster cocktails (bread in autumn); roach – maggot, casters.
Facilities   Shops/food/toilets in city centre/embankment. Nearest pub Peacock Inn, London Road (1 mile).

Disabled facilities   Easy access to embankment for disabled and wheelchair anglers.

Hotspot Tips

- When flow is moderate, groundbait by hand and fish a straight leger.
- The old flour mill opposite provides the most consistent winter pegs.

NORTH BANK
Atlas Page 202 C.9/1.9

A man-made section – wide but straight, with good access, comfortable banks and a shallow ledge either side of a central channel (11–13ft). Mostly roach and skimmer bream , but bream can appear anywhere all season. Good carp (20lb+, caught at night) and pike have been known here too! Overall, top-class fishing.

How to get there   Take the A605 east from Peterborough to Whittlesey; turn north on B1040. After 1 mile, turn left on river-side road which crosses the river at Dog in a Doublet sluice. Park on the verge.
Day tickets   £2.50; available from the bailiff on the bank.
Best methods   Roach – pole or small waggler fished just over marginal weed. Bream – use bulk-shotted waggler or leger, three-quarters across.
Best baits   Roach, skimmer bream – hemp, tares in summer, bronze/red maggot. Bream – caster/worm cocktail.
Facilities   Food/toilets at the Dog in a Doublet pub.

River Nene, North Bank.

Hotspot Tips

- The first 40-odd pegs upstream of the road are good for summer roach.
- Later in the season, pegs 300–320 always produce good bream.

THE OFFORDS AND BUCKDEN
Atlas Page 202 C.8/2.7

Two fisheries – one a very wide (40 yards) section of the River Ouse, the other a weir pool. Expect roach, dace, bream and chub in the river; chub, carp, barbel in the pool. Members only fishing in the mill race. Excellent fishing, especially in extra flow, with 100lb catches possible. The tree-lined river provides excellent cover for chub.

How to get there   At Buckden roundabout on the A1, turn through the village and head east towards Offord Cluny. Look for signpost directions (Offord & Buckden A.S.) to the fisheries. Free car parking near the river.
Day tickets   Adult £2; junior/OAP 50p. Available from the bailiff on the bank or Tim's Tackle, 88 High Street, Huntingdon; Tel. 0480 450039.
Best methods   Most methods work well here; groundbait is essential for good results. Waggler or pole are best in the river.
Best baits   Maggots (double red), casters, hemp, bread, cheese.
Facilities   Nearest shop Offord Cluny (½ mile); nearest pub, Swan Inn, Offord Cluny (¼ mile).
Disabled facilities   Some swims suitable for disabled anglers; phone for advice; Tel. 0480 810166.

ORTON WATER TROUT FISHING
Atlas Page 202 C.8/1.8

Don't be misled by the name! A 25-acre gravel pit, providing excellent pike fishing. Boat fishing (17 boats) October–March; bank fishing also available. Best fish to date, 25lb.

How to get there   At Orton Waterville, on the A605 Oundle-Peterborough road. Adjacent to Ferry Meadows Country Park (signposted).

Day tickets   Adult £6/rod. Available
from Orton Water Trout Fishing Lodge,
Oundle Road, Peterborough; Tel. 0733
239995. Opening times 08.30–dusk;
booking is advised.
Best methods   Floatfish with deadbait,
trolling, leger, spinning.
Best baits   Deadbaits (smelt, roach,
trout).
Restrictions   Spinner max length 3″; all
fish over 10lb returned.
Facilities   Shops/toilets/food/tackle/bait
available on site. Also caravan park,
steam train, golf courses. Nearest pubs
The Granary and Gordon Arms (½ mile
each).
Disabled facilities   Swims accessible for
disabled and wheelchair anglers.

Good mixed coarse fishing at Raveley Drain.

RAVELEY DRAIN
Atlas Page 202 C.9/2.2

A small, secluded drainage channel midway between Peterborough and
Huntingdon. Good mixed coarse fishing
with roach, tench and bream.

How to get there   From the A1 south of
Peterborough take B660 east (signpost
Peterborough Business Airport) to
Ramsey St Marys; turn right onto
B1040, then minor road towards
Upwood. At sharp left-hand bend (about
2½ miles), look for the drain
immediately on the right. Park at top of
lane and walk to water.

Day tickets   Adult £6; junior/OAP £1.
Available from Ken Burt, 55 Windsor
Road, Yaxley, Peterborough;
Tel. 0733 241119.
Best methods   Use any recognised coarse
technique.
Best baits   Summer roach – pinkies,
bronze maggots; tench, bream – casters.
Winter roach – bread punch.
Restrictions   No bloodworm or jokers.
Facilities   Nearest shop Ramsey Heights
(1 mile); nearest pub, The White Lion,
Ramsey St Marys (2 miles).
Disabled facilities   Poor access; ¼ mile
walk from car park to fishery may
prohibit disabled angling

ST. IVES
Atlas Page 202 D.1/2.4

A group of 10 lakes located at Fen
Drayton, to the east of St Ives, and ranging
from ½ to 20 acres in area and 4–25ft in
depth. Plenty of good coarse fishing, with
tench and carp, plus large bream shoals
that provide excellent catches all season.
Also very good pike fishing in winter.

How to get there   Take the A604 west
from Cambridge and turn onto the St
Ives by-pass (signposted B1040). Drive
over the river and turn right at
roundabout. Look for directions to the
fisheries. Free car parking on site.
Day tickets   Adult £3; junior/OAP £1.50.
Season tickets: adult £18; junior/OAP
£9. Available from St Ives Angling
Centre, 5 Crown Street, St Ives;
Tel. 0480 301903.
Best methods   Most methods work but
waggler is preferred.
Best baits   Mixed species – maggot,
hemp. Tench, carp – sweetcorn, worms.
Facilities   Nearest shops/pubs, St Ives
town centre (10–15 mins walk).

SILVER LAKE
Atlas Page 202 C.8/1.8

Part of Orton Water Trout Fishing in the
Nene Park fishing complex. An attractive,
4-acre lake with tree-lined banks and
cobble stones. No mud! Expect carp, tench
and roach, with 50lb catches common-
place.

How to get there   Located at Orton
Waterville, on the A605 Oundle-
Peterborough road. Just follow the signs.

Day tickets   Adult £4.50 (evening £3); child/OAP £4; weekly (5-day) ticket £18. Available from The Fishing Lodge, Goldie Lane, Oundle Road, Orton Waterville, Peterborough; Tel. 0733 239995.

Best methods   Float or leger.

Best baits   Maggots, sweetcorn, casters.

Facilities   Shop/toilets/food on site, plus caravan park, steam trains and golf. Nearest pubs – The Granary and Gordon Arms (½ mile each).

Disabled facilities   Swims accessible for disabled and wheelchair anglers.

THE STEW POND
Atlas Page 202 C.8/2.8

A small gravel pit which forms part of the Wyboston Lakes complex, near St. Neots. Expect a good catch of coarse fish, including small carp (2–3lb) plus a few larger fish of about 18lb.

How to get there   Head north on the A1 and at junction with A45 to Cambridge look for signs to Wyboston Lakes. Follow signs to the fishery and car parks.

Day tickets   Adult £2; junior/OAP £1. Available from the Club House of the adjacent golf course. Night fishing permitted; for details, ask at the Club House.

Best methods/baits   Use any recognised coarse technique and baits.

Facilities   Toilets/bar/food at Wyboston Sports Complex.

Disabled facilities   Some swims suitable for disabled anglers.

THORNEY DRAIN
Atlas Page 202 D.3/1.7

A small Fenland drain, part of the North Level system, midway between Peterborough and Wisbech. Expect mainly bream, tench and roach, plus some large pike. Fishing is best at the bottom end basin (where it widens), or through the gravels in winter.

How to get there   From Peterborough, drive east on the A47, through Thorney to Thorney Toll (about 9 miles from Peterborough). Turn down the road opposite the Black Horse pub and park on the roadside, near the water.

Day tickets   Adult/junior/OAP £1.50. Available on the bank, or from the garage nearby.

Best methods   Short pole is best, with styl rig for roach on the drop. Or try an Olivette rig (half-depth, with two No. 8s to allow a slow fall of the bait). Float fishing – use small canal grey with styls or dust shot down the line.

Best baits   Roach – bread punch, pinkie or squatt. Bream – pinkie or caster hookbait. Loosefed squatts are also effective. Pike – deadbait.

Restrictions   No bloodworm or jokers. No livebaiting.

Facilities   Nearest shop in Thorney; nearest pub, the Black Horse.

Disabled facilities   Some swims may be suitable for disabled anglers; phone for advice; Tel. 0733 270773.

Twenty Foot Drain.

TWENTY FOOT DRAIN
Atlas Page 202 D.2/1.7

A section of the fen drain system located between Whittlesey and March, and running close to the A605 road. Good fishing, with plenty of bream and roach, plus a few tench.

How to get there From Peterborough, take the A605 east to Whittlesey, then Coates and turn right to Turves village. Turn over the drain at the first bridge and park (free) along the water-side.

Day tickets Adult/junior/OAP £1.50. Available from local tackle shops or Mr C. Smith, 36 Linley Road, Whittlesey; Tel. 0733 202588.

Best methods/baits Roach – float or pole; bream – leger.

Restrictions No bloodworm or jokers.

Facilities Nearest shop Whittlesey; nearest pub, Carpenter's Arms, Coates (1–3 miles according to fishing site).

Rivers

RIVER WELLAND

Along its last few miles from Market Deeping to the Wash, the Welland provides a host of excellent fishing spots which are the venue for many angling competitions. Closely accompanied by its companion waterway, the Coronation Channel, these two move slowly through flat, featureless country, each being pegged throughout their length and providing specimen examples of bream, roach and tench, as well as pike weighing over 20lb.

CROWLAND BRIDGE, UPSTREAM
Atlas Page 202 D.2/1.8

A 45–50-yard wide stretch with 4–5ft close in, dropping to 8–10ft in the middle.. Weed at both edges and mid-river makes far bank tactics difficult. Expect bream (to 7lb) and tench (to 5lb) in summer, with 100lb nets possible. Winter sport is often poor.

How to get there From Crowland, take the B1166 west about 1 mile. The road runs alongside the river; park on the verge, access is via a series of stiles.

Day tickets £2; available from bailiffs on the bank, or from local tackle shops.

Best methods Leger three-quarters across with an open-ended feeder or straight lead. Begin with small groundbait balls loaded with squatts or casters; top up with feeder. Use brown groundbait with red additive/squatts.

Best baits Bream – bread, sweetcorn, worm, casters, red maggots. Summer roach – seed baits, bronze maggots later in year.

River Welland, Crowland Bridge Downstream.

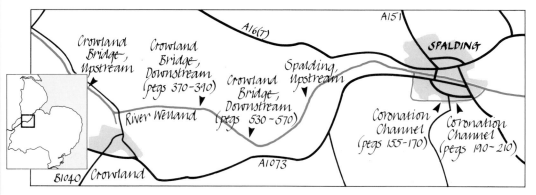

Crowland Bridge, Upstream.

and groundbait. Roach – hemp, bronze maggot plus loosefeed.

Facilities   Shops/food/toilets in Crowland.

Hotspot Tips

- When float fishing for bream, try adding a small amount of cereal.
- Pegs 381 and 388 are the best for bream.

 CROWLAND BRIDGE DOWNSTREAM:

PEGS 530–570
Atlas Page 202 D.2/1.8

A 45-yard-wide section, 9–11ft deep mid-river with 5–6ft nearer the banks. Weed growth can extend almost one-third across. Mainly bream (6–7lb), roach, plus some tench. Expect a typical bag of 50–60lb.

How to get there   Take the B1166 west from Crowland; at the bridge, turn right alongside the river, towards Spalding. Peg numbers are marked on the fence at each stile.
Day tickets   £2; available from bailiffs on the bank, or from local tackle shops.
Best methods   Bream – leger beyond the middle; roach – float fish just short of the middle.
Best baits   Bream, tench – bread, worms, red maggots, casters and groundbait. Roach – hemp, bronze maggot.
Facilities   Shops/food/toilets in Crowland.

Hotspot Tips

- Locals rate peg 543 as one of the best on the river.

Facilities   Shops/food/toilets in Crowland.

Hotspot Tips

- Early season pleasure anglers should use bread or sweetcorn; match anglers will use worm, caster or red maggot.
- Float fishing can be very productive, but the wind can be tricky.
- All the pegs are good, but 812 is a real flyer!

 CROWLAND BRIDGE, DOWNSTREAM:

PEGS 370–390
Atlas Page 202 D.2/1.8

A very consistent section, fairly wide with 6ft depth nearside and 10ft far-side. Marginal weed and a clear bottom. In summer, expect big chub, bream, roach and tench, with 100lb nets possible; in winter, roach provide the action.

How to get there   Take the B1166 west from Crowland; at the bridge, turn right alongside the river, towards Spalding. Peg numbers are marked on the fence at each stile.
Day tickets   £2; available from bailiffs on the bank, or from local tackle shops.
Best methods   Leger three-quarters across with straight bomb or feeder; floatfish the nearside or middle; polefish nearside.
Best baits   Bream, tench – bread, worms, red maggots, casters with red squatts

 SPALDING, UPSTREAM
Atlas Page 202 D.0/1.2

A fairly wide section, with 6ft at the middle, dropping to 11ft far side, and a shelf from one-third out, deepening to the far bank. Plenty of bream and roach, plus some tench. A real hotspot could net 50lb+.

How to get there   Take the A16 south from Spalding; after about 1 mile, turn left onto the bankside road. Watch for peg numbers on fence. Park on the roadside, cross the stile and walk over the flood bank.

Day tickets £2; available from bailiffs on the bank, or from local tackle shops.

Best methods Roach – waggler, with feed to encourage fish from the bottom. Bream – leger at the far bank.

Best baits Roach – hemp, maggot; bream – bread, worms, red maggots, casters and groundbait.

Facilities Shops/food/toilets in Spalding.

Hotspot Tips

- Pegs 220–225 (on the point of the bend) produce bream most of the year.
- Watch for bites on the drop when feeding.

Coronation Channel.

 CORONATION CHANNEL:

PEGS 100–120
Atlas Page 202 D.0/1.2

A 50-yard-wide stretch, average depth 7–8ft, deepening from one-third across to middle. Usually little or no flow. Mainly roach, eels, skimmer bream, plus some big bream and tench, with typical nets of 15lb. Winter catches are mostly roach and skimmer bream.

How to get there From Spalding take the B1165 Wisbech road. Park on the bridge over the Welland and walk to the pegs.

Day tickets £2; available from bailiffs on the bank.

Best methods Polefish the near side, or waggler fished one-third to two-thirds out.

Best baits Skimmer bream – red/bronze maggots hookbait plus groundbait balls packed with squatts. Summer roach – hemp, tares.

Restrictions Match fishing from south bank only.

Facilities Shops/food/toilets in Spalding town centre.

Hotspot Tips

- When using a pole, fish a 10-metre line for the eels.
- Use casters as bait for eels – they're deadly!

 CORONATION CHANNEL:

PEGS 130–150
Atlas Page 202 D.0/1.2

A stretch with minimal flow, depth 8–11ft, marginal weed in summer and a shelf 2 yards out from the match bank. Mainly bream (to 8lb), roach, skimmer bream, eels and some tench in summer, with nets up to 70lb; in winter, expect only bream and roach. *Note:* there are no pegs on the north side.

How to get there From Spalding take the B1165 Wisbech road. Park on the bridge over the Welland and walk about 30 pegs downstream of the bridge.

Day tickets £2; available from bailiffs on the bank.

Best methods Bream – leger, casting just beyond the middle, or waggler fished one-third to middle if conditions are good.

Best baits Roach, eels – red/bronze maggots. Bream – bread, worm/caster.

Facilities Shops/food/toilets in Spalding town centre.

Hotspot Tips

- Use a pole for roach and eels.
- For bream, red squatts in red groundbait is a good tactic.

WERRINGTON LAKES
Atlas Page 202 C.9/1.8

A tidy, well-kept group of lakes a few miles north of Peterborough. Good sport, with regular 20lb catches of rudd and carp, plus some bigger carp, tench and bream.

How to get there Take the A15 north from Peterborough to Werrington (about 2 miles); on the by-pass, look for signposts to the lakes. Free car parking on site.

Day tickets   Adult/junior/OAP £4 (dawn-dusk). Available from local tackle shops or Nick Cesare (owner); Tel. 0733 70226.

Best methods   Use any recognised coarse technique. A float in the marginal water is preferred.

Best baits   Boilies preferred for big fish.

Restrictions   Use a minimum 4lb line.

Facilities   Nearest shop/pub Werrington (1½ miles).

WIMBLINGTON PITS
Atlas Page 202 D.3/2.3

A three-lake complex just north of Chatteris – Brown's Pond, Honey Pond and Wimblington Mere. Plenty of roach, bream (skimmers) and tench, plus some large carp. Fishing is best where bushes overhang the water. Double-figure nets common if the Crucian carp feed well.

How to get there   From Huntingdon, follow the A141 north-east through Chatteris (14 miles) and look for right turn onto B1093 to Manea. The entrance to the lakes is about 2 miles on the right; plenty of parking on site.

Day tickets   Adult/junior/OAP £3. Available on the banks. Also season tickets: adult £15; OAP/disabled £10; juniors £8.

Best methods   Roach, tench, bream, Crucian carp – use pole or waggler. Carp – fish at long range.

Best baits   Roach, bream – maggots, sweetcorn. Carp – boilies.

Restrictions   No cereal groundbait. No bloodworm or joker.

Facilities   Nearest shop/pub in Wimblington or Manea.

Disabled facilities   Some swims may be suitable for disabled anglers; please phone for advice; Tel. 0354 53223.

RIVER WISSEY, HILGAY BRIDGE
Atlas Page 202 D.8/1.7

A narrow, 5ft deep, slow-flowing section of the River Wissey, weedy in summer but clear and even-bottomed in winter. Roach predominate here, with specimen fish, especially in the mild, wet winter months. Some large bream may also appear.

How to get there   Leave the A10 at Hilgay village (3 miles south of Downham Market); head for the old river bridge. Be prepared for a long walk!

Day tickets   £2; available in advance from Colin's Tackle, 55 London Road, King's Lynn. Also from Bridge Stores, Hilgay; Roses Tackle, Bridge Street, Downham Market; The Tackle Box, Tower Street, King's Lynn.

Best methods   Summer – stalk individual fish with freelined and link-legered bread or natural baits; winter – stick float or waggler.

Best baits   Bronze maggots, casters. Avoid cereal groundbait.

Disabled facilities   Some swims are a long walk from the access point making disabled fishing difficult.

Hotspot Tips

- When roach are rampaging, loosefeed with plenty of hookbait.
- When the roach want static bait, try using a pole.
- The bend upstream of Hilgay Bridge can produce some slab-sided bream.

Woolpack Fisheries.

WOOLPACK FISHERIES
Atlas Page 202 C.9/2.4

Excellent day-ticket fishing on one lake of an 8-lake complex (former gravel pits) set in rural surroundings at Godmanchester, near Huntingdon. Quite deep water (10ft) producing good mixed coarse fishing, with bream (to 9lb), carp (to 25lb), rudd, roach, perch, pike and large tench (to 6lb).

How to get there   Take the A604 from Cambridge towards Huntingdon and turn right at the Huntingdon/Godmanchester turn-off. As you leave the roundabout, turn right (signposted to waste tip) and bear left down track. Turn right at the crossroads, use the car park on the left (½ mile) and walk to the water.

Day tickets   Available only for Lake 8: adult/junior/OAP £2.50 when purchased in advance from Stanjay Fishing Tackle, 7 Old Court Hall, Godmanchester, Huntingdon; Tel. 0480 453303; £5 when purchased on the bank.

Best methods/baits   Use general coarse techniques and baits.

Restrictions   Maximum 2 rods per person. Only fish under 5lb to be held in keepnets. No night fishing.

Facilities   Nearest shop (Spar) and pub, The Black Bull (good food) in Godmanchester (about 1 mile).

Disabled facilities   Two swims are located in the car park allowing fishing from the car for disabled or wheelchair anglers; for any advice, please contact Stanjay Fishing Tackle (see above).

WYBOSTON LAKE
Atlas Page 202 C.9/2.8

Located at Wyboston Leisure Complex, Wyboston, Cambs. A man-made lake with a cut through to the River Great Ouse. Expect good bags of bream and small fish, plus larger pike and carp.

How to get there   Take the Eaton Socon turn-off from the A1. The leisure complex is signposted. Free car parking.

Day tickets   £2; available from the Site Manager; Tel. 0480 219200.

Best methods   Float and leger.

Best baits   Maggots, worm, boilies.

Facilities   Club house/toilets/bar on site. Nearest village Eaton Socon (1 mile); nearest pub The Crown (½ mile).

ESSEX

BOREHAM, CHELMSFORD A.C.
Atlas Page 203 E.1/4.1

Three lakes about 4 miles north-east of Chelmsford, 7 acres, 1½ acres and 1 acre in size. Expect good general coarse fishing, with bream, tench and roach, (particularly good carp and pike in Boreham Mere).

How to get there   Take A12 to Chelmsford, then B1137 (via slip road/traffic lights) to Boreham village. At the Cock Inn, turn left over the A12 and drive 1½ miles to Anglia Building Supplies (on left). The car park is signposted on the left.

Day tickets   Membership only, £20 annually and £5 joining fee. Application form from Edward's Tackle, 16 Broomfield Road, Chelmsford, Essex; Tel. 0245 357689 (other waters available).

Best methods/baits   Use any recognised coarse technique and baits.

Restrictions   Fishing dawn to dusk only. No night fishing.

Facilities   Nearest shop/pub in Boreham village.

Disabled facilities   Some swims suitable for disabled anglers.

BOREHAM, MARCONI
Atlas Page 203 E.1/4.1

Three small lakes of variable size with good general coarse fishing and some nice carp and pike. Situated 4 miles north east of Chelmsford on the A12.

How to get there   Directions from Edward's Tackle, with membership.

Day tickets   Fishing available to members only, £20 annually from Edward's Tackle, 16 Broomfield Road, Chelmsford, Essex; Tel. 0245 357689 . Limited night fishing facility for an extra £5, available after joining.

Best methods/baits   Use any recognised coarse technique and baits.

Restrictions   Fishing dawn to dusk only.

Facilities   Nearest shop/pub in Boreham village (1½ miles).

Disabled facilities   Some swims are suitable; consult Edward's Tackle.

BULPHAN CARP FISHERIES
Atlas Page 203 D.8/4.4

A fairly small (2-acre) park lake, a few miles south of Brentwood, where carp fishing is the speciality. The largest 1991 specimen was 24lb.

How to get there   From Brentwood, take the A128 south; cross the A127 and continue about 3 miles to Bulphan village. The fishery is signposted just south of the village.Free car parking on site.

Day tickets   Adult/junior/OAP £5–6.
Available on the bank.

Best methods/baits   Use any recognised
coarse technique.

Facilities   Nearest shop West Horndon (2
miles); nearest pub, Dog & Partridge,
Bulphan (½ mile).

CHURCHWOOD FISHERIES
Atlas Page 203 D.8/4.4

Two estate lakes on private land about 5
miles north of Brentwood. The smaller
(½-acre) lake is carp only; the larger (3-acre)
lake has mixed fishing, with tench, roach
and perch, plus some smaller carp and
rudd.

How to get there   Take the A128 north
from Brentwood towards Ongar and at
Kelvedon Hatch (about 4 miles) turn
right into Blackmoor Road. The fishery
is 1 mile on the right-hand side. Free car
parking on site.

Day tickets   Adult/junior/OAP £7.50.
Available from Brentwood Angling
Centre, 118 Warley Hill, Brentwood;
Tel. 0277 200985.

Best methods/baits   Use any recognised
coarse technique.

Facilities   Nearest shop/pub, The Swan,
Kelvedon Hatch (½ mile).

COBBLERS MEAD LAKE
Atlas Page 203 D.9/4.8

A quite large (5 acres) gravel pit at
Corringham, near Stanford-le-Hope. A
mixed fishery, with a good head of bream,
tench and roach, but better known for
some large carp, with records of 20lb+
specimens taken.

How to get there   Take the A13 east from
London to Stanford-le-Hope and bear
right onto A1014 to Corringham and the
fishery. For details of access and parking,
contact G. Hyde, Box 18, Canvey Island;
Tel. 0268 683946; or Basildon Angling
Centre, Whitmore Way, Basildon.

Day tickets   Season tickets only:
adult/junior £21.50 (plus gate key £2);
OAP £13. Available from G. Hyde (see
above).

Best methods/baits   Use any recognised
coarse technique and baits.

Facilities   Nearest shop/pub in
Corringham.

Disabled facilities   Some swims may be
suitable for disabled anglers; please
phone for advice (see above).

DOGGETTS FARM, ROCHFORD
Atlas Page 203 E.4/4.6

A very irregularly-shaped pit with small
bays and peninsulars, plus high ground at
one end. Many species, including perch
and rudd, plus some very large Crucian
carp and pike. A very busy angling venue
in the holiday season.

How to get there   Take the A127 past
Southend Airport, turn left on B1013 to
Rochford, then bear right towards
Stambridge. Park in the road and
approach the fishery via a farm track,
close to the recreation grounds. *Note*: no
parking by the lake.

Day tickets   Free fishing.

Facilities   Shops in Rochford (8 mins
walk); many pubs nearby.

GOSFIELD LAKE
Atlas Page 202 E.1/3.7

A very large gravel pit of 45 acres, a few
miles north of Braintree. A good mixed
fishery providing reasonable sport, with
perch, roach, pike and tench, as well as a
good head of carp.

How to get there   From Chelmsford, take
the A130, then A131 through Braintree;
after about 3 miles, bear left onto A1017
to Gosfield. Follow signs to the lake and
park near the fishery.

Day tickets   Adult £4; junior/OAP £2; no
night fishing available. Available from
the shop on site or from C.W. Turp,
Gosfield Lake, Church Road, Gosfield;
Tel. 0787 475043.

Best methods/baits   Use any recognised
coarse technique and baits.

Facilities   Boat hire available on site.
Nearest shop/pub in Gosfield.

Disabled facilities   Some swims may be
suitable for disabled anglers; contact the
fishery for advice.

GREAT MYLES LAKE
Atlas Page 203 D.7/4.2

A small (5-acre) lake near Chipping Ongar,
with plenty of small bays that provide
excellent mixed coarse fishing.

How to get there   Take the A128 from
Brentwood north to Chipping Ongar;
look for a small sign to the fishery on
the right-hand side, just after leaving
Chipping Ongar. Free car parking on
site.

Day tickets   Adult/junior/OAP £6.
Available on the bank.
Best methods/baits   Use any recognised
coarse technique.
Restrictions   Use only barbless hooks.
Facilities   Nearest shop/pub, The Stag,
Chipping Ongar (1 mile).

LAKE MEADOWS, BILLERICAY
Atlas Page 203 E.0/4.4

A large park lake on the outskirts of the
town; a very busy fishery, with plenty of
bream, carp (to 23lb), roach and perch.
Late autumn/early winter carp fishing is
good, with several double-figure fish being
taken in late 1991 during an afternoon.

How to get there   From Brentwood, take
the A129 to Billericay; from the railway
station, follow signs to 'Lake Meadows
Park'. No car parking available on site.
Day tickets   Adult £1.40 per rod;
junior/OAP 70p per rod. Available on
the bank.
Best methods/baits   Use any recognised
coarse technique.
Facilities   Nearest shop/pub Billericay.

NEWLAND HALL
Atlas Page 203 E.1/4.1

A pleasant, secluded, 2-acre spring-fed
lake near Chelmsford, providing top-class
carp fishing, with specimen fish to 38lb.

How to get there   From Chelmsford, head
north-west on the A1060 towards
Bishop's Stortford; Newland Hall is
about 4 miles from Chelmsford, on the
left, 1 mile past the Cross Keys pub.
Day tickets   Adult: weekend £8;
weekday £6; junior/OAP half-price.
Small lake available for juniors at £2.
Night fishing £5. Available on site. For
details; Tel. 0245 31463.
Best methods/baits   Mainly specialist
carp methods will be required. Use
standard carp baits for best results.
Facilities   Nearest shop/pub 1 mile.
Breakfast facilities on site.

PIPPS HILL FISHERIES
Atlas Page 203 E.1/4.4

A large, 25-acre lake fishery set within a
country club near Basildon. Contains
general mixed coarse fish, together with
some large carp of between 20–30lb. Often
difficult fishing due to surrounding noise
and activity.

Newland Hall.

How to get there   Take the A13 east from
London to Basildon (about 15 miles)
and look for Cranes Farm Road and the
Pipps Hill Country Club (formerly
'Aquatels'). Parking on site. For details
of access, contact the Country Club
direct; Tel. 0268 523456.
Day tickets   12 hour: adult, £2.20 per
rod, £1 per extra rod; under 16/OAP, £1
per rod, £1 per extra rod. 24 hour:
adult/junior, £4 per rod, £1.50 per extra
rod. Available on the bank.
Best methods/baits   Use any recognised
coarse technique and baits.
Restrictions   No sacking of carp.
Toilets/cafe/bar on site.
Disabled facilities   Some swims may be
suitable for disabled anglers; contact
the Country Club for advice (see above).

PRIORY PARK LAKES
Atlas Page 203 E.4/4.6

A busy, council-controlled park lake in
the centre of Southend; a popular fishery
which produces good catches of coarse
fish, including large carp that often reach
well over 20lb.

How to get there Take the A127 from London to Southend and in the town centre follow signs to Priory Park and the lakes. Parking available on site.

Day tickets Adult £1.80; junior/OAP 90p. Available on site.

Best methods/baits Use any recognised coarse technique and baits. Modern carp methods may be required. Toilets/cafe on site. Nearest shops/pub in Southend.

Disabled facilities Some swims may be suitable for disabled anglers.

ROCHFORD RESERVOIR
Atlas Page 203 E.4/4.5

A small reservoir with open swims and fairly easy angling conditions. A prolific fishery, very popular with local anglers, with most coarse fish, with large carp, occasionally to 20lb. Weekday fishing, out of holiday season, is usually quieter.

How to get there Take the A127 past Southend Airport, turn left on B1013 towards Rochford. The reservoir is visible on the left of the Rochford by-pass, near the railway station (about 2 miles). Free parking nearby.

Day tickets Adult £1.50; junior/OAP 70p; available on the bank.

Best methods/baits Use recognised techniques and baits.

Restrictions Maximum 2 rods per person.

Facilities Shops in town centre (5 mins walk); several pubs within 5 mins walk.

Disabled facilities Fishing by disabled and wheelchair anglers is possible in some swims.

SHOEBURY PARK
Atlas Page 203 E.5/4.7

This small public park lake in Shoeburyness is sometimes very busy and is very popular with juniors. Dense areas of lily pads. Expect most coarse species, with tench (to 5lb+) and very big common carp (to 25lb+).

How to get there Take the A127 through Southend to Sea Front Road and drive towards Shoebury. Enter Ness Road (as the road veers away from the sea); the fishery is at the top of the road, close to the Asda supermarket. Free car parking.

Day tickets Adult £1.70; junior/OAP 80p; available on the bank.

Best methods/baits Use general coarse fishing tackle and baits; heavy tackle will be needed to land the larger carp.

Facilities Shops/garage within 5 mins walk. Pubs (The Cambridge; Captain Mainwaring) within 10 mins walk.

SOUTH OCKENDEN CARP FISHERY
Atlas Page 203 D.9/4.8

The fishery, located near Grays and not far from the M25, comprises three gravels pits, each of about 3 acres. The pike, perch, tench and roach all reach good sizes, but carp are the speciality here – 25lb+ fish are quite common.

How to get there Take the A127 east from London; just after M25 junction turn right on B186 to South Ockenden. Look for signs to the fishery and park on site.

Day tickets Adult £2.50; junior/OAP £1.50. Available on the bank.

Best methods/baits Most species – use recognised coarse techniques. Carp – use specialist methods and baits

Facilities Nearest shop/pub in South Ockenden.

SOUTH WEALD PARK
Atlas Page 203 D.8/4.3

A good-sized, square lake set amongst parkland near Brentwood. The lake has a good local fishing reputation, with excellent mixed sport, including big carp, bream and tench.

How to get there At the western end of Brentwood High Street, turn right at traffic lights into Weald Road; the third car park is the nearest to the lake.

Day tickets Adult/junior/OAP £2 per rod. Available on the bank.

Best methods/baits Use any recognised coarse technique.

Facilities Toilets are a long walk away. Nearest shop Brentwood; nearest pub, The Tower Arms, South Weald.

Disabled facilities Some swims suitable for disabled and wheelchair anglers. Vehicular access to the lake is possible.

STAMBRIDGE TROUT AND COARSE FISHERIES
Atlas Page 203 E.4/4.5

A small, commercial fishery offering both coarse and game fishing (trout). Prolific fishing, with a wide variety of species.

How to get there Take the A127 past Southend Airport, turn left on B1013 to Rochford, then bear right towards Stambridge. The fishery is visible from the road, after about 4 miles. Free car parking on site.

Day tickets Adult: 0600–1800 £5, 1800–0600 £5; under 12 free. Prices on application to Stambridge Trout & Coarse Fisheries, Stambridge, Nr Rochford, Essex; Tel. 0702 258274.

Best methods/baits Advice available from fishery owners.

Facilities Baits available on site. Shops/toilets on site or in Rochford (4 miles); nearest pub (Royal Oak; Cherry Tree) 5 mins drive.

Disabled facilities Good access to swims for disabled anglers.

STANFORD-LE-HOPE, THE WARREN
Atlas Page 203 D.9/4.8

A 46-acre lake with islands and walkways out to the islands, which you can fish off. Mixed fishery of good standard with recent extensive restocking – carp to 26lb, one or two 2lb 13oz roach, perch to 3lb, bream to 5–6lb, and tench 5–7lb.

How to get there From the M25, jct 30, take A13 east, then A1014 to Stanford-le-Hope and Coryton. Follow Stanford signs to Southend Road, fork left (at Burmah Garage) and take Wharfe Road under railway bridge on to unmade road. The fishery entrance is on the right.

Day tickets Adult £2 per rod; junior/OAP £1 per rod. Available on the bank.

Best methods/baits Use any recognised coarse technique and baits.

Restrictions No night fishing.

Facilities Nearest shops/pubs in Stanford-Le-Hope.

Disabled facilities Two concreted swims with railings available.

STANFORD-LE-HOPE, LEISURE SPORTS
Atlas Page 203 D.9/4.8

Two adjacent gravel pits of 6 and 7 acres, not far from Basildon. Plenty of large pike, Crucian carp, perch, roach, bream, rudd, tench and eels, but common and mirror carp are few and far between. A good coarse venue, nevertheless.

How to get there From the M25, jct 30, take the A13 east, then A1014 to Stanford-le-Hope and Coryton. Follow Stanford signs to Southend Road, fork left (at Burmah garage) and take Wharfe Road under railway bridge onto un-made road. The fishery entrance is on the left; use either car park – no parking on central causeway.

Day tickets Season tickets only: adult £22; junior/OAP/disabled £11. Available from Leisure Sport, Thorpe Park, Staines Road, Chertsey.

Best methods/baits Use any recognised coarse technique and baits.

Facilities Nearest shop/pub in Stanford-le-Hope.

STAR LANE, GREAT WAKERING
Atlas Page 203 E.4/4.6

A very popular (especially in school holidays), general coarse fishery, with two pits on day-ticket fishing and one lake on syndicate fishing. Expect carp (possibly to 20lb), tench, roach, bream, roach and pike. Best fishing is weekdays, out of holiday season. Night fishing is permitted.

How to get there Follow the A127 through Southend and follow signs to Thorpe Bay and Shoeburyness. From Bournes Green (Thorpe Bay) take North Shoebury Road; Star Lane and the fishery are about 3 miles on the left. Free parking on site.

Day tickets Adult £2.50; junior/OAP £2.50. Also season tickets: day £30; day/night £35. All tickets available on the bank.

Best methods/baits Use general coarse fishing techniques; heavy tackle for large carp.

Restrictions Maximum 2 rods per person.

Facilities Shops/pubs Great Wakering (8 mins drive).

THORNDON PARK
Atlas Page 203 D.8/4.4

A 3-acre, quite shallow lake, surrounded by trees, located in a park south of Brentwood. A good coarse fishing venue, with most species, including good-sized carp and pike up to 15lb.

151

How to get there   From Brentwood, take the A128 south to Herongate (about 4 miles). The fishery car park is visible from the road on the right; park (free) and walk ½ mile to the lake.

Day tickets   Adult £2; junior/OAP £1. Available on the bank.

Best methods/baits   Use any recognised coarse technique; float fishing is preferred.

Facilities   Toilets near car park. Nearest shop/pub, The Cricketer's Arms, Herongate.

HUMBERSIDE

A good result on still water.

BARTON BROADS
Atlas Page 205 G.8/3.5

A mixed fishery of some 11 acres – formerly a clay pit – near the southern approach to the Humber Bridge. Mainly roach, bream, tench and catfish, plus large carp – some to 20lb+.

How to get there   Take the A15 north to the Humber Bridge; the fishery is just before the bridge, close to the road. Follow signs for access and parking.

Day tickets   Adult £2; junior/OAP £1.25; 24-hour ticket £2.50. Available from the house near the lake; for details; Tel. 0652 32237.

Best methods/baits   Use any recognised coarse technique and baits.

Restrictions   No hempseed baits.

Facilities   Toilets/cafe/ tackle & bait shop on site. Also holiday caravans for hire. Nearest shop/pub in Barton-on-Humber.

THE NEST
Atlas Page 205 G.4/3.6

A man-made lake of just over 1 acre, close to the Humber estuary, north of Scunthorpe. Contains some good quality mirror and common carp of 6–8lb, plus Crucians, grass carp, tench, rudd, roach and perch. A popular, but small fishing venue

How to get there   From Scunthorpe, take the A1077 towards Barton-on-Humber; after about 7 miles, bear left to Winteringham and follow signs to the fishery. Parking on site.

Day tickets   Adult/junior/OAP: Monday–Friday £2, Saturday and Sunday £3. Available on the bank. Maximum 20 anglers; advance booking is advised. For details; Tel. 0724 732465.

Best methods/baits   Use any recognised coarse technique and baits.

Restrictions   No night fishing.

Facilities   Nearest shop/pub in Winteringham.

Disabled facilities   Slippery banks generally prevent access by disabled anglers, but phone to check (see above).

LINCOLNSHIRE

The River Ancholme.

ABY POND
Atlas Page 205 F.5/4.2

A 2-acre lake, situated at South Thoresby, near Aby, Lincolnshire. Expect roach, bream, tench, carp and rudd. Fishing available all year. Best fish caught was 25lb carp.

How to get there   Take the A16 south from Louth; after 10 miles turn left to South Thoresby.

Day tickets   Adult £2; from A Harrop, Belleau Bridge Trout Farm, Belleau, nr Alford; Tel. 05216 225.

Best methods/baits   Use general coarse methods and baits.

Restrictions   No night fishing.

Facilities   Nearest shop/pub in Alford, 2 miles.

Rivers

RIVER ANCHOLME

On the bank.

The old adage that appearances can be deceptive is certainly true of the River Ancholme. Although largely uninspiring in its canalised and almost featureless form as it flows from Snitterby weir to the Humber Estuary, the river holds a good head of fish, although distracting them from the river's vast supplies of natural food can be difficult for the angler. That being the case, apart from finding a bream shoal, the likelihood of a really big catch along the river is somewhat limited. However, six *Angling Times* Hotspots have been identified along the Ancholme.

SNITTERBY
Atlas Page 205 G.6/4.3

A narrow stretch, poor flow, average depth 5–6ft and a slightly deeper boat channel. Lily beds and dense summer weed. Expect bream and tench (both to 4lb) plus small roach and skimmer bream. Winter sport consists of pike (to 8lb) or roach if water is coloured. Pleasure nets of 10–12lb – much bigger if bream or tench show.

How to get there   Take the A15 north from Lincoln for about 15 miles and turn right to Snitterby. Go 1 mile east through the village, turn right, then left, to Snitterby Bridge. Walk upstream (both banks) to Snitterby Weir or Harlam Lock.

Day tickets   £1.80; available on the bank. Also yearly ticket: adult £6; junior/OAP £2.50. Available from Scunthorpe Fishing Tackle; Tel. 0724 849815.

Best methods   Waggler or pole; fish fine (22 hooks, 1lb bottoms), but scale up (to 20 hook, 2lb line) if bream or tench show.

Best baits   Tench – bread, sweetcorn, worm or maggots; roach - seed baits, maggot or casters.

Disabled facilities   Good banks may enable access by disabled anglers.

Hotspot Tips

- For tench, fish just off the lily beds.
- Bream prefer white maggots here.
- For fun, try a spinner or plug for small pike.
- Using some groundbait can be a big advantage if tench or bream are about.

BRANDY WHARFE
Atlas Page 205 G.6/4.3

A canal-like section, depth 5–7ft, with shelf 6 yards from bank; heavily-weeded swims. A popular summer spot; mainly tench, bream, skimmer bream and roach; pleasure nets rarely exceed 6lb. Pike are small, numerous – and a nuisance! Winter sport is modest.

How to get there   Take the A15 north from Lincoln for about 16 miles; take the B1205 east through Waddingham village until you cross the river (at Brandy Wharfe). Park at the bridge, or drive down track to east bank car park. Fish from either bank.

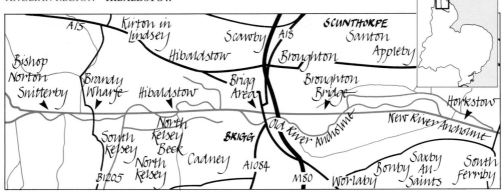

Day tickets £1.80; available on the bank.
Also yearly ticket: adult £6; junior/OAP
£2.50. Available from Scunthorpe
Fishing Tackle; Tel. 0724 849815.

Best methods Use a short pole on the
ledge, or a feeder/waggler in the middle
or at the far bank.

Best baits Tench, bream, roach – bread,
sweetcorn, worm or maggots.

Facilities The Cider House pub.

Disabled facilities Good vehicular
access close to the east bank fishery.

Hotspot Tips

❧ The bream hotspots are on pegs
140–150.

❧ If you're looking for perch, try chopped
worms.

HIBALDSTOW
Atlas Page 205 G.3/3.9

A wider stretch, with 7-yard ledge either
side and 9ft centre boat channel. Flow
minimal; weed can cause problems in
early summer when perch and bream are
plentiful near the ledge and bream in mid-
channel. Typical catches 6–8lb, 30–50lb if
bream arrive. Winter sport poor (except
Cadney, 1 mile downstream, with good
roach (in clear water) or perch (in coloured
water).

How to get there Take the A15 south
from Brigg, about 4 miles; turn left at
Hibaldstow towards Hibaldstow Bridge.
Follow the road for 2½ miles to the river;
fishing is from both banks.

Day tickets £1.80; available on the bank.
Also yearly ticket: adult £6; junior/OAP
£2.50. Available from Scunthorpe
Fishing Tackle; Tel. 0724 849815.

Best methods Bream – groundbait feeder
in the boat channel with maggot or
squatt hookbait. Perch – pole and fish

just off the shelf. Roach – standard light
tactics.

Best baits Tench, bream, roach – bread,
sweetcorn, worm or maggots.

Hotspot Tips

❧ For skimmer bream, try a long pole
with maggots, or a short pole close to
the weeds.

❧ There are plenty of tench – try using
bread flake.

❧ On this stretch, early and late sessions
are the most productive.

BRIGG AREA
Atlas Page 205 G.4/3.8

Here the river splits into old and new
courses. New river: shelving at edges, plus
8–10ft boat channel, ledges and lilies.
Flow is mainly slow. Old river: 5ft deep,
weedy. Expect tench, bream, skimmer
bream, roach and perch in each stretch
during summer, plus good roach and perch
at Cake Mills. Winter sport includes
perch, roach and bream.

How to get there In Brigg town centre,
access to the old river is via Cadney
Road; Grandways car park and the
leisure centre are both nearby. The
'island' formed by the old and new
rivers leads to Cake Mills Point; park on
the rough ground (NOT ON THE
ROAD).

Day tickets £1.80; available on the bank.
Also yearly ticket: adult £6; junior/OAP
£2.50. Available from Scunthorpe
Fishing Tackle; Tel. 0724 849815.

Best methods Summer – waggler and
pole; fish light (size 22 hooks, 2–2½ lb
bottom). Also use a groundbait feeder.

Best baits Roach, bream – white and red
maggots or casters.

Facilities   Shops/food/toilets in Brigg town centre.

Hotspot Tips

🐟 Red maggots with a pole are ideal for winter roach.
🐟 The new river attracts most attention – above the railway ridge is a good bream area.
🐟 Chopped worm is an ideal bait for perch here.

Netting the catch on the Ancholme.

BROUGHTON BRIDGE
Atlas Page 203 E.9/1.3

A wider stretch, shelves 8–9ft deep 6 yards out. Main channel (12ft) provides moderate flow. Mainly skimmer bream, roach and perch in summer; 12–20lb catches using three lines – near ledge, middle and right across. Bream improve in autumn/winter as the level drops.

How to get there   Just north of Broughton, turn off the B1207 onto the B1208. Follow signs to Broughton Bridge and the river (about 1½ miles). Access to the river is from the parking area; fish from either bank (footbridge access to the far bank).
Day tickets   £1.80; available on the bank. Also yearly ticket: adult £6; junior/OAP £2.50. Available from Scunthorpe Fishing Tackle; Tel. 0724 849815.
Best methods   Use similar tactics to the other Ancholme Hotspots. Skimmer bream, roach – use 9-metre pole.
Best baits   Bream – maggots, casters/worms cocktail, and bread. Breadcrumb groundbait (plus loosefeed) is effective if used carefully.
Disabled facilities   Good access is available from the car park.

Hotspot Tips

🐟 Maggots work well for bream and roach, but don't overlook casters or small worms.
🐟 In winter, squatts and pinkies are very effective.
🐟 Count eight telegraph poles down from the bridge – that's where you'll find the bream!

HORKSTOW
Atlas Page 205 G.4/3.8

A ditch-like section with a very deep (14ft) central channel. Expect bream from July to October only, with roach, perch and tench later in the season. A large bream shoal can net 70lb+, with some fish 5lb+, but otherwise, 7lb is good.

How to get there   Take the B1204 from Brigg north towards South Ferriby; after 2 miles, look for signs to Horkstow Bridge. Park at the bridge and walk downstream on either bank.
Day tickets   £1.80; available on the bank. Also yearly ticket: adult £6; junior/OAP £2.50. Available from Scunthorpe Fishing Tackle; Tel. 0724 849815.
Best methods   Groundbait in the middle and far side; look for roach in the margins.
Best baits   Bream – maggots, casters, bread; roach – seed baits. Use cereal groundbait moderately.

Hotspot Tips

🐟 Fish the west bank for bream, downstream of the bridge.
🐟 Use worm as bait when the water is coloured.

BAINSIDE NURSERIES LAKE
Atlas Page 202 C.7/0.1

Located at Kirkby on Bain, near Woodhall Spa, Lincolnshire. A 1-acre lake containing roach, tench and carp (including grass carp). Fishing available all year; best fish caught – 13lb carp.

How to get there   Take the A53 south from Horncastle; after 5 miles, turn right towards Woodhall Spa and Kirkby on Bain. Look for signs to the fishery.
Day tickets   Adult £2; from Mr Rickwood; Tel. 0526 52050.

Best methods   General coarse methods.
Best baits   Maggots, bread, sweetcorn, boilies for carp.
Restriction   No junior fishing.
Facilities   Shop/pub in Kirkby on Bain.

BELL'S YARD LAKE, HORNCASTLE
Atlas Page 205 H.1/4.6

Excellent fishing available all year with Horncastle AC. Mainly roach, bream, pike, perch, tench and rudd. Expect top bag weights close to 25lb.

How to get there   Located at Horncastle, on the A158, east of Lincoln city.
Day tickets   Annual permits – adult £6; ladies/juniors/OAPs £2.50. Permit holders may fish in the close season at Bell's Yard Pit. Available from K. Dannatt (Club Secretary), 95 Tennyson Gardens, Horncastle; Tel.0507 527277.
Best methods/baits   Use general coarse methods and baits.
Facilities   Nearest shop/pub in Horncastle.

BRICKYARD FISHERY
Atlas Page 205 H.5/4.3

A 4-acre brick pit at South Somercotes, a few miles east of Louth and next to a small caravan site. Expect mixed general coarse fishing, plus some large carp to 20lb. Fishing is available all year round.

How to get there   From Louth, take the B1200 east to meet the A1031 and turn left to Saltfleet. Turn left on minor road to South Somercotes and follow signs to the fishery. Park nearby.
Day tickets   Adult/junior/OAP £3. Available on site from Mrs Cartwright; Tel. 0507 358331.
Best methods/baits   Use any recognised coarse technique and baits.
Facilities   Toilets on site at caravan park. Touring caravans welcome. Nearest shop/pub in South Somercotes.

BROOKSIDE STUD FISHERIES
Atlas Page 205 G.3/4.7

This ¾-acre lake is situated at Eagle Lane, North Scarle, Lincolnshire. Mainly carp, rudd, tench and roach; carp may reach 25lb+.

How to get there   Take the A46 south-west from Lincoln; after about 4 miles,

look for right turn to Eagle and then North Scarle (about 6 miles).
Day tickets   Adult £2; available from the house on site, or from Mrs O Blow; Tel. 052277 234.
Best methods   Use general coarse methods.
Best baits   Use recognised baits.
Facilities   Toilets on site. Nearest shops and pub in village (1 mile).

CARLTON LAKES
Atlas Page 205 H.7/4.2

A group of recently-dug lakes, situated between Louth and Mablethorpe. Stocked with quality fish.

How to get there   From Mablethorpe take the A1031 Saltfleet road, then the B1200 Louth road. At Saltfleetby St. Peter, turn left (it's the 2nd left along that road) cross the river, turn right and the lake's ¾ mile on the right.
Day tickets   Adult £2.50; details available from Pets 'n' Plants, Mablethorpe; Tel. 0507 473104.
Best methods   Use general coarse methods and baits.
Best baits   Floating bread, sweetcorn, punch bread for rudd, etc.
Facilities   Shop in Saltfleetby and The Kings Head in Theddlethorpe, both about 3¼ miles.

CASTLE LEISURE PARK
Atlas Page 205 G.7/5.0

A group of four lakes located at Sleaford Road, Tattershall. Three lakes contain mainly tench, bream, mirror and common carp, rudd, perch and pike; the fourth lake contains mainly rudd. Expect bream to 7lb+. Fishing is available all year.

How to get there   Take the A153 south from Tattershall towards Sleaford; look for signs for Castle Leisure Park on the right.
Day tickets   Adult £2.50; junior/OAP £2 (entrance to Leisure Park £1); also details available from Mr Dickinson, Tel. 0526 43193.
Best methods/baits   Use general coarse methods and baits.
Facilities   Toilets/food available in the Leisure Park.
Disabled facilities   Good access to lakesides.

CLEETHORPES BOATING LAKE
Atlas Page 205 H.2/3.8

A 5-acre lake in Cleethorpes, containing roach, rudd, carp, tench and perch. Fishing is available all year.

How to get there Follow the main A46 from Lincoln, north to Cleethorpes (about 40 miles). In the town centre, look for signs to the lake.
Day tickets Adult 1.70; junior/OAP 80p,. Also annual permits available: adult £10; junior/OAP £7; available from the water bailiff at the boating lake.
Best methods/baits Use general coarse methods and baits.
Facilities Toilets/food available near the lake.
Disabled facilities Good access to swims.

CULVERTHORPE HALL
Atlas Page 205 G.4/5.3

Two estate lakes at Culverthorpe Hall, near Grantham. Depth ranges from shallow to deep at dam wall. Both lakes contain most coarse fish; the larger mainly bream, the smaller mainly roach.

How to get there From Grantham, take the B6403 to Ancaster; turn left through Welby and then Oasby. The lakes are on the left, after about 2 miles. Free car parking.
Day tickets Adult £3; available from the bailiff on the bank.
Best methods Bream – use feeder; roach – use pole.
Facilities Shops/food and nearest pub in Oasby (2 miles).
Disabled facilities Good access to swims enables disabled and wheelchair angling (but no special constructions).

CYPRINIDS ANGLING CLUB
Atlas Page 205 H.5/4.2

A 2-acre lake in North Somercotes, containing carp, tench, roach, bream, rudd and perch, with carp to 19lb possible. Fishing is available all year.

How to get there Take the B1200 east from Louth, then A1031 north. Look for signs to North Somercotes on right.
Day tickets 7-day (Mon-Sat, except Bank Holidays) tickets: adult £3; available from the bungalow next to the lake, or from Mrs Marshall; Tel. 0507 358662.
Best methods/baits Use general coarse methods and baits.
Restrictions No Sunday day-ticket fishing.
Facilities Shop/food in North Somercotes village.

DAM BOTTOM RESERVOIR
Atlas Page 205 H.2/3.9

A 3½-acre reservoir on the Yarborough Estates, Brocklesby, containing roach, plus tench to 4lb+. Fishing in season only: 16th June to 16th August.

How to get there Take the A46 north from Market Rasen towards Grimsby; after 15 miles, turn left on A18. At Keelby, take B1211 to Brocklesby (2 miles).
Day tickets Adult minimum £1.50 (donation to church fund); day permits (Mon-Sat) available from Brockleby Estate Office, Monday-Friday (0845–1700); Tel. 0469 60214.
Best methods/baits Use general coarse methods and baits.
Restrictions Only 12 permits allowed each day.
Facilities Shop/pub in Brocklesby.

DENNIS'S RAINWATER LAKE
Atlas Page 202 D.7/0.1

A 1-acre lake in Low Road, Croft Bank, Skegness, containing carp, rudd and tench. Fishing is available all year. Carp may reach 30lb+

How to get there Take the A158 east from Lincoln to Skegness; Croft Bank lies to the south of the town.
Day tickets Adult £1.50; junior/OAP £1 (under 14s must be accompanied by an adult); evening permits (after 1600) £1. All available on site from S. Dennis; Tel. 0754 765783.
Best methods/baits Use general coarse methods and baits.
Restrictions Under 14s must be accompanied by an adult.
Facilities Shops/food/toilets in Skegness town centre.
Disabled facilities Good access to swims allows disabled angling.

DYKES COTTAGE LAKE
Atlas Page 202 C.8/0.5

A ½-acre lake containing bream, roach, rudd, tench and carp, at Chapel Hill, near Coningsby. Fishing available all year. Expect carp to 9lb+.

How to get there   Take the A153 north from Sleaford towards Coningsby; at Billinghay (about 9 miles), look for right turn to Chapel Hill.

Day tickets   Adult £2; junior/OAP £1.50; available from Mrs Webster, Dyke Cottage, Chapel Hill; Tel. 0526 43315.

Best methods/baits   Use general coarse methods and baits.

Restrictions   No keepnets allowed.

Facilities   Shop/food in Chapel Hill village.

RIVER EAU
Atlas Page 205 H.8/4.3

A 2½-mile length of river bank, with shallows 3–4ft deep, and which contains small skimmers, roach, rudd, the odd tench, and some big bream. In the winter, roach to 2½lb and pike to 20lb.

How to get there   Details from Pets 'n' Plants.

Day tickets   Adult £1.50; available only from Pets 'n' Plants, High Street, Mablethorpe; Tel. 0507 473104.

Best methods/baits   Use general coarse methods. Most baits work well here; use caster for good quality fish.

Facilities   Shops in Mablethorpe; bait available from Pets 'n' Plants.

FARLESTHORPE BRICK PITS
Atlas Page 205 H.2/4.6

Three acres of brick pits which contain roach, bream, carp, tench, perch, dace and rudd. Fishing rights are owned by Burgh Angling Society (Secretary D. Hatson, West End, Hogsthorpe; Tel. 05212 73680.

How to get there   From Lincoln, take the A158 to Horncastle, then Splisby; turn left on to A1104 to Alford (7 miles), look for B1196, bear left for Farlesthorpe.

Day tickets   Adult £1.50; junior/OAP £1 (under 14s must be accompanied by an adult); evening permits (after 1600) £1. All available on site from S. Dennis; Tel. 0754 765783.

Best methods/baits   Use general coarse methods and baits.

Facilities   Shop/pub in Farlesthorpe.

FOSTON LAKES
Atlas Page 202 C.2/0.6

Three lakes (also known as Willow Lakes) situated at Foston; one lake carp only, other lakes contain roach, tench, bream etc. There is no close season, but fishing here is best in the hottest months.

How to get there   Take the A1 north beyond Grantham by-pass (about 3 miles); turn right to Foston, drive through village. The lakes are on the left, after the pub. Free car parking at the lakes.

Day tickets   Adult £3/rod (evenings £2); available on the banks.

Best methods/baits   Use any recognised technique or bait.

Restrictions   Use barbless hooks only; no groundbait. No boilies.

Facilities   Shop/toilets at caravan site (also caravans for hire). Bait for sale at bungalow nearby or at Bait Farm nearby. Nearest shops/pub in Foston village.

Disabled facilities   Good access to swims for disabled and wheelchair anglers.

GRANGE FARM
Atlas Page 205 H.8/4.3

A group of three lakes, each 1 acre. Two lakes coarse fishing, one carp only. Although stillwater, with high banks, the breezes cause a gentle movement of water.

How to get there   Located on the A1104 Alford-Mablethorpe road, about 1 mile west of Mablethorpe. Well signposted.

Day tickets   Adult £2.50; available on site. Details available from Pets 'n' Plants, Mablethorpe; Tel. 0507 473104.

Best methods/baits   Use general coarse methods and baits.

Facilities   Tackle shop at venue; bait available on site. Shops/toilets/food available in Mablethorpe.

GROOBY'S PIT
Atlas Page 202 D.7/0.2

A 2-acre lake at Bridge Foot Farm, Thorpe Culvert, Wainfleet, near Skegness. Contains tench (to 3lb), roach, bream, carp, pike and perch. Fishing available all year.

How to get there   From Skegness, head south on the A52 towards Wainfleet. Look for signs to Thorpe Culvert/ Wainfleet Bank.

Day tickets   Permits (0600–1700): adult £1.50 (50p from 1700–2100); available from Mr Grooby; Tel. 0754 880216.

Best methods/baits   Use general coarse methods and baits.

Facilities   Nearest shop/pub in Wainfleet All Saints.

HALL FARM MOAT
Atlas Page 205 G.4/4.3

A farm moat which provides good all-round coarse fishing – all year round! Contains a good head of most species, but is particularly well stocked with carp up to 15lb.

How to get there   From Lincoln, drive north on the A15 about 11 miles and turn left onto A631 towards Gainsborough. Hall farm and the fishery are about 4 miles along this road, just after Harpswell village. Parking on site.

Day tickets   Adult £1.50; junior/OAP 75p. Available from Hall Farm.

Best methods/baits   Use any recognised coarse technique and baits.

Restrictions   No night fishing.

Facilities   Nearest shop/pub in Harpswell village.

Disabled facilities   Some swims suitable for disabled anglers.

HARTSHOLME LAKE
Atlas Page 205 G.5/4.6

This 25-acre lake (of which 12 acres is accessible to anglers) lies in Hartsholme Park, off Skellingthorpe Road, near Lincoln. Contains roach, bream, pike, tench and carp. Fishing only within season: 16th June to 14th March.

How to get there   Take the A46 south from Lincoln; at North Hykeham, bear right onto B1190 towards Skellingthorpe. Look for signs to Hartsholme Park and Lakes.

Day tickets   Adult £2; under 16/OAP £1; available on the bank.

Best methods/baits   Use general coarse methods and baits.

Facilities   Food/toilets available in Park.

Disabled facilities   Good access to swims for disabled anglers.

HILL VIEW FISHERIES
Atlas Page 205 H.9/4.5

A coarse-fishing lake of about ¾ acre, situated at Hogsthorpe, just west of Chapel St Leonards. The lake contains carp (up to 23lb), roach, bream, rudd and tench. Seasonal fishing only: 28th March–17th October.

How to get there   From Skegness, head north on the A52 towards Mablethorpe. Hogsthorpe is about 1 mile beyond the turn to Chapel St Leonards.

Day tickets   Adult £2.50 plus £2 per extra rod; junior/OAP £1.50 per rod; evening: adult/junior/OAP £1.50. Available on site (after 0900hrs) or from K. Raynor; Tel. 0754 72979.

Best methods/baits   Use general coarse methods and baits.

Restrictions   Children under 12 must be accompanied by an adult.

Disabled facilities   Good access to swims for disabled anglers.

HOE HILL POND
Atlas Page 205 G.8/3.4

These 10 acres of fishable waters near Barton on Humber contain large stocks of tench (up to 7lb), common bream, roach, rudd, chub and perch, plus mirror and Crucian carp. Fishing is available all year.

How to get there   Take the A15 north from Lincoln to Barton on Humber (about 35 miles, via M180). Look for signs to Pasture Road North.

Day tickets   Adult £2; junior/OAP £1.50. Night fishing permits £3 (by appointment only). Permits available from Pasture House Fishery, Pasture Road North; Tel. 0652 635119 (Mrs K Smith).

Best methods/baits   Use general coarse methods and baits.

Facilities   Shops/toilets/food available in Barton on Humber.

Disabled facilities   Good access for disabled and wheelchair anglers.

HOLME LAKE, MESSINGHAM

Atlas Page 205 G.4/3.8

A 15-acre lake containing large carp (up to 27lb), plus bream (9lb), roach (2lb), rudd, perch and dace. Fishing in season only 15th March to 16th June.

How to get there   Take the A15 north from Lincoln; at Kirton in Lindsey (about 18 miles) look for B1400 on left to Messingham (about 8 miles).

Day tickets   Adult £2.50 (12 hours) or £5 (24 hours). Enquiries for permits to G. Denton (Tel. 0724 855972) or J. Foster (Tel. 06737 453).

Restrictions   No keepnets to be used.

Best methods/baits   Use general coarse methods and baits.

Facilities   Shop/pub in Messingham village.

HOMESTEAD LAKE, IMMINGHAM

Atlas Page 205 H.0/3.7

This 2½-acre coarse fishery was first opened in April 1985 and contains rudd, tench, bream and carp. Fishing is available all year.

How to get there   From Lincoln, take the A15 north to beyond Brigg, then M180/A180 towards Grimsby. Look for signs to Immingham on the left (about 8 miles).

Day tickets   Dawn to 1630, £2, 1630 to dusk, £1; junior/OAP half price. UB40s, Monday to Friday (excl. Bank Holidays) £1.60 per week, Saturday/Sunday, normal rates. Children of UB40s 80p per week, excl. Bank Holidays. Saturday/ Sunday normal junior rate. Further details from Civic Centre, Pelham Road, Immingham; Tel. 0469 572763.

Best methods/baits   Use general coarse methods and baits.

Facilities   Shops/toilets/food in Immingham.

Disabled facilities   Two wheelchair-bound anglers can be accomodated each day.

LAKESIDE FARM, CAYTHORPE

Atlas Page 202 C.3/0.7

Two lakes, the smaller of which is reserved for coarse fishing. Most species, including quality tench in summer and large pike (20lb+) in winter.

How to get there   From Grantham, take the A607 north towards Lincoln. After Normanton (8 miles) the lake entrance is on the left, just after a hump-back bridge. Drive down to the house before fishing. Free parking.

Day tickets   Adult/junior/OAP £3. Available at the site, or contact Lakeside Farm; Tel. 0400 72758.

Best methods/baits   All recognised techniques and baits may be used.

Facilities   Toilets on site; nearest shop in Caythorpe village.

Disabled facilities   Swims suitable for wheelchairs, but with caution (no specially designed facilities).

LAKESIDE HOLIDAY PARK

Atlas Page 205 H.5/4.3

A 6-acre lake at North Somercotes, near Louth, containing rudd, carp (26lb+), tench, bream, roach and pike. Fishing available only April to October.

How to get there   Take the B1200 east from Louth, then A1031 north. Look for signs to North Somercotes on right.

Day tickets   For details, contact Mr P Reed, Lakeside Holiday Park, North Somercotes; Tel. 0507 358315.

Best methods/baits   Use general coarse methods and baits.

Restrictions   Fishing for campers only; not available to the general public.

Facilities   Shop/toilets on camp site.

LEGBOURNE MILL FISHING POND

Atlas Page 205 H.5/4.3

A small fishing pond containing tench, carp and rudd. Fishing is available all year.

How to get there   From Louth, take the A157 south-east for about 3 miles to Legbourne.

Day tickets   Season ticket only, £75 per annum plus VAT; available from R. Oliver, Legbourne Mill, Louth; Tel. 0507 607432.

Best methods/baits   Use general coarse methods and baits.

Facilities   Shops/food in Louth or Legbourne.

Rivers

THE LINCOLNSHIRE DRAINS

The Lincolnshire Drains are a man-made, criss-cross of water courses which protects the Eastern flatlands from North Sea floodwaters. Around the Boston area, four Drains – the Sibsey Trader, the South Forty Foot, the West Fen drain and the Upper Hobhole – each provide excellent sport with significant numbers of quality fish. Although bream and roach predominate, carp of up to 20lb are quite common, while the pike population is steadily increasing, with 20lb+ specimens a major attraction for the enthusiast. Six *Angling Times* Hotspots are to be found on the stretch.

The Lincolnshire Drains.

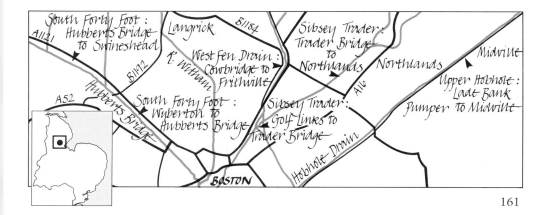

SIBSEY TRADER, GOLF LINKS TO TRADER BRIDGE
Atlas Page 202 D.1/0.6

A wide (30-yard) stretch with almost no flow in summer, depth 2–3ft and marginal weed growth. Mainly bream and roach, plus perch, dace and bleak. Pleasure nets are often 70lb+, mainly bream. Typical roach nets are 4–20lb, and an odd big carp may also appear!

How to get there   From Boston, take the B1183 north towards Horncastle. Just outside Boston, turn down Willow Lane towards Stonebridge. Vehicular access is above and below the bridge, or via the golf club.

Day tickets   Adult £1.50; junior/OAP 75p; available from bailiffs on the bank, or in advance from local tackle shops.

Best methods   Bream – leger or waggler close to the far bank; roach – light canal rig or pole.

Best baits   Casters, worm, bread, maggots, squatts or pinkies.

Hotspot Tips

- For good roach, use seed baits in summer, but punched bread in winter.
- Look for bream shoals upstream and downstream of Stonebridge.
- Catch the best summer roach between Stonebridge and the Golf Links.

SIBSEY TRADER, TRADER BRIDGE TO NORTHLANDS
Atlas Page 202 D.1/0.5

A very slow flowing, 30-yard-wide stretch, 2–3ft deep, with summer marginal weed and lilies. Typical catches include bream and roach, with perch, dace, bleak and carp. Expect 20–30lb bream nets, or 8–10lb roach nets, but 100lb+ catches are also quite common!

How to get there   Follow the B1183 Boston to Horncastle road north to Frithville (about 4 miles). Before the bridge, turn right towards Trader Bridge; the road runs alongside the drain. Or, take the A16 north to Sibsey; turn left opposite the school, towards Trader Bridge.

Day tickets   Adult £1.50; junior/OAP 75p; available from bailiffs on the bank, or in advance from local tackle shops.

Best methods   Bream – leger or waggler at the far bank; roach – pole just beyond the marginal weed.

Best baits   Casters, worm, red and bronze maggots, plus hemp. tares and various seed baits.

Hotspot Tips

- For the best fishing, look for coloured water.
- Pegs 261–290 and 351–400 give the best sport.
- A weed rake can be useful for clearing the swim in summer.

Netting the bream.

WEST FEN DRAIN, COWBRIDGE TO FRITHVILLE
Atlas Page 202 D.1/0.5

A typical Lincoln Drain stretch; up to 40 yards wide, fairly deep (4–6ft), minimal flow and minimal weed. Excellent roach, some reaching 2lb; typical bream catches are 10–50lb (individual fish to 7lb); perch to 2lb. Pike fishing also provides good sport.

How to get there Follow the B1183 north from Boston to Cowbridge. The drain runs alongside the road; the left bank had good vehicular access and is the most popular among anglers.

Day tickets Free fishing.

Best methods Bream – waggler or leger; roach – use pole tactics.

Best baits Bream – breadflake, or occasionally a caster-worm cocktail; roach – seed baits and maggots.

Disabled facilities Vehicular access close to swims.

Hotspot Tips

- The best fish normally locate in the middle of the drain.
- Find coloured water and you'll find feeding bream.
- Cowbridge Locks to Richardson Bridge is the most likely area for good bream.

SOUTH FORTY FOOT: WYBERTON TO HUBBERTS BRIDGE
Atlas Page 202 D.1/0.6

A 40-yard-wide section, depth 6–8ft. Heavy marginal weed (a swim drag may be a useful here). Mainly roach, with summer dace and some unpredictable bream catches. Typical roach nets are 7–8lb, although 20lb is possible if they're feeding well on seed baits.

How to get there Take the A1121 from Boston west towards Sleaford. The first bridge after the mini-roundabout is Wyberton Bridge. For Hubberts Bridge, follow the A1121 for about 3 miles.

Day tickets Adult £1.50; junior/OAP 75p; available from the bailiff on the bank, or in advance from either the shop at Hubberts Bridge or local tackle shops.

Best methods Fish a waggler, first on the shelf, just over the weed; move to the middle as fish go off the feed.

Best baits Bread, casters, worm, squatts, pinkies, large maggots, hemp or tares.

Facilities Shop at Hubberts Bridge.

Hotspot Tips

- Stick with the waggler – leger tactics are generally unsuccessful here.
- Roach are best above and below Wyberton Bridge, or at Hubberts Bridge.
- Most of the fish are in a distinct channel, beyond the marginal weed.

SOUTH FORTY FOOT: HUBBERTS BRIDGE TO SWINESHEAD
Atlas Page 202 D.1/0.6

A 35-yard-wide, 4–7ft deep section. Poor flow; bottom shelves away beyond marginal weed. Mostly roach, skimmer bream and dace; better bream are elusive. Fishing often poor early season, but improves later, with 10lb+ roach nets and pike of 30lb+. Recently-dredged Donington reaches are unpredictable, but worth a try!

How to get there Follow the A1121 from Boston towards Sleaford. At Swineshead (about 6 miles), the Bridge is immediately on the left by the Barge Hotel.

Day tickets Adult £1.50; junior/OAP 75p; available from bailiffs on the bank, or in advance from tackle shops at either Hubberts Bridge or in Boston.

Best methods Waggler between marginal weed and middle.

Best baits Casters, bread, worms, squatts, pinkies, large maggots and seed baits in summer.

Facilities Food/toilets at the Barge Hotel; shops in Hubberts Bridge or Boston.

Hotspot Tips

- In windy conditions, the leger will come into its own.
- At Swineshead in winter, roach and perch shoals pack in close to the bridge; but beware – the pike often follow them!

UPPER HOBHOLE: LADE BANK PUMPER TO MIDVILLE
Atlas Page 202 D.2/0.3

A 20-yard wide, 5–6ft deep section with minimal weed. Huge stocks of common and silver bream, plus roach, dace and bleak. An average bream net is 20lb, but 90lb is possible! Excellent pike fishing in winter.

How to get there Take the A16 north from Boston towards Spilsby. At Stickney (8 miles), turn right to Midville and Eastville, then to Midville Bridge (3 miles). Vehicular access is to both banks, downstream from the bridge.

Day tickets   Free fishing, but matches are held here by New Leake AC; check with Tom Cuttleditch, Bass Farm, Stickford, Boston for dates.

Best methods   In most conditions use a pole, but light leger is best in a bream shoal.

Best baits   Bread, casters, worm, squatts and pinkies.

Disabled facilities   Good vehicular access, but beware of steep banks.

Hotspot Tips

❦ If you locate a bream shoal, a light leger will be most successful.

❦ The best swims are midway along the section, or from Midville Bridge to the Duke of Wellington pub.

LOUTH C.A.W.A.C. LAKE
Atlas Page 205 H.5/4.3

A 1-acre, club-owned lake in Louth which contains roach, Crucian carp and tench (up to 5lb). Fishing is available all year.

How to get there   From Lincoln, take the A158 east to Horncastle, then the A153 north-east to Louth.

Day tickets   Annual permits: £30; for details, contact the Club Secretary, P. Collins, 18–20 Upgate, Louth.

Best methods/baits   Use general coarse methods and baits.

Facilities   Shops/toilets/food in Louth town.

MILL ROAD FISHING LAKES
Atlas Page 205 H.9/4.7

A two-lake complex in Addlethorpe, near Skegness, totalling 2¼ acres and containing large tench (to 7lb), large carp (to 29lb), roach, rudd, perch and bream. Fishing in season only – March to December.

How to get there   From Lincoln, head east on the A158 via Horncastle towards Skegness. At Burgh le Marsh (5 miles before Skegness), turn left to Addlethorpe.

Day tickets   Adult /junior/OAP £2.50; available from Mr P. Cumberworth (Tel. 0754 767586).

Best methods/baits   The hotter the weather, the better bread works.

Restrictions   No boilies or groundbaits. No night fishing.

Facilities   Shops in Addlethorpe village.

NORTH INGS FARM LAKE
Atlas Page 202 C.7/0.3

A 1-acre lake which provides fishing all year. Mainly roach, tench, rudd, tench and carp (up to 9lb).

How to get there   From Sleaford, take the A153 north (about 3 miles), then B1188 to Ruskington and Dorrington (3 miles).Look for signs to North Ings Farm.

Day tickets   Adult £2; junior/OAP £1; available from the farmhouse; Tel. 0526 832327.

Best methods/baits   Use general coarse methods and baits.

Restrictions   No groundbait.

Facilities   Shop in Dorrington village.

OASBY LAKES
Atlas Page 202 C.3/0.7

Located at Oasby village, near Grantham. Three small lakes, all inter-connected. Mainly carp (up to 20lb), plus large roach.

How to get there   From Grantham, take the A52 east, then B6403 north and turn right to Welby, then left into Oasby village. Bear left at the pub; fishing is ¼ mile on the left. Free car parking.

Day tickets   Adult £3 for two rods; junior/OAP £1.50; available on the bank, or from Gilbert's Fuschias and Fishing garden centre.

Best methods   Carp or roach – use standard techniques.

Best baits   Roach – maggots, sweetcorn.

Restrictions   No keepnets for carp. Hemp or particle baits must not be used.

Facilities   Drinks available at garden centre. Nearest shop and pub in Oasby village (¼ mile).

OHAM LAKE
Atlas Page 205 H.8/4.4

A small coarse fishery of just over ¼ acre, located in the village of Maltby le Marsh, near Mablethorpe.

How to get there   From Louth, take the A157 south-east for about 12 miles to Maltby le Marsh. Look for signs to Oham Lake.

Day tickets   Adult £2.50; available on
   site. Details available from Mr
   Beckenham; Tel. 05074 50623.
Best methods/baits   Use general coarse
   methods and baits.
Restrictions   Use barbless hooks only.
Facilities   Tackle shop at venue;
   shops/toilets/food in Maltby le Marsh or
   in Mablethrope (2½ miles).
Disabled facilities   Perfect for disabled
   and wheelchaired anglers.

ORCHARD FISHERIES, WINTERINGHAM
Atlas Page 202 G.3/3.8

This ½-acre pond offers dawn until dusk
coarse fishing all year. Expect mainly
tench roach and bream, plus carp to 14lb.

How to get there   From Scunthorpe, take
   the A1077 north for about 6 miles; look
   for signs to Winteringham on the left.
Day tickets   Adult £1.50/junior/OAP £1;
   available from T. Smith, Sycamore
   House, Silver Street, Winteringham;
   Tel. 0724 732498.
Best methods/baits   Use general coarse
   methods and baits.
Facilities   Shop in Winteringham village.
Disabled facilities   Only in dry
   conditions.

PASTURE HOUSE FISHERY
Atlas Page 205 G.7/3.5

A 10½-acre lake situated at Barton-on-
Humber, and which contains common
bream, tench, roach, perch, rudd and carp.
Fishing is available all year.

How to get there   Take the A15 north
   from Lincoln to Barton-on-Humber
   (about 35 miles, via M180). Look for
   signs to Pasture Road North.
Day tickets   Adult £2; junior £1.50;
   available on the bank, from the house,
   or contact Mrs K. Smith; Tel. 0652
   635119.
Best methods/baits   Use general coarse
   methods and baits.
Facilities   Shops/toilets/food in Barton-
   on-Humber.
Disabled facilities   Good access for
   disabled and wheelchair anglers.

PICKWORTH HALL LAKES
Atlas Page 202 C.3/0.9

A picturesque venue providing excellent
fishing. Mainly roach, bream and tench,
plus large carp (to 20lb).

How to get there   Leave Grantham on the
   A52 (east); turn right after 3 miles and
   follow road through Ropsley, then
   Sapperton, to Pickworth. Free car
   parking.
Day tickets   Adult £2.50; available on the
   site (collect tickets from Pickworth Hall
   before fishing) or in advance from the
   Hall.
Best methods   Carp – use floating bait in
   warmer weather, otherwise recognised
   carp techniques. In cooler weather, pole
   fishing with pinkies can be very
   effective.
Facilities   Nearest shop and pub in
   Pickworth village.

REVESBY RESERVOIR
Atlas Page 205 H.4/4.7

Two large lakes situated near Horncastle.
Totalling over 42 acres, containing
excellent bream, roach and tench, plus
large carp and pike (to 20lb+). Fishing is
available only in season – 16th June to
14th March.

How to get there   From Horncastle, take
   the A153 south, then B1183 east (after 2
   miles). Revesby is at the B1183/A155
   junction.
Day tickets   Adult £3; junior £1.50; OAP
   £2; available from Revesby Estate Office,
   Revesby; Tel. 0507 568395.
Best methods/baits   Use general coarse
   methods and baits.
Restrictions   No night fishing. Sundays
   are reserved for match fishing, but
   remaining pegs are available for day
   tickets.
Facilities   Shop in Revesby.

RICHMOND LAKES
Atlas Page 205 G.6/4.6

Three lakes at North Hykeham, totalling
almost 40 acres. One lake contains carp
and mixed species, the second contains
mixed species, the third contains
principally pike. Fishing is available all
year.

Day tickets   Adult £2; available on the bank. Details from L. Kirk, Richmond Lakes, Richmond Drive, North Hykeham; Tel. 0522 681329.

Best methods/baits   Use general coarse methods and baits. Pink maggots work well here.

Facilities   Shops in North Hykeham.

Disabled facilities   Access to some swims available for disabled anglers.

ROD AND LINE CARAVAN PARK
Atlas Page 202 D.7/0.2

A 1-acre lake, located in a caravan park at Lymm Bank, Thorpe St Peter, which provides free fishing for anglers staying at the site. Mainly roach, tench (to 3lb), rudd, bream and chub, plus mirror and common carp. Fishing is available all year.

How to get there   From Skegness, head south on the A52 towards Wainfleet. Turn onto the B1195 and look for signs to Thorpe St Peter.

Day tickets   (Non-residents): adult £2 per rod; available from the house at the caravan park. Booking by phone (Mrs Shaw; Tel. 0754 880494) is advisable in peak summer periods.

Best methods/baits   Use general coarse methods and baits.

Facilities   Shop/toilets at the site.

Disabled facilities   Suitable for disabled and wheelchair anglers.

ROSSWAYS WATER
Atlas Page 202 D.1/0.8

An attractive, 1-acre tree-lined former clay pit, a few miles south of Boston. A difficult fishing venue, with perch, roach, tench, rudd and bream, in addition to some very large carp of up to 25lb.

How to get there   Drive south from Boston on the A16 towards Spalding and after about 2 miles, signposted opposite Murco garage. The fishery is at 189, London Road; parking available on site.

Day tickets   Adult/junior/OAP £2 per rod. Available on site, but numbers are limited and advance booking is advised. Night fishing by arrangement only.

Best methods/baits   Use any recognised coarse technique and baits. Carp fishing is best with float tackle at the near bank.

Restrictions   No nut baits; no groundbait; no particle baits. No sacking of carp.

Facilities   Toilets/cafe/tackle & bait on site. Nearest shop/pub in Wyberton village.

Disabled facilities   Some swims suitable for disabled anglers.

SWAN LAKE
Atlas Page 202 D.7/0.2

A 1¼-acre lake located on a caravan site at Thorpe Culvert, near Wainfleet; fishing available all year, for caravan site patrons only.

How to get there   From Skegness, head south on the A52 towards Wainfleet. Turn onto the B1195 and look for signs to Thorpe Culvert.

Day tickets   Available only to park residents; for details, contact Mrs Caton; Tel. 0754 880469.

Best methods/baits   Use general coarse methods and baits.

Facilities   Shop/toilets on caravan site.

Disabled facilities   Very suitable for disabled and wheelchair anglers.

SYCAMORE LAKES, BURGH LE MARSH
Atlas Page 202 D.6/0.1

Three lakes totalling 4 acres, containing carp (to 20lb), tench, rudd, roach and golden orfe. Expect particularly large bags of tench. Fishing available during season, March to November.

How to get there   From Horncastle, take the A158 east to Skegness; Burgh le Marsh is about 4 miles before Skegness.

Day tickets   Adult £3 per rod, 0600–dusk; £5 for two rods; juniors £1.50 per rod; available on the bank, or contact Mrs J. Giraldez; Tel. 0754 810749. Evening permits (1700hrs to dusk) £1.50 per rod.

Best methods/baits   Use general coarse methods and baits.

Restrictions   No particle baits.

Facilities   Bait available on site.

Disabled facilities   Suitable near car park for disabled and wheelchair anglers.

TOTHBY LAKE, ALFORD
Atlas Page 205 H.9/4.7

This 2-acre lake is available for coarse fishing all year, and contains carp, roach, bream, tench and perch (to 3lb).

How to get there   From Skegness, head north on the A52; at Mumby, bear left onto B1449 to Alford.

Day tickets   Adult £1.50; available from Alford tackle shops: H.N. Thorley, Market Place, or Windmill Pet Stores, High Street, Alford; Tel. 0507 463505.

Best methods/baits   Use general coarse methods and baits.

Restrictions   Under 16s may only fish when an adult is in attendance at the lake.

Facilities   Shops/toilets in Alford.

Disabled facilities   Several pegs are available for disabled and wheelchair anglers.

THE UPPER WELLAND
Atlas Page 202 C.5/1.6

A 19-mile stretch of the Welland, upstream and downstream of Stamford. Fishing rights along this stretch are owned by Stamford Welland AAA. An excellent winter fishery, lots of summer weed due to shallowness. The stretch down Water Street and the first three meadows upstream is free fishing.

How to get there   Access to the river banks is from Stamford town centre, or at points along the river. For details contact Stamford Welland AAA, Mr Bates; Tel. 0780 51060, or Bob's Tackle Shop, 13A Foundry Road, Stamford; Tel. 0780 54541.

Day tickets   No day tickets: club book only; adult £10; juniors £2.50.

Best methods/baits   Casters and bronze maggots trotted through on the stick-float, or pole in the bays and eddies where the roach and chub hold up.

Facilities   Shops/toilets in Stamford town centre.

Disabled facilities   A couple of places along Water Street are suitable for disabled and wheelchair anglers.

WELLINGTON ANGLING CLUB LAKE
Atlas Page 205 H.5/4.3

A ½-acre lake at Linden Walk, Louth; fishing rights are owned by Wellington Angling Club, with fishing available all year. Main species include roach, bream, Crucian carp, tench, rudd and perch.

How to get there   From Sleaford, take the A153 north-east to Louth (about 37 miles).

Day tickets   Annual permits only: adult £6; ladies/junior/OAP £3; family £8.50. Membership includes access to 400-yard stretch of the River Witham. Details from the Club Secretary, Mr Foster; Tel. 0507 602581.

Best methods/baits   Use general coarse methods and baits.

Restrictions   Members must live within 10-mile radius of Louth.

Facilities   Shops in Louth town centre.

WEST ASHBY LAKES
Atlas Page 205 H.4/4.7

These two gravel pits – one of 5 acres, one of 2 acres – lie just north of Horncastle and are basically carp fishing waters, though some good-sized tench, chub and roach may be taken. Typical carp here range from 10–25lb, with an average of about 13lb.

How to get there   From Lincoln, take the A158 east to Horncastle (about 21 miles) and turn north onto A153. West Ashby is about 2 miles north of Horncastle; look for signs to the lakes and park nearby.

Day tickets   Adult/junior/OAP £4. Available on site; prior booking is necessary.

Best methods/baits   Use any recognised coarse technique and baits. Use permitted specialist methods for carp.

Restrictions   Use only barbless hooks. No hair rigs. No boilies. No particle baits.

Facilities   Nearest shop/pub in West Ashby or Horncastle.

Disabled facilities   Some swims suitable for disabled anglers; please phone for further advice (see above).

WESTFIELD LAKES
Atlas Page 205 G.7/3.5

A two-lake complex at Far Ings Road, Barton-on-Humber, available for fishing all year. The 10-acre Hotel Lake contains common bream, roach, mirror carp, tench, perch and rudd. The 8-acre Bridge Lake has similar species.

How to get there   Take the A15 north from Lincoln to Barton on Humber (about 35 miles, via M180). Look for signs to Pasture Road North.

Day tickets   Adult £2; juniors/OAPs/
disabled £1; tickets must be obtained
from Westfield Lake Hotel before
fishing; Tel. 0652 32313.

Best methods/baits   Use general coarse
methods and baits.

Facilities   Shops/toilets in Barton-on-
Humber and in hotel complex.

WINTER BROTHERS LAKES
Atlas Page 205 H.0/3.7

A small, privately-owned (but available for
public angling) lake containing bream (to
9lb), tench (to 4lb), roach, rudd, perch and
very big carp – a 21lb specimen has been
taken here. Fishing available all year.

How to get there   From Scunthorpe, take
the M180/A180 east; 3 miles before
Immingham, turn left onto A160, then
left to East Halton.

Day tickets   Adult £1.50; junior/OAP
75p; available from the house on the
site. Also 5-day (Monday-Friday) permits
for disabled and OAPs: £2. For bookings,
contact Mr Winter; Tel. 0469 40238.

Best methods/baits   Use general coarse
methods and baits.

Disabled facilities   Good access to
swims for disabled.

Rivers

RIVER WITHAM

The wide and featureless, slow-flowing
Witham, with its man-made banks and
flat fenland stretches, is a river of many
moods as catches vary from non-existent
to mind-blowing. In summer, the roach
are big and the bream even bigger, but as
winter draws near, roach begin to predominate and float fishing supersedes leger
tactics.

The River Witham.

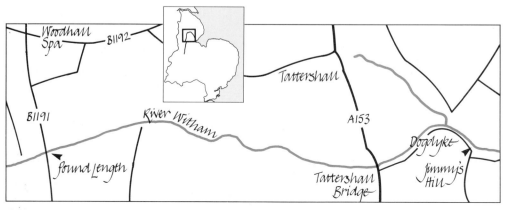

POUND LENGTH
Atlas Page 205 H.0/4.8

A wide, steep-banked section with some well cut-away spots. Most pegs have 12ft depth at casting distance; pole anglers use the inside ledge. Careful fishing is needed, but expect roach and bream, hopefully in 10lb+ quantities.

How to get there   Take the B1191 west from Woodhall Spa; turn on to the west bank at Kirkstead bridge (by the pub and caravan site). Pound Length begins where the road and river meet.
Day tickets   Adult £2; junior/OAP £1; available on the bank.
Best methods   Bream – leger; roach – lightly shotted waggler or pole.
Best baits   Maggots (bronze or red), casters, red worm.
Facilities   Food/toilets at the pub.

Hotspot Tips

❧ Some hemp loosefeed will tempt some good roach.
❧ The first 6 pegs near the pub can produce good winter roach.
❧ The fish here are smart – use a small hook and a fine bottom, well presented, and you'll get a good net!

JIMMY'S HILL
Atlas Page 205 H.1/4.9

A featureless section where plumbing is needed to check variable depths (average 10ft). Winter levels are low, so standing just off the bank edge is possible. Mainly roach, with 1lb fish and 20lb nets possible.

How to get there   At Tattershall Bridge on the A153, turn south through Dogdyke and drive beyond the mouth of the River Bane. Jimmy's Hill is between Dogdyke and Chapel Hill.
Day tickets   Adult £2; junior/OAP £1; available on the bank.
Best methods   Most species – waggler with conventional shotting and bait close to bottom. Loosefeed as necessary.
Best baits   Maggots (mainly bronze, try red for a change).

Hotspot Tips

❧ For best results, keep a trickle of feed going in.
❧ The roach here like a slowed down bait, so light shotting may need changing for 3BB bulk.

WOODTHORPE HALL LAKE
Atlas Page 205 H.9/4.5

A 1-acre lake at Strubby, near Alford, providing coarse fishing all year. Mainly rudd, tench, Crucian, mirror and common carp.

How to get there   From Skegness, head north on the A52; at Mumby, bear left onto B1449 to Alford.
Day tickets   Adult season ticket only, £25; details from Pets 'n' Plants, Mablethorpe; Tel. 0507 473104.
Best methods/baits   Use general coarse methods and baits.
Restrictions   There is no bait for sale on site.
Facilities   Shop/toilets at caravan park.

NORFOLK

Wood Lakes near Downham Market.

ALDERFEN BROAD
Atlas Page 202 F.3/1.2

A 'challenging' water, situated just outside Neatishead on the Norfolk Broads. An ideal fishery for the angler wishing to specialise. Expect a large head of good-sized tench (to 7lb+), plus plenty of big bream (to 11lb).

How to get there   Take the A1151 north-east from Norwich; after Hoveton (8 miles), look for right turn to Neatishead and signs to Alderfen Broad.

Day tickets   Adult £5/boat/day; available from Wroxham Angling Centre, Station Road, Wroxham; Tel. 0603 782453.
Best methods/baits   Use recognised techniques/baits.
Restrictions   Boat fishing only.
Facilities   Shops/pubs in Neatishead.

BARTON BROAD
Atlas Page 202 F.3/1.2

A very large broad providing excellent coarse fishing for mixed species. Large bream shoals which are hard to track down, plus plenty of roach and eels which frequent the boat channels. Also good pike fishing in autumn and winter.

How to get there   Take the A1151 north-east from Norwich; after Hoveton (8 miles), look for right turn to Neatishead and signs to Barton Broad.
Day tickets   Free fishing but boat hire is essential; for hiring, contact Tom King at the Barton Angler pub; Tel. 0692 630740.
Best methods/baits   Use recognised techniques, or ask at the boat hire site.
Facilities   Nearest shop – Neatishead; nearest pub – Barton Angler.

BEESTON LAKE, NEATISHEAD
Atlas Page 202 F.3/1.2

A pleasant fishery, mainly tench (to 7lb+) fishing plus an occasional good-sized carp or bream; also hoardes of small rudd. Winter pike fishing is also good, with recent 28lb+ specimens taken.

How to get there   Take the A1151 north-east from Norwich; after Hoveton (8 miles), look for right turn to Neatishead and signs to Beeston Lake.
Day tickets   Adult £1; available from Mr Jeckell; Tel. 0692 630688.
Best methods/baits   Ask for advice from Mr Jeckell.
Facilities   Shops/toilets/food in Neatishead.

BLICKLING LAKE
Atlas Page 202 F.2/1.0

A small lake close to Blickling Hall (National Trust); fishing here is predominantly bream (4–9lb possible), plus tench (to 8lb+). Also very good fishing for roach, perch and eels, and some large carp of over 10lb.

How to get there   From Norwich take the A140 north to Aylsham, then bear left on B1354 to Blickling. Look for signs to Blickling Hall and the lake.
Day tickets   Adult £2.50; available on the bank from Mr Cooper (on behalf of the National Trust).
Best methods/baits   Use recognised techniques.
Facilities   Toilets/food at Blickling Hall.

BUXTON CLAY PIT
Atlas Page 202 F.1/1.2

An attractive, quite deep former clay pit of about 4 acres, with reed-beds and sand-bars, located near Buxton, near Norwich. Expect a good head of tench, roach, rudd, pike and bream, but only a few carp – although these are very big – perhaps in the upper 30lb region!

How to get there   Take the B1149 north-west from Norwich and after about 8 miles turn right on minor road towards Buxton and Hevingham. The pit is located behind some trees, after about 1½ miles. Parking on site.
Day tickets   Adult/junior/OAP £2.50 per rod. Available from the bailiff on bank.
Best methods/baits   Use any recognised coarse technique and baits.
Facilities   Nearest shop/pub in Buxton village.

RIVER BURE
WOODBASTWICK
Atlas Page 202 F.2/1.4

A 25-yard-wide section, with 5–8ft depth, steady tidal flow and very little weed. No shelves or channels. An ideal spot for autumn and winter fishing, with all swims providing good catches of roach – up to 30lb is possible.

How to get there   Take the A1151 Norwich-Wroxham road. At Rackheath (3 miles), turn right to Woodbastwick village, then follow sign to 'Marshes'. Park on the river bank, which is boarded to Cockshoot Broad.
Day tickets   Free fishing.
Best methods   Waggler, stick or pole. Use loosefeed.
Best baits   Maggots, casters.
Facilities   Nearest shop/pub, Woodbastwick.
Disabled facilities   Easy access for disabled via boarded walkways.

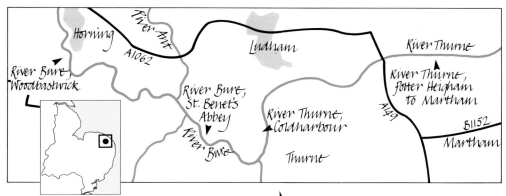

Hotspot Tips

❧ You'll catch roach from summer to Christmas, but September to November is best.

RIVER BURE
ST BENET'S ABBEY
Atlas Page 202 F.3/1.3

Between the confluences of the Ant, Thurne and Bure; strong tidal flow, 5–10ft depth. Downstream bed is littered with stone from abbey ruins; upstream is snag-free. Summer/autumn fishing is best, with roach, bream and eels; due to boats, early/late fishing is essential. Expect 10lb+ roach catches, plus bream and hybrids.

How to get there Take the A1151 from Norwich to Hoveton; turn east on A1062 to Ludham village. Turn right at The Dog pub, first right on concrete road across marshes. Park by abbey ruins – OFF the road.

Day tickets Annual ticket £4; day ticket 50p. Available from the Thrower Store in Ludham village (plus £3 signing fee for first year). Tickets must be obtained *before* fishing.

Best methods Stick float, waggler or loosefeed. Pole or feeder as alternatives.

Best baits Hemp, casters, maggots; mixed hook maggots for feeder.

Hotspot Tips

❧ Old-style groundbait bombardment is useless today.

❧ The best swims are in a 300-yard section by the rocks just left of the abbey.

RIVER BURE, WROXHAM
Atlas Page 202 F.3/1.3

A pleasant stretch of the Bure, but one which often provides only mediocre sport. Fishing from the bank, but is better from a boat. Most species, including roach and bream during summer and autumn.

How to get there Take the A1151 north-east from Norwich to Wroxham (8 miles). Enquire at local tackle shops for best access to river.

Day tickets Free fishing. Boat hire is available from local boatyards, or enquire at tackle shops.

Best methods/baits Use recognised techniques.

Facilities Shops/toilets/food available in Wroxham town.

BURE VALLEY LAKES FISHERIES
Atlas Page 202 F.2/1.0

A fishing complex near Aylsham, north Norfolk, comprising 10 acres of lakes (8–25ft deep) plus 1 mile of river, offering coarse fishing in a 2-acre lake set in quiet, beautiful country. Coarse fishing includes most species, but especially mirror carp (10–30lb specimens).

How to get there Take the A140 north from Norwich, and on the city outskirts bear left onto B1149 to Saxthorpe (about 15 miles), then turn right onto B1354. The fisheries are on the left (about 2 miles),

Day tickets Adult £3/rod/session (sessions are 0800–2000hrs or 2000-0800hrs). Booking essential; Tel. 026387 666.

Best methods/baits Use recognised techniques.

Restrictions   Carp fishing only until 1st October; general coarse fishing thereafter. Sessions limited to 20 rods only.

Facilities   Clubhouse/toilets/hot food on site; for non-anglers, Blickling Hall and other NT properties nearby.

Disabled facilities   Good access to some swims.

CHISWICK PIT
Atlas Page 202 E.2/1.5

A small farm pond, just north of Downham Market, with good numbers of roach and tench, plus mirror and common carp in the double-figure range.

How to get there   Take A47 west from Norwich via East Dereham to Swaffham, then A1122 to Stradsett (total 39 miles). Turn right onto A134, left at Shouldham Thorpe (2 miles) and after 1 mile take farm track on left. The pond is on the left, opposite the farmhouse.

Day tickets   Adult/junior/OAP £2.50. Only 3 permits issued daily; these must be purchased in advance during office hours from Stow Estates Office, Stow Bardolph; Tel. 0366 383194.

Best methods/baits   Use any recognised coarse technique and baits.

Restrictions   Fishing dawn to dusk only; no night fishing.

Facilities   Nearest shop/pub in Stow Bardolph.

CRANWORTH-WOODRISING CARP LAKE
Atlas Page 202 E.4/1.6

A fairly small farm pond (man-made), south of East Dereham. A mainly carp lake, but also containing some tench in shallow, coloured water.

How to get there   Take the B1108 west from Norwich towards Watton and at Hingham (about 16 miles) turn right on minor road to Shipden, then Cranworth. The lake is just after Jubilee Farm in Cranworth village.

Day tickets   Adult £2.50; junior/OAP junior/OAP £2. Available from Jubilee Farm; Tel. 0362 820702.

Best methods/baits   Use any recognised coarse technique and baits. Specialist carp methods may be required.

Facilities   Nearest shop/pub in Cranworth.

DOCKING POND
Atlas Page 202 E.1/0.9

The village pond at Docking, mid-way between Hunstanton and Fakenham. A 1-acre former clay pit, providing good mixed coarse fishing for Crucian carp, roach and tench. Also common carp to 10lb.

How to get there   From King's Lynn, take the A148 Fakenham road and bear left onto B1153 after about 8 miles. At Great Bircham, turn left to Docking; the pond is in the village. Parking available nearby.

Day tickets   Adult £2; under 16/OAP £1. Only eight tickets are issued daily and must be purchased on the day of fishing, from Roy's Shop in the village; Tel. 0485 518430 (the shop opens at 0730).

Best methods/baits   Use any recognised coarse technique and baits.

Restrictions   Fishing only from 0830–2300. No Sunday fishing.

Facilities   Nearest shop/pub in Docking village.

Disabled facilities   Disabled anglers may fish here; contact Roy's shop for availability.

GRANARY LAKES
Atlas Page 202 E.5/1.5

A village fishing 'complex' comprising four interconnected lakes, three small, one large, close to a hotel near Swaffham. Plenty of smaller coarse fish, including tench and Crucian carp, plus commons and mirrors of well over 10lb in all the lakes.

How to get there   Take the A47 west from Norwich through East Dereham to Necton village (total 22 miles) and turn right on minor road to Little Dunham. The lakes are close to the Granary Hotel in the village centre. Parking nearby.

Day tickets   Adult/junior/OAP £3.50. Available from the Granary Hotel (only in advance); Tel. 0328 701310.

Best methods/baits   Use any recognised coarse technique and baits.

Facilities   Accommodation/food/sports facilities available at hotel. Nearest shop in village.

Disabled facilities   Some swims suitable for disabled anglers.

GREAT MASSINGHAM VILLAGE POND
Atlas Page 202 E.3/0.9

A typical Norfolk village pond, mid-way between Fakenham and King's Lynn. Good angling for wild carp of small to fair-sized fish.

How to get there From the King's Lynn by-pass, drive west on the B1145, through Gayton (about 6 miles) and continue about 5 miles to left turn to Great Massingham. The pond is in the village centre; park nearby.
Day tickets Free fishing.
Best methods/baits Use carp methods and baits.
Facilities Nearest shop/pub in the village.
Disabled facilities Access is possible at some swims for disabled anglers.

HEACHAM RIVER
Atlas Page 202 E.2/0.9

A three-mile stretch of river water, containing dace (to 1lb), chub (to 3lb) and roach. Also occasional trout, dabs and flounders due to the water disgorging to the sea via a culvert.

How to get there Follow the A149 north from King's Lynn for about 9 miles; at Heacham, turn into the village and enquire at Heacham Tackle, 31 Kenwood Road, Heacham; Tel. 0485 70333, about various fishable sections.
Day tickets Free fishing.
Best methods/baits Use recognised techniques or ask at Heacham Tackle.
Facilities Shop/pub in Heacham village.

HEVINGHAM LAKES
Atlas Page 202 F.1/1.2

A pleasant holiday centre combined with three small lakes, a few miles north of Norwich. Mixed coarse fishing, with Crucians, roach, rudd, bream and tench, plus some common carp in the 10–20lb range.

How to get there From Norwich, head north-west on the B1149 about 6 miles and turn right on minor road to Hevingham. Continue for 1 mile; the fishery is on the left. Parking on site.
Day tickets Adult £2 per rod; under 16 £1.50 per rod. Available only in advance from the bungalow on site. For details of availability, contact Mr. Matthewson; Tel. 060548 368.

Best methods/baits Most species – use coarse techniques. Carp – use carp methods and baits.
Facilities Toilets/showers/caravan hire on site. Also touring caravan/camping holiday site. Nearest shop/pub in Hevingham village.
Disabled facilities Some swims suitable for disabled anglers.

HORSTEAD MILL
Atlas Page 202 F.2/1.2

A pleasant fishery, situated just outside Horstead village, with fast flowing water – an exception for this area! Good general coarse fishing with large shoals of dace (to 8oz) which feed all year.

How to get there Take the B1150 north from Norwich; Horstead is about ½ mile before Coltishall (8 miles).
Day tickets Free fishing.
Best methods/baits Use recognised techniques.
Facilities Shops/toilets/food in Horstead village.

HOVETON HALL LAKE
Atlas Page 202 F.2/1.2

An ideal lake for the younger angler, with plenty of small roach and tench (2–3lb) which are relatively easy to catch. Also some large carp (10–20lb). Located near Wroxham, Norfolk. Shallow, well-coloured water in summer provides the best sport.

How to get there From Norwich, take the A1151 north-east to Wroxham and Hoveton (8 miles); look for signs to Hoveton Hall and fishing lake.
Day tickets Adult £1.50; available from the cottage by the lake.
Best methods/baits Use recognised techniques.
Facilities Shops/toilets in Hoveton. Also Hoveton Hall (NT) available for non-anglers.

MARTHAM PITS
Atlas Page 202 E.9/1.5

A group of small, shallow, heavily-weeded pits containing plenty of tench (2–5lb) and hordes of small rudd and jack pike. Tench fishing is best early season but declines later as fishing increases. An occasional carp may also appear.

How to get there   From Norwich, head east on the A47; at Acle, take the A1064, then B1152 north to Martham. Look for signs to the fishery, or ask in Martham village.

Day tickets   Adult £3; available from 'Molly's Sweet Shop' in Martham village.

Best methods/baits   Use recognised techniques.

Facilities   Shops/food in Martham village.

MERE FARM POND
Atlas Page 202 E.9/1.2

Mere Farm is at Saxthorpe, about 5 miles south from Holt. A 1-acre farm pond, providing roach and eels, with wild carp (some up to 6lb+) as sport.

How to get there   From the northern outskirts of Norwich take the B1149 north-west to Saxthorpe village (about 16 miles). Drive over the River Bure, over crossroads, and the fishery is 1 mile on the left. Parking on site.

Day tickets   Adult £1.50, half day 90p, evening 60p; junior 50p all day; OAP 70p all day. Available from the farmhouse; Mrs Harris; Tel. 026 387883.

Best methods/baits   Use any recognised coarse technique and baits.

Facilities   Nearest shop/pub in Saxthorpe.

Disabled facilities   Very suitable for disabled and wheelchair anglers.

RINGLAND LAKES
Atlas Page E.9/1.6

A group of seven gravel pits of different sizes and containing a varied assortment of coarse fish – perch, pike, bream, rudd, tench and Crucian carp – about 8 miles west of Norwich. Expect mixed fishing in all the lakes, but mainly carp in the largest – Days Water.

How to get there   Head west on the A47 from Norwich and just after Taverham (about 6 miles) turn right towards Ringland via Longwater Lane (by The Roundwell pub). Go downhill, turn left at bottom, bear left and continue 1 mile. The fishery is on the right; parking on site.

Day tickets   Adult/junior/OAP £2. Also season tickets. Available from the bailiff on the bank.

Best methods/baits   Use any recognised coarse technique and baits.

Facilities   Nearest shop/pub Ringland village.

SCOULTON MERE
Atlas Page 202 E.6/1.7

A typical Norfolk mere – shallow and reeded, with excellent coarse fishing – tench in summer and very good pike in winter, with numerous jacks and large specimens.

How to get there   Take the B1108 west from Norwich to Hingham (about 15 miles), then Scoulton. The mere is on the right hand side of the road. Free car parking on site.

Day tickets   Adult/junior/OAP £2.50; available on the bank.

Best methods   Tench, roach – float; pike – leger with deadbait.

Best baits   Most baits are effective here.

Facilities   Shops and pub in Hingham (2 miles).

Disabled facilities   Disabled and wheelchair access to some swims.

SHROPHAM LAKES
Atlas Page 202 E.7/1.8

A large lake situated just west of Attleborough, containing a huge head of bream – a single day net in 1991 reached 139lb! Also plenty of tench and small pike which create an ideal venue for junior anglers.

How to get there   Follow the A11 south-west from Norwich to Attleborough (15 miles); then after 3 miles look for right turn to Shropham. In village, turn left after Watton Produce; the lake is 200 yards on the left. Free parking on site.

Day tickets   Season tickets (Wymondham & District AC) only; adult £17; junior/OAP £5; available from Wymondham Angling Centre, 17 Town Green, Wymondham; Tel. 0953 605417.

Best methods   Float or leger.

Best baits   Sweetcorn, casters, maggots, bread.

Facilities   Shop and pub in Shropham village (¼ mile).

Disabled facilities   Disabled (and some wheelchair) access to some swims.

SNETTERTON PITS
Atlas Page 202 E.6/1.8

Three large lakes in Snetterton village. The largest – Swan Lake – holds a very large head of bream, plus roach and very big carp. Excellent pike fishing in winter, with 20lb+ fish taken every season on deadbait.

How to get there   Follow the A11 south-west from Norwich, through Attleborough to Snetterton (about 19 miles). Turn right into village (opposite race-track), then left at T-junction. A track on the right leads past houses to the lakes. Free parking on site.

Day tickets   Adult/junior/OAP £4 for one rod, £5 for two rods; available on the bank.

Best methods   Bream, roach – use feeder.

Best baits   Sweetcorn, maggots, bread, boilies, hemp, peanuts.

Restrictions   No night fishing.

Facilities   Shops and pub in Snetterton village (½ mile).

Disabled facilities   Excellent access for disabled and wheelchair anglers on one lake.

 ## STALHAM BOATYARD
Atlas Page 202 F.7/1.2

An out-and-out winter fishery comprising docks and boatsheds. Average depth is 4ft, with no flow, weed or shelves. Expect roach, some bream and hybrids, with 10lb catches common when fish are located.

How to get there   Follow the A149 north from Potter Heigham. After 5 miles (just before Stalham) the location can be seen on the left.

Day tickets   Adult/junior/OAP £1; available from the boatyard offices.

Best methods   Loosefeed with small waggler; or, use a short line pole with elastic.

Best baits   Casters, maggots; use very small amounts.

Facilities   Shop/toilets at the boatyard.

SWANGEY LAKES
Atlas Page 202 E.7/1.8

Two lakes at Swangey, near Attleborough. The larger lake has a good head of carp, plus several large catfish (recently caught on cockles, intended for carp). The smaller lake has good tench (to 6lb+); day nets can reach 25lb.

How to get there   Follow the A11 south-west from Norwich to Attleborough (15 miles); turn right into West Carr Road, take first left, cross ford, take the track on the left to the lakes. Free parking on site.

Day tickets   Adult £5; evenings £3; available on the bank.

Best methods   Tench, roach – float; carp – leger.

Best baits   Sweetcorn, maggots, boilies.

Restrictions   No keepnets. No night fishing.

Facilities   Shops/toilets/food at Attleborough (2 miles); nearest pub Breckland Lodge (on A11, Attleborough, 1½ miles).

SWANTON MORLEY FISHERIES
Atlas Page 202 E.5/1.6

A group of three gravel pits – 65 acres in all – just north of East Dereham. Plenty of good-sized perch, rudd and tench, plus some large pike which provide excellent sport. Also some carp of various sizes.

How to get there   Take the A47 west from Norwich to East Dereham (16 miles) and turn right onto B1147. At Swanton Morley village (4 miles), go past The Papermakers pub, left at T-junction, then sharp right. Waterfall Farm is on the left; the fishery entrance is ¼ mile on the right. Parking on site. *Note*: be careful NOT to use the work's entrance.

Day tickets   Adult £1.50; junior/OAP 75p. Evening ticket: 75p. Also season tickets: adult £12; junior/OAP £6. Day tickets (after 0800) from Waterfall Farm; advance day tickets (SAE please) from Mrs Marsham, at the farm; or from Rod & Gun, Norwich Street, Dereham.

Best methods/baits   Use any recognised coarse technique and baits.

Restrictions   Fishing only from sunrise to sunset; no night fishing.

Facilities   Nearest shop/pub in Swanton Morley.

Disabled facilities   Some swims suitable for disabled anglers.

TASWOOD LAKES
Atlas Page 202 F.2/1.6

A group of four privately-owned, man-made lakes ranging from 1 to 3½ acres, due south of Norwich. A surprisingly good mixed fishery with roach, rudd, bream, tench, perch and pike, plus Crucian carp. Expect mirror carp in all the lakes, but the biggest (20–30lb) in the biggest lake!

How to get there   Head south from Norwich on the A140 to Newton Flotman (about 8 miles) and bear right on minor road through Flordon. After 1½ miles, take left turn towards Tasburgh; the lakes are about 200 yards on the left. Parking on site.

Day tickets   Adult/junior/OAP £2. Available from the owner on site. Also season tickets.

Best methods/baits   Use any recognised coarse technique and baits.

Facilities   Nearest shop/pub in Tasburgh village.

Disabled facilities   Some swims suitable for disabled anglers; please phone to check availability (see above).

Hooked!

THOMPSON WATER
Atlas Page 202 E.6/1.6

A very large, 30-acre lake near Watton, close to the Peddars Way. Plenty of roach, rudd, bream, tench and pike, with Crucian and common carp. By using selective baits, the water may well produce some carp in the 20lb region.

How to get there   Drive west from Norwich via the B1108 to Watton (22 miles) and turn left onto A1075. After about 1 mile, bear right to Merton, then Thompson village. At Thompson, take the road to Peddars Way (signposted); the lake is visible on the left. Park nearby and walk to the fishery.

Day tickets   Adult/junior/OAP £2. Available from the bailiff on the bank. For further information, contact Merton Estate Office, Watton, Thetford; Tel. 0953 883370.

Best methods/baits   Most species – use coarse techniques and baits. Carp – use specialist tackle and baits.

Facilities   Nearest shop/pub in Thompson.

Disabled facilities   The long walk to the water may be a deterrent to disabled anglers; phone for advice.

RIVER THURNE COLDHARBOUR
Atlas Page 202 F.3/1.2

A wide section (20 yards) with a steady tidal flow and depth of 4–8ft. No pronounced shelves or channels, a clean bottom and marginal weed in places. Expect summer and autumn roach, with pleasure nets approaching 20lb. Winter sport is often poor.

See p. 171 for location map.

How to get there   Take the A1151 from Norwich to Hoveton; turn east on A1062 to Ludham village. Turn right at The Dog pub, then at lane-end, turn right onto track to the river.

Day tickets   50p. Annual ticket £4 from the Thrower Store in Ludham village (signing fee of £3 for first year). Tickets must be obtained *before* fishing.

Best methods   Stick float or waggler with loosefeed.

Best baits   Maggots, casters. No groundbait required.

Facilities   Food/toilets at The Dog pub.

Hotspot Tips

- Fish just off the bottom to avoid troublesome eels.
- Fish early or late to avoid those boats!
- The best swims are 300 yards downstream of the access point.

RIVER THURNE POTTER HEIGHAM to MARTHAM
Atlas Page 202 F.3/1.4

A nicely paced water, with 5–8ft depth and some marginal lily pads in summer. Expect roach, bream and pike, although sport can vary as salt tides move the fish in and out. Check with local tackle shops before fishing.

See p. 171 for location map.

How to get there   Take the A1151 from
Norwich to Hoveton; turn east on
A1062 to Potter Heigham. A footpath
runs the length of the bank upstream to
Martham.
Day tickets   Free fishing.
Best methods   Roach – loosefeed casters
or maggots. Bream – open feeder or plain
leger with cereal bait.
Best baits   Summer – bread; winter –
worm.
Disabled facilities   Good access via the
footpath.

Hotspot Tips

❦ If you're looking for pike, first find the
roach – the pike will follow!
❦ For good bream, try the swims around
High's Mill.
❦ A winter hotspot for roach is around
the village bridges.

RIVER TIFFEY
Atlas Page 202 F.1/1.7

A slow-flowing river stretch, average depth
4ft, located just east of Wymondham.
Mainly good quality roach and some chub
(to 7lb), plus very large pike; a recent
specimen was 22lb, caught on legered
deadbait.

How to get there   Take the A11 south-
west to Wymondham (9 miles); turn
right onto B1135 to Kimberley, then
onto B1108. Take next right turn; after
200 yards, the river runs under the road.
Free parking near the site.
Day tickets   Season tickets only: adults
£12; juniors/OAPs £6. Available from
Kimberley Hall Estate, Carleton
Forehoe, Wymondham, Norfolk.
Best methods   Light float or waggler.
Best baits   Maggots, casters.
Facilities   Nearest shop/pub (The Cock)
in Barford (2 miles).
Disabled facilities   Stiles prevent access
to disabled anglers.

TRINITY BROADS
Atlas Page 202 F.8/1.4

A fishing complex, comprising broads at
Ormesby St Margaret, Ormesby St
Michael, Rollesby and Filby. Excellent
fishing from the bank or boat. Large bream
shoals (fish to 8lb+) plus roach, tench and
perch. Also very good pike, with 20-
pounders each year and the odd 30lb+ fish.

How to get there   Take the A47 east from
Norwich; at Acle, take the A1064 to
Filby (6 miles). Ormesby and Rollesby
are to the north.
Day tickets   Free fishing from the bank;
boat hire available from John Barnes,
Filby Bridge Cafe; Tel. 0493 368142.
Best methods/baits   Use recognised
techniques.
Facilities   Shop/food in local villages.

WAVENEY VALLEY LAKES
Atlas Page 202 F.2/1.8

A commercial fishery near Harleston, on
the Norfolk-Suffolk border. Eight mature
gravel pits, from 2–5 acres, providing
excellent coarse fishing, renowned for
huge carp of 20–30lb. Expect also Crucian
carp, tench, roach, rudd, bream, perch,
pike and eels. Fishing for smaller fish is
generally quite easy; the monster
specimens can be a lot more difficult!

How to get there   Head south from
Norwich on the A140 for about 12 miles
and turn left onto the B1134 via Pulham
Market to Harleston. Bear left onto the
A143 to Wortwell (about 2 miles), where
the lakes entrance is signposted. Parking
on site.
Day tickets   Adult/junior/OAP £3.50 one
rod; £6 two rods per 12-hour session.
Weekly ticket £65 for 2 rods (seven 24-
hour sessions). Available from the
site shop when open; if closed, bailiffs patrol
the banks. *Note*: a second ticket must be
purchased for night fishing. For details;
Tel. 098 686 676.
Best methods/baits   Most species – use
coarse techniques and baits. Carp – use
advanced rigs with boilies or multiple
baits.
Restrictions   No dogs allowed on site.
Facilities   Toilets/showers on site. Also
caravan (touring and static)/camping
facilities for hire. Food/tackle & bait
sold on site. Nearest shop/pub in
Wortwell.
Disabled facilities   Some swims suitable
for disabled anglers; phone for advice
(see above).

WEYBREAD GRAVEL PITS
Atlas Page 202 F.2/1.8

A complex of five large gravel pits, near
the Waveney Valley Lakes. Only three pits
offer day tickets – No. 1 (58 swims), No. 2
(36 swims) and Ocean Pit (95 swims). Nos.

1 and 2 are mixed fisheries – expect bream, carp, roach and skimmers. Ocean Pit is known better for its roach and bream.

How to get there   Take the A140 south from Norwich and after about 14 miles turn left onto B1134 to Harleston. Continue on B1116 to Weybread; after crossing the river, the pits are on either side of the road. Follow signs to the separate car parks for each lake.

Day tickets   Adult £2.50; junior/OAP £1. Membership £10 for the two club lakes; £24 to fish all five lakes. Available only in advance from Waveney Tackle, Harleston; Tel. 0379 852248, or other local tackle shops.

Best methods   No. 1 pit – waggler or tip. No. 2 – as for No. 1, but also pole. Ocean Pit – feeder or waggler.

Best baits   Maggot, casters, corn and boilies work well in all pits.

Facilities   Nearest shops/pubs in Harleston or Weybread.

Disabled facilities   Ocean Pit and Middle Pit have very good swims for disabled and wheelchair anglers.

WOOD LAKES
Atlas Page 202 D.8/1.7

A group of four lakes – one large, three small – totalling 20 acres, near Downham Market. An excellent 'family-fishing' water, with a good head of roach, rudd, bream and tench, and also for the carp specialist, with some very big carp in the 20–30lb region.

How to get there   Take the A10 south from the King's Lynn by-pass for about 12 miles to Stow Bardolph; turn right onto minor road and at sharp bend (500 yards before bridge) drive straight on. The lakes are on the right, just before Stow Bridge.

Day tickets   Two 12-hour shifts, 0800–2000 and 2000–0800: adult £4.50; junior/OAP £3.50. 24 hours £6 and £5 respectively. Available from the kiosks when open; if closed, bailiffs patrol the banks; Tel. 0366 810585 for details.

Best methods/baits   Most species – use coarse techniques and baits. Carp – use specialist methods and baits.

Restrictions   None, just use common-sense!.

Facilities   Toilets and showers available. Camping/caravan facilities on site.

Nearest shop/pub in Stow Bardolph or Downham Market.

Disabled facilities   Many swims suitable for disabled and wheelchair anglers.

RIVER YARE, MARLINGFORD
Atlas Page 202 F.1/1.5

A pleasant fishery situated only a few miles west of Norwich, comprising a shallow mill pool holding large chub, dace, roach and silver bream (to 1½lb), but with roach and dace in the deeper holes in the downstream river.

How to get there   Take the A47 west from Norwich; at Easton (about 7 miles), turn left at Easton Dog pub and cross minor road at The Bell pub. The Mill House and the fishery are about ½ mile on the right. Free (but limited) parking.

Day tickets   Adult £1; available from The Mill House, Marlingford, Norwich.

Best methods   In pool – use swimfeeder; in river – use stick float.

Best baits   Maggots, casters.

Facilities   Nearest shop and pub, The Bell, at Marlingford (½ mile).

RIVER YARE, CRINGLEFORD
Atlas Page 202 F.2/1.5

An area known as the Yare Valley Walk, with public footpath running through University of East Anglia grounds; well used by walkers and dogs! A mainly shallow river section with several deep holes where large roach (2lb+) are often taken. Also occasional tench and chub.

How to get there   Take the A11 south-west from Norwich; at Cringleford (after about 2 miles), turn into the village, cross the traffic light and use the free car park on the right, just before the bridge.

Day tickets   Free fishing from Cringleford road bridge north west to Earlham road bridge.

Best methods   Summer – light float or waggler; winter – stick float.

Best baits   Maggots, casters, bread.

Restriction   Fishing is restricted to the north bank.

Facilities   Nearest shop/pub in Cringleford; shop 200 yards from car-park; pub, The Red Lion, 100 yards.

Disabled facilities   Some swims suitable for disabled and wheelchair anglers.

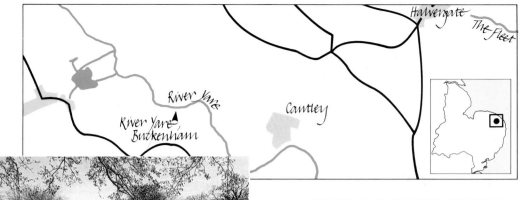

River Yare, Marlingford.

NORTHAMPTONSHIRE

Ditchford Lake.

RIVER YARE, BUCKENHAM
Atlas Page 202 F.3/1.5

A powerful, tidal, 80-yard-wide stretch; mostly 8–15ft deep, with centre (20ft deep) channel; reed-lined banks and lily patches in bays. Summer/autumn venue for large bream, roach (to 2lb), hybrids (to 4lb) and eels. Peak fishing in August/September, with 20lb+ catches likely.

How to get there Take the A146 from Norwich-Beccles road; at Trowse, turn left at Crown Point pub and continue through Rockland (5 miles) and Staithe. After a half-mile, turn left to Buckenham sailing club and Beauchamp Arms pub; pay in pub for parking.
Day tickets Free fishing.
Best methods Float or pole in deep water/slow flowing areas. Other swims – open-end feeder filled with groundbait and casters/red maggots.
Best baits Casters, red maggots; bread and corn as alternatives.
Facilities Food/toilets at Beauchamp Arms pub.

Hotspot Tips

- Topper floats up to 10BB, or a pole rig of 10g, are ideal.
- Holding back can score while feeding hard, small balls of groundbait every cast – loosefeed is useless.
- For good results, groundbait must be stiff.

BILLING AQUADROME
Atlas Page 202 B.5/2.9

A holiday complex just outside Northampton, with several lakes suitable for fishing. Expect most coarse species, including pike, perch, roach, tench, carp and bream, but fishing is notoriously difficult due to excessive noise and activity. Fishing season from 16th June–1st November.

How to get there Take the A45 east from Northampton and follow signs to Little Billing and the Aquadrome, on the eastern outskirts of the town. Plenty of parking on site.
Day tickets Adult £1.50 if paid at the gate; £2 if collected at the water; £3.50 entry fee to Aquadrome; junior/OAP half-price. Adult: weekly £10; season £25; junior/OAP half-price; no entry fee required to Aquadrome; available on site. For information; Tel. 0604 45255.

179

Best methods/baits   Use any recognised coarse technique and baits.

Restrictions   Fishing only through summer until mid-October. Fishing from 0600–2100. No night fishing.

Facilities   Toilets/cafes/bars/amusements on site.

Disabled facilities   Some swims suitable for disabled anglers.

CASTLE ASHBY LAKES
Atlas Page 202 B.6/3.0

A cluster of four lakes on an estate about 8 miles east of Northampton. Good general coarse fishing, with plenty of carp (to 10lb) in two lakes and most other coarse species in all four. One lake has been recently designated as carp-only fishing.

How to get there   Leave Northampton via the A45, then take the A428 south-east towards Bedford, and after about 6 miles turn left onto minor road to Castle Ashby. Follow signs to the Castle and the fishery. Parking on site.

Day tickets   Adult £1.50; junior/OAP £1. Available from Castle Ashby Estate Office, Castle Ashby, Northampton; Tel. 0601 29232.

Best methods/baits   Use any recognised coarse technique and baits.

Restrictions   Fishing only from dawn until dusk. No night fishing.

Facilities   Nearest shop/pub in Castle Ashby village.

Disabled facilities   Some swims suitable for disabled anglers.

DITCHFORD LAKE
Atlas Page 202 C.1/2.7

A pair of mature gravel pits, one of 30 acres, the other 6 acres, near Rushden. Both contain most coarse species, plus a large number of double-figure common and mirror carp. There are also some very big carp here – possibly up to 30lb.

How to get there   From the A45 Northampton to St. Neots road, take the Rushden exit and at the first roundabout turn left into Ditchford Lane. The lake is on the right.

Day tickets   Season tickets only: adult £8; junior/OAP £3. Available from Jack Leach Tackle, Church Street, Rushden, or Ron's Tackle, 18 Park Road, Wellingborough; Tel. 0933 226913.

Best methods/baits   Use any recognised coarse technique and baits.

Facilities   Nearest shops/pubs in Rushden.

Disabled facilities   Some swims suitable for disabled anglers.

KIMBOLTON, SCHOOL WATER
Atlas Page 202 C.5/2.5

A town-centre lake of about 1½ acres, close to Kimbolton Castle. Mainly general coarse fishing, but plenty of small carp (to 5lb) likely.

How to get there   From Northampton, drive eastwards on the A45, through Rushden to Kimbolton (about 27 miles). In the town, follow signs to the castle; the fishery is nearby. Parking available in the town.

Day tickets   Adult/junior/OAP £1. Available on site.

Best methods/baits   Use any recognised coarse technique and baits.

Facilities   Nearest shops/pub/toilets/food in Kimbolton.

Disabled facilities   Some swims suitable for disabled anglers.

MAXEY NO. 2 PIT
Atlas Page 202 C.9/1.8

A small, disused gravel pit – one of a group – just north of Peterborough. Average 5–10ft depth, with summer marginal weedbeds and some willow fringes. Plenty of roach, rudd and tench, plus a large shoal bream that will suit the bream specialist.

How to get there   From Peterborough, head north on the A15 and after 4 miles turn left onto B1162 to Maxey. Drive down the village High Street and follow signs to No. 2 Pit, opposite Tuckers Nook. Limited free car parking on site.

Day tickets   Adult/junior/OAP £1.75. Available on the bank.

Best methods   Float and leger both work well here. In summer, fish a waggler overdepth, two rod-lengths out.

Best baits   Most baits work well. Summer tench – sweetcorn. Roach, rudd – maggots, casters, bread.

Restrictions   No bloodworm or joker.

Facilities   Nearest shop/pub in Maxey village.

Disabled facilities   For advice on disabled angling here; Tel. 0778 343691.

MAXEY NO. 4 PIT/GERARD'S PIT
Atlas Page 202 C.9/1.8

Two large pits in a village near Market Deeping. Recognised for top quality carp fishing, with 100lb+ day catches possible.

How to get there From Peterborough, head north on the A15 and turn left after 4 miles to Maxey. Take 1st left to Woodgate Lane; No. 4 Pit is on the right, Gerard's Pit is signposted on the left. Free car parking on site.
Day tickets Adult/junior/OAP £7. Available from the bailiff on the bank.
Best methods Use carp tackle; minimum 5lb breaking strain line with small maggot feeder.
Best baits Luncheon meat, sweetcorn.
Restrictions Owners keepnets only on Gerard's Pit.
Facilities Nearest shop Maxey (½ mile); nearest pub corner of Woodgate Lane.

RANSOME ROAD GRAVEL PIT, NORTHAMPTON
Atlas Page 202 B.9/2.7

A mature gravel pit with depth of 3–10ft. Good heads of roach and tench, with a few good carp and some decent pike.

How to get there Leave the M1 at jct16 and take A45 to Swallow Hotel on the left. The lake is in front of the hotel.
Day tickets Adult £2; junior/OAP £1. Available on the bank.
Best methods/baits Use maggot on the float for roach. For the bigger fish, use boilies.
Facilities Shops and pubs in Northampton (1 mile to town centre).
Disabled facilities If there is no skiing on the water, then the jetty is suitable for disabled and wheelchair anglers.

SIBSON FISHERIES
Atlas Page 202 C.9/1.7

A 14-acre complex of lakes at Stibbington, just north of Peterborough. Plenty of bream, tench, rudd and roach, in addition to some good-sized carp. Even an occasional trout!

How to get there Head north on the A1 past Peterborough turn-off and just after Sibson House Hotel (on left) look for signs to Stibbington. In the village, look for New Lane and the fishery. Parking on site.

Day tickets Adult/junior/OAP £3 for 12-hour ticket; Tel. 0780 782621.
Best methods/baits Use any recognised coarse technique and baits.
Restrictions Maximum 10 advance day tickets.
Facilities Cottage hire (with river) available. Nearest shop/pub in Stibbington or Wansford.
Disabled facilities Some swims are very suitable for disabled and wheelchair anglers; phone for advice (see above).

THRAPSTON GRAVEL PITS
Atlas Page 202 C.4/2.6

This is reputed to be the largest gravel pit in England – over 300 acres and 3 miles around. Good quality general coarse fishing. Some very big carp are thought to inhabit some regions of the pit.

How to get there From Northampton, take the A45 east to Higham Ferrers (about 16 miles), then A605 north to Thrapston. The pits are on the left, just after passing through Thrapston. Follow signs to the fisheries; parking on site.
Day tickets Adult £3, season ticket £20; junior/OAP half-price. Available from Jack Leach Fishing Tackle, Church Street, Rushden; Tel. 0933 53007, or Ron's Tackle, 18 Park Road, Wellingborough; Tel. 0933 226913.
Best methods/baits Use any recognised coarse technique and baits.
Facilities Nearest shops/pub in Thrapston.
Disabled facilities Some swims may be suitable for disabled anglers; for advice, contact Jack Leach Fishing Tackle.

WEEDON ROAD GRAVEL PITS
Atlas Page 202 B.9/2.7

A mature gravel pit in Northampton town, containing most coarse species, especially large tench. Rumour has it that carp up to 25lb inhabit these waters!

How to get there In Weedon Road, Northampton. Details from tackle shop on application for membership.
Day tickets Available only to members of Northampton Nene AC: £20.
Best methods/baits Use any recognised coarse technique and baits.
Facilities Nearest shops/pubs in Northampton.
Disabled facilities Some swims suitable for disabled anglers.

SUFFOLK

Water proofed.

How to get there   Take the A12 from Ipswich north-east towards Wickham Market; access to the river is at various points near the town and at villages to the west. For details of access/parking and the best fishing, contact Geoffrey Abbott at The Rod & Gun Shop, 18 Church Street, Woodbridge, Suffolk; Tel. 0394 382377.

Day tickets   Adult £2; junior/OAP £1. Available from local tackle shops.

Best methods/baits   Use general coarse methods and baits.

Facilities   Shops/pubs/toilets/food in various villages and in Wickham Market.

Disabled facilities   Some swims are suitable for disabled and wheelchair anglers; please contact The Rod & Gun Shop for advice (see above).

ALTON WATER
Atlas Page 202 F.0/3.3

A vast reservoir with distinctive, irregularly-shaped banks, located about 5 miles south of Ipswich. A very popular fishery which provides some excellent fishing, mainly consisting of massive bream shoals and good roach. Catches between 40 to 100lb are regular here.

How to get there   Heading west on the A12 Ipswich by-pass, drive across Orwell Bridge and turn immediately left onto the B1080 direct to Alton Water. Alternatively, turn left on the A137 for about 3 miles, then turn left to Tattingstone and follow signs to the reservoir. Free car parking on site.

Day tickets   Adult £1.50; junior/OAP 75p. Available from local tackle shops.

Best methods/baits   Use general coarse techniques and baits.

Facilities   Toilets/food at various points around the water. Plenty of shops and pubs in villages in the area.

Disabled facilities   Some swims may be suitable for disabled and wheelchair anglers; for advice, contact The Rod & Gun Shop, 18 Church Street, Woodbridge, Suffolk; Tel. 0394 382377.

RIVER DEBEN
Atlas Page 202 F.1/3.1

A 5-mile river stretch extending from the new A12 bridge near Woodbridge to Glevering Bridge. Plenty of bream, roach, perch and rudd, plus some large pike. The best fishing is near the Wickham Market area.

RIVER GLEN
Atlas Page 202 E.4/3.2

A very narrow river section near Sudbury. The water becomes very weedy in the summer, but still produces quite good nets of roach, plus a few dace and chub – and pike up to 10lb.

How to get there   From Sudbury, head north on the A134 to Long Melford (3 miles) and turn left on the A1092 towards Clare and Haverhill. After about 1½ miles, the road crosses the river; use the large car park (free) on the left and walk to the water. The signs indicate the fishing boundaries.

Day tickets   Adult £2; junior/OAP £1. Available from local tackle shops or from Norman Mealham, Long Melford AA; Tel. 0787 77139.

Best methods/baits   Use general coarse methods and baits.

Facilities   Cafe/toilets/shop/pub at Long Melford (2 miles).

GOSLINGS FARM CARP LAKES
Atlas Page 202 F.1/3.2

Two lakes lying just north of the main A45 Ipswich-Felixstowe road. The first, general, coarse fishing lake contains rudd, tench, bream, tench and Crucian carp. The second lake contains mainly carp, with Crucians to 20lb+, plus some tench and rudd.

How to get there   Take the A45 south-east from Ipswich for about 6 miles; look for the turning to Kirton and Trimley St Martin on the left. In the village, the carp lakes are in Grimston Lane. Free car parking on site.

Day tickets   Adult/junior/OAP £2.60 per rod. Night fishing (£6/rod) is available on alternate weekends. Tickets available on site.

Best methods/baits   Use recognised techniques.

Restrictions   No groundbait.

Facilities   Shop/pub in Trimley St Martin (½ mile).

GUNTON HALL LAKE
Atlas Page 202 F.8/1.5

A 2-acre lake which forms part of a holiday centre just north of Lowestoft. A shallow, weedy lake with reasonable catches of tench, roach and rudd, plus some larger mirror carp (to 10lb+).

How to get there   From Lowestoft, head towards Great Yarmouth on the A12; after about 2 miles, look for Gunton Hall on the right (just before Corton village). Parking available at the fishery.

Day tickets   Fishing available to holiday residents only – for details; Tel. 0502 730283.

Best methods/baits   Use any recognised coarse technique and baits.

Facilities   Golf/tennis/archery/clay pigeon available for residents. Toilets/food also available. Nearest shops/pubs in Corton or Lowestoft.

Disabled facilities   Some swims suitable for disabled anglers.

HENHAM DAIRY POND
Atlas Page 202 F.7/1.5

A shallow, 1-acre lake on an estate a few miles south of Beccles. A mixed bag of tench, roach, Crucian carp and rudd, in addition to some small mirror carp. Some mirrors may reach double figures.

How to get there   Take the A145 south from Beccles for about 6 miles and turn right on minor road to Brampton. Continue for 2 miles, then turn left into Henham Park Estate. The pond is on the left; parking nearby.

Day tickets   Adult/junior/OAP £2. Limited tickets, available from the farmhouse *before* fishing.

Best methods/baits   Use any recognised coarse technique and baits.

Restrictions   Only one rod per person. No night fishing.

Facilities   Nearest shop/pub in Brampton village.

Disabled facilities   Some swims suitable for disabled anglers.

HOLTON PIT
Atlas Page 202 F.4/2.4

A very attractive water, with roach, rudd, crucian, mirror carp – in fact a popular match venue.

How to get there   Take A12 Woodbridge road, beyond Saxmundham. Then take A144 to Halesworth and as you come into the town, turn right on to new bypass. Pass a pub and turn right into a lane. Follow that to the pond.

Day tickets   Adult £2; junior/OAP £1;

Best methods/baits   Use any recognised coarse technique and baits.

Restrictions   Under 16s must be accompanied by an adult.

Facilities   Shops and pubs in Halesworth (½ mile).

LAKESIDE CARAVAN PARK
Atlas Page 202 F.4/2.6

A caravanning and camping site near Saxmundham, with a 3-acre lake providing good coarse fishing for roach, bream, perch and tench. Mirror carp of double-figure size have also been taken from these waters.

How to get there   Head south on the A12 from Lowestoft to Saxmundham (about 25 miles) and turn right onto the B1119. At Rendham village (about 3 miles), look for signs to the caravan park and lake. Parking available on site.

Day tickets   Fishing available only to campers and caravanners at the site. For information, contact the Park Manager; Tel. 0728 603344.

Best methods/baits   Use any recognised coarse technique and baits.

Facilities   Shop/food/toilets available on site. Nearest pub in Rendham.

Disabled facilities   Some swims may be suitable for disabled anglers; for advice, please phone (see above).

MELTON RESERVOIR
Atlas Page 202 F.1/3.1

An old gravel pit, quite large and about 15ft deep. Carp, bream, tench and many other species provide good fishing. Restocking continues regularly.

How to get there   From Ipswich, head north-east on the A12 and turn right at Woodbridge onto the A1069, signposted Melton. Look for signs to the reservoir. Car park on site.

Day tickets   Adult £2; junior/OAP £2; available from Rod & Gun Shop, 18 Church Street, Woodbridge; Tel. 0394 382377.

Best methods/baits   Use recognised techniques, or enquire at Rod & Gun Shop.

Facilities   Nearest pub, 100 yards.

Disabled facilities   Some swims are suitable for disabled and wheelchair anglers.

Putting back a mirror carp.

STARFIELD PIT
Atlas Page 202 E.4/3.2

A large, irregularly-shaped gravel pit near Long Melford, west of Sudbury. A weedy water, ranging from 2–10ft deep, with several islands, but good mixed fishing for bream, roach and pike. Also some double-figure mirror carp.

How to get there   From Sudbury, take the A134 about 2 miles, then turn left (at Rodbridge Corner) onto B1064 towards Foxearth. Drive through Liston (right of chemical factory) and take the track on the right, through Liston Gardens. The pit is at the end of the track, on the right.

Day tickets   Adult £3; junior/ladies/OAP £1.50. Season tickets: adult £18; junior/ladies £9; OAP no charge. Available (in advance) *only* from Mr. Mealham, 6 Springfield Terrace, East Street, Sudbury; Tel. 0787 77139.

Best methods/baits   Use any recognised coarse technique and baits.

Facilities   Nearest shop/pub in Foxearth.

Disabled facilities   Some swims may be suitable for disabled anglers; please phone for advice (see above).

RIVER STOUR, BLACK BARN
Atlas Page 202 E.4/3.2

A fairly short river section near Long Melford, but one which contains lots of interesting bends, narrows and glides. Mainly chub, roach and dace, plus a few large carp and bream in the lower field.

How to get there   From Bury St. Edmunds, take the A134 south past Long Melford and turn right at Rodbridge picnic area. Cross the river and shortly turn right towards Liston. Park at the gate by the Black Barn (100 yards) and walk over the field to the water.

Day tickets   Adult/junior/OAP £2. Available from local tackle shops or from Norman Mealham, Long Melford AA; Tel. 0787 77139.

Best methods   Use general coarse methods.

Best baits   Use hemp and tares in summer; casters in winter.

Facilities   Nearest shop and pub, Long Melford (1½ miles).

RIVER STOUR, THE CONVENT
Atlas Page 202 E.4/3.2

A town centre river stretch at Sudbury, about 12 yards wide with a depth of 8–9ft in the middle. Expect moderate fishing, with mainly roach, plus a few chub and carp.

How to get there   The fishery is in Sudbury town centre; for details of access and/or parking and the best places to fish, contact The Tackle Box, 42 North Street, Sudbury; Tel. 0787 312118.

Day tickets   Adult £2; junior/OAP £1. Available from The Tackle Box.

Best methods/baits   Use general coarse methods and baits.

Facilities   Toilets/shops/pubs/food all available in Sudbury town centre.

Disabled facilities   The bank is tarmacked for between 200–300 yards, allowing fishing by disabled and wheelchair anglers.

RIVER STOUR, KIPLING'S MEADOW
Atlas Page 202 E.4/3.2

A quite small section of the Stour, close to Sudbury town centre. Expect good coarse fishing for roach and bream, plus some tench and good-sized chub (5lb+). Also expect perch and pike – and some very large carp of over 20lb, which live in the lower length on the left, just over the bridge.

How to get there   Take the A134 south from Bury St. Edmunds to Sudbury. On approaching Sudbury (downhill), bear left and turn left into Chaucer Road, then immediately left into Canterbury Road. Use the free car park on the left (100 yards), walk across the road and through to the river.

Day tickets   Adult £2; junior/OAP £1. Available at The Tackle Box, 42 North Street, Sudbury; Tel. 0787 312118.

Best methods/baits   Use general coarse methods and baits.

Restrictions   No fishing directly in front of the bungalow.

Facilities   There is a small shop and a pub (The Red Cow) on the road back to Sudbury.

RIVER STOUR, LISTON MILL
Atlas Page 202 E.4/3.2

A secluded fishery to the east of Sudbury, and where the water is variable. Expect dace, chub and roach on the lower stretches, where width is about 12 yards and depth 4ft. On the bends, which may be 16 yards wide and up to 8ft deep, expect mainly chub and roach, with some particularly big shoals!

How to get there   From Bury St. Edmunds, take the A134 south past Long Melford and turn right at Rodbridge picnic area. Cross the river and shortly turn right towards Liston. Continue past the Black Barn, turn right

and follow the road to the Mill Pool on the left. Free car parking on site.

Day tickets   Adult £2; junior/OAP £1.Available from local tackle shops or from Norman Mealham, Long Melford AA; Tel. 0787 77139.

Best methods/baits   Use general coarse methods and baits.

Facilities   Nearest shop and pub, the Cock and Bell, in Long Melford.

RIVER STOUR, MILL MEADOWS
Atlas Page 202 E.4/3.2

A pleasant river stretch at Sudbury, about 2 minutes' walk from the town centre. Mainly roach and chub, but the occasional perch and dace might spring a surprise!

How to get there   The fishery is in Sudbury town centre; for details of access and/or parking and the best places to fish, contact The Tackle Box, 42 North Street, Sudbury; Tel. 0787 312118.

Day tickets   Adult £2; junior/OAP £1. Available from The Tackle Box.

Best methods/baits   Use general coarse methods and baits.

Facilities   There are plenty of shops and pubs in Sudbury town centre.

RIVER STOUR, PECK'S MEADOW
Atlas Page 202 E.4/3.2

A very pleasant, fairly wide and deep river stretch, south of Sudbury, where good catches of quality roach and bream are often taken, especially during the summer months.

How to get there   From Sudbury town centre, take the B1508 south towards Bures. On leaving Sudbury, park (free) outside the Ernest Doe factory (on the right), walk down the side of the factory and cross over the railway line. Follow the footpath to the water, keeping left of the concrete bridge.

Day tickets   Adult £2; junior/OAP £1. Available from The Tackle Box, 42 North Street, Sudbury; Tel. 0787 312118.

Best methods   Use general coarse methods.

Best baits   Use seed for summer roach; use worm or maggot for bream.

Facilities   Nearest shops and pubs, in Sudbury (½ mile).

THORPENESS MERE
Atlas Page 202 F.7/2.8

A very big but very shallow (2–3ft) lake with many islands, all of which forms part of a 'childrens playground' near Leiston. Expect some roach, rudd and eels, together with a few common carp – some in the 10lb region. Fishing can be difficult due to activity and noise.

How to get there   From Ipswich, take the A12 north through Woodbridge and Wickham Market and at Farnham (about 20 miles) turn right onto the A1094. After 4 miles, turn left on B1069 to Leiston and Thorpeness. Follow signs to the mere and park nearby.
Day tickets   Free fishing over a 100-yard stretch.
Best methods/baits   Use any recognised coarse technique and baits.
Restrictions   No fishing from most of the bank. No night fishing.
Facilities   Childrens playground/boat hire available. Also toilets/food on site. Nearest shop/pub in Leiston.
Disabled facilities   Some swims suitable for disabled anglers.

WALDRINGFIELD SWALE PITS
Atlas Page 202 F.1/3.1

A fair sized, squarish pit, dropping deep on one side, and shallow on the tree side. Provides good bream fishing with bags up to 30lb when you find them.

How to get there   From Ipswich, head north-east on the A12 and turn right at Woodbridge onto the A1069, then B1083 to Sutton and Waldringfield. Look for signs to the pits. *Note*: there is NO car parking on site.
Day tickets   Adult £2; available from Rod & Gun Shop, 18 Church Street, Woodbridge; Tel. 0394 382377.
Best methods   Float or leger.
Facilities   Nearest shop/pub 2 miles.

WICKHAM MARKET RIVER
Atlas Page 202 F.1/3.0

A beautiful stretch of the River Deben, with a bit of everything for fishing, with a lot restocked last year. Crucian, carp, perch, roach, massive pike and lots of others.

How to get there   From Ipswich, take the A12 north-east to Wickham Market (13 miles). Look for signs to the River Deben, or phone for directions from the Rod & Gun Shop, Woodbridge.
Day tickets   Adult £2; available from Rod & Gun Shop, 18 Church Street, Woodbridge; Tel. 0394 382377.
Best methods   Float
Best baits   Maggots, bread, worms.
Facilities   Nearest shop/pub 1 mile.

WICKHAM SKEITH MERE
Atlas Page 202 E.9/2.3

A shallow and weedy common pond mid-way between Diss and Needham Market. An ideal venue for youngsters and beginners alike, with plenty of small carp and pike.

How to get there   From Ipswich, take the A45 to Needham Market, then bear right onto A140 towards Diss. Turn left to Wickham Skeith about 10 miles after Needham Market, and in the village follow signs to the mere. Parking available on site.
Day tickets   Free fishing.
Best methods/baits   Use any recognised coarse technique and baits.
Facilities   Nearest shop/pub in Wickham Skeith village.
Disabled facilities   Some swims may be suitable for disabled anglers.

Crucian carp.

186

PIKE LEGENDS

WEIGHT	CAPTOR	VENUE	DATE	
49 lb 14 oz	C. Thornton	Loch Alva	June	1784
47 lb 11 oz	T. Morgan	Loch Lomond	July	1945
46 lb	C. F. Giffard	Chillington Pool	Sept	1940
45 lb 6 oz*	G. Edwards	Llandegfedd	March	1990
44 lb 14 oz	M. Linton	Ardleigh	Jan	1987
44 lb 8 oz	C. Garret	Llandegfedd	Oct	1988
44 lb	S. Gilham	Llandegfedd	Oct	1988
43 lb 2 oz	P. Wright	Castle Howard		1988
43 lb 2 oz	B. Ingrams	Llandegfedd	Oct	1988
42 lb 5 oz	P. Climo	Llandegfedd	Oct	1988
42 lb 2 oz	D. Amies	River Thurne	Aug	1985
42 lb	J. Nudd	Wroxham Broad		1901
41 lb 8 oz	D. Amies	Thurne System		
41 lb 6 oz	N. Fickling	River Thurne	Feb	1985
41 lb 4 oz	J. Mills	River Thurne	Feb	1986
40 lb 6 oz	M. Hopwood	Kent water	Nov	1979
40 lb 4 oz	K. Vogel	Loch Ken		1972
40 lb	P. Hancock	Horsey Mere		1967
40 lb	J. Young	River Don		1866
39 lb 12 oz	D. Leary	Lyng		1985
39 lb 8 oz	R. Miller	Lyng	Dec	1989
39 lb 7 oz	G. F. Parrott	Dorset Stour	Mar	1909
39 lb 4 oz	L. Tyler	Broadlands		
39 lb	C. Loveland	Knipton		1967
38 lb 8 oz	T. Cottis	Abberton	Mar	1980
38 lb 4 oz	P. Emmings	Abberton	Dec	1969
38 lb 1 oz	John Watson	Thurne System		
38 lb	E. Harrison	Castle Howard		
38 lb	Capt C. Yard	Overstone Park Lake	Mar	1941
38 lb	S. Lambard	River Thurne	Nov	1985
38 lb	R. Stone	Thurne System	Oct	1979
37 lb 12 oz	J. R. J.	Private Warks Lake	Mar	1882
37 lb 10 oz	P. Woodhouse	River Thurne	Feb	1984
37 lb 8 oz	R. Arabin	Dorset Stour		1876
37 lb 8 oz	C. Warwick	Hants Avon	Oct	1944
37 lb 8 oz	E. Turner	London chalk pit		1989
37 lb 4 oz	L. Tyler	Broadlands		
37 lb 4 oz	Lord Gainsborough	Exton Park Lake	June	1796
37 lb	E. Turner	London chalk pit		1989
37 lb	Lord Gainsborough	Private pond		1796
37 lb	A. Jardine	Amersham Park Lake	Sept	1879
37 lb	A. Jardine	Hants Avon		1879
37 lb	Maj W. Booth	River Wye		1910
37 lb	L. Jones	Loch Gelly	Nov	1970
36 lb 10 oz	P. Tomsett	Grafham Water	Oct	1981
36 lb 8 oz	Col Atherton	Vandervells Lake	Feb	1957
36 lb 8 oz	Tom the Pole	Loch Fitty		1967
36 lb 8 oz	D. Chilman	Llandegfedd	Oct	1988
36 lb 6 oz	D. Amies	Thurne System		1982
36 lb 4 oz	J. Bailey	Lyng	Dec	1984
36 lb 2 oz	M. Rouse	Llandegfedd	Oct	1988
36 lb 1 oz	S. Martin	Theale	Mar	1985
36 lb	G. Forbes	Luton Hoo		1875
36 lb	A. Jardine	Leeds Castle Moat	Feb	1879
36 lb	F. Thorne	Haveringland Lake	Feb	1878
36 lb	G. Keen	Rapley Lake		1874
36 lb	J. Birch	Barrow on Soar	Feb	1912
36 lb	M. Halliday	River Yare		1939

* Current record

Barbel

Scientific name: Barbus barbus.

British Record: 14 lb 6 oz, A. Tryon, Royalty Fishery, Hants Avon, 1934.

Other notable fish: 14 lb 4 oz, F. W. K. Wallis, Hants Avon, 1933; 14 lb 3 oz, B. Shaw, Hants Avon, 1991.

Characteristics: Streamlined body, with an underslung mouth and four barbules. Its pectoral fins are well-developed. Colour varies but the flanks are golden, changing to brown along the back. The pectoral, anal and pelvic fins are orange, tail and dorsal are dark brown.

Habitat: A lover of fast water, the barbel is found in rivers such as the Hants Avon, Kennet, Thames, Severn and some Yorkshire rivers. The River Severn received its first stock of barbel in 1956 when 500 fish were released. The fish thrived and today it is a prolific barbel water.

Feeding habits: A bottom feeder which browses over gravel beds, using its four barbules to root for food. Baits such as bread, worms, maggots and casters, along with meat based products, all work well.

Perch

Scientific name: Perca fluviatilis.

British Record: 5 lb 9 oz, caught by J. Shayler, private lake, Kent.

Characteristics: Broad, dark vertical body stripes earn the perch its 'sergeant major' nickname. Its erect, spikey dorsal fin and cavernous mouth give it an almost prehistoric appearance.

Habitat: Although disease decimated perch stocks throughout Britain a few years ago they are once again returning in force to waters of all descriptions. A lover of deep, dark pools where there is plenty of cover, old tree roots, bank sheathing and reed beds. But perch can be found in murky canals, ponds, lakes and rivers.

Feeding habits: Small specimens feed on all forms of water creatures from bloodworms to fry. As they grow, perch become even more predatory and will stalk shoals of small fish until close enough to charge through them and grab a meal.

Best fishing time: Summer and Autumn produce a lot of big perch but they can be caught throughout the season. Periods of mild, overcast weather usually trigger off a feeding spree.

Pike

Scientific name: Esox lucius.

British Record: 45 lb 6 oz, Gareth Edwards, Llandegfedd Reservoir, Gwent, 1990.

Characteristics: Nobody could ever confuse the pike with any other species swimming in our waters. Long, lean and boasting a huge mouth lined with thousands of needle-sharp teeth, the pike's function and feeding habits are obvious at a glance.

Britain's supreme predator, it is the top target for thousands of specialist anglers who know that it can thrive in any venue with a sufficient stock of prey fish.

The biggest pike are females, which can grow to more than 40 lb in the right environment. Male pike, however, seldom exceed 7 lb.

Habitat: Pike are found everywhere except in the tiniest of highland streams. They thrive best in lowland waters – rivers and stillwaters – which boast a large head of other species for them to prey upon.

Feeding habits: The pike is the victim of old wives' tales. Contrary to folklore, they do not attack livestock at the water's edge, nor eat their own weight in other fish every day. The pike is, in fact, a wary feeder which is every bit as difficult to catch as any other species. Deadbaits are very effective for the larger specimens, although the use of artificial lures is increasing in popularity.

Rudd

Scientific name: Rutilus erythrophthalmus.
British Record: 4 lb 8 oz, caught by the Rev E. C. Alston, Thetford, Norfolk.
Characteristics: At first glance the rudd can be mistaken for a roach, but closer inspection will show the rudd has a protruding lower lip while a roach has an underslung one. Coloration is also similar to the roach but the flanks have a golden tinge and all the fins are red, the ventral ones in particular are brilliant.

While the mouth is the easiest distinguishing feature, a really positive identification between roach and rudd will involve lateral line scale counts.

Habitat: A lover of lakes and gravel pits, the rudd is far more at home in these waters than in rivers, although some are found in slow-moving areas, such as canals.

A shoal fish, the rudd will spend time at all levels from the bottom to cruising right on the surface. Spawning takes place between April and June, when sticky eggs are laid on water plants. Hatching will take between eight and 15 days, depending on temperature.

Feeding habits: When young the rudd feeds on algae and small insects but as it grows so its attentions turn to larger prey.

Best fishing times: A Summer species which is best fished for when water temperature is fairly high. Evening often sees a lot of surface activity as the rudd puts on a trout-like act to sip flies from the surface.

When they are close to the surface try a small piece of floating crust or a dark caster which will also float.

Chub

Scientific name: Leuciscus cephalus.
British Record: 8 lb 4 oz, caught by G. F. Smith, Hants Avon, Christchurch in 1913.
Characteristics: Most striking thing about the chub is its gigantic mouth which deals with all sorts of food ranging from small insects to young fish. The back is dark green but the flanks range from silver to golden. Fins are dark, except the pelvic and anal fins which are orange. In good waters chub often survive for more than 10 years.

Habitat: A lover of snaggy swims. Widely spread throughout rivers ranging in pace from slow-running to powerful. The turbulent water of weir pools is another haunt of this powerful, streamlined fish which is equally at home in large stillwaters where it can grow to near-record proportions. During spawning the chub will move into the shallows to lay its eggs on water plants and rocks.

Feeding habits: As a young fish the chub feeds on tiny aquatic insects but later in life it makes maximum use of its large mouth and formidable pharyngeal (throat) teeth. As an adult fish it will devour small fish, worms and crayfish. Good chub baits include luncheon meat, worms, waspgrub, bread, cheese, maggots and casters.

Best fishing time: Chub can be caught throughout the season. During the heat of Summer they pack into the fastest water where oxygen content is high. In Winter they continue to feed and can be caught in sub-zero temperatures but under these conditions bait size may need to be small and tackle fine.

Fish File

Common carp

Scientific name: Cyprinus carpio.

British Record: 45 lb 12 oz, Damian Clark, Snake Pit, Essex, 1991.

Characteristics: The common carp is the fully scaled cousin of the mirror and leather carp. All three varieties are, in fact, the same species and all are descendants of the so-called wild carp.

For centuries, the carp has been an important food source for man – especially on the continent, where fish farmers embarked on a selective breeding programme. The long, lean wild carp seldom exceeded 10 lb, but the progeny from the specialised stewponds grew fat and fast to 20, 30 and even 40 lb-plus.

Today's prized specimen mirror, leather and common carp are all descendants of fish grown for the European table. Among carp anglers, the common carp is regarded as the wiliest and hardest-fighting of the three varieties.

Habitat: The carp thrives in waters ranging from stagnant farm ponds to fast-flowing rivers. The biggest specimens are generally found in rich still-waters, but carp specialists are now starting to explore the major rivers – and coming up with some weighty surprises. The River Trent has already produced many specimens, while the Thames is reputed to hold fish capable of toppling the record.

Britain's canal systems hold vast numbers of carp, including some 20 lb-plus specimens, but for some reason this ubiquitous species has not yet colonised the Fenland drains or the Norfolk Broads.

Feeding habits: The carp grows big and fast because it is a versatile feeder, taking full advantage of a fishery's food supplies. It is happy both rooting in the bottom mud for bloodworm and cruising on the surface, sipping in floating insects.

Crucian carp

Scientific name: Carassius carassius

British Record: 5lb 10^1/$_2$ oz caught by G. Halls from a lake near King's Lynn, Norfolk, in 1976.

Characteristics: Unlike other carp the crucian has no barbules at its mouth. It is also much smaller and a fish of 3 lb would be considered a very good fish from most waters. The body is deep and a rich golden bronze. The fins are an orange red, except the large convex dorsal, which is a deep brown to grey.

Habitat: The crucian can survive in poor quality waters, some of which would not sustain other species. But the better the water quality the more this sporting fish will thrive. A lover of old lakes where there is plenty of weed growth.

Feeding habits: A varied diet which includes small insects, water plants and almost anything else it can find as it browses around weed patches. It is a species with the ability to exist in waters where food is very limited and of poor quality.

Breeding habits: Between May and June sticky, deep golden-coloured eggs are laid on water plants. Hatching takes five to seven days according to water temperature, after which the newly-hatched fish stay attached to the plants for a further two days while they absorb their yolk sacs.

Best fishing times: Early and late sessions during Summer are by far the best times to fish for crucians. If conditions are overcast they may continue to feed well throughout the day. If the water temperature rises much above 21C (70F) crucians move into deeper water. Most baits are acceptable, from maggots and casters to sweetcorn and bread.

Mirror carp

Scientific name: Cyprinus carpio.

British Record: 51lb 8oz, Chris Yates, Redmire Pool, Hereford and Worcs, 1980.

Characteristics: Common carp, mirror carp and leather carp are all classed scientifically as the same species but there are obvious visible differences.

In the case of the mirror carp the body has a leathery appearance except for a row of very large 'mirror' scales running along the lateral line and stretching across the root of the tail. Other 'mirrors' often run along the body beneath the dorsal fin. The mirror carp has four barbules, two long ones below the mouth and two shorter ones above.

Colour can vary but generally it will be a variation of browns and bronze. Fins will be grey to reddish.

Habitat: Carp grow largest in stillwaters but will live happily in rivers and canals. They do particularly well in warm water and for that reason often congregate close to power station outfalls. Breeding takes place when the water temperature reaches at least 18C.

Feeding habits: Mainly a bottom feeder. Its natural food includes a high proportion of insect larvae, water snails and other bottom dwellers. Most active at night but carp are caught throughout the day too. Baits include everything from maggots and worms to bread, meat baits, sweetcorn and specially prepared boilies.

Fish File

Dace

Scientific name: Leuciscus leuciscus.
British Record: 1 lb 4¼ oz, J. L. Gasson, Little Ouse, Thetford, Norfolk 1960.
Characteristics: Easily mistaken for a young chub, the dace has a streamlined, slim body. Unlike the chub it has a narrow head and small mouth. It can be distinguished from the chub by the shape of its fins. On the dace the dorsal and anal fins are concave, while on the chub they are convex. Flanks are silver with greyish fins except for the pectorals, pelvics and anals which are yellow to orange. The eye is yellowish.

Dace shoal in large numbers, usually of similar size to each other. A dace of eight inches long would be considered a nice fish from many waters and one weighing a pound is exceptional.

Habitat: A lover of well-oxygenated, fast-flowing water, it does best in clean conditions and is often found in the upper reaches of rivers where it can shoal between streamer weed and intercept food items being washed downstream.

In slower water it will survive but does not thrive so well as its faster water cousins.

Breeding usually takes place during hours of darkness, beginning in early Spring over areas of gravel. The eggs, which are small and pale orange, can take between three and four weeks to hatch. The young take two years to become mature and will live no longer than seven years.

Feeding habits: Natural food includes a lot of small insects, larvae and adult flies. In the case of flies it will either intercept them as they rise to the surface of the water to emerge as adults or take them from the surface. Some vegetable matter, such as silkweed washed from weir sills, is also included in its diet.

Baits for dace need to be small. Among the most popular are maggots and casters, small pieces of worm or tiny pinches of bread flake, Bites can be very fast and small hooks and fine tackle are needed.

Roach

Scientific name: Rutilus rutilus.
British Record: 4 lb 3 oz, Ray Clarke, Dorset Stour, 1990.
Characteristics: Although one of our most widespread and popular species of coarse fish, the roach is often the subject of mistaken identity. The roach looks similar to its close cousin, the rudd, with which it also inter-breeds to produce hybrids. Just to confuse matters, the roach also inter-breeds with bream – resulting in another hybrid that the inexperienced angler can mistake for a true roach.

A true roach has silvery flanks, usually with a blue tinge but occasionally bronze. The fins are a bright crimson-red. The rudd is generally a bronze-golden colour, with bright vermillion fins.

The rudd is also a deeper-bodied fish than the roach. The leading edge of the roach's dorsal fin is level with the leading edge of the pelvic fins, while the rudd's dorsal fin is set much further back. The rudd's bottom lip protrudes, while the roach's lips are level.

Habitat: The roach is Britain's favourite fish, because it is found everywhere. Rivers, stillwaters, canals and drains all hold shoals of these obliging fish. It feeds throughout the season, although most anglers would agree that it is at its best in the Autumn and Winter.

Feeding habits: Mainly a bottom feeder, the roach's natural diet comprises insect larvae and water snails. But on most waters, of course, anglers' baits form an important part of the roach's diet – and there are few that the roach won't sample. Bread, maggots, casters, worms and seed baits will all score.

Roach feed throughout the day, but the period of fading light in the evening is the very best time for the bigger specimens.

DREAM BREAM

Fish File

WEIGHT	CAPTOR	VENUE	DATE
16lb 6 oz	A. Bromley	Staffs Mere	Aug 1986
16 lb 3 oz	A. Mundy	Queenford	Aug 1990
16 lb 0 oz	D. Quirk	Queenford	July 1989
15 lb 14 oz	P. Smith	Queenford	Aug 1989
15 lb 14 oz	M. Chivers	Queenford	Unknown
15 lb 12 oz	D. Sharps	Ches. Mere	Sept 1988
15 lb 12 oz	D. Quirk	Queenford	July 1988
15 lb 11 oz	P. Coates	Queenford	Aug 1988
15 lb 11 oz	D. Quirk	Queenford	July 1989
15 lb 10 oz	G. Dixon	Queenford	June 1988
15 lb 10 oz	J. Knowles	Queenford	July 1985
15 lb 9 oz	D. Quirk	Queenford	July 1988
15 lb 8 oz	D. Quirk	Queenford	July 1988
15 lb 6 oz	P. Smith	Queenford	July 1989
15 lb 6 oz	T. Bromley	Staffs Mere	July 1984
15 lb 6 oz	A. Nicholson	Queenford	Aug 1984
15 lb 6 oz	A. Nicholson	Queenford	June 1985
15 lb 6 oz	A. Mundy	Queenford	Sept 1990
15 lb 5 oz	A. Wilson	Queenford	Aug 1988
15 lb 4 oz	P. Coates	Queenford	Unknown
15 lb 3 oz	P. Smith	Queenford	July 1986
15 lb 3 oz	A. Mundy	Queenford	Aug 1990
15 lb 2 oz	A. Mundy	Queenford	July 1990
15 lb 2 oz	E. Edwards	Queenford	July 1985
15 lb 2 oz	M. Chivers	Queenford	July 1988
15 lb 2 oz	A. Miles	Queenford	Aug 1988
15 lb 0 oz	D. Quirk	Queenford	July 1988
14 lb 15 oz	P. Smith	Queenford	Aug 1985
14 lb 14 oz	A. Nicholson	Queenford	Sept 1984
14 lb 14 oz	J. Knowles	Queenford	July 1985
14 lb 13 oz	D. Quirk	Queenford	Aug 1990
14 lb 12 oz	A. Nicholson	Queenford	Sept 1984
14 lb 12 oz	L. Strudwick	Queenford	Unknown
14 lb 12 oz	A. Moy	Watford Lake	July 1988
14 lb 11 oz	G. Brandwood	Queenford	Unknown
14 lb 10 oz	J. Mills	Queenford	Unknown
14 lb 10 oz	L. Strudwick	Queenford	Unknown
14 lb 10 oz	D. Quirk	Queenford	Aug 1990
14 lb 9 oz	K. Palmer	Queenford	Unknown
14 lb 7 oz	P. Smith	Queenford	Aug 1989
14 lb 6 oz	Unknown	Standlake	Unknown
14 lb 6 oz	D. Quirk	Queenford	July 1988
14 lb 4 oz	P. Smith	Queenford	Sept 1990
14 lb 4 oz	E. Ewards	Queenford	July 1985
14 lb 4 oz	J. Mills	Queenford	Aug 1989
14 lb 4 oz	A. Miles	Queenford	Aug 1990
14 lb 3 oz	K. Salter	Leics. Res	July 1988
14 lb 3 oz	P. Smith	Queenford	July 1988
14 lb 3 oz	A. Miles	Queenford	June 1987

Chris Yates enjoying the scenery and atmosphere of the Lake District.

1 BOTTOM END

THIS simple little float can be made from
scrap pieces of quill and cocktail sticks and
it can be deadly if conditions are right.

On still waters and canals it will cope well
with a difficult wind which has proved too
much for a more conventional top and
bottom pole rig.

2 BALSA

BALSA floats are best in those swims which
have too much turbulence for a stick float.
Use it as a close in float and space the
shot down the line to make the bait rise if
the float is checked back.

3 INSERT WAGGLER (heavy)

IF your venue is a wide, deep and
windswept water then a heavy insert
waggler may be needed to beat the effects
of a downstream skim.

4 ZOOMER

Under the right conditions it's a float to use
at long range on big, slow rivers where fish
such as skimmer bream are the target.

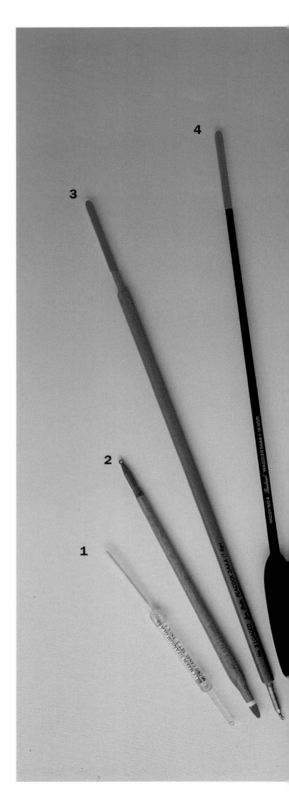

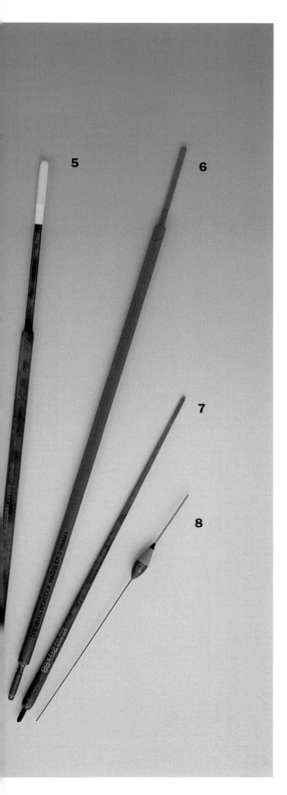

5 WAGGLER (with long insert)

INSERT tips on wagglers limit their use to stillwater or slow moving rivers. But on days when fish are feeding well off the bottom they are deadly for detecting bites from fish which may be intercepting the bait as it descends.

6 INSERT WAGGLER (light)

THIS is the float for still or very slow waters when conditions are good. But don't use one which is so light it makes casting to the required spot difficult.

7 CANAL WAGGLER

THOSE nasty skimming winds which have a habit of skating along exposed canals need to be tackled with a waggler so that line can be sunk beneath the surface. Casting range will be limited but by using most of the shot load to lock the float it will travel well enough for most canals.

8 LIGHT POLE

AT the delicate end of the float scale are the ultra light pole patterns. A good basic pattern is one with a slim balsa body and a fine tip bristle.

9 CROWQUILL AVON

IN deep water this float can be deadly. And if your swim has overhanging trees you'll find the crowquill Avon casts beautifully with an underarm swing.

10 DART

It casts really well and will cope reasonably well with a slight surface skim. But because it can be shotted very lightly down the line it is perfect for casting close to the far bank or beaneath overhanging trees.

11 SLIDER

THIS versatile float-fishing method can be used in all depths of water but is particularly useful in deep water. Use it whenever the depth is approaching the length of your rod, setting the stop knot at the required depth.

12 SIGHT-TIP

LONG range fishing on slow or stillwaters calls for a sight-tip waggler, a pattern which is basically a normal insert waggler with a thicker tip to the insert waggler.

13 STRAIGHT WAGGLER

ON those days when the wind is downstream, a double rubber float, such as a stick, will be difficult to control. This is where the straight waggler, comes into play. By attaching it bottom end only line can be sunk beneath the surface where it will not be affected by wind.

14 STICK

THE running water float for use when conditions are good. But don't try to fish this float at long range. It is best when casting can be done as a sideways, underarm swing.

15 WIRE-STEM STICK

FACED with a running water swim which doesn't call for a pacemaker but looks too pacey and turbulent for a conventional cane-stemmed stick, a good choice would be a wire-stemmed stick pattern.

16 HEAVY POLE

THE heavy pole float is a pattern chosen for its ability to cope with deep and flowing water where there's a need to get a bait down quickly to fish such as bream.

Steve Simmonds on the Nene Embankment.

MAP SECTION

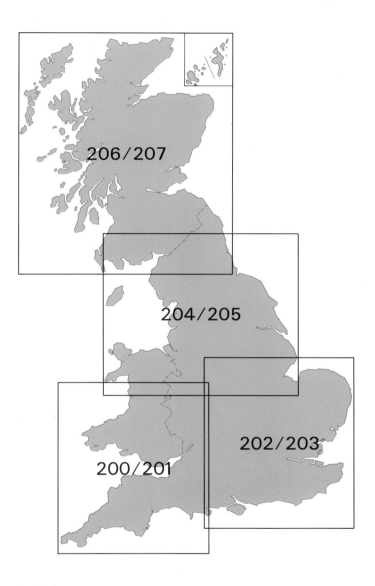

Grid References

To locate a grid reference position for any fishery:

1. Read the page number.
2. Read *eastings* (letters west to east, along the top and bottom of the map).
After the oblique:
3. Read *southings* (numbers north to south down the side of the map).

Letters or numbers *preceding* the decimal point refer to the marked grid;
numbers *following* the decimal point refer to one-tenth units within the grid
square. For example, the grid reference for Hereford is Atlas Page 200 E.9/2.1

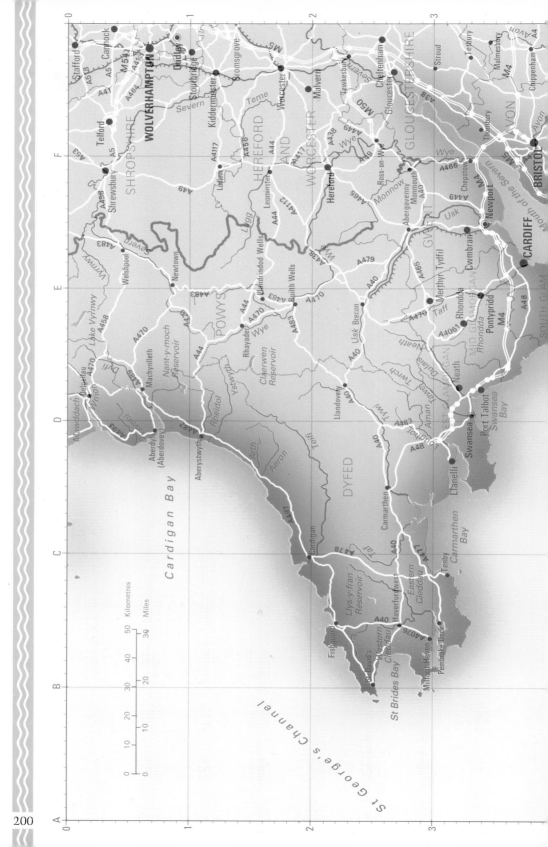

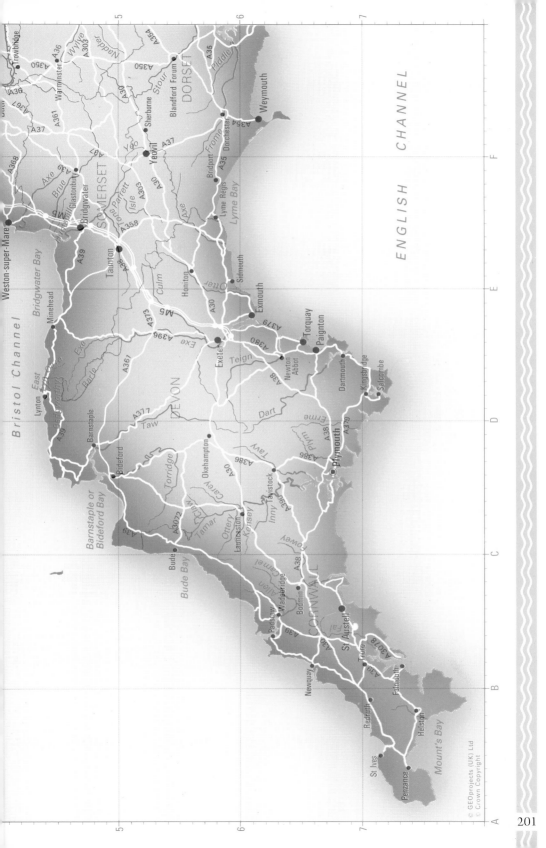

ENGLISH CHANNEL

Bristol Channel

DORSET

SOMERSET

DEVON

CORNWALL

Weymouth
Dorchester
Bridport
Lyme Regis
Lyme Bay
Sidmouth
Exmouth
Torquay
Paignton
Newton Abbot
Dartmouth
Kingsbridge
Salcombe
Plymouth
Tavistock
Okehampton
Launceston
Wadebridge
Bodmin
St Austell
Truro
Falmouth
Newquay
Padstow
Bude
Bideford
Barnstaple
Lynton
Minehead
Taunton
Bridgwater
Glastonbury
Weston-super-Mare
Yeovil
Sherborne
Blandford Forum
Trowbridge
Warminster
Honiton
Exeter
Redruth
Helston
Penzance
St Ives

Mount's Bay
Bude Bay
Barnstaple or Bideford Bay
Bridgwater Bay

Wylye
Nadder
Stour
Piddle
Frome
Yeo
Brue
Axe
Parrett
Tone
Isle
Axe
Otter
Culm
Exe
Teign
Dart
Erme
Plym
Tavy
Carey
Ottery
Tamar
Inny
Kensey
Camel
Allen
Fowey
Taw
Torridge
Lyn East

A36
A350
A303
A36
A361
A37
A303
A37
A350
A354
A35
A30
A358
A39
A368
A361
M5
A39
A396
A373
A30
A380
A379
A38
A390
A39
A386
A30
A377
A3072
A388
A39
A30
A3058
A39
A367

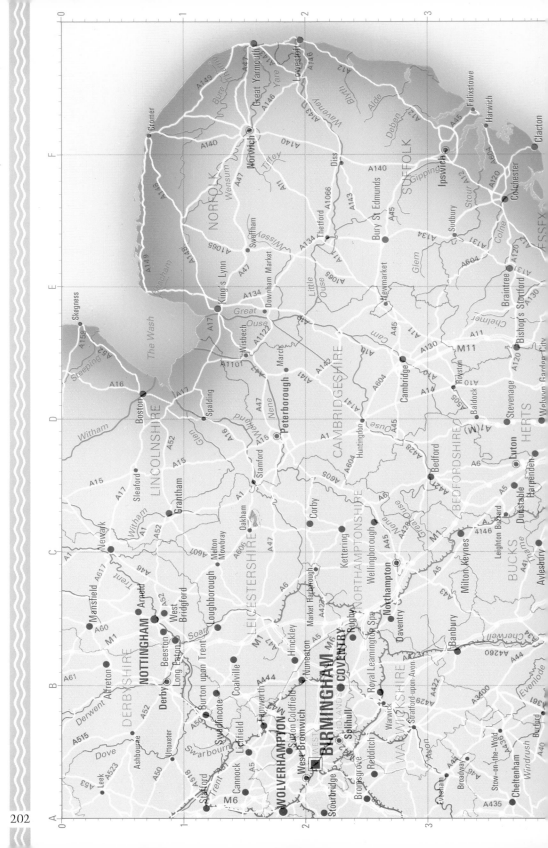

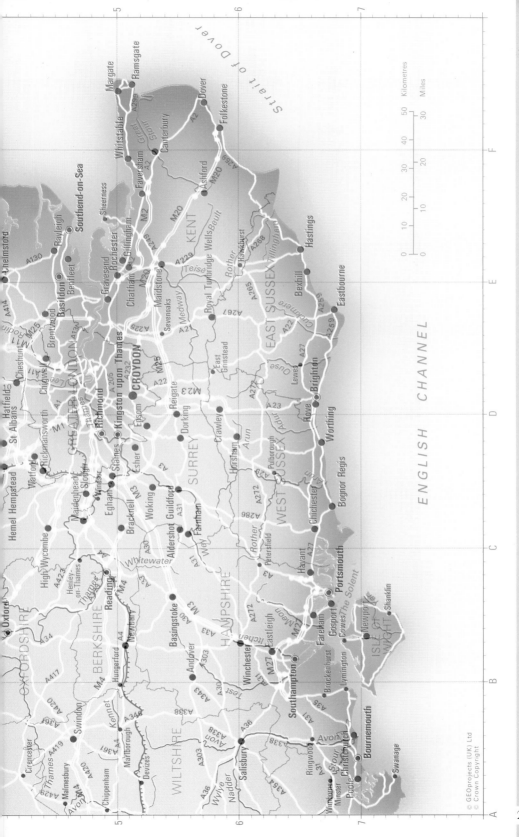

ENGLISH CHANNEL

Strait of Dover

Kilometres
Miles

KENT

EAST SUSSEX

WEST SUSSEX

SURREY

HAMPSHIRE

BERKSHIRE

WILTSHIRE

OXFORDSHIRE

GREATER LONDON

ISLE OF WIGHT

Margate
Ramsgate
Dover
Folkestone
Whitstable
Canterbury
Faversham
Ashford
Sheerness
Southend-on-Sea
Rayleigh
Rochester
Gillingham
Gravesend
Chatham
Maidstone
Sevenoaks
Royal Tunbridge Wells
Hawkhurst
Hastings
Bexhill
Eastbourne
Basildon
Benfleet
Brentwood
Chigwell
Cheshunt
Hatfield
St Albans
Rickmansworth
Watford
Hemel Hempstead
Chelmsford
East Grinstead
Crawley
Horsham
Brighton
Hove
Worthing
Bognor Regis
Chichester
Reigate
Dorking
CROYDON
Kingston upon Thames
Richmond
Epsom
Esher
Staines
Egham
Windsor
Slough
Maidenhead
High Wycombe
Henley-on-Thames
Reading
Bracknell
Woking
Aldershot
Guildford
Farnham
Petersfield
Havant
Portsmouth
Gosport
Fareham
Cowes
The Solent
Newport
Shanklin
Eastleigh
Winchester
Southampton
Brockenhurst
Lymington
Bournemouth
Christchurch
Poole
Swanage
Wimborne Minster
Ringwood
Salisbury
Basingstoke
Andover
Newbury
Hungerford
Marlborough
Devizes
Swindon
Cirencester
Malmesbury
Chippenham
Lewes
Pulborough

Great Stour
Teise
Rother
Medway
Beult
Cuckmere
Ouse
Adur
Arun
Rother
Wey
Whitewater
Thames
Itchen
Meon
Test
Avon
Stour
Nadder
Wylye
Kennet
Thames
Roding

M25
M20
M2
M26
M23
M1
M11
M4
M3
M25
M27
M40
A2
A20
A299
A28
A252
A251
A256
A259
A267
A268
A265
A21
A229
A130
A127
A12
A414
A411
A1
A205
A232
A22
A23
A24
A3
A31
A30
A33
A34
A36
A303
A338
A343
A303
A354
A35
A31
A27
A272
A286
A29
A259
A286
A272
A212
A417
A420
A429
A419
A361
A346
A344
A340
A332
A308
A329
A4
A404
A413
A423
A3400

© GEOprojects (UK) Ltd
© Crown Copyright

203

© GEOprojects (UK) Ltd
© Crown Copyright

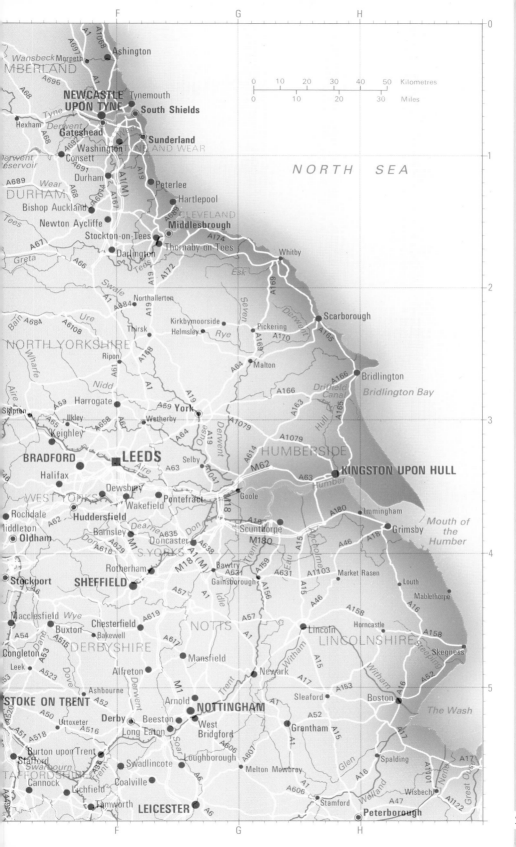

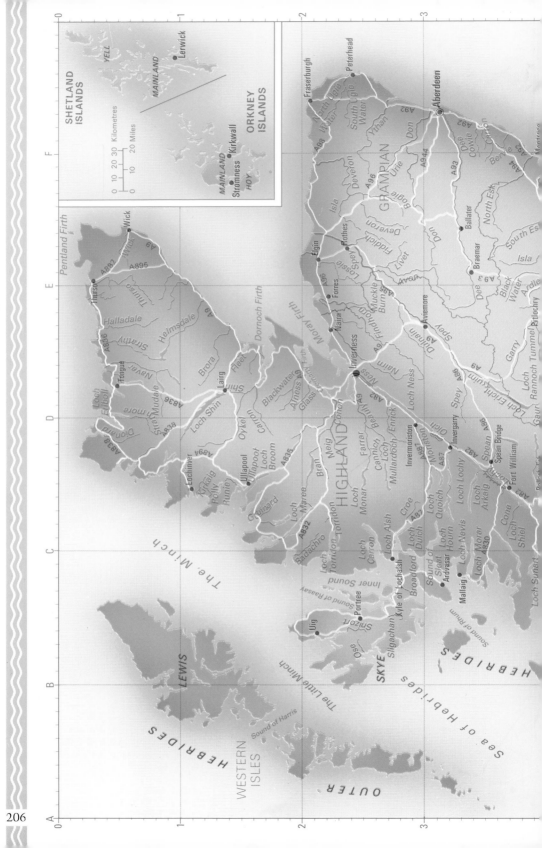

Sunset at Fordingbridge on the Hampshire Avon.

Thames Region

In the Capital.

Although very much a 'hybrid' by including waters from 11 counties spread around the capital, the Thames Region of the NRA comprises two distinct fishery types – namely those urban venues of Greater London, and those of the surrounding, rural areas.

Outside Greater London, river fishing concentrates largely on the River Thames, which flows west-to-east through the region, providing a wide spectrum of coarse fishing venues, from beautiful surroundings in Oxfordshire, to the partly-tidal reaches of Surrey at Richmond and Kingston-upon-Thames. Despite such variation, the Thames offers good quality, consistent fishing, with catches of roach, perch, chub and bream, plus barbel in the upper reaches. Some good river fishing is also available in Surrey on the Wey, which flows into the Thames at Weybridge. Canal fishing is also catered for, with the Basingstoke, Oxford and Grand Union Canals each offering many miles of fishing, while the many stillwater ponds, reservoirs and lakes – many of which specialise in specimen carp or pike fishing – can be an angler's dream!.

Within the Greater London area, coarse fishing venues are (perhaps) surprisingly frequent, with river fishing focused on the Thames at Staines or Laleham, or on the River Lea, which extends north into Hertfordshire and includes the more industrialised areas of the capital's waterways.

Non-river fishing is also easy-to-find, whether at the multi-reservoir Walthamstow complex, on the small canal sections which criss-cross the capital, or on the many lakes and ponds in the public parks. All can yield surprisingly good catches, despite the hubbub of the metropolis!

BERKSHIRE

ALDERMASTON
Atlas Page 203 B.4/5.2

A group of seven gravel pits at Paices Hill, near Aldermaston. Six lakes (all less than 1 acre each) contain mixed coarse fish; lake No. 6 (almost 4 acres) is carp only – with some to 25lb. A very good fishery providing a good day's sport.

How to get there Leave the M4 at jct 12 and take A4 towards Newbury. After 4 miles, bear left onto A340 to Aldermaston; the fishery entrance is just after the village. Parking on site.

Day tickets Adult £3; junior/OAP: £1.50 (dawn to dusk); available from Youngs Garden Centre at the entrance. Also season tickets: adult £26; junior/OAP/disabled £13; (allows night fishing) available from Leisure Sport Angling, Thorpe Park, Staines Road, Chertsey, Surrey; Tel. 0932 564872.

Best methods/baits   Use any recognised coarse technique and baits. Specialist carp methods may be needed in Lake 6.

Restrictions   Carp over 3lb must not be retained.

Facilities   Toilets/food on site. Nearest shop/pub in Aldermaston.

Disabled facilities   Some swims may be suitable for disabled anglers; phone for advice; Tel. 0932 564872.

CALIFORNIA COUNTRY PARK
Atlas Page 203 C.3/5.4

A country park located mid-way between Reading and Camberley, with a 6-acre lake that contains bream, roach, perch, tench, rudd and pike, plus some very big carp (specimens of 30lb have been taken). A pleasant holiday spot for anglers and families.

How to get there   Leave the M3 at jct 4 and turn right onto the A321 towards Wokingham. At Crowthorne, turn left to Finchampstead and follow signs to 'California-in-England' and the fishery. Parking on site.

Day tickets   Adult £3; junior/OAP/ disabled £1.50. Also season tickets: adult £17, concessions £12. Available on site; for details; Tel. 0734 730028.

Best methods/baits   Use any recognised coarse technique and baits.

Facilities   On-site holiday chalet hire available. Toilets/cafe on site. Nearest shop/pub in Finchampstead.

Disabled facilities   Some swims may be suitable for disabled anglers.

DINTON PASTURES COUNTRY PARK (WHITE SWAN LAKES)
Atlas Page 203 B.8/4.9

A 21-acre gravel pit, plus 50 pegs on the River Lodden, near Reading. The lake provides specialist fishing for carp and pike to 30lb, tench and bream 11lb, and good heads of roach, rudd and perch. The Lodden is fairly fast flowing, about 25 yards wide. Expect a good barbel, with fish to 11lb. Also chub to 6lb, some trout and most other general river coarse fish.

How to get there   Leave the M4 at jct 10 and take A329M to Reading. The Park is signposted from this road.

Day tickets   Adult £3; junior/OAP/disabled/UB40 £1.50. Also season permits: adult £17, concessionary £12. Tickets available on site.

Best methods/baits   Use general coarse fishing techniques. Specialist carp methods may be needed.

Facilities   Toilet/cafe on site. Food available at the garage opposite. Nearest shop, 300 yds; nearest pub, Finchampstead (1 mile).

Disabled facilities   The entire lake is suitable for disabled and wheelchair anglers, but not the river.

BUCKINGHAMSHIRE

A good selection on the Grand Union Canal.

BLACK PARK
Atlas Page 203 C.4/4.7

A fairly large park lake (about 7 acres) near Iver town centre, with good fishing for carp, bream and pike. Some carp are especially large, with 28lb specimens reported.

How to get there   Leave the M4 at jct 5 and take Slough exit (A4); turn immediately onto B470 to Iver and in the town, follow signs to Black Park. Park nearby.

Day tickets   Free fishing.

Best methods/baits   Use any recognised coarse technique and baits.

Facilities   Toilets/cafe in park. Nearest shops/pub in Iver.

Disabled facilities   Some swims suitable for disabled anglers.

COMMON POND
Atlas Page 203 C.2/4.5

This compact (1 acre) lake is on common land near Gerrards Cross. Expect easy fishing for roach, tench and a few large carp, with some up to 20lb.

How to get there   Leave the M40 at jct 2 and turn right onto the A40, then right again towards Gerrards Cross. In the town, follow directions to the common and the fishery. Parking nearby.

Day tickets   Free fishing.

Best methods/baits   Use any recognised coarse technique and baits.

Facilities   Nearest shops/pub in Gerrards Cross.

Disabled facilities   Some swims suitable for disabled anglers.

FARLOW'S LAKE
Atlas Page 203 C.5/4.7

A 40-acre lake lying just off the M25 at Iver. Expect some very good fishing, with predominantly very large carp (over 30lb), bream, tench and big pike (to 30lb). There are also some very good winter roach nets taken here.

How to get there   Leave the M4 at jct 4 and take the A408 through West Drayton; at the first roundabout, turn left towards Iver, and just before crossing over the M25, turn left into Ford Lane. Free car parking on site.

Day tickets   Adult/junior/OAP £2.50. Available on the bank.

Best methods/baits   Use general coarse methods and baits.

Facilities   Toilets/cafe/bar/shop and bait all available on site.

Disabled facilities   Some swims are suitable for disabled and wheelchair anglers.

GRAND UNION CANAL –
AYLESBURY ARM
Atlas Page 203 C.2/3.9

A picturesque, 3½-mile long, but very narrow, stretch of the canal, from Aylesbury boat basin to Red House, Aston Clifton. Average depth is 3–4ft, with heavy water plant growth and no boat traffic. Expect most species, but mainly carp, plus some roach and gudgeon.

How to get there   From Aylesbury, take the A41 east towards Tring; Aston Clifton is about 4 miles from Aylesbury. Access to the canal is along various roads to the left.

Day tickets   £2; available from local tackle shops.

Best methods   Carp – leger in the middle; roach, gudgeon -pole or light waggler.

Best baits   Carp – boilies, sweetcorn, meat; roach, gudgeon – maggots.

ESSEX

Newland Hall.

CLAVERHAMBURY LAKE
Atlas Page 203 D.4/4.2

This pleasant, tree-lined, 2-acre, stream-fed fishery is located at Waltham Abbey, just off the northern side of the M25. Variable depth (2–8ft) but well stocked with carp of double-figure size which provide reasonable sport.

How to get there   Leave the M25 at jct 26 and take slip road to Waltham Abbey. Locate Galley Hill Road, then Claverhambury Road and the fishery. Parking available nearby.

Day tickets   Adult/junior/OAP £6 (two rods). Limited tickets; advance booking recommended. Available from P. & B. Hall, 44 Highbridge Street, Waltham Abbey; Tel. 0992 711932.

Best methods   Use modern carp methods.
Best baits   Boilies or multiples.
Restrictions   Maximum 10 anglers per day.
Facilities   Nearest shops/pub in Waltham Abbey.
Disabled facilities   Some swims may be suitable for disabled anglers; contact P. & B. Hall for advice.

Best methods/baits   Use any recognised coarse technique and baits.
Restrictions   No groundbait.
Facilities   Nearest shop/pub in Takeley. Also toilets/food on site.
Disabled facilities   Some swims may be suitable for disabled anglers; check with Warden. From Easter to the end of October, vehicular access is available to the lake.

CONAUGHT WATER
Atlas Page 203 D.5/4.4

A fairly large lake, situated in Epping Forest, which has been recently deepened around its islands and margins but suffers badly from summer weed. Expect a wide variety of coarse fish, including a few wild carp.

How to get there   Leave the M11 at its southern end and take the 3rd exit, signposted Epping. After 1 mile turn into Rangers Road; the fishery is 150 yards on the right; use the gravel car park on the right.
Day tickets   Adult/junior/OAP £1.50. Available from the Hollow Pond Society bailiff on the bank.
Best methods/baits   Use any recognised coarse technique and baits.
Facilities   Occasional snack food available on site. Nearest shop Chingford (¾ mile); nearest pub, The Royal Forest Hotel (½ mile).
Disabled facilities   Some swims suitable for disabled and wheelchair anglers.

HATFIELD FOREST LAKE
Atlas Page 203 D.6/3.7

A National Trust property which includes a large fishing lake, not far from Stansted Airport. A mixed fishery – pike, tench, roach and rudd, plus some large carp. For more information, contact the Warden (see below).

How to get there   Leave the M11 at jct 8 and turn right onto the A120; Hatfield Forest is on the right before the B183 junction (Takeley) to Hatfield Broad Oak. Look for directions to the Forest and fishery; parking available on site.
Day tickets   Adult £2.50; junior/OAP £1.25. Available only in advance, from The Warden, The Shell House, Takeley, Bishop's Stortford; Tel. 0279 870678.

HIGHAMS PARK LAKE
Atlas Page 203 D.5/4.4

A park lake close to Woodford Green, brimming full of tench, plus good numbers of carp and also jack-pike in the winter. Summer fishing can be difficult unless a swim is raked.

How to get there   Leave the M11 at its southern end, take the 3rd exit (signposted Epping/South Woodford). Turn left at Chingford Lane traffic lights, fork immediately left (Charter Road) and continue to end of road; the lake is on the right. Park on the roadside.
Day tickets   Adult/junior/OAP £1.50. Available on the bank.
Best methods   Float fishing preferred for tench.
Best baits   Tench – sweetcorn, breadflake. Other species – most baits work well.
Facilities   Nearest shop/pub Highams Park (1 mile).

HOLLOW PONDS
Atlas Page 203 D.5/4.6

Considering its location (close to Whipps Cross Hospital) a very picturesque lake, weed-free and with plenty of tench in the hollows. Also three big bream shoals, good carp and large eels (to 7lb), and excellent pike fishing in winter.

How to get there   Leave the M11 at its southern end, bear left to the roundabout and take the 1st exit; look for Snaresbrook Road on left after 1½ miles. At road end, bear left and turn left opposite Whipps Cross Hospital. Park in the layby at the roadside.
Day tickets   Adult/junior/OAP £1.50. Available from the Hollow Pond Society bailiff on the bank.
Best methods   Bream, tench – use leger or swim feeder.

Best baits   Roach – hemp, casters; carp – boilies.

Facilities   Food available from mobile shops; nearest static shop ¼ mile; nearest pub, The Alfred Hitchcock, Whipps Cross Road.

Disabled facilities   Some swims suitable for disabled and wheelchair anglers.

THE CHASE
Atlas Page 203 D.6/4.7

A large gravel pit, to the east of Dagenham, providing good sport for roach, perch, bream, tench, pike and Crucian carp, plus some good-sized common carp.

How to get there   Take the A13 east from London and at Dagenham, turn left (A1112) to Dagenham East underground station. Look for signs to the fishery and car park

Day tickets   Adult £1.50; junior/OAP 75p. Available from the bailiff on the bank.

Best methods/baits   Use any recognised coarse technique and baits.

Restrictions   No night fishing.

Facilities Nearest shops/pubs in Dagenham.

Disabled facilities   Some swims may be suitable for disabled anglers.

WALTHAM ABBEY
Atlas Page 203 D.4/4.2

A short stretch of the Horsemill Stream in Waltham Abbey which has been developed solely for use by disabled anglers. The site is kept locked; access is by key only (see below). Expect some good fishing, with most coarse species in reasonable numbers.

How to get there   Leave the M25 at jct 26 and take the A121 to Waltham Abbey. Follow the road through the town and at the 2nd roundabout turn right along Highbridge Street. The fishery entrance is just on the right; there is a small car park on the roadside.

Day tickets   For disabled anglers, a free seasonal permit and key is available on written application to Mr. Baldwin, Fisheries Manager, Lee Valley Park, P.O. Box 88, Enfield, Middlesex. *Note:* the key also enables access to the Dobbs Weir fishery (see Hertfordshire, below).

Best methods/baits   Use general coarse methods and baits.

Facilities   Nearest shops and pubs are in Waltham Abbey.

Disabled facilities   All paths are made up to allow access by wheelchair and disabled anglers.

GLOUCESTERSHIRE

A 4lb common carp

BRADLEY'S PIT
Atlas Page 203 A.4/4.4

A 100-acre, mature gravel pit located south-east of Cirencester. Mainly tench, with huge catches every season, but most species present. There is a restricted area for day-ticket anglers. Fishing is best with overcast, light conditions and wind.

How to get there   From Cirencester, head south-east on the A419; after about 4 miles, turn right towards South Cerney and the Cotswold Water Park. Take 2nd right into Broadway Lane; entrance is 600 yards on right. Free parking on site.

Day tickets   Adult £2; junior/OAP £1; available from machine at Fishermans Rest, Broadway Lane, South Cerney; or South Cerney Clubhouse, at Ham Pool, Broadway Lane, in South Cerney. Season tickets also available, adult £17.50; junior/OAP £5.

Best methods   Float fish down the marginal shelf.

Best baits   Casters plus groundbait.

Facilities   Shop and 3 pubs in South Cerney village. Licensed club house open evenings Mon-Fri; lunch and evenings Sat/Sun.

Disabled facilities   Some swims suitable for disabled anglers.

HAM POOL
Atlas Page 203 A.4/4.4

An 11-acre gravel pit at South Cerney village, adjacent to Bradley's Pit (see above). A good general coarse fishery, plus some generally small carp.

How to get there Follow directions as for Bradley's Pit; follow signs to the fishery and parking.

Day tickets Adult £2; junior/OAP £1; available from machine at Fishermans Rest, Broadway Lane, South Cerney; or South Cerney Clubhouse, in Broadway Lane, by the pool. Season tickets also available – adult £17.50; junior/OAP £5.

Best methods/baits Use any recognised coarse technique and baits.

Facilities Shop and 3 pubs in South Cerney village. Licensed club house open evenings Mon-Fri; lunch and evenings Sat/Sun.

Disabled facilities Some swims suitable for disabled anglers.

HORSESHOE LAKE
Atlas Page 203 A.7/4.3

A nationally-renowned, prolific, 70-acre carp fishery just north of Lechlade and controlled by the Carp Society. Multiple catches of 12–18lb fish plus plenty of 25lb+ specimens – some of the hardest fighters going! Best fishing in summer.

How to get there Take the A361 north from Lechlade towards Burford. After about ½ mile, go past roundabout; Horseshoe Lake is on the right. Free car parking on site.

Day tickets Adult/junior/OAP £3: 24-hour ticket £6: weekly ticket £20. Tickets (available only to Carp Society members) from Chase Newsagents, Burford Road, Lechlade.

Best methods/baits Use any recognised carp technique or bait.

Restrictions No bent-hook rigs. Some particle baits are banned.

Facilities Shop/toilets/food and pubs in Lechlade (½ mile).

Disabled facilities Some swims suitable for disabled anglers; also some platforms for disabled.

KEYNES PARK
Atlas Page 203 A.4/4.4

Two fairly large gravel pits set in a country park south of Cirencester. Excellent fishing for tench, especially in the 'Top Pit' in winter; also bream, plus some big roach. Weedy swims can cause problems. Usually very busy on summer weekends.

How to get there Take the A419 south-east from Cirencester towards Cricklade. After about 4 miles, look for right turn to Somerford Keynes and Ashton Keynes; look for signs to Keynes Country Park (on right). Free car parking on site.

Day tickets Adult £2; junior/OAP £1; available from the Warden's Office on site.

Best methods Use recognised techniques.

Best baits Casters, groundbait.

Facilities Toilets/food in park; also children's play area/paddling pool. Nearest shops Ashton Keynes/South Cerney (1 mile); nearest pub Baker Arms, Somerford Keynes (½ mile).

Disabled facilities Some swims suitable for disabled anglers.

SOUTH CERNEY, NO. 1 LAKE
Atlas Page 203 A.4/4.4

One lake of a fishing complex near Cirencester. Good quality coarse fishing in fairly shallow (5–6ft) water, with carp, bream, tench, roach and pike. No closed season; fishing available all year round. A ¾-acre section has just been fenced off and restocked with small carp, so sport should improve next year!

How to get there Head north-west from Swindon on the A419 and about 2 miles after Cricklade take left turn on minor road to Cerney Wick and South Cerney. In South Cerney, turn left at the War Memorial; the lake is on the right. Free car parking on site.

Day tickets Anglers must become members of Isis A.C. There is no subsequent charge for fishing on No. 1 lake. Membership £15.50; available from Rob's Tackle, Chippenham; Tel. 0249 659210, or Swindon Angling Centre, Sheppard Street, Swindon; Tel. 0793 619909.

Best methods Waggler is best, but lead or feeder also work well.

Best baits All baits work well here; maggots are preferred.

Restrictions No groundbait during closed season.

Facilities Nearest shop, South Cerney
(1½ miles).
Disabled facilities Some swims are
suitable for disabled and wheelchair
anglers.

GREATER LONDON

Inner City ponds can be overcrowded.

BURGESS PARK LAKE
Atlas Page 203 D.3/4.7

In South London (not far from the
Elephant & Castle), a public park lake, not
picturesque but suitable for fishing. Most
species, including roach, tench and carp.

How to get there From the Old Kent
Road (A2), look for signs to Burgess Park
and the fishery.
Day tickets Adult £1.50; junior/OAP
£1.25; available only from the bank.
Best methods Use leger and float as
necessary.
Best baits Maggots, boilies, worms.
Facilities Toilets on site; shops/food
locally.
Disabled facilities Some swims suitable
for disabled anglers.

CLAPHAM COMMON POND
Atlas Page 203 D.3/4.9

A quite large (2 acre) pond in south-east
London. A good mixture of coarse fish,
including mirror and common carp to
20lb, but a very busy, often crowded
venue, making fishing difficult. Night
fishing can be more productive.

How to get there Follow the South
Circular (A205) to Clapham Common.
The pond is visible from the road; park
on the roadside near the fishery.Or
travel to Clapham Common
underground and walk to the pond.
Day tickets Free fishing.
Best methods/baits Use any recognised
coarse techniques and baits.
Facilities Nearest shops/pub near
Clapham Common underground
station.
Disabled facilities Easy access makes
most swims suitable for disabled and
wheelchair anglers.

COPPERMILL STREAM
Atlas Page 203 D.3/4.5

A surprisingly good London fishery
consisting of a 1-mile river section, close
to Tottenham Hale underground station.
Contains barbel, bream, roach, chub, dace,
grayling and pike; also some large carp (to
16lb).

How to get there Follow the A10 north
from London city centre to Seven Sisters
and turn right along Broad Lane, then
Ferry Lane to the underground station;
use the car park nearby and walk to the
water. Or travel directly by underground.
Day tickets Adult/junior/OAP £3
Available from the machine on the
bank. Correct money is necessary.
Best methods/baits Use any recognised
coarse technique and baits.
Restrictions No groundbaiting. Fishing
only from 0730 until 30 mins after
sunset; no night fishing.
Facilities Nearest shops, Ferry Lane;
nearest pub, the Ferry Boat Inn.
Disabled facilities Some swims may be
suitable for disabled anglers.

EAGLE POND
Atlas Page 203 D.4/4.5

A high-banked fishery fed by a stream, and
with a weir exit, located at Snaresbrook,
near Wanstead. Expect mainly tench,
roach and bream, plus some fairly large
carp near the Court House bank in
summer.

How to get there Leave the M11 at its
southern end, bear left to the
roundabout and take the 1st exit; look
for Snaresbrook Road on left after 1½
miles; the road runs alongside the pond.
Free car parking on the roadside.

Day tickets Adult/junior/OAP £1.50. Available on the bank.

Best methods Tench, roach, bream – use waggler or feeder. Carp – use floaters in summer.

Best baits Most baits work well here.

Restrictions No fishing from the far bank. No night fishing. Use only lead-free weights.

Facilities Nearest shop/pub, The Eagle, Snaresbrook (½ mile).

HAINAULT LAKE
Atlas Page 203 D.6/4.5

A small lake set within Hainault Country Park near Loughton. Expect mostly carp (which provide very good sport), plus a few tench, roach and pike.

How to get there From Romford, head north on the A1112 towards Loughton. Look for signs to Hainault Country Park, opposite the Broad Oak pub; park (free) at the roadside and walk down hill to the lake.

Day tickets Adult/junior/OAP £1.50. Available on the bank.

Best methods/baits Use any recognised coarse technique. Carp respond to most methods.

Restrictions No night fishing.

Facilities Nearest shop/pub, The Broad Oak, Hainault (¼ mile).

Disabled facilities Some swims suitable for disabled and wheelchair anglers.

Rivers

RIVER LEA

The River Lea flows – in natural and canalised forms – through Hertfordshire into North London. It is mostly slow, but may become pacey, notably at King's Weir fishery. Most coarse species swim in profusion in the Lea, where tackle-shy shoals offer a challenge to matchmen, and specimen hunters seek pike, carp, barbel and chub. Listed here are six *Angling Times* Hotspots situated along the Lea's length.

The River Lea.

216

KING'S WEIR & LANGUAGE LAKE
Atlas Page 203 D.3/4.5

A 40–50ft wide section, with average depth about 4ft. The stretch is pacier than most reaches of the Lea, with the streamer weed-filled runs containing good shoals of chub and roach; barbel over 10lb are also taken each season. Typical nets are 30–40lb. Adjacent to King's Weir is Language Lake, a large water with 5 or 6 swims for day fishing and a further 15 on the season ticket. With depth from 5 foot to 15 foot and a good mixture of fish, it can be hard going, but it can also be good going.

How to get there Take the Wormley exit off A10, onto A1170 into Wormley. At roundabout turn left, then right into Wharf Road (about ½ mile), Walk 400 yards downstream to weirpool.
Day tickets On the lake, £1. At the weir pool, £5 per rod, but this must be booked in advance. Season ticket for river and lake (but not the weirpool) £30 plus £4 for a key. Details from Bill Newton, Tel. 0992 468394.
Best methods Roach – stick float with fine tackle; chub and barbel – fish the lead with heavier tackle to extract specimens from the streamer weed.
Best baits Roach – maggots, casters; chub, barbel – luncheon meat.

Hotspot Tips

- Fish the weirpool itself for the best chub and barbel.
- Fish fine to tempt the tackle-shy shoals.

WALTHAM COMMON
Atlas Page 203 D.3/4.5

Here, the Lea is slow-flowing, 30–45ft wide, with average depth 5ft. Fishing is generally superior on the far bank, despite rush beds. Expect skimmer bream (to 1lb), tench and roach. Typical roach nets are 10lb+; long poles can produce 20lb+ nets of bream.

How to get there Leave the M25 at junction 25 or 26; follow the signs to Waltham Abbey. Take the Abbey Road and park by the Olde English Gentleman pub.

Day tickets Adult £1.50; junior/OAP 50p; available on the bank.
Best methods Summer – short pole (3–5 metres) for roach, 12-metre pole for skimmer bream and tench. Light tackle (1lb bottoms, 18–24 hooks) is essential.
Best baits Summer roach – hemp; bream, tench – maggots, casters, pinkies.
Facilities Food/toilets at the Olde English Gentleman pub.

Hotspot Tips

- Popular hotspots are the first 5 pegs above the lock, and either side of the footbridge.
- For far bank specimens, try a light waggler rig.

PONDERS END
Atlas Page 203 D.3/4.6

A wide (50–60ft) stretch, with poor flow, but strong currents in the first 10 swims. Average depth 7ft; minimal weed growth. A good, all-year-round fishery including roach, dace, perch, bream, carp, chub and tench. Expect nets of 10lb for roach, or 20lb for chub.

How to get there Leave the M25 at junction 25, follow the A1010 to Ponders End. Take Wharf Road, off the main Lea Valley Road.
Day tickets Adult £1.50; junior/OAP 50p; available on the bank.
Best methods Short pole for inside lines, or a long pole for quality fish further out. Fine tackle only.
Best baits Summer roach – hemp; casters, maggots for all species.

Hotspot Tips

- Try a bomb rig for the far bank – or a 2 or 3AAA waggler set-up.
- For chub and an occasional carp, try luncheon meat or sweetcorn.
- The best swims are opposite the Ford factory; mixed nets of 30lb+ are common.

COOKS FERRY
Atlas Page 203 D.3/4.6

A wide (40–50ft), shallow, slow-flowing region, average depth 7ft. Cooks Ferry fishes well all season, but opposite Tottenham playing fields is best in summer. Catches of roach, chub, perch, bream, tench and bleak can reach 10lb+, with 20lb+ possible.

How to get there   Turn off the A406 North Circular Road into Lea Valley Trading Estate and follow the road to the river.
Day tickets   Adult £1.50; junior/OAP 50p; available on the bank.
Best methods   Chub, bream–fish under the far bank with light waggler rig or bomb. Use a short whip for smaller fish on the inside. Light tackle is essential.
Best baits   Casters ideal all season; for summer roach – use hemp. Luncheon meat and corn are useful change baits.

Hotspot Tips

- For quality roach and skimmer bream, use a long pole, laying on over-depth.
- The two barge-turning bays are hotspots for bream and carp.

The River Lea.

STONEBRIDGE
Atlas Page 203 D.3/4.7

A good, all-year-round stretch, with a slight flow, full width (40–60ft) and little weed. Average depth 7ft, with shelves either side, 9ft out. Main species include chub, roach, bream and perch, plus some large carp. Typical nets 10–20lb, but the far bank may produce 20lb+, mainly chub.

How to get there   From Northumberland Park station, drive over the level crossing and follow Marsh Lane down to the river.

Day tickets   Adult £1.50; junior/OAP 50p; available on the bank.
Best methods   Roach, bream – short poles in summer, long poles for all-year. Roach, chub – light waggler rig fished on the drop at the far bank. Light tackle is essential.
Best baits   Casters, hemp, red maggot.

Hotspot Tips

- A light bomb rig or block-end feeder is ideal for chub, bream and roach.
- The best swims are just below the lock, or anywhere near moored boats.

TOTTENHAM HALE
Atlas Page 203 D.3/4.7

A medium flow fishery, average depth 8ft, average width 50ft, with a distinct far-bank shelf, 3ft out. The bottom is snaggy, with a fine weed. Good catches of roach, chub, dace and bream are common, with mixed nets of over 25lb. An occasional specimen carp is taken.

How to get there   From Walthamstow, follow the Ferry Lane down to the river.
Day tickets   Adult £1.50; junior/OAP 50p; available on the bank.
Best methods   Large roach – lay over-depth with a long pole; small roach, dace – stick float.
Best baits   Casters or maggots for quality roach.

Hotspot Tips

- For consistent sport, fish the Pymmes Brook outfall and Stamford Hill Marina.
- A waggler or leger fished tight against the far shelf may produce good bream and chub.

LEE PARK WAY, EDMONTON
Atlas Page 203 D.3/4.7

This fishery is on the western bank of the River Lee navigation, alongside Lee Park Way, and extends from the car park (northern end) to the bridge of the Lee Park Way over the river. Expect good-sized bream (to 5lb+), roach, carp (to 10lb), tench, bleak, dace and pike from these waters, with some good sport available.

How to get there   From the North Circular road at Upper Edmonton, turn along Montagu Road (near Angel Road station) and turn right into Picketts Lock Lane, then into Lee Park Way. Follow the road to the car park at the north end of Lee Park Way.

Day tickets   Adult £2; junior/OAP £1. Available on site.

Best methods/baits   Use general coarse methods and baits.

Restrictions   Security gates open 0700–2300 Monday-Saturday; 1400–2300 Sunday. Fishing only sunrise until sunset (all season).

Facilities   Refreshments available at Picketts Lock Centre.

Disabled facilities   A special area adjoining the car park has been reserved for disabled and wheelchair anglers.

LIMEHOUSE CUT
Atlas Page D.4/4.7

A tidal canal running through east London. Fishing is possible throughout the tide, though on very high tides the towpath may be under 3″ of water. Expect most species in large numbers.

How to get there   The fishery is approached at points along its length, from the north end near Blackwall Tunnel Approach Road (A11) to the south end at Limehouse (on the A13). Limited, free roadside parking.

Day tickets   Adult £1; junior/OAP 50p. Season tickets: adults £7.50; junior/OAP £5. Available from local tackle shops.

Best methods/baits   Use recognised methods and baits.

Restrictions   No bloodworm or joker.

Facilities   Shops/toilets/food available locally; most open late. Nearest pub 150 yards from any exit.

LITTLE BRITAIN
Atlas Page 203 C.7/4.7

A square-shaped, 35-acre lake lying close to West Drayton and the M4. A pleasant fishery providing good general coarse sport covering most species. Expect to catch almost anything here!

How to get there   Leave the M4 at jct 4 and take the A408 through West Drayton. Turn left at the Paddington Packet Boat pub (about 1 mile) and continue to the lake at the bottom of the road. Free car parking on site.

Day tickets   Adult/junior/OAP £2. Available on the bank.

Best methods/baits   Use general coarse methods and baits.

Facilities   Nearest shop, West Drayton (2 miles); nearest pub, Paddington Packet Boat.

LOW MAYNARD/NO.2/NO.3
Atlas Page 203 D.3/4.6

A trio of Walthamstow reservoirs – Low Maynard (25 acres), No. 2 (13 acres) and No. 3 (12 acres) – near Blackhorse Road underground station. Expect tench, bream, roach and carp in good numbers, but sport can vary. Winter fishing is generally good here.

How to get there   At Crooked Billet roundabout on the A406 North Circular road, take Billet Road to Walthamstow (Blackhorse Road station). Turn right at underground station, the reservoir is just on the right; main gates are on the left. Free car parking on site. Or travel to either Tottenham Hale or Blackhorse Road station and walk to the water.

Day tickets   Adult/junior/OAP £3 Available from the machine on the bank. Exact money is necessary.

Best methods   Use any recognised coarse technique and baits.

Restrictions   Fishing only from 0730 until 30 mins after sunset; no night fishing. Closed Christmas Day.

Facilities   Toilets on site. Nearest shops, Ferry Lane; nearest pub, the Ferry Boat Inn.

Disabled facilities   Some swims may be suitable for disabled anglers.

NEW CUT
Atlas Page 203 D.3/4.6

A ¾-mile long river cut, close to the Walthamstow reservoir complex and Tottenham Hale underground station. Roach, chub and bream have been reported in these waters, plus the occasional carp – some quite large!

How to get there   Follow the A10 north from London city centre to Seven Sisters and turn right along Broad Lane, then Ferry Lane to the underground station; use the car park nearby and walk to the water, or travel directly by underground.

Day tickets   Adult/junior/OAP £3. Available from the machine on the bank. Exact money is necessary.

Best methods/baits   Use any recognised coarse technique and baits.

Restrictions   Fishing only from 0730 until 30 mins after sunset; no night fishing.

Facilities   Nearest shops, Ferry Lane; nearest pub, the Ferry Boat Inn.

Disabled facilities   Not suitable for disabled anglers.

REGENTS CANAL
Atlas Page 203 D.3/4.7

A picturesque stretch of canal, set in the heart of London, which attracts anglers and sightseers alike. Generally good roach sport, plus some bream and dace for variety. Fishes best in winter.

How to get there   At the junction of Mile End Road (A11) and the North Circular (A406), near Woodford, follow Grove Road to Bethnall Green, where it meets Old Ford Road. The entrance to Victoria Park is close by; park nearby and walk.

Day tickets   Adult £3; junior/OAP 50p. Available on the bank.

Best methods/baits   Winter roach – use pole (or waggler) with punched bread with liquidised bread feed. Use squatts or pinkies as alternative.

Facilities   Shops, pubs and toilets are nearby, depending on where you fish!

Disabled facilities   Reasonable access for disabled anglers.

RODING VALLEY LAKE
Atlas Page 203 D.5/4.4

A smallish lake situated within a sports complex in Loughton. The lake has a good supply of natural food making fishing generally hard. Expect large carp (to 24lb), bream (to 10lb+), perch and roach (to 2lb).

How to get there   At Loughton near the M11, jct 5. Access (via a housing estate) and parking details are complicated; contact A1 Angling, 176 High Road, Woodford Green, Essex; Tel. 081 504 4848 for further information.

Day tickets   Adult £1.50; junior/OAP £1 (max 2 rods per person). Also day season tickets £10 per annum. Available on the bank or from A1 Angling (see above).

Best methods   Most species – pole or swim feeder; carp – leger.

Best baits   Most baits work well here.

Restrictions   No bloodworm or jokers.

Facilities   Nearest shops 400 yards;

nearest pub, The Old Mother Hubbard 300 yards.

Disabled facilities   Some swims suitable for disabled and wheelchair anglers.

SAVAY LAKE
Atlas Page C.7/4.4

One of the premier fisheries around London, set in a mature 60-acre gravel pit near Denham. Expect mixed fish, with bream, tench, perch, roach and pike – all very large, plus some very big carp. Only very experienced carp anglers should attempt fishing here – even so, the latest techniques are vital.

How to get there   Take the A40 west from London and turn right onto the A412 at Denham (start of the M40). Drive past Denham station (½ mile) and turn right into Moorfield Road (towards Harefield). The lake entrance is ½ mile on the right.

Day tickets   Adult £2; junior/OAP £1. Evening ticket £1. All available from Peverills Newsagents, 3 Moorhall Road, Harefield; or Balfours Newsagents, 12 Station Parade, Denham. Season tickets: adult £25; junior/OAP £12.50; only from the Fishery Manager, 309 Shirland Road, London W9 (SAE please).

Best methods/baits   Use any recognised coarse techniques and baits. Modern carp methods and baits will be required.

Restrictions   Fishery open 0800 until sunset. No night fishing. Public access is restricted to 100 pegs on the open part. Juniors must be accompanied by an adult (unless season ticket holders).

Facilities   Nearest shop/pub in Harefield.

Disabled facilities   Some swims may be suitable for disabled anglers.

SOUTH NORWOOD LAKES
Atlas Page 203 D.3/4.8

A group of lakes located in a south London public park, between Norwood and Croydon. Good general fishing for most species, including large bream and carp. Some boating activity at weekends can cause problems.

How to get there   From central London, follow the A281 from Upper Norwood (near ITV television tower) down South Norwood Hill. After traffic lights, turn left into Wood Vale Avenue; the lakes

are at the end of the road. No car parking on site, use adjacent roads.
Day tickets   Adult £1.80; junior/OAP £1.40; available only from the bank.
Best methods   Smaller species – float; larger species – legering.
Best baits   Maggots, worm, plus general carp baits.
Facilities   Cafeteria/toilets in park.
Disabled facilities   Some swims suitable for disabled and wheelchair anglers.

Rivers
RIVER THAMES

LALEHAM
Atlas Page 203 C.5/5.0

North bank, a shallow area with a gentle slope to the far bank (6–7ft); width 40 yds. Little weed growth but many houseboats. Dace and roach all season; large summer chub (to 5lb). Day catches can exceed 25lbs, especially if chub are located.

How to get there   Between Staines and Shepperton. Access is via the B376 Staines-Shepperton road; take the turn towards Laleham Park.
Day tickets   Free fishing
Best methods   Summer chub – feeder with bronze maggot; roach and dace – waggler in mid-river with maggot or caster on size 18–22 hook. Use fine tackle whenever possible.
Best baits   Bronze maggots, caster, hemp; groundbait is not recommended.

Hotspot Tips

☙ For big summer chub, use a feeder with bronze maggot and fine tackle; cast to the far bank.

☙ For best results, loosefeed maggot/hemp or caster/hemp every cast.

STAINES
Atlas Page 203 C.5/4.9

North bank, very low flow in summer, but good in winter. Average depth 8–10ft; width 30–35yds. Weed growth minimal; no pronounced shelves or channels. Good spot for dace, roach, perch, chub, barbel; perch may produce 20lb day-catches.

How to get there   Leave the M25 at jct 13; follow signs to Staines Town (via B376). Access north bank of river via various riverside roads.
Day tickets   Free fishing
Best methods   Summer – waggler or stick float. Feeders give good results.
Best baits   Roach – hemp, tares in summer; maggot, hemp, caster all season.

Hotspot Tips

☙ Best swims are downstream of road bridge, upstream of Staines Bridge.
☙ Use fine end tackle – 1lb bottoms and hooks 18–22 range.
☙ Keep shotting light down the line; look for bites on the drop.

River Thames, near Staines.

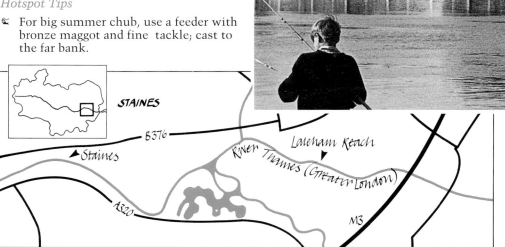

WAKE VALLEY LAKE
Atlas Page 203 D.5/4.4

Located in Epping Forest, a very deep, very 'snaggy' lake which provides hard fishing, but when they bite, the pike, tench and carp are all very big!

How to get there   From Chingford, take Epping New Road north, through Robin Hood (pub) roundabout towards Epping. After 2 miles, turn left shortly after passing the lake. Free parking at the lakeside.
Day tickets   Free fishing.
Best methods/baits   Use any recognised coarse technique.
Facilities   Nearest shop Chingford (2–3 miles); nearest pub, The Robin Hood (2 miles).

WALTHAMSTOW NO. 1 RESERVOIR
Atlas Page 203 D.3/4.6

A 19-acre reservoir in the Walthamstow 'complex', close to Tottenham Hale underground station. Expect tench, roach and bream, and a good head of 6–12lb carp, though larger fish have been recorded here.

How to get there   At Crooked Billet roundabout on the A406 North Circular, take Billet Road to Walthamstow (Blackhorse Road station). Turn right at station, the reservoir is on the left, through the main gates. Free car parking on site. Or travel direct by underground railway.
Day tickets   Adult/junior/OAP £3 (two rods). Also weekend tickets £3.50 (two rods). Available from the machine on the bank. Exact money is necessary.
Best methods   Use any recognised coarse technique and baits.
Restrictions   Fishing only from 0730 until 30 mins after sunset; no night fishing.
Facilities   Toilets on site. Nearest shops, Ferry Lane; nearest pub, the Ferry Boat Inn.
Disabled facilities   Wheelchair anglers may fish from a platform built into the lake; also suitable for disabled anglers.

WANSTEAD LAKE
Atlas Page 203 D.5/4.6

A lake fishery at Wanstead, close to the Redbridge roundabout. An ideal spot for Crucian carp, but a mixed bag is to be expected. Virtually any tactics or bait will provide a good catch here.

How to get there   Turn off the A12 onto the A127 and head towards Wanstead underground station. At next traffic lights turn left into Blake Hall Road; turn left at mini-roundabout into Primrose Road, take 3rd left (opposite Flats) and drive to road end. Park near the lake.
Day tickets   Adult £1.50; junior/OAP 75p. Available on the bank.
Best methods/baits   Use any recognised coarse technique and baits.
Facilities   Nearest shops Wanstead Flats (¼ mile); nearest pub, Three Rabbits, Romford Road (about 1 mile).
Disabled Facilities   Some swims are suitable for disabled and wheelchair anglers.

WEST WARWICK
Atlas Page 203 D.3/4.6

A 34-acre reservoir at Walthamstow, near Tottenham Hale or Blackhorse Road underground stations. A carp-only fishery, with average size about 10lb, and some fish to 25lb+.

How to get there   At Crooked Billet roundabout on the A406 North Circular road, take Billet Road to Walthamstow (Blackhorse Road station). Turn right at station, the reservoir is on the left, through the main gates. Free car parking on site. Or travel direct by underground railway.
Day tickets   Adult/junior/OAP £3. Available from the machine on the bank. Exact money is necessary.
Best methods   Use any recognised coarse technique and baits.
Restrictions   Fishing only from 0730 until 30 mins after sunset; no night fishing. No groundbait.
Facilities   Toilets on site. Nearest shops, Ferry Lane; nearest pub, the Ferry Boat Inn.
Disabled facilities   Some swims are suitable for disabled and wheelchair anglers.

WRAYSBURY
Atlas Page 203 C.5/4.9

These two gravel pits – Lake 1 is 61 acres, Lake 2 is 76 acres – are located near Staines, and both offer excellent coarse fishing for most species. Lake 1 is particularly renowned for its very big carp, though few such fish have been landed. A venue for the specialist carp angler only!

14lb 5oz tench, taken at Wraysbury.

How to get there   Take the A30 past Staines, go under the M25 (at jct 13) and take the B376 towards Wraysbury. Go through village (Station Road), turn left on Douglas Lane to Lake 1 car park. The Lake 2 entrance is where the B376 turns left in Wraysbury village centre (near the school).

Day tickets   Adult £2; junior/OAP £1. Also season tickets: adult £24; junior/OAP/disabled £12. Available (in advance only) from Wraysbury Newsagents in the High Street; or Davies Angling, 47 Church Street, Staines.

Best methods/baits   Use any recognised coarse technique and baits. Advanced methods (long casting) may be required for carp.

Restrictions   No fishing within casting distance of trout pens.

Facilities   Nearest shop/pub in Wraysbury village.

Disabled facilities   Some swims may be suitable for disabled anglers.

HAMPSHIRE

BASINGSTOKE CANAL: CHEQUERS BRIDGE
Atlas Page 203 C.2/5.3
A stretch of the Basingstoke Canal, near Church Crookham in Hampshire. Excellent general coarse fishing for roach, tench and carp, plus some pike.

How to get there   Turn off the west-bound M3 at jct 5 and take the A287 east for 5 miles. Turn left into Crondall Road, cross the canal and turn left. Car parking on site.

Day tickets   Adult £1.50; junior/OAP 75p; available from B.B.C. Tackle, 3 Elmfield Court, Lindford, Bordon, Hants; Tel. 0420 472573.

Best methods   Pole and waggler.

Best baits   Roach – bread punch; tench, carp, skimmer bream – feed casters to weed; perch, pike – chopped worm on inside line.

Restrictions   No bloodworms to be used.

Facilities   Nearest shop 1½ miles; nearest pub 300 yards.

Disabled facilities   Some swims suitable for disabled and wheelchair anglers.

BASINGSTOKE CANAL: CLAYCART BRIDGE
Atlas Page 203 C.2/5.2
A 15-mile canal stretch, recently restored, running from Aldershot to Fleet. Expect plenty of mixed coarse fish and some fairly large carp, with some fish reaching 20lb+.

How to get there   From Aldershot, drive west on the A323 towards Fleet. Access to the water is possible (among other sites) at Claycart Bridge; park nearby and walk to the fishery.

Day tickets   In advance: adult £1; junior/OAP 50p. On the bank: adult £1.50; junior/OAP 75p. Available from local tackle shops, such as Raison Brothers in Farnborough; Tel. 0252 543470.

Best methods/baits   Use any recognised coarse technique and baits.

Facilities   Nearest shop/pub in Aldershot or Fleet.

Disabled facilities   Access is generally difficult, preventing use by disabled anglers.

HOLLYBUSH LANE PIT NO. 3
Atlas Page 203 C.3/5.2
One of three lakes, just to the west of Farnborough. A mature, picturesque fishery, 5–15ft deep, tree-lined and with islands, which provides very good coarse fishing from about 40 pegs. Expect bream, tench, roach, perch and pike, plus some large carp. Best fishing is in the deeper water near the car park.

How to get there   Leave the south-bound M3 at jct 4 and take A325 towards Farnborough. At Queens Hotel (3 miles), turn left onto A3011. The entrance is 1 mile further on, opposite the Fir Tree pub. Park 300 yards down the lane on the left.

Day tickets   Adult £3; junior/OAP £150. Evening ticket £1.50. Available from J.& A. Newsagents, 201 Lychford Road (300 yds from fishery). Tickets must be obtained *before* fishing.

Best methods   Most methods work; pole or waggler preferred. Use groundbait feeder for bream. Advanced carp methods may be required.

Best baits   Carp and tench – use sweetcorn. Other species – most baits work well.

Restrictions   No night fishing. No sacking of fish.

Facilities   Nearest shop/pub in Farnborough.

Disabled facilities   Some swims may be suitable for disabled anglers.

WILLOW PARK FISHERIES
Atlas Page 203 C.3/5.3

A complex of lakes lying adjacent to the Basingstoke Canal at Ash Vale, near Aldershot. Main species include roach, bream, tench and carp, with most fishing methods providing excellent sport.

How to get there   Leave the M3 at jct 4 and take the A325 to Queens Hotel roundabout; turn left onto A3011, then right at Ash railway station onto Ash Dale Road. Cross the canal, take next right (Shawfield Rd) at mini-roundabout, then 2nd right, Youngs Drive. Free car parking on site.

Day tickets   Adult/junior/OAP £6; available from Willow Park Fisheries; Tel. 0252 25867. Gates open 0700 hrs. Night fishing by arrangement.

Best methods/baits   Most species – pole on inside line with groundbait feeder; carp – luncheon meat hair-rigged over hemp.

Restrictions   No keepnets; no bait colourings or flavourings. Only barbless hooks to be used; no bent hooks.

Facilities   Shop/toilets/food/tackle/bait/instruction all available on site. Nearest pub, The Cricketers, Shawfield Rd.

Disabled facilities   Some swims suitable for disabled and wheelchair anglers.

HERTFORDSHIRE

Pike.

BROOKFIELD LANE LAKE
Atlas Page 203 D.4/4.3

A 6-acre, tree-lined lake in Cheshunt, just north of the M25. Average depth 5ft, providing good mixed fishing, with large bream (to 5lb), tench (5–6lb), roach, carp (to 20lb), perch and some quite big pike.

How to get there   Take the A10 north from London and turn right to Cheshunt (shortly after the M25 junction). The lake is behind the Tesco and Marks & Spencer stores. Park (free) on the road, near Cheshunt golf course car park and walk to the water.

Day tickets   Adult £2.35; junior/OAP £1.17. Only 10 day tickets issued each day; booking is advisable in summer, at Simpson's, Nunsbury Drive, Turnford, Herts; Tel. 0992 468799.

Best methods/baits   Use general coarse techniques and baits.

Facilities   Nearest shop Tesco (10 mins walk); nearest pub, The White Horse (top of Brookfield Lane).

Disabled facilities   Some parking is also available by the water; also flat concrete areas suitable for wheelchair anglers.

BROXBOURNE MEADOWS
Atlas Page 203 D.4/4.0

An extensive fishery at Broxbourne, near Hoddesdon, producing good mixed fishing for chub, roach, dace, bream, pike and bleak. Various Millstream sites available: western bank, opposite the holiday chalets; eastern bank, from Broxbourne Mill upstream to the footbridge; the Millstream banks; southern bank to Broxbourne boatyard.

How to get there   Leave the north-bound A10 at Cheshunt and take the A1170 to Broxbourne. In the High Street, turn right into either Mill Lane or Station Road and continue to one of three car parks (Meadows, Boatyard or Leisure Pool).

Day tickets   Adult £2; junior/OAP £1. Available on site from the Broxbourne Meadows Warden.

Best methods/baits   Use general coarse methods and baits.

Restrictions   Fishing only from sunrise until sunset (all season).

Facilities   Food/toilets at Broxbourne Meadows.

Disabled facilities   Some swims are suitable for disabled and wheelchair anglers. Disabled toilets also available.

CARTHEGENA FISHERY
Atlas Page 203 D.4/4.1

A short (¾-mile) section of river which forms part of the adjacent gravel works, near Broxbourne. Expect a good mixed bag, including mainly chub and roach, but also some large carp (some to 20lb) and superb perch. The chub are really good – a recent net of nine fish weighed 27lb!

How to get there   Leave the north-bound A10 at Cheshunt and take the A1170 to Broxbourne. Turn left at the traffic lights and follow signs to the Lido Centre. The river is on the left, forming part of the gravel works. Free car parking on site.

Day tickets   Adult/junior/OAP £2. Available from Peter Brill at the fishery; Tel. 0992 463656.

Best methods   A waggler or fairly light quiver tip work best here.

Best baits   Most baits work well.

Restrictions   Fishing only available on the river; NOT in the pits.

Facilities   Refreshment on site in summer. Nearest pub, The Crown (a few hundred yards).

DOBBS WEIR
Atlas Page 203 D.5/4.0

Located to the east of Hoddesdon, this fast-flowing but fairly shallow stretch of water provides excellent mixed coarse fishing, with large carp (20lb+) just above – and chub just below – the weir. Also chub, roach, perch, dace, bream and the odd barbel. Fishing can be difficult due to snaggy conditions.

How to get there   Leave the A10 at Hoddesdon (about 7 miles north of the M25 junction), drive straight on at the 1st roundabout and turn left at the next. Follow the road, over a level crossing, until it passes over the weir. Free car parking nearby in Essex Road or at Dobbs Weir cafe.

Day tickets   Adult/junior/OAP £2. Available on the bank. Free seasonal permit and key available for disabled; apply (writing) to Mr. Baldwin, Fisheries Manager, Lee Valley Park, P.O. Box 88, Enfield, Middlesex; Tel. 0992 717711.

Best methods/baits   Use general coarse techniques and baits.

Facilities   Toilets/cafe on site. Nearest shop, 5 mins walk; nearest pub, The Fish & Eels, next door!

Restrictions   Fishing from sunrise to sunset only.

Disabled facilities   Specially adapted parking/swims/toilets available for disabled and wheelchair anglers.

KINGS WEIR, WORMLEY
Atlas Page 203 D.3/4.2

A combined fishery of a fast-flowing weirpool and river stretch (day tickets on pool only), a few miles north of Cheshunt. Expect mainly barbel (to 12lb), chub (to 6lb) and bream, plus some roach and pike for variety. Best fishing is from pegs 1 and 2 on the weir cill.

How to get there   Take the A10 north to Turnford (about 3 miles beyond the M25) and bear left at 1st roundabout (signposted Wormley). Drive down to the bottom of Wharfe Road and park (free) at the river. The weir is on the right.

Day tickets   Adult/junior/OAP £5 for weirpool tickets. *Note*: bookings must be made before fishing. Also season tickets for the river only, £30 per annum plus £4 for the key. For tickets and availability, contact Bill Newton; Tel. 0992 468394.

Best methods/baits   Use general coarse techniques and baits.

Facilities   Nearest shop/pub, about 1 mile.

FAIRLAND PARK
Atlas Page 203 C.9/3.6

An estate park lake of about 16 acres, located in Stevenage. Expect a reasonable catch of roach, rudd, bream, tench and pike, together with quite large carp – double-figure fish here are quite common.

How to get there   From the A1(M) take the A602 towards Stevenage Town Centre. Continue over two roundabouts; the park is in front of you. Follow signs to the lake.

Day tickets   Adult £2.50; junior/OAP/ UB40 £1.25. Available from the bailiff on the bank.

Best methods/baits   Use any recognised coarse techniques and baits.

Restrictions   Fishing is only permitted from one bank.

Facilities   Nearest shops/toilets/food/ pubs in Stevenage.

Disabled facilities   Some swims suitable for disabled anglers.

GRAND UNION CANAL, TRING
Atlas Page 203 C.3/3.8

A short section of the Canal, providing 'fun' fishing with good numbers of roach, bream, perch and catfish. Also plenty of common and mirror carp, mostly in the 5–7lb region, but with the odd double-figure fish.

How to get there   From Tring town centre, take the B489 north to Marsworth; access to the water is available at various points along the road; check with local tackle shops for details, or contact Tring A.C.; Sec. David Rugg, 175 Aylesbury Road, Andover, Bucks; Tel. 0296 622534.

Day tickets   Adult £2.50; junior/OAP £1. Available on the bank.

Best methods   Float or leger. No specialist carp methods needed.

Best baits   Sweetcorn, maggots or bread.

Facilities   Nearest shops/pub in Tring.

Disabled facilities   Check with local tackle shops for access to disabled anglers.

HOLWELL HYDE LAKE
Atlas Page 203 C.9/3.9

This compact, 2-acre lake is located at Cole Green, near Welwyn Garden City. A pleasant mixed fishery with some good sport – tench, roach and rudd – plus some reasonably-sized carp which are still growing!

How to get there   From the north-bound A1 at Hatfield, turn right onto the A414 towards Hertford. After 3 miles, turn left on B195, continue 1½ miles, then turn left into Holwell Hyde Lane. The fishery is ½ mile on the left. Parking *only* in the allotted car park.

Day tickets   Adult £2.50; junior/OAP £1.25. Available on the bank, or in advance from the Fishery Manger. Fishing from sunrise to sunset; non-ticket holders must not fish before 0830.

Best methods/baits   Use any recognised coarse techniques and baits.

Restrictions   No night fishing. No sacking of fish.

Facilities   Nearest toilets/shop/pub in Welwyn Garden City.

Disabled facilities   Some swims may be suitable for disabled anglers.

NORTH METROPOLITAN PIT
Atlas Page 203 D.3/4.3

A fair-sized pit (48 swims) at Cheshunt; recently stocked with good carp, plus tench of 9lb+, roach, bream, chub and pike to provide excellent fishing sport. Fishing is best around the underwater features – and in the case of large tench in the early morning.

How to get there   Leave the A10 at Cheshunt and drive to the town centre. Turn left at the fountain, go past 3–4 mini-roundabouts, past church and use the (free) car park at the pit. Walk over, then alongside, the railway line to the pit (on the left).

Day tickets   Adult £2; junior/OAP £1. Available on the bank.

Best methods/baits   Fishing for tench is best close in. Use a waggler or swim-feeder. Most baits work well here.

Restrictions   No peanuts. No flattened barbs for pike fishing.

Facilities   Nearest shop/pub/toilets/food at the Cheshunt Country Walk car park (3 mins walk).

Disabled facilities   Five sites have been specially adapted for disabled and wheelchair anglers.

STANBOROUGH LAKE
Atlas Page 203 C.9/3.9

A very busy lake, with sailing and other watersports, close to the A1(M), just south of Welwyn Garden City. An easy-fishing venue, with roach, rudd, tench and catfish – and surprisingly large carp, with many 10–20lb fish, and some approaching 30lb!

How to get there   Take the A1 north from London and exit the A1 (M) at jct 4. The lakes are visible on the right of the motorway. Follow signs to the lake and park nearby.

Day tickets   Adult £2.50; junior/OAP £1.50. Available on the bank.

Best methods/baits   Use any recognised coarse techniques and baits.

Restrictions   Maximum one rod per person (two after 1st November).

Facilities   Toilets/cafe on site. Nearest shops/pub in Welwyn Garden City.

Disabled facilities   Good access for disabled anglers.

KENT

Ready for the day.

STARTOPS, TRING
Atlas Page 203 C.3/3.9

This fairly large reservoir (30 acres) lies just north of Tring and is regarded as a difficult fishing venue. Expect bream, roach, tench, perch, pike and catfish in reasonable numbers, and a few carp – some in the 20–30lb range.

How to get there   Take the Tring bypass (A41) and at the western end turn right onto the B489 towards Dunstable. The reservoir is on the right, after about 2 miles. Follow signs to the fishery and use the car park.

Day tickets   Adult/junior/OAP £2.50. Available from the bailiff on the bank.

Best methods/baits   Use any recognised coarse techniques and baits.

Restrictions   No night fishing.

Facilities   Nearest shops/pub in Tring.

BROOKLANDS LAKES
Atlas Page 203 D.8/4.8

A complex of four lakes, a short distance from Dartford town centre. Expect mixed species, with roach, tench, bream and some large carp. Good fishing for carp specialists and pleasure anglers alike.

How to get there   Take the A2 from Dartford town centre. Turn left at traffic lights, into Princes Way, then immediately right by DIY store. Pay for parking on site.

Day tickets   Adult £2.50; junior/OAP £1.25; available only from the bank.

Best methods/baits   Smaller species – float; bream, tench – leger; carp – use modern rig.

Facilities   Shops/toilets/food in Dartford town centre.

Disabled facilities   Some swims suitable for disabled and some (3) wheelchair anglers.

Startops Reservoir.

DANSON PARK
Atlas Page 203 D.7/4.9

A small council-controlled park midway between Welling and Bexleyheath, just off the main A2 road. The shallow lake contains mainly roach and carp, with some quite large fish being taken.

How to get there Take the A2 south-east from London to Welling; at Blackfen (East Rochester Way), look for signs on the left to the Park and lake. Parking nearby.

Day tickets Adult £2.50; junior/OAP £1.10. Available on the banks.

Best methods/baits Use any recognised coarse techniques and baits .

Restrictions No night fishing.

Facilities Nearest shops/pub in Rochester way or Welling.

Disabled facilities Good access for disabled anglers.

ORPINGTON & DISTRICT
Atlas Page 203 D.6/5.3

Two lakes located just off the main A20, near Sidcup. A fairly well stocked mixed fishery, with bream, tench, raoch and pike. Also some large carp – specimens of 20lb+ have been reported here.

How to get there Take the A20 east from London to Sidcup; the lakes are near Klingers roundabout.

Day tickets Adult £3; junior/OAP £1.50. Tickets must be bought in advance from Orpington Angling Supplies, 304 High Street, St. Mary Cray; Tel. 0689 834905 (open from 0800).

Best methods/baits Use any recognised coarse techniques and baits.

Facilities Nearest shop/pub in Sidcup or St. Pauls Cray.

Disabled facilities Some swims may be suitable for disabled anglers; check at tackle shops.

Success on the lakes.

OXFORDSHIRE

Oxford Canal.

BLENHEIM PARK LAKES
Atlas Page B.3/3.9

A boat-fishing only venue situated in the grounds of Blenheim Palace, near Oxford. Expect excellent fishing with large bags of bream (to 7lb), tench (to 9lb) and roach (to 2lb+). Winter pike fishing also provides great sport.

How to get there From Oxford, take the A34 north-west towards Woodstock. After about 5 miles, follow signs to Blenheim Park Estate and the lakes.

Day tickets Boat fishing only. Adult/junior/OAP £27 per boat. **Applications in writing only** to: The Lodge, Blenheim Palace, Woodstock, Oxford.

Best methods/baits Use recognised techniques.

Restrictions Boat fishing only.

Facilities Toilets at Blenheim Palace.

RIVER CHERWELL
Atlas Page 203 B.4/4.0

A pleasant stretch of the River Cherwell, just north of Oxford. Expect excellent coarse fishing, with good roach and chub, plus some specimen barbel of 10lb+.

How to get there From Oxford, take the A4260 north through Kidlington; the river is located just behind the church. Free car parking near the swims.

Day tickets   Adult £2; junior/OAP 50p; available from local tackle shops. Bookings available from T. Lester, 11 Morton Close, Kidlington; Tel. 08675 6943.

Best methods   Roach – stick float; chub, barbel – stick float, leger.

Best baits   Roach, chub – maggot, bread.

Facilities   Shops/food in Kidlington.

DORCHESTER-ON-THAMES LAKES
Atlas Page 203 B.3/4.3

A mature gravel pit complex near Oxford, comprising The Creek (2 acres), Dorchester Lagoon (40 acres) and Orchid Lake (17 acres). Dorchester provides mixed fishing including very large carp, roach, tench and bream; Orchid has carp to 33lb, with ten 30lb+ fish taken in 1991; The Creek is more a novice water, packed with little fish. Expect superb sport, whichever lake you choose!

How to get there   From Oxford, head south-east on the A423 about 7 miles; approaching the village of Dorchester, the lakes are on the right. Follow signs to Burcot and the fishery and park on site.

Day tickets   Fishing 0800-sunset: one rod – adult £4, junior £3; two rods – adult £6, junior £5. Night ticket £10 (two rods); 24-hour ticket £15 (two rods). Concessions for long stays and pre-purchased tickets. All tickets available from the office in the main car park.

Best methods/baits   Boilies preferred for carp; sweetcorn or hemp as alternatives. Mixers on the surface can work well. Most baits work well for other species.

Restrictions   No particle baits. No keepnets to be used.

Facilities   Toilets/showers/cafe/shop on site. Nearest pub, The Chequers, Burcot (½ mile).

HORSE AND GROOM INN
Atlas Page B.3/3.3

Two small lakes, 4½ acres and 2½ acres, close to a 16th century inn near Banbury. A mixed fishery with most species and some good-sized carp to provide the sport. An ideal site for a 'country sports' holiday.

How to get there   Leave the M40 at jct 11 and take the A361 south-west towards Chipping Norton. After about 4 miles, look for signs on right to Milcombe

village and the Horse and Groom Inn. Follow signs to the fishery and car park.

Day tickets   Adult £5; junior/OAP £2 (Free to residents of the inn). Available from the Horse and Groom; Tel. 0295 720471.

Best methods/baits   Use any recognised coarse techniques and baits.

Facilities   B&B facilities at the inn; also rough shooting arranged. Nearest shop in Milcombe; nearest pub, the Horse and Groom.

Disabled facilities   Some swims may be suitable for disabled anglers; phone for advice.

LINCH HILL LEISURE PARK
Atlas Page 203 B.2/4.1

A coarse-fishing complex located within Linch Hill Leisure Park, comprising three lakes – Stoneacres (52 acres, with mixed species and large pike); Christchurch (6 acres, with bream, roach and large carp); Willow Pool (7 acres, with *very* large carp).

How to get there   Take the A40 west from Oxford and at Eynsham (about 6 miles) follow the signs to Linch Hill Leisure Park. Free car parking on site.

Day tickets   Adult/junior/OAP £2.50; £3.50; £6 respectively for the three lakes. Also boat hire £6/day. Tickets available on site, or from Linch Hill Leisure Park, Stanton Harcourt, Eynsham, Oxford; Tel. 0865 882215.

Best methods/baits   Use recognised techniques.

Facilities   Cafe/garden centre/toilets/ children's play area/sailboarding available on site. Nearest shop and pub Harcourt Arms, Stanton harcourt (1½ miles).

Disabled facilities   Some swims suitable for disabled and wheelchair anglers.

MANOR FARM, KIRTLINGTON
Atlas Page 203 B.4/3.9

An extremely picturesque 6-acre lake set in beautiful countryside a few miles north of Oxford. Well stocked with carp, small chub and barbel, plus some very good-sized tench, roach and pike. An ideal fishery for the family day-out.

How to get there   Take the A34 (by-pass) north from Oxford for about 3 miles and turn left onto the B4027 towards Shipton-on-Cherwell. Look for right turn on minor road to Kirtlington. For details of access/parking, contact Catch 1 Tackle, 14 The Parade, Kidlington, Oxon; Tel. 08675 2066.

Day tickets Adult/junior/OAP £3.50. Available from Catch 1 Tackle.

Best methods/baits Use general coarse methods and baits.

Facilities Family barbecue/picnic area on site. Nearest shop and pub, Kirtlington (½ mile).

MARSH WATER
Atlas Page 203 B.8/4.6

A small, but well-stocked venue, situated a few miles east of Henley-on-Thames. Good fishing, with common, mirror, ghost, grass and Crucian carp, some of 20lb+. Also plenty of tench, roach, rudd and perch.

How to get there From Marlow, take the A4155 west towards Henley-on-Thames. Approaching Henley, look for the signs to Toad Hall Garden Centre. The fishery is located behind the garden centre. Free car parking on site.

Day tickets Adult/junior/OAP £4 (max 2 rods); available from Marsh Tackle, 4 Cross Court, Plomer Green Avenue, Downley, High Wycombe; Tel. 0494 437035.

Best methods Leger preferred; float alternative.

Best baits Maggots, corn, bread, meat, dog biscuits.

Restrictions Use barbless hooks only; no keepnets. No night fishing permitted.

Facilities Shop in garden centre.

MILTON COMMON
Atlas Page 203 B.5/4.1

Three quite small lakes – 3, 2 and 1½ acres respectively – close to the M40, just east of Oxford. Mainly carp, but other species are present here. A relatively new venue; further advice can be obtained from local tackle shops.

How to get there Leave the north-west-bound M40 at jct 7 and take the A329 towards Goring. Great Milton, Milton Common and the lakes can be seen from the road. Follow signs to the car park.

Day tickets Adult/junior/OAP £1.50 per rod. Available from the owner on site.

Best methods/baits Use any recognised coarse technique and baits.

Facilities Nearest shop/pub in Great Milton.

Disabled facilities Access for disabled anglers may be possible; check with local tackle shops.

OXFORD CANAL – THRUPP
Atlas Page 203 B.5/3.9

A stretch of the Oxford Canal, a few miles north of the city. Fishing is best early season, with predominantly bream. Catches have been known to top 100lb!

How to get there From Oxford, take the A4260 north through Kidlington; the turn to Thrupp is on the right. Free car parking near the swims.

Day tickets Adult/junior/OAP £2.50; available on the bank or from local tackle shops.

Best methods/baits Waggler or pole with recognised baits.

Facilities Toilets at boat yard. Nearest pub, The Boat (½ mile).

Disabled facilities Some swims suitable for disabled and wheelchair anglers.

OXFORD CANAL – WOLVERCOTE
Atlas Page 203 B.5/3.9

A stretch of the Oxford Canal just to the north east of Oxford. Mainly bream fishing, with catches of 30lb+. Also winter chub bags of 40lb+, and occasional carp of 15–18lb.

How to get there From Oxford, head west on the A40 to the city's northern outskirts; look for signs to Wolvercote at the roundabout just before the A43 fly-over. Free car parking on site.

Day tickets Adult £3; junior/OAP £1.50; available from local tackle shops. Also bookings from P. Jackman; Tel. 08675 79582.

Best methods/baits Pole is preferred method; use recognised baits.

Facilities Shop in Wolvercote (1 mile); nearest pub, The Plough (200 yards).

OXFORD QUARRY
Atlas Page 203 B.2/4.1

This large (16-acre) gravel pit is located about 8 miles west of Oxford. Shallow, and with a gravelly bottom, it provides good coarse fishing, with large chub, tench, catfish and pike, plus some carp in the 25lb region.

How to get there   Take the A40 west from Oxford and at Eynsham (about 6 miles) bear right onto B4449 to Stanton Harcourt. In the village, look for signs to the fishery and car park.

Day tickets   Season tickets only: £20; available from State Tackle, 19 Fettiplace Road, Witney; Tel. 0993 702587.

Best methods/baits   Use any recognised coarse techniques and baits.

Facilities   Nearest shop/pub in Stanton Harcourt.

Disabled facilities   Access may be difficult for disabled anglers.

SEACOURT STREAM
Atlas Page 203 B.4/4.2

This pleasant fishery lying close to the A43 Oxford by-pass provides fantastic mixed fishing with roach, bream, tench, pike and specimen chub, barbel and dace. A 'must' for the enthusiast.

How to get there   From Oxford, head west on the A40 to the city's northern outskirts; look for signs to Wolvercote, then Wytham, at the roundabout just before the A43 fly-over. Free car parking on site.

Day tickets   No day tickets. Details of availability from Catch 1 Tackle, 14 The Parade, Kidlington, Oxford; Tel. 08675 2066.

Best methods/baits   Use recognised techniques.

Facilities   Shop in Wytham.

T.C. PIT
Atlas Page 203 B.3/4.0

A 50-acre coarse fishery near the main A40/A34 junction. The pit contains a large head of roach and perch, plus specimen tench and bream. Also pike to 30lb+.

How to get there   Off the A40/34 junction, just before Oxford, or near the A34 lay-by. Park in the lay-by. The lake is on the roadside. Possibly soon to become club water; check with tackle shops.

Day tickets   Free fishing.

Best methods/baits   Use recognised techniques.

Facilities   Shop in Kidlington.

Rivers
THE UPPER THAMES

The Upper Thames.

Along its upper reaches, the Thames is mainly slow-flowing, with plenty of variety in both width and depth. Weed growth can cause problems to summer anglers – as can the heavy boat traffic. The section of the river from Lechlade to Clifton Hampden holds many large carp and barbel for the specialist angler, plus a large head of pike for excellent winter sport. Six *Angling Times* Hotspots have been identified along this Thames stretch.

WATER EATON
Atlas Page 203 A.5/4.4

An extremely pleasant stretch of the Thames which extends from near Cricklade to Castle Eaton (about 2½ miles). Expect very good coarse fishing, with roach, dace, chub and barbel in plentiful numbers.

How to get there   Take the A419 south-east from Cirencester to Cricklade (about 7 miles) and turn left onto minor road giving access to the river. For more details of access/parking, contact House of Angling, Commercial Road, Swindon; Tel. 0793 693460.

Day tickets   Adult/junior/OAP £2.50. Available from local tackle shops or from Peter Gilbert, 31 Havelock Street, Swindon; Tel. 0793 535396.

Best methods/baits   Use general coarse methods and baits.

Facilities   Nearest shop and pub in Cricklade.

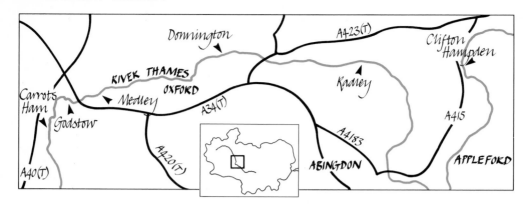

KELMSCOT
Atlas Page 203 B.0/4.5

A 1½-mile long stretch of the Thames, just east of Lechlade. Expect usual Thames species, but predominantly chub and bream. There is a large, but elusive, resident bream shoal near Grafton Lock.

How to get there From Lechlade, take the A417 east towards Faringdon; after ½ mile turn left at Trout Inn on minor road towards Clanfield. Kelmscot is about 1 mile on the right. Free parking near the swims; fish upstream and downstream of main access point.
Day tickets Adult/junior/OAP £2; available on the bank, or from local tackle shops.
Best methods Waggler preferred when water is clear; feeder later in the year (especially for chub).
Best baits Maggot, bread.
Facilities Nearest shops Lechlade (2 miles); nearest pub The Plough, Kelmscot (½ mile).

TADPOLE
Atlas Page B.2/4.5

A 2-mile stretch of the Thames, a few miles east of Lechlade and downstream of Tadpole Bridge. Mainly chub, with best fishing when the water is coloured, plus an occasional barbel in September/ October. Summer boat traffic can cause problems.

How to get there From Swindon, head north-east on A420 through Faringdon; after about 4 miles, turn left towards Bampton. At Tadpole Bridge (2½ miles), the fishery is downstream, on the right bank. Free car parking near the swims.

Day tickets Adult/junior/OAP £2; available from the booth in The Trout pub car park (near Tadpole Bridge).
Best methods/baits Waggler with maggot, or feeder; best results are obtained when the water is coloured.
Facilities Toilets/food at The Trout pub.
Disabled facilities There is only limited access to the swims.

DUXFORD
Atlas Page 203 B.3/4.3

A two-part fishery, about 10 miles west of Oxford. Part one is a 1½-mile backwater, about 15 yards wide and 5–6ft deep, with streamy water and reedbeds in summer. Part two, the link from Shifford Weir to the main Thames, provides another 1-mile section of bank. Good fishing in both parts, with mainly bream, chub, roach and dace, but also some very good spots for barbel sport.

How to get there From the A34 Oxford by-pass, take the A420 towards Swindon. At about 1 mile after Kingston Bagpuize, turn right to Hinton Waldrist and follow the road to Duxford. Park (free) in the large lay-by.
Day tickets Adult/junior/OAP £2. Available from local tackle shops, or from Roger Bateman, 16 The Gap, Marcham, Abingdon, Oxon, OX13 6NJ.
Best methods Use float or waggler in summer; stick in winter.
Best baits Use maggots, casters in summer, or worm/caster cocktail for the bream shoals.
Facilities Nearest shop and pub in Hinton Waldrist.

CARROTS HAM
Atlas Page 203 B.4/4.4

This 25–35-yard-wide, 10–12ft deep section has a reputation for quality fish. Typical catches include chub, roach and – when the water is coloured – bream. Common weights are 10–15lb, with some pleasure catches – mainly chub – topping 30lb.

How to get there Take the A34 Oxford 'by-pass'; just south of the A40 intersection, turn into Wytham village and follow the signs to the University Field Station. Park on the left and walk through the gate to the farm.

Day tickets £2; available from local tackle shops; also Dells Fishing Tackle, 136 Oxford Road, Cowley, Oxford; Tel. 0865 711410

Best methods Maggot feeder, tight across; alternatively, a waggler in the middle or at the far bank.

Best baits Maggots plus pinkies as hookbait; bream – casters and red worms.

Facilities Shop in Wytham village.

Hotspot Tips

- The best groundbait is brown crumb, mixed with continental groundbait of your choice.
- With a feeder, fishing from the middle to two-thirds across can be productive.
- Good chub appear upstream of the brook, where the telegraph poles cross the river.

GODSTOW
Atlas Page 203 B.4/4.4

A typical Upper Thames fishery, 25–30 yards wide and 6–10ft deep. Chub, roach, perch and bream are caught all year, but bream are best in summer. When the water is clear, sport can be patchy, but average match nets range from 8–10lb+.

How to get there Take the A34 Oxford 'by-pass'; just south of the A40 intersection, turn through Wytham village and follow the road under the flyover. Park on the right before the river and go through the gate on the left.

Day tickets £2; available from local tackle shops.

Best methods Waggler down the middle to tight across, with 22 hook and 12–16oz bottom.

Best baits Summer – maggots, hemp; winter – maggots.

Facilities Food/toilets at the Trout Inn; shops in Wytham village.

Hotspot Tips

- A loosefeed of maggot and hemp with single or double maggot hookbait can produce some good fish.
- The first peg above the Trout Inn on the point at the island produces regular 10lb+ nets.
- For large chub, try big bait, fished tight against a feature.

A night-fished carp.

MEDLEY
Atlas Page 203 B.4/4.4

A popular, slow-flowing section; gravel bottom, 6ft depth. Summer weed can cause problem; no cover on the far side, few trees on the near. Expect chub, bream, roach, perch, bleak and gudgeon in summer, plus carp and barbel; pleasure nets can reach 30lb. Winter catches comprise roach and chub (2–3lb). Expect pike from October onwards.

How to get there   Take the A34 Oxford 'by-pass' and turn off towards Botley. Turn left at traffic lights (Botley Road), then (¼ mile) to Botley Lane. Drive down, park on the right, just before The Perch pub. Access is possible up- or down-stream.
Day tickets   £2; available from local tackle shops (not weekends).
Best methods   Waggler fished short of middle or two-thirds across. Summer – use 22 hook with 12–16oz bottom; winter – use waggler fished 1–3ft overdepth.
Best baits   Chub, roach – maggots and hemp; bream – casters with groundbait and red worms.
Facilities   Food/toilets at The Perch pub.

Hotspot Tips

- A small Drennan feeder fished two-thirds across works well in winter, but not in summer, due to weed growth.
- Punched bread, fished with liquidised bread, can be a winner with winter bream.
- When the water is coloured, the bream will feed – so try an open-end feeder.

Day tickets   £2; available from local tackle shops (not weekends).
Best methods   Roach, perch, skimmer bream – waggler with maggot fished to the middle, or maggot feeder down the middle. Bream – open-end feeder fished from middle to two-thirds across.
Best baits   Summer – maggots and hemp; winter – maggots plus liquidised bread.
Facilities   Food/toilets at the Fox & Hounds, or Isis pubs.

Hotspot Tips

- Try a few red worms for summer bream.
- After the first frost, punched bread fished with a waggler or feeder can provide a 10lb+ roach net.
- Downstream, outside the Isis pub, is a productive area.

Radley.

DONNINGTON
Atlas Page 203 B.4/4.2

A fairly wide, slow-flowing venue, with 6–8ft depth. Mainly roach (over 1lb), bream (to 2lb+) and perch in summer, but early starts are needed to avoid boat traffic. The best fishing is available later in the year, with typical winter match weights of 12–15lb.

How to get there   From the A34 south of Oxford take the A4144; turn right at traffic lights next to The Fox and Hounds pub. Park at the side of the bridge.

RADLEY
Atlas Page 203 B.4/4.3

A widish, slow-flowing fishery, 6–10ft deep, that is known for its roach, although chub, bream and perch may appear, plus the odd barbel! Expect a match net of 12–15lb, but higher if the bream arrive.

How to get there   Turn off the A34 south of Oxford and follow signs to Radley. Cross the railway, follow the lane and take the left fork. Park on the left, by the gate to Radley boat station.
Day tickets   £2; available from local tackle shops.

Best methods   Waggler and feeder for most catches; stick when there is extra water.

Best baits   Chub/roach – maggots and hemp; bream – casters and red worms.

Hotspot Tips

- For pleasure fishing, try hemp and tares for good summer roach.
- A pole fished over nearside weed can produce some great sport.
- A waggler fished from the middle to the far side will find you some big roach and chub.

NUNEHAM COURTENAY
Atlas Page 203 B.5/4.3

A straight and pleasant Thames fishery near Radley, south of Oxford, with very wide (up to 45 yards) and deep (8–9ft) water, and with a wooded far bank. Expect virtually all coarse species here, with bream, perch and roach in large shoals, plus the occasional 20lb+ carp and very big pike. A good 'all-method' water.

How to get there   From the southern side of the A34 Oxford ring-road, take the minor road to Radley. Drive over the railway line in Radley and park (free) at the top of Boat House Road. Walk along the footpath to Nuneham Courtenay.

Day tickets   Adult/junior/OAP £2. Available from local tackle shops, or from Roger Bateman, 16 The Gap, Marcham, Abingdon, Oxon, OX13 6NJ.

Best methods/baits   Use general coarse methods and baits.

Facilities   Nearest shop and pub, Bowyers Arms, in Radley.

CLIFTON HAMPDEN
Atlas Page 203 B.5/4.5

A slow-flowing stretch renowned for very big chub and bream, 30–45 yards wide, 6–10ft deep, with tree and bush cover for the fish. Mainly roach, chub and bream, plus perch, gudgeon, bleak, dace, and an odd barbel. Most match nets reach 15lb – some have topped 100lb!

How to get there   Take the A423 south from Oxford and turn west on the A415 to Clifton Hampden. Cross the river, use the car park on the left. Walk back onto the bridge, go through the fence and walk downstream. Fish the first five fields.

Day tickets   £2; available from local tackle shops (not weekends).

Best methods   Waggler down the middle or right across; feeder on same line.

Best baits   Roach and chub – maggots and hemp; bream – casters and red worms.

Hotspot Tips

- Don't forget the pole – fished at 6–10 metres, it can account for some good catches.
- For really good sport, try mixing groundbait (3–4 pints) with casters.
- Pegs by the fourth (pig) field can throw up huge bream weights when the conditions are right.

Chub.

DORCHESTER-ON-THAMES
Atlas Page 203 B.7/4.4

A clear, shallow weedy stretch of the Thames, close to the Dorchester-on-Thames lakes complex (see above). A very productive fishery with roach, dace and perch in plentiful numbers, plus some really big barbel (8lb+) and chub (up to 5lb). Also a few really big pike in the weirpool – a 27lb specimen was taken recently.

How to get there   From Oxford, head south-east on the A423 about 7 miles; approaching the village of Dorchester, the lakes are on the right. Follow signs to Burcot and the fishery and park on site.

Day tickets   Fishing 0800-sunset: one rod – adult £4, junior £3; two rods – adult £6, junior £5. All tickets available from the office in the main car park.

Best methods/baits   Use general coarse methods and baits.

Restrictions   No keepnets to be used.

Facilities   Toilets/showers/cafe/shop on site. Nearest pub, The Chequers, Burcot (½ mile).

SURREY

A wintery Frensham Ponds.

ASH VALE
Atlas Page 203 C.4/5.4

Three gravel pits ranging from 1¼ to 7½ acres in size, about 5 miles west of Guildford. Expect good mixed coarse fishing for tench, roach, perch, rudd, Crucian carp and pike, together with some 20lb carp.

How to get there Leave the M3 at jct 4 (Camberley) and take the A321 to Frimley and Frimley Green. After 3 miles, take the A3013 (Ash Vale road) and turn right on Lakeside Road. Enter the fishery under the railway bridge, on the left. Parking on site.
Day tickets Adult £2.50; junior/OAP £1.50. Available from Leisure Sport Angling, Thorpe Park, Staines Road, Chertsey; Tel. 0932 564872.
Best methods/baits Use any recognised coarse techniques and baits.
Restrictions No radios. No camping.
Facilities Nearest shop/pub at Ash Vale.
Disabled facilities Some swims may be suitable for disabled anglers; please phone for advice (see above).

BRITTENS POND
Atlas Page 203 C.4/5.5

A very popular fishery, close to Guildford city centre. About 4 acres, dredged and restocked within the last few years to provide good mixed coarse fishing, with small specimens of most species, but some large common carp (several 20lb+ this season) and quality roach.

How to get there At Jacobs Well, in Salt Box Road, Guildford. Park nearby.

Day tickets Adult/junior/OAP £3. Membership of Guildford A.S. £30 (including £10 joining fee); junior: 12–16 £5; 8–12 £2.50. Available from Guildford Angling Centre; Tel. 0483 50633.
Best methods/baits Use any recognised coarse techniques and baits.
Facilities Nearest shops/toilets/food/ pubs in Guildford.
Disabled facilities Access is possible for disabled anglers, but check with local tackle shops.

CHERTSEY
Atlas Page 203 C.5/5.2

A fairly small (4½-acre) gravel pit, close to the M3 at Chertsey. Plenty of fish available, including perch, roach and bream, plus the odd large pike. Very few carp, but those present are reputed to exceed 20lb.

How to get there Leave the M25 at jct 13 and take the A320 towards Egham and Chertsey; turn right (onto B388) at the mini-roundabout, to Thorpe. The fishery entrance is just before the M3 flyover, on the right. Use the car park on site (do NOT drive round the lake).
Day tickets Season tickets only: adult £21; junior/OAP/disabled £10.50. Available from Leisure Sport Angling, Thorpe Park, Staines Road, Chertsey; Tel. 0932 564872.
Best methods/baits Use any recognised coarse techniques and baits.
Restrictions No night fishing. No trespassing onto Thorpe Park property.
Facilities Nearest shop/pub in Thorpe or Chertsey.
Disabled facilities Access may be possible for disabled anglers; please phone for advice (see above).

EARLSWOOD LAKES
Atlas Page 203 D.0/5.5

Two lakes located just south of Reigate. The lower lake (2 acres) is deepest on its southern side and is weedy, but produces some good-sized carp (20lb+) and tench (to 6lb). The water has been recently stocked with 2,000 Crucian carp; further stocking is planned shortly.

How to get there From Reigate, take the A217 south towards Crawley. After about 1 mile, turn left at traffic lights

(The Angel pub) and continue for ¾ mile. The fishery is on the left; car parking available on site.

Day tickets Adult £2; junior/OAP 50p. Season tickets: adult £10; junior £2. Available at Woodhatch Tackle, 10 Doversgreen Road, Woodhatch, Reigate; Tel. 0737 244772.

Best methods/baits Use general coarse methods and baits.

Facilities Toilets/food & drinks kiosk on site. Nearest shop and pub, The Angel (¾ mile).

Disabled facilities Some pathways have been tarmacked to allow use by disabled and wheelchair anglers.

EVERSLEY LAKE
Atlas Page 203 C.2/5.2

A mixed fishery at Yateley; a good general coarse fishing venue, with mostly tench and Crucian carp.

How to get there Leave the M3 at jct 4. Take the A327 to Yateley and turn right onto the Sandhurst Road (at the Royal Oak pub). The entrance is on the right.

Day tickets Adult £3; junior/OAP/ disabled £1.50.

Best methods/baits Use any recognised coarse technique and baits.

Restrictions No night fishing.

Facilities Nearest shop in Yateley; nearest pub, the Royal Oak.

FRENSHAM PONDS
Atlas Page 203 C.2/5.6

Two shallow, clear lakes but with dense reedbeds. Sport is best in early morning or late evening. Expect good roach (to 2lb+) and big tench (to 9lb) plus some large, elusive, carp and good winter pike (to 30lb).

How to get there Leave the A31 at Farnham and turn south on the A287 to Frensham village. The Great Pond is adjacent to the road; follow signs towards the River Wey to find the Little Pond. Car parking available (charge in summer).

Day tickets Adult £5; junior/OAP £2.50 (one rod only); available from local tackle shops.

Best methods Open-end feeder and waggler.

Best baits Casters, maggots, sweetcorn, worms.

Restrictions An unhooking mat is essential.

Facilities Toilets/food on site; nearest shop and pub (Mariner's) Frensham (1 mile).

Disabled facilities Some swims suitable for disabled and wheelchair anglers.

An 8lb tench taken on Frensham Ponds.

HENFOLD LAKES
Atlas Page 203 C.8/5.7

A small fishery comprising two lakes – one of 1 acre, the other of ½ acre – midway between Dorking and Horsham. Expect good mixed coarse fishing with everything present – from gudgeon to large carp of 15lb+.

How to get there Take the A24 south from Dorking towards Horsham and after about ¾ mile (at the brow of a hill) turn left into Mill Lane. Continue for about 5 miles; Henford Lakes are signposted about ¼ mile after the railway bridge. Free car parking on site.

Day tickets Adult/junior/OAP £3.50. Available on the bank.

Best methods/baits Use general coarse methods and baits.

Facilities Toilets/food & drink on site. There is a bar in the Club House.

Disabled facilities Some swims in front of the club house are suitable for disabled and wheelchair anglers.

LODGE POND, NR. FARNHAM
Atlas Page 203 C.2/5.6

A small lake, about 10 miles south of Farnham, with some areas deepened by a dam wall, containing roach, bream, skimmer bream, tench and carp.

How to get there   From Farnham, take the A325 south towards Bordon Camp. Alice Holt is about 1½ miles beyond this point. Look for signs to the pond. Free car parking on site.

Day tickets   Adult £5; junior/OAP £2.50; available from BBC Tackle, 3 Elmfield Court, Lindford; Tel. 0420 472573.

Best methods   Roach, skimmer bream – long waggler. Bream – open-end feeder with groundbait.

Best baits   Maggots, sweetcorn, meat, boilies, worms.

Facilities   Nearest shop Bordon Camp (2 miles); nearest pub 1 mile.

Disabled facilities   Some swims suitable for disabled and wheelchair anglers.

NEWDIGATE
Atlas Page 203 C.8/5.7

Two clay pits – Lake 1, of over 8 acres, and lake 2, of over 3 acres – midway between Dorking and Horsham. Experience indicates this to be carp-only water, with good catches of smaller fish from Lake 2, but much bigger specimens in Lake 1. Fishing at night produces best results here.

How to get there   Take the A24 south from Leatherhead, through Dorking and at Beare Green, fork left towards Newdigate. Turn left at the church and take the left fork; the lakes are 400 yards on the right. Park *only* in the car park on site.

Day tickets   Season tickets only: adult £21; junior/OAP/disabled £10.50. Available from Leisure Sport Angling, Thorpe Park, Staines Road, Chertsey; Tel. 0932 564872.

Best methods/baits   Use any recognised coarse techniques and baits.

Restrictions   No swimming or boating.

Facilities   Nearest shop/pub in Newdigate village.

Disabled facilities   Please phone for advice on suitability for disabled anglers.

OLD BURY HILL LAKE
Atlas Page 203 C.7/5.5

A 12-acre lake near Dorking, providing excellent general coarse fishing, especially in summer. Mainly tench and bream (each to 7lb), plus large carp (including Crucians) and perch. Also pike (to 30lb) and zander (to 16lb).

How to get there   Take the A25 from Guildford towards Dorking; Old Bury Hill Lake is about 1 mile before Dorking, opposite Milton Heath House. Free car parking on site.

Day tickets   Adult £6; junior/OAP £3; available from Lakeview, Old Bury Hill, Dorking; Tel. 0306 883621. Rowing-boat hire also available (adults only;£3). Times: weekdays 0800-sunset; weekends/Bank Holidays sunrise-sunset.

Best methods/baits   Use recognised techniques, or ask for advice from the bailiff on the bank.

Facilities   Toilets/food/bait/tackle all available on site. Nearest shop Dorking (2 miles); nearest pub Prince of Wales, Westcott (2 miles).

Disabled facilities   Some swims suitable for disabled and wheelchair anglers.

PRIORY FARM, NUTFIELD
Atlas Page 203 D.0/5.5

Two lakes – Priory and Hungerford – each with 36 swims providing excellent fishing in all weathers. Fishing **Tuesdays only** in season (16th June–30th September). Mainly carp (to 10lb+), roach, rudd, perch and Crucian carp. No advance booking; first come, first served, so best to arrive well before gates open. A very easy water which fishes well.

How to get there   Leave the M25 at jct 6 and take A25 towards Redhill. At Nutfield (4 miles), turn left into Mid Street, then right to Priory Farm. Free parking on site.

Day tickets   Adult/junior/OAP one price. Priory: day (0700–2100 or dusk) £4.50; evening (1600–2100 or dusk) £2.50. Hungerford: day £7.50; evening £5.50.

Best methods   Float, leger, feeder.

Best baits   White maggots, boilies, sweetcorn, luncheon meat.

Restrictions   No keepnets. No groundbait (loosefeed only); no coloured maggots; no hemp. Maximum 1 rod/person. Use only barbless hooks. No unaccompanied under–16s; spectators must not sit with anglers.

Facilities   Toilets.

Disabled facilities   Some swims suitable for disabled anglers.

RIVER VALLEY FISHERY
Atlas Page 203 C.2/5.4

A very attractive, tree-lined lake in the Blackwater Valley, near Camberley. A very deep mixed fishery, with large rudd, perch, pike and tench, in addition to large carp which are reputed to reach 30lb+. Recommended for the experienced angler.

How to get there   Leave the M3 at jct 4 and take the A327 to Yateley (about 4 miles); in the village, bear right onto Sandhurst Road. Follow signs to the fishery which is at the end of the road and park on site.

Day tickets   Adult/junior/OAP £3.50. Night ticket: adult/junior/OAP £5. Both available on site. Season tickets also available.

Best methods/baits   Use mainly carp methods and baits.

Facilities   Nearest shop/pub in Yateley.

Disabled facilities   Some swims suitable for disabled anglers; phone for advice (see above).

A quieter time at Richmond.

Rivers

RIVER THAMES

Sometimes like fishing on a regatta day at Kingston.

As it flows through Surrey, the Thames is a wide, medium-paced river with good, tow-path style, banks. Boats may be a problem at weekends. Among the major catches, dace are most common, but bream, chub, roach and perch will also figure high on the list; also expect the occasional large barbel or carp. Most methods will work, but tackle must be kept fine, with small hooks and 1lb bottoms. There are six *Angling Times* Hotspots along this stretch.

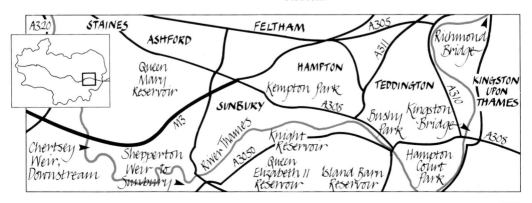

CHERTSEY WEIR DOWNSTREAM
Atlas Page 203 C.6/5.1

A wide (40–50yds) section; slow to medium flow. Depth is 8ft only two rod-lengths out, shallows (6ft) at far bank; centre boat channel is deeper. Chub, dace and roach all season; chub rarer after November. Day catches to 20lbs (will include chub).

How to get there   Leave the M25 at jct 12; take the B388, then join the B375 towards the river. Park near the water.
Day tickets   Free fishing
Best methods   Roach and dace – fish 2–3 rod lengths out with waggler; chub – fish close to far bank, using feeder. Fine tackle/small hooks essential.
Best baits   Bronze maggots consistent; hemp, caster productive. Loosefeed, but no groundbait is needed.

Hotspot Tips

✎ For dace, head for Chertsey Bridge; for chub, head for trees and houseboats on the far bank.
✎ Hemp and caster may produce a better fish in midwater.

Chertsey.

SHEPPERTON WEIR TO SUNBURY
Atlas Page 203 C.7/5.1

A 40–60 yard wide stretch with medium flow and some weed growth and a centre, deep boat channel. Barbel and dace provide sport in summer; roach are very good in winter; bream shoals are also located. Expect day catches to 15lbs, but may reach 80lbs if bream and barbel turn up.

How to get there   Turn off the M3 at jct 1 and take the A244 to Walton on Thames. Cross the river bridge, turn right, and follow signs to Weybridge. The road follows the river.
Day tickets   Free fishing
Best methods   Roach, dace, barbel – use stick float on running line or pole with 6–8yds line. Barbel – use feeder.
Best baits   Red or bronze maggots effective; hemp and caster in summer.

Hotspot Tips

✎ Fish two-thirds across the river for barbel, using fine tackle if possible.
✎ Best swims are Chinese Bridge downstream, Desborough Channel and towards Walton Bridge.
✎ For bream, try brown crumb in the feeder.

MOLESEY
Atlas Page 203 C.7/5.0

A picturesque stretch of the river, with depth 12ft about 8 rod lengths out. Fishing is over 100 pegs, from Molesey Cricket Club to Cherry Orchard, with best sport at this latter end. Expect mainly dace and some roach, with catches often reaching 18lb.

How to get there   Approach Hampton Court from the south on the A309 (leave the A3 at Hook interchange), drive over the river and turn left onto the A308 towards Sunbury. Use Saddlers Road car park, off Hurst Road.
Day tickets   Free fishing.
Best methods/baits   Use either pole or waggler with maggot. Loosefeed with hempseed. If flow picks up, use stick float and maggot. For chub, use feeder.
Facilities   Nearest shops/pubs in Hampton Court.
Disabled facilities   Some swims may be suitable for disabled anglers.

KINGSTON BRIDGE
Atlas Page 203 C.8/5.0

A slow running section in summer, more pacey later in season. Depth from 6–10ft, very little weed growth. Mainly roach, dace and bream; day catches to 15lbs – but if bream appear, anything can happen!

How to get there   Follow either the A307, A308 or A310 to Kingston town centre. Parking is difficult; best river access is from the bridge, or from road running close to the river (downstream).

Day tickets   Free fishing

Best methods   Roach, dace – use float (waggler in summer; stick later); loosefeed at every cast. Bream – use open-end feeder from middle to two-thirds out. Always use fine tackle and tiny hooks.

Best baits   Summer – hemp, caster, with maggot standby.

Hotspot Tips

- Look for the flow and fish its edge with a rig set overdepth.
- Roach and dace are best where the road is close to the river; bream are best close to Kingston Bridge.
- A breadflake-hook/brown-crumb feeder combination works well for bream.

RICHMOND
Atlas Page 203 C.8/4.8

A wide, tidal section of the Thames, with slow summer flow which rises in winter. Very little weed growth. Summer, dace, roach, perch and bream are plentiful; day catches to 30lbs common when dace are feeding. Best fishing in winter.

How to get there   Take the A307 Ham to Richmond road (heavy traffic can cause problems at Richmond). Parking is available at Ham or Richmond.

Day tickets   Free fishing

Best methods   Summer – waggler; a feeder can be very effective for bream. For winter dace, use stick float on running line or 6–7-metre pole. Use 18–22 hooks with 1lb bottoms.

Best baits   Maggots for everything; flake for bream. Use a hemp/caster combination in summer.

Facilities   Food/shops/toilets in Richmond town centre.

Hotspot Tips

- Be prepared to cast wagglers some distance to find the flow.
- Swims close to Richmond Bridge and The Pigeons pub are very good.
- Fishing is best at the bottom of the tide, when close-in depth is 3–5ft.

TRILAKES
Atlas Page 203 C.2/5.3

A popular, commercial fishery in an 11-acre gravel pit near Camberley. A pleasant, rural venue in which tench, perch, roach, rudd, bream and chub abound. Sport is often dominated, however, by very big carp specimens, with a record fish of over 35lb. A venue for the real enthusiast!

How to get there   Leave the M3 at jct 4, take the A321 towards Sandhurst and turn into Yateley Road at Yateley. The entrance to TriLakes is on the right, just beyond Yateley Match Lake (see below). Car parking on site.

Day tickets   Adult/junior/OAP £5 per rod. Available at the entrance, or from C. Homewood, TriLakes, Yateley Road, Sandhurst; Tel. 0252 873191. *Note*: tickets must be purchased *before* fishing.

Best methods/baits   Use any recognised coarse techniques and baits, including advanced carp methods.

Restrictions   No night fishing.

Facilities   Toilets/cafe/bar/tackle & bait on site. Nearest shop/pub in Yateley.

Disabled facilities   Some swims suitable for disabled anglers.

Rivers
RIVER WEY

Fishing on the Wey.

241

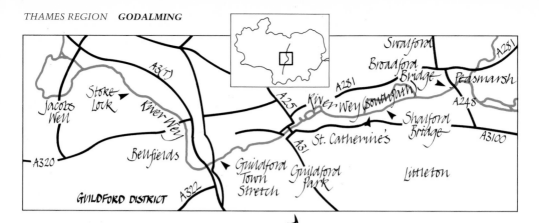

The Wey is a medium-sized river with a steady flow, and is at its best in autumn when an increased flow brings it to life. The Wey represents an excellent venue for match and pleasure anglers alike, with very good access to the river banks, but frequent problems with heavy summer boat traffic. Expect a varied head of fish, including chub, roach and bream.

GODALMING
Atlas Page 203 C.4/5.6

A 2–3-mile stretch of river bank providing excellent fishing, especially in winter, but generally poor when the river is in flood. Mainly chub (to at least 5lb), dace and roach, plus an occasional barbel. Plenty of jack pike (to 20lb).

How to get there From Guildford, head south on the A3100 to Godalming (about 4 miles). Access to the left bank of the river is at various points in the town, from the town bridge, downstream towards Broadford Bridge, Shalford. Car parking available at various locations along the stretch.

Day tickets Adult/junior/OAP £3; season tickets (Guildford A.S.): adult £30 (incl. £10 joining fee); juniors: 12–16 £5; 8–12 £2.50. Available from Guildford Angling Centre; Tel. 0483 506333.

Best methods Use float or leger when river is at good height.

Best baits Hempseed, casters, maggots, plus loosefeed.

Facilities Shops/toilets/food in Godalming town; nearest pub The Three Lions (½ mile).

BROADFORD BRIDGE
Atlas Page 203 C.5/5.6

A 50–60ft-wide section, a steady flow, some marginal weed and varying depth but a central channel of 6–8ft. Expect a mixed catch (mostly chub), with best sport in autumn and winter. Nets of just over 10lb are likely, unless the chub appear.

How to get there Take the A281 Guildford-Horsham road. At Shalford village (2 miles), turn right to Broadford Bridge, just past The Parrot pub.

Day tickets Adult/junior/OAP £3; season tickets (Guildford A.S.): adult £30 (incl. £10 joining fee); juniors: 12–16 £5; 8–12 £2.50. Available from Guildford Angling Centre; Tel. 0483 506333.

Best methods Stick float or waggler down the centre channel; loosefeed with hemp or casters.

Best baits Hempseed, casters, maggots, plus loosefeed.

Facilities Food/toilets at The Parrot pub.

Disabled facilities There is good access to river banks for disabled anglers.

Hotspot Tips

❧ For good sport, be prepared to fish on the drop.

SHALFORD PARK
Atlas Page 203 C.6/5.4

A wide (50–60ft) river loop providing escape from summer boats. Picturesque – shallows, deeps, marginal weed, steady flow, and depths of 2–12ft. Good sport all year, with chub, bream, roach and carp, plus big winter pike (20lb) from deep water. Always good double-figure nets.

How to get there   Take the A3100 from
  Guildford towards Godalming; at St
  Catherine's village (1 mile) pass the
  kennels on the left and take the next
  lane to Shalford Lock.
Day tickets   Adult/junior/OAP £3;
  season tickets (Guildford A.S.): adult
  £30 (incl. £10 joining fee); juniors: 12–16
  £5; 8–12 £2.50. Available from
  Guildford Angling Centre;
  Tel. 0483 506333.
Best methods   Most species – stick float
  or waggler or lead. Pike – deadbaits.
Best baits   Maggots, hemp, casters, flake;
  loosefeed as groundbait.

Hotspot Tips

✂ Avoid feeders – even a small one can
   frighten off the fish.
✂ Look for shallow water in summer,
   deeper in winter.

Wey Navigation Canal.

ST CATHERINE'S
Atlas Page 203 C.4/5.6

A quite deep (8–10ft) section with some
marginal weed. Fishing is from both
banks, with excellent roach, plus dace,
bream and chub. The best sport is in
winter, with 20lb+ roach nets common.

How to get there   Take the A3100
  Guildford-Godalming road; at St
  Catherine's village (1 mile) pass the
  kennels on the left and take Ferry Lane;
  access is at the footbridge. Or, walk
  upstream from Guildford city centre.

Day tickets   Adult/junior/OAP £3;
  season tickets (Guildford A.S.): adult
  £30 (incl. £10 joining fee); juniors: 12–16
  £5; 8–12 £2.50. Available from
  Guildford Angling Centre;
  Tel. 0483 506333.
Best methods   Stick float or waggler
  overdepth in centre channel.
Best baits   Hemp, casters, maggots;
  loosefeed only as groundbait.
Facilities   Shops/food/toilets in the city
  centre.

Hotspot Tips

✂ Use a hemp/caster combination for
   quality roach.

GUILDFORD TOWN STRETCH
Atlas Page 203 C.4/5.5

A 50-ft wide stretch with steady flow;
mostly 5–6ft deep, but some 12ft deep
areas. Best fishing in autumn and winter,
with roach, chub, dace, bream, plus some
carp and barbel. Mixed nets of 30–40lb are
always likely.

How to get there   Take the A3 into
  Guildford; the best access is at Severn
  Arches in Walnut Tree Close.
Day tickets   Adult/junior/OAP £3;
  season tickets (Guildford A.S.): adult
  £30 (incl. £10 joining fee); juniors: 12–16
  £5; 8–12 £2.50. Available from
  Guildford Angling Centre;
  Tel. 0483 506333.
Best methods   Stick float in centre or
  waggler far side.
Best baits   Hemp, caster, maggot;
  loosefeed only as groundbait.
Facilities   Food/shops/toilets in town
  centre.

Hotspot Tips

✂ As the chub come up to feed, look for
   drop bites on the waggler.
✂ For big roach, use overdepth bait, put
   through slowly.

STOKE LOCK
Atlas Page 203 C.5/5.4

A slow-flowing section with a 12ft centre
depth, 50–60 ft wide. Expect chub, roach,
bream, carp and some very big perch (to
3lb). Nets up to 30lb (mostly bream) are
possible, with best fishing in autumn and
winter.

How to get there   Take the A320 Guildford-Woking road to Slyfield Green industrial estate; access to the river is via Moorfield Road. There is additional access at Burpham.

Day tickets   Adult/junior/OAP £3; season tickets (Guildford A.S.): adult £30 (incl. £10 joining fee); juniors: 12–16 £5; 8–12 £2.50. Available from Guildford Angling Centre; Tel. 0483 506333.

Best methods   Stick float in the centre, waggler at the far bank (where there is cover).

Best baits   Hemp, casters, maggots, worms; loosefeed only as groundbait.

Hotspot Tips

- Try using brown crumb as groundbait for bream on a feeder.
- Look for bream on the deep bends.

but above all huge carp, in most of the lakes. North Lake contains at least one 45lb+ specimen.

How to get there   Leave the M3 at jct 4, take the A327 to Yateley and turn right onto Sandhurst Road (at The Royal Oak pub). The West Lakes entrance is on the left; the East Lakes entrance is on the right. Car parking on site.

Day tickets   Season tickets only: adult £30; junior/OAP/disabled £15. Available (first come – first served) from Leisure Sport Angling, Thorpe Park, Staines Road, Chertsey; Tel. 0932 564872.

Best methods/baits   Use any recognised coarse techniques and baits. Specialist carp methods may be needed.

Facilities   Nearest shop in Yateley; nearest pub, The Royal Oak.

Disabled facilities   Some swims suitable for disabled anglers; please phone for advice (see above).

WILLINGHURST COARSE FISHERY
Atlas Page 203 C.5/5.6

Two small, but very well stocked lakes situated a few miles south of Guildford. Large numbers of small fish, with most species and individual catches often 10–16lb. Matches are fished on Sundays.

How to get there   Take the A281 south from Guildford, then at Bramley take B2128 towards Shamley Green and Cranleigh. At Willinghurst, look for Gaston Gate garage and signs to the fishery. Free car parking on site.

Day tickets   Adult/junior/OAP £5; available only from Mark Syms, in Willinghurst; Tel. 0483 275048.

Best methods/baits   Float best, but use any recognised technique.

Facilities   Toilets on site; nearest shop Shamley Green; nearest pub The Red Lion (2 miles).

Disabled facilities   Some swims suitable for disabled and wheelchair anglers.

YATELEY
Atlas Page 203 C.2/5.3

One of the foremost fishing complexes in Britain, renowned for its excellent (though very difficult) carp fishing. A 14-lake fishery, with lakes from ¾ to 12 acres. Expect mixed coarse fish, with Crucian carp, tench, roach, bream, rudd and pike,

Yateley, carp lake.

WILTSHIRE

COATE WATER COUNTRY PARK
Atlas Page 203 A.6/4.6

A 70-acre former reservoir now included in a country park. Well landscaped, providing excellent fishing. Most species, but predominantly bream; also carp (to 27lb) in recent seasons. Fishing is best when a strong south-westerly wind blows onto the dam.

How to get there   Leave the M4 at jct 15 and take A419 towards Swindon; at next roundabout take first exit, then first exit at second roundabout (by the Sun Inn) into Coate Water car park. Pay for parking on site.

Day tickets   Adult £1.10; junior/OAP 55p; available from the ticket machine at the entrance. Boat hire also available. Bookings and information from Arts & Recreation Dept., Thamesdown Borough Council, Swindon; Tel. 0793 526161.

Best methods   Use pole, float; use open-ended feeder when windy.

Best baits   Most species – maggots, casters; carp – boilies.

Facilities   Toilets on site; some food in summer only. Also children's sand pit/paddling pool. Nearest pubs – Sun Inn or Post House Hotel – outside main entrance.

Disabled facilities   Some swims suitable for disabled and wheelchair anglers.

WICK WATER
Atlas Page 203 A.4/4.4

A difficult-to-fish 17-acre gravel pit a few miles from Cirencester. Well stocked with most coarse species, including some large carp (to 18lb+).

How to get there   From Cirencester, head south-east on the A419 towards Cricklade and after about 3 miles take minor road on right to South Cerney. Follow road towards Cerney Wick and turn right on Spine Road (at the 1st crossroads). The fishery is just on the left. Car parking on site.

Day tickets   Adult/junior/OAP £2. Season tickets adult £17.50; junior/OAP £5. Available from South Cerney A.C.; Sec. Mrs Reynolds, Melville, Siddington Road, Cirencester (SAE please); Tel. 0285 655251. Also available in clubhouse at Ham Pool in Broadway Lane, South Cerney, or local tackle shops.

Best methods/baits   Use any recognised coarse techniques and baits.

Restrictions   No night fishing.

Facilities   Nearest shop/pub in Cerney Wick.

Disabled facilities   Some swims suitable for disabled anglers.

A 20 lb carp.

Southern Region

Waggoners Wells.

The Southern Region of the NRA extends from the industrial low-lying Thames Estuary in the north to the New Forest in the west, and includes the Weald of Kent, together with areas south and east of London, to the coast.

River fishing within the region is confined mainly to Kent, with the Medway, which flows to the Thames Estuary at Sheerness, the Rother, which rises at Rotherfield and enters the sea at Rye, and the Stour, which rises near Ashford and flows to the coast near Sandwich. All three provide reasonable coarse sport, with winter fishing most productive. River fishing – on the Yar – is also available on the Isle of Wight (where several lake fisheries also offer good sport as variety), and on the River Test, which drains part of Hampshire and enters the sea at Southampton. All offer very good coarse fishing for all-comers.

In addition, the region is also rich in still-water fisheries, with many lakes and ponds in Hampshire, Sussex, Surrey and Kent. A large number of these operate as commercial fisheries for the specialist, as well for the enthusiast, with specimen carp and bream often the major attraction.

HAMPSHIRE

BROADLANDS LAKE
Atlas Page 203 B.1/6.4

One of the finest fisheries in Britain. A 27-acre fishery on the Broadlands Estate, fed from the River Test. Huge carp (35lb), pike (39lb) and eels (8lb), plus roach and bream, with bags up to 50lb in summer. Fishing in season only 16th June to 31st December (pike and eels from 1st October).

How to get there   Leave the M27 at jct 2 and take the A36 towards Southampton. After 1½ miles, turn left into Hill Street; the lake entrance is ½ mile further on, immediately before the bridge over the M27. Free car park.

Day tickets   (June-Sept 0700–2100; Oct-Dec 0700–1800) Adult £4.50; junior/OAP/disabled £2.25. Evening ticket (June-Sept 1600–2100; Oct-Dec 1400–1800): £2.25. 24-hour ticket: £7. Weekly ticket £35.Available only from Broadlands Lake (Tel. 0703 869881) or local tackle shops. *Note:* Tickets must be purchased before fishing.

Best methods/baits   Use general coarse techniques and baits.

Restrictions   Maximum 2 rods/person; a third may be used on payment of 50p surcharge.
Facilities   Shop/toilets/food available on site.
Disabled facilities   Disabled platforms; lakeside car park.

CADMAN'S POOL
Atlas Page 203 A.6/6.5

Cadman's Pool, in the New Forest, was formerly a quarry providing gravel for local roadworks, but now provides good mixed coarse fishing. Fishing in season only – 16th June–14th March.

How to get there   From Ringwood, take the A31 north-east and turn left towards Fritham after about 8 miles. Before Fritham, take a left turn to Cadman's pool. West-bound A31 traffic must approach the fishery through Fritham via the B3078 Downton road. Parking only in officially designated car parks.
Day tickets   All max 2 rods/person. Adult £3.20; junior £1.60. Weekly ticket: adult £7.20; junior £3.60. Monthly/season tickets also available. Tickets from local tackle shops, Forestry Commission Offices and some Post Offices.
Best methods/baits   Use only recognised techniques and baits.
Restrictions   Use only barbless hooks. No lead weights. Keepnets must be fully immersed and fish not retained for over 3 hours (or as directed). No fish to be removed.
Facilities   Shop/pub in Fritham. Toilets/food on site.
Disabled facilities   Some swims suitable for disabled anglers.

GILLIES POND (I.O.W.)
Atlas Page 203 B.4/7.1

A disused reservoir, just outside Newport, Isle of Wight, which contains only about five swims. Mixed coarse fishing, mainly carp but also roach and rudd.

How to get there   Take the A3020 Newport to Cowes road; just beyond the prison (about 2 miles), turn right at The Stag pub down Stag Lane; the fishery is 100 yards on the right. Free car parking on site.

Day tickets   Adult £2; junior/OAP £1; available only from A.P. Scott & Sons, 11 Lugley Street, Newport; Tel. 0983 522115.
Best methods/baits   Use recognised techniques and baits.
Facilities   Shops in Newport (2 miles); nearest pub, The Stag (100 yards).
Disabled facilities   Some swims suitable for disabled and wheelchair anglers.

GUNVILLE POND (I.O.W.)
Atlas Page 203 B.4/7.2

A 3-acre mixed coarse fishery at Carrisbrooke, the ancient capital of the Isle of Wight. Well stocked to include carp, perch, tench, rudd and pike. A good, straightforward holiday fishery.

How to get there   From Newport, drive west towards Carrisbrooke village and look for signs to the fishery. Parking on site.
Day tickets   Members of I.O.W. Fresh Water AA only: adult £18, junior/OAP £10; from Ray Kirby; Tel. 0983 529617.
Best methods/baits   Use general coarse techniques and baits.
Facilities   Nearest shops in Newport; nearest pub in Carrisbrooke.
Disabled facilities   Some swims may be suitable for disabled anglers; contact local tackle shops for advice.

HATCHET POND
Atlas Page 203 A.7/6.7

Hatchet Pond is one of the few large expanses of water in the New Forest. It is derived from old marl pits which flooded to form a pond and provides good mixed coarse fishing. Fishing in season only - 16th June–14th March.

How to get there   From Brockenhurst, take the B3055 west about 6 miles. Hatchet Pond is at the B3055/B3054 junction, near Beaulieu.
Day tickets   All max 2 rods/person. Adult £3.20; junior £1.60. Weekly ticket: adult £7.20; junior £3.60. Monthly/season tickets also available. Tickets from local tackle shops, Forestry Commission Offices and some Post Offices.
Best methods/baits   Use only recognised coarse techniques and baits.

Restrictions   Use only barbless hooks.
No lead weights. Keepnets must be fully
immersed and fish not retained for over
3 hours (or as directed). No fish to be
removed.
Facilities   Shops/pubs in Beaulieu.
Toilets/food on site.
Disabled facilities   Some swims suitable
for disabled anglers.

HEATH LAKE, PETERSFIELD
Atlas Page 203 B.8/6.3

A large (20-acre) but shallow lake just
south of Petersfield. Good mixed fishing,
with bream (to 6lb), carp (to 18lb) and pike
(to 24lb). Also plenty of skimmer bream.

How to get there   Turn off the southbound A3 at Petersfield onto the B2146
Chichester road; the lake is about 500
yards on the left. Free car parking on
site.
Day tickets   Adult £3.50; junior/OAP £2;
available on the bank.
Best methods   Floating baits. Also
waggler or feeder for bream.
Best baits   Bream – maggots, corn; carp –
long range boilies; pike – deadbait.
Restrictions   Maximum 2lb groundbait/
day. Only sea deadbaits to be used for
pike.
Facilities   Toilets/food on site. Nearest
shops Petersfield (½ mile); nearest pub,
the Red Lion (¼ mile).
Disabled facilities   Some swims suitable
for disabled and wheelchair anglers.

HORDLE LAKES
Atlas Page 203 A.7/6.8

A complex of 6 lakes in a tree-lined valley
at New Milton, near Christchurch, with
depth ranging up to 18ft. Large (Bob's) lake
has big carp, roach and bream; smaller
lakes hold tench, roach, perch and small
carp; a 'Tiddlers pool' is ideal for juniors.
Fishing in season only, 25th March to
15th June, dawn to dusk.

How to get there   From Christchurch,
head north-east on the A35 and bear
right onto B3035 to New Milton (about
4 miles). Look for signs to Hordle Lakes.
Free car parking on site.
Day tickets   Bob's Lake: adult £5; other
lakes £3. Junior £2. Available on the
bank or from local tackle shops. Details
from Mike Smith; Tel. 0590 672300.
Best methods   Float or leger; also pole
from the dam on Bob's Lake.

Best baits   Bream – sweetcorn; carp –
luncheon meat. 'Smelly' baits do well
here.
Restrictions   No boilies. Keepnets by
arrangement only.
Facilities   Shops/toilets/food in New
Milton.
Disabled facilities   Fishing platforms
suitable for disabled anglers.

ISLAND FISH FARM (I.O.W.)
Atlas Page 203 B.3/7.3

A purpose-built fishing complex next to
Yafford Mill on the south coast of the Isle
of Wight, including a coarse fishing lake.
Good mixed coarse fishing available. Open
from 16th June.

How to get there   From Newport, take
the B3323 south and after about 4 miles
bear right towards Brightstone and
Limestone; follow the white-on-brown
signs for the fish farm. Free car parking
on site.
Day tickets   Adult/OAP £3.50; junior £2;
tickets and bookings available from the
fish farm at Muggleton Lane,
Limestone, I.O.W.; Tel. 0983 740941.
Best methods/baits   Use recognised
techniques and baits.
Facilities   Fishing lodge with toilets/
tackle/bait/instruction on site. Nearest
shop 2 miles; nearest pub 2½ miles.
Disabled facilities   Some swims suitable
for disabled and wheelchair anglers.

KINGFISHER LAKE, NR. SOUTHAMPTON
Atlas Page 203 B.1/6.4

A pleasant, 3-acre gravel pit on the
western outskirts of Southampton. Mainly
roach, tench, perch, chub and pike, plus
some good-sized carp that average about
15lb. Larger carp have been reported here,
however.

How to get there   Take the A35 west
from Southampton and at Totton (about
2 miles) bear right onto the A36 towards
Salisbury. At Testwood (about 1½ miles),
look for the Salmon Leap pub and take
the track on the right to the lake.
Parking on site.
Day tickets   Membership only: £28.
Apply to Mike Felbrich;
Tel. 0703 782545.

Best methods/baits Use general coarse techniques and baits.
Facilities Nearest shop in Testwood; nearest pub, the Salmon Leap.
Disabled facilities Some swims may be suitable for disabled anglers; please phone for advice (see above).

LONGBRIDGE LAKE
Atlas Page 203 B.0/6.3
An ideal fishery for the pleasure angler; 2 acres, well stocked, with plenty of carp (common, mirror, ghost, koi and Crucian) plus roach, bream, tench, rudd, chub, dace, perch, goldfish, grass carp and eels. Also grayling near October. Fishing in season only,16th June to 31st December.

How to get there Leave the M27 at jct 3 and take the M271 towards Romsey. At next roundabout take first left to Lee; at T-junction turn right, then left at 50 yards. The lake entrance is 50 yards on the left.
Day tickets Adult/junior/OAP/disabled £5. 24-hour ticket (Jun-Sept only) £9. Tickets available only from Broadlands Lake (Tel. 0703 869881) or local tackle shops. *Note:* tickets must be purchased before fishing.
Best methods Use any recognised coarse technique.
Best baits Carp, tench – sweetcorn, bread, luncheon meat, maggots.
Restrictions Maximum 2 rods/person. No boilies. Fishing times vary with season: June-Sept: 0700–2100; Oct-Dec: 0700–1800.
Facilities Shop/toilets/food available on site.

M.B.K. LEISURE, LISS
Atlas Page 203 B.8/6.2
Two very prolific coarse fishing lakes situated a few miles north of Petersfield. Excellent fish including chub (to 7lb), carp (to 24lb), Crucians (3–4lb), tench (to 6lb), plus plenty of roach and rudd.

How to get there Take the A3 south-west from Guildford; after about 18 miles turn right at Rake village, next to the Flying Bull pub. Follow the road to Liss and look for St. Patricks Lane and the fishery.
Day tickets Adult £4; junior/OAP £2; available from The Bait Box, 2A Chapel Street, Petersfield; Tel. 0730 66999.

Best methods Fish close in with feeder.
Best baits Tench, roach – maggots, corn; carp – luncheon meat, boilies.
Restrictions Use only barbless hooks. No floating baits; no hemp.
Facilities Nearest shop and pub, The Flying Bull, Rake village (½ mile).
Disabled facilities Some swims suitable for disabled anglers.

PETERSFIELD HEATH LAKE
Atlas Page 203 B.9/6.3
A park lake on the eastern side of Petersfield town. This 8-acre fishery provides mixed coarse sport with most species and large carp (to 27lb).

How to get there Take the A3 south-west from Haslemere to Petersfield (about 12 miles) and in the town centre turn right onto the B2146 Chichester road. The lake is on the right, on the town outskirts; follow signs to the fishery and parking areas.
Day tickets Adult £3.50; junior/OAP £2. Available from local tackle shops.
Best methods/baits Use general coarse techniques and baits.
Facilities Toilets/cafe in the park. Nearest shop/pub in Petersfield.
Disabled facilities Some swims may be suitable for disabled anglers.

ROOKLEY COUNTRY PARK (I.O.W.)
Atlas Page 203 B.4/7.2
A country caravan park at Rookley, about 4 miles south of Newport. A small holiday fishery, consiting of several small lakes, containing most coarse species, including carp, roach and perch.

How to get there From Newport, drive south (or take the bus!) on the A3020 about 4 miles to Rookley village. Follow signs to the Country Park and fishery and park on site.
Day tickets Adult/junior/OAP £3 (under 14s must be accompanied by an adult). Available on application to the Park owner; Tel. 0983 721606.
Best methods/baits Use general coarse techniques and baits.
Facilities Toilets/bar/restaurant on site. Also games facilities and luxury caravan hire. Please phone for details (see above).
Disabled facilities Some swims may be suitable for disabled anglers; please phone for advice (see above).

SOMERTON RESERVOIR(I.O.W.)
Atlas Page 203 B.4/6.8

A large man-made reservoir located outside Cowes, Isle of Wight, with a central causeway dividing the two sections – one 8–9ft deep, the other 13–14ft. Mixed coarse fish, including carp (to 8lb), roach, rudd, perch and tench.

How to get there　Take the A3020 from Newport to Cowes; drive past the Plessey factory (left), garage and supermarket (right). Somerton reservoir is on the right approaching Cowes.

Day tickets　Adult £3 junior/OAP £1.50; available from the visiting bailiff or from local tackle shops.

Best methods/baits　Use any recognised technique or bait.

Restrictions　No floating baits.

Facilities　Nearest shop ¼ mile; nearest pub 500 yards.

Disabled facilities　Some swims suitable for disabled and wheelchair anglers·

SWAY LAKES
Atlas Page 203 A.7/6.8

A long, narrow lake of varying depth up to 10ft, with a bridge in the middle. Good mixed coarse fishing, but expect mainly carp, perch, tench and roach. The bailiff, Mr Clark, is usually around to give help and advice.

How to get there　Leave the M27 at jct 1 and take the A337 to Brockenhurst, then B3055 to Sway. Just outside Sway, at the bottom of the hill, turn left into Barrows Lane. Free car parking on site.

Day tickets　Adult/junior/OAP £3.50 (day or night). Available on the bank.

Best methods/baits　Use any recognised coarse technique.

Restrictions　Use only barbless hooks. No keepnets. No tiger nuts or peanuts to be used.

Facilities　Nearest shop/pub In Sway (½ mile).

Disabled facilities　Some swims suitable for disabled and wheelchair anglers.

WAGGONERS WELLS
Atlas Page 203 C.1/5.8

A National Trust property which includes three lakes, two of which provide good coarse fishing, with perch, roach and tench as well as some small carp. Located just west of Haslemere.

How to get there　Take the A3 south-west from Guildford to Hindhead (about 14 miles) and at Grayshott, look for right turn onto the B3002 towards Headley. Follow National Trust signs (on the left) for Waggoners Wells (also known as Hammer Ponds) and park near the fishery.

Day tickets　Adult £3 per rod; junior/OAP £1.50. Also season ticket: £15. Available from the Ranger on site; for details; Tel. 0428 723722.

Best methods/baits　Use general coarse techniques and baits.

Facilities　Toilets/cafe on site. Nearest shop/pub in Grayshott or Headley.

Disabled facilities　Some swims may be suitable for disabled anglers; please check with the Ranger.

Carp from Waggoners Wells.

RIVER YAR, ALVERSTONE (I.O.W.)
Atlas Page 203 B.5/7.2

Two narrow stretches of the River Yar, near Sandown, I.O.W., controlled by the Isle of Wight Freshwater Angling Assn. Mainly carp (including koi), bream, roach, rudd, dace, perch and eels. Fishing can be 'patchy' here.

How to get there　From Newport take the A3056 towards Sandown; turn left after about 5 miles to Alverstone. At Alverstone, park on road and follow signs to the river; fish from the Mill to the stile, or from the bridge to the S.W.A plant. No car parking at the swims.

Day tickets   Adult £3; junior/OAP £1.50; available from Scotties, Sandown; Tel. 0983 404555; or Newport; Tel. 0983 522115.

Best methods/baits   Use any recognised technique.

Facilities   Nearest shop and pub, ½ mile.

RIVER YAR, YARBRIDGE (I.O.W.)
Atlas Page 203 B.4/7.2

A short stretch of the River Yar, controlled by the Isle of Wight Freshwater Angling Assn. Mainly carp (including koi), bream (to 7lb), roach, rudd, dace, perch and eels, plus large tench. Fishing can be unpredictable along this stretch.

How to get there   Take the A3055 Ryde to Sandown road; at Brading (about 4 miles), turn left at The Anglers pub and drive over the railway; park in the area on the left and walk to the fishery. Fish between the pumphouse and sluice (south bank only).

Day tickets   Adult £3; junior/OAP £1.50; available from Scotties, Sandown; Tel. 0983 404555; or Newport; Tel. 0983 522115.

Best methods/baits   Use any recognised technique.

Facilities   Nearest shop 50 yards; nearest pub 5 (five) yards!

KENT

The serenity of Kent lake fishing.

ASHBY FARM LAKES
Atlas Page 203 E.7/5.8

A holiday centre in beautiful woodland surroundings, about 12 miles south of Ashford, which offers mixed coarse fishing to residents. Two lakes, each of 2 acres, containing most species (including some large carp of 15lb+).

How to get there   Take the A2070 south from Ashford to Brenzett village (about 12 miles) and turn right onto the B2080 to Appledore. In the village, follow signs to the holiday centre and lakes; parking available on site.

Day tickets   Fishing available to holiday residents only. For details; Tel. 0233 83378.

Best methods/baits   Use general coarse techniques and baits.

Restrictions   Fishing by residents only (exclusive of holiday charges).

Facilities   Self-catering Scandinavian chalet accommodation available at the water's edge. Toilets/shop on site; nearest pub, Appledore village.

Disabled facilities   Some swims may be suitable for disabled anglers; please phone for advice.

CAPSTONE LAKE
Atlas Page 203 E.1/5.1

A small (only 28 pegs) fishing lake located in Capstone Leisure Park at Chatham. Expect a good head of carp, plus some very nice-sized roach, together with a few tench and perch.

How to get there   Leave the M2 at jct 3 and take the A229 towards Chatham. Turn left at the 2nd roundabout and take the 1st left, which leads directly to the Park. Free car parking on site.

Day tickets   Adult/junior/OAP £2. Available from Medway Bait & Tackle, 64B St Johns Road, Gillingham, Kent; Tel. 0634 856948.

Best methods/baits   Use general coarse methods and baits.

Facilities   Cafe/toilets on site. Nearest shop in Capstone; nearest pub, The Wagon at Hale, nearby.

Disabled facilities   Platforms have been erected at some swims to enable disabled and wheelchair angling.

CHIDDINGSTONE CASTLE LAKE
Atlas Page 203 D.4/5.4

Located on the Chiddingstone Castle
Estate, a few miles west of Tonbridge.
This peaceful, tree-lined, 3-acre lake with
its lilies and reedbeds provides plenty of
fishing for roach, perch, bream, gudgeon
and rudd, as well as carrying a good stock
of common carp, with some fish in the
10lb region.

How to get there   Leave the M25 at jct 6
and take the A25 east to Limpsfield
(about 4 miles). Turn right onto B269
through Crockham Hills and Four Elms
and look for signs (on right) to
Chiddingstone Castle. The lake is in the
castle estate; parking available on site.
Day tickets   Adult/junior/OAP £6 (dawn
until dusk). Available from the bailiff on
the bank. Advance booking suggested;
for details of availability, contact
Chiddingstone Castle Estate;
Tel. 0892 870347.
Best methods   Mixed species – use
general coarse techniques. Carp – use
specialist carp methods.
Best baits   Carp – use bread.
Restrictions   No night fishing.
Facilities   Nearest shop/pub in
Chiddingstone village or Edenbridge.
Disabled facilities   Some swims may be
suitable for disabled anglers; please
phone for advice (see above).

HIGHAM LAKES
Atlas Page 203 E.2/4.8

A group of lakes on the grounds of
Nuralife's factory, providing mixed coarse
fishing but particularly good carp sport.

How to get there   Take the A226
Rochester to Gravesend road, and after
2½ miles turn right to Lower Higham.
Go through the village to Church Street,
turn left into Canal Road. The factory is
at the bottom.
Day tickets   Membership fee £7.50 a
season plus £5 per day fishing. Tickets
from the main gate at Nuralife (UK) Ltd,
Canal Road, Higham, Rochester, Kent;
Tel. 0474 823451.
Best methods/baits   Use general coarse
techniques and baits.
Facilities   Fishing weekends and holidays
available at hotel. Toilets/food/bar at
the hotel. Nearest shops in Maidstone.

Restrictions   No under 16s fishing the
lakes.
Disabled facilities   Some swims may be
suitable for disabled anglers; please
phone for advice.

JOHNSONS PIT
Atlas Page 203 E.2/5.4

These two gravel pits, which total about
20 acres, lie close to the M20 near
Maidstone. Expect a good head of roach
and tench plus some large pike. Also some
very big carp – fish in the high 20s have
been taken from these waters.

How to get there   Leave the M20 at jct 4
(New Hythe) and follow signs to
Larkfield and the gravel pits. Parking
available on site.
Day tickets   Adult/junior/OAP £1.50.
Available from the bailiff on the banks.
Best methods/baits   Use general coarse
techniques and baits.
Facilities   Nearest shop/pub in Larkfield.
Disabled facilities   Difficult access to
the water may prohibit disabled angling.

Rivers
RIVER MEDWAY

Dace.

Between Tonbridge and Allington, the
Kentish Medway is a wide and weed-free
river, its flow in summer being controlled
largely by a series of locks. In fact, current

may flow downstream and then reverse upstream – all in one session! Despite this and the heavy summer boat traffic, the Medway provides excellent fishing, with not only roach, chub, carp, dace, perch, pike and gudgeon, but also prime bream. Six *Angling Times* Hotspots have been identified on the Medway's Tonbridge–Allington stretch.

TONBRIDGE
Atlas Page 203 D.7/5.6

A 30–50ft wide section; minimal weed growth. Water depth variable – over 5ft at rod tip, 14ft in some swims. Expect good season-long fishing for chub and roach, with 10lb+ catches for most anglers. If bream are feeding, expect a 'heavyweight' catch.

How to get there   Approach Tonbridge from the north via the A227 and park in the Cannon Bridge area.
Day tickets   Available to members only of Maidstone Victory, c/o 33 Hackney Road, Maidstone. Membership cost first year is £37.50.
Best methods   Waggler in middle or near far bank. Shotting patterns allow bites to be detected on the drop. In winter, when pace and level are low, fish over-depth with stick float.
Best baits   Hemp, casters, maggots, worms, bread; brown crumb groundbait.
Facilities   Shops/toilets in Tonbridge.

Hotspot Tips

&   For bream, use a small, open-ended swimfeeder with crumb and caster, and a maggot-worm or caster-worm cocktail hookbait.
&   Fish near Cannons Bridge for roach, and in the deep water (where a stream enters opposite) for bream.

YALDING
Atlas Page 203 D.8/5.4

A winding section with limited tree cover on far bank, depths 5–12ft, minimal weed growth. Late summer, autumn and a mild winter provide best fishing; good roach (to 2lb+), bream (to 4lb+), plus carp, perch and chub. Expect only 10lb roach nets, but better bream.

How to get there   Take the A20 west from Maidstone; after 10 miles, turn south on B2016 to Nettlestead Green. The follow the B2162 to Yalding where the site is located.
Day tickets   Available to members of Maidstone Victory, c/o 33 Hackney Road, Maidstone or from local tackle shops. Membership cost first year is £37.50 .
Best methods   Aim for static or slow-moving bait. Pole on nearside (5–10yds out), or waggler at far bank.
Best baits   Hemp, casters, maggots, worm, flake.
Facilities   Shop in Yalding.

Hotspot Tips

&   For quality fish, shot to get the bait down quickly.
&   A small, open-ended feeder can be very productive.

TESTON
Atlas Page 203 E.1/5.4

Plenty of far bank cover on this 40–50ft-wide section; depth from 5–20ft. Fishing for roach, chub and bream good all year, but best in autumn. Expect a 12lb mixed pleasure bag, but when big bream begin feeding, expect really big catches!

How to get there   Follow the A26 south-west from Maidstone for about 2 miles to Teston. Then turn onto the B2163 and head for the river.
Day tickets   Available to members of Maidstone Victory, c/o 33 Hackney Road, Maidstone or from local tackle shops. Membership cost first year is £37.50 .
Best methods   Open-ended feeder for bream; use waggler to fish between the middle and far bank.
Best baits   Hemp, casters, maggots and flake.
Facilities   Shop/toilets/food in Teston.

Hotspot Tips

&   Try a worm-caster cocktail to tempt the bream.
&   Set your float overdepth and let the bait drag on the bottom.
&   For the best roach, chub and bream, fish in the first field below Teston Bridge.

EAST FARLEIGH
Atlas Page 203 E.1/5.4

A wide (40–50ft), fairly deep (5–12ft) tree-lined stretch with little weed growth, but always flow due to East Farleigh weir. Fishing best in autumn/winter; good catches of roach and chub, plus bream and dace. A typical 10lb net consists of roach and chub.

How to get there   Approach Maidstone along the A26 from Tonbridge. On the outskirts of Maidstone, turn right to East Farleigh station. Parking is limited.
Day tickets   Free fishing.
Best methods   Bream – open-ended feeder and cast to the far bank; roach – waggler at far bank.
Best baits   Hemp, casters.

Hotspot Tips

- In warmer weather, look out for bites on the drop.

MAIDSTONE
Atlas Page 203 E.2/5.3

A 40–60ft-wide section, little weed growth, depth 5–9ft and holes to 15ft. Fishing good all season, very good in autumn/winter. Mostly roach, plus perch, dace and bream and some big carp (to 20lb). A typical mixed net is 10–20lb, bigger if bream are feeding.

How to get there   Take either of the Maidstone exits from the M20 (junctions 5, 6 or 7) and drive to the town. Park on the market place.
Day tickets   Free fishing.
Best methods   Bream – open-ended feeder at the far bank; roach – waggler at the far bank, using any cover.
Best baits   Bream – worm, casters; other species – maggot, casters, hemp.
Facilities   Shops/toilets/food in Maidstone town centre.

Hotspot Tips

- In summer, fish will take bait on the drop, but prefer it on the bottom in winter.
- Don't forget some brown crumb for the feeder.

River Medway below Tonbridge.

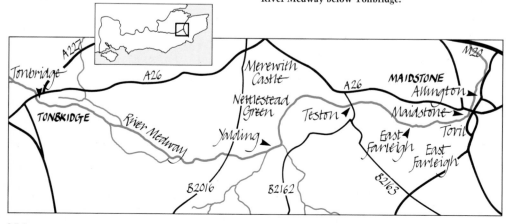

ALLINGTON
Atlas Page 203 E.2/5.4

A wide section (to 60ft), some deep water (10–12ft at rod tip), and a centre channel 15ft. Good fishing season-long, but excellent in autumn/winter. Plenty of roach, dace and perch, plus large chub or carp. Expect a day net of 10–12lb – more if bream are feeding well.

How to get there   Take either junction 5, 6 or 7 from the M20 into Maidstone. Follow the one-way system through the town and park at Monktons Lane.
Day tickets   Free fishing.
Best methods   Roach – fish nearside swims with a pole at 8–9 metres; present bait at 6–24″ overdepth. Bream – feeder.
Best baits   Hemp, casters, maggots.
Facilities   Shops/toilets/food in Maidstone town centre.

Hotspot Tips

❦ Medway fish like static bait, so hold the float back when the river is running.
❦ For good sport, fish the centre channel overdepth with a sliding float.
❦ The best spots are downstream of Monktons Lane.

NICHOLLS PIT
Atlas Page 203 F.0/5.8

A large gravel pit, near the south coast at Hythe. Contains most mixed species – roach, tench, bream – in addition to some big carp in the 10–20lb range.

How to get there   From Folkestone, drive west along the A259 coast road through Hythe towards Dymchurch and St. Mary's Bay. Look for signs to the Army firing ranges; the fishery is nearby. Car parking available on site.
Day tickets   Members of Cinque Ports AC only. Cost £25; apply to Mr R. MacGregor, Honorary Secretary, 31 Ermarsh Road, Hythe, Kent; Tel. 0303 269094.
Best methods/baits   Use general coarse techniques and baits.
Facilities   Nearest shop/pub in Hythe or Dymchurch.
Disabled facilities   Some swims may be suitable for disabled anglers.

Rivers
RIVER ROTHER

The Rother rises near Rotherfield, East Sussex and runs to the sea at Rye. Despite its straight, canalised, featureless appearance and steeply sloping banks, it provides excellent fishing. In general, the flow is slow, so fine tackle is essential, the key to success being location of shelves, although the shallows can also yield good catches. In its upper reaches, chub predominate, while plenty of bream and roach appear lower downstream.

Five *Angling Times* Hotspots are located along the stretch of the Rother from Bodiam to Iden.

BODIAM
Atlas Page 203 E.3/6.2

A narrow stretch of river, average depth 5–6ft, with a good flow but possibly very weedy in summer. A good venue all season, particularly in winter. Expect roach (up to 1lb; nets of 10–12lb) and some chub.

How to get there   Take the A21 London-Hastings road; at Flimwell, turn east on the A268 to Hawkhurst, then Sandhurst. At Sandhurst, turn south, signposted Bodiam Castle.
Day tickets   Edenbridge AC members only: £35 from PO Box 544, Purley, Surrey, CR18 1XJ. (Membership includes access to waters in Kent, Surrey and Sussex). Members can obtain day tickets for guests.
Best methods   Stick float or waggler, plus small hook sizes and fine hooklengths.
Best baits   Maggot, casters; loosefeed only.

Hotspot Tips

❦ Look for flows and swims where a float can be run between weed beds.

NEWENDEN
Atlas Page 203 E.4/6.2

A stretch with minimal flow and depth of 6–7ft; weed growth can be heavy in summer. Sport can be patchy, but summer provides the best fishing. Expect roach, bream, chub and tench, with mixed nets of up to 30lb.

How to get there   Take the A21 London-Hastings road; at Flimwell, turn east on the A268 to Hawkhurst, Sandhurst, then Newenden.

Day tickets   Adult £1.50; junior/OAP £1; available on the bank for most areas.

Best methods   Waggler with 2–3 AAA close to far-bank weed; light end tackle and loosefeed are essential.

Best baits   Casters better than maggot; breadflake is worth trying.

Hotspot Tips

🐟 Try using a pole on the inside line, using the weed beds to locate fish.

🐟 Possible holding areas are often weed covered.

WITTERSHAM
Atlas Page 203 E.5/6.3

A 20-yard-wide section with pronounced shelves on both banks and very little flow. Summer fishing is best here. Main species are roach, bream (3–5lb) and chub (to 4lb), plus a few tench.

How to get there   Take the A21 – A268 route through Hawkhurst to Newenden. Follow signs for Camber and Rye, then turn left towards Wittersham and the river.

Day tickets   Adult £1.50; junior/OAP £1; available on the bank.

Best methods   Fish the far bank, just off the shelf; use standard float or waggler up to 4AAA to fish on the drop. For the near bank and middle, use a pole.

Best baits   Maggot, casters, worm; brown crumb for bream.

Facilities   Shops/food available in Wittersham.

Hotspot Tips

🐟 The bigger fish stay close to the far-side shelf.

🐟 Try using a small leger or feeder as an alternative to float.

🐟 The best pegs are where the shelf is pronounced and holding weed cover.

NEWBRIDGE
Atlas Page 203 E.5/6.4

A 20-yard-wide stretch, with wooded banks and shelf on each bank; depth 10ft in the middle to 6ft just off the shelf. Very much a summer fishery, with roach, bream, chub and tench. A 10lb catch is likely, but with good shoals, hefty mixed nets are quite possible.

How to get there   From the southbound A21, turn left on the A268 to Rye. Go through Peasmarsh and turn towards Rye Foreign. Take the first left; follow the road to the river.

Day tickets   Adult £1.50; junior/OAP £1; available on the river bank.

Best methods   Waggler or leger at the far bank. Bites may come on the drop – shot float accordingly. In extra flow, use pole on inside line, close to shelf.

Best baits   Maggots, casters, worm; use brown crumb for bream.

Hotspot Tips

🐟 When legering for bream, use a long tail – up to 8ft.

🐟 Don't ignore the shelf, even though it may be very shallow!

🐟 The best swims have that little extra bit of cover.

The River Rother.

IDEN
Atlas Page 203 E.6/6.4

A wide, slow-flowing stretch, with shelves either side, depth from 6ft at the bank to 10ft in the middle. Summer fishing for roach, chub, bream and tench is best, with 'staggering' catches from good bream shoals. Expect a pleasure catch of 10–20lb.

How to get there   Take the A268 east towards Rye; just before the town, turn left into Military Road and follow the road to Iden Lock.

Day tickets   Adult £1.50; junior/OAP £1; available on the bank.
Best methods   Waggler or leger at the far bank.
Best baits   Maggot, casters, worms; use brown crumb for bream.

Hotspot Tips

- For some big roach, fish the nearside.
- A second/third line in the centre/nearside can be productive.

ROYAL MILITARY CANAL
Atlas Page 203 E.8/5.9

A shallow canal which runs westward from Hythe to join the River Rother near Rye; the best fishing is between Hythe and Hamstreet (about 10 miles). Expect most coarse species plus some good quality carp, with 30lb+ specimens possible.

How to get there   From Ashford, head south on the A2070 to Hamstreet (about 6 miles) and turn left onto B2067 towards Hythe. Access to the canal is possible at various points on the right; check with local tackle shops for details.
Day tickets   Adult £2; junior/OAP £1.. Available on the bank.
Best methods/baits   Use general coarse techniques and baits.
Facilities   B&B accommodation at pubs/hotels, plus shops/pubs/toilets/food at various points along the canal.
Disabled facilities   Disabled/wheelchair angling may be possible at some venues; please phone for advice (see above).

SCHOOL POOL
Atlas Page E.7/5.2

A popular 'town-centre' gravel pit of about 11 acres, surrounded by houses, roads and factories, at Faversham. Nevertheless, expect very good mixed coarse fishing for tench, bream and pike, in addition to some very big carp (commons and mirrors) that may reach over 30lb.

How to get there   Directions from Mick Kennett; Tel. 0795 534516.
Day tickets   Adult/junior/OAP £4; available Monday to Friday. Tickets must be bought in advance from Mick Kennett (see above).

Best methods/baits   Use general coarse techniques and baits; advanced methods are needed for carp.
Restrictions   No night fishing.
Facilities   Nearest shops/pubs in Faversham.
Disabled facilities   Some swims may be suitable for disabled anglers; please phone for advice (see above).

Rivers

RIVER STOUR

The River Stour.

Running through the Kentish countryside from the vale of Ashford to the sea at Sandwich, the Great Stour is a swift-flowing river, whose lower stretches are tidal. The stretch from Canterbury to Plucks Gutter, which includes five *Angling Times* Hotspots, is perhaps less prolific than many years ago, but still provides very enjoyable fishing – especially for the float fisherman. Large catches of bream, chub, roach and dace are the 'norm', with pike and perch adding to the excitement.

VAUXHALL BRIDGE UPSTREAM
Atlas Page 203 F.1/5.3

A 30–40ft-wide, brisk-flowing stretch; heavy summer weed, average depth 5ft. Fishing fairly even, catches average 10lb. Mainly bream, roach and dace; bigger catches are likely when the bream appear. Some chub, perch and pike may be taken.

How to get there   From Canterbury city centre, take the A28 towards Sturry and Margate. On the city outskirts, turn left

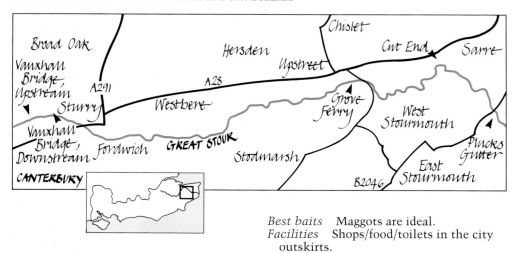

Best baits   Maggots are ideal.
Facilities   Shops/food/toilets in the city
   outskirts.

Hotspot Tips

☙ Working bait down channels between
   the streamer weed works very well
   here.
☙ You may need a roving approach to
   find the fish.
☙ Swims on the bends often provide
   especially good sport.

Day tickets   Free fishing.
Best methods   Use a double rubber float
   approach with a large stick or Avon. For
   bream at the bottom end, use a waggler
   at the far bank.
Best baits   Maggot.
Facilities   Shops/food/toilets in the city
   outskirts.

Hotspot Tips

☙ When float fishing, you'll need a 3BB
   bulk down the line; ease it between the
   weed channels.
☙ Legering can be a good alternative for
   bream.

GROVE FERRY
Atlas Page F.3/5.2

A tidal, 40ft wide, weedy stretch with
shelves off both banks. Depth ranges from
7–12ft. Chub and bream are best in winter,
with 40lb catches possible; a 12lb mixed
net is likely in summer. There is also a
good head of pike.

How to get there   Take the A28 from
   Canterbury towards Margate; at
   Upstreet (6 miles) turn right to Grove
   Ferry Bridge.
Day tickets   £3; available from the bailiff
   on the bank.
Best methods   Double rubber on running
   line or pole; work between the near
   shelf and mid-river. Use bulk shooting
   to get the bait down.
Best baits   Maggot and casters; for bream
   also use worm and flake.

VAUXHALL BRIDGE
DOWNSTREAM
Atlas Page 203 F.2/5.3

A 30–40ft-wide stretch, very weedy in
summer, with strong flow. Average depth
4–6ft. The length fishes well all season,
but hits peak form during autumn/winter.
Expect roach, dace, chub and bream, with
10lb+ catches always possible, plus a
chance of 3–4lb bream!

How to get there   From Canterbury city
   centre, take the A28 towards Sturry and
   Margate. On the city outskirts, turn left
   to Vauxhall Bridge.
Day tickets   Free fishing.
Best methods   Double rubber float
   tactics (stick or Avon) are effective;
   heavy shotting is vital to get bait down
   quickly.

Hotspot Tips

☙ For best results, fish overdepth and
   ease it through slowly.
☙ The best winter areas are just
   downstream of the bridge, or the
   boathouse bend.

CUT END
Atlas Page 203 F.4/5.3

An even-fishing stretch, with 50ft width, tidal flow and shelves on either side. Good weed growth, with a 7–11ft depth. Bream and roach are best in summer, but sport can be patchy, with only 6lb some days. Expect much better nets if the bream are feeding.

How to get there   From Canterbury, take the A28 Margate road. About 2 miles after Upstreet, turn right down Cut End.

Day tickets   £3; available from the bailiff on the bank.

Best methods   Fish overdepth with stick float bulk shotted and eased over the shelf. Bream – open-ended feeder or straight lead.

Best baits   Maggot, or for summer bream, use bread flake.

Hotspot Tips

- For a change, try using a pole with a stick float, bulk shotted.

PLUCKS GUTTER
Atlas Page 203 F.4/5.4

This wide (up to 50ft), tidal stretch has a strong downtide flow, a depth of 8–11ft, and is well reeded at the edges. It is noted for its bream and roach, with large catches when the bream feed; otherwise, expect a mixed catch of perhaps 12lb.

How to get there   Follow the A28 Canterbury-Margate road. After 9 miles, turn right on the B2046; Plucks Gutter is about 1½ miles down this road.

Day tickets   £3; available from the bailiff on the bank.

Best methods   Bream – straight leger or open-ended feeder at the far bank. Other species – float with bulk shot.

Best baits   Maggot or caster; worm or flake are best for bream.

Hotspot Tips

- When legering, a long tail gives best results.
- The best bream pegs are just above the first bend, on the upstream side.
- The bream shoals tend to patrol the opposite bank!

SUNDRIDGE LAKE
Atlas Page 203 D.7/5.4

A single, 5-acre gravel pit very close to the M25, midway between Westerham and Sevenoaks. The lake contains few mixed coarse fish, but is reputed to carry a good head of carp – with some in the 20lb+ region.

How to get there   Leave the M25 at jct 5 via the A21 and at 1st junction turn right onto the A25 to Sundridge (about 1½ miles) down the road, the lake is on the right. Car parking available on site.

Day tickets   Newly taken over by Holmesdale Angling Society. Membership £35 plus £15 joining fee; two guests tickets daily allowed at £2.50 with membership. Send SAE to Mr S. Banks, 58 Chevening Road, Chipstead, Sevenoaks, Kent TN13 2SA for details. Membership allows access to many other club waters.

Best methods/baits   Use general coarse techniques and baits.

Facilities   Nearest shop/pub in Sundridge.

Disabled facilities   Some swims may be suitable for disabled anglers; please phone for advice (see above).

Many large carp on Surrey lakes.

SURREY

KINGFISHER LAKES
Atlas Page 203 C.3/5.6

Three small ponds located a few miles
west of Haslemere. Mainly mixed species,
especially small carp and tench, plus some
larger carp.

How to get there   Take the A3 south from
   Guildford through Hindhead (about 10
   miles) and turn right onto B3002 towards
   Grayshott after ½ mile. Look for Hammer
   Lane and signs to the fishery. Free car
   parking on site.
Day tickets   Adult £5; junior/OAP £3;
   available on site; details from the fishing
   lodge; Tel. 0428 604928.
Best methods/baits   Use any recognised
   technique.
Facilities   Toilets/bait available on site.
   Nearest shops Hindhead (2 miles);
   nearest pub, The Mill Tavern, Shotter
   Mill (2 miles).

SUSSEX

Special effects in Sussex.

BEAVERS FARM, FELBRIDGE
Atlas Page 203 D.4/5.7

Four lakes just outside East Grinstead,
each well stocked with mixed coarse fish,
including carp (to 10lb) and some rare
catfish. Also a pike lake on site.

How to get there   Take the A22 from
   East Grinstead north-west to Felbridge
   (about 1 mile); the turning to the lakes
   is on the left, just past the church and
   restaurant. Free car parking on site.

Day tickets   Adult/junior/OAP £5;
   available on the bank.
Best methods/baits   Use recognised
   techniques.
Facilities   Shops/toilets/food in
   Felbridge; nearest pub at Wire Mill
   Lake.

CHALLENGE OUTDOOR PURSUITS CENTRE
Atlas Page 203 D.8/5.8

A group of lakes within an Outdoor
Pursuit Centre near Tunbridge Wells.
Some lakes fished by syndicates; others
fished on day tickets. Mixed coarse
fishing, with large carp, plus good tench,
roach and perch.

How to get there   Take the A21 beyond
   Tunbridge Wells to Lamberhurst, then
   turn right on B2169 towards Bells Yew
   Green. At crossroads, turn right towards
   Kippins Cross. Free car parking on site.
Day tickets   Adult/junior/OAP £3;
   available on site.
Best methods/baits   Use any recognised
   technique.
Facilities   Toilets/food at fishing lodge
   on site.
Disabled facilities   Some swims suitable
   for disabled and wheelchair anglers.

CHICHESTER LEISURE CENTRE
Atlas Page 203 C.2/6.7

An eleven-lake complex – the largest (Ivy
Lake) is 50 acres – which forms part of
Chichester Leisure Centre. Fishing can be
difficult, but the lakes contain some good
fish; carp to 30lb+, tench to 11lb, pike to
30lb+, bream to 13lb. Recently restocked.

How to get there   Take the A27
   Chichester by-pass and turn south onto
   B2145 towards Selsey. Park in the lay-by
   and walk along the footpath (through
   the Leisure Complex) to the lakes.
Day tickets   Adult £3; junior/OAP £1.50.
   Available on site.
Best methods   Use recognised techniques
   (match preferred).
Best baits   Maggots, bread.
Facilities   Shops/toilets/food in Leisure
   Centre complex.
Disabled facilities   Some swims are
   suitable for disabled and wheelchair
   anglers.

CLIVE VALE AND ECCLESBOURNE RESERVOIRS
Atlas Page 203 E.3/6.5

Two small reservoirs near Hastings, each well stocked with most coarse species and good-sized carp. Ecclesbourne is more of a specialist carp lake, with fish to 30lb, plus bream (to 8lb) and tench (to 7lb).

How to get there For Ecclesbourne, take Barley Lane from Hastings Old Town and park by Shearbarn Caravan Park. For Clive Vale, take the Harold Road out of the Old Town; the reservoirs are on the right, after about ¾ mile.
Day tickets Ecclesbourne: £4 on the bank, £3 from tackle shops. Clive Vale: adults £2; juniors £1. Membership also available: adult £18; ladies/OAP £10; junior £9. Other waters on the Rivers Rother and Brede.
Best methods/baits Use general coarse techniques and baits.
Restrictions No junior anglers allowed at Ecclesbourne.
Facilities Plenty of shops and pubs in Hastings.

DITCHLING POOL
Atlas Page 203 D.3/6.2

A small pond on Ditchling Common, adjacent to Burgess Hill. Contains most coarse species, including carp, but the heavy weed growth causes problems for the angler and sport is 'patchy'.

How to get there From Haywards Heath, take the B2112 south towards Burgess Hill (about 4 miles). The fishery is just before the B2112/B2113 junction. Park nearby.
Day tickets Free fishing.
Best methods/baits Use general coarse techniques and baits.
Facilities Nearest shops/pub in Burgess Hill.
Disabled facilities Some swims may be suitable for disabled anglers.

FAYGATE WOOD PONDS
Atlas Page 203 C.8/5.8

Two 'easy-fishing' ponds located just north of Horsham. The larger, carp pond contains large carp plus many roach. The smaller, general coarse pond has only 14 swims and contains carp (to 12lb), bream (to 8lb), lots of roach plus chub and barbel, all in great condition.

How to get there Take the A264 from Crawley towards Horsham; at Faygate roundabout (3 miles) turn right past Holmbush Inn and continue to Amberly Court. Take 2nd driveway into farmyard and park in corner near gates marked 'Pond'. Follow signs across the field.
Day tickets Adult £4.50; junior/OAP £2 (under 14s must be accompanied by an adult). Fishing must be booked with the owner. Phone for availability; Tel. 0306 712627.
Best methods Float, leger, feeder and pole all work well.
Best baits Maggots (red preferred), sweetcorn, luncheon meat in summer only. Red groundbait brings roach, bream and barbel.
Restrictions No keepnets; one rod only. Use only barbless hooks; no boilies. All gates must be kept shut, and NO LITTER.
Facilities Shops/pubs in Horsham or Faygate.

FURNACE BROOK FISHERIES
Atlas Page 203 D.8/6.5

A small lake fishery lying just north of Hailsham, East Sussex. Well stocked, with mirror carp (to 12lb), Crucians and very big common carp (to 20lb). Also roach, bream and tench.

How to get there From Heathfield, take the A267 south for 7 miles; at Hailsham turn left onto A271 towards Hastings. Look for the turn to Cowbeech on the left, after about 1 mile.
Day tickets Adult/junior/OAP £3 per day or night; 24-hour ticket £6.50. Tickets available on site. For details; Tel. 0435 830298.
Best methods/baits Use recognised techniques.
Facilities Lodge facilities on site. Shop/pub in Cowbeech.

HAWKINS POND
Atlas Page 203 C.8/5.9

This beautiful 15-acre woodland lake, not far from Horsham town centre, is a former clay pit and tin mine. Good mixed fishing in an average 8ft of water which produces large pike, tench and bream, plus roach, rudd, perch and chub. Also a good head of small carp, and some bigger fish, possibly to 20lb+.

How to get there   Take the A24 south from Dorking into Horsham town centre. From Horsham Town Centre take A281 Brighton Road (just outside town centre). Turn left, then right at bottom of hill. The Pond is on the left, where the road narrows.

Day tickets   Season tickets only: £25. Available from Horsham & District A.A., Secretary Alan Giess; Tel. 0323 895741.

Best methods/baits   Use general coarse techniques and baits; specialist methods may be needed for carp.

Restrictions   Fishing only from 0400–2300. No night fishing. No pre-baiting.

Facilities   Nearest shops/pubs in Horsham.

Disabled facilities   Some swims may be suitable for disabled anglers.

HOLBEAM WOOD FARM
Atlas Page 203 D.8/5.8

Two lakes – large and small – a few miles south-east of Tunbridge Wells. Each stocked with mixed coarse fish, including carp (largest in large lake), tench, perch and roach. Especially suitable for young anglers (accompanied).

How to get there   From Tunbridge Wells take the A267 south; after 3 miles, bear left onto B2099 to Wadhurst, then Ticehurst. At Wallcrouch (on main road), the small lake is by the roadside; for the large lake, take first farm drive on right after entering Wards Lane. Free car parking on site.

Day tickets   Large lake: adult/junior £4. Small lake: adult/junior £3. Tickets available from Holbeam Wood Farm, Wallcrouch, nr Wadhurst; Tel. 089288 3231.

Best methods/baits   Use recognised techniques.

Restrictions   Use only barbless hooks. Juniors must be accompanied by an adult.

Facilities   Nearest shop Wadhurst village.

LITTLE DECOY LAKE
Atlas Page 203 D.5/6.4

A single, general coarse fishing lake located at Halland, just north of Lewes. Contains a good head of carp (to 10lb) plus roach, tench and rudd.

How to get there   From Lewes take the B2192 north-east to Halland (about 7 miles); at crossroads turn right to East Hoathly. The lake entrance is 400 yards on the right, in woodland. Free car parking on site.

Day tickets   Adult/junior/OAP £4.50; night ticket £7.50; available from Lagoon Bait & Tackle Shop, 327 Kingsway, Hove; Tel. 0273 415879.

Best methods   Floatfishing.

Best baits   Luncheon meat, sweetcorn.

Restrictions   No boilies; use only barbless hooks.

Facilities   Nearest shop and pub ½ mile. A fishing lodge with facilities is planned for the near future.

Disabled facilities   Some swims are suitable for disabled and wheelchair anglers.

MILTON MOUNT LAKE
Atlas Page 203 D.1/5.8

A small lake at Three Bridges, near Crawley, just off the M23. A pleasant location, providing some good fishing; well stocked with most coarse fish, including carp.

How to get there   Leave the southbound M23 at jct 10 and take the A264 towards Crawley. Follow signs to Three Bridges and the lake; car parking available nearby.

Day tickets   Members only of Horsham Angling Club; £25 from Alan Giess; Tel. 0323 895741.

Best methods/baits   Use general coarse techniques and baits.

Facilities   Nearest shops/pub at Three Bridges.

Disabled facilities   Some swims may be suitable for disabled anglers.

PASSIES POND
Atlas Page 203 C.8/6.6

A fairly recently-opened (June 1990) 4-acre lake at Coombes, near Lancing in West Sussex. Well stocked with all coarse species: mirror and ghost carp to 16lb, plus roach, rudd, tench (to 6lb) and chub (to 4lb).

How to get there   From Horsham, take the A24 south about 12 miles, then turn left onto A283. At Steyning, turn right on minor road to Coombes (about 2 miles).

Day tickets   Adult £5 junior/OAP £2.
Mid-week tickets: adult £3; junior/OAP
£1. Available from Trevor Passmore,
Church Farm, Coombes, Lancing,
Sussex; Tel. 0273 465257.

Best methods/baits   Use recognised
techniques.

Restrictions   Use only barbless hooks.
No groundbait; no boilies, peanuts or
dried dog or cat food. No keepnets to be
used for carp.

Facilities   Shops/toilets/food in Steyning.
Nearest pub, Sussex Pad, at top of
Coombes Road. Information centre on
site.

Disabled facilities   Most swims suitable
for disabled and wheelchair anglers.

PETT POOLS
Atlas Page 203 E.4/6.4

A group of three gravel pits – Western,
Northern and Eastern – which form an
excellent fishery. Plenty of large bream in
all three, but especially good carp, tench,
pike and eels in Western and Northern,
with particularly big bream bags (to 50lb)
in Northern. Eastern contains plenty of
carp and bream. A difficult choice to make
between the three!

How to get there   From Hastings, drive
east on the A259 towards Winchelsea;
after about 6 miles, bear right on minor
road to Pett Level. The lakes are
signposted (about 2 miles from
Winchelsea); use either of the three car
parks in front of the lakes.

Day tickets   Adult £4; junior/OAP £2.
Available only in advance from Market
Stores, Pett Level.

Best methods   Float and feeder both
work well here.

Best baits   Carp – boilies. Tench –
lobworms. Bream, perch - maggots.

Facilities   Nearest shop/pub in Pett
Level.

Disabled facilities   Some swims may be
suitable for disabled anglers; for advice,
contact Peter McLaine;
Tel. 0424 715218.

PILTDOWN POND
Atlas Page 203 D.4/6.1

This small pond, which is located on
common land near Uckfield, contains
mixed coarse fish along with some quite
large carp (to 10lb), but heavy weed
growth can make fishing difficult.

How to get there   From Haywards Heath,
take the A272 east through Newick
(about 6 miles) and turn left at Piltdown
Common. The pond is 100 yards on the
left; car parking nearby.

Day tickets   Free fishing.

Best methods/baits   Use general coarse
techniques and baits.

Facilities   Nearest shop/pub in Newick.

Disabled facilities   Some swims may be
suitable for disabled anglers.

ROOSTHOLE
Atlas Page 203 C.8/5.9

A very peaceful 3¼-acre lake, close to
Horsham town centre. Formerly a clay pit,
with clear, deep (22ft) water, providing
plenty of coarse fishing with bream, roach,
rudd, perch and pike, plus some large carp
– 22lb+ has been recorded here.

How to get there   From Horsham town
centre take A281 to Brighton. Turn left
at garden centre outside town, then
right at the bottom of the hill.
Roosthole is on the right.

Day tickets   Season tickets only: £25.
Available from Horsham & District
A.A., Secretary Alan Giess;
Tel. 0323 895741.

Best methods   Use general coarse
techniques; specialist methods may be
needed for carp.

Best baits   Most baits work well here;
floaters are preferred.

Restrictions   Fishing only from
0400–2300. No night fishing. No pre-
baiting.

Facilities   Nearest shops/pubs in
Horsham.

Disabled facilities   Some swims may be
suitable for disabled anglers.

SCARLETTS LAKE
Atlas Page 203 D.7/5.7

A picturesque 3-acre lake situated in a
beautifully wooded and sheltered valley
on the Kent/Sussex border, close to East
Grinstead. Well stocked, with carp, tench,
rudd, roach, bream and perch. Open daily;
an ideal venue for a quiet day's fishing.

How to get there   From East Grinstead,
take the A264 east towards Tunbridge
Wells; at Hammerswood (4 miles), turn
left into private road opposite
Steadleaze House (near church). Access

is also possible from local Cowden-Dormansland road. Free parking on site.

Day tickets   0800-sunset: adult £3.50; junior/OAP/disabled/unemployed £2. 1400-sunset: adult £2.50; junior/OAP/disabled/unemployed £1.50. Tickets available at the lakeside. All prices per rod until 31st October; thereafter 2 rods per ticket. Season tickets/club bookings available: contact the fishery for details; Tel. 0342 850414.

Best methods/baits   Use recognised techniques.

Facilities   Shop/pub in Cowden.

Disabled facilities   Most swims suitable for disabled and wheelchair anglers.

RIVER TEISE
Atlas Page 203 D.8/5.8

A small river section from Wadhurst to Lamberhurst via Bayham and Hook Green. Contains deeper pools and shallow glides, with a good head of medium-sized pike, chub, perch, minnows and some trout. Best fishing time is just after the rain.

How to get there   From Tunbridge Wells town centre, take the B2169 east for about 5 miles; at Lamberhurst, look for Forge Garage (opposite Bayham Abbey ruins). Details of river access available from the Garage. No car parking at the swims.

Day tickets   Adult/junior/OAP £3; available from Forge Garage, Lamberhurst Road, Lamberhurst.

Best methods/baits   Use recognised techniques. Worm, maggots or freelined minnow are preferred.

Facilities   Nearest shop/pub in Lamberhurst.

TILGATE PARK LAKE
Atlas Page 203 D.1/5.8

A public park lake in Crawley, well used by canoeists, windsurfers and the public in general – hence quite difficult fishing. Expect most coarse fish, together with some common and mirror carp which may reach double figures.

How to get there   Leave the southbound M23 at jct 10 and take the A264 towards Crawley. Follow signs to Tilgate Park and the lake; car parking available nearby.

Day tickets   Adult/OAP £3.50; junior half price. Available from park keepers on the banks.

Best methods/baits   Use general coarse techniques and baits.

Restrictions   No night fishing.

Facilities   Toilets/cafe in the park. Nearest shops and pubs in Crawley.

Disabled facilities   Good access to swims; some may be suitable for disabled anglers.

WEIR WOOD RESERVOIR
Atlas Page 203 D.3/5.8

A huge reservoir located south of East Grinstead, totalling some 300 acres. Contains many mixed species – roach, perch, rudd – and thousands of small carp which provide plenty of sport, although catches are not big. Finding the larger fish can be difficult.

How to get there   From East Grinstead, take the B2110 south-west about 2 miles and look for left turn onto minor road to Saint Hill and the reservoir. Follow the signs (about 3 miles) to the fishery and use the car park on site.

Day tickets   Adult/junior/OAP £5 for one rod. Available on the bank.

Best methods/baits   Use general coarse techniques and baits.

Restrictions   No night fishing.

Facilities   Nearest shop/pub/toilets/food in East Grinstead.

Disabled facilities   Disabled fishing may be possible at some swims; check at local tackle shops.

WILDINGS FARM, CHAILEY
Atlas Page 203 D.2/6.3

A long, thin, secluded lake situated on a farm near Haywards Heath and owned by Hassocks & District A.C. Mainly carp (including Crucians), tench, rudd, perch and roach. Summer fishing here is generally good, but is harder in winter.

How to get there   From Haywards Heath, take the A272 east, then A275 south towards Lewes. Chailey is about 1½ miles south of the A272/A275 junction. Look for signs to Wildings Farm.

Day tickets   Adult £5; available only in advance from the Club Secretary, Hassocks & District A.C.

Best methods   Float, leger and feeder.

Best baits Maggots, bread, sweetcorn, luncheon meat, boilies.

Restrictions Maximum 2 rods per angler.

Facilities Shop/pub in Chailey village.

WIRE MILL LAKE, FELBRIDGE
Atlas Page 203 D.3/5.7

A single lake situated at Felbridge, just outside East Grinstead. Most fishing is from wooden jetties; sport includes bream, tench, carp and roach. Boaters and water-skiers can cause problems.

How to get there Take the A22 from East Grinstead north-west to Felbridge (about 1 mile); Wire Mill Lake is signposted on the left, after the Mormon temple. Car parking (pay) on site.

Day tickets Adult/junior/OAP £3; available only on the bank.

Best methods/baits Feeder generally successful; or use recognised techniques.

Facilities Shops/toilets/food in Felbridge. Nearest pub at the lake.

WYKE LAKE
Atlas Page 203 C.2/6.7

One of three gravel pits to the south of Chichester, alongside the bypass. This 8-acre lake contains most coarse species and in good sizes, plus some large carp in the 20–25lb region.

How to get there From Bognor Regis, take the A259 to Chichester and at the bypass turn left towards Portsmouth. Wyke Lake is the third lake on the right; follow signs to the fishery and car park.

Day tickets Season tickets only: adults £28 per year plus £28 entry fee. Juniors/OAPs £14 per year plus £14 entry. Available from Chichester & District A.S. Secretary: Mrs C. Luffman, 3 Birdham Close, Bognor Regis; Tel. 0243 867673 or from Fisherman's Den; Tel. 0243 866663.

Best methods/baits Use general coarse techniques and baits.

Facilities Nearest shops/pubs in Chichester.

Disabled facilities Some swims may be suitable for disabled anglers.

WYLAND LAKES
Atlas Page 203 E.2/6.4

A six-lake complex on a working farm, just outside Battle. Five lakes contain mixed coarse fish, with rudd, tench, bream, perch and some carp; the sixth lake is designated a specialist carp lake, with mirrors and commons, and specimens approaching 30lb.

How to get there Head north-west from Hastings on the A2100 and at Battle, turn left onto the B2095. Wyland Farm and the fishery is on the left, shortly after turning. Look for the signs; free car parking on site.

Day tickets Adult/junior/OAP £5; specimen carp lake £6.

Best methods/baits Mixed species – use general coarse techniques and baits. Carp – use modern methods and baits.

Facilities Toilets on site. Nearest shop/pub in Battle.

Disabled facilities Some swims may be suitable for disabled anglers; please phone for advice (see above).

Wessex Region

River Avon at Bisterne.

The Wessex NRA region, which incorporates parts of Hampshire and Wiltshire, as well as Dorset, before extending north to include Somerset and much of Avon, offers a variety of top quality coarse fishing to suit all needs.

The region's river sport is dominated by the Hampshire Avon, which flows south from Devizes to enter the English Channel at Christchurch. This quite slowly-flowing river has many famous and prolific fisheries on its lower reaches near the south coast, with large barbel, roach, dace, chub and grayling being the order of the day. To the west of the Avon lies the Stour – another prolific fishery whose lower reaches, with their much faster-flowing water, provide roach, chub and bream. Further north, in Somerset, the Frome also offers good fishing, though catches tend to be smaller than those taken from the southern rivers.

To the north of the region lies the Bristol Avon, which as it flows from its source near Malmesbury to the Severn Estuary, offers consistent fishing for most coarse species. Somerset also offers good river angling, with the Huntspill, Brue, Yeo, Parrett and the Kings Sedgemoor Drain each contributing to the fisherman's fun.

Of course, fishing in Wessex is not limited to the rivers. There are plenty of still-water fisheries available in the region's many lakes, reservoirs and disused clay and gravel pits – mainly in Hampshire and Somerset – which now provide top quality sport, including specimen carp, bream or pike.

AVON

Rivers

THE BRISTOL AVON

BATHEASTON
Atlas Page 201 F.4/4.0

A very pleasant section of the Bristol Avon which includes the 'Quarter Mile Field', just north of Bath. Good coarse fishing, with bream, rudd, roach, pike, perch, chub and some quality barbel.

How to get there   Take the A4 west from Chippenham towards Bath and turn right (towards Batheaston) at the A4/A46 junction. Continue for about ½ mile and look for 'Avon Rugby Club' sign on the right, just before the Amoco garage. Drive down the track 100 yards to free parking area. Fish from the upstream boundary of the rugby field, downstream, to the riding stables.

Day tickets   Adult £2; junior/OAP 50p. Available at local tackle shops.

Best methods/baits   Use general coarse methods and baits.

Restrictions   The car park is closed to anglers on Saturday afternoons during games. No vehicles are to be taken onto the rugby fields.

Facilities   Nearest shop and pub, in Batheaston.

Disabled facilities   Some swims may be suitable for disabled and wheelchair anglers; for advice, please contact Bristol, Bath & Wiltshire Amalgamated Anglers, Hon. Sec. Jeff Parker; Tel. 0272 672977.

BATHAMPTON
Atlas Page 201 F.4/4.0

A 2-mile, left-hand river stretch to the east of Bath, which includes Bathampton Weir, Bathampton Meadow Farm and Bathampton Manor waters, downstream to one field below Grosvenor Bridge. Expect some good quality coarse fishing, with bream, rudd, roach, pike, perch, chub and some large barbel. Fishing from the weir is allowed, but should be attempted only when SAFE to do so.

How to get there   Take the A4 west from Chippenham towards Bath, turn left at the A4/A363 junction to Bathampton. Parking is at various points. For the weir, park at the Beefeater Inn (by the toll bridge). For Meadow Farm, fork left off the A36 out of Bath into Bathampton Lane, then 1st left via the Canal Bridge, cross the cattle grid and park by the hedge.

Day tickets   Adult £2; junior/OAP 50p. Available at local tackle shops.

Best methods/baits   Use general coarse methods and baits.

Restrictions   No fishing from pontoons or outside the restaurant at the weir.

Facilities   Food at the Beefeater Inn. Nearest shop and pub, in Bathampton.

Disabled facilities   Some swims may be suitable for disabled and wheelchair anglers; for advice, please contact Bristol, Bath & Wiltshire Amalgamated Anglers, Hon. Sec. Jeff Parker; Tel. 0272 672977.

UPPER BATHFORD
Atlas Page 201 F.4/4.0

A fishery covering four large meadows at a farm on the southern outskirts of Bath. A popular fishery which produces high quality fish – expect bream, rudd, roach, pike, perch and chub – and in good numbers.

How to get there   From Bath, take the A4 east to Bathford and take A363 towards Bradford-on-Avon. At ¼ mile after Bathford railway bridge, turn right (signposted Warleigh). Follow the lane for 600 yards and turn into farm on the right (look for adjacent bungalow), bear left by the hay barn and park behind it. Walk to the river (200 yards) and fish for two fields upstream and downstream of the farm.

Day tickets   Adult £2; junior/OAP 50p. Available at local tackle shops.

Best methods/baits   Use general coarse methods and baits.

Restrictions   **No smoking in the farmyard**.

Facilities   Nearest shop and pub, in Bathford.

Disabled facilities   Difficult access to the water would probably prevent disabled and wheelchair angling, but for advice, please contact Bristol, Bath & Wiltshire Amalgamated Anglers, Hon. Sec. Jeff Parker; Tel. 0272 672977.

CLAVERTON
Atlas Page 201 F.4/4.1

This left-hand bank fishery, which is located south of Bath, occupies a long, narrow field below the Dundas Aqueduct downstream to the railway embankment – ¾ mile in all. Expect typical Bristol Avon coarse fishing, with plenty of bream, rudd, roach, pike, perch and chub. Also the occasional barbel.

How to get there   From Bath, take the A36 south towards Warminster. After passing through Claverton village (about 2¼ miles), park in the first lay-by on the left. *Note:* do not park in the Canal bridge gateway or farm entrance. Walk across the Canal via the swingbridge nearby and go through the tunnel under the railway.

Day tickets   Adult £2; junior/OAP 50p. Available at local tackle shops.

Best methods/baits   Use general coarse methods and baits.

Facilities   Nearest shop and pub, in Claverton village.

Disabled facilities   Some swims may be suitable for disabled and wheelchair angling; for advice, please contact Bristol, Bath & Wiltshire Amalgamated Anglers, Hon. Sec. Jeff Parker; Tel. 0272 672977.

Chub taken on the Avon.

WARLEIGH
Atlas Page 201 F.4/4.1

A typical Avon stretch, to the south-east of Bath, extending downstream from Dundas Aqueduct to within one field of Warleigh weir, and upstream to the farm fence below Limpley Stoke bridge (all right-hand bank). Expect good quality fishing, with perch, pike, bream, rudd, roach and chub, plus some barbel.

How to get there   From Bath, take the A36 south towards Warminster. Approaching Monkton Combe (about 4 miles), park in the long lay-by just before the garage. Walk down the field from the far end of the lay-by, turn left at the bottom and go over the canal footbridge. Cross the river via the aqueduct, using path behind the boathouse. Access to the top of the fishery is in front of the boathouse.

Day tickets   Adult £2; junior/OAP 50p. Available at local tackle shops.

Best methods/baits   Use general coarse methods and baits.

Restrictions   No fishing from the steps on the right of the aqueduct.

Facilities   Nearest shop and pub, in Monkton Combe village.

Disabled facilities   Some swims may be suitable for disabled and wheelchair angling; for advice, please contact Bristol, Bath & Wiltshire Amalgamated Anglers, Hon. Sec. Jeff Parker; Tel. 0272 672977.

MONKTON COMBE
Atlas Page 201 F.4/4.2

A shortish river stretch, midway between Bath and Bradford-on-Avon, extending from the arches over Midford Brook downstream to Dundas Aqueduct. Mainly perch, pike, bream, rudd, roach and chub, plus some barbel.

How to get there   From Bath, take the A36 south towards Warminster. At Monkton Combe (about 4 miles, opposite the Viaduct Hotel), turn left onto the B3108. Turn left again after 50 yards and look for signs to Monkton Combe Mill Furniture and Carpet Warehouse. Access to the water is next to this turning. Park (tidily) on the roadside.

Day tickets   Adult £2 junior/OAP 50p. Available at local tackle shops.

Best methods/baits   Use general coarse methods and baits.

Facilities   Nearest shop and pub, in Monkton Combe village.

Disabled facilities   For advice on disabled and wheelchair angling, please contact Bristol, Bath & Wiltshire Amalgamated Anglers, Hon. Sec. Jeff Parker; Tel. 0272 672977.

LIMPLEY STOKE, HAYDENS FIELD
Atlas Page 201 F.4/4.2

A large fishery which also includes 'The Cabbage Patch', a few miles west of Bradford-on-Avon. Fishing is on the left-hand bank, downstream of Limpley Stoke river bridge, from just below the restaurant gardens. Expect a good catch of roach, perch, bream, chub and rudd, plus a few pike and barbel.

How to get there   From Bath, take the A36 south to Limpley Stoke (about 6 miles); park near the railway bridge and walk along the base of the railway embankment, NOT through the restaurant garden. For the lower end, turn left onto the B3108 and park to the left of the level crossing (about 400 yards). Walk through the crossing to the water.

Day tickets   Adult £2; junior/OAP 50p. Available at local tackle shops.

Best methods/baits   Use general coarse methods and baits.

Restrictions   No bank digging at this venue.

Facilities   Nearest shop and pub, in Limpley Stoke village.

Disabled facilities   For advice on disabled and wheelchair angling, please contact Bristol, Bath & Wiltshire Amalgamated Anglers, Hon. Sec. Jeff Parker; Tel. 0272 672977.

LIMPLEY STOKE TO AVONCLIFFE
Atlas Page 201 F.4/4.2

A left-hand bank fishery which extends from Limpley Stoke bridge to just below Avoncliffe weir, near Bradford-on-Avon. A picturesque location which provides good catches of roach, perch, bream, chub and rudd, plus a few pike and barbel.

How to get there   From Bath, take the A36 south to Limpley Stoke (about 6 miles), turn left onto B3108 and park in the left-hand lay-by on the Winsley Hill side of Limpley Stoke bridge. Or continue on the B3108 through Winsley Hill and turn right through Turleigh. After ¾ mile, turn sharp right for Avoncliffe; park in the village and walk to the water (behind the railway station).

Day tickets   Adult £2; junior/OAP 50p. Available at local tackle shops.

Best methods/baits   Use general coarse methods and baits.

Restrictions   No fishing in Avoncliffe weir hole.

Facilities   Nearest shops and pubs are at either Limpley Stoke or Avoncliffe villages.

Disabled facilities   For advice on disabled and wheelchair angling, please contact Bristol, Bath & Wiltshire Amalgamated Anglers, Hon. Sec. Jeff Parker; Tel. 0272 672977.

BITTERWELL LAKE
Atlas Page 200 F.2/3.6

A small pit at Coalpit Heath, between Bristol and Yate. A mixed fishery which is very popular at weekends, producing roach, rudd, tench, bream and eels, as well as mirror carp in large numbers. The odd 20lb mirror has also been taken here.

How to get there   Leave the M4 at jct 18 and take A46, towards Stroud, then A432 to Chipping Sodbury and Yate. Continue along A432 to Coalpit Heath and follow signs to the lake. Car parking on site.

Day tickets   Adult £1.50; junior/OAP 75p. Available direct from Bristol Corporation or from the caravan on site.

Best methods/baits   Float fishing preferred. Otherwise, use general coarse techniques and baits.

Restrictions   No night fishing (although permission may be obtained for occasional night sessions).

Facilities   Nearest shop/pub in Coalpit Heath or Yate.

Disabled facilities   Some swims may be suitable for disabled anglers.

CAM BROOK, DUNKERTON (SECTION 1)
Atlas Page 201 F.2/4.2

A pleasant section of the Brook, located close to the Bath–Radstock road. Access to the water is from either end of the stretch, with fishing on the Bath side (right bank upstream from Combe Hay, left bank downstream from Dunkerton). Plenty of good quality mixed coarse fish to provide a good day's sport.

How to get there   From Bath, head south on the A367 towards Radstock and at Dunkerton (about 4 miles), park in the lay-by on the Radstock side of the bridge. Access to the water is by steps on the Bath side. Or, on leaving Bath, turn left at the Burnt House pub and follow signs to Wellow; fork right at Combe Hay, park by the lower bridge and walk to the water.

Day tickets   Adult £2; junior/OAP 50p. Available at local tackle shops.

Best methods/baits   Use general coarse methods and baits.

Facilities   Nearest shops and pubs, in Dunkerton and Combe Hay villages.

Disabled facilities For advice on disabled and wheelchair angling, please contact Bristol, Bath & Wiltshire Amalgamated Anglers, Hon. Sec. Jeff Parker; Tel. 0272 672977.

CAM BROOK, DUNKERTON (SECTION 2)
Atlas Page 201 F.2/4.2

A second stretch of the Cam Brook which extends from the access point in Dunkerton upstream to the next road bridge (except for the sewerage works) – about 1½ miles in all. Fishing is also permitted from the right-hand bank downstream to the Church bridge. A pleasant fishery which produces good-sized catches of quality fish, and of most species.

How to get there From Bath, head south on the A367 towards Radstock and at Dunkerton (about 4 miles), turn right just before the bridge. Drive past the cricket ground and church and park where the road widens (space for only 3 cars). Access to the fishery is via a gate and farm bridge on the left (10 yards from the road).

Day tickets Adult £2; junior/OAP 50p. Available at local tackle shops.

Best methods/baits Use general coarse methods and baits.

Facilities Nearest shops and pubs, in Dunkerton and Combe Hay villages.

Disabled facilities For advice on disabled and wheelchair angling, please contact Bristol, Bath & Wiltshire Amalgamated Anglers, Hon. Sec. Jeff Parker; Tel. 0272 672977.

HUNSTRETE LAKE
Atlas Page 201 F.2/4.1

This 5-acre dammed estate lake, which lies a few miles south-west of Bath, is well known for its carp fishing, with several 20–30lb fish present and offering excellent sport. Coarse fishing is also good, with plenty of roach, tench and bream.

How to get there From Bath, head west on the A4 and bear left onto the A368 at Newton St Loe and Marksbury, then bear right onto A368. After about 1 mile, turn right on minor road to Hunstrete. Access to the fishery (on the left) is via a path as you enter the village. Park nearby.

Day tickets £1. Bathampton Anglers licence required (£14). Only limited tickets available. For details, contact Bathampton A.A. Secretary D. Crookes; Tel. 0225 427164.

Best methods/baits Most species – use general coarse techniques and baits. Carp – advanced methods and baits will be needed.

Restrictions No night fishing.

Facilities Nearest shop/pub in Hunstrete village.

Disabled facilities Some swims may be suitable for disabled anglers; check with Club Secretary (see above).

SHACKELL'S LAKE
Atlas Page 200 F.8/3.8

A recently-opened fishery (June 1991) which lies a few miles north-west of Bath. Compact, with only 40 pegs, but expect good sport with plenty of carp, tench, roach, rudd and bream.

How to get there Take the A420 from Chippenham towards Bristol and turn left (just after A46 junction) into Freezing Hill at the top of Tog Hill. Continue about ½ mile and turn left to Lower Hamswell (10 mph; no speeding). Drive to the 2nd cattle grid, park on the left and follow signs to the lake. *You must not deviate from this route.*

Day tickets No day tickets; fishing here requires Full Membership of Bristol, Bath & Wiltshire Amalgamated Anglers: £16.50 from Jeff Parker (Hon. Sec.); Tel. 0272 672977. There is no subsequent charge for fishing these waters.

Best methods/baits Use general coarse methods and baits.

Facilities Nearest shop and pub in Kingswood.

WOODBOROUGH PARK LAKE
Atlas Page F.4/4.2

A peaceful fishery – largely due to the limits on day tickets – consisting of a 2 acre, dammed estate lake, near Midsomer Norton. A good head of roach, perch and tench, together with large numbers of mirror carp about 10lb, plus some 10–15lb fish.

How to get there From Bath, head south-west on the A367 towards Radstock. After about 6 miles, look for left turn to Woodborough Court. Use the car park on the right and walk (½ mile) across fields to the water.

Day tickets £1. Bathampton Anglers licence required (£14). Contact Bathampton A.A. Secretary D. Crookes; Tel. 0225 427164 or local tackle shops. Only limited tickets available.

Best methods Carp – use specialist methods. Most species – use general coarse techniques and baits.

Best baits Carp – floating crust works well.

Restrictions No night fishing. No fishing from the dam.

Facilities Nearest shop/pub in Peasedown St John.

Disabled facilities The ½-mile walk may prohibit (or discourage) access by disabled anglers.

DORSET

CANFORD PONDS
Atlas Page 203 A.4/6.8

A small Wessex NRA-controlled coarse fishing lake a few miles east of Wimborne Minster. Most common species present, with some good sport.

How to get there Take the A31 south-west to Ringwood, then Ferndown; bear left at Canford Bottom roundabout onto A348 Longham road. After 25 yards turn right onto Wessex NRA site; the lake is on the left. Free car parking on site.

Day tickets Season ticket only: adult £28.70; junior/OAP £14.40. Details from NRA at Rivers House, Blandford, Forum; Tel. 0258 456080.

Best methods/baits Use any recognised technique.

Facilities ·Nearest shop Canford Bottom (1 mile); nearest pub, Fox and Hounds (½ mile).

Disabled facilities Some swims suitable for disabled anglers.

DORSET SPRINGS LAKES
Atlas Page 203 A.4/6.8

A unique combination of easily accessible fishing and landscaped lakes near Wimborne Minster. For coarse fishing, Tolpuddle Lake (3 acres) offers carp (to 23lb), roach, perch, rudd and tench. Open daily (except Xmas) from 16th June to 14th March (0800-dusk).

How to get there Take the A31 Wimborne by-pass to the A31/A350 junction (about 4 miles from town centre). Turn right onto A350 Blandford road; the lakes are on the right at Sturminster Marshall. Free car parking.

Day tickets Adult £3; junior (under–14) £2. Available on site. For details; Tel. 0202 857653.

Best methods/baits Use any recognised technique.

Restrictions No keepnets. Only single hooks to be used. All fish must be returned. Only 1 rod per ticket. Under–14s must be accompanied by an adult.

Facilities Shop/toilets/food available on site.

Disabled facilities Some swims suitable for disabled anglers.

RIVER FROME UPPER WATER
Atlas Page 201 F.3/5.8

A 1½-mile stretch of the Frome, just to the north of Dorchester, upstream from Loder's Garage. Controlled by Dorchester Fishing Club. Good mixed coarse fishing.

How to get there From the roundabout at the north of the town drive towards Charminster and Stratton (A356). River access is available at various points; park near Loder's Garage, Round House and Gascoyne Bridge and walk .

Day tickets Fishing members only of Dorchester District Angling Society. £23 senior – £11 junior.

Best methods/baits Use any recognised technique.

Facilities Shops/toilets/food in Dorchester or at points along the river.

Disabled facilities Some swims suitable for disabled anglers; check with tackle shops.

RIVER FROME MIDDLE WATER
Atlas Page 201 F.3/5.8

A ¾-mile stretch of the Frome, downstream from Loder's Garage to Grey's Bridge. Controlled by Dorchester Fishing Club. Good mixed coarse fishing.

How to get there From the roundabout at the north of the town drive towards Puddletown and Blandford (A35). River access is available at various points;

park near Loder's Garage, Swan Bridge or Prince's Bridge and walk to the river.

Day tickets   Fishing members only of Dorchester District Angling Society; £23 senior, £11 junior.

Best methods/baits   Use any recognised technique.

Facilities   Shops/toilets/food in Dorchester or at points along the river.

Disabled facilities   Some swims suitable for disabled anglers; check with tackle shops.

RIVER FROME LOWER WATER
Atlas Page 201 F.3/5.8

How to get there   From the roundabout at the north of the town drive towards Puddletown (A35) and bear right at Swan's Bridge towards Prince's, Standfast and Long Bridges, and Loud's Mill. River access is available at various points; park near any of the bridges and walk to the river.

Day tickets   Fishing members only of Dorchester District Angling Society; £23 senior, £11 junior.

Best methods/baits   Use any recognised technique.

Facilities   Shops/toilets/food in Dorchester or at points along the river.

Disabled facilities   Some swims suitable for disabled anglers; check with tackle shops.

HYDE LAKE
Atlas Page 203 A.3/6.9

A secluded and very peaceful country lake of just over 1 acre, near Bovington Camp, west of Poole. Expect most coarse species, including roach, rudd, tench and Crucian carp, plus a good stock of mirrors and commons that may reach 20lb.

How to get there   From Wareham, near Poole, head west on the A352 towards Bovington Camp. The lake is at Hyde, about 4 miles from Wareham. Look for signs to the fishery and car park.

Day tickets   Season tickets only: £22. Available from Hyde A.C. Chairman Steve Alderson; Tel. 0929 463127.

Best methods/baits   Use general coarse techniques and baits.

Restrictions   Maximum 3 rods per person.

Facilities   Nearest shop/pub in Bovington Camp.

Disabled facilities   Some swims may be suitable for disabled anglers.

LUCKFIELD LAKE, BROADMAYNE
Atlas Page 201 F.3/5.8

A very quiet and exclusive 1½-acre lake set in beautiful surroundings with overhanging trees and lily pads, 4 miles east of Dorchester. Specimen coarse fish of all sizes, with carp (to 20lb), tench (to 9lb) and roach (to 2lb+). Limited availability (10 swims); only 6–7 tickets issued daily.

How to get there   From Dorchester, take the A352 south-east to Broadmayne (4 miles). Turn left into West Knighton road, then right into Watergates Lane; the lake is at the end of the gravel lane. Free parking in the lane.

Day tickets   Adult/junior/OAP £4. Evening ticket £2; night ticket £6. Also season ticket £55. Available from John Aplin Specialist Angling Supplies, 1 Athelstan Road, Dorchester; Tel. 0305 266500.

Best methods   Float or leger.

Best baits   Most every-day baits; boilies, particle baits.

Restrictions   No keepnets. No cereal groundbait. All fish to be returned immediately. Maximum 2 rods/angler.

Facilities   Nearest shop and pub, Black Dog, Broadmayne (¼ mile).

Disabled facilities   Some swims suitable for disabled anglers.

OSMINGTON MILLS LAKE
Atlas Page 201 F.1/6.0

A popular summer fishery of about 1½ acres, close to a caravan park on the coast, just east of Weymouth. Contains mainly carp (some to double figures) and tench; fishing improves considerably in winter.

How to get there   From Dorchester, head south-east on the A352 to Warmwell (about 4 miles) and turn right onto the A353 towards Weymouth. Look for a left turn to Osmington Mills and the fishery after about 2½ miles. Car parking on site.

Day tickets   Adult/junior/OAP £4 for 12 hours only. Available on the bank or from The Ranch House on the caravan park at Osmington Mills.

Best methods/baits   Use general coarse techniques and baits.

Facilities   Toilets at the caravan park. Nearest shop/pub in Osmington village (1½ miles).

Disabled facilities   Some swims suitable for disabled anglers.

PALLINGTON LAKES, TINCLETON
Atlas Page 201 F.2/5.9

A 3-lake complex located about 6 miles east of Dorchester, in very pleasant surroundings. Plenty of specimen fish – carp (to 22lb), tench (to 7lb) plus roach, chub, perch and bream. Coarse fishing in season only, 16th June to 14th March.

How to get there   Take the A352 south-east from Dorchester, turn right onto B3390 at Warmwell (about 5 miles) and continue to Waddock Cross. Turn left on minor road to Tincleton village. Turn left towards the river and park (free) at the fishery.

Day tickets   Adult £4; junior/OAP half-price. Carp and tench lake £5.50 (no juniors) (0800–2100 or dusk). Available on site but booking advisable (Tel. 0305 848141).

Best methods/baits   Use any recognised technique.

Facilities   Toilets/picnic and leisure areas on site.

Disabled facilities   Some swims suitable for disabled anglers.

REVELLS FARM
Atlas Page 201 F.3/5.5

A pleasant, rural fishery midway between Dorchester and Sherborne, comprising three lakes totalling almost 2 acres. Good fishing for perch, tench, roach, rudd and bream, plus carp of all varieties and sizes.

How to get there   From Dorchester, take the A35 towards Poole but after about 1 mile bear left onto the B3143 to Buckland Newton (10 miles) and follow signs to the fishery. Car parking on site.

Day tickets   Adult £4.50; junior/OAP £2. Available on the bank, or from the house on site.

Best methods/baits   Use general coarse techniques and baits.

Facilities   Nearest shop/pub in Buckland Newton.

Disabled facilities   Some swims may be suitable for disabled anglers.

Rivers
RIVER STOUR

The Dorset Stour produces record fish of several species, its variety of swim types appealing mainly to the angler seeking consistent, quality fish. The river is subject to flash-floods which usually recede within 24 hours – during which time sport is excellent. Roach, barbel, chub and dace are the main species, with the occasional pike; all may reach immense proportions in this fertile fishery. Six *Angling Times* Hotspots are located in this region.

KINGS MILL, STALBRIDGE
Atlas Page 201 F.3/5.2

About 2 miles of winding river, leading to a large mill pool by the bridge at Stalbridge, east of Sherborne. Several deep holes near the bends provide very good roach, tench (to 4lb+) and chub, plus large pike (to 18lb) in the mill pool.

How to get there   From Blandford Forum take the A357 north-west and just before Stalbridge (about 13 miles) follow minor road (at T-junction) to Marnhull. Kings Mill is about 1 mile beyond the T-junction. Free roadside parking near the river.

Day tickets   Adult £2; junior/OAP £1. Weekly ticket: adult £5; junior/OAP £2.50. Available at Corner Cottage Tackle, High Street, Stalbridge; Tel. 0963 62025.

Best methods   Leger or float according to conditions.

Best baits   Most baits work well; use deadbait for pike.

Restrictions   No livebait to be used.

Facilities   Nearest shop and pub, Stalbridge (1½ miles).

 ## STURMINSTER NEWTON
Atlas Page 201 F.6/5.3

A contrasting stretch of water, narrow above the mill and weir, but widening and deepening below this point. Roach, perch, chub, dace and pike (20lb+) all season; tench (to 8lbs) may appear in summer. Normal nets 5lb, but may reach 10lbs.

How to get there   From Blandford Forum, follow the A357 to Sturminster Newton. Parking is on the roadside, running alongside the river.

273

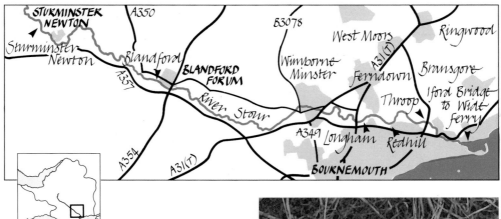

Day tickets   Adult £2; junior/OAP £1.
  Weekly ticket: adult £5; junior/OAP £1.
  Available from Hart's Garden Supplies,
  Sturminster Newton (Tel. 0258 72788),
  or from Corner Cottage Tackle,
  Stalbridge (Tel. 0963 62025).
Best methods   Roach, dace – stick float
  in streamy swims or medium waggler at
  the far bank.
Best baits   Bread, maggots, caster, hemp.
  Use deadbaits for big pike.
Restrictions   No livebaiting
Facilities   Nearest shop, ½ mile; nearest
  pub, The Red Lion, on the A357, near
  the Mill Pool.
Disabled facilities   Some swims are
  suitable for disabled and wheelchair
  anglers.

Roach.

Hotspot Tips

🐟 Tackle big summer tench with baits
  laid hard on the bottom.
🐟 The best swims are immediately below
  the weir.

BLANDFORD
Atlas Page 201 F.8/5.4

In summer, a shallow, slow-flowing,
weedy stretch with excellent fishing.
Sport is best after October as waters
deepen, flow rises and weeds die back.
Mainly roach, dace, perch, bream, chub
and pike. Catches from 2–30lbs according
to the river's state; typical catches under
10lbs.

How to get there   Take the A350 or A354
  to Blandford Forum. Park in car park
  beside bridge; fish upstream from the
  bridge.
Day tickets   Adult £3, junior (under 16)
  £1; OAP £2 from Conyers Guns &
  Fishing Tackle, Main Street, Blandford;
  Tel. 0258 452307.
Best methods   Summer – light tackle,
  laying among the weedbeds. Winter –
  stick and wagglers, according to
  conditions.
Best baits   Hemp, caster, maggots,
  pinkies, sweetcorn, or luncheon meat.
Facilities   Food/shops/toilets in
  Blandford Forum.

Hotspot Tips

🐟 For successful summer fishing, early
  mornings and late evenings are best.
🐟 Fishing here is at its very best in
  winter, especially after heavy flooding.
🐟 The best swims are at Crown
  Meadows, close to the Kissing Gate.

LONGHAM
Atlas Page 203 A.4/6.9

An 800-yard stretch on the south bank below Longham Bridge. Shallow at first, then deepens. Expect barbel, roach, chub, bream, dace and pike. A day catch averages 10lbs (mostly dace); up to 50lbs is possible if larger species appear.

How to get there   At the junction of the A341 and A348, turn towards Longham Bridge. Park in the lay-by on the Poole (south) side of the Bridge; walk across the road to the river.

Day tickets   Free fishing.

Best methods   Roach, dace – use stick, Avon and waggler floats; barbel and chub – use leger.

Best baits   Hemp, maggot, caster, bread, worms, luncheon meat, sweetcorn; tares for good roach and chub.

Hotspot Tips

🐟 Caster fished over hemp is very effective for summer float angling.

🐟 In summer, fish the deeper water at the lower end of the stretch.

REDHILL
Atlas Page 203 A.4/6.8

A typical Stour fishery with deeps, shallows and streamer weed. A busy summer area, but quiet, vacant swims are always available. Mainly barbel, chub, roach, dace and pike; record-breaking barbel and pike are likely, plus big roach. Average day catch 15lbs but often more.

How to get there   Take the A3060 towards Ensbury. Follow Castle Lane to the Horse & Jockey pub; turn right into Muscliffe Lane. Park in the public car park; the fishery is 50 yards away.

Day tickets   Free fishing

Best methods   Big fish – feeder, or fish straight lead and feed with dropper or catapult. Float or leger for 3lb chub; stick float (or waggler if windy) for roach.

Best baits   Hemp, maggot, caster, luncheon meat, sweetcorn, bread, lobworms.

Facilities   Food/toilets at the Horse & Jockey.

Hotspot Tips

🐟 For best roach, fish the top end of the stretch, where swims are deeper.

🐟 Heavy tackle is essential for specimen fish.

🐟 In summer, head for the Muscliffe Shallows; from autumn onwards, fish deeper water.

THROOP
Atlas Page 203 A.4/6.8

The complete fishery, with shallows, deeps, glides and a small lake. Most swims hold 2–4ft in summer, 4–6ft in winter. Extensive weedbeds. Bream, tench, carp in the lake; barbel, chub, roach, dace, bream and pike in the river (all season). Catches include 10lb+ barbel, 5lb+ chub, 2lb roach – and 20lb pike!

How to get there   Turn off the A31 at Ringwood, take the A338 spur road towards Bournemouth. At the Stour crossing, the Throop Fishery extends upstream and downstream of the road.

Day tickets   Adult £5; junior £2.50; OAP £3; afternoon and evening tickets available from The South Lodge at nearby Holdenhurst village; Tel. 0202 395532.

Best methods   Pleasure fishing – stick float or waggler. Fish fine in summer (18 hook, 1.7lb bottom); heavier in winter.

Best baits   Maggots, caster, bread, sweetcorn, luncheon meat, lobworms.

Hotspot Tips

🐟 Fish below the weir in summer; move upstream later in the year for less pacey water.

🐟 When specimen hunting for barbel and chub, use heavy feeder tackle and up to 8lb line.

🐟 For best fishing, head for the river rather than the lake.

IFORD BRIDGE TO WICK FERRY
Atlas Page 203 A.6/6.9

A tidal stretch with 12ft depth at high water. Little weed growth but some boat problems in summer. A prolific fishery, with bream, roach, dace and mullet in summer, and roach, dace and pike in winter. A 20lb-plus day catch is a realistic target.

How to get there At Christchurch, park along Iford Lane, which runs parallel to the river; walk across to river. Or, use public car park at Wick (close to boats), with direct access to fishery.

Day tickets Adult £4; junior/OAP £2 from all local tackle shops.

Best methods Use a cork-on-quill float with 3AAA if there is a push on the water; if slack, use light waggler with 2AAA and 8 hook.

Best baits Maggot, caster, hemp; roach – use lump flake.

Hotspot Tips

- In summer, use a swimfeeder for the best bream.
- Best fishing is in winter floods; use heavy groundbaiting.

HAMPSHIRE
Rivers
THE HAMPSHIRE AVON

The Hampshire Avon, with its powerful flow – often three feet deep and going like a train – is a hard river to fish, but is one of the best. Although its glory days are long gone, with the advent of swimfeeders and heavy baiting with hemp and casters, today's angler is at last beginning to reap the rewards to which the fishermen of yesteryear were accustomed. The lower reaches of the river, from Christchurch Harbour to Fordingbridge, provide a variety of swim types, where specimen roach, barbel and chub have been taken in recent years.

Fishing for barbel on the Royalty.

CHRISTCHURCH HARBOUR
Atlas Page 203 A.6/6.9

Shallow water (even at high tide), with limited bank fishing due to marshland (the firm bank space at one end is occupied by sea trout anglers). Mainly roach, bream and dace, with 30lb mixed nets possible. Chub and pike are rare, but occasional mullet, bass and flounder provide varied sport.

How to get there Drive over the two bridges in Christchurch and use the swimming pool car park. Walk down the lane by Waterloo Stream to the fishery's top boundary. Or, turn right at Purewell into Stoney Lane and park at the recreation ground; walk across the marsh to the bottom boundary.

Day tickets Adult £3; junior/OAP £1.50. Also weekly tickets £9; annual tickets £15 (junior/OAP half-price). Available from local tackle shops.

Best methods Trotting is best method, but check bait trips the bottom (adjust for tidal changes). Heavy groundbaiting required.

Best baits Bread or maggot hookbaits; cereal-based groundbaits.

Restrictions Some deep spots are out of bounds to day-ticket holders.

Hotspot Tips

- Keep the groundbait trickling in, or the shoals will go!
- Try using harbour ragworm or lugworm for bass and flounder.
- The best way to fish the harbour is by boat – hire one at Chub Keynes, on Christchurch quay.

Royalty Fishery.

ROYALTY FISHERY
Atlas Page 203 A.6/6.9

A famous fishery, partly tidal at the bottom end. Many swim types: shallow runs between thick weed beds; deep areas upstream. Famous for specimen barbel and chub, specimen carp to over 30 lb, plus roach, dace, bream and pike – and salmon and sea trout. The best swims – Parlour, the Railway Pool and the Pipes – can each be brilliant on their day!

How to get there At Mill Lane, Bargates, in the centre of Christchurch.

Day tickets Summer – Upper stretch £11; lower stretch £6.50; Winter – both stretches £5.50 available from Davis Tackle, Bargates, Christchurch (close to the fishery); Tel. 0202 485169. Parlour is a seperate booking – call first.

Best methods Use either a block-end feeder or a float with trotting tackle.

Best bait Maggots, casters are ideal; bread, luncheon meat, worms and sweetcorn also successful.

Facilities Shops/food/toilets in Christchurch.

Hotspot Tips

- A skilled float angler using trotting tackle will catch plenty.
- Use plenty of bait to get the big barbel feeding furiously.

A quiet moment at Christchurch.

277

WINKTON
Atlas Page 203 A.7/6.9

Winkton fishery has less pace than most Avon swims, but is very weedy, with an average depth of 5ft. Expect roach – perhaps a 30lb net – plus dace, chub, barbel, and the occasional 20lb+ pike.

How to get there From the Christchurch by-pass, take the Stony Lane exit towards Highcliffe. The fishery lies at the end of the road, on the left, before the B3347 Burton-Ringwood road.

Day tickets £3.50 from 1st August to 28th February only available from Davis Tackle, Bargates, Christchurch (close to the fishery). For details; Tel. 0202 485169.

Best methods Use long trotting (especially after October, when weed has declined).

Best baits Bread is best, but hemp, sweetcorn, casters, maggots, worms are all effective. Use cereal groundbait in winter; loosefeed at other times.

Hotspot Tips

☙ Look for good chub, barbel and large pike at the top end, opposite Sopley Stream.

SEVERALS FISHERY, RINGWOOD
Atlas Page 203 A.5/6.6

A 3-mile Avon stretch with everything – weedy shallows, steady glides, powerful deeps, boiling eddies. Mainly barbel – big individuals and nets – but chub, roach and dace are also excellent. Pike fishing is very good. Choice of peg depends on conditions and target species.

How to get there Take the A31 from Ringwood towards Bournemouth; take the first slip road (signposted Verwood and Matchams). Car park is on the left; walk over the railway line to the fishery's bottom end. Or, take the B3347 towards Christchurch and turn down lane by Kingston village shop; go past the Nag's Head pub, over the stream.

Day tickets Adults £5; junior/OAP £2.50 available from Ringwood Tackle; Tel. 0425 475125.

Best methods Some swims suit trotting, others legering; try either.

Best baits Bread, casters, maggots, sweetcorn, luncheon meat or worms; use cereal groundbait when water is coloured.

Restrictions Day tickets available only after 1st July

Severals Fishery, Ringwood.

Facilities   Food/toilets at the Nags Head
pub. Nearest shop, Windmill Garage
(½ mile).

Hotspot Tips

✎ Early morning or late evening fishing is
most productive.

LIFELANDS, RINGWOOD
Atlas Page 203 A.5/6.6

A 1-mile fishery, on both banks. Shallow
and fast, but slightly steadier at the top
end. Good catches are always likely, with
barbel the main species – 8 in a session is
quite normal! Also expect dace, chub,
roach and pike.

How to get there   Park in the lay-by at
the junction of the A31/A338 Salisbury
road, just north of Ringwood.
Day tickets   Adult £5; junior/OAP £2.50;
available from Ringwood Tackle;
Tel. 0425 475125.
Best methods   Barbel – leger tactics;
chub, dace – float.
Best baits   Hemp, casters, maggots,
sweetcorn, luncheon meat or worms.
Restrictions   Coarse fishing begins here
on 16th June.
Facilities   Nearest shop, Windmill garage
(½ mile); nearest pubs, three within
¾ mile.
Disabled facilities   Some swims are
suitable for disabled and wheelchair
anglers; please phone for advice (see
above).

Hotspot Tips

✎ For good barbel, fish the weir pool at
the fishery's bottom end.
✎ Stick float or Trent trotter tactics work
well; hold back the float for quick
bites.

FORDINGBRIDGE
RECREATION GROUND
Atlas Page 203 A.5/6.4

This stretch is shallow at the top end, but
deep and powerful further downstream,
with plenty of weed growth. All spots are
good, and can produce good catches of
roach (up to 40lb), with specimen fish up
to 1.5lb. Large barbel and chub are also
likely in this stretch.

How to get there   Take the A338 north
from Ringwood. On entering
Fordingbridge, the recreation centre and
car park are on the left.
Day tickets   Free fishing.
Best methods   Float and swimfeeder,
including trotting with heavy tackle.
Best baits   Hemp, casters, maggots,
sweetcorn, luncheon meat or worms.
Facilities   Shops/food/toilets in
Fordingbridge.

Hotspot Tips

✎ For brilliant catches, fish from early
morning to 10am.

HIGHTOWN LAKE
Atlas Page 203 A.5/6.6

A single large pit of 23 acres lying just to
the south of Ringwood town centre.
Contains most coarse species.

How to get there   Take the A31 from
Southampton to Ringwood town centre
and bear left onto B3347. Drive past
Nags Head pub (on right), then turn left
past garage and follow minor road to
Hightown village; the fishery is on the
left. Free car park available on site.
Day tickets   Adult/junior/OAP £5.
Available from Ringwood Tackle, 5 The
Bridges, Ringwood; Tel. 0425 475125.
Best methods/baits   Use any recognised
coarse technique and baits.
Facilities   Nearest shop and pubs, Nags
Head or Elm Tree, in Hightown
(½ mile).

HURST POND, RINGWOOD
Atlas Page 203 A.5/6.6

A small but well stocked pond on the
town's northern outskirts, providing good
general coarse fishing for carp, roach,
chub, tench, perch and pike.

How to get there   From Ringwood town
centre head north on the A338 and on
the outskirts turn right just before
Windmill garage. Drive through the
gates; the pond is further down on the
right. Free car park on site.
Day tickets   Adult/junior/OAP £4.
Available from Ringwood Tackle, 5 The
Bridges, Ringwood; Tel. 0425 475125.
Note: limited tickets available; do not
enter the fishery without a ticket.

Best methods/baits   Use any recognised coarse technique and baits.
Facilities   Nearest shop Windmill garage; nearest pubs in Ringwood.

SOMERLEY LAKES
Atlas Page 203 A.5/6.6

A group of three lakes – Meadow, Vincents and Kings – located just north of Ringwood, providing very good carp fishing, plus tench and most other coarse species.

How to get there   Take the A31 to Ringwood, then turn north onto A338 towards Salisbury.The lakes are a short distance on the left; the car park entrance is just beyond the lakes.
Day tickets   Adult £5; junior/OAP £3. Available from Ringwood Tackle, 5 The Bridges, Ringwood; Tel. 0425 475125.
Best methods/baits   Use any recognised coarse technique or baits.
Facilities   Nearest shops/pubs in Ringwood.
Disabled facilities   Some swims may be suitable for disabled anglers.

SOMERSET

APEX PONDS
Atlas Page 201 E.4/4.4

A group of ponds on the outskirts of Burnham, providing good coarse fishing; very good roach and skimmer bream, plus good carp (7–8lb). Expect good fishing in most conditions, with 10lb+ catches common.

How to get there   Leave the M5 at jct 22 and take A38 to Highbridge; turn right through town centre towards Burnham. Look for signs to Apex ponds. Free car parking on site.
Day tickets   Adult/junior/OAP £2. Weekly ticket: adult/junior/OAP £5; available from Thyers Tackle, 1A Church Street, Highbridge; Tel. 0278 786934.
Best methods   Roach, skimmer bream – pole and waggler. Smallish carp – often taken on light tackle.
Best baits   Loosefed casters, pinkies.
Restrictions   No boilies or coloured maggots.

Facilities   Shops/toilets/food in Highbridge or Burnham.
Disabled facilities   Some swims suitable for disabled and wheelchair anglers.

RIVER AXE, BLEADON
Atlas Page 201 E.5/4.1

A deep stretch of the Axe, with 13ft above the bridge and 6–8ft below. An excellent roach venue, with always a good head, plus hybrids and some big bream. Penned in early season.

How to get there   Leave the M5 at jct 21 and follow the A370 through Weston-super-Mare to Bleadon. The fishery is about ½ mile south of Bleadon village. Free parking on site.
Day tickets   Adult/junior/OAP £2. Weekly ticket: adult/junior/OAP £5; available from local tackle shops or from Weston A.A.
Best methods   Waggler or pole preferred.
Best baits   Roach – hemp, tares in summer. Bream – hemp. maggots, (sometimes bread).
Restrictions   No coloured maggots.
Facilities   Nearest shop at garage (100 yards); nearest pub, Hobb's Boat (½ mile).
Disabled facilities   There is a disabled platform just below Bleadon bridge.

BOLHAM WATER
Atlas Page 201 E.3/5.4

Three fairly isolated ponds in the Black Down Hills, several miles south of Taunton. Superb fishing all year round, with roach, tench, carp and bream, plus barbel up to 2lb.

How to get there   From Taunton, take the B3170 south towards Honiton; after about 10 miles, look for minor road on right to Churchinford and Bolham Water (about 6 miles).
Day tickets   Adult £3; junior/OAP £2; available from local tackle shops, or details from Enterprise Angling, East Reach, Taunton; Tel. 0823 282623.
Best methods   Float (rod or pole) and leger.
Best baits   Maggots, particle baits.
Facilities   Toilets on site.
Disabled facilities   Some swims suitable for disabled and wheelchair anglers.

BRIDGWATER AND TAUNTON CANAL
Atlas Page 201 E.5/4.6

A long canal stretch, from Bridgwater to Taunton, with plenty of good access points providing excellent but typical canal fishing, and with little boat traffic. Most species, including big carp (to 28lb), bream (to 8lb) plus roach, rudd and tench.

How to get there   Leave the M5 at jct 24 and follow the A38 south towards Taunton. Access points via minor roads on the left occur at intervals along this stretch of the A38. Check with Thyer's Tackle, Highbridge for local hotspots; Tel. 0278 426789.

Day tickets   Adult £3; junior/OAP £2. Season ticket: adult £14; junior/OAP £7; available from local tackle shops and angling clubs.

Best methods   Most methods, including pole, waggler and leger.

Best baits   Maggots, pinkies, punched bread for tench and bream. Luncheon meat or boilies for carp.

Facilities   Many shops/food/toilets/pubs at various points along the canal.

Disabled facilities   Some towpath sites are suitable for disabled anglers, but best accompanied by able-bodied.

RIVER BRUE, BASON BRIDGE
Atlas Page 201 E.5/4.6

A quite short river section, just east of Highbridge and close to the M5. The fishery extends continuously from Bason Bridge to two fields above the Cripps Corner confluence, in addition to two fields on the upstream bank, from the Cripps Corner footbridge. Expect most coarse species in these waters, and reasonably-sized catches.

How to get there   Leave the M5 at jct 22 and take the A38 into Highbridge. In the town, turn left onto the B3139 to Bason Bridge; at the bridge turn left into Merry Lane and continue to the gate across the road. Park on the river side of the road and walk through the gate to the water. Access to the Cripps Corner section is via the footbridge.

Day tickets   Adult £2; junior/OAP 50p. Available at local tackle shops.

Best methods/baits   Use general coarse methods and baits.

Facilities   Nearest shops and pubs, in Bason Bridge.

Disabled facilities   Some swims may be suitable for disabled and wheelchair angling; for advice contact Bristol, Bath & Wiltshire Amalgamated Anglers, Hon. Sec. Jeff Parker; Tel. 0272 672977.

RIVER BRUE, GLASTONBURY
Atlas Page 201 E.9/4.7

The upper reaches of the River Brue between Street and Glastonbury, with especially good chub in 24 hours following winter spate, when sport is 'hectic'! Mainly chub and roach, but dace can be prolific. Bags of 20lb+ are common here.

How to get there   Leave the M5 at jct 23 and head east on the A39 to Street and Glastonbury. Ask at local tackle shops for best access points. Car parking near the fishery may be difficult.

Day tickets   Adult/junior/OAP £2. Weekly ticket: adult/junior/OAP £4. Available from local tackle shops; details from Street Angling Centre; Tel. 0458 47830.

Best methods   All recognised methods work here.

Best baits   All baits work; casters preferred.

Facilities   Shops/toilets/food/pubs in Street or Glastonbury.

RIVER BRUE, HIGHBRIDGE
Atlas Page 201 E.5/4.4

A tidal stretch of the Brue, near Burnham-on-Sea, with fishing best when the tide is on the way out. Plenty of roach, dace and skimmer bream, plus some chub and carp.

How to get there   Leave the M5 at jct 22 and take A38 to Highbridge. Turn left onto the B3139, then right on B3141 towards East Huntspill; enquire at local tackle shops about access to the river. Free car parking near the swims.

Day tickets   Adult/junior/OAP £2. Weekly ticket: adult/junior/OAP £5; available from local tackle shops.

Best methods   Most methods work well here.

Best baits   Roach, dace, chub – hemp, tares, bread punch, maggots, casters. Bream – sweetcorn, breadflake, worms.

Restrictions   No coloured maggots.

Facilities   Post office 200 yards; nearest pub, Bason Bridge Inn, 100 yards.

COMBWICH PONDS
Atlas Page 201 E.4/4.6

A fairly small pond, just off the River Parrett estuary, best known for its carp but also with a large head of bream, roach and tench. Excellent fishing in the right conditions.

How to get there   From Bridgwater, take the A39 west towards Minehead; at Cannington (3 miles), turn right by war memorial onto Hinckley Point road. The pond is on the right (2 miles). Free parking on site.

Day tickets   Adult/junior/OAP £1.75; weekly £5. Season tickets: adult £13.50; junior/OAP/disabled £4.60. Available from Thyers Tackle, 1A Church Street, Highbridge; Tel. 0278 786934.

Best methods   Use feeder, waggler or pole.

Best baits   Most baits work well here.

Facilities   Nearest shop Cannington (2 miles).

Disabled facilities   Some swims suitable for disabled anglers.

DUNWEAR PONDS
Atlas Page 201 E.5/4.6

A group of ponds lying just east of Bridgwater, with plenty of good roach, perch, rudd, bream and tench, but most well known for its carp fishing. Not an easy water to fish, but produces large specimens every season.

How to get there   Take the A372 east from Bridgwater Westonzoyland for 1 mile; Dunwear is off a lane on the right hand side. Free parking on site.

Day tickets   Adult/junior/OAP £1.75. Weekly £5. Season tickets: adult £13.50; junior/OAP £4.60. Available from Thyers Tackle, 1A Church Street, Highbridge; Tel. 0278 786934.

Best methods/baits   Use any recognised technique.

Facilities   Nearest shop/food/toilets Bridgewater (1 mile).

RIVER FROME, BECKINGTON
Atlas Page 201 F.6/4.4

A ¾-mile river stretch, about 2 miles north of Frome. Fishing extends from the small brook, one field above the weir, for five fields downstream to the next weir. Expect most coarse species here, and in

plentiful numbers. Fishing from the weir is allowed (when **safe**).

How to get there   From Bath, take the A36 south to Beckington (about 13 miles) and just after the A36/A361 junction, turn right down Mill Lane. Continue ¼ mile to the car park on the left (if locked, lift the gate from its hinges, but **replace** it; do **not** drive any further). Walk across the field to the water, behind the sewerage works.

Day tickets   Adult £2; junior/OAP 50p. Available at local tackle shops.

Best methods/baits   Use general coarse methods and baits.

Facilities   Nearest shop and pub, in Beckington village.

Disabled facilities   Some swims may be suitable for disabled and wheelchair angling; for advice, please contact Bristol, Bath & Wiltshire Amalgamated Anglers, Hon. Sec. Jeff Parker; Tel. 0272 672977.

RIVER FROME, RODE ISLAND AND WEIRPOOL
Atlas Page 201 F.7/4.3

A fairly short (½-mile), right-hand bank river section midway between Trowbridge and Frome, which extends from one swim below Woolverton bridge upstream to, and including, the weir pool. Fishing is allowed from the weir, but only when it is SAFE to do so. Fishing is also permitted in the mill stream which isolates the top field. Expect a good catch of mixed coarse species.

How to get there   From Bath, take the A36 south to Woolverton (about 11 miles) and turn left at the Red Lion pub. Drive past the Tropical Bird Gardens and use the small parking area on the left. Access to the water is on the right, between the derelict mill and the bridge.

Day tickets   Adult £2; junior/OAP 50p. Available at local tackle shops.

Best methods/baits   Use general coarse methods and baits.

Facilities   Nearest shop and pub, in Woolverton village.

Disabled facilities   For advice on disabled and wheelchair angling, please contact Bristol, Bath & Wiltshire Amalgamated Anglers, Hon. Sec. Jeff Parker; Tel. 0272 672977.

RIVER HUNTSPILL, HIGHBRIDGE
Atlas Page 201 E.4/4.4

One of the best pleasure venues in the west country. Wide and shallow, with large bream shoals, roach and eels, and day catches up to 100lb+ (when the bream feed).

How to get there   Leave the M5 at jct 22 and take A38 south through Highbridge to Huntspill (3 miles). Access to the river is at various points from Gold Corner to Sloway Bridge (both banks). Free car parking near the swims.
Day tickets   Adult/junior/OAP £1.75. Weekly £5. Season ticket adult £13.50; junior/OAP/disabled £4.60. Available from Thyers Tackle, 1A Church Street, Highbridge; Tel. 0278 786934.
Best methods   Bream – feeder; roach, hybrids – float, waggler or pole.
Best baits   Worms, casters, but most baits work well; too much will bring the eels!
Facilities   Nearest shop East Huntspill; nearest pub Bason Bridge.

RIVER KENN, CLEVEDON
Atlas Page 201 E.6/4.0

A comfortable venue a few miles south of Clevedon, which provides unpredictable fishing with mixed species – from large perch to flatfish!

How to get there   Leave the M5 at jct 20 and take the B3133 through Clevedon towards Congresbury. Ask at local tackle shops for access points to river. Free car parking near the swims.
Day tickets   Adult/junior/OAP £2. Weekly ticket: adult/junior/OAP £5; available from local tackle shops.
Best methods   Most methods, straight lead to waggler.
Best baits   Summer – hemp; all baits produce tench, bream, roach, rudd, perch and pike.
Restrictions   No coloured maggots.
Facilities   Shops/toilets/food in Clevedon.

KINGS SEDGEMOOR DRAIN, BRIDGEWATER
Atlas Page 201 E.5/4.6

A good all-round fishery that stretches from Bridgwater east towards Street. Noted for tench in the early season, but also holds large bream above Bradney, rudd at the bottom end at Dunball, and skimmer bream, hybrids and roach throughout.

How to get there   Leave the M5 at jct 23 and take A39 east towards Street. Access to the river is at Dunball and via bridges at Crandon, Parchey, Greylake and Bradney. Free car parking at swims.
Day tickets   Adult/junior/OAP £1.75; available from local tackle shops.
Best methods   Waggler, pole or feeder.
Best baits   Red maggots, casters, sweetcorn plus groundbait.
Restrictions   There is a close season for pike.
Facilities   Shops/toilets/food in Bridgewater (2 miles).

LOWER LOVELYNCH FARM
Atlas Page 201 E.1/5.1

A well-stocked lake located at Milverton, 8 miles west of Taunton. Good fishing, with plenty of roach, perch, bream and tench, plus some small carp.

How to get there   From Taunton, head west on the A361 and turn left on B3187 to Milverton (8 miles). Lower Lovelynch is signposted on the left. Pay for car parking on site.
Day tickets   Adult £3; junior/OAP £2; available from local tackle shops.
Best methods   Float and leger.
Best baits   Maggots (coloured), floating crust.
Restrictions   No night fishing. Juniors must be accompanied by adult.
Facilities   Toilets/food on site.
Disabled facilities   Some swims suitable for disabled and wheelchair anglers.

NEWTOWN PONDS, HIGHBRIDGE
Atlas Page 201 E.4/4.4

Surrounded by houses, this 7-acre lake is in the Newtown district of Highbridge, near Burnham-on-Sea. Good mixed fishing with roach, rudd, bream, eels and pike. The lake has been stocked with mirror and common carp, with some fish in the 10–20lb range.

How to get there   Leave the M5 at jct 23 and take the A38 towards Burnham-on-Sea. Just after passing through Highbridge, turn left into a housing estate; the lake is on the left. Car parking nearby.

Day tickets   Only limited numbers of day tickets: £2. Available from the newsagent in Newtown High Street, or from Veals of Bristol, Old Market, Bristol; Tel. 0272 260790.

Best methods/baits   Use general coarse techniques and baits.

Restrictions   Maximum 1 rod per person. No floating crust. No night fishing (2230-0530).

Facilities   Shops/pubs/toilets/food in Newtown.

Disabled facilities   Some swims may be suitable for disabled anglers; check at local tackle shops.

NORTH DRAIN, BRIDGWATER
Atlas Page 201 E.5/4.6

A small, often weedy venue but good fishing with plenty of bream, tench, roach, perch and pike. For success here a gentle approach is needed. Ideal for young anglers, not deep and lots of small fish – but also plenty of big specimens.

How to get there   Leave the M5 at jct 22 and take A38 to Highbridge, then B3139 east to Wedmore (about 8 miles). Access to North Drain is on the B3151 Wedmore-Meare road and at villages west of this point. Free parking near the swims.

Day tickets   Adult/junior/OAP £1.75. Weekly ticket: adult/junior/OAP £5; available from local tackle shops.

Best methods   Small waggler or pole with cloud groundbait.

Best baits   Squat, hemp, casters.

Restrictions   No coloured maggots.

Facilities   Shops/food in Wedmore.

OXENLEAZE FARM, WIVELISCOMBE
Atlas Page 201 E.2/5.0

A small farm pond of under 1 acre, on a caravan park, located a few miles west of Taunton. Mainly tench and carp, with some large fish of either species.

How to get there   Take the A361 west from Taunton towards Wiveliscombe. At Milverton roundabout (about 6 miles), turn right on minor road signposted to Wiveliscombe. As you approach Wiveliscombe, look for signs to Oxenleaze Farm and the fishery. Car parking on site.

Day tickets   Free fishing for caravan park residents. For details, contact Mrs. Rottenbury; Tel. 0984 23427.

Best methods/baits   Use general coarse techniques and baits.

Facilities   Caravan (static) hire available on site. Nearest shop/pub in Wiveliscombe.

Disabled facilities   Caravan accommodation may not be suitable for disabled; please phone for advice (see above).

RIVER PARRETT, BRIDGWATER TO SOMERTON
Atlas Page 201 E.5/4.6

The River Parrett flows through some pleasant countryside, including this 12-mile stretch from Bridgwater, east to Somerton. Fishing sport will vary according to the location, but expect plenty of good quality mixed coarse fishing for most species, including common carp that may reach 20lb+.

How to get there   Access is at various points along the river from Bridgwater to Somerton, via (or close by) the villages of Northmoor Green, Moorland, Burrow Bridge, Stathe and Langport. Check with local tackle shops for further details of access and parking.

Day tickets   Adult/junior/OAP £1.75; weekly £5. Season tickets, adult £13.50; junior/OAP/disabled £4.60. Available from Thyers Tackle, 1A Church Street, Highbridge; Tel. 0278 786934.

Best methods/baits   Use general coarse techniques and baits.

Facilities   Plenty of holiday or B&B accommodation close to the river banks. Various shops/pubs/toilets/eating places along the route.

Disabled facilities   Check with local tackle shops for points allowing disabled anglers access to the river.

SOUTH DRAIN, BRIDGWATER
Atlas Page 201 E.5/4.6

A stretch similar to the North Drain. Peaty water that appears coloured, with lots of bream, plus tench, roach, gudgeon, ruff and some carp. Often excellent fishing – mostly bream – but sport can vary from day-to-day.

How to get there   Leave the M5 at jct 22 and take A38 to Highbridge, then B3139 east; after 2 miles turn right onto B3141 and at East Huntspill look for turns on left to Burtle and Westhay. Access to South Drain is at points along this road. Free parking near the swims.

Day tickets   Adult/junior/OAP £1.75. Weekly ticket: adult/junior/OAP £5; available from local tackle shops.

Best methods   Most methods work; try pole, or waggler and feeder.

Best baits   Roach, hybrids – hemp, bread punch. Bream – casters, worms.

Restrictions   No coloured baits.

Facilities   Shops in East Huntspill and Bason Bridge; nearest pub, Burtle Inn (500 yards).

RIVER TONE
Atlas Page 201 E.4/5.0

A 1½-mile stretch of the River Tone in Taunton, from the town centre to French Weir. Expect good shoals of bream and chub (to 6lb), plus carp up to 26lb.

How to get there   Various access points in the town centre; check details with local tackle shops. Pay for parking in town centre.

Day tickets   Free fishing on this stretch. *Note*: the remainder of the river is controlled by Taunton A.A.

Best methods   Float, leger or spinning.

Best baits   Most baits work well; legered boilies are preferred for carp.

Facilities   Shops/toilets/food in Taunton town centre (¼ mile).

Disabled facilities   Some swims suitable for disabled and wheelchair anglers.

WALROW PONDS
Atlas Page 201 E.4/4.4

A small but deep (12–13ft) water, just outside Highbridge. A mixed fishery with plenty of small fish, plus good bream and tench and the odd carp.

How to get there   Leave the M5 at jct 22 and take A38 to Highbridge; Walrow Ponds are about 2 minutes' drive south of Highbridge on the A38. Free parking near the ponds.

Day tickets   Adult/junior/OAP £1.75; weekly £5; season tickets, adult £13.50; junior/OAP/disabled £4.60. Available from Thyers Tackle, 1A Church Street, Highbridge; Tel. 0278 786934.

Best methods   Most methods work; try pole, waggler or feeder.

Best baits   Most baits work well; don't overdo the groundbait or eels will appear!

Restrictions   No coloured maggots; no boilies.

Facilities   Shops/toilets/food/pubs in Highbridge (5 mins walk).

Disabled facilities   Some swims suitable for disabled and wheelchair anglers.

RIVER YEO, BRIMSCOMBE
Atlas Page 201 E.6/4.3

A picturesque fishery, just south of Axbridge and not far from Cheddar Reservoir. Fishing extends along the left-hand bank both downstream and upstream (three fields), plus a field adjacent to the New River Yeo relief channel. Expect a good day's sport, with some fair-sized fish of most species, and quite large nets.

How to get there   Take the A38 south-west from Bristol and about ½ mile after the A38/A371 junction (at Axbridge) turn left through Upper Weare. Bear left at the church and follow the 'No Through Road'. After about 1 mile, turn down the lane on the left and continue to the river. Park near the water. Access to the New River Yeo is via the footbridge.

Day tickets   Adult £2; junior/OAP 50p. Available at local tackle shops.

Best methods/baits   Use general coarse methods and baits.

Facilities   Nearest shops and pubs, in Upper Weare.

Disabled facilities   For advice on disabled and wheelchair angling, contact Bristol, Bath & Wiltshire Amalgamated Anglers, Hon. Sec. Jeff Parker; Tel. 0272 672977.

WILTSHIRE

RIVER AVON, KELLAWAYS TO CHRISTIAN MALFORD
Atlas Page 201 F.8/3.8

Another good quality, all-weather, Avon fishery just north of Chippenham. Plenty of large tench (to 7lb), bream (6–8lb), barbel (to 10lb), roach and perch in water which varies little from 8–10 ft in depth. Most matches are won here with 15–20lb (mainly roach), but nets rise to 20–30lb if the bream and tench appear.

How to get there   Take the A420 from Chippenham towards Swindon and turn right onto the B4279 to Langley Burrell. Continuing upstream to Kellaway Bridge and Christian Malford there are two parking areas (marked), each only a short walk from the river.

Day tickets   No day tickets; fishing here requires Full Membership of Isis A.C: £15.50 from Pete Gilbert (Hon. Sec.); Tel. 0793 535396. There is no subsequent charge for fishing these waters.

Best methods   Pole, waggler, stick float and crowquill are best here.

Best baits   Use casters, hemp, tares and bronze maggots.

Facilities   Nearest shop, Chippenham (2½ miles); nearest pub, about ½ mile.

RIVER AVON, TOWN WEIR TO MORTIMERS WOOD
Atlas Page 201 F.8/3.8

A town-centre stretch of the Avon at Chippenham, with typical water about 5ft deep. A very popular fishery for all ages, with most species being caught here, but some very good barbel (to 13lb) taken at the weir and also downstream near Mortimers Wood. Large pike also inhabit these lower reaches to provide some excellent mixed fishing.

How to get there   In Chippenham town centre, drive past 'Goldigger's' Night Club down to the river weir. Parking (mostly free) at various points; fishing is available over a 2–2½ mile stretch downstream, on both banks.

Day tickets   Free fishing.

Best methods/baits   Use general coarse methods and baits.

Facilities   Nearest shops and pubs, in the town centre.

Disabled facilities   Some swims are suitable for disabled and wheelchair anglers; contact Rob's Tackle, 22 Marshfield Road, Chippenham for advice; Tel. 0249 659210.

RIVER AVON, LACOCK
Atlas Page 201 F.8/3.8

A pleasant section of the Avon, midway between Chippenham and Melksham. Water depth is consistent at 4–5ft. Expect roach, barbel, bream, perch, gudgeon and

pike in large numbers providing good quality sport.

How to get there   From Chippenham, drive south on the A350 towards Melksham; at Lacock village (about 2½ miles) use the free car park by Lacock Abbey and walk across the field to the river.

Day tickets   Adult £2.50; junior/OAP £1.50. Available from Rob's Tackle, 22 Marshfield Road, Chippenham; Tel. 0249 659210.

Best methods   Float is preferred method, but feeder works well in some areas.

Best baits   Maggots, casters or hemp.

Restrictions   Maximum pole size 7 metres.

Facilities   Nearest shop and pub, The Red Lion, in Lacock (½ mile).

The peace and quiet of the Wiltshire Avon.

RIVER AVON, BEANACRE TO MELKSHAM
Atlas Page 201 F.8/3.8

A very good fishery on the Avon, extending about 2 miles north from Melksham. Typical water depth is between 5–6 ft all along, producing good quality roach, bream and chub, with average match weights of 7–8lb.

How to get there   From Chippenham, drive south on the A350 towards Melksham; at Beanacre (about 5 miles) the road runs close to the river. Park on the grass verge on the left hand side of the road, where the route to the water is marked.

Day tickets   Adult £1; junior/OAP 50p. Available from Rob's Tackle, 22 Marshfield Road, Chippenham; Tel. 0249 659210.

Best methods   All float, feeder and lead methods work well here.

Best baits   Bronze maggot, casters, hemp and tares are best in summer.

Facilities   Nearest shop in Melksham (1 mile); nearest pub in Lacock (1½ miles).

RIVER AVON, BARTON FARM
Atlas Page 201 F.7/4.1

A pleasant fishery located at Bradford-on-Avon, Barton Farm is noted for its large shoals of quality bream, particularly from Avoncliffe End to the middle of the stretch. Expect mainly roach and chub from the middle to Tithe Barn. Water depth along the stretch is consistent and generally 8–10ft.

How to get there   From Bath, take the A4 east, then A363 south-east to Bradford-on-Avon town centre and use the car park at the railway station. Walk under the railway bridge and along the river to Barton Farm. Alternative parking is available at Tithe Barn. For details, contact West Tackle, Trowbridge; Tel. 0225 5472.

Day tickets   Adult £2.50; junior/OAP £1.25. Weekly tickets: adult £8.50; junior £3.50. Available from local tackle shops.

Best methods/baits   Bream – use feeder. Roach – use float. Most baits work well here.

Facilities   Nearest shops within 100 yards; nearest pub, about ½ mile.

Disabled facilities   Some swims are suitable for disabled and wheelchair anglers.

BURTON HILL LAKE
Atlas Page 200 F.9/3.5

A pleasant lake just south of Malmesbury, which is well stocked with good quality common, mirror and Crucian carp, plus plenty of roach, tench and perch.

How to get there   Take the A429 north from Chippenham, cross the M4 (jct 17) and continue through Corston village. After 1 mile (high wall on left) look for Burston Hall; the car park is where the wall turns away from the road (Bath

A.A. sign). Park and follow the path over the stile to the lake (about 100 yards).

Day tickets   No day tickets; fishing here requires Full Membership of Bristol, Bath & Wiltshire Amalgamated Anglers: £16.50 from Jeff Parker (Hon. Sec.); Tel. 0272 672977. There is no subsequent charge for fishing these waters.

Best methods/baits   Use general coarse methods and baits.

Restrictions   Groundbait limited to 1lb dry crumb per person per day. No night fishing. Juniors must be accompanied by an adult. The concrete platform at the right-hand end is out-of-bounds. Access to the far bank is via the dam bridge – not over the feeder stream.

Facilities   Nearest shops and pubs, Malmesbury.

Disabled facilities   Some swims may be suitable for disabled anglers; please contact the Club Secretary for advice.

Tench.

FLAMSTONE COTTAGE
Atlas Page 203 A.5/6.0

Generally considered as a specialist carp fishery, this stream-fed pool is located about 5 miles south west of Salisbury. Expect some large fish up to 25lb, plus some big tench, roach, chub, orfe and grayling. There are also very large brown trout here!

How to get there   From Salisbury, head south-west on the A354 to Coombe Bissett (about 2½ miles) and turn right on minor road to Bishopstone village. Follow signs to the fishery; car parking available nearby,

Day tickets   Adult/junior/OAP £10.
Best methods/baits   Carp – use recognised methods and baits. Other species – use general coarse techniques and baits.
Restrictions   Use only barbless hooks, not bigger than size 12. No keepnets.
Facilities   Nearest shop/pub in Bishopstone village.
Disabled facilities   Some swims may be suitable for disabled anglers; please check when purchasing tickets.

HIGH PENN
Atlas Page 203 A.2/5.0

A secluded pit lake located on a working farm in a rural area just north of Calne. Mainly carp, but also some tench, roach and perch – among others. Best fishing is in the summer.

How to get there   From Calne, head north on the A3102 towards Swindon; High Penn Farm is about ½ mile outside Calne, on the right-hand side. Look for the signpost at the top of the lane. Free car parking available on site.
Day tickets   Adult £2; junior/OAP £1 (weekdays only). Weekly tickets (excluding weekend): adult £5; junior £2.50. Available from T. K. Tackle, 123A London Road, Calne; Tel. 0249 659210.
Best methods   Most methods work well; float is preferred.
Best baits   Breadcrumb is effective in summer.
Facilities   Nearest shop, Calne (½ mile); nearest pub, at the bottom of the lane (½ mile).

IVY HOUSE FARM LAKES
Atlas Page 203 A.3/4.7

Two lakes situated on a farm close to Wootton Bassett and the M4. Both have a good depth of water (10–12ft) and are well stocked with carp, bream, roach and tench, providing mixed sport in pleasant surroundings.

How to get there   From Chippenham, take the A420 towards Swindon and at Tockenham Wick (about 12 miles) turn left to Grittenham. Follow the road to the end junction and turn right; the lakes are on the right. Free car parking on site.

Day tickets   Adult £3; junior/OAP £1.50. Evening ticket: £1.50. Available from Pete Warner at Ivy House Farm; Tel. 066641 368.
Best methods/baits   Roach, tench – use float with waggler/maggot, or feeder/lead with worm, casters or maggots.
Restrictions   No boilies or tiger nuts.
Facilities   Nearest shop, Wootton Bassett (2 miles); nearest pub, the Suffolk Arms, Brinkworth (1½ miles).

Success on the Kennet.

KENNET AND AVON CANAL, PEWSEY
Atlas Page 203 A.6/5.2

From Milkhouse Bridge to Lady's Bridge, a typical canal stretch, with both near- and far-side shelves, just over 12 yards width and 2½ to 3 ft depth. Expect mainly skimmer bream and roach, plus tench, perch and some carp. With 190 pegs there is plenty of choice, but pegs 70–75 are best for bream; peg 80 is good for tench.

How to get there   Leave the M4 at jct 15 and take the A345 south through Marlborough to Pewsey (about 12 miles). In Pewsey, park at Pewsey Wharfe and walk to the canal.
Day tickets   Adult £2; junior/OAP £1. Available from the black 'honesty box' on the warden's fence, near Pewsey Wharfe. Day tickets are available only from Milkhouse Bridge to Wilcot Bridge.

Best methods/baits Skimmer bream, perch, roach – use pole or waggler, with pinkie hookbait and squatts in groundbait. Tench – use caster, fished tight to the bank reeds.

Restrictions No bloodworm or jokers from 16th June until 1st October.

Facilities Nearest shops/pubs/toilets/food in Pewsey.

Disabled facilities Access for disabled anglers is possible at some pegs; for details, phone Don Underwood (0672 62541) or Kevin Chubb (0722 339457).

KENNET AND AVON CANAL – SEAMINGTON TO WILCOT
Atlas Page 201 F.7/4.2

A very productive canal stretch (about 15 miles) between Pewsey and Trowbridge, generally about 4ft deep and providing really big catches, from gudgeon, roach and skimmer bream to big bream, tench and carp of 20lb+. Best areas are Pile Stretch, Willows, Magpies, Seend Park and Seamington. Catches often exceed 30lb.

How to get there From Marlborough, head south on the A345 towards Pewsey and after about 5 miles, bear right on minor road to Wilcot. Access to the water is westward through villages to Devizes and then along the A341 towards Trowbridge. For details of access/parking, contact Rod & Reel, Sidmouth Street, Devizes; Tel. 0380 725431.

Day tickets Adult £2; junior/OAP £2. Night tickets available on application to Devizes A.A., Terry Fell (Hon. Sec.); Tel. 0380 725189.

Best methods Use general coarse methods; most work well.

Best baits Sweetcorn, pinkies, squatts, casters, punched bread and meat all work well here.

Facilities Plenty of shops and pubs in villages along the stretch.

Disabled facilities Fishing by disabled and wheelchair anglers is possible at most sites; please contact Rod & Reel for advice (see above).

KENNET AND AVON CANAL, WHADDON TO AVONCLIFFE
Atlas Page 201 F.5/4.2

Another scenic canal stretch of about 5 miles, fairly shallow (3½ ft) but containing large numbers of fish. Expect good-sized carp, roach and skimmer bream, with particularly large tench and bream at the Whaddon (eastern) end. Plenty of large pike have also been taken from these waters.

How to get there From Melksham, head west on the B3107 to Holt and Bradford-on-Avon, or alternatively, take the A350 south, then A366 towards Trowbridge. Access to the water is at various points along the route(s). For details, contact either West Tackle, Trowbridge; Tel. 0225 5472; or Rob's Tackle, 22 Marshfield Road, Chippenham; Tel. 0249 659210.

Day tickets Adult £2.50; junior/OAP £1.25. Weekly tickets: adult £8.50; junior £3.50. Available from local tackle shops (see above).

Best methods/baits Use general coarse methods and baits.

Facilities Various shops and pubs in villages along the routes.

Disabled facilities Fishing by disabled and wheelchair anglers is possible at most sites; please contact local tackle shops for advice (see above).

LONGLEAT PARK
Atlas Page 201 F.7/4.5

Three very mature lakes – Top, Middle and Bottom – situated within the Longleat Estate, near Warminster. An excellent carp fishery, particularly in the deeper, 3½-acre Top lake, with lots of double-figure specimens present, but even the Middle and Bottom lakes will produce nets of 40–50lb.

How to get there From Warminster, head west on the A362 and after about 2 miles follow signs to Longleat Estate and the fishery; the car parks for anglers are signposted.

Day tickets Adult/junior/OAP £3. Available from the bailiff on the bank.

Best methods/baits Top lake – use specialist methods for large fish; boilies with white seed mix or strawberry yoghurt-flavoured baits are best. Middle/Bottom lakes – use pole or waggler with maggot feed for small carp.

Restrictions No peas, nuts or beans. No boilies on the Middle and Bottom lakes.

Facilities Toilets/cafes/bars on site.

Disabled facilities Some swims may be suitable for disabled anglers; for advice, phone Pete Bundy; Tel. 0985 215082.

RIVER MARDEN, HAZELANDS MILL TO TYTHERTON
Atlas Page 200 F.9/3.9

A very narrow river section, a few miles north-west of Calne. Fairly deep (5–6ft), and containing a good head of large chub, roach, dace and barbel – especially at the Tytherton end. Also the biggest gudgeon you're likely to see!

How to get there   Take the A4 from Marlborough west to Calne (about 13 miles) and turn left after the Soho pub. Follow the road and take the right fork to Hazelands Mill on the river. Free parking available at the mill.

Day tickets   Adult £2; junior/OAP £1. Weekly ticket: £3.50. Available from either TK Tackle, London Road, Calne; Tel. 0249 812003; or Rob's Tackle, 22 Marshfield Road, Chippenham; Tel. 0249 659210.

Best methods/baits   Use stick float with bronze maggot, casters, or hemp lead. Feeder is best in pool areas.

Facilities   Nearest shop, Calne (1¼ miles); nearest pub, Dumbpost Inn (1 mile).

Disabled facilities   Some swims are suitable for disabled and wheelchair anglers.

Barbel.

ROWDE LAKE
Atlas Page 203 A.2/5.2

A small lake of about 1 acre, located at a caravan site in Rowde, just west of Devizes. Good coarse fishing for most species, including Crucian carp.

How to get there   From Devizes, take the A342 west towards Chippenham; at Rowde village (about 1 mile) look for signs to the caravan park and lake. Car parking available on site.

Day tickets   Adult/junior/OAP £3 per rod. Available from the house near the lake.

Best methods/baits   Use general coarse techniques and baits.

Restrictions   No keep nets.

Facilities   Toilets on site. Also caravan hire/parking available. Nearest shop/pub in Rowde village.

Disabled facilities   Some swims may be suitable for disabled anglers.

SABRE LAKE
Atlas Page 200 F.9/3.9

A fairly deep (10–12ft), privately-owned farm lake, at Cheerhill, just west of Calne. Good coarse fishing, with carp, bream, roach and tench in quite large numbers. A pleasant venue for both family and angler alike.

How to get there   Take the A4 from Marlborough west to Calne (about 13 miles). On leaving Calne, Sabre Lake is visible on the left-hand side of the road. Free car parking available on site.

Day tickets   Adult £3; junior/OAP £1.50. Available from the owner, Paul Candy, on site at Quemerford Gate Farm; Tel. 0249 812388.

Best methods   Float fishing is preferred method.

Best baits   Use big baits on the lead for roach and carp.

Facilities   Toilets/barbecue area on site. Nearest shop (Spar, 1 mile); nearest pub, The Black Horse (1 mile).

Disabled facilities   Some swims are suitable for disabled and wheelchair anglers.

SHEARWATER LAKES
Atlas Page 201 F.7/4.5

Two extremely picturesque lakes forming a fishing complex, just south of Warminster. Shearwater is a large, dammed estate lake with depth ranging from about 3 to 25ft (at the dam), providing 80 pegs for top-class angling – roach, tench, bream and thousands of carp from under 1lb to 10lb+. Little Shearwater provides plenty of roach, bream, skimmer bream and golden rudd.

How to get there Drive south from Warminster on the A350 through Crockerton (about 1½ miles) and take right turn on minor road signposted Maiden Bradley. Look for the entrance to Shearwater Lake on the right (well signposted), and park in one of the purpose-built bays around the lake.

Day tickets Adult/junior/OAP £3. Available on the bank.

Best methods/baits Shearwater lake: in winter, fish from the dam, with caster or maggot at 12 metres. In summer, floatfish close in, using any bait. Little Shearwater lake: use pole or waggler with white maggot.

Restrictions No keepnets for pleasure anglers.

Facilities Toilets/cafes/shop/bar on site.

Disabled facilities Good vehicular access to the lakeside for disabled and wheelchair anglers; for advice, phone the Water Bailiff, Nick Robbins; Tel. 09853 496.

SILVERLANDS LAKE
Atlas Page 203 A.1/5.2

A mature, 35-year-old, comfortable and easy-to-fish lake at Wick Farm, near Melksham. The typical depth of 5ft provides excellent mixed coarse fishing, with many very big carp (30lb+), large bream and tench, plus roach, skimmer bream, perch, crucian carp and eels. Also the most popular pike fishery in the area, with some specimen fish available.

How to get there Take the A350 south from Chippenham to Melksham and turn right immediately after the Whitehall Garden Centre. Follow the road and take the 1st right turn, then 1st left turn and follow the signs to the lake. Free parking available next to the lake.

Day tickets Adult £3; junior/OAP £2. Also available: half-day £1.90; evening £1.90; weekend £10; season £45. Night fishing tickets: adult £3; junior/OAP £2. All tickets available *only* at Rob's Tackle, 22 Marshfield Road, Chippenham; Tel. 0249 659210.

Best methods/baits Use general coarse methods and baits. Use specialist methods for pike.

Restriction No tickets available on site; only from Rob's Tackle in Chippenham.

Facilities Nearest shop and pubs, in Lacock (1 mile).

Disabled facilities Some swims are suitable for disabled and wheelchair anglers.

TOCKENHAM RESERVOIR
Atlas Page 203 A.4/4.8

A large, very pleasantly-sited lake, a few miles west of Wootton Bassett and close to the M4. Quite deep (average 10–12ft) and containing all species of coarse fish, providing good all-round sport for anglers.

How to get there Take the A420 from Chippenham north-east towards Swindon and at Lyneham (about 10 miles) look for a white house on the left-hand side. Turn left down the hill; the lake is on the right. Free parking (members) on site.

Day tickets No day tickets; fishing here requires Full Membership of Bristol, Bath & Wiltshire Amalgamated Anglers: £16.50 from Jeff Parker (Hon. Sec.); Tel. 0272 672977. There is no subsequent charge for fishing these waters.

Best methods/baits Most species – float fish with maggots and casters. For large fish – use feeder and lead with big baits.

Restrictions Maximum pole size 7 metres.

Facilities Nearest shop, Lyneham (2 miles); nearest pub, 1 mile.

Disabled facilities Many fishing stages have been fitted for use by disabled and wheelchair anglers.

WOOTTON BASSETT LAKE
Atlas Page 203 A.4/4.8

A 2-acre lake, with depth to 12 ft and a single island, lying just off the M4. Having been recently drained, dredged and restocked, the lake offers good sport for up to 35 anglers, with mainly tench, roach, carp and perch. Day catches of up to 40lb are possible here.

How to get there Leave the M4 at jct 16 and take the A420 to Wootton Bassett. At the roundabout, take the B4042 towards Brinkworth and Malmesbury. The fishery entrance is a short distance on the left; parking is available on site.

Day tickets Adult £2; junior/OAP £1. Available (Monday to Friday only) from Canon Sports, High Street, Wootton Bassett; Tel. 0793 853760.

Best methods   Most methods work, but leger and float are best. Use a 2AA waggler with caster, and groundbait little and often.

Best baits   Most baits work, but casters are best.

Restrictions   No boilies or nuts.

Facilities   Nearest shop/pub in Wootton Bassett.

Disabled facilities   Some swims may be suitable for disabled anglers; please phone for advice; Tel. 0793 853760.

Chris Yates with a 24lb carp.

South-West Region

The scenic but rugged terrain of Dartmoor.

The South-West NRA Region, which incorporates all of Devon and Cornwall, plus parts of Somerset and Dorset, contains perhaps the greatest number of 'scenic' fisheries in Britain – from the rugged terrains of Dartmoor and Exmoor, to the gentle and very picturesque rural areas nearer the coast.

Although there is a small amount of river fishing in the region – the River Taw and Tamar each offer limited sport – fisheries here are mainly confined to lakes and reservoirs. The majority of these – many of which are commercially-operated – offer superb fishing for good quality fish, with a great and well-deserved reputation for specimen carp, bream and roach, in addition to large catches of perch and rudd. Another advantage, largely due to the warmer climate enjoyed in the south-west, is that many such fisheries have no closed season, so fishing is available all year round!

Also, with the region's strong accent and extensive experience in the holiday and tourist industries, the South-West region welcomes visitors, with day-ticket angling being very popular, and many fisheries and hotels also providing good-value fishing holiday packages – ideal for families!

CORNWALL

BILBERRY POOL
Atlas Page 201 B.5/6.6

A fairly secluded pit – about 6 acres – near Roche, midway between St. Austell, Bodmin and Newquay. Exceptionally deep – up to 90 ft – providing good fishing for bream, perch, eels, tench and rudd, supported by some double-figure carp. Best fishing in summer.

How to get there   Take the A30 Bodmin bypass and after about 3 miles bear left onto the A391 St. Austell road. At Bilberry (about 3 miles), turn right on minor road towards Roche and look for signs to the fishery. Car parking on site.

Day tickets   Adult £3.50; junior/OAP £1.75. Weekly tickets: adult £15; junior/OAP £7.50. Available from The Angling Centre, St. Austell; Tel. 0726 63377.

Best methods/baits   Use general coarse techniques and baits.

Facilities   Nearest shop/pub in Bugle, near St. Austell.

Disabled facilities   Some swims are suitable for disabled anglers; (on an open stretch near the car park).

BILLINGSMOOR FARM
Atlas Page 201 D.8/5.3

Three farm ponds near Cullompton, near Tiverton. A fishery offering a good variety of sport – two ponds contain plenty of mixed coarse fish, the third is well stocked with good-sized carp, some in double figures. Fishing available all year round.

How to get there   Leave the M5 at jct 28. In Cullompton centre turn right onto road between Manor House Hotel and bank, 1½ miles to crossroads, turn left, bear right at junction, left at next crossroads, through Butterleigh, left onto Silverton Road, continue 1 mile, ignoring first left turning, first farm on the left is Billingsmoor. Parking on site.

Day tickets   Adult/junior/OAP £3. Available from the farm; for details, contact Mr. Berry; Tel. 0884 855248. Tickets are valid for all three ponds.

Best methods/baits   Use general coarse techniques and baits.

Facilities   Nearest shop/pub in Butterleigh village.

Disabled facilities   Some swims may be suitable for disabled anglers; check in advance by phone.

BOSCATHNOE
Atlas Page 201 A.4/7.3

A 4-acre reservoir on the northern outskirts of Penzance, containing a good head of carp, tench, bream, roach, rudd, perch and gudgeon. Plenty of good quality fishing all year round; open from 1 hour before sunrise until 1 hour after sunset.

How to get there   Off the A30 ring road at Penzance take the B3312 Heamoor Road, immediately before the school. After 300 yards, turn left into an unclassified road. The lake is ½ mile on the left.

Day tickets   Adult £3; junior/OAP/ disabled £1.50. Available from Newtown Angling Centre, Germoe, Penzance; Tel. 0736 763721. For all other information; Tel. 0752 766897.

Best methods/baits   Use any recognised coarse technique and baits.

Restrictions   No carp in keepnets. No lead weights to be used. All fish must be returned to the water.

Facilities   Nearest shops, Penzance (2 miles). Nearest pub, Heamoor (½ mile).

BOLINGEY LAKE
Atlas Page 201 B.0/6.8

A small lake on the north Cornish coast, near Perranporth. Suitable for conventional match fishing styles, with 100lb catches of carp, tench, roach and perch taken regularly.

How to get there   In Perranporth, at Riley's Garage, follow the B3284 Truro road 1 mile to a small crossroads (look for bus shelter on left) and turn right. The lake is 400 yards on the left. No car parking available.

Day tickets   Adult £4; junior/OAP £3. Available from the lake at Penwartha Road, Bolingey, nr Perranporth; Tel. 0872 572388.

Best methods/baits   Use any recognised coarse fishing technique.

Restrictions   Use no hooks above size 8.

Facilities   Toilets/tackle on site; campsite 100 yards. Nearest shop (post office/grocer) 150 yards; nearest pub, Bolingey Inn (60 yards).

Disabled facilities   Five swims suitable for disabled anglers; also staging for wheelchairs.

BUDE CANAL
Atlas Page 201 C.0/5.5

A 2-mile stretch of canal flowing inland from the sea at Bude, now disused and overgrown with weed, but producing some good coarse fish. Expect roach, perch and tench, plus some big eels and carp – said to be in the 10–20lb range.

How to get there   In Bude town centre, locate the canal as it flows inland from the sea. For details of access points and parking facilities, check with tackle shops in Bude.

Day tickets   Adult £2; /junior/OAP 50p or £10 for seven day week. Available on the bank or from Bude tackle shops.

Best methods/baits   Use general coarse techniques and baits (including carp methods as necessary).

Restrictions   No fishing from 1st April to 31st May.

Facilities   Shops/pubs/toilets/food all in Bude town centre.

Disabled facilities   Some swims may be suitable for disabled anglers; check at tackle shops.

BUSSOW
Atlas Page 201 A.5/7.4

A 7-acre reservoir, lying close to St. Ives and Penzance. First opened in 1990 and very popular with holiday anglers. Mainly carp, tench, bream, rudd, roach and eels. Open all year round, 24 hours a day.

How to get there   Take the B3306 west from St. Ives, then left onto B3311 towards Hasletown. Turn right almost immediately onto minor road; the reservoir is a short distance on the left. Park nearby.

Day tickets   Adult £2.75; junior/OAP/ disabled £1.75. Also 24-hour ticket: £5.50. Available from local tackle shops. For all other information; Tel. 0752 766897.

Best methods/baits   Use any recognised coarse technique and baits.

Restrictions   No carp in keepnets. Use only barbless hooks. No lead weights to be used. All fish must be returned to the water.

Facilities   Nearest shop, St. Ives (1 mile). Nearest pub, The Shire Horse Inn, Towednack Road (½ mile).

CHOONE FARM, ST. BURYAN
Atlas Page 201 A.3/7.5

A small farm lake south-west of Penzance. Good mixed coarse fishing, with carp (to 20lb), tench, perch and rudd. Fishes well all year round; no closed season.

How to get there   Take the A30 south-west from Penzance and bear left onto B3283 just after Drift (about 3 miles). Continue to St. Bunyan, and turn left into Rectory Road (opposite church). The fishery is 1 mile on the left; look for signposts. Free car parking on site.

Day tickets   Adult/junior/OAP £2.50 (two rods). Available from Mr. Case, Choone Farm, St. Buryan, nr Penzance; Tel. 0736 810220.

Best methods/baits   Use any recognised coarse technique. Most baits work well; use dog biscuits or bread for carp.

Restrictions   No night fishing. No keepnets; use only barbless hooks. No cereal groundbait to be used.

Facilities   Toilets/self-catering facilities on site. Nearest shop and pub St. Buryan (1 mile).

COLLEGE, NR. FALMOUTH
Atlas Page 201 A.5/7.5

A very large reservoir (38 acres) renowned for its carp fishing, with regular catches of 20lb+ fish. Also excellent sport with rudd and roach, plus skimmer bream. Best carp 32lb, best bream 8lb, best tench 8lb+. Open all year round, 24 hours a day.

How to get there   Head west from Falmouth on the A394 towards Helston and after 3 miles turn left to Mabe Burnthouse. Drive over crossroads (inn on left) and bear left to car park which serves College and Argal reservoirs. Park and take footpath to College.

Day tickets   Adult £3.25; junior/OAP/ disabled £2.25. Also 24-hour ticket: £6.50. Available from the machine at the car park, or from local tackle shops. For all other information; Tel. 0752 766897.

Best methods/baits   Use any recognised coarse technique and baits. Float is recommended.

Restrictions   No carp in keepnets. Use only barbless hooks. No lead weights to be used. No cereal groundbaiting by hand (loosefeed with hookbait and feeders). All fish must be returned to the water.

Facilities   Nearest shops and pubs are in Penryn (1 mile).

CRAFTHOLE, NR. TORPOINT
Atlas Page 201 C.7/6.8

A quite small (2 acres) but very popular water, well stocked with carp and tench. Open all year round, from 1 hour before sunrise to 1 hour after sunset.

How to get there   From Liskeard, head east on the A374 towards Torpoint; at Sheviock (about 12 miles), turn right to Crafthole, then left onto B3247 and park nearby. Entry to the lake is by footpath from behind the pub.

Day tickets   Adult £3.25; junior/OAP/ disabled £2.25. Available from Crafthole Post Office Store; Tel. 0503 30225. Phone in advance to check availability. For all other information; Tel. 0752 766897.

Best methods/baits   Use any recognised coarse technique and baits.

Restrictions   No carp in keepnets. Use only barbless hooks. No lead weights to be used. All fish must be returned to the water. Children must be accompanied by an adult.

Facilities   Nearest shop in Crafthole (1 mile); nearest pub, Finnygook Inn, Crafthole.

DUTSON WATER
Atlas Page 201 B.3/6.0

A ¾-acre lake just north of Launceston. Fish first introduced in the late 1960s; carp – mirrors, Crucians, commons – now into double figures. Also bream, tench (green and gold), rudd, roach and golden orfe.

How to get there   From Launceston, head north on the A388; after 1 mile, look for signpost outside Lower Dutson Farm. Free car parking on site.

Day tickets   Adult/junior/OAP £3. Available from Mr. Broad, Tamar View, Lower Dutson Farm, Launceston; Tel. 0566 772607.

Best methods/baits   Float or leger; most baits work well.

Restrictions   No carp in keepnets. No groundbait.

Facilities   Toilets/self-catering/B&B facilities on site. Nearest shop/pub Launceston (1 mile).

Disabled facilities   Some swims suitable for disabled and wheelchair anglers.

FORDA HOLIDAY LODGES
Atlas Page 201 C.0/5.5

A small fishing lake within a complex of Scandinavian-style, self-catering holiday lodges, a few miles north of Bude and only 10 minutes from the beaches. A mixed fishery, with bream, tench, rudd and carp. No close season – open all year for fishing.

How to get there   From Bude, take the A39 north about 4 miles to Kilkhampton and follow signs in the village to the Holiday Lodges and fishery. Car parking is available on site.

Day tickets   Fishing for residents only. For details; Tel. 0288 82413.

Best methods/baits   Use general coarse techniques and baits.

Facilities   Toilets/shop on site. Nearest pub in Kilkhampton village.

Disabled facilities   Some swims may be suitable for disabled anglers; please phone for advice.

MEADOWSIDE COARSE FISHERIES
Atlas Page 201 B.4/6.6

A 2-acre mixed coarse fishery a few miles east of Newquay. Good fishing, with carp (mirror, Crucian and common to 15lb), tench (to 7lb), perch and roach.

How to get there   From St. Columb Major take the A39 north for about 1½ miles. The fishery is signposted on the roadside. No car parking available.

Day tickets   Adult £3.50 per rod (£4 for two rods); junior/OAP £2. Available from the fishery at Winnards Perch, St. Columb Major, Cornwall; Tel. 0637 880544.

Best methods/baits   Float or feeder; most baits work well, but luncheon meat and sweetcorn are preferred.

Restrictions   No boilies. No groundbait. Use only barbless hooks. No keepnets after Easter.

Facilities   Toilets (disabled access)/food/B&B available on site. Nearest shop/pubs, St. Columb Major (1½ miles).

Disabled facilities   Some swims suitable for disabled or wheelchair anglers (dependent on weather).

OAKSIDE FISHERY
Atlas Page 201 B.3/6.6

A 3½-acre lake, complete with four islands, a few miles east of Newquay. Plenty of fishing available, with tench, rudd and crucian carp, plus some large roach (to 2lb+) and carp of up to 15lb.

How to get there   From Newquay, take the A3058 east towards St. Austell. Continue through Kestle Mill (about 1½ miles), past Dairylands and turn left to St. Columb. The lake is ½ mile down this road; free car parking on site.

Day tickets   Adult £3; junior/OAP £1.50. Two rods per person. Available from Oakside Fishery, 89 Pyda Close, Newquay, Cornwall TR7 3BT.

Best methods/baits   Use general coarse methods and baits.

Facilities   Nearest shop and pub, the Two Clomes, in Quintrell Down.

Disabled facilities   Cars can be driven to one side of the lake in summer, allowing access by disabled and wheelchair anglers.

PERRANPORTH LAKE
Atlas Page 201 B.0/6.8

A 4½-acre lake just outside Perranporth, providing good quality mixed coarse fishing, including roach, tench and carp. Specimen carp of 20lb+ are also thought to patrol these waters! No close season – open all year for fishing.

How to get there   From Newquay, drive south on the A3075 for about 6 miles and turn right to Perranporth at Goonhavern. Turn left at Riley's garage, go past fire station to small crossroads, turn right, and follow road to pool.
Day tickets   Adult £4. (one rod), £4.50 (two rods); junior/OAP £3 and £3.50 respectively. Available from bailiffs on the bank. For details of availability, contact Mr. Phillips; Tel. 087257 2388.
Best methods/baits   Use general coarse techniques and baits.
Facilities   Nearest shops and pubs in Perranporth.
Disabled facilities   Some swims may be suitable for disabled anglers; please phone for advice.

PORTH RESERVOIR
Atlas Page 201 B.2/6.6

A large, 40-acre reservoir just east of Newquay. A very consistent fishery, providing very large bream (to 9lb+) and enormous tench (to 10lb). Also good roach, rudd, perch, eels and carp. Open all year round, 24 hours a day.

How to get there   From Newquay, head east on the A3059 and at St. Columb Minor (about 1 mile) bear right on minor road to the reservoir (about 1 mile). Car parking on site.
Day tickets   Adult £3.25; junior/OAP/disabled £2.25. Also 24-hour ticket: £6.50. Available from the machine at the car park, or from local tackle shops. For all other information; Tel. 0752 766897 or 0637 879481.
Best methods/baits   Use any recognised coarse technique and baits.
Restrictions   No carp in keepnets. Use only barbless hooks. No lead weights to be used. No cereal groundbaiting by hand (loosefeeding with hookbait and feeders allowed). All fish must be returned to the water.
Facilities   Nearest shop and pub, Quintrell Inn, in Quintrell Downs (3 miles).

ROSEWATER LAKE
Atlas Page 201 B.0/6.8

Two secluded lakes situated in a valley at Rose, near Perranporth. Expect most coarse species, including carp (to 20lb), tench, roach, bream, chub and rudd. Some very big bags were taken in 1991!

How to get there   From Perranporth, take the B3285 west towards Goonhavern; Rose is about 2 miles from Perranporth. Look for signposts to the lake. Free car parking on site.
Day tickets   Adult £3; junior/OAP £1.50. Evening ticket: £1.50. Available from Mr Mike Waters, Hendravossan Farm, Rose, nr Perranporth, Cornwall; Tel. 0872 573992/572216/573040.
Best methods/baits   Use any general match-fishing technique.
Facilities   Toilets at the farm; also B&B/food available. Nearest shop Perranporth (1½ miles); nearest pub, The New Inn, Goonhavern.

SHILLAMILL LAKES
Atlas Page 201 B.8/6.6

A commercial fishery comprising three small dammed lakes and providing holiday accommodation, midway between Looe and Lostwithiel. Plenty of perch, tench, rudd and roach to produce good sport, plus lots of common and mirror carp, some of 20lb+. No close season – fishing available all year round.

How to get there   Drive west from Liskeard on the A390 towards Lostwithiel and at East Taphouse (about 4 miles) turn left onto the B3359 Polperro road. At Lanreath (about 4 miles) follow signs to Shillamill Lakes; car parking on site.
Day tickets   Adult £5; junior under 14s/OAP £4. Available on site, but advisable to book in advance; for details of availability, contact John Facey: Tel. 0503 220271.
Best methods/baits   Use general coarse techniques and baits. Specialist methods may be needed for carp.
Facilities   Toilets on site. Also caravan/flat/cottage accommodation for hire. Nearest shop/pub in Lanreath.
Disabled facilities   Some swims may be suitable for disabled anglers; phone for advice.

TINDEEN FISHERY
Atlas Page 201 A.5/7.5

Three separate pools (each up to 1½ acres) set in several acres of secluded woodland between Penzance and Helston. Good mixed fishing with roach, rudd and tench, plus some very big carp – a 24lb+ specimen was taken in 1991.

How to get there   From Penzance, take the A30 east and bear right onto A394 after 3 miles. Drive over next roundabout to Coach & Horses pub (2 miles); at Newtown (¼ mile) turn left at signpost 'Millpool/Trescowe'. The fishery is signposted, 1 mile further on (No Through Road). Drive to the waterside for free car parking.

Day tickets   Adult £2; junior/OAP £1.50. Extra rod £1. Available at the fishery, Millpool, Goldsithney, Penzance; contact Mr Laity; Tel. 0736 763486.

Best methods/baits   Use any recognised coarse technique.

Facilities   On site caravan accommodation available. Nearest shop/garage Newton (1 mile); nearest pub, The Crown Hotel or Trevelyan Arms, Goldsithney (2½ miles).

Disabled facilities   Some swims suitable for disabled and wheelchair anglers.

TREDIDON BARTON LAKE
Atlas Page 201 C.4/6.0

A ¾-acre stretch of water just outside Launceston. Excellent mixed fishing, including carp (Crucians, commons and mirrors, some to 20lb+), tench and some rudd. Just bring a rod, line and hook!

How to get there   From Launceston, take the A30 west, then (after 4 miles) bear right onto A395 towards Camelford. Take the first right after joining the A395 and look for signs to the fishery. Free car parking on site.

Day tickets   Adult £3; junior/OAP £2.50. Available from Mr Jones at the fishery; Tel. 0566 86288.

Best methods/baits   Use any recognised coarse technique; most baits work well here.

Restrictions   Use only barbless hooks. No carp in keepnets. No groundbait.

Facilities   Toilets/food/tackle/ on site. Also B&B (fishing inclusive)/self-catering/camping/caravanning facilities available. Nearest shop/pub, The Elliott Arms, Tregadillet (3½ miles).

Disabled facilities   Some swims suitable for disabled anglers; wheelchair angling in dry conditions.

WHITE ACRES HOLIDAY PARK
Atlas Page 201 B.2/6.5

A holiday park at White Cross, near Newquay, with three ponds – 10 acres in all – providing excellent mixed coarse pleasure fishing, plus a 60-peg matchwater. The specimen carp lake contains fish up to 25lb.

How to get there   From Newquay, head east on the A395 towards Indian Queens; White Acres is well signposted (near White Cross) after about 3 miles. Free car parking on site.

Day tickets   Adult £3.50; junior/OAP £2 (two rods). Available at the holiday park.

Best methods/baits   Use pole or waggler with loose-fed maggots.

Restrictions   No carp in keepnets. Use only barbless hooks. No shelf-life boilies.

Facilities   Toilets/tackle/food available on site. Also holiday park for children. Shop and pub on site.

Disabled facilities   Some swims suitable for disabled and wheelchair anglers.

WHEAL RASHLEIGH & WALDON POOL
Atlas Page 201 B.6/6.8

A pair of lakes at St. Blazey, just east of St. Austell. Wheal Rashleigh is 8 acres, surrounded by rhododendrons and is very deep (30–40ft) in the middle. Waldon Pool is smaller (2 acres) but also deep. Expect good sport in both lakes, with some large carp (20lb+), roach, perch, rudd, crucian carp and tench. Also big eels for variety!

How to get there   From St. Austell, take the A390 east through St. Blazey (about 2½ miles) and turn left opposite the petrol station. The two pools are about ¾ mile on the left. Free car parking available on site.

Day tickets   Adult £3.50; junior/OAP £1.75. Two rods per person. Weekly tickets: adult £15; junior £7.50. Available from The Angling Centre, St. Austell; Tel. 0726 63377 or from N&D Tackle, St. Austell; Tel. 0726 67394.

Best methods/baits   Use waggler in summer; pole in winter. Most baits work well here.

Facilities   Nearest shop and pub in St. Blazey.

WOODLEY FARM
Atlas Page 201 C.3/7.6

A holiday farm providing self-catering accommodation and mixed coarse fishing from two small lakes, in very pleasant surroundings between Liskeard and Looe. Mainly tench, roach and carp. No close season – fishing available all year round.

How to get there   From Liskeard take the B3254 Looe road and at St. Keyne (about 2 miles) turn right on minor road to Herodsfoot. In the village, look for Woodley Farm and the fishery; car parking on site.

Day tickets   Available only to residents – details from Mrs. Hawke; Tel. 0503 220221.

Best methods/baits   Use general coarse techniques and baits.

Facilities   Nearest shop/pub in Herodsfoot or Duloe.

Disabled facilities   Some swims may be suitable for disabled anglers; phone for advice.

DEVON

Tench.

ANGLER'S ELDORADO
Atlas Page 201 C.9/5.7

Four lakes of between 1 and 3 acres, midway between Okehampton and Holsworthy. Top lake (with island) has tench (to 5lb) plus golden orfe and, imminently, carp. Second lake has quite large carp, tench and rudd. The general (3-acre) lake has golden orfe, carp and tench. Excellent fishing at all venues.

How to get there   From Okehampton, take the A386 south-west and outside the town turn right onto B3218 towards Holsworthy. At Halwill (about 12 miles) look for Tourist Board signposts to the fishery. Free car parking on site.

Day tickets   Adult £3.50 per rod; junior/OAP £2.50 per rod. Available from the fishery at The Gables, Winsford, Halwill, Beaworthy, Devon; Tel. 0409 221559, or from Mike Summers Angling Centre, Unit 1, Southern Court, Newport Ind. Estate, Launceston; Tel. 0566 776532.

Best methods/baits   Use any recognised coarse technique. Landing nets are vital.

Restrictions   No keepnets. Use only barbless hooks (minimum size 14, minimum 3lb line).

Facilities   Tackle shop/bar at fishing centre (½ mile). Nearest shop ¾ mile; nearest pub, The Junction Inn, Halwill Junction (¾ mile).

Disabled facilities   Some swims suitable for disabled and wheelchair anglers.

COFTON PARK FARM
Atlas Page 201 D.6/6.0

A holiday caravan site with a small lake providing good mixed coarse fishing, located just north of Dawlish. Well stocked with roach, tench, skimmer bream and carp. Open all year round (no closed season).

How to get there   From Exeter take the A379 south towards Dawlish. Just after Starcross (after about 7 miles), look for signs to Cofton Park Farm and the fishery. Car parking available on site.

Day tickets   Adult £2.25; junior/OAP £1.50. Available on site; for details of availability, contact Mrs. Jeffery; Tel. 0626 890358.

Best methods/baits   Use general coarse techniques and baits.

Facilities   Caravan hire (static/touring) and camping on site. Also toilets/shops/swimming pool. Nearest pub in Starcross village.

Disabled facilities   Some swims may be suitable for disabled anglers; please phone for advice.

COOMBE WATER FISHERY
Atlas Page 201 C.9/6.9

A picturesque, 1-acre lake near Kingsbridge in south Devon, which provides excellent mixed fishing for bream, tench and carp.

How to get there   Head south-west from Totnes on the A381 to Kingsbridge. From Kingsbridge take the Loddiswell road. The lake is ½ mile on the right. (Well signposted).

Day tickets   Adult £4; junior/OAP £2. Available on site; for details of availability, contact the site owner, Mr. Robinson; Tel. 0548 852038.

Best methods/baits   Use general coarse techniques and baits. Specialist methods may be needed for carp.

Facilities   B&B available on site. Nearest shop/pub in Kingsbridge. Toilets on site.

Disabled facilities   Some swims are very suitable for disabled anglers; please check in advance.

DARRACOTT RESERVOIR, NR. TORRINGTON
Atlas Page 201 C.6/5.0

This 3-acre lake was re-opened in 1990 and produces good sport, with quality bags of roach, carp (to 14lb), tench and bream. Open all year, 24 hours a day.

How to get there   Take the A386 south-east from Bideford to Torrington; turn left opposite the church on minor road, bear right and follow signs to Huntshaw. The fishery is on the right; car parking on site.

Day tickets   Adult £2.75; junior/OAP/ disabled £1.75. 24-hour ticket: £5.50. Available from local tackle shops. For all other information; Tel. 0752 766897.

Best methods/baits   Use any recognised coarse technique and baits.

Restrictions   No carp in keepnets. Use only barbless hooks. No lead weights to be used. All fish must be returned to the water.

Facilities   Nearest shops and pubs in Torrington (2 miles).

HOGSBROOK LAKE
Atlas Page 201 D.5/5.8

Two lakes at a campsite at Salterton, just east of Exeter – one of 2½ acres and one of 1½ acres – open all year for mixed coarse fishing. Expect tench, roach and bream, plus some large carp up to 15lb.

How to get there   Leave the M5 at jct 30 (Exeter) and turn left onto the A3052 to Woodbury Salterton. Look for signs to the fishery. Car park (charged) on site.

Day tickets   Adult £3; junior/OAP £2. Evening ticket: £2. Available from Enterprise Angling, East Reach, Taunton; Tel. 0823 32855.

Best methods   Float or leger.

Best baits   Coloured maggots.

Restrictions   No fish under 1lb allowed in keepnets.

Facilities   Toilets/food available on the camp site.

Disabled facilities   Some swims suitable for disabled and wheelchair anglers.

INDIO POND
Atlas Page 201 D.5/5.8

An estate lake of 2 acres providing excellent coarse fishing plus top-class accommodation in Greywalls Lodge, near Bovey Tracey. Lots of perch, rudd, eels, trout and tench – added to very big carp approaching 30lb – means quality fishing. No closed season – open all year round.

How to get there   Take the M5 past Exeter onto the A38 and continue to Chudleigh roundabout (about 8 miles). Turn right onto the Bovey Tracey road (Newton Road) and continue for 1½ miles. The entrance to Greywalls Lodge is on the right, 200 yards after the old railway bridge. Car parking on site.

Day tickets   Fishing available for residents of Greywalls Lodge only. Details from the owner, Mr. Charlier, at his home on site; Tel. 0626 832508.

Best methods   Mixed species – use general coarse techniques and baits. Carp – use specialist carp methods.

Best baits   Carp – use hard boilies to deter tench.

Restrictions   No bolt rigs. Use only barbless hooks. No keepnets for carp. Fishing is from 0600 until dusk (night fishing only by arrangement).

Facilities   First class holiday accommodation available on site (B,B & EM). Nearest shops and pubs in Bovey Tracey.

Disabled facilities   Some swims may be suitable for disabled anglers; please phone for advice (see above).

JENNETTS, NR BIDEFORD
Atlas Page 201 C.6/5.0

An 8-acre reservoir which has gained a national reputation for its carp fishing, with consistent 20lb+ mirrors and commons, plus quality catches of roach. Open all year round, 0630–2200.

How to get there   Take the A386 south-east from Bideford towards Torrington; after about 1 mile look for a right turn to the lake. Car parking nearby.

Day tickets   Adult £3.25; junior/OAP/disabled £2.25. Available from local tackle shops. For all other information; Tel. 0752 766897.

Best methods/baits   Use any recognised coarse technique and baits. Pole and float preferred for roach.

Restrictions   No carp in keepnets. Use only barbless hooks. No lead weights to be used. All fish must be returned to the water.

Facilities   Nearest shops/pubs in Bideford (2 miles).

LITTLE COMFORT FARM
Atlas Page 201 C.5/4.5

A small (1 acre) farm lake situated at West Down, a few miles south of Ilfracombe. Quite deep, with 6ft in the middle, providing plenty of rudd, roach, bream, beautiful green tench and big perch, plus some very large carp (up to 20lb). A peaceful and very enjoyable fishery.

How to get there   From Barnstaple, take the A361 north towards Ilfracombe. Turn right at Headen Mill crossroads and continue for just over 1 mile. Turn left at the 2nd full crossroads, then left again at crossroads (after 100 yards). The farm is ¾ mile along this road. Free car parking on site.

Day tickets   Adult/junior/OAP £5. Half-day £4. Evening ticket £3. Charge covers two rods per person. Available from the farm in West Down, Braunton; Tel. 0271 812414. Please phone to check availability.

Best methods/baits   Use general coarse methods and baits.

Restrictions   Maximum 8 anglers on the lake.

Facilities   Toilets on site. Nearest shop and pub, The Crown, in West Down (¾ mile).

Disabled facilities   Some swims are suitable for disabled and wheelchair anglers.

LOWER TAMAR LAKE
Atlas Page 201 C.0/5.5

This 40-acre lake lies just south of Upper Tamar Lake, north-east of Bude on the Devon-Cornwall border. Expect good mixed fishing, with large carp (to 26lb+), tench, bream, rudd and roach. Bream nets of 50lb+ are quite common. Open all year round, 24 hours a day.

How to get there   From Bude, take the A39 north and turn right at Kilkhampton towards the lakes. Lower Tamar Lake is on the right; follow signs to car parks and access points to fishery.

Day tickets   Adult £3.25; junior/OAP/disabled £2.25. Also 24-hour tickets £6.50. Available from the machine in the car park, or from local tackle shops. Season tickets from the Ranger at Upper Tamar Lake; Tel. 0288 82262. For all other information; Tel. 0752 766897.

Best methods/baits   Use any recognised coarse technique and baits.

Restrictions   No carp in keepnets. Use only barbless hooks. No lead weights to be used. No cereal groundbaiting by hand (loosefeeding with hookbait and feeders allowed). All fish must be returned to the water.

Facilities   Nearest shop and pubs at Kilkhampton or Bradworthy (3 miles).

MELBURY, NR. BIDEFORD
Atlas Page 201 C.6/5.0

A 12-acre reservoir first opened in summer 1990. Excellent coarse fishing, with mirror carp (to 24lb+), plus good mixed bags of roach, rudd and bream. Open all year round, 0630–2200.

How to get there   Take the A39 west from Bideford to Fairy Cross (about 4 miles); turn left and follow signs to Parkham, then Melbury. At Melbury village, look for signs to the reservoir. Car parking nearby.

Day tickets   Adult £3.25; junior/OAP/ disabled £2.25. Available from local tackle shops. For all other information; Tel. 0752 766897.

Best methods/baits   Use any recognised coarse technique and baits.

Restrictions   No carp in keepnets. Use only barbless hooks. No lead weights to be used. All fish must be returned to the water.

Facilities   Nearest shop, Powlers Place Garage & Store (1 mile); nearest pubs, in Melbury or Parkham.

MILEHEAD
Atlas Page 201 C.6/6.3

A picturesque lake which is rich in wild life, on the outskirts of Tavistock. Excellent coarse fishing, including large tench (3lb+), roach, mirror carp (to 14lb) and ghost carp (to 5lb). Fishing is available all year round.

How to get there   Take the A384 from Tavistock towards Launceston; just on leaving Tavistock, take left turn (signposted Mill Hill) and continue for 1 mile. Entering the valley, Mill Hill Quarry is immediately ahead; the fishery entrance is on the right. Free car parking on site.

Day tickets   Adult/junior/OAP £3.50. Evening ticket: £2.35. Available on the banks.

Best methods/baits   Legered luncheon meat (small portions) is the best method here. Floatfish with maggot or caster also works well; floating crust is also effective in spring/summer.

Restrictions   No keepnets. Use only barbless hooks.

Facilities   Nearest shops and pubs in Tavistock.

Disabled facilities   Some swims may be suitable for disabled anglers; for advice, contact Andrew or Paul Evenden; Tel. 0822 610888.

MILL POND, BERRYNARBOR
Atlas Page 201 C.7/4.7

A 1½-acre lake set within a picturesque site at the lower end of a valley near Ilfracombe. Expect bream, carp, roach, perch, tench and an occasional brown trout – plus competition from herons!

How to get there   From Barnstaple, head north on the A39 to Blackmoor Gate (about 10 miles) and turn left onto A399 to Berrynarbor. Take 1st right after Watermouth Castle; Mill Park is on the left hand side. No car parking available.

Day tickets   Adult £3; junior/OAP £1.50. Available from Mill Park Touring Site, Berrynarbor, nr Ilfracombe, Devon; Tel. 0271 882647.

Best methods/baits   Use any recognised coarse technique.

Facilities   Toilets/showers/shop/food available on site; also 2 self-contained flats and 2 caravans for hire. Nearest pubs, The Globe and The Sawmill (5 mins walk each).

Disabled facilities   Some swims suitable for disabled and wheelchair anglers.

OLD MILL, DARTMOUTH
Atlas Page 201 D.5/6.8

A secluded, peaceful 4-acre reservoir which will provide a memorable day's fishing. Contains mirror and common carp (20lb+), roach (to 2lb) and tench. Also recently stocked with bream. Open all year round, 24 hours a day.

How to get there   From Dartmouth town centre, head north towards Chipton and Bruckton. The Old Mill is on the left as you approach the Dittisham road. Car parking nearby.

Day tickets   Adult £3.25; junior/OAP/ disabled £2.25. Also 24-hour tickets £6.50. Available from The Sport'n'Fish, 16 Fairfax Place, Dartmouth; Tel. 0803 833509. For all other information; Tel. 0752 766897.

Best methods/baits   Use any recognised coarse technique and baits.

Restrictions   No carp in keepnets. Use only barbless hooks. No lead weights to be used. No cereal groundbaiting by hand (loosefeeding with hookbait and feeders is allowed). All fish must be returned to the water.

Facilities   Nearest shops in Dartmouth; nearest pub, the Sportsmans Arms, Old Mill (1 mile).

RACKERHAYES
Atlas Page 201 D.5/6.3

This mature pit of about 5 acres is close to Newton Abbott racecourse, and provides some good fishing, with heavy stocks of carp from 10–30lb, plus most coarse species to add to the fun!

How to get there From Exeter, take the A38, then A380 to Newton Abbott. Approaching the town, bear right and follow signs to the racecourse. The entrance to the fishery is down a track, opposite the racecourse entrance. Car parking available on site.

Day tickets Adult/ junior/OAP £3. Available from Drum Sports, 47a Courtenay Street, Newton Abbott; Tel. 0626 65333 or Newton Abbot Angling Centre; Tel. 0626 55153. Associate Membership, adult £17; junior/OAP £4, from Dave Horder, 22 Mount Pleasant Road, Newton Abbot; Tel. 0626 64173.

Best methods/baits Use any recognised coarse technique and bait.

Restrictions Tickets are generally restricted to people living within 25 miles of Newton Abbott.

Facilities Nearest shops and pubs in Newton Abbott.

Disabled facilities Some swims may be suitable for disabled anglers; ask for advice at local tackle shops.

RIVERTON FISHERIES, SWIMBRIDGE
Atlas Page 201 C.8/4.8

Two lakes situated a few miles east of Barnstaple. One lake has predominantly roach, bream, perch and dace, plus some carp up to 5lb. The second lake has specimen carp (to 28lb), plus tench, rudd and a few bream and perch.

How to get there From Barnstaple, take the A36 east for about 5 miles to Swimbridge; look for signs to the fishery in the village. Free car parking on site.

Day tickets Adult £2.50; junior/OAP £2. Weekly ticket: £12. Available from Mr Cork, Riverton Fisheries, Swimbridge, Barnstaple, Devon.

Best methods/baits Use any recognised coarse technique.

Restrictions No carp under 2lb in keepnets.

Facilities Nearest shop in village (½ mile); nearest pub, The Jack Russell (1½ miles).

SIMPSON VALLEY FISHERY
Atlas Page 201 C.5/5.5

A multi-lake complex, three of ¼ acre, one of 1 acre, one of 1½ acres, set in a peaceful village east of Holsworthy. Plenty of tench, roach and rudd, some fairly large carp, with 16lb specimens taken in 1991.

How to get there From Holsworthy, head east on the A3072 towards Hatherleigh. Drive past the Water Board depot (on the right, after 1 mile), and turn into the next farm on the right (well signposted). Free parking on site.

Day tickets Adult £3; junior/OAP £1.50. Evening ticket: adult £2; junior/OAP £1. Available from Mr Simpson at the fishery; Tel. 0409 253593.

Best methods/bait Use any recognised coarse technique.

Restrictions No carp in keepnets. Use only barbless hooks. No cereal groundbait; boilies on hook only.

Facilities Some tackle/bait on site. Nearest shop/pubs: Holsworthy (1 mile).

Disabled facilities Some swims suitable for disabled and wheelchair anglers.

SLADE RESERVOIRS, NR. ILFRACOMBE
Atlas Page 201 C.5/5.4

A pair of lakes totalling 10 acres, both providing good coarse fishing. Upper Slade has carp, tench and huge roach (to 3½lb!); Lower Slade has carp, tench, bream, roach (to 2lb) and rudd. Bream nets alone can reach 40lb. Open all year, 24 hours a day.

How to get there From Ilfracombe, head south on the B3231 (signposted Lee); the fishery is near Slade village, about 1 mile on the left. Car parking on site.

Day tickets Adult £2.75; junior/OAP/ disabled £1.75. 24-hour ticket: £5.50. Available from Slade Post Office or local tackle shops. For all other information; Tel. 0752 766897.

Best methods/baits Use any recognised coarse technique and baits.

Restrictions No carp in keepnets. Use only barbless hooks. No lead weights to be used. No cereal groundbaiting by hand (loosefeeding with hookbait and feeders allowed). All fish must be returned to the water.

Facilities Nearest shop, the Post Office and Store, in Slade. There are several pubs nearby, and in Ilfracombe.

SOUTH FARM PONDS
Atlas Page 201 E.2/5.6

Two small farm ponds, a few miles north-west of Honiton, in a complex offering holiday homes for hire in addition to good coarse fishing. Expect plenty of tench, roach and carp. No closed season – fishing available all year round.

How to get there   Leave the M5 at jct 28 and take the A373 towards Honiton. After about 1½ miles, turn left on minor roads to Kentisbeare and Blackborough. At Blackborough, look for South Farm and follow signs to the fishery. Car parking available on site.

Day tickets   Available only to holiday home residents; contact Mr. Donnithorne at the farm; Tel. 0823 681078.

Best methods/baits   Use general coarse techniques and baits.

Facilities   Holiday homes (games room/swimming pool etc) for hire on site. Also toilets. Nearest shop/pub in Blackborough.

Disabled facilities   Some swims may be suitable for disabled anglers; please phone for advice.

SOUTH REID FISHERIES
Atlas Page 201 C.8/5.8

A 3½-acre lake for general mixed coarse fishing, plus a similar-sized carp lake, located just west of Okehampton. Expect bream (to 4lb), roach and rudd, but very large carp (to 23lb) and good-sized tench.

How to get there   From Okehampton, drive westward on the B3218 (about 5 miles) to Boasley Cross; the fishery is well signposted in the village. Free car parking on site.

Day tickets   Adult/junior/OAP £4. Carp lake £6. Available from Bill Gray, South Reid Fisheries, Boasley Cross, Bratton Clovelly, Okehampton; Tel. 083787 295.

Best methods   Pole is preferred method.

Best baits   Most baits work well.

Restrictions   No carp in keepnets. Use only barbless hooks.

Facilities   Camping and caravanning facilities available. Nearest shop and pub, Royal Oak in Bridestowe (2 miles).

Disabled facilities   Some swims suitable for disabled and wheelchair anglers.

SQUABMOOR
Atlas Page 201 E.0/6.0

A picturesque, 4-acre lake set on Woodbury Common, in the heart of a site of special scientific interest (SSSI). Expect some very big fish, with 20lb carp, 5lb+ tench and huge roach of 3lb+! Open all year round, 24 hours a day.

How to get there   Within Budleigh Salterton town centre, take the B3179 north for about 1½ miles; turn right on minor road towards East Budleigh. The lake is on the right; car parking nearby.

Day tickets   Adult £2.75; junior/OAP/ disabled £1.75. 24-hour ticket: £5.50. Available from Knowle Post Office or local tackle shops.For all other information; Tel. 0752 766897.

Best methods/baits   Use any recognised coarse technique and baits.

Restrictions   No carp in keepnets. Use only barbless hooks. No lead weights to be used. No cereal groundbaiting by hand (loosefeeding with hookbait and feeders allowed). All fish must be returned to the water.

Facilities   Nearest shops and pubs are in Woodbury or East Budleigh.

RIVER TAW, NEWBRIDGE
Atlas Page 201 C.8/4.8

A stretch of the River Taw, ½ mile downstream from the bridge, on the right bank. Fairly fast water, with pools; muddy water at high tide, but clears rapidly (within 2 hours). Expect mainly roach.

How to get there   Take the A377 south-east from Barnstaple to where the road crosses the River Taw (Newbridge, about 1 mile). Free road parking by the gates.

Day tickets   Free fishing from the notice 'End of Club Water'.

Best methods/baits   Use any recognised coarse technique.

Restrictions   No worms.

Facilities   Nearest shop/pub in Bishop's Tawton (1 mile).

TRENCHFORD
Atlas Page 201 C.8/6.8

A scenic, 33-acre reservoir on the eastern edge of Dartmoor, providing specialist pike fishing for specimens up to 30lb. Fishing in season only, 1st October to 14th March (incl.); from 1 hour before sunrise to 1 hour after sunset.

How to get there   From Exeter, take the A38 south-east to Chudleigh and bear right to Bovey Tracey. Turn right onto minor road and follow signs to reservoirs. Car parking on site.

Day tickets   Adult £3.25; junior/OAP/disabled £2.25.Available from the ticket machine at Kennick Reservoir (adjacent). For all other information; Tel. 0752 766897.

Best methods/baits   Specialist pike-fishing tackle. Use spinner, plug, worm or dead seafish bait.

Facilities   Nearest shop/pub in Bovey Tracey.

UPHAM FARM
Atlas Page 201 D.6/5.8

A six-pond complex on a farm a few miles east of Exeter. A good mixed fishery in a secluded spot, producing mainly tench and large carp (20lb+). The record to date is a 24lb 6oz common. No closed season – fishing available all year round.

How to get there   Leave the M5 at jct 30 and head east on the A3052 towards Seaton. After about 3½ miles, look for left turn to Farringdon village. Follow signs to Upham Farm and the fishery. Car parking available on site.

Day tickets   Adult £3; junior under 14s £2; OAP/disabled £1.50. Additional charge of £1 for second rod. Available at the farm; for details, contact Mr. Willcocks; Tel. 0395 32247. Parties welcome, but if more than 20, advance booking needed.

Best methods/baits   Use general coarse techniques and baits.

Facilities   Nearest shop/pub in Farringdon.

Restrictions   Limited groundbait. No peanuts or tiger nuts.

Disabled facilities   Some swims are suitable for disabled anglers; please phone for advice.

VENN POND
Atlas Page 201 C.8/4.8

A disused quarry, very deep and steep-sided, a few miles outside Barnstaple. Good fishing, but essentially all bottom-feeders, with plenty of carp, tench and bream.

How to get there   Take the A361 south-east from Barnstaple about 3 miles to Landkey; turn right at Venn Farms and drive over Venn Stream to the pits. Free parking, but very limited.

Day tickets   Adult £1.50; junior/OAP 50p. Weekly (Mon-Fri) ticket: adult £5; junior/OAP £2.Available from North Devon Angling Centre, Bear Street, Barnstaple; Tel. 0271 45191.

Best methods   Carp, tench, bream – feeder.

Best baits   Most baits work well.

Facilities   Nearest shop and pubs, The Castle and The Ring o' Bell, Landkey (1 mile).

WEST PITT FARM POOL
Atlas Page 201 D.5/5.4

This small farm pool, about 5 miles north-east of Tiverton, provides some good coarse fishing sport for roach, rudd, tench and carp – mirrors caught here in recent years have weighed well over 20lb.

How to get there   Leave the M5 at jct 27 and take the A373 towards Tiverton. After about ½ mile, turn right on minor road, signposted to Whitnage and Uplowman. Follow the road to Uplowman and to West Pitt Farm. Car parking available on site.

Day tickets   Adult/junior/OAP £3.50. Available at the farm; for details, contact Mrs. Bent; Tel. 0884 820296.

Best methods/baits   Use general coarse techniques and baits, plus carp methods as required.

Facilities   Farmhouse accommodation available on site. Also toilets. Nearest shop/pub in Uplowman.

Disabled facilities   Some swims suitable for disabled anglers.

Welsh Region

Wintery scenery showing the inaccessible side to Welsh fishing.

Coarse fishing in the Welsh NRA region, which incorporates most – though not all of Wales – is limited mainly to the extreme southern and northern areas of the country – perhaps not surprisingly since the centre of Wales is dominated by fairly inaccessible mountainous areas where coarse fishing sites are few and far between.

In south Wales, fishing sport is concentrated around Glamorgan and Gwent, with river angling centred on the River Wye, which rises in mid-Wales and flows to the Severn Estuary, providing excellent coarse fishing in its lower reaches. Similarly, a tributary of the Wye – the Monnow – which meets the Wye at Monmouth, also produces top quality coarse fish. In addition to the river fisheries, a number of small lakes have recently become available, with surprisingly good results which should improve.

In the north, lake fishing predominates, with Anglesey and Gwynedd the main areas of interest. All such stillwater venues enjoy good reputations for containing large carp and also pike, while – if required – many of the fisheries can also provide fishing holiday packages for the family or enthusiast angler alike.

CLWYD

BANGOR-ON-DEE
Atlas Page 204 C.9/5.1

A pleasant stretch of the River Dee, almost 2 miles using both banks, from the village to the old railway bridge. Good coarse fishing, with lots of chub, grayling, dace and eels, plus some very good pike. Also the occasional perch and trout.

How to get there   From Wrexham, head south-east on the A525 for about 5 miles to Bangor-is-y-Coed (generally referred to as Bangor-on-Dee). Parking and access to the river is at various points along the stretch; check at Brunner's Newsagent; Tel. 0978 780073.

Day tickets   Adult/junior/OAP £1.75. Season ticket £8.50. Available from Brunner's (see above).

Best methods/baits   Use general coarse methods and baits.

Restrictions   From 1st January to 1st April, fishing is limited to between the two town bridges.

Facilities   Nearest shops and pubs, The Buck House or the Royal Oak, in the village.

BRICKWORKS, PARK DERWEN
Atlas Page 204 C.2/4.4

A fairly large area of water (7½ acres) which has been split into two pools, on the outskirts of Rhyl. A pleasant fishery providing good sport, with roach, rudd, Crucian carp, tench and eels. Some very big carp have been taken in these waters.

How to get there   From Rhyl town centre drive over the railway bridge to Dale Road and take 1st right into Marsh Road. Continue to Fford Derwen Road, when the pool will be visible from the road. Free car parking on site.

Day tickets   Free fishing.

Best methods/baits   Use general coarse methods and baits.

Restrictions   No bloodworm.

Facilities   Marsh Road caravan site (with shops and pub) is nearby. Nearest shop, Ceavend Road (5 mins walk); nearest pub, 'Caskky's' (2 mins walk).

Disabled facilities   The concrete jetty has ramps suitable for use by disabled and wheelchair anglers.

LLANGOLLEN CANAL
Atlas Page 204 C.6/5.2

A very long canal – about 35 miles in all – flowing from Llangollen east to Nantwich in Cheshire. Fishing is variable along the canal's length, but expect mainly roach, dace, gudgeon, chub, perch and eels. A particularly good section is at Chirk (on the A5, north of Oswestry), where 50lb match nets have been taken recently.

How to get there   From Llangollen, the canal heads east to Nantwich, generally along the A539/A525/A530 roads. For details of best access and parking points, check with local tackle shops along the route.

Day tickets   Adult/junior/OAP £1. Available on the bank.

Best methods/baits   Use general coarse methods and baits.

Facilities   Various shops and pubs along the route.

Disabled facilities   Some swims may be suitable for disabled and wheelchair anglers; check with local tackle shops before fishing.

LLYN ALED
Atlas Page 204 B.9/4.7

A large 110-acre lake about 10 miles south-west of Denbigh. Good quality coarse fishing, with large numbers of roach, rudd, perch, Crucian carp, tench and pike. No fishing in the closed season, 14th March to 16th June.

How to get there   Take the A5 west from Llangollen to Cerrigydrudion (about 20 miles) and turn right onto B4501. Drive past the Llyn Brenig Information Centre and continue to the junction with the A543. Turn left, past the Sportsman's Arms pub and turn right (opposite Alwen Reservoir); Llyn Aled is the first lake. Free car parking on site.

Day tickets   Adult £2; junior/OAP £1.50. Available from Llyn Brenig Information centre; Tel. 049082 463 (if closed, tickets may be purchased from the car park).

Best methods/baits   Use general coarse methods and baits. Legering on swimfeeder is most successful method. Most baits work well here.

Restrictions   Fishing only from 0800 until 1 hour after sunset.

Facilities   Nearest shop, in Pentrefoelas (4 miles); nearest pub, The Sportsman's Arms (really good food, 2 miles).

Disabled facilities   Some swims are suitable for disabled and wheelchair anglers (with assistance).

DYFED

The peace and quiet.

LILY PONDS, BOSHERSTON
Atlas Page 200 B.5/3.1

A group of three lakes (only two fishable), about 6 miles south of Pembroke. In all, about 40–50 acres of fishing, with mainly roach, tench (up to 6lb) and big eels, plus some good-sized pike of up to 26lb.

How to get there   From Pembroke, take the B4319 south through St. Petrox and follow signs to Stackpole and Bosherston. Bear left towards Stackpole and The Court Site. Limited parking is available on the east side.

Day tickets   Adult £2; junior/OAP/unemployed £1. Available from Mr Gregson at the Olde Worlde Cafe, Bosherston; Tel. 0646 661216, or from local tackle shops.

Best methods/baits   Use general coarse methods and baits.

Restrictions   No fishing in the middle lake, which is an SSSI.

Facilities   Cafe/toilets at Bosherston. Also self-catering group accommodation (Nov-March). Nearest shops, Pembroke (6 miles); nearest pub, St. Govan's Inn, Bosherston.

Disabled facilities   Some swims are suitable for disabled and wheelchair anglers, with assistance. There is also a disabled centre adjacent to the lakes; facilities are available with notice.

LLYN CARFAN
Atlas Page 200 B.9/2.7

A small, picturesque, 1½-acre, kidney-shaped pool, with tree cover on one side, about 8 miles north-east of Tenby. Quite deep (12–13ft) at one end, but shallowing to 6ft in general. Expect large carp (to 20lb) plus good roach, tench (6lb+), mirror carp, rudd and grass carp. A very pleasant fishery providing good sport.

How to get there   Take the A40 west from Carmarthen to Whitland. In the town centre, turn right into St. John's Street, drive over the level crossing and turn right to Lampeter Velfrey. After 2 miles, turn left to Tavernspite; the lake is 1 mile further on. Free car parking on site.

Day tickets   Adult £3.50; junior/OAP £1.50. Available from Hugh John, Carfan-y-Ddol, Whitland, Dyfed; Tel. 0994 240819.

Best methods/baits   Use general coarse methods and baits.

Facilities   Nearest shops and pubs, in Tavernspite or Whitland (2 miles).

Disabled facilities   Some swims are suitable for disabled and wheelchair anglers. In good weather, parking is possible very close to the water.

RAIN PONDS
Atlas Page 200 B.9/2.6

A long, narrow, 2-acre natural pond which has been landscaped to provide plenty of tree and shrub growth, just north of Tenby. Well stocked for over 3 years with large carp (25lb+), tench (8lb+) and roach, plus some smaller Crucians and perch. Natural food levels are high here in summer, making fishing more of a problem.

How to get there   Take the A477 west from Carmarthen towards Pembroke. Continue for about 1 mile beyond the Broadmoor crossroads (about 14 miles from Carmarthen) and look for signs on right-hand side to Rain Ponds. Free car parking on site.

Day tickets   Adult £3; junior/OAP £1.50. Two rods per person. Available on the bank.

Best methods/baits   Use general coarse methods and baits.

Restrictions   No boilies (shelf-life). Use only barbless hooks. Use only lead-free weights.

Facilities   Nearest shop and pub, The Cross Inn, Broadmoor crossroads (½ mile).

Disabled facilities   Some swims are suitable for disabled and wheelchair anglers. Parking is possible close to the water.

WEST ORIELTON LAKE
Atlas Page 200 B.4/3.2

A boot-shaped lake which has woodland on the lower side and fields on the upper side. A popular, peaceful fishery, just south-west of Pembroke, with good-sized tench, roach, perch and eels, plus some very big pike (to 22lb). In dry summers, the noise from the irrigation pumps can be a pain!

How to get there   From the ring road at Pembroke head west on the B4320, signposted to the Texaco refinery and the Power Station. At Hundleton (about

1½ miles) park (free) at the Speculation Inn and walk (about ¼ mile) to the lake.

Day tickets Adult £2; junior/OAP/ unemployed £1. Available from the Speculation Inn, Hundleton, nr Pembroke; Tel. 0646 661306.

Best methods Use general coarse methods. Spinning preferred for pike.

Best baits Tench – use luncheon meat or sweetcorn. Pike – use livebait.

Facilities Nearest shop, Hundleton (1 mile); nearest pub, Speculation Inn (½ mile).

Disabled facilities Fishing from the dam is suitable for disabled and wheelchair anglers; assistance is needed for access.

GLAMORGAN

A long night ahead.

BRYNMILL PARK
Atlas Page 200 D.1/3.3

A busy park just outside Swansea where fishing is good but too much interest from passers-by can cause problems! An excellent variety of fish, with carp (to 25lb), tench (to 6lb) and bream (to 8lb).

How to get there Brynmill is just in the outskirts of Swansea, on the A4067 Swansea-Mumbles road. Look for signs to the park. No parking available.

Day tickets Adult/junior/OAP £2.50. Season ticket: adult £16; junior/OAP £5. Limited pegs (25). Tickets available from P. E. Mainwaring, 9 Dillwyn Road, Sketty, Swansea; Tel. 0792 202245.

Best methods Float, leger and feeder are best methods.

Best baits Maggots, sweetcorn, worms.

Restrictions No spinning.

Facilities Toilets/childrens play area in park plus small wildlife park. Nearest shop/pub in Brynmill village.

Disabled facilities Some swims suitable for disabled anglers.

BUTE TOWN RESERVOIR
Atlas Page 200 D.9/2.9

A fairly small (80 pegs) reservoir which lies about midway between Merthyr Tydfil and Ebbw Vale. A good mixed fishery containing roach, bream, perch, chub, tench and carp. Expect a good day's sport here.

How to get there From Merthyr Tydfil, head east on the A465 towards Ebbw Vale. The reservoir is on the right, after about 4 miles. Free car parking on site.

Day tickets Adult/junior/OAP £2. Available from Bute Post Office; fishing is allowed only on the day of purchase.

Best methods Use waggler, pole or feeder with groundbait and maggots.

Best baits Use bread, maggots, caster and hemp.

Facilities Nearest shop, ¼ mile; nearest pub, ½ mile.

CAERPHILLY CASTLE LAKES
Atlas Page 200 E.2/3.6

A combined fishery comprising two lakes and the castle moat, in the centre of Caerphilly. Expect mixed fishing, including tench, bream, roach, carp and pike.

How to get there Drive to Caerphilly town centre and follow signs to the castle. Car parking nearby.

Day tickets Adult £2; junior/OAP £1. Available from Tony's Tackle, 14 Castle Street, Caerphilly; Tel. 0222 885409/867513.

Best methods/baits Use any recognised coarse technique and baits.

Facilities Nearest toilets/shops/pubs in Caerphilly.

CLYNE VALLEY POND
Atlas Page 200 D.0/3.3

A newly-opened fishery near Swansea. Although small, the pond has a good head of roach, rudd and skimmer bream. Also excellent leisure facilities in pleasant surroundings.

How to get there   Take the A4067 Swansea-Mumbles road and at Black Pill look for signs to the Clyne Valley Bike Track. Car parking available (charged).
Day tickets   Adult/junior/OAP £2.50. Season ticket: adult £16; junior/OAP £5. Available from P. E. Mainwaring, 9 Dillwyn Road, Sketty, Swansea; Tel. 0792 202245.
Best methods/baits   Use any recognised coarse technique and baits.
Restrictions   No spinning.
Facilities   Picnic area/bike track/nature walks on site. Nearest shop/pub at Black Pill (½ mile).
Disabled facilities   Some swims suitable for disabled anglers.

DOLYGAER RESERVOIR
Atlas Page 200 D.9/2.9

A small reservoir located at the southern end of the main Pontsticill reservoir, about 3 miles north of Merthyr Tydfil. Quite deep water (8–12ft), providing good-sized roach, bream, carp and a good head of tench, plus some large pike between 30–40lb.

How to get there   Take the A465 from Ebbw Vale to Merthyr Tydfil and follow signs to Dolygaer reservoir. Free car parking on site.
Day tickets   Adult £2; junior/OAP £1.50. Available from Cefn Coed Fishing Tackle, 185 High Street, Cefn Coed, West Glamorgan; Tel. 0685 79809.
Best methods   Use pole with sliding float or leger with feeder.
Best baits   Maggots or bread. Use hemp and casters in feeder.
Restrictions   Only seafish and artificial spinners to be used for pike.
Facilities   Nearest shop and pub, 1 mile.

GNOLL POND
Atlas Page 200 D.2/3.2

A small mixed fishery comprising only 20 pegs, located on a municipal golf course at Gnoll Park, just outside Neath. Most species are taken here, but catches also include some very big carp of 20lb+.

How to get there   From Neath town centre, take the road to Tonmawr; Gnoll Park and the golf course are signposted on the left hand side (after about ½ mile). Free car parking on site.
Day tickets   Adult £2.50; junior/OAP £1. Available on the day, from the golf hut. For details, contact Ann's Pantry, 63 Old Road, Neath; Tel. 0639 645784.
Best methods/baits   Use a pole or waggler for most species. Specialist methods may be needed for carp.
Best baits   Maggots, bread and boilies.
Restrictions   No night fishing.
Facilities   Toilets on site.

LADBROKES
Atlas Page 200 D.1/3.3

Swansea's newest fishing water, with plenty of swims (over 80 pegs) and good background cover. Stocking is currently being carried out, so sport is steadily improving.

How to get there   From Swansea city centre, head for the northern outskirts of Morriston. Follow the main road into Llansamlet Industrial Estate; the lake is just beyond the Morganite factory. Free car parking on site.
Day tickets   Adult/junior/OAP £2.50. Season ticket: adult £16; junior/OAP £5. Available from P. E. Mainwaring, 9 Dillwyn Road, Sketty, Swansea; Tel. 0792 202245; or from Tourist Information Centre, Swansea.
Best methods/baits   Use any recognised coarse technique and baits.
Restrictions   No spinning.
Facilities   Nearest shops/pubs in Llansamlet.
Disabled facilities   Some swims suitable for disabled anglers.

NEATH CANAL
Atlas Page 200 D.3/3.2

A 6-mile stretch of canal along which facilities are currently being improved and weed cleared. Having been fished very lightly for 10 years, the water has developed some very good specimen fish, including large tench (to 8lb), bream (to 5lb), perch and double-figure carp. Fishing is best in coloured water, after the rain.

How to get there Leave the M4 at jct
41A and take A474 to Briton Ferry and
Neath by-pass. Access to the canal (and
parking in adjoining streets) is at various
points along the water's length; for
details, contact Ann's Pantry, 63A Old
Road, Melyn, Neath; Tel. 0639 645784.
Day tickets Adult £1; junior/OAP 50p.
Available from Ann's Pantry (see above).
Best methods Use pole or waggler. Light
leger is best in winter.
Best baits Maggots, squatts, flake,
boilies, hemp, tares, worms.
Restrictions No bloodworm.
Facilities Various facilities/shops
currently under construction. Nearest
pubs, four within 1 mile.
Disabled facilities Some swims nearer
the town centre are suitable for disabled
and wheelchair anglers (caution needed
– there are no barriers).

OGILVIE LAKE
Atlas Page 200 D.9/3.1
A recently-created lake on the site of the
old Ogilvie Quarry at Bargoed. Expect
reasonable mixed coarse fishing from new
water.

How to get there From Tredegar, take
the A469 south towards Bargoed and
turn off to Deri (about 6 miles). Turn
right by the Bargoed Inn and follow
signs to the lake.
Day tickets Adult £1.50; junior/OAP
70p. Available on the bank.
Best methods/baits Use any recognised
coarse technique and baits.
Facilities Nearest shop in Deri; nearest
pub, Bargoed Inn.

PLUCK POND
Atlas Page 200 D.0/3.3
A small (17 pegs only) but up-and-coming
angling venue, in Swansea city, next to
the Morfa athletics stadium. An excellent
variety of small coarse fish, including
skimmer bream (to 2lb) and eels (to 3lb).

How to get there In Swansea city, follow
signs to the athletics stadium. Park
nearby.
Day tickets Adult/junior/OAP £1.
Available from Sports & Recreation
Department of Swansea City Council, at
the Guildhall. Tickets cover fishing at
all Swansea City-controlled venues.

Best methods/baits Use any recognised
coarse technique and baits.
Facilities Nearest shop/pub in Swansea.

PONTSTICILL RESERVOIR
Atlas Page 200 D.9/2.9
A very large (365 acres) reservoir which
lies about 4 miles north of Merthyr Tydfil.
Very deep water (up to 60ft), providing
some very large roach approaching 2½lb,
plus good quality bream, carp and tench.
The occasional monster pike – some in
the region of 40lb – may also put in an
appearance!

How to get there Take the A465 from
Ebbw Vale to Merthyr Tydfil and follow
signs to Pontsticill reservoir. Free car
parking on site.
Day tickets Adult £2; junior/OAP £1.50.
Available from Cefn Coed Fishing
Tackle, 185 High Street, Cefn Coed,
West Glamorgan; Tel. 0685 79809.
Best methods Use pole with sliding float
or leger with feeder.
Best baits Maggots or bread. Use hemp
and casters in feeder.
Restrictions Only seafish and artificial
spinners to be used for pike.
Facilities Nearest shop and pub, 1 mile.

PWLL-Y-WYNE
Atlas Page 200 D.4/3.7
A small (20 pegs), shallow lake, situated
on the outskirts of Porthcawl. Contains
plenty of summer bream, tench, roach and
rudd, as well as double-figure carp; the
record carp here is 18lb+. Fishing is best
when there is a ripple on the water.

How to get there Leave the M4 at jct 35
(approaching Bridgend) and follow the
A4106 towards Porthcawl. After about 8
miles, turn right towards Newton; the
lake is about ½ mile on the left-hand
side, visible from the road. Free car
parking on site.
Day tickets Adult £3; junior/OAP £1.50.
Available from A & J Ivey, The Mace
Shop, 2 Cilparc, Porthcawl;
Tel. 0656 783371.
Best methods Most species – use
waggler or pole. Carp – use leger rig.
Best baits Maggots, casters and hemp.
Try boilies for carp (but in moderation).
Restrictions No floating baits. Carp
must not be kept in keepnets. No night
fishing.

Facilities   Nearest shop, 300 yards;
nearest pub, about ½ mile.
Disabled facilities   Some swims are
suitable for disabled and wheelchair
anglers.

ROATH PARK LAKE
Atlas Page 200 E.3/3.8

A large, oval, 4-acre park lake controlled
by Cardiff Corporation. Quite well
stocked, mainly with roach but also
containing tench and rudd. Also some
good-sized carp (to 20lb+) but these are
difficult to catch.

How to get there   Take the A48 from
Bridgend to Cardiff and turn off at Heath
Hospital to City Centre/Merthyr Tydfil.
At the roundabout, head towards Roath
and turn left at The Heath pub. Follow
the road alongside the cemetery, take
1st right (Wedal Road), then left past
park to the lake. Free parking on site.
Day tickets   Adult £1.50; junior/OAP
75p. Available on the bank, or from the
park-keeper.
Best methods/baits   Good water for pole
or float fishing. Most baits work well
here. Specialist methods may be needed
for carp.
Restrictions   No night fishing. No fishing
on the islands.
Facilities   Toilets on site. Nearest shops
and pub, The Discovery, in Lakeside (20
mins walk).
Disabled facilities   Fishing stage at one
end of the lake is suitable for disabled
and wheelchair anglers.

SINGLETON BOATING LAKE
Atlas Page 200 D.0/3.3

A well-established fishery with a wide
selection of coarse fish, just to the west of
Swansea. Also a boating lake (hire boats
available), an ideal venue for family days
out.

How to get there   Take the A4067
Swansea-Mumbles road; the boating
lake is midway between the University
and the hospital. Car parking available
(50p).
Day tickets   Adult/junior/OAP £2.50.
Season ticket: adult £16; junior/OAP £5.
Available from P. E. Mainwaring, 9
Dillwyn Road, Sketty, Swansea;
Tel. 0792 202245; or from Tourist
Information Centre, Swansea.

Best methods   Most methods work; float
or leger preferred.
Best baits   Maggots, boilies, worms.
Restrictions   No spinning or lures.
Facilities   Toilets/cafe/bar/childrens play
area/crazy golf on site. Nearest shop/
pub in Sketty.
Disabled facilities   Some swims suitable
for disabled and wheelchair anglers.

SKEWEN ANGLING
Atlas Page 200 D.2/3.2

A fishing 'complex' incorporating a stretch
of the Tennant Canal and two ponds (4
and 6 acres). An excellent choice of coarse
fishing, with large carp (to 18lb), rudd,
bream (to 5lb+), perch and dace, plus quite
big pike (to 14lb).

How to get there   Leave the M4 at jct
41A and take A474 to Briton Ferry and
Neath by-pass. Fish either on the
Tennant Canal or on ponds. For details,
contact Ann's Pantry, 63A Old Road,
Melyn, Neath; Tel. 0639 645784.
Day tickets   Season tickets: adult £10;
junior/OAP £3.50. Available from Ann's
Pantry (see above).
Best methods   Use any recognised coarse
technique.
Best baits   Bread flake, maggots, boilies.
Restrictions   No bloodworm. Maximum
2 rods per person.
Facilities   Nearest pubs, four within
½ mile.

SQUARE POND
Atlas Page 200 D.2/3.2

A small mixed fishery at Briton Ferry, just
outside Neath. Contains plenty of large
bream (to 6lb), roach, perch, tench, rudd
and some large eels. Best sport is for carp,
with several over 20lb and lots of fish into
double figures.

How to get there   Leave the M4 at jct 43
(Briton Ferry) and follow the A474
towards Neath town centre. Drive past
the hospital on the right-hand side and
park (free) in the side road opposite the
railway crossing. Follow the footpath
over the canal bridge to the pond.
Day tickets   Adult £3; junior/OAP £1.50.
Available from Ann's Pantry, 63 Old
Road, Neath; Tel. 0639 645784.

Best methods   Use pole or waggler for most species; use specialist methods for carp.

Best baits   Maggots, bread, casters or hemp. Special baits may be needed for carp.

Facilities   Nearest shop, 300 yards; nearest pub, the Eaglesbush Inn, 500 yards.

TENNANT CANAL
Atlas Page 200 D.2/3.2

Several miles of canal fishing in a rural area; a favourite with both pleasure and match anglers. A shallow stretch, but good bags expected, with 30–40lb of bream and tench quite common. Also some large pike (to 15lb).

How to get there   Access to the canal is at points from Neath to Skewen, along the line of the A465. For details of access and parking, contact Ann's Pantry, 63 Old Road, Neath; Tel. 0639 645784.

Day tickets   Season tickets only. Adult £12; junior/OAP/disabled £3.50. Available from Ann's Pantry (see above).

Best methods/baits   Use any recognised coarse technique and baits.

Facilities   Various shops/pubs along the canal stretch.

WILDERNESS POOL
Atlas Page 200 D.3/3.7

A fairly small (35 pegs), shallow pool on the outskirts of Porthcawl. Contains plenty of summer bream, tench, roach and rudd. Fishing is best when there is a ripple on the water.

How to get there   Leave the M4 at jct 35 (approaching Bridgend) and follow the A4106 towards Porthcawl. After about 8 miles, turn right towards Newton; the pool is about ¾ mile on the left-hand side, visible from the road and just beyond Pwll-y-Wyne lake. Free car parking on site.

Day tickets   Adult £3; junior/OAP £1.50. Available from A & J Ivey, The Mace Shop, 2 Cilparc, Porthcawl; Tel. 0656 783371.

Best methods   Most species – use waggler or pole. Carp – use leger rig.

Best baits   Maggots, casters and hemp. Try boilies for carp (but in moderation).

Restrictions   No floating baits. Carp must not be kept in keepnets. No night fishing.

Facilities   Nearest shop, 150 yards; nearest pub, about ¾ mile.

GWENT

Rudd.

BRYN BACH PARK
Atlas Page 200 D.9/2.9

A popular 36-acre lake, with three islands, all in a pleasant setting, at Tredegar. Water sports on the far side do not interfere with fishing. Expect roach, bream, carp, tench, gudgeon and a few dace. An excellent 'family' fishery.

How to get there   Take the A465 east from Merthyr Tydfil and at the Tredegar roundabout (about 4 miles) follow signs to Bryn Bach Park. Turn towards the town and after about 60 yards turn right; the park is further down the road, on the left. Free car parking on site.

Day tickets   Adult £1; junior/OAP 50p. Available on the bank, or at the Clubhouse.

Best methods/baits   Use general coarse methods and baits.

Facilities   Toilets/food/childrens facilities/souvenir shop on site. Nearest shop, Tredegar (½ mile); nearest pub, just across the road.

CEFN GOLAU
Atlas Page 200 D.9/2.9

A pleasant, spoon-shaped, 3½-acre lake (with an island) at Tredegar, which provides good quality carp, roach, tench, rudd and gudgeon in quite large numbers.

How to get there   Located on the outskirts of Tredegar; directions can be confusing, so for advice, contact Tiles & Tackle, 108 Commercial Street, Tredegar; Tel. 0495 717001.

Day tickets   Adult/junior/OAP £1.50; available from Tiles & Tackle (see above). Or £3 at the lakeside.

Best methods/baits   Use general coarse methods and baits.

Restrictions   No night fishing.

Facilities   Nearest shop and pub, in Tredegar (½ mile).

Disabled facilities   In summer, some swims are suitable for disabled and wheelchair anglers.

RIVER MONNOW, MALTHOUSE FARM
Atlas Page 200 E.7/2.6

A small farm lake located midway between Abergavenny and Ross-on-Wye, with deep water (up to 15ft) with good catches of chub, dace, carp, roach and grayling, plus king-sized gudgeon!

How to get there   From Abergavenny, take the B4521 north-east to Skenfrith (about 10 miles). In the village, turn left; Malthouse Farm is 150 yards past the church, on the right. Park on the roadside by the farm.

Day tickets   Adult/junior/OAP £1.50. Available from Mr. W. Price at the farm; Tel. 060084 219.

Best methods/baits   Use general coarse methods and baits.

Facilities   Nearest shop, Broad Oak garage (2 miles); nearest pub, The Bell, in Skenfrith village.

Disabled facilities   Some swims are suitable for disabled and wheelchair anglers.

RIVER MONNOW, SKENFRITH BRIDGE
Atlas Page 200 E.7/2.6

An excellent river fishery at Skenfrith, near Monmouth, with left-bank fishing 100 yards above the bridge and 250 yards

below, to the weir. The water is deep and slow-moving to the weir, but quickens after leaving the weirpool. Expect large fish here, with double-figure carp and chub approaching the Welsh record.

How to get there   From Abergavenny, take the B4521 north-east to Skenfrith (about 10 miles). In the village, access to the river is near the bridge; for details of best fishing, contact The Priory Motel in the village; Tel. 060084 210.

Day tickets   Adult £2.50; junior/OAP £1.25. Available from The Priory Motel (see above).

Best methods/baits   Use general coarse methods and baits.

Restrictions   Use any coarse method until the trout season begins; thereafter, fish only to the weir.

Facilities   Nearest shop, Broad Oak garage (2 miles); nearest pub, The Bell, in Skenfrith village.

RIVER MONNOW, MONMOUTH
Atlas Page 200 E.7/2.7

Two river stretches close to Monmouth town centre: the first extends from the Old Town Bridge upstream for ¾ mile; the second from above the weir for ¾ mile. Expect deep (up to 12ft), slow-moving water which contains 34 varieties of fish, including carp, tench, bream, pike, dace and large chub.

How to get there   The first stretch is in Monmouth town centre. To reach the second, take the B4233 north-west towards Rockfield; after about 150 yards look for a track signposted as a footpath – drive down this to the weir. Free car parking near the water.

Day tickets   Adult £2; junior/OAP £1. Available from either Mr. Holloway, Monnow Lodge; Tel. 0600 714381; or from The Monmouthshire Sportsman, St. James Street, Monmouth; Tel. 0600 715289.

Best methods/baits   Use general coarse methods and baits.

Facilities   Nearest shops and pubs in Monmouth town centre.

RIVER MONNOW, ROCKFIELD
Atlas Page 200 E.7/2.7

A very pleasant river fishery, which extends about 2 miles north from Monmouth. Deep, slow-moving water containing a good selection of coarse fish, including carp, bream, tench, pike and chub.

How to get there   From Monmouth, drive north-west on the B4233, then B4347 towards Rockfield. On the outskirts of Monmouth, look for signs to Osbaston Farm; the fishery extends upstream from the Farm for 2 miles.

Day tickets   Adult £2; junior/OAP £1. Available on the bank, or at Osbaston Farm.

Best methods/baits   Use general coarse methods and baits.

Facilities   Nearest shops and pubs in Monmouth.

ST. JAMES PARK, TREDEGAR
Atlas Page 200 E.1/2.8

A 2-acre, round lake located within Tredegar town. A popular fishery, with crucian carp, roach, perch, tench, rudd and gudgeon, in addition to some large, good quality bream in the 5lb region.

How to get there   Directions to the lake are complex. Contact Tiles & Tackle, 108 Commercial Street, Tredegar; Tel. 0495 717001 for details of where – and how – to fish.

Day tickets   Adult £1.50 (£3 on the bank); junior/OAP 75p. Season tickets: adult £7.50; junior £2. Available at Tiles & Tackle (see above).

Best methods/baits   Use general coarse methods and baits.

Facilities   Nearest shops and pub, in Tredegar (½ mile).

Disabled facilities   Some swims are suitable for disabled and wheelchair anglers.

RIVER WYE, MONMOUTH
Atlas Page 200 E.7/2.7

A very good river fishery, near the bridge in Monmouth town centre. A wide (90 yards) stretch where the initial slow flow quickens through the bridge, and depth is 4–5ft. Expect good chub, perch, pike and barbel, plus some quite large eels, particularly around the bridge arch.

How to get there   Drive to Monmouth town centre via the A40 and park (free) by the river. For details of access and parking, contact either Monmouth

Borough Council Offices; Tel. 0495 762311 or The Monmouthshire Sportsman, St. James Street, Monmouth; Tel. 0600 715289.

Day tickets   Adult/junior/OAP £1.50. Available from the Borough Council or Monmouthshire Sportsman (see above).

Best methods/baits   Use general coarse methods and baits.

Facilities   Toilets within 300–400 yards. Plenty of shops and pubs in Monmouth town centre.

RIVER WYE, BIGSWEIR
Atlas Page 200 E.9/3.1

A pacey stretch, 5–7ft depth, plus shallows, fords, glides and slower, deeper sections. Some steep banks, plus tree-lined areas. Expect chub in summer, autumn and winter, roach and dace only late in the year. Lots of elusive barbel and large pike. Match nets of 50lb+ are quite common.

How to get there   Approach on the A466 Monmouth-Chepstow road. The stretch begins at Redbrooke (after 3 miles) and runs to Wyeseal Farm, and on to Llandogo (after 8 miles). Various access points from the road. See p. 318 for location map.

Day tickets   Adult £3, junior OAP £1; available from Tump Farm, nr Llandogo; membership books from Mr L Clarke, 14 Allt-y-ryn Ave., Newport, Gwent NP9 5DB; Tel. 0633 267047.

Best methods   Chub – fish under trees with big baits or with maggots and waggler or big balsa; also swimfeeders with meat, sweetcorn, maggots or casters.

Best baits   Maggots, casters, hemp plus usual big baits.

Hotspot Tips

- The steadier, deeper swims produce roach on the stick with normal maggots or casters.
- The sewer pipe swim – a big eddy 50 yards below the railway bridge – produces lots of chub.
- Huge barbel have been seen in the Cadorra salmon pool – also a great place for chub and dace.
- The chub are particularly good as the river runs off after a normal spate.

GWYNEDD

Eel.

Disabled facilities   Some swims at the northern end of the lake are suitable for disabled and wheelchair anglers.

CARNA
Atlas Page 204 A.6/4.3

A scenic, 2-acre lake located on a farm, a few miles from Valley, at Llanfairyneubwll. The water contains plenty of perch, roach and rudd, as well as some very big tench. Fishing is available only from the end of March until November.

How to get there   Take the A5 to Anglesey and just after Caergeiliog (about 5 miles before Holyhead) turn left at the toll gate. Cross the railway line; Carna Farm is directly ahead (there is a red light on the roof!). Park on the roadside nearby.

Day tickets   Adult/junior/OAP £2. Available from Mr. Owen at Carna Farm; Tel. 0407 741044.

Best methods/baits   Use general coarse methods and baits.

Facilities   Nearest shop, on the campsite; nearest pub, at Caergeiliog (2 miles).

LLYN TRAWSFYNYDD
Atlas Page 204 B.4/5.2

A huge, 1200-acre lake set amid beautiful scenery just south of Ffestiniog. Excellent coarse fishing for large perch (3lb+), rudd (2lb+) and grass carp (National record site). Also huge eels to 8lb+. Expect a catch of anything up to 60lb!

How to get there   From Ffestiniog, head south on the A470 for about 5 miles to Trawsfynydd village. Access to the lake and free parking places are to be found at intervals around the lake. For details, contact Mitch Atherton, Manchester House, Trawsfynydd; Tel. 076687 234.

Day tickets   Adult £7; OAP £5; junior £4. Weekly tickets: adult £30; OAP £20; junior £16. Available from Mitch Atherton (see above).

Best methods   Use float or leger.

Best baits   Sweetcorn or maggots.

Restrictions   No livebaiting.

Facilities   Toilets in the village. Nearest shop, at Mitch Atherton's; nearest pubs (2) in the village (both do B&B).

Disabled facilities   Some swims are suitable for disabled and wheelchair anglers.

BALA LAKE
Atlas Page 204 C.6/5.2

An excellent lake fishery set amid the Welsh mountains. The water can be rough when the south-westerly wind blows, but fishing remains good. Roach and pike are the most productive species, with 50–70lb roach nets possible, though the average is 10–15lb.

How to get there   From Llangollen, head west on the A494 to Bala (about 26 miles); access to the fishery is on either side of the lake, via the A494 or B4403. Free parking at various sites along the route.

Day tickets   Adult £2; junior/OAP £1. Available on the bank, or from Eryr's Sports & Tackle, 33 High Street, Bala; Tel. 0678 520370.

Best methods/baits   Use general coarse methods and baits. Swim feeder is most successful.

Restrictions   No fishing at the extreme southern end (conservation area).

Facilities   Nearest shops and pubs, in Bala.

LLYN-Y-GORS
Atlas Page 204 A.7/4.1

A 3-acre carp lake, complete with three islands. Excellent carp fishing, with mirror (24lb) and common (21lb+) carp in abundance. Open all year round.

How to get there Leave the A5 at Menai Bridge and take the A5025 towards Amlwch. After about 1 mile (at Mazda garage), turn right, then left at cross-roads by church. The fishery is 2 miles on the right. Free car parking on site.

Day tickets Adult £6; junior/OAP £4. Also 24-hour ticket: £8. Available from Llyn-y-Gors, Llandegfan, Menai Bridge, Anglesey; Tel. 0248 713410.

Best methods Use normal carp fishing methods.

Best baits Boilies, mixers.

Restrictions No particle baits.

Facilities Toilets/food & drink/bait & tackle available on site. Also self-catering cottages/caravans/tents. Nearest shop, ½ mile; nearest pub, 1 mile.

Disabled facilities Some swims suitable for disabled and wheelchair anglers.

LLYN EURONWY
Atlas Page 204 A.7/4.6

A small (1½-acre) lake situated on Ty-Heh Farm, on the west coast of Anglesey. Good mixed coarse fishing; large common, mirror and Crucian carp, plus good-sized rudd, tench (to 7lb) and roach.

How to get there Leave the A5 at Menai Bridge and take the A4080 to Rhosneigr (about 20 miles). Turn right at cross-roads, then left after railway bridge. Free car parking on site.

Day tickets Adult/junior/OAP £6. Evening ticket: £3. Available on the banks, or from Ty-Heh Farm, Rhosneigr; Tel. 0407 810331.

Best methods Most methods work, but float preferred.

Best baits Maggots, casters, sweetcorn, meat.

Restrictions No hemp, boilies or groundbait. No keepnets. No lead weights or barbed hooks to be used. No night fishing.

Facilities Toilets on site. Nearest shop ¼ mile; nearest pub, 5 mins walk. Also self-catering cottages available.

Disabled facilities Some swims suitable for disabled and wheelchair anglers.

HEREFORD & WORCESTER

A cold cast.

DOCKLOW POOLS
Atlas Page 200 E.9/1.6

A private fishery comprising eight pools with islands, margins and tree stumps, plus a canal stretch – all about 4 miles east of Leominster. Day-ticket fishing on three lakes only; anglers staying at the complex can fish all eight venues. Excellent fishing, with tench, chub, bream, roach and perch, plus some really big carp in the 30lb+ region. The best 1-day catch here is 305lb!

How to get there Take the A44 west from Worcester through Bromyard and after about 7 miles look for signs on the right to Docklow Pools. Free car parking on site.

Day tickets Adult/junior/OAP £3; extra rod £1. Available from the shop on site.

Best methods In summer, use crystal waggler or pole. In autumn and winter, use feeder and pole.

Best baits Maggot, sweetcorn, luncheon meat and bread work well for mixed species. Use boilies or Pedigree Chum mixer for carp.

Restrictions No hemp, nuts, groundbait or keepnets on Moby Dick Pool.

Facilities Tackle and bait available at shop on site. Nearest shop and pub, Docklow village.

Disabled facilities Some swims may be suitable for disabled and wheelchair anglers; please contact Mike Bozward at the Pools for advice; Tel. 056882 256.

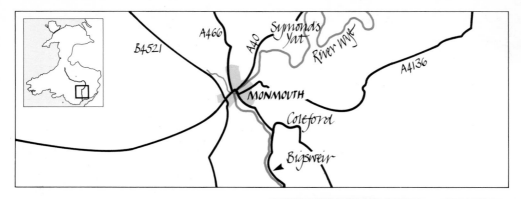

Rivers

RIVER WYE

Although the Wye is primarily a game-fishing river, it is also one of Britain's premier coarse fisheries, with its steep banks, shallow fords, fast gravel runs, steady glides and deep pools. Most coarse fishing occurs during autumn and winter, with huge catches of roach, chub, dace, plus specimen barbel and monster pike routinely taken. On many stretches, coarse fishing is allowed only during the salmon close season (October 25-January 26), with larvae baits (maggots and casters) being restricted between March 14 and September 14.

BELMONT
Atlas Page 200 E.8/2.1

A wide, open fishery; level bottom, depth 7ft upstream and 10ft downstream, where flow is steadier. Heavy summer weed growth. Mainly chub, roach, dace and bleak in winter, plus carp, bream and an occasional barbel. Winter bags approach 65lb roach, or 30lb chub. Winter pike are big – up to 35lb!

How to get there   In Hereford city centre, downstream access is via a car park at the A49 road bridge; walk upstream from the rowing club. Middle access is via the road past the Antelope Inn and waterworks. Upstream access is at the new bridge at Breinton (park nearby).

Day tickets   Adult £3; junior/OAP £1. Weekly ticket £5. Available from Hatton's and Perkins tackle shops in Hereford.

Returning a good barbel.

Best methods   Summer bream, carp – pole; roach, dace – stick float with maggot or caster; chub – waggler down the middle with maggot, or balsa with breadflake.

Best baits   Summer – sweetcorn, worms, breadflake; winter roach – maggots or casters.

Facilities   Food/shops/toilets in Hereford city centre. Food/toilets at the Antelope Inn (200 yards).

Hotspot Tips

- Simple breadcrumb groundbait can be a valuable weapon.
- Swimfeeders can produce large catches of roach and chub.
- In high water, a link leger down the side will catch roach.
- The best chub swims are left bank, by the rowing club.

WYELEA/BRIDSTOW
Atlas Page 200 F.1/2.5

A 1-mile, right-bank fishery with good access and partly tree-lined banks. Depths range from 5–16ft, with some fast swims. Mainly chub, roach, dace, plus some barbel (to 9lb), carp and big pike. One match net here topped 65lb.

How to get there   From Ross-on-Wye, take the A49 towards Hereford. Turn first right after the A49/A40 junction, to Bridstow. Wyelea House is on the riverside.

Day tickets   Adult £5; junior/OAP £5. Tickets and swim maps available from the owner, Mr Colin Bateman, Wyelea House, Bridstow, Ross-on-Wye HR9 6PZ.

Best methods   Summer bream, carp – use pole; roach, dace – use stick float with maggot or caster; chub – use waggler down the middle with maggot, or balsa with breadflake.

Best baits   Maggots, casters, bread, worms, sweetcorn.

Restrictions   Salmon rods take preference in season.

Disabled facilities   Good access; some swims may be suitable for disabled anglers.

ROSS-ON-WYE
Atlas Page 200 F.1/2.5

A pacey stretch with weed patches and a central shelf, 8ft in places, shallower at the far bank. Excellent roach in autumn/winter when levels are 2–3ft above normal, plus lots of chub, dace, carp (to 30lb) or elusive pike (to 35lb). A 100lb net is likely – notably as the river runs down after a spate.

How to get there   From Ross-on-Wye town centre, approach the river via Wilton Bridge. Use the car park at the bridge, where there is access to the left bank.

Day tickets   Adults/OAP £3, weekly £10. Juniors – best join Ross Angling Club £2. Available on the bank, or from tackle shops in the town.

Best methods   Roach, dace – use waggler when water is slow, pole and stick float when swollen but falling. Chub – use 4 or 5SSG balsa float with 10p-sized breadflake on 8–10 hook.

Best baits   Roach, dace – maggots, casters, hempseed. Chub – as for roach/dace, plus bread or meat.

Facilities   Food/shops/toilets in town centre, or the Hope & Anchor pub.

Hotspot Tips

- Attract the chub shoals with breadcrumb groundbait laced with hemp and casters.
- For chub, swimfeeders are worth a try, but legered meat is a good alternative.
- The biggest nets of roach and dace are taken immediately upstream of the bridge.

LYDBROOK
Atlas Page 200 F.1/2.6

A pleasant fishery with a 1-mile right bank and ¾-mile left bank. Deep water upstream (11ft); shallows at lower end. Tree-lined banks and close car parking all along. Good catches of autumn/winter chub, roach, dace and barbel, plus large pike (30lb) and perch (2lb). Summer bleak are a nuisance.

How to get there   Take the B4228 south from Ross-on-Wye; after 5 miles look for Courtfield Hotel. The bailiff (George Crouch) lives in Greenway Cottage on the river bank, 150 yards beyond the hotel.

Day tickets   £2; available on the bank, or from the bailiff's cottage.

Best methods   Roach, dace – use float tactics; chub – use leger.

Best baits   Roach, dace – use maggots, casters, hemp. Chub – meat, sweetcorn, bread.

Facilities   Food/toilets at the Courtfield Hotel.

Disabled facilities   Good vehicular access along the fishery for disabled anglers.

Hotspot Tips

- It's worth trying a swimfeeder for chub.
- George Crouch knows his river – he'll point you in the right direction!

SYMONDS YAT
Atlas Page 200 F.0/2.7

A double-bank fishery set in a famous beauty spot. Streamy, with shallows and deeps (to 12ft), producing roach, dace and large chub in late autumn and winter, plus some summer barbel. A winter roach net here can top 50lb.

How to get there   Take the A40 Ross-Monmouth road. At Symonds Yat (6 miles) turn left, use public car park for upstream, right bank section, or go through village for downstream section. For left bank, take B4229 (1 mile), turn right over Huntsham Bridge.

Day tickets   No day tickets; fishing free to patrons of the Saracen's Head pub; Tel. 0600 890435.

Best methods   Roach – use stick float with casters as feed. Chub – trot down the middle with waggler or balsa float.

Best baits   Most species – maggots, casters, hemp. Chub – breadflake, meat or sweetcorn.

Facilities   Shops in village; food/toilets at Saracen's Head pub.

Hotspot Tips

- Hold the shoals with breadcrumb, hemp and caster feed.
- For chub, try using a swimfeeder with sweetcorn.
- Stick float or pole tactics can produce good dace.
- The best roach area is outside the Saracen's Head.

The end of a long hard fight.

Scottish Region

River Tweed at Coldstream.

Coarse fishing in the Scottish NRA region is affected by similar constraints to those seen in Wales – namely that the terrain is often inaccessible for angling, although many of the very fast-flowing waters of the region are limited to game fishing, with coarse fishing available only in some lochs and private lakes and ponds.

The majority (though not all) of coarse fisheries are concentrated in southern Scotland, in Dumfries and Galloway, on or near the west coast. Here, there are many small lochs which can provide good mixed fishing for perch and roach, but the very large pike which also inhabit such waters are often the main target. For this reason, the area is a pike specialist's dream! Further north, several very large lochs – some between 25–30 miles long – and forming part of the Caledonian Canal are also pleasant and productive fisheries, though most fall into the 'pike' category.

Of course, stillwater fishing in Scotland is not confined to the Highland areas; Edinburgh and Glasgow each provide lake fishing in public parks, as well as canal fishing of reasonable quality.

Despite this domination by the lochs,

coarse river fishing in Scotland is available, but is largely confined to the Borders, and to the Tweed specifically, which offers good quality fishing for most species in its lower reaches, through Kelso and Coldstream to meet the sea at Berwick-on-Tweed.

BORDERS

ALEMOOR LOCH
Atlas Page 207 E.5/6.4

A large loch-cum-reservoir about 9 miles west of Hawick. A very scenic setting where the coarse fishing is very good. Expect some roach, perch and eels, plus some trout. Also some very big pike (20lb+), with the best fish at the top end of the loch.

How to get there   Take the A7 south from Hawick and after about 1½ miles turn right onto the B711. Follow the road through Roberton until it crosses the Loch (about 7 miles from the A7). Free car parking on site.

Day tickets   Adult/junior/OAP £5.
Season tickets: adult £12.50; junior
£2.Available from The Pet Shop, Union
Street, Hawick; or from Mr. Sutherland,
20 Longhope Drive, Hawick;
Tel. 0450 75150.

Best methods/baits   Use general coarse
methods and baits. Use deadbait for
pike.

Restrictions   No worms or maggots. No
boat fishing.

Facilities   Nearest shop and pub, in
Hawick (9 miles).

RIVER ANNAN
Atlas Page 207 E.1/7.2

A twisting stretch of river, some 3 to 4
miles long, flowing south from Lockerbie
towards the Solway Firth. Deep pools
occur along the entire length, providing
excellent fishing, mainly for chub. A
specialist chub pool is to be found at about
midway, near Hightae. Mrs. Ratcliffe will
supply a local map (see below).

How to get there   From Lockerbie, head
west on the A709 and follow signs via
minor roads on the left to Greenhill,
Hightae or Smallholm. Park (free) in any
of these villages and walk to the water.
For details of best access and best
fishing, contact the local tackle shops.

Day tickets   Adult/junior/OAP £5 (25th
February to 1st October). Weekend
ticket £10 (1st October to 15th
November). Available from Mrs. K.
Ratcliffe, Clerk to the Commissioners
of Royal Four Towns, Fishing, at Jay-Ar,
Hightae, Lockerbie; Tel. 0387 810220.

Best methods/baits   Use general coarse
methods and baits.

Restrictions   No Sunday fishing.

Facilities   Nearest shops and pubs, in
Lockerbie (3–4 miles).

RIVER TWEED, KELSO
Atlas Page 207 F.0/6.1

A town-centre fishery which is divided
into several sections, north and south of
the town. Expect most species of coarse
fish here, but the local specialities are
roach and grayling.

How to get there   In Kelso town centre.
Fishing is available on the south of the
town at Junction Pool to Kelso Bridge,
and from Mellendean Burn to Broase
Stream. On the north side, fish from

Kelso Cauld to Broase Stream (except for
two private stretches). For more details,
ask at the local tackle shop (see below).

Day tickets   Adult £2; junior (13–16) £1;
under 13s, free. Weekly ticket £6.
Available from Teeside Tackle, 32
Woodmarket, Kelso; Tel. 0573 25306.

Best methods/baits   Use general coarse
methods and baits.

Restrictions   No maggots or groundbait.
No spinning. No Sunday fishing.

Facilities   Nearest shops, pubs and
toilets, in Kelso.

RIVER TWEED, COLDSTREAM
Atlas Page 207 F.2/6.0

A very wide river stretch, punctuated by
big pools, together with a number of
islands and shallows. Quite good coarse
fishing once the shoals have been located,
with roach, perch and grayling
predominant. A popular region is near the
caravan site, or the pool upstream of the
bridge. Leet Point can also produce some
good fish.

How to get there   Take the A698 from
Kelso into Coldstream and park (free) in
the town centre. Access to the river is at
various points from the Tweed Bridge to
Leet Point. For more details, ask at the
local tackle shop.

Day tickets   Adult £3; junior/OAP £1.50.
Weekly ticket £15. Available from The
Sports Shop, in the town centre, or from
The Crown Hotel, Market Square;
Tel. 0890 2558.

Best methods/baits   Use general coarse
methods and baits.

Best baits   Sweetcorn and meat work
well here.

Restrictions   Coarse fishing only from
the north bank of the river. No
spinning. No baits associated with
salmon fishing allowed.

Facilities   Nearest shops and pubs, in
Coldstream town centre.

RIVER TWEED, LADYKIRK
Atlas Page 207 F.3/5.8

An excellent coarse fishery comprising 2½
miles of river bank, midway between
Coldstream and Berwick-upon-Tweed.
Expect some very good sport, with
grayling, roach, perch and dace the main
attraction.

How to get there   Take the A698 from Berwick-upon-Tweed towards Coldstream and after about 6 miles turn right on the B6470, signposted Norham. Park in the village (free) and fish anywhere downstream to Horncliffe.

Day tickets   Adult/junior/OAP £3. Available from The Mason's Arms pub at Norham; Tel. 0289 382326.

Best methods/baits   Use general coarse methods and baits – most are successful here.

Restrictions   No groundbaiting. No spinning.

Facilities   Nearest shop and pub, The Mason's Arms, in Norham (also toilets).

Disabled facilities   Some swims are suitable for disabled and wheelchair anglers; please contact The Mason's Arms for advice (see above).

RIVER TWEED, HORNCLIFFE
Atlas Page 207 F.3/5.7

A tidal stretch of the river, extending about 8 miles inland from Berwick-upon-Tweed. A very pleasant fishery which contains good stocks of roach, dace, perch and grayling, plus some quite large eels for variety!

How to get there   Take the A698 from Coldstream towards Berwick-upon-Tweed and after about 8 miles look for signs to Horncliffe on the left. Either follow the road to its end, or turn right and carry on to the bridge on the Fishwick road. Fish anywhere between here and the sea, all year round (no closed season).

Day tickets   Free fishing.

Best methods/baits   Use general coarse methods and baits.

Facilities   Various shops and pubs along the route, or in Berwick-upon-Tweed.

CENTRAL

FORTH AND CLYDE CANAL
Atlas Page 207 C.9/5.4

A 38-mile canal running from Dumbarton, on the west coast of Scotland to Falkirk on the east. The canal produces excellent coarse fishing along its length, with most species taken at various points. Some of the most popular fishing spots are at Castle Cary, near the M80/A80 intersection.

How to get there   Access to the Canal is available at numerous points between Dumbarton (Bowling Basin) on the Firth of Clyde, to Falkirk, on the Firth of Forth. For the best access points and fishing, consult either British Waterways (see below) or the local tackle shops along the route.

Day tickets   Season tickets only, £5.88 per annum. Available from British Waterways, Rosebank House, Main Street, Camelon, Falkirk; Tel. 0324 612415.

Best methods/baits   Use general coarse methods and baits. Most baits are successful on these waters.

Facilities   Plenty of shops, pubs and toilets along the route.

Disabled facilities   Some swims are suitable for disabled and wheelchair anglers; additional improvements to the towpath are currently being made. Contact British Waterways for advice (see above).

LOCH ACHRAY
Atlas Page 207 D.2/4.9

A large but fairly shallow loch located in The Trossachs, about 10 miles west of Callander. Fish from the south side of the loch, and also on the south side of the river (all within the Forestry Commission's boundaries). Expect some good coarse sport, especially from the big pike which live among the reeds at the forest end.

How to get there   Take the A81 north from Glasgow to Aberfoyle (about 27 miles) and bear left onto the A821 to Loch Achray. The road runs alongside the loch for several miles. Park on the main road and walk to the water. Entry to the loch is also above the Visitor's Centre.

Day tickets   Adult/junior/OAP £2.50. Available from Bain's Tackle in Callander (10 miles) or from the Queen Elizabeth Forest Park Visitor's Centre in Aberfoyle; Tel. 08772 383.

Best methods/baits   Use general coarse methods and baits.

Restrictions   Fishing available only from 15th March until 1st October.

Facilities   Nearest shop/food at Brig o'Turk (2 miles); nearest pubs, the Achray Hotel and Trossachs, on the loch side.

LOCH LOMOND
Atlas Page 207 C.9/5.4

A vast loch which extends from just east of Helensburgh in Strathclyde, north for some 30 miles to Ben Vorlich in the Central Region. Expect some very active sport in a very scenic setting, with big pike the main target, although other coarse species are present. Also occasional trout and salmon catches.

How to get there   Take the A82 west from Glasgow and follow the road north to Alexandria. The main road then runs alongside the loch for about 30 miles, offering many fishing points. For details of access and parking, contact the local tackle shops along the route.

Day tickets   Adult/junior/OAP £9. From 11th February until 31st October a game ticket must be purchased in case of any unintended salmon or trout catches. Outside these dates coarse fishing is free. Tickets are available from local hotels, shops and tackle dealers along the loch.

Best methods/baits   Use general coarse methods and baits. Use specialist methods for pike.

Restrictions   No Sunday fishing. Fishing on west bank only. Fishing on the east bank is strictly subject to ownership.

Facilities   Various shops/pubs/food/toilets along the loch.

DUMFRIES AND GALLOWAY

Craighlaw Loch.

AUCHENREOCH LOCH
Atlas Page 207 D.6/7.2

A long, narrow 80-acre loch located about 10 miles west of Dumfries. The surrounding farmland and forests provide a sheltered site, especially at the Castle Douglas (southern) end of the loch. Mainly pike and perch, plus an abundance of good quality roach.

How to get there   From Dumfries, head south-west on the A75 towards Castle Douglas. At Crocketford (after about 9 miles) look for the Lochview Hotel, which is 1 mile beyond the A75/A712 junction. Free parking at the Hotel, or at the Loch.

Day tickets   Adult £3; junior/OAP £2. Available at the Lochview Hotel at Crocketford; Tel. 055669 281.

Best methods/baits   Use general coarse methods and baits.

Facilities   Hotel accommodation/caravan & camping at Lochview. Nearest shop, Crocketford (1 mile); nearest pub, the Lochview Hotel.

Disabled facilities   Some swims near the Hotel are suitable for disabled and wheelchair anglers.

BARNBARROCH LOCH
Atlas Page 207 C.9/7.5

A totally secluded 12-acre lake set within 180 acres of forest and woodland, just south of Wigtown. Good mixed coarse fishing, with perch, tench, carp, roach, rudd and bream.

How to get there   Take the A714 south from Newton Stewart through Wigtown to Whauphill. Turn right and the entrance to the forestry is 600 yards on the right. Follow the track for ½ mile to the loch. Park near the water.

Day tickets   Adult £3.50 (£2.50 to hotel residents); junior/OAP £1.75. Available from David Canning at Torwood House Hotel, Glenluce, Newton Stewart; Tel. 05813 468.

Best methods/baits   Use general coarse methods and baits.

Restrictions   No livebaiting. Use only semi-barbless hooks.

Facilities   Nearest shop and pub, in Whauphill.

BLACK LOCH
Atlas Page 207 C.5/7.4

A fairly small, 15-acre loch, a few miles east of Stranraer, renowned for its big perch, as well as some good-sized tench and eels.

How to get there Take the A75 west from Newton Stewart towards Stranraer, and at Castle Kennedy (about 21 miles) follow signpost (on the right) to the Black Loch. Car parking available on site.

Day tickets Adult £3.50 (£2.80 for hotel residents); junior/OAP £1.75. Available from David Canning at Torwood House Hotel, Glenluce, Newton Stewart; Tel. 05813 468.

Best methods/baits Use general coarse methods and baits.

Facilities Nearest shop and pub, in Castle Kennedy.

CARLINGWARK LOCH
Atlas Page 207 D.5/7.5

A square-shaped loch on the south-western outskirts of Castle Douglas, offering good quality pike and perch fishing.

How to get there From Castle Douglas, take the A75 west towards Bridge of Dee. The loch is on the left as you leave Castle Douglas. Park (free) on the roadside.

Day tickets Free fishing on the west bank.

Best methods/baits Use general coarse methods and baits.

Facilities Nearest shops and pubs in Castle Douglas.

CLATTERINGSHAWS LOCH
Atlas Page 207 D.3/7.3

A big loch of some 150 acres, surrounded by woodland and very deep, about 5 miles west of New Galloway. Mainly pike fishing, with some big fish being taken from the region of the River Dee inlet (the southern corner). Also perch and brown trout.

How to get there Take the A712 north-east from Newton Stewart towards New Galloway. The loch is on the left of the road, after about 15 miles. Plenty of free parking on the roadside, but 50p in the Visitor's Centre.

Day tickets Adult £2; junior/OAP 50p (one rod per person). Available from Clatteringshaws Visitor's Centre in New Galloway; Tel. 06442 285.

Best methods/baits Use general coarse methods and baits. Specialist pike methods may be needed.

Restrictions No livebaiting. No boat fishing.

Facilities Toilets/food/shop on site. Nearest pub, in New Galloway (5 miles).

COWANS LOCH
Atlas Page 207 D.7/7.4

A small (1-acre) loch on a farm just north of Dalbeattie, with superb panoramic views. Quite deep water (up to 8ft), well stocked with double figure carp, tench and roach to provide good, all-round sport.

How to get there From Dalbeattie, drive north-east on the A711 to Kirkgunzeon (about 4 miles). Look for the farm's signpost on the roadside and park where indicated.

Day tickets Adult/junior/OAP £3. Available from Mr. Hamlet, Cowan's Farm, Kirkgunzeon, nr Dalbeattie.

Best methods/baits Use general coarse methods and baits.

Restrictions No groundbaiting. No keepnets to be used.

Facilities B & B available at the farm. Nearest shop, Dalbeattie; nearest pub, in Kirkgunzeon.

CRAIGHLAW
Atlas Page 207 C.8/7.3

A small loch, complete with lily beds, set in a beautifully landscaped estate, about 5 miles west of Newton Stewart. Expect good fishing for tench, roach, bream and brown trout.

How to get there From Newton Stewart, take the A75 towards Stranraer. After about 5 miles, turn left onto the B733; the fishery entrance is about ½ mile on the left. Parking nearby.

Day tickets Adult/junior/OAP £4 (£3 for hotel residents). Available from David Canning at Torwood House Hotel, Glenluce, Newton Stewart; Tel. 05813 468.

Best methods/baits Use general coarse methods and baits.

Facilities   Nearest shop and pub, in Kirkowan.

Disabled facilities   Some swims are suitable for disabled and wheelchair anglers; contact the hotel for advice.

DERNAGLAR LOCH
Atlas Page 207 C.6/7.4

A fair-sized loch located high on open moorland within a Site of Special Scientific Interest (mainly for rare plants), about 4 miles east of Glenluce. A shallow, but productive water, with good catches of pike and perch, plus some very big eels.

How to get there   From Newton Stewart, take the A75 towards Stranraer. After about 12 miles, look for signs to Derskelpin Farm. Turn off the road and continue for about 1½ miles to the loch. Parking nearby.

Day tickets   Adult/junior/OAP £3.50 (£2.50 for hotel residents). Available from David Canning at Torwood House Hotel, Glenluce, Newton Stewart; Tel. 05813 468.

Best methods/baits   Use general coarse methods and baits.

Facilities   Nearest shop and pub, in Glenluce.

GARWACHIE LOCH
Atlas Page 207 C.7/7.4

A compact and fairly secluded 5-acre loch, partially surrounded by woodland, about 6 miles from Newton Stewart. A very good coarse fishing venue, with a good head of pike, perch, tench, roach and rudd.

How to get there   From Newton Stewart, take the A714 north-west towards Girvan, and after about 2 miles turn left on the B7027 towards Knowe. The loch is about 4 miles further on, just after the Spectacle Lochs, on the left-hand side. Free parking on site.

Day tickets   Adult £2.50; junior/OAP £1.50. Available from any Forestry Commission Office, or from D. G. Guns & Tackle in Newton Stewart, or from Torwood House Hotel, Glenluce; Tel. 05813 468.

Best methods/baits   Use general coarse methods and baits.

Restrictions   Fishing only available from the roadside bank. No boat fishing.

Facilities   Nearest shop and pub, in Newton Stewart (6 miles).

KELHEAD QUARRY
Atlas Page 207 E.1/7.3

A boomerang-shaped lake of about 6 acres, in a very pleasant setting between Annan and Dumfries. Plenty of top quality coarse fishing (50 pegs) with catches of roach, bream, carp, tench, perch, pike, eels and also a few brown and rainbow trout!

How to get there   From Annan (near Gretna) take the A75 west for about 3 miles to Kelhead (on the right). Look for two cottages which are set together, just where the woods start. Miss Ross' cottage is the second. Park (free) nearby.

Day tickets   Adult/junior/OAP £2. Available from Miss Ross at Kelhead Bungalow, Cummertrees; Tel. 04617 344.

Best methods/baits   Use general coarse methods and baits.

Facilities   Picnic area and woodland walks for the family. Nearest shop and pub, in Annan (3 miles).

Disabled facilities   There are excellent facilities for disabled and wheelchair anglers.

LOCH DORNAL
Atlas Page 207 C.8/7.3

Located about 12 miles from Newton Stewart, this fairly large, but irregularly-shaped loch contains a large number of big pike which will provide an excellent day's fishing for the pike specialist. Also some good-sized trout for variety.

How to get there   From Newton Stewart take the A714 north-west and after 2 miles turn left onto the B7027 towards Knowe and Barrhill. The loch is about 12 miles on the right-hand side, opposite Loch Maberry. Free parking on site.

Day tickets   Adult/junior/OAP £10. Available from The Keeper at The Kennels, Drumlamford Estate; Tel. 046582 256.

Best methods/baits   Use specialist pike fishing methods and baits.

Facilities   Nearest shop and pub, in Barrhill (5 miles).

LOCH ELDRIG
Atlas Page 207 C.8/7.4

A large loch of 35–40 acres, a few miles west of Newton Stewart. Plenty of cover, with one-third of the banks tree-lined.

Expect some top-class coarse fishing, with good stocks of perch, pike and brown trout.

How to get there From Newton Stewart take the A714 north-west and after 2 miles turn left onto the B7027 towards Knowe and Barrhill. After a further 2 miles, turn left (opposite a house) onto a forestry track. Continue 2 miles to the loch and park (free) nearby.

Day tickets Adult £2.50; junior/OAP £1.50. Available from any Forestry Commission Office, or from D. G. Guns & Tackle in Newton Stewart.

Best methods/baits Use general coarse methods and baits.

Restrictions Fishing only available from the banks where there are trees. No boat fishing.

Facilities Nearest shop and pub, in Newton Stewart.

LOCH HERON
Atlas Page 207 C.7/7.4

A 40-acre loch lying in a pine forest, about 8 miles west of Newton Stewart. Heavily weeded water on the west side but still with good access. Expect good-sized pike, plus roach and tench. Carp, bream and rudd may be here too, but have not been taken – yet!

How to get there Take the A75 west from Newton Stewart for about 6 miles and look for right turn on minor road, signposted Loch Heron and Loch Ronald. Follow the road to the water and park nearby.

Day tickets Adult £3.50 (£2.80 for hotel residents); junior/OAP £1.75. Available from David Canning at Torwood House Hotel, Glenluce, Newton Stewart; Tel. 05813 468.

Best methods/baits Use general coarse methods and baits.

Facilities Nearest shop and pub, in Newton Stewart, or Torwood House Hotel.

LOCH KEN
Atlas Page 207 D.4/7.4

A very long fishery which extends from Castle Douglas, north-west to New Galloway. The loch has recently acquired a reputation as a top roach water, with 2lb+ fish taken regularly during spring and winter. Also perch, plus the well-known large pike, with several 30lb+ specimens taken in recent years.

How to get there From Castle Douglas, take the A713 north-west towards New Galloway. The road runs alongside the loch for several miles; for details of the best fisheries and parking, contact Paraphernalia, in the High Street, New Galloway; Tel. 06442 632.

Day tickets Adult £1; junior/OAP 50p. Available from Paraphernalia, in New Galloway (see above). Also boat hire £12.

Best methods/baits Use general coarse methods and baits. Use leger off-shore for good-sized roach.

Restrictions No livebaiting.

Facilities Nearest shop, in New Galloway; nearest pubs, in New Galloway, Laurieston, Crossmichael and Castle Douglas.

Disabled facilities Only a limited number of swims are suitable for disabled and wheelchair anglers; check at Paraphernalia for advice.

LOCH MABERRY
Atlas Page 207 C.8/7.2

A fairly large loch of over 100 acres, complete with a number of islands, close to Loch Dornal, and about 12 miles north-west from Newton Stewart. Mainly perch and eels for 'small' fishing, but there are also plenty of very big pike for the specialist – with several approaching 30lb!

How to get there From Newton Stewart take the A714 north-west and after 2 miles turn left onto the B7027 towards Knowe and Barrhill. Loch Maberry is about 12 miles on the left-hand side; free parking by the loch-side.

Day tickets Adult/junior/OAP £3. Available from The Keeper at The Kennels, Drumlamford Estate; Tel. 046582 256.

Best methods/baits Use specialist pike-fishing methods and baits.

Facilities Nearest shop and pub, in Barrhill (5 miles).

Disabled facilities Some swims are suitable for disabled and wheelchair anglers.

LOCH RONALD
Atlas Page 207 C.7/7.4

A large, 140-acre loch situated among pine forests to the west of Newton Stewart. Mainly fairly shallow water (15ft maximum), but with good stocks of pike, perch and eels. Lots of jack-pike here, but fish up to the 20lb mark can also be expected.

How to get there   Take the A75 west from Newton Stewart for about 6 miles and look for right turn on minor road, sign posted Loch Ronald and Loch Heron. Follow the road to the water and park nearby.

Day tickets   Adult £3.50 (£2.80 for hotel residents); junior/OAP £1.75. Available from David Canning at Torwood House Hotel, Glenluce, Newton Stewart; Tel. 05813 468.

Best methods/baits   Use general coarse methods and baits. Specialist pike methods may be needed.

Facilities   Nearest shop and pub, in Newton Stewart, or Torwood House Hotel.

SPECTACLE LOCHS
Atlas Page 207 C.8/7.3

A pair of small lochs (4–5 acres each) which are almost totally surrounded by spruce woodland, except for the roadside sections. Good quality coarse fishing venue, with plenty of roach, dace, perch and pike (to 14lb). Large tench are also quite common here – about 3 years ago, the Scottish record was held by a fish from these waters.

How to get there   From Newton Stewart, take the A714 north-west towards Girvan, and after about 2 miles turn left on the B7027 towards Knowe. The Spectacle Lochs are about 4 miles further along the road, on the left-hand side. Free parking by the loch.

Day tickets   Adult £2.50; junior/OAP £1.50. Available from any Forestry Commission Office, or from D. G. Guns & Tackle in Newton Stewart.

Best methods/baits   Use general coarse methods and baits.

Restrictions   Fishing only available from the roadside bank. No boat fishing.

Facilities   Nearest shop and pub, in Newton Stewart (6 miles).

LOCH STROAM
Atlas Page 207 D.4/7.4

A smallish loch, roughly oval in shape and surrounded by reed beds, in a secluded position with lovely views, just south of New Galloway. Water depth is 7–10ft, and fed by the Black Water of Dee. Mainly pike and perch, with plenty of large specimens of both.

How to get there   From Castle Douglas, take the A713 north, then turn left onto B795. At Laurieston, turn right onto A762 and continue to Mossdale (about 5 miles further). Soon after Mossdale, turn left into Raiders Road Forest Drive and continue to the loch. Use the car park (£1) near the loch.

Day tickets   Adult £2.50; junior/OAP £1.50. Available from the ticket machines on the roadside, or from any Forestry Commission Office.

Best methods/baits   Use general coarse methods and baits.

Restrictions   Fishing only from 1st April until 21st October.

Facilities   Nearest shop, in Mossdale (2 miles); nearest pub, in New Galloway (4 miles).

TORWOOD LOCHS
Atlas Page 207 C.6/7.4

A group of three lochs at Glenluce, a few miles east of Stranraer. Superb scenery and top quality sport, with one tench, one carp and one general fishery. Expect carp up to 18lb, plus roach, bream and perch. Plenty of variety for the angler.

How to get there   Take the A75 from Newton Stewart west to Glenluce (about 15 miles) and in the village, turn right at the tourist sign to the Motor Museum. Continue for 5 miles to Torwood House Hotel. Park at the hotel; the lochs are nearby.

Day tickets   Adult £3.50; junior/OAP £1.75. Available from David Canning at Torwood House Hotel, Glenluce, Newton Stewart; Tel. 05813 468. Fishing is free to hotel residents.

Best methods/baits   Use general coarse methods and baits.

Restrictions   No livebaiting.

Facilities   Toilets at the hotel. Nearest shop, at the caravan site (1 mile); nearest pub, at the hotel.

Disabled facilities   Fishing by disabled and wheelchair anglers is possible in some areas; contact the hotel for advice (see above).

WHITE LOCH
Atlas Page 207 D.7/7.5

A small loch close to the banks of the Solway Firth near Dalbeattie. A pleasant fishery with sport confined mainly to perch and large pike, with plenty of 20lb+ fish to provide the sport.

How to get there   From Dalbeattie, head south on the A710 for about 5 miles to Colvend village. Park (free) by the Post Office and walk to the loch (2 minutes).
Day tickets   Adult £1.50; junior (under 12s) 75p. Available from Colvend Post Office; Tel. 05563 228.
Best methods/baits   Use general coarse methods and baits.
Restrictions   Fishing is only available over a 200-yard section.
Facilities   Nearest shop, the Post Office; nearest pub, The Clonyard (10 minutes, and good food).

HIGHLAND

Loch Leven.

LOCH A'CHROISG (LOCH ROSQUE)
Atlas Page 206 C.5/2.2

A very picturesque loch, about 3 miles long and 500 yards wide, in the middle of the Highlands. The water is very deep on the mountain side, but much shallower near the road. Expect mainly perch and brown trout, plus some very big pike. The history books record a 56lb monster being caught here in the 1960s!

How to get there   From Dingwall, head west on the A835 and just after passing Loch Garve (about 12 miles), bear left onto the A832. Continue about 16 miles to Achnasheen (get your permit here!) and follow the road to the loch side. Free parking on the verge.
Day tickets   Free fishing, but a permit must be obtained (*before* fishing) from the Ledgowan Lodge Hotel at Achnasheen.
Best methods/baits   Use general coarse methods and baits. Specialist pike methods may be needed.
Restrictions   No boat fishing.
Facilities   Nearest shop, at Achnasheen filling station; nearest pub, the Ledgowan Lodge Hotel.

LOCH ALVIE/LOCH BEG
Atlas Page 206 D.6/3.1

A pair of beautiful lochs totalling 100 acres, a few miles south of Aviemore, and fed by a small burn. Surrounded by marvellous countryside and rushes, the Loch Alvie produces excellent coarse fishing. Loch Beg, which is adjacent, provides some ferocious specimens of pike.

How to get there   From Aviemore, drive south on the B9152 and after about 4 miles, turn right under the A9 underpass. Keep bearing right and drive to the back of Alvie House. Free parking on site.
Day tickets   Bank fishing: £8. Boat fishing with one rod: £14 per day, plus £9 for each extra rod. Available from Dalraddy Caravan Park, Aviemore; Tel. 0479 810330; or from Mr. Lewtas, at the Alvie Estate Office, Kincraig, by Kingussie; Tel. 0540 651255. (The Estate Office is opposite the caravan park on the B9152 about 3 miles south of Aviemore; look for the huge signs.)

329

Best methods/baits Use general coarse methods and baits. Specialist pike methods may be needed.

Facilities Self-catering cottages on site. Nearest shop, at the caravan park (¾ mile); nearest pub, the Ossian Hotel, and food, in Kincraig (2 miles).

LOCH ARKAIG
Atlas Page 206 C.4/3.4

A very beautiful loch, over 13 miles long and up to 1½ miles wide, about 8 miles north of Fort William. Best fishing is in summer to late autumn, when some very big fish appear. For the biggest specimens, local anglers suggest fishing the western end between Murlaggan and Strathan, where the marshy land floods. Winter fishing here can be poor.

How to get there From Fort William, take the A82 north-east through Spean Bridge (about 8 miles) and take the B8004 (Mucomir Road). At Gairlochy, turn right onto the B8005 to Clunes and follow the road alongside the loch. Free car parking near the loch.

Day tickets Adult/junior/OAP £2.50. Available from Locheil Estate Fishings, West Highland Estate Office, 33 High street, Fort William; Tel. 0397 702433.

Best methods/baits Use specialist pike methods and baits.

Facilities Nearest shop and pub, in Spean Bridge (18 miles).

LOCH LOCHY
Atlas Page 206 C.6/3.4

A long loch forming part of the Caledonian Canal, north-east of Fort William. Fairly deep water (up to 15ft) with mainly pike fishing, and some really big fish (25lb) present. Rumour also suggests some even bigger, duck-eating specimens!

How to get there From Fort William, take the A82 north-east through Spean Bridge towards Fort Augustus. The road runs alongside the loch; free parking nearby.

Day tickets Free fishing (subject to riparian rights).

Best methods/baits Use specialist pike methods and baits.

Facilities Nearest shop, Invergarry or Spean Bridge; nearest pubs, at various hotels along the loch side.

LOCH MORLICH
Atlas Page 206 D.8/3.0

A very picturesque fishery with over 100 acres of water and some very deep spots, high up to the east of Aviemore. Mainly pike fishing, with some very enjoyable sport, plus the occasional brown trout.

How to get there Follow the ski-lift road from Aviemore for about 6 miles and look for the loch on the right. Free parking on site.

Day tickets Adult/junior/OAP £5 (maximum four rods). Available from Rothiemurchus Fish Farm, Aviemore; Tel. 0479 810703.

Best methods/baits Use specialist pike methods and baits.

Restrictions No boat fishing.

Facilities Tea-room/toilets/small shop on site; nearest pub, The Woodshed, in Aviemore.

LOCH PITYOULISH
Atlas Page 206 E.0/2.8

A 40-acre, pear-shaped loch with a flat bank on one side and bays on the other, just south of Grantown-on-Spey. Some deep water which produces large fish, with brown trout and large pike – some up to 20lb.

How to get there From Aviemore, take the B970 north to Nethy Bridge (about 12 miles) and continue for about 1 mile. Loch Pityoulish is on the right; free parking nearby.

Day tickets Boat fishing only: £15 including two rods. Available from Rothiemurchus Fish Farm, Aviemore; Tel. 0479 810703.

Best methods/baits Use specialist pike methods and baits.

Restrictions No fishing from the banks.

Facilities Nearest shop and pub, in Aviemore.

Setting out.

LOTHIAN

Sunset on the loch.

DUDDINGSTON LOCH
Atlas Page 207 E.3/5.4

An oval, 7-acre loch situated within a 650-acre highland park in the outskirts of Edinburgh. A very pleasant but also very productive fishery in which large carp – up to 22lb – provide most of the sport. Also some small rudd.

How to get there   Approach Edinburgh from the south on the A68 (Old Dalkeith Road) and look for the Royal Commonwealth Pool on the right. Take the right turn (Holyrood Park Road) and follow signs to Holyrood Park. Enter the park, turn right at the roundabout and follow signs to the loch. Free car parking on site.

Day tickets   Free fishing, but an annual permit is required from the Park Constabulary, Holyrood Park, Holyrood Road; Tel. 031 556 3407.

Best methods/baits   Use general coarse methods and baits. Specialist carp methods may be needed.

Restrictions   No lead weights. Fishing is restricted to a 500-yard section.

Facilities   Nearest shops, in Portobello (1½ miles); nearest pub, The Sheep's Head Inn (2 minutes).

UNION CANAL
Atlas Page 207 E.2/5.4

A very long canal stretch of some 25 miles running from Edinburgh through to Falkirk in Central Region and which is accessed by a criss-cross of roads. However, the water provides some good quality fishing, with pike, perch, tench, roach, carp and bream, plus some eels. A very good fishery for the beginner as well as the experienced angler.

How to get there   Access points are available along the canal stretch. For a detailed map and advice, contact Helen Rowbotham, British Waterways, Rosebank House, Main Street, Camelon, Falkirk; Tel. 0324 612415. Parking is generally difficult and charged for.

Day tickets   Free fishing, but an annual permit is required from Lothian District Council, 12 St. Giles Street, Edinburgh; Tel. 031 229 9292.

Best methods/baits   Use general coarse methods and baits.

Facilities   Various shops/food/toilets/ pubs in towns and villages along the route.

Disabled facilities   Some areas may be suitable for disabled and wheelchair anglers; contact Helen Rowbotham for advice.

STRATHCLYDE

Castle Loch.

CASTLE SEMPLE LOCH
Atlas Page 207 C.8/5.7

Located about 15 miles south-west of
Glasgow, this large, but fairly shallow
loch has a mainly silty bottom but also
some stony stretches which suit the
roach. Also lilies and reeds at the south
end, where the pike live. As a bonus,
expect a good catch of perch and eels.

How to get there   From Glasgow, head
west on the A737 through Paisley;
continue for about 9 miles and turn
right onto the A760. Lochwinnoch is
about 1½ miles further on; turn right on
the B786 and follow signs to the loch.
Free car parking on the lochside.

Day tickets   Adult 65p; junior/OAP 40p;
unemployed free. Available from The
Country Park, Castle Semple,
Strathclyde; Tel. 0505 842882.

Best methods/baits   Use general coarse
methods and baits. Use specialist
methods for pike.

Restrictions   No boat fishing. No fly
fishing. No fires.

Facilities   Toilets at the Information
Centre and along the lochside. Nearest
shop/food/pubs (3), in Lochwinnoch.

Disabled facilities   Some swims are
suitable for disabled and wheelchair
anglers, but only with assistance.

LOCH AWE
Atlas Page 207 C.4/4.7

A very long loch – 27 miles in all –
situated in Argyll, to the north of
Inveraray. A very scenic venue, which
contains reasonable numbers of good-sized
perch (2–3lb) but is recognised mainly for
its pike fishing. Specimen fish of over 30lb
are not uncommon here.

How to get there   From Dalmally, at the
northern head of the loch, head south on
the A819 to Cladich (about 6 miles) and
turn right onto the B840. Continue for
about 2 miles and look for signposts on
the right to the loch. Free car parking
nearby.

Day tickets   Free fishing. Boat hire
available: £10 rowing, £20 motor. From
Mr. Wilson at Loch Awe Boats,
Ardbrecknish House, Dalmally;
Tel. 08663 223.

Best methods   Use general coarse
methods. Use specialist methods for
pike.

Best baits   For pike, use deadbait from
the loch.

Facilities   Nearest shop, Dalmally;
nearest pub, at Loch Awe Boats.

Disabled facilities   Some swims are
suitable for disabled and wheelchair
anglers. Some boats have also been
adapted for use by wheelchair anglers.

STRATHCLYDE COUNTRY PARK LOCH
Atlas Page 207 D.5/5.7

A fishing complex comprising a 200-acre
loch, three small ponds and a stretch of
the River Clyde, all in a Country Park at
Motherwell. Expect plenty of bream,
roach, perch, dace, tench, pike and large
carp (to 20lb) in the loch. The ponds are
popular for good catches of rudd, while the
river produces quality chub and pike. A
very interesting venue all-round for the
angler!

How to get there   Leave the M74 at jct 6
and take the A723 to Motherwell. At
the first traffic lights, turn left into the
Park and left again to the Water Sports
Centre and fishery. Free car parking on
site.

Day tickets   Adult £1; junior/OAP 50p
(maximum two rods per person).
Available from the Water Sports Centre
Booking Office in the park;
Tel. 0698 66155.

Best methods   Use general coarse
methods.

Best baits   Maggots (pink or bronze),
sweetcorn, worm; use boilies for carp.

Facilities   Toilets/showers/cafe on site;
nearest pub, at the golf driving range, or
in Motherwell.

Disabled facilities   Some swims are
suitable for disabled and wheelchair
anglers.

Loch Ken.

Many thanks to the following *Angling Times* Report Stations for the recommendations and assistance in compiling this Guide.

AVON

Weston Angling Centre, 25A Locking Road, Weston super Mare, Avon; Tel. 0934 31140

S Veal & Son Ltd, 61 Old Market Street, Bristol, Avon BS2 0EE; Tel. 0272 260790

Colin's Angling Centre, 11 Nightingale Court, Meadvale, Worle, Weston super Mare, Avon; Tel. 0934 518251

BEDFORDSHIRE

Dumpleton's, 15 The Parade, Hill Rise, Sundon Park, Luton, Bedfordshire; Tel. 0582 582715

CAMBRIDGESHIRE

Tim's Tackle, 88 High Street, Huntingdon, Cambridgeshire; Tel. 0480 450039

Chas W Shelton Ltd, South Street, Stanground, Peterborough, Cambridgeshire; Tel. 0733 65287

Don's Fishing Tackle, 721 Lincoln Road, New England, Peterborough, Cambridgeshire; Tel. 0733 344899

Orton Water Fishery Tackle, The Fishing Lodge, Goldie Lane, Oundle Road, Peterborough, Cambridgeshire; Tel. 0733 239995

Wade's, 247 High Street, Old Fletton, Peterborough, Cambridgeshire PE2 9EH; Tel. 0733 65159

St. Neots Angling Centre, 28A Hardwick Road, Eynesbury, St. Neots Cambridgeshire PE19 2UE; Tel. 0480 212108

CHESHIRE

Dave's of Middlewich, 67 Wheelock Street, Middlewich, Cheshire CW10 9AB; Tel. 0606 843853

Trev's Tackle, 16 Altrincham Road, Wilmslow, Cheshire SK9 5ND; Tel. 0625 528831

CLWYD

William Roberts (Rhyl) Limited, 123–131 High Street, Rhyl, Clwyd LL18 1UA; Tel. 0745 353031

CORNWALL

Mike Summers Angling Centre, Unit 1, Southern Court, Newport Industrial Estate, Launceston, Cornwall PL15 8EX; Tel. 0566 776532

Newton Angling Centre, The Shop, Newton, Germoe, Penzance, Cornwall; Tel. 0736 763721

Ken's Fishing Tackle, 9 Beachfield Court, The Promenade, Penzance, Cornwall TR18 4NQ; Tel. 0736 61969

CUMBRIA

Carlsons Fishing Tackle, 64/66 Kirkland, Kendal, Cumbria; Tel. 0539 724867

DEVON

North Devon Angling Centre, 48 Bear Street, Barnstaple, Devon EX32 7DB; Tel. 0271 45191

The Kingfisher Rod 'n' Tackle Shop, 22 Castle Street, Barnstaple, Devon; Tel. 0271 44919

DORSET

Corner Cottage Tackle, High Street, Stalbridge, Sturminster Newton, Dorset DT10 2LH; Tel. 0963 62025

Bournemouth Fishing Lodge, 904 Wimborne Road, Moordown, Bournemouth, Dorset; Tel. 0202 514345

EAST SUSSEX

Lagoon Bait & Tackle, 327 Kingsway, Hove, East Sussex; Tel. 0273 415879

Polegate Angling Centre, 101 Station Road, Polegate, East Sussex; Tel. 03212 6379

Wadhurst Rod & Line, 2 Highbury Place, Sparrows Green, Wadhurst, East Sussex TN5 6SJ; Tel. 089 288 3231

ESSEX

Brentwood Angling Centre, 118 Warley Hill, Brentwood, Essex CM14 4BN; Tel. 0277 200985

Jim's Tackle Box, 509 Ashingdon Road, Ashingdon, Rochford, Essex; Tel. 0702 545688

Southend Angling Centre, 5–6 Pier Approach, Western Esplanade, Southend-on-Sea, Essex SS1 2EH; Tel. 0702 611066

A1 Angling, 176 High Road, Woodford Green, Essex IG8 9EF; Tel. 081 504 4848

GLOUCESTERSHIRE

D & J Sports Ltd, 75 Cricklade Street, Cirencester, Gloucestershire; Tel. 0285 652227

GWENT

Tiles & Tackle, 108 Commercial Street, Tredegar, Gwent; Tel. 0495 717001

GWYNEDD

Eyr Sports & Tackle, 33 High Street, Bala, Gwynedd LL23 7AF; Tel. 0678 520370

Llyn-y-Gors Tackle Shop, Llandegfan, Menai Bridge, Anglesey, Gwynedd LL59 5PN; Tel. 0248 713410

HAMPSHIRE

BBC Tackle, 3 Elmfield Court, Lindford, Bordon, Hampshire; Tel. 0420 472573

The Bait Box, 2A Chapel Street, Petersfield, Hampshire GU32 4JD; Tel. 0730 66999

HERTFORDSHIRE

Johnson Ross, 3 Amwell Street, Hoddesdon, Hertfordshire EN11 8TP; Tel. 0992 462044

HUMBERSIDE

Lightwoods of Grimsby, 172 Cleethorpe Road, Grimsby, Humberside DN31 3HW; Tel. 0472 43536

ISLE OF WIGHT

A P Scott & Son, 11 Lugley Street, Newport, Isle of Wight; Tel. 0983 522115

KENT

Medway Bait & Tackle, 64B St. John's Road, Gillingham, Kent; Tel. 0634 856948

LANCASHIRE

The Anglers Den, 17 Rosegrove Lane, Burnley, Lancashire BB12 6HX; Tel. 0282 21837

Charlton & Bagnall Ltd, 3–5 Damside Street, Lancaster, Lancashire LA1 1PD; Tel. 0524 63043

Leigh Angling Centre, 261 Twist Lane, Leigh, Lancashire WN7 4EH; Tel. 0942 670890

Morecambe Angling Centre, Grand Garage, Thorinton Road, Morecambe, Lancashire LA4 5PB; Tel. 0524 832332

Elton Tackle, 51 Church Street, Radcliffe, Lancashire; Tel. 061 724 5425

Dave's Tackle Box, 211 Yorkshire Street, Rochdale, Lancashire OL12 0DS; Tel. 0706 861219

LINCOLNSHIRE

The Pet Shop, 21 High Street, Long Sutton, Lincolnshire PE12 9DB; Tel. 0406 363683

Pets 'n' Plants, Clifton House, High Street, Mablethorpe, Lincolnshire; Tel. 0507 473104

Bob's Tackle Shop, 13A Foundry Road, Stamford, Lincolnshire; Tel. 0780 54541

LONDON

Jim's Tackle, 49 Ben Johnson Road, Stepney, London E1 4BQ; Tel. 071 791 2961

MERSEYSIDE

Taskers Grandstand Sports, 29 Utting Avenue, Liverpool, Merseyside; Tel. 051 260 6015

MID GLAMORGAN

Tony's Tackle, 14 Castle Street, Caerphilly, Mid Glamorgan CF8 1NY; Tel. 0222 885409

Porthcawl Angling Centre, 10 Dock Street, Porthcawl, Mid Glamorgan; Tel. 0656 772404

MIDDLESEX

Catchit Tackle, 40 Coldharbour Lane, Hayes, Middlesex UB3 3EB; Tel. 081 561 7169

NORFOLK

Heacham Tackle, 31 Kenwood Road, Heacham, Norfolk; Tel. 0485 70333

Wroxham Angling, Station Road, Wroxham, Norfolk; Tel. 0603 782453

Wymondham Angling Centre, 17 Town Green, Wymondham, Norfolk NR18 0PN; Tel. 0953 605417

NORTH YORKSHIRE

C J Fishing Tackle, 182 Kings Road, Harrogate, North Yorkshire HG1 5JG; Tel. 0423 525000

G B Angling Store, 131 Victoria Road, Scarborough, North Yorkshire YO11 1SP; Tel. 0723 365000

Thirsk Angling Centre, 7 Sowerby Road, Thirsk, North Yorkshire YO7 1HX; Tel. 0845 524684

NOTTINGHAMSHIRE

Whitegate Fishing Tackle, 86 Waterdown Road, Clifton, Nottinghamshire NG11 9JR; Tel. 0602 216044

Ken Ward Limited, 6 Carlton Road, Worksop, Nottinghamshire; Tel. 0909 472904

OXFORD

Didcot Angling Centre, 36 Wantage Road, Didcot, Oxon OX11 0BT; Tel. 0235 817005

Catch 1 Fishing Sports, 14 The Parade, Kidlington, Oxford, Oxon; Tel. 08675 2066

POWYS

Brian's Tackle & Bait Supplies, Canalside, Llanymynech, Powys SY22 6EA; Tel. 0691 830027

SHROPSHIRE

Shrewsbury Bait Centre, 198 Whitchurch Road, Harlescott, Shrewsbury, Shropshire; Tel. 0743 236759

Rod & Gun Co. Ltd, 3 High Street, Dawley, Telford, Shropshire; Tel. 0952 503550

SOMERSET

Peter Thyer, 1A Church Street, Highbridge, Somerset; Tel. 0278 786934

Enterprise Angling, 5 Silver Street, Taunton, Somerset TA1 3DH; Tel. 0823 282623

SOUTH YORKSHIRE

Dave Parkes Fishing Tackle, 28 Westgate, Rotherham, South Yorkshire; Tel. 0709 363085

The Bait Bar, 156 Doncaster Road, Rotherham, South Yorkshire; Tel. 0709 362317

STAFFORDSHIRE

Mullarkey & Sons, 184–185 Waterloo Street, Burton-on-Trent, Staffordshire DE14 2NH; Tel. 0283 66777

SUFFOLK

Saxmundham Angling Centre, Rear of Market Place, Saxmundham, Suffolk IP17 1AH; Tel. 0728 603443

Rod and Gun Shop, 18 Church Street, Woodbridge, Suffolk; Tel. 0394 382377

Tackle & Guns, 2A Bent Hill, Felixstowe, Suffolk; Tel. 0394 285318

SURREY

The Fishing Shop, 32 Meadrow, Godalming, Surrey GU7 3HT; Tel. 0483 426956

Woodhatch Tackle, 10 Doversgreen Road, Woodhatch, Reigate, Surrey RH2 8BS; Tel. 0737 244772

Salfords Angling Centre, 34 The Parade, Brighton Road, Salfords, Surrey RH1 5BZ; Tel. 0293 773976

WEST GLAMORGAN

Ann's Pantry, 63 Old Road, Neath, West Glamorgan SA11 2BU; Tel. 0639 645784

Mainwaring's Fishing Tackle, 9 Dillwyn Road, Sketty, Swansea, West Glamorgan SA2 4AL; Tel. 0792 202245

WEST MIDLANDS

Fosters Fishing Tackle, 266 Kings Road, Kingstanding, Birmingham, West Midlands B44 0SA; Tel. 021 355 3333

W H Lane & Son, 31–33 London Road, Coventry, West Midlands CV1 2JP; Tel. 0203 223316

Hingleys of Dudley, 46 Wolverhampton Street, Dudley, West Midlands; Tel. 0384 234780

Castlecroft Tackle, 122 Castlecroft Road, Wolverhampton, West Midlands WV3 8LU; Tel. 0902 761763

WEST YORKSHIRE

Wibsey Angling Centre, 208 High Street, Bradford, West Yorkshire BD6 1QP; Tel. 0274 604542

WILTSHIRE

T K Tackle, 123A London Road, Calne, Wiltshire SN11 0AQ; Tel. 0249 812003

Rob's Tackle, 22 Marshfield Road, Chippenham, Wiltshire; Tel. 0249 659210

The Angler's Code

Courtesy

Please take into account other river users and:

* take care not to block the footpath with your fishing tackle
* look out for others when casting
* appreciate some boats may need to come close to the bank

Conservation

Conservation of our rivers benefits everyone especially anglers so:

* take all your tackle home. Hooks and line are lethal to wildlife
* don't leave food or bait when you leave. This encourages vermin and increases the health risk
* leave your peg tidy. Litter, especially plastic, will stay around for years and is a danger to wildlife and livestock
* help conserve fish stocks by following the National Federation of Anglers keep net code and match rules

Safety

* Water can be very dangerous – do not take unnecessary risks.
* Fishing near overhead power lines can be extremely dangerous – do not take any unnecessary risks. More information can be obtained from the National Federation of Anglers.

Health

Weil's Disease (Leptospirosis)

All rivers and fresh waters can contain pathogenic organisms which are harmful to health.

Organisms that cause Leptospirosis can be present wherever rodents have been on banks or in the water. Leptospirosis can result in serious illness or death. Principal routes of infection are open cuts, scratches and abrasions. In the event of illness, inform your doctor of the potential contact so that he can consider Leptospirosis in any diagnosis.

Blue-green algae

The Department of Health has stated: "Illnesses including skin rashes, eye irritation, vomiting, diarrhoea, fever, and pains in muscles and joints have occurred in some recreational users of water who swallowed or swam through algal scum.

There have been no reports of long-term effects or deaths in humans, but in some cases the illnesses were severe.

Although algal scum is not always harmful, it is a sensible precaution to avoid contact with the scum and the water close to it."